The Postcolonial State
in Africa

Africa, 2012

The Postcolonial State
in Africa

Fifty Years of Independence, 1960–2010

CRAWFORD YOUNG

THE UNIVERSITY OF WISCONSIN PRESS

The University of Wisconsin Press
1930 Monroe Street, 3rd Floor
Madison, Wisconsin 53711-2059
uwpress.wisc.edu

3 Henrietta Street
London WC2E 8LU, England
eurospanbookstore.com

Printed in the United States of America

Library of Congress Cataloging-in-Publication Data
Young, Crawford, 1931–
The postcolonial state in Africa : fifty years of independence, 1960–
2010 / Crawford Young.
p. cm. — (Africa and the diaspora: history, politics, culture)
Includes bibliographical references and index.
ISBN 978-0-299-29144-0 (pbk. : alk. paper) — ISBN 978-0-299-29143-3 (e-book)
1. Africa—Politics and government—1960– 2. Africa—History—1960–
3. Postcolonialism—Africa. I. Title. II. Series: Africa and the diaspora.
DT30.5.Y686 2012
960.3′2—dc23
2012015295

To
Rebecca Young
In Memoriam

Contents

Tables

Preface

In a real sense, this volume is a product of the half century of engagement with Africa, beginning with graduate study in 1955, that roughly overlaps the fifty years of African independence. Teaching and research concerning African politics was my primary mission during my academic career at the University of Wisconsin–Madison from 1963 until 2001 and has continued to be my main interest in my emeritus years. The present book became my primary (though not the only) research focus after publication of the work intended as a predecessor, *The African Colonial State in Comparative Perspective*, in 1994. One may only hope that the volume is worthy of its protracted period of gestation.

Over such an extended time period, the number of debts I have accumulated far exceeds the space available to acknowledge them all. Looming over all others is the diverse support I have received from the university I have been privileged to serve: a pair of research professorships, one bearing the name of my doctoral mentor, Rupert Emerson, and the other that of the retired chancellor and president of the university, H. Edwin Young, as well as sundry grants from the Graduate School Research Committee. Beyond material support, the superb intellectual environment provided by the university, especially my colleagues in the Department of Political Science and in the African Studies Program, and the resources of the university libraries have been of immense benefit. The extraordinary erudition and scholarly contribution of my colleague Jan Vansina have been a particular inspiration.

Over the years, I have enjoyed research awards from the Ford Foundation, Rockefeller Foundation, Guggenheim Foundation, Fulbright Program, Social Science Research Program, and most recently the Mellon Foundation.

Visiting years at the Institute for Advanced Study (Princeton), and the Wood-row Wilson Center (Washington) were memorable opportunities. Of partic-ular value were visiting professor years at Makerere University in Uganda (1965–66) and Cheikh Anta Diop University of Dakar in Senegal (1987–88), and a term as dean of the Social Science Faculty at the former Lubumbashi campus of the Université Nationale du Zaire (now University of Lubumbashi) in Congo (1973–75). The latter service fell within the frame of an African uni-versity development program of the Rockefeller Foundation, whose field rep-resentative (and dean of African politics scholarship), the late James Coleman, was a priceless support.

A number of graduate students have provided invaluable help as research assistants; in the years during which this volume was my primary goal, they include Gwen Bevis, Brandon Kenthammer, Cédric Jourde, Bruce Magnus-son, Geraldine O'Mahoney, Laura Singleton, and Ric Tange. Beyond direct research assistance, these pages reflect the intellectual contributions of the sixty outstanding graduate students whose doctoral programs I have been privileged to help supervise; perhaps less directly, but no less importantly, the stimulation provided by the intellectual curiosity of the hundreds of graduate students and thousands of undergraduates enrolled in my courses over the years plays a part as well. Several of my former students served as coauthors on various books and articles over the years, notably Thomas Turner, Neal Sherman, Tim Rose, and Mustafa Mirzeler.

My teaching and research years in Uganda, Congo-Kinshasa, and Senegal were likewise enriched by colleagues and students. In Uganda, these in-clude Okello Oculi, E. A. Brett, Edward Kannyo, and Nelson Kasfir. In the Lubumbashi years, my debt is great to Munzadi Babole and Ileka Nkiere, my colleagues in the dean's office, as well as fellow faculty members Mwabila Malela, Pascal Payanzo, Georges Nzongola Ntalaja, Johannes Fabian, Jean-Claude Willame, Jean-Luc Vellut, Bogumil Jewsiewicki, and Benoît Verhae-gen. In Senegal, special thanks are due to my colleagues Babacar Kante, El Hadj Mbodj, Tafsir Ndiaye, Mamadou Diouf, and Richard Siegwalt.

Over the past five decades, I have benefited from regular contact with sev-eral fellow African politics scholars entered the field about the same time as I did: Goran Hyden, René Lemarchand, Richard Sklar, William Foltz, and Herbert Weiss. I am especially grateful to my colleagues who provided in-valuable critiques of the manuscript draft: Michael Schatzberg, Thomas Spear, Aili Mari Tripp, Scott Straus, Louise Young ,and Ralph Young. So also did the press readers, notably Catherine Boone and Pierre Englebert.

Our four daughters, Eva, Louise, Estelle, and Emily, all assisted with the manuscript at one stage or another. Greatest of all is my debt to my beloved late wife Becky, who passed away while the manuscript was in process. Her remarkable political career as long-serving state legislator, former member of the Madison School Board and Dane County Board of Supervisors, and occupant of other high state offices was an inspiration to her family. She was always the first to see manuscript drafts, including the first two chapters of the present work. I dedicate the volume to her indelible memory.

Glossary and Acronyms

ABAKO	Alliance des Bakongo (Congo-Kinshasa)
AEF	Afrique équatoriale française
ADB	African Development Bank
AFDL	Alliance des forces démocratiques pour la libération du Congo-Zaire
ANC	African National Congress (South Africa)
Anya-nya	guerrilla forces; southern Sudanese insurgents
AOF	Afrique occidentale française
AQIM	Al Qaeda in the Islamique Mahgreb
AFRC	Armed Forces Revolutionary Council (Sierra Leone)
AU	African Union
BDP	Botswana Democratic Party
bula matari	crusher of rocks, Congolese term for Belgian colonial state
CFA franc	communauté financière d'Afrique (currency)
DUP	Democratic Unionist Party (Sudan)
ECOMOG	West African Military Advisory Group
ECOWAS	Economic Community of West African States
ELF	Eritrean Liberation Front
EPLF	Eritrean People's Liberation Front (Eritrea)
Estado Novo	Portuguese "New State" under the 1933–75 dictatorship

FDLR	Front démocratique pour la libération du Rwanda
FIS	Front islamique de salut (Algeria)
FLN	Front de libération nationale (Algeria)
FNLA	Frente nacional para a libertaçâo de Angola
forces vives	vital forces of society
Françafrique	former French territories in sub-Saharan Africa
FRELIMO	Frente da libertação de Moçambique
GDP	gross domestic product
Gécamines	Générale des carrières et des mines (Congo-Kinshasa mining corporation)
GNP	gross national product
Herrenvolk	master race
ICC	International Criminal Court
ICU	Islamic Courts Union
IGAD	Inter-African Governmental Agency for Development
IMF	International Monetary Fund
Interahamwe	Rwandan Hutu youth militia
jamahariyya	state of the masses, Muammar Qadhafy's term for his Libyan autocracy
Kamajors	traditional militia in Mende region, Sierra Leone
KANU	Kenya African National Union
loi-cadre	1956 French framework law providing territorial reorganization for decolonization
LRA	Lord's Resistance Army (Uganda)
LURD	Liberians United for Peace and Democracy
MASSOB	Movement for the Actualization of the Sovereign State of Biafra (Nigeria)
MDC	Movement for Democratic Change (Zimbabwe)
MFDC	Mouvement des forces démocratiques de Casamance (Senegal)
MMD	Movement for Multi-Party Democracy (Zambia)

MPLA	Movimento para a libertaçâo de Angola
MPR	Mouvement populaire de la révolution (Congo-Kinshasa)
mukhabarat	national security state, referring to Arab states
NARC	National Alliance Rainbow Coalition (Kenya)
NCP	National Congress Party (Sudan)
NEPAD	New African Partnership for Development
NIF	National Islamic Front (Sudan)
NP	National Party (South Africa)
NPFL	National Patriotic Front of Liberia
NRA	National Resistance Army (Uganda)
NRC	National Republican Convention (Nigeria)
OAU	Organization of African Unity
ODM	Orange Democratic Movement (Kenya)
PAIGC	Partido africano da independência de Guiné e Cabo Verde
POLISARIO	Frente popular para la liberación de Saguia el-Hamra y Rio de Oro
RCD	Rassemblement congolais pour la démocratie
RENAMO	Rêsistencia nacional moçambicana
RPF	Rwandan Patriotic Front
RUF	Revolutionary United Front (Sierra Leone)
SADC	Southern African Development Community
SAPs	structural adjustment programs
SDP	Social Democratic Party (Nigeria)
shari'a	Islamic law
SLPP	Sierra Leone People's Party
SNM	Somali National Movement
SPLA/M	Sudan People's Liberation Movement/Army
SSDF	Somali Salvation Democratic Front
SSDF	Southern Sudan Defense Force
TPLF	Tigray People's Liberation Front (Ethiopia)

TFG	Transitional Federal Government (Somalia)
UDF	United Democratic Front (South Africa)
UDSG	Union démocratique et sociale gabonaise
ULIMO	United Liberation Movement of Liberia
UNAMSIL	United Nations Mission in Sierra Leone
UNDP	United Nations Development Program
UNECA	United Nations Economic Commission for Africa
UNITA	Uniâo para a independência total de Angola
UNOSOM	United Nations Operation in Somalia
UPC	Union des populations du cameroun
UPDF	Uganda People's Defense Force
UPS	Union progressiste sénégalaise
USC	United Somali Congress
ZANU	Zimbabwe African National Union
ZANU-PF	Zimbabwe African National Union-Patriotic Front

PART ONE

Setting the Frame

1

A Half Century of African Independence

Three Cycles of Hope and Disappointment

Baseline for Independence

The symbolic date of African independence is commonly acknowledged to be 6 March 1957, when the colonial Gold Coast became the sovereign state of Ghana. Some might choose 1956, when Morocco, Tunisia, and Sudan all emerged from colonial occupation. But these transitions lacked the continental resonance of Ghanaian independence. The commanding importance of Ghana lies in its having traced a path along which former British territories would soon follow, setting in turn a precedent that other European colonial powers could not escape, even if Portugal resisted militarily for nearly two decades.[1] Above all, Ghanaian independence was decisive in creating a sense of the inevitability of imminent decolonization, which was not present even a year or two earlier. Still, the more customary baseline for marking the independence era is 1960, when no less than seventeen countries achieved sovereignty.

Five turbulent decades have followed, producing an African political landscape in which there was strikingly little change in the set of state actors but a dramatic transformation in their institutional content and social environment. Outcomes well beyond the outer bounds of analytical imagination when Ghana celebrated its independence are legion. If one accepts as valid measure of state performance a stable democratic regime politically and sustained robust development economically, then none could forecast that two of the least promising territories in 1957, Botswana and Mauritius, would top the tables five decades hence. Conversely, at that base point Somalia was frequently celebrated as a rare African example of a genuine nation-state whose cultural coherence held promise for effective rule; yet since 1991—for nearly a third of the postcolonial era—the country has been a morass of civil strife pitting subclans and warlord factions against one another in an effectively stateless environment. In 1957, many Africans and observers perceived in the mass single party of anticolonial combat the potential for societal mobilization for rapid development once independence was won. Armed liberation movements combined progressive ideologies with apparent iron discipline, presumed applicable to the tasks of development. These illusions have an archaic ring today.

Scope and Objectives: Seeing Africa Whole

The object of this volume is to examine the political trajectories of the fifty-three African states over the course of the past half century. This period covers my academic career, which has been devoted to the study of African politics, as researcher, as teacher, as visiting professor in three African countries (Senegal, Uganda, and Congo-Kinshasa), as faculty dean in Congo, and as occasional policy consultant.[2] I include the entire continent rather than restricting "Africa" to its sub-Saharan regions, which is a frequent analytical practice, and I have made this choice for several reasons. History argues for a continental perspective; deep cultural, economic, religious, and political links unite the Arab tier of states in the north to the lands to the south. As G. N. Sanderson has noted, the colonial partition that defined the contemporary territorial map operated in interactive competitive manner with the entirety of the continent as its frame.[3] Ali Mazrui adds that "Africa is at once more than a country and less than one. . . . Africa is a *concept*, pregnant with the dreams of millions of people."[4] The two major recent collective works synthesizing African history from its earliest days, the Cambridge and UNESCO eight-volume histories of Africa, both aspire to seeing Africa whole. Official Africa claims standing as a constituted region of intercommunicating states with a commonality of goals; the pan-African dream is surprisingly robust in the face of its institutional shortcomings and disappointments. Not least important, the most popular sport in Africa, football (soccer), operates organizationally on an all-Africa basis.

On a more personal note, my first engagement with Africa came in 1956 with the opportunity to observe a national congress of the Union générale des étudiants tunisiens in Tunis. Subsequently, a study year in Paris in 1956–57 brought me into close connection with the Union générale des étudiants musulmans algériens. The exposure I gained through my association with the Mahgreb student movements to the two faces of anticolonial nationalist action throughout Africa left enduring memories of mass mobilization around the political party led by the charismatic *combattant suprême* Habib Bourguiba in Tunisia, the fierce military discipline and moral determination of an armed liberation movement in Algeria.

Still, the continental ambition is not without its problems. Although in the first postindependence decades there were close similarities in the political patterns north and south of the Sahara, in more recent times the North African states have been less afflicted by the state decline that overtook most of sub-Saharan Africa by the 1980s. The Mediterranean orientation, the Middle East connections, and the depth of the Arab-Islamic cultural heritage are other distinguishing features.

South Africa is another outlier until the 1990s. The British decision to transfer unrestricted power in 1910 to a white minority that never constituted more than a quarter of the population reflected the deeply embedded presumptions of white racial supremacy of the day; indeed, Britain basked in the approval of liberal opinion of the time for permitting white Afrikaners to share power with British settlers. Rather than a colonial state, what endured was an exclusionary settler state with a surface layer of liberal constitutional structures fastened atop an apparatus of systematic subordination and exploitation ruling the African majority. Thus the patterns of politics predominant elsewhere in the first three decades of African independence could not emerge in South Africa until the dissolution of the racial state, which occurred between 1990 and 1994.

Notwithstanding these limitations, I believe that Africa as a whole, more than any other world region save possibly Latin America, lends itself to a broadly comparative approach, owing to similarities among the countries on numerous fronts. There are large similarities in cultural patterns, similarities that underpin the regular invocation of an "African society" as a generic entity by leaders and analysts. Historians find an elaborated tradition constructed over broad areas.[5] African philosophers postulate a distinctively African view of the world and its causative mainsprings.[6] The premise of a common African culture was a staple of nationalist discourse, from Julius Nyerere to Léopold Senghor.[7] Michael Schatzberg shows that the similarities of distinctive African notions of power, leadership, and authority across what he terms "Middle Africa," situated in a widely shared cultural realm, constitute a common "moral matrix of legitimacy."[8] An engagement with Africa as a whole characterizes the Organization of African Unity (OAU) and its successor body, the Africa Union (AU), as well as an array of continental and regional organizations from finance to football.

A second crucial commonality is the defining impact of the colonial occupation. In my earlier book on the African colonial state, intended as a forerunner to the present volume, I argued that, despite some variation in ideology and practice of rule, the seven colonial powers (Britain, France, Portugal, Belgium, Italy, Germany, and Spain) were driven by the imperatives of hegemony, revenue, and security into broadly similar patterns of rule.[9] Critical in the African instance was the time frame: colonial occupation both began and ended significantly later than in Asia or the Americas. The technologies of conquest and rule—weaponry, transportation, communication—were far more potent than in earlier centuries.[10] The intensely competitive "scramble for Africa" in the late nineteenth century led to the invocation of the doctrine of "effective occupation" as a means of confirming international recognition of proprietary title, requiring rapid establishment of a skeletal network of military garrisons and administrative outposts. Metropolitan treasuries demanded that the new territorial domains be self-financing: in most areas, sustenance for the colonial occupation could only be generated from the newly subjugated African through taxation, obligatory labor for the state, or muscular recruitment to work European mines and plantations. This in turn necessitated the construction of a frugal but brutal command state, with a thin layer of European agents operating through a denser network composed of chiefly intermediaries and indigenous armed auxiliaries. The establishment of the colonial state coincided with the historical zenith of virulent racism, which permeated government policy reason with a premise of African inferiority. "African culture," I wrote, for the colonizer "had no redeeming value; only a wholly new African might be worthy of the colonial order, tailored from imported cloth."[11]

At the end of colonial rule, rapidly rising postwar revenues and a new ideology of developmentalism gave momentum to a state expansion that was to endure. Even Ethiopia and Liberia, the two polities that escaped full colonial subjugation (save for the ephemeral 1935–41 Italian occupation in Ethiopia), drew on the African colonial state for its metaphors and practices of rule. The mentalities, routines, and quotidian modes of operation were inevitably embedded in the postcolonial successor states, lodged within a legacy of autocratic practice.

A third shared feature is that most African countries decolonized at the same time. Once the dam broke, decolonization was quite rapid; thirty-five of the fifty-three states achieved independence during the decade between 1956 and 1966.[12] Their crucial early policy choices were deeply influenced by the ascendant developmental thinking and ideological discourse of the day. Planned development, socialism in different forms, and the imagery of "take-offs" and "big pushes" were in the air. In 1957, the Soviet Union for many African intellectuals was not the derelict corpse it became by 1991 but an inspiring example of successful state-led development. The Chinese "Great Leap Forward" was not the catastrophic famine that took thirty million lives as the world came to learn much later but a shining path of peasant mobilization for revolutionary transformation. The Nyerere catechism—"We must run while they may walk"—found an echo in the confident summons to "bruler les étapes" (leap over the stages) to rapid development, an expression I recollect being used in many conversations with young African intellectuals at the time.

A fourth common element is the similarity of regime structures at the point of departure. Aside from the handful of transitions that were directly determined by liberation wars (Algeria, Guinea-Bissau, Mozambique, and Eritrea), the decolonization process grafted onto the robust trunk of colonial autocracy weakly implanted constitutional frames modeled on the imperial centers. The schooled elites that emerged as leaders of independence movements were almost all young, nearly all less than fifty.[13] Their success grew from a capacity to master simultaneously two disparate discourses: an idiom of anticolonial protest blended with enticing images of the life more abundant that independence would bring, on the one hand, and a language of developmental rationality and postcolonial comity directed toward reassuring the withdrawing powers. The impossible task of reconciling the institutional frame of the decolonization settlements—what Bertrand Badie and others have labeled the "imported state"—and the urgent need to meet the aroused expectations of the campaign for independence shaped the early stages of postcolonial politics.[14]

Finally, a major factor in the similarity in trajectories until the 1990s was the high degree of political diffusion in the African arena. Ideological debates bounced from one end of the continent to another. Reciprocal interaction was strong, particularly among neighboring states. Through multiple forums, intercommunication among leaders and intelligentsias was extensive; one might speak of a continental epistemic community. In the most recent period, negative contagion has been critical; protracted civil conflict in a given country has inevitably drawn in its neighbors, through refugee flows, militia cross-border sanctuaries, or military support by nearby states for embattled governments or sometimes insurgent forces.

The core ambition of this work is thus comparative. The aim is to capture the unfolding dynamic of African politics across five decades, situating evolving tendencies within their temporal frame of reference. Retrospectively one can easily identify some huge miscalculations in policy choice; however, the paths taken at different stages were often not obviously misguided at the time of decision. For each phase of political evolution save the most recent, I suggest the dominant patterns of rule. From the independence moment until the early 1990s, the similarities in the trajectories are particularly striking. Only since then have the itineraries diverged sharply, from moderately successful political and economic liberalization to state failure and collapse.

Finally, I consider the haunting question of why African developmental performance has fallen well short of other world regions. To cite but a couple of dispiriting statistics, Ghana in 1957 was more prosperous than South Korea; by 2000, Korean gross national product (GNP) per capita was over twenty times that of Ghana. Though Nigeria has received more than $600 billion in oil revenues since production began at the beginning of the 1960s, a 2004 study found that 54.2% of Nigerians lived on well under a dollar a day; some suggest that as much as $400 billion has disappeared.[15]

There is no ambition to cover all dimensions of African politics or to provide an encyclopedic political history. My focus follows from the dimensions of African politics on which I have specialized: the state, ethnicity and nationalism, ideology, democratization, and civil conflict. I walk in the footsteps of several other Africanist political scientists of the first generation who have contributed valuable recent works that serve as summary statements of a lifetime: Goran Hyden, William Tordoff, Victor Le Vine, René Lemarchand, Patrick Chabal.[16] The book draws on, adapts, and amends the framework for grasping the state as a conceptual variable set forth in my earlier work, *The African Colonial State in Comparative Perspective*. Although my primary analytical mode is qualitative, I benefit from the proliferating quantitative measures of state performance by diverse organisms (Freedom House, Transparency International, Mo Ibrahim Index, among others) and use these to reflect on the range of outcomes. I begin by proposing an analytical narrative intended to frame the portion of the book that explores the itineraries of the postcolonial state in Africa over its first half century.

PERIODIZATION: SIX MOMENTS, THREE CYCLES

Six distinctive though overlapping moments of the postcolonial trajectories can be identified, which will serve as a means of periodizing. The first, decolonization and the independence settlement, extended from the late 1950s to the early 1960s. A second phase opened in the early 1960s and becomes visible with the wave of military coups in 1965–66 and the hardening of regimes into single party monopolies. A third period marked by a quest for state expansion began at the end of the 1960s: in politics, it took the form of a pervasive presidentialism, often textured by personality cults, and in economics the form of a wave of nationalizations, bringing a comprehensive parastatalization of production processes. At the outer limits of this phase, regimes appeared on the verge of a comprehensive hegemony, realizing a vision of what some termed an "integral state."[17] In a fourth phase, stretching from the late 1970s to the late 1980s, most African states were in a downward spiral on all fronts, and a widespread sense of profound state crisis took hold. During the fifth moment, bridging the late 1980s and the early 1990s, an astonishing wave of democratization swept the continent; only Libya, Sudan, and Swaziland stood completely outside the surge of pressure from an awakening civil society below and an international community suddenly hostile to patrimonial autocracy as an entrenched mode of rule. The first five periods exhibited remarkably parallel patterns across the continent.

Only the sixth, most recent, from the early 1990s to the present, displays a striking divergence in the pathways. On the one hand, a number of countries that had sunk into dilapidated condition have recovered dramatically (Ghana, Mozambique, Tanzania). But elsewhere large zones of interpenetrated civil conflict have appeared, and "state failure" has emerged as a conceivable outcome (Sierra Leone, Liberia, Congo-Kinshasa for extended periods, and Somalia throughout this phase).

One may compare this periodization with that proposed by Hyden, who divides the same historical period into three phases of state evolution: the first period, from 1958 to 1968, was dominated by a party-state aimed at instituting order, the second, from 1969 to 1981, by a developmental state whose goal was progress, and the third, from 1982 to the present, by a contracting state seeking better control.[18] The dimension that I wish to add, through doubling the number of distinct phases, is the dramatic mood shift in analytical perspectives over the course of the postcolonial half century. The half dozen periods form three cycles, which fluctuate between high optimism, even euphoria, followed by disappointment, even a despairing "Afropessimism," in the first two and a mingling of hope, even audacious, and skeptical uncertainty in the current stage, reflecting the sharply divergent itineraries. In the remainder of this chapter, I offer an initial analytical summary of these oscillations, by way of introduction to the overall themes of the volume. Chapters 4, 5, and 6 pursue the analytical narrative of the half century of African independence in greater detail.

Superimposing a periodization on the ongoing flow of events does not imply that the transitions were clearly demarcated. The wave of democratization marking the sixth phase was relatively abrupt and sweeping; the transition from the second moment of dispiriting authoritarian drift into ambitious state expansion at the beginning of the 1970s was more gradual, unfolding on varying timetables in different polities and evident mainly in retrospect. Deploying periodization as analytical device does not imply that there were no underlying continuities in political culture, social differentiation, or economic process; the chronological template is primarily an organizational convenience.

PHASE I: THE EUPHORIA OF INDEPENDENCE

The dawn of independence seemed full of promise. The euphoria I encountered in Tunisia in 1956 was widely shared across the continent. In the context of the times, there were solid grounds for expecting better days ahead. For the most part, decolonization was a bargained process, whose consummation was an independence mostly celebrated in a mutually reciprocated goodwill between former colony and former colonizer. This stood in stark contrast to the turbulence of power transfer in Asia—the million fatalities and twelve million refugees resulting from the partition of India, the protracted liberation wars in Indochina and Indonesia, the violent collapse of the Palestine

TABLE I.I. Six Phases of Postcolonial Evolution

Phase	Mood	Time period	Main attributes
1	Optimism	1956–60s	Decolonization, independence
2	Pessimism	Early 1960s–70s	Authoritarian drift, single parties, military coups
3	Optimism	1970s	Civil wars end, state expansion, nationalizations, radicalization
4	Pessimism	1980s	Economic decline, political decay, state crisis
5	Optimism	early 1990s	Democratization
6	Mixed	1990s–	Varying itineraries: consolidating democracy, semidemocracy, civil war, state collapse

mandate in 1948, the failed Dutch wars of reconquest in Indonesia from 1946 to 1949. The two most important departing colonizers, Britain and France (accounting for thirty-eight of the fifty-three African territories) developed, if partly by accident, pathways to independence that permitted mainly peaceful power transfer. This stood in stark contrast to the perils of sudden and unscripted sovereignty illustrated by the instant disaster that overwhelmed the former Belgian Congo in 1960. British rule had begun initially in the "old dominions," or settler colonies, and then extended in the 1930s to Sri Lanka and India, a pattern involving gradual extension of "representative government" through elected majorities in legislatures to "responsible government" when executives were indigenized and made subject to legislative majorities. Beginning in West Africa, faced with rapidly expanding nationalist mobilization, Britain abandoned gradualism for an abridged version of the preceding model. In East and Central Africa, the presence of settlers and introduction of a jarring new principle of "racial partnership" delayed—for a decade in Central Africa—the political evolution toward full self-government based on universal suffrage. By 1960, however, the notion that the small immigrant minorities, European and Asian, could claim equal footing with the huge African majorities had been abandoned.[19]

In the French case, there was no initial postwar disposition to decolonize; the lapidary 1944 Brazzaville declaration on the future of the African territories was categorical: "The eventual formation, even in the distant future, of self-government in the colonies must be excluded."[20] But the 1946 constitution provided for African representation in the French parliament, and later, ministerial chairs in Paris even opened for Africans; the 1956 Guy Mollet government had four African cabinet members, including future heads of state Modibo Keita and Félix Houphouët-Boigny. The 1956 *loi-cadre* (framework law) created elected territorial assemblies with African executives, which by 1958 were self-governing. Although in a constitutional referendum in that year all French-ruled territories but Guinea voted by large margins for a quasi-federal French Community, with important functions reserved for Paris (defense, finance, justice, foreign affairs), by 1960 the already functioning and autonomous territorial governments quietly assumed full sovereignty.[21]

Thus, in most of these cases independence was celebrated in a mood of optimism and of anticipated postcolonial partnership. The British Commonwealth, to which all but Egypt and Sudan acceded, was redolent with the imagery of a postcolonial family, whose historic kinship softened the sharp edges of new sovereignty. Less formalized but more intimate ties were maintained between the former sub-Saharan French territories and Paris, lubricated by budget subsidies, security guarantees, and close personal ties of most new rulers with the inner elite circles of the French state. The harsh treatment of Guinea, unceremoniously cut off from all French assistance after its defiant "no" vote in the 1958 Fifth Republic constitution referendum, was a solitary exception.

The youthful generation of nationalist leaders included a number of individuals whose charismatic appeal extended internationally: Nkrumah, Senghor, Houphouët-Boigny, Bourguiba, Sékou Touré, Jomo Kenyatta, and Kenneth Kaunda. In negotiated decolonizations, aspiring rulers were required to demonstrate the legitimacy of their claims through electoral processes; although administrative manipulation of balloting was frequently encountered early in the terminal colonial period, the independence elections were fairly conducted. The mood of the time internationally was captured by the high optimism of then UN general secretary Dag Hammarskjöld following an extended tour of Africa in early 1960; enchanted by the energy and enthusiasm of the young African leadership, Hammarskjöld returned convinced that Africa was "a continent launched on the road to cooperative success by new and able young leaders with the help and advice of the UN."[22]

But acceptance of decolonization by the key colonizers within an ever-foreshortening time frame was not simply a matter of forward-looking statesmanship; it was driven above all by an incapacity to contain swelling African protest and a growing apprehension that violent struggle would punish procrastination. The astonishing speed with which emergent nationalist leaders mobilized rural populations that still seemed quiescent at the close of World War II contributed to the growing sense of the imperial centers (excepting the two dictatorships, Spain and Portugal) that decolonization was inevitable; timetables shrank from decades in the 1940s to months by the 1960s. Another critical vector driving the process forward was the enormous cost of containing armed challenge or even waves of violent protest; rioting in Gold Coast capital Accra in 1948 and in Malawi in 1959 were detonators of change; urban turbulence in Tunisia and Morocco in 1954 similarly sped independence in 1956, while France concentrated its military resources to confront the Algerian revolution. The bitter Mau Mau uprising in Kenya from 1952 to 1958 and the sporadic guerrilla actions of the Union des populations du cameroun (UPC) in Cameroon from 1955 to 1959 compelled official minds to seek accommodation with African leadership, even though the rebellions failed. On the African side, the multifaceted mobilization reinforced a sense of the invincibility of anticolonial nationalism. At the All-African People's Conference convened by Nkrumah in Accra in December 1958, the Kenyan conference chair, Tom Mboya, expressed the intoxication of the times by warning the colonial occupants that "your time is past. Africa must be free. Scram from Africa."[23]

The costly failure of France and Netherlands to recapture Southeast Asian colonies seized militarily by Japan during the war was a compelling lesson. Even more instructive was the Algerian war. Though the French army was able to contain the Front de libération nationale (FLN) uprising, the liberation army could never be defeated. The toll of the war was immense: a million Algerian casualties, the dislocation of hundreds of thousands who were regrouped in "protected villages," the massacre at the end of the war of a large number of the Algerian auxiliaries recruited by the French army (estimates range up to 150,000).[24] A half dozen premiers lost their posts, the Fourth Republic collapsed, and French rule in Algeria nearly succumbed to coup plots by military and settler conspiracies in 1960 and 1961. A million French settlers fled, the more extreme of these wreaking havoc in a final paroxysm in 1962.[25]

The Algerian war cast a long shadow over the decolonization process; I recollect Algerian leaders in 1960 ruefully noting that all sub-Saharan former French territories painlessly achieved sovereignty while their struggle continued. Belgium was particularly influenced by events in Algeria, acutely conscious that a small and divided nation could not sustain an insurgent war in Congo. The remarkable tenacity of the Algerian liberation struggle was a crucial dimension of the dramaturgy of independence as well: an epic heroic combat pitting revolutionary vision against retrograde colonial exploitation, the future against the past. The triumph against overwhelming odds served as avatar to the dreams of independence.

The high expectations for independence were also a product of the exceptional prosperity of the postwar years, particularly the 1950s. The final colonial decade was the only period since the occupation had begun when there was a substantial increase in real wages. The commodity demand of the World War II years and then the Korean War brought soaring prices for African exports. The imperial centers, for the first time on any scale, put metropolitan public capital to work in support of an invigorated discourse of developmentalism and colonial welfare. A rapid expansion of the social and other infrastructure was enabled by extraordinary expansion in state revenue: Belgian Congo expenditures increased elevenfold from 1939 to 1950, then tripled in the final colonial decade; in the same period in Ghana, state expenditures multiplied by ten; in Nigeria, public revenues were a mere £7 million in 1937, but £71 million in 1957.[26] In French West and Equatorial Africa, the obligatory fiscal self-sufficiency of prewar years was replaced by a bountiful flow of funds from Paris: from 1946 to 1958, some 30% of operating costs and 70% of the investment budget.[27]

The independence leadership assumed power convinced that progress was much too slow and was critical of the cautious management of the public purse. The successor elite was acutely aware as well of the soaring expectations aroused by promises made on the electoral circuit. The dilemma had only one remedy: forceful state action, through comprehensive planning, large-scale public investment, and united effort. "At the present stage of Ghana's economic development, the whole community must act in the national interest," wrote Kwame Nkrumah at the time. "In fact most of our development had to be carried out by the government itself. There is no other way out."[28] Few then questioned the capacity of the new states to take on this expanded role.

The emergent discipline of development economics provided important support for these perspectives.[29] To slay the dragon of underdevelopment, the sword of industrialization was indispensable. This in turn required a "big push" in mobilizing capital and marshaling resources, with the state as central actor. Import substitution was the key to a self-reliant, domestically focused industrial expansion. The role of the agricultural sector was to generate a surplus that through state planning and management could provide the requisite investment resources. With varying degree of nuance, the founding generation of development economists—W. W. Rostow, Albert Hirschman, Albert Waterston, Andrew Kamarck, Arthur Lewis, among others—provided intellectual support for the thesis of state-led and directed development as the necessary choice.[30]

The crucial new institutional vehicle for fulfilling the hopes vested in independence was the nationalist political party. Even at the moment of decolonization, in many countries the upper ranks of the civil service remained well populated with expatriate personnel; Congo-Kinshasa was an extreme case, with only 3 Congolese among the 4,636 serving in the top three grades as independence approached.[31] Access to the senior grades of the bureaucracy normally required a university degree, a credential still found among only a modest number of Africans in many countries by 1960. Parties, by definition, were African, and had no formal qualifications beyond a gift for politics and mastery of the colonial language. The first wave of academic studies of African politics found an elective affinity for political parties, the first domain of political action to be Africanized. The striking rapidity with which in the last

colonial years parties mobilized a national following, once the arsenal of repressive regulations was relaxed, captured the analytical imagination. Hodgkin, Morgenthau, and others developed an influential distinction between
mass movements, which sought an unmediated popular mobilization, and
patron parties, organized as a coalition of local notables or organizations.[32]
Key monographs of the time validated the reality of a mass base in several
key cases: Guinea, Ivory Coast, Tunisia, Mali, Tanzania, parts of Congo-
Kinshasa.[33] In the Tanzania case, Hyden in 1965 found in rural Bukoba a high
degree of political penetration by the Tanganyika African National Union
(subsequently renamed Chama Cha Mapinduzi, or Revolutionary Party); the
party then enjoyed a capacity for sustained mobilization of a rural following
and had built "a strong political organization that made a difference" with
respect to "both political awareness and orientation."[34]

The blessings of new sovereignty included access to international financial
institutions and external assistance from sources other than the imperial
treasuries. Inspired by the novelty of African independence, the dominant
mood of optimism, and the global competition for favor and influence in this
newly opened arena, the world at large at first offered aid that stood as a
generous supplement to the pledges of postcolonial succor from the withdrawing colonizers. American aid, for example, reached an early peak in the
Kennedy years that was not surpassed for decades.[35] The international markets for African commodities, less favorable than in the 1950s, were nonetheless reasonably remunerative.

Thus the new leaders initially had resources to respond to popular expectations. They could hardly fully meet them; the pledges on the campaign
trail were often lavish, and ordinary voters had not yet learned to discount
the promissory notes issued on the hustings. In the first postindependence
years, across the continent major investments were made in basic social infrastructure—schools, clinics, roads, water supply—which constituted the core
of popular expectations.

The mood of the independence moment was partly framed by the larger
global context. Conquest of sovereignty coincided with a period of peak intensity in the cold war and the American obsession with the threat of Communist expansion. Insurgent movements of Communist inspiration were active
across Southeast Asia, prompting exaggerated apprehensions of African vulnerability. At the same time, the mystique of Soviet and Chinese success in
transforming backward societies enhanced the seduction of the five-year plan
for many African leaders. They were keenly aware that Africa would become

a terrain for cold war rivalry, and some hoped that at least nominal non-alignment would serve as a shield; others briefly perceived an opportunity to benefit from playing one side off against the other, a difficult course to sustain in the face of the disparities of power and resources.

PHASE 2: SINGLE PARTIES, MILITARY RULE

The first phase of postcolonial politics began to end not long after independence, and with it the mood of unreal euphoria that attended African sovereignty evaporated. The first symptom was the shift to political closure that set in quickly. Ghana was a pacesetter in this respect. The leading chronicler of Ghanaian independence, David Apter, notes that a mere year into sovereignty there was "a flaunting of authority in the face of opposition groups" by the ruling party, and party leaders who "reveled in their power and made it clear" that they had " no intention of relinquishing it."[36] That same year, Ghana adopted a preventive detention act, and a new constitution in 1960 empowered Nkrumah to rule by decree. By 1964, Ghana became officially a one-party state.[37] A similar sequence of democratic erasure took place in much of Africa. The arsenal of repressive colonial legislation was dusted off and enhanced with further restrictions on opposition; the prison cells that had once housed nationalist organizers now began to fill with outspoken critics of postcolonial rulers. For many, the less perilous path of co-optation into the dominant party or prudent retreat into exile was more inviting than the risks of determined opposition.

The single-party system initially had a number of influential defenders.[38] Partisans of single-party rule pointed to the clear tendency of political party divisions in terminal colonial elections to reflect ethnic and regional cleavages that threatened a fragile national unity. African leaders argued that the deep class divisions that shaped party divisions in European democracies were absent in Africa; thus there was no social need for more than one party. Further, African societies were by nature communal, operating by consensus, and thus adversarial institutions were inappropriate. A more meaningful democracy could emerge within the nurturing frame of the single party, once the threat of formal opposition was removed. Moreover, the single party unconstrained by partisan warfare could pursue a process of political education of an unschooled populace new to the ways of self-government.

The most elaborate and elegant brief for the single party as instrument of democracy was the 1965 Tanzania Presidential Commission on the Establishment of a Democratic One-Party State. The document endorsed a range of basic freedoms, though resisted codifying them as a bill of rights. Processes of candidate selection and internal party procedures were designed to ensure full and free debate. Party membership was open to all without ideological screening; "any citizen of good will can participate in the process of Government," the document claimed. The party was grounded in "the principle of democracy as understood in traditional African society."[39]

However, even as this well-reasoned and persuasive document was being published, the actual practice of single-party rule was steadily eviscerating the initial democratic impulse. Rulers perceived the party to be a core agency for imposing at center and periphery the developmental vision of the leaders. Party and state flowed together into an exclusionary political monopoly, well characterized by Aristide Zolberg as a "party-state," raising questions about whether the mass mobilization had been partly illusory.[40] Reproducing incumbent rule and preserving power were the overriding imperatives, eclipsing the political rights of the citizen. Immanuel Wallerstein had perceived the mass single party as a potent instrument of liberation and development in 1960 but by 1969 was dismissing single parties as merely "the politics of ination" in really no-party states.[41] The "routinization of charisma" identified as a core dynamic for newly independent Ghana in Apter's classic study had become the crystallization of authoritarian practice in the major monograph by Dennis Austin that followed Apter's book. "Patriotism," asserted Nkrumah in a 1962 address to the Winneba party ideological institute, is founded in discipline: "The whole nation from the President downwards will form one regiment of disciplined citizens."[42]

A broader mood of skepticism, even deep pessimism, began to supplant the earlier euphoria in influential works. French agronomist René Dumont entered an early jarring note in 1962, already suggesting Africa was off to a bad start; more far-reaching pessimism followed from Albert Meister in 1966, suggesting a more permanent blockage to development.[43] Martin Kilson offered an early and prescient critique of the single-party system, noting its tendency to descend into authoritarianism.[44] Perhaps the most pungent dissection of the brief for the single party came from renowned West Indian economist Arthur Lewis, who had observed its performance from the privileged vantage point of economic advisor to Nkrumah: "The single-party thus fails in all its claims. It cannot represent all the people; or maintain free discussion; or give stable government; or above all, reconcile the differences between various regional groups. It is not natural to West African culture, except in the sense in which cancer is natural to man."[45] Lewis adds a telling jab at the first-generation political science literature: "To be a Minister is to have a lifetime's chance to make a fortune. It is necessary to remember all this when we read in the political science books about the 'charisma' of the great men now engaged in modernizing backward societies. Almost any charming rogue can get himself written up in the political journals of the western world."[46]

The first harbinger of looming problems was the crisis that engulfed Congo-Kinshasa five days after its 30 June 1960 independence, when its army mutinied against the still entirely Belgian officer corps. Over the following week, the administration lost most of its top cadres when a panic flight of Belgians ensued, and the richest province (Katanga) declared its secession, leaving the new government of Patrice Lumumba bereft of its bureaucratic and security instruments and much of its revenue. The crisis quickly took on global dimensions, with the UN hastily assembling a peacekeeping force to hold the ring. Within a year, Lumumba had been assassinated with the complicity of the Belgians and the Americans, and UN general secretary Hammarsjköld perished in a plane crash while on a futile negotiating mission.[47] The Congo crisis, and its instant translation into the central front in the global cold war, gave dramatic illustration to the vulnerability of the new African states. Though as a living politician Lumumba was a controversial figure, the circumstances of his murder transformed his memory into pan-African icon of an unequal combat against predatory imperialism.

Above all, the deflation of the sanguine expectations concerning independence came with the wave of military coups in the mid-1960s that swept away some of Africa's pacesetter regimes of the anticolonial struggle. Military intervention had occurred earlier in Egypt in 1952, leading to the ouster of a corrupt monarch and a discredited liberal order; in 1958, the Sudan army was virtually invited to take power by civilian leaders at political impasse. Short-lived military interventions took place in 1960 in Congo-Kinshasa and Togo in 1963, but power was returned to civilians. More portentous was the 1963 military power seizure in Congo-Brazzaville, introducing nearly three decades of uninterrupted army rule. But these military actions seemed isolated incidents attributable to specific local circumstances and were not contagious. Most African armies at independence were small, were often still commanded by European officers, had played no role in anticolonial liberation, and had slender social prestige. Thus most observers in 1960 discounted armies as future political actors, even though military coups were already endemic in Latin America and Asia.

But then within the space of a few months in late 1965 and 1966, a wave of successful military power seizures occurred in Algeria, Benin, Burkina Faso, Burundi, Central African Republic, Congo-Kinshasa, Ghana, and Nigeria. Not only was there no resistance, but the new army rulers were greeted with exuberant popular demonstrations of welcome. The shock wave of the overthrow of independence hero Nkrumah, which was celebrated by dancing in the Accra streets, reverberated through the continent. The wave of coups took down regimes in three of Africa's largest and most important countries (Algeria, Congo-Kinshasa, and Nigeria).[48] A fundamental reconfiguration of political institutions had occurred. From the end of the 1960s to the end of the 1980s, at any given point almost 40% of African regimes were of military origin; some reversions to civilian rule occurred, but until 1990 the army always remained the primary alternative to incumbent rulers. In the process, confidence in the viability of the carefully negotiated independence constitutional settlements evaporated.

By the mid-1960s, then, a more skeptical mood concerning African prospects took hold. Three African giant states were torn by civil conflict. Congo-Kinshasa, after an apparent recovery from 1961 to 1963, descended into a wave of rebellion affecting a third of the country in 1964–65.[49] Nigeria was torn by a bitter civil war from 1967 to 1970, when the Igbo-dominated Eastern Region tried unsuccessfully to secede.[50] The discontents of the southern provinces of Sudan over their marginalization were congealing into a broadening separatist insurgency.[51] Single-party systems that escaped military intervention hardened into autocracies. Though there was still no sign of generalized economic crisis, the anticipated "takeoff" was nowhere visible. The term "Afropessimism" had not yet been coined and in any case would have been too strong to capture the sense of unease creeping into the prognosis for African development. But the sunny optimism of 1960 was gone.

PHASE 3: STATE EXPANSION

However, by the late 1960s a number of positive developments opened a second cycle of more modulated hopefulness. The fires of civil war in Sudan, Congo-Kinshasa, and Nigeria were not only extinguished but an era of high hope held sway in this pivotal trio of megastates; indeed in retrospect all three enjoyed a moment of great expectations that was never again matched. The "new regime" of Mobutu Sese Seko that seized power in November 1965 in Congo-Kinshasa had remarkable accomplishments to its credit in its early years. The remnants of the rebellions were eliminated, and most of the political elite rallied to the regime. Mobutu's project of reinventing the vast country as a centralized, unitary nation-state commanded broad support and initially seemed to succeed. A successful International Monetary Fund (IMF) program in 1967 had eliminated inflation and created a strong currency. Grandiose projects such as the giant Inga dam and Inga-Katanga power line were launched, and foreign-financed projects proliferated: a steel mill and automobile assembly plant were built and copper expansion and oil production went into high gear. Mobutu felt secure enough in 1973 to spend 150 days out of the country, visiting twenty-six countries. A once-critical Belgian journal marveled at the Mobutu-led resurrection: "Both in the domestic field and in the pan-African and international arenas, General Mobutu exhibits an extraordinary energy and dynamic activity, which leaves one wondering what its outer limits might be."[52]

In Nigeria, the bitter civil war pitting the secessionist Biafra southeastern region against the federal government lasted thirty-one months, ending when Nigerian army forces overran the last separatist redoubt in January 1970. Starvation and hostilities took a heavy toll during the war itself, with more than a million fatalities in the Igbo regions.[53] The active Biafran information services gave dire warnings of a likely genocide if Nigeria succeeded in defeating the secession. However, Nigerian ruler Yakubu Gowon chose the path of reconciliation. Those who fomented and led the separatist attempt were not punished, nor was any vengeance wreaked on the Igbo who had supported the Biafra venture. Igbo bureaucrats and officers who had deserted the federal side to join the secession were given the opportunity to reintegrate into the Nigerian civil service and military. Igbo elites could not recover the leading position they once held in the national bureaucracy, but the ethos of reconciliation was remarkably effective. The oil fields discovered just before independence began to yield a large revenue bonanza following the civil war, permitting a moment of dramatic increase in infrastructure investment and educational expansion. Good feeling and confidence in consolidated nationhood marked the Nigeria of the early 1970s.

In Sudan, with the active mediation of Ethiopian emperor Haile Selassie, a 1972 accord between the Khartoum regime of Jaafar Nimeiri and southern rebels promised to bring at last a peaceful resolution to long-simmering rebellion in the southern region, whose antecedents dated from before the 1956 independence. The north appeared to abandon its earlier insistence on Arab-Islamic culture and religion as the privileged basis for national unity, accepting a southern regional government with some autonomy, integration of Anya-nya rebels into the national army, and southern region control over army units garrisoning the south. Southern scholar-diplomat Francis Deng notes a striking surge of attachment to a united Sudan in the south following the settlement: "No observer," he writes, "could fail to see a genuine feeling of solidarity with the North under the leadership of Nimeiri, and a desire for national unity." Nimeiri himself underlined the broader African significance of the reunification: "Divergence in cultures and origins is a common factor in all African countries. . . . Our success in settling this problem is a victory for our continent. It will give them new hope and new belief in national unity despite cultural and other differences."[54]

The shock of the growing military intervention in politics that served the final deflator of independence moment optimism concerning new African states was by the late 1960s ironically inverted into a symbol of hope. A legend was spun by an array of influential analysts presenting the military as uniquely suited by its institutional properties to serve as instrument of modernity. Armies, ran the argument, embody the qualities of hierarchy and discipline required for effective developmental leadership. As armed servants of the nation, they have a unique vocation to nurture unity. Meritocracy is embedded in the ethos of the military, ensuring selection mechanisms that guarantee leadership qualities at the summit.[55] Samuel Huntington provided a compelling gloss for these theses with the broader argument that the crucial vector for development was authority.[56] The vogue of the military as privileged developmental agent did not encounter systematic challenge until the Samuel Decalo monograph on military rulers in 1976.[57]

As African countries found themselves buoyed by a sense of renewed self-confidence and a sharpened economic nationalism, by the end of the 1960s a wave of nationalizations and indigenization measures swept the continent. In 1968, the Algerian state took over marketing of gas and oil products, and sixty-six of the three hundred foreign firms then operating in Algeria; the total takeover of the oil sector was completed in 1971.[58] Congo-Kinshasa nationalized its giant copper company in 1969, and Zambia followed suit the same year by taking 51% control of its copper mines. Mobutu then raised the ante in November 1973, suddenly announcing the virtual confiscation of a huge array of foreign-owned commercial and agricultural enterprises for redistribution by the state to politically favored Congolese.[59] In Nigeria, the Second National Development Plan in 1970 struck a newly assertive economic nationalist tone: "It is vital, therefore, for Government to acquire and control on behalf of the Nigerian society the greater proportion of the productive assets of the country. To this end, the Government will seek to acquire, by law if necessary, equity participation in a number of strategic industries that will be specified from time to time."[60]

Far-reaching indigenization decrees of 1972 and 1977 gave substance to this declaration of intentions. President Milton Obote in Uganda proclaimed a "move to the Left" in 1969, proclaiming an intent to take a 60% state equity in the eight-four leading foreign firms; his successor, Idi Amin, took the seizure of foreign assets a giant step further in 1972 with the sudden expulsion of Asians who controlled much of the commercial sector. The 1967 Arusha Declaration in Tanzania proclaimed a more socialist course; by the mid-1970s, then Tanzanian economic advisor Reginald Green noted with satisfaction that 80% of Tanzania's medium- and large-scale economic activity lay in the public sector, a higher figure than for the former Eastern Europe Soviet bloc states at a comparable time after imposition of Stalinist socialism.[61] Parastatalization of much of the economy swept Africa during these years.

Such measures drew sustenance from a more radical moment in the ebb and flow of ideological currents in Africa and the third world more broadly. Dependency theory, which originated in Latin America, migrated across the Atlantic to Africa, and had a major intellectual impact, not least among the political leadership. Powerful texts translated the premise of a relentlessly extractive Western capitalism draining resources from the underdeveloped world to the African context; Dakar-based Egyptian Marxist Samir Amin and the late Guyanese scholar Walter Rodney were especially influential.[62] Socialism as a doctrine of African development had held rhetorical sway in the first postcolonial moment but often had had only modest policy impact. A second wave of socialist orientation now washed over Africa, much more influenced by "scientific socialism" of Marxist derivation; a number of states declared Marxism-Leninism to be regime ideology.[63] "Third worldism" was in full intellectual flower, and a summons to a "New International Economic Order" reverberated in international forums. The stunning effectiveness of the 1973 Arab oil embargo on the West fostered a momentary sense of possible empowerment.

Notwithstanding the leftward shift in ideological discourse, for a brief period in the early 1970s the major international lending agencies were keen to lend to African states, particularly those with major resources as implicit collateral. Western economies were stagnant, and large Eurodollar surpluses swashed around in the books of the biggest banks. African debt was still small, and thus a number of giant projects such as the Inga-Katanga dam and power line in Congo-Kinshasa could find finance.

A final factor contributing to a sense of African momentum was the 1974 collapse of the Portuguese dictatorship, opening the door to swift independence for the five Portuguese colonies (Angola, Mozambique, Guinea-Bissau, Cape Verde, and Sao Tome and Principe). Suddenly the stalled campaign for the liberation of southern Africa took on new life, as the Zimbabwe and Namibia guerrilla armies were presented with new open frontiers. Even the ultimate redoubt of white racial domination, South Africa, suddenly lost its large buffer zone; its rulers began to talk of an impending "total Communist onslaught" on the apartheid state. At the other end of the continent, the collapse of the millennial imperial order in Ethiopia and its replacement by a radical socialist regime opened new vistas of African transformation.

The international context perhaps impinged less on African evolution during this phase than it had in earlier phases, at least until the Angolan civil war that erupted in 1975 created a new terrain of direct cold war confrontation. The Vietnam War was winding down, the Sino-Soviet bloc had split, and China, in the turmoil of the cultural revolution, mostly withdrew from Africa, save for the Tanzania-Zambia railway project. The Soviet Union was entering what was retrospectively known as the Leonid Brezhnev "era of stagnation," and the United States was convulsed with Watergate.

PHASE 4: DECLINE AND STATE CRISIS

By the end of the 1970s, the African mood pendulum was swinging back toward its pessimistic pole. A sense of impasse took hold on multiple fronts: economic, political, institutional. The term "state crisis" (not yet "state failure") began to enter the analytical vocabulary, initially with reference only to the most spectacular cases. I recall first invoking this phrase in a paper presented at a 1977 conference, to some skepticism, and in a 1978 article concerning Congo-Kinshasa in *Foreign Affairs*. However, I applied the term only to what seemed some egregious cases at that moment (Uganda and Ghana, in addition to Congo).[64]

Across the continent single-party autocracy or military rule had degenerated into personal rule, a phenomenon given early recognition by Robert Jackson and Carl Rosberg. "Personal rule," they suggested, "is a system of relations linking rulers not with the 'public' or even with the ruled (at least not directly), but with patrons, associates, clients, supporters, and rivals who constitute the 'system'. . . . The fact that it is ultimately dependent upon persons rather than institutions is its ultimate vulnerability."[65] Soon this flowered into the concept of "neopatrimonialism" as the defining attribute of African regimes. The notion of patrimonialism, borrowed from Max Weber, was first deployed in 1972 by Jean-Claude Willame to characterize the Mobutu regime in Congo-Kinshasa.[66] Its reformulation and systematization as "neopatrimonialism" was especially shaped by Jean-François Médard as life presidency by a "big man."[67]

Corruption on a grand scale became a defining feature of the African state. One of its major practitioners, Congo-Kinshasa president Mobutu declared in a 1977 address to a party congress that every encounter with the state was subject to an "invisible tax": "In a word, everything is for sale, anything can be bought in our country. And in this flow, he who holds the slightest cover of public authority uses it illegally to acquire money, goods, prestige or to avoid all kinds of obligations."[68]

Although the term "kleptocracy" was coined by Stanislav Andreski in 1968 to characterize a system of government in which "the use of public office for private enrichment is the normal and accepted practice," in the first postcolonial cycle its scale was still modest and often received indulgent academic treatment as mere machine politics that lubricated the wheels of government.[69] In 2002, Nigerian president Olusegun Obasanjo told an OAU meeting that $140 billion was secretly exported annually by African rulers and leading politicians, a figure frequently invoked since that time by international financial institutions and others.[70]

Another measure of a deepening infirmity of the postcolonial state was the emergence in the later 1970s of a widespread debt crisis. Until 1970, African external debt was negligible. The lending conduits were wide open for a few years, as international banks suddenly flush with Eurodollars and petrodollars sought to recycle their holdings. By 1980, African external debt neared $300 billion, and a number of countries were in acute distress. At this untimely moment, a sea change took place in ascendant global economic ideology with a resurrection of neoclassical doctrines. Beset by unpayable debts and negative trends in international primary commodity markets and shunned by foreign capital, African states had little choice but to accept the stringent market-oriented conditions of the "structural adjustment programs" (SAPs) whose contours were first delineated in the 1981 World Bank Berg Report.[71] SAPs were made more irresistible by the Soviet decision by the early 1980s to move away from costly African commitments. State socialism as an alternative pathway to development progressively lost its élan, as the stagnation of the Soviet bloc became more evident. The dictates of the market economy became ineluctable.

Through the 1980s, these painful therapies fell well short of delivering the promised relief. Negative growth rates had appeared in a number of countries by the later 1970s; through the 1980s, across the continent declining per capital gross domestic product (GDP) was the norm. For the sub-Saharan countries, the World Bank reported an average annual negative growth rate of 2.8% from 1980 to 1987.[72] The 1979 OAU Summit took official cognizance of the developmental impasse, receiving a report that offered the sobering conclusion that "Africa . . . is unable to point to any significant growth rate or satisfactory index of general well-being." The then director of the UN Economic Commission for Africa (ECA), Adebayo Adedeji, captured the widespread mood of disappointment in asking sadly, "How had we come to this sorry state of affairs in the post-independence years which seemed at the beginning to have held so much promise?"[73]

Analysts began to speak of state decline as a widespread African pathology.[74] Naomi Chazan, in an influential 1982 monograph examining Ghana at the deepest moment of existential crisis, concluded: "By the early 1980s it was apparent that Ghana had forfeited its elementary ability to maintain internal or external order and to hold sway over its population. Although its existence as a *de jure* political entity on the international scene was unquestionable, these outward manifestations did raise doubts as to its *de facto* viability. . . . Indeed, some kind of disengagement from the state was taking place[,] . . . an emotional, economic, social, and political detachment from the state element."[75] Others went further and raiseed questions as to the empirical reality of the weakened African states. Robert Jackson and Carl Rosberg suggested that the postcolonial state was artificially sustained by the international system, which accorded African polities a juridical sovereignty that served as shield concealing their lack of empirical "stateness." In this view, African nations were mere "quasi states."[76]

By the late 1980s, the postcolonial state was the target of scornful criticism. Leading African novelists such as Sony Lebou Tansi and Ayei Kwei Armeh portrayed the state as a predator. A former senior official of the Bank of Ghana, Jonathan Frimpont-Ansah, published an insider analysis of government operations terming his erstwhile employer as a "vampire state."[77] The metamorphosis of the state from privileged agency of development to predator preying on civil society was deeply anchored in the public mind by the end of the 1980s.

PHASE 5: DEMOCRATIZATION WAVE

At the very moment when Afropessimism was at its darkest, a new morning of hope and expectation was about to dawn. The miracle of the marketplace touted by the "Washington Consensus" as therapy for state crisis proved wanting; redemption required a profound reworking of the political realm, a virtual reinvention of the state. Through an extraordinary confluence of events, such an outcome came within the realm of possibility. A veritable tsunami of democratization swept over Africa at the end of the 1980s, the final act in what Samuel Huntington memorably labeled the "third wave" of democracy that opened with the collapse of dictatorships in Greece and Iberia in the mid-1970s and then swept through Latin America and parts of Asia in the 1980s before washing up in Africa.[78]

Profound changes in the international environment facilitated the third wave. The collapse of the Berlin Wall in 1990 and the Soviet Union itself the following year obliterated the cold war security logic that had motivated the superpower competitive quest for client regimes in Africa, whatever their internal deficiencies. The former Soviet bloc, which had progressively withdrawn from costly African engagement under the impetus of the "new thinking" of premier Mikhail Gorbachev during the 1980s, vanished as an alternative to reliance on the Western donor community and international financial institutions. The West, for a brief moment at the beginning of the 1990s, insisted on democratization. Unusually outspoken American ambassadors in Cameroon, Central African Republic, Kenya and Congo-Kinshasa pushed publicly and aggressively for political liberalization. France, usually indulgent toward its most faithful clients, warned at the Franco-African summit in August 1990 that Françafrique was not exempt from the democratization imperative. Within the World Bank, a significant current of opinion held that political reform was a necessary companion to economic liberalization.[79] "Governance" became a password in the discourse of structural adjustment, overlapping notions of democratization with such aspects as citizen influence and oversight, responsible and responsive leadership, decentralization, and meaningful accountability and transparency.

Internally conditions were likewise exceptionally propitious for political change. The old order of life presidents and single parties was utterly delegitimated. Ideologies rooted in Afromarxism or other forms of socialist orientation or anti-imperial revolution rang hollow in the face of continuing decline in living standards. The institutional fabric of the state was corroded by long years of fiscal crisis; bankrupt governments slashed spending on basic social services. The "vampire state" was at bay, its hegemony now subject to challenge from a long-silenced society.[80]

The capacity of the urban street to force a seemingly impregnable regime into retreat first became manifest in Algeria in October 1988. For a new generation of unemployed urban youth, the liberation struggle and the Algerian revolution were remote abstractions; emigration or "trabendo" (underground economy) seemed the only survival alternatives. An emergent Islamist movement offered new hope to them in their social despair. Riots sweeping Algerian cities forced the ruling FLN to abandon it claim to political monopoly and to accept multiparty elections. When in 1992 the Islamist challengers, the Front Islamique de salut (FIS), were poised to sweep the elections, the army intervened to block their ascent to power. But the psychological shock wave generated across the continent by the spectacle of a once-invincible revolutionary movement humbled by street protest was electrifying.[81]

The next source of diffusion was Benin. Veteran ruler Matthieu Kérékou, a pioneer of Afromarxism, by late 1989 was cornered. His creditors refused further advances; the government payroll was deep in arrears. Abandoned by his former clientele, he faced growing isolation, escalating street protest, and a chorus of denunciation from intellectuals, teachers, civil servants, unions, and students. They demanded a "national conference" of the *forces vives* of the nation: the major interest categories of the country. Once convened, the *forces vives*, echoing the 1789 French États-Généraux, seized effective power through a declaration of its sovereignty and created transitional institutions leading to multiparty elections and a new constitution. This stunning coup by civil society resonated powerfully through Africa, especially its francophone states. Elsewhere, without benefit of national conferences, single-party rulers were compelled by the confluence of internal and external pressures to yield to competitive elections and constitutional redrafting. About a third of the rulers in power in 1988 were driven out, voluntarily or involuntarily, by the democratic wave. By my count, thirty-nine African constitutions were either entirely replaced or substantially revised in this period.[82]

A final dimension of the democratization dynamic was its revival as necessary element in the final stage of liquidating white minority rule. Constitutional democracy was a crucial aspect of the international diplomacy leading to the long-delayed independence of Namibia in 1989. Even more decisively, the democratizing process that was initiated by the release of Nelson Mandela and the legalizing of the African National Congress (ANC) in 1990, leading to the achievement of universal suffrage majority rule in 1994, anchored constitutionalism in the final redoubt of exclusionary white rule. The same year, an admirably democratic constitution was adopted (although never implemented) in newly independent Eritrea, after painstaking consultation of the populace and a global search for appropriate models.[83]

PHASE 6: DIVERGENT PATHWAYS

The sweep of the democratization wave was astonishing. Though a number of the more wily incumbents (for example, Paul Biya in Cameroon as well as Gnassingbé Eyadéma in Togo and Omar Bongo Ondimba in Gabon until their deaths in 2005 and 2009, respectively) were able to ride out the storm, in almost all cases important concessions were made. The single-party model was abandoned, and opposition parties became legal. State media monopolies were abandoned, and a political space opened up for civil society, even if the former ruling party remained dominant. Only three countries managed to preserve autocratic forms virtually unscathed: Libya, Sudan, and Swaziland. For a brief moment at the beginning of the 1990s, an exhilarating sense of African renewal took hold, reminiscent of the euphoria accompanying independence. The hopes vested in this third cycle of African political evolution as a durable democratic dispensation, however, crested quickly and began to deflate by the mid-1990s. In contrast to the first two cycles, however, emergent patterns proved remarkably divergent. The most widespread pattern was a partial and incomplete political liberalization, usually matched by half-hearted economic reform. Yet there were a significant number of pacesetter states that achieved impressive results and that appeared to have secured sustainable constitutional democracies, usually accompanied by effective economic reform. At the other end of the spectrum, large zones of protracted internal war emerged, and total state collapse emerged as a possible outcome.

By the mid-1990s, the term "semidemocracy" (or "semiauthoritarianism") had emerged to describe a system of rule whereby incumbents adapted to the new rules of the game by adopting the formalities of a liberalized polity but restricted their application to assure retention of power. Marina Ottaway defines such regimes as "ambiguous systems" not easily classified as democratic or authoritarian.[84] William Case had earlier coined the phrase to capture the political essence of such durable Southeast Asian regimes as Malaysia, Singapore, and Thailand.[85] Richard Joseph proposes a different metaphor, "virtual democracy," driven by the twin imperatives of retaining power and securing "external presentability."[86]

Such hybrids of democracy and authoritarianism appeared a durable regime type by the early twenty-first century; well over a third of African states fell in this category. By 2004, eighteen rulers who held power on the eve of the democratic wave in 1988 were still in office. Opposition forces that sprang to life at the peak of the transition in 1990s over time became demoralized by their inability to oust such governments in countries like Gabon and Cameroon, among others. With the spread of civil wars in Africa, stability regained its standing as a policy determinant for the Western donor community. Cooperation on Western donor community proposals for market-based economic reform soon became an effective means for semidemocracies to fend off political conditionalities. After the 2001 George Bush proclamation of a "war on terror" security collaboration proved another avenue for reducing external pressures on the political front. Soon after, the emergence of China as a major partner opened yet further opportunities for circumscribing liberalization.

Still, semidemocracy was in most respects a clear improvement on the patrimonial autocracy that preceded it. There was some opportunity for an opposition voice in the legislature or through a freer media. Human rights groups organized and became forceful voices, linked to an international network that amplified their message. National and international nongovernmental organizations could take root and provide alternative forums and mechanisms for social action.

In a number of countries, the democratic wave produced much more favorable outcomes. A genuine transition to a regime type more closely approximating classical definitions of democracy seems consolidated in a number of countries.[87] By my count, in 2010 some sixteen countries had maintained reasonable standards of polyarchy without interruption since the moment of third-wave transitions.[88] Two, Botswana and Mauritius, have had sustained liberal democratic regimes since independence (1965 and 1968 respectively), although in the former one dominant party has held power continuously. In all these cases, rulers have turned over, though in nearly half the same party has held the majority. In the best cases (for example, Benin, Cape Verde, and Ghana), the successful democratization has been accompanied by dramatic improvement in economic performance; in 2007, once-impoverished Cape Verde moved into the category of middle-income countries, despite the complete absence of high-value resources.[89] Worthy of note is the fact that the two continuously democratic states stand far ahead of the field in terms of economic performance since independence.

Juxtaposed to these positive developments after 1990 were some profoundly negative trends: the spread of internal wars. Some were already in course: Angola, Somalia, and Sudan had long endured violent civil strife. But in the years that followed another fifteen countries were torn by insurgencies or, in the case of Eritrea and Ethiopia, by bitter border wars.[90] Comoros and Guinea-Bissau were beset with repeated episodes of internal turbulence. At the extreme edge of possible disastrous outcomes was the 1991 dissolution of the state in Somalia, which was replaced by a chaotic pattern of warlord competition and clan-based militias vying for control of local areas, relief resources, and trade routes. Even devoid of a government, Somalia remained nonetheless an internationally recognized juridical entity, a potential state in perpetual rebirth. Analytical prophecy in 1960 never included the possibility of total state failure and dissolution into anarchy.

Even in instances where state failure was less total, constituted authority all but vanished for periods of time (Congo-Kinshasa, Liberia, Sierra Leone in particular). As the patterns of internal war spread through the 1990s, they coalesced into two large zones of interpenetrated conflicts: one extending southwestward from the Horn of Africa to the two Congos and Angola and the other from Senegal and Mali to Ivory Coast. Insurgents sought shelter and supplies in neighboring countries, which in turn intervened on behalf of governments or sometimes rebels. In the most complex of these civil wars, Congo-Kinshasa from 1996 to 2003, no less than eight other African armies at one time or another took part in the fighting and in several cases took advantage of the opportunity for large-scale plunder.[91]

A number of novel factors appeared in this wave of violence. Militias without legible political agendas took root, replacing the liberation movements of an earlier age that had identifiable political programs. They found weapons supply readily available because weakened states were less able to control arms flow. The collapse of former Soviet bloc armies led to the funneling of large quantities of now-surplus weaponry into international markets. In a number of instances, rebel forces from the periphery seized power, resulting in the dissolution of existing security forces, who often vanished into the countryside with their weapons and military knowledge. Insurgents also developed revenue sources by seizing high value resources: the "blood diamonds" syndrome. They found a ready source of recruits in unemployed young men, and they augmented their ranks through the use of child soldiers, frequently recruited by kidnapping. For all these reasons, once launched, internal wars proved singularly difficult for debilitated regimes to bring to an end.

By the turn of the century, efforts within Africa and through the international community to resolve such conflicts began to bear fruit, and the number diminished significantly. But several simmered on (notably those in Sudan and Somalia), and others verged on reigniting. Restoration of an effectively functioning state capable of providing basic services to its population was an evident necessity.

PLAN OF THE VOLUME

In the remainder of this volume, I turn first to the problematic of analytical capture of the African state, suggesting a framework for its analysis and exploring the avenues of conceptual debate seeking purchase on this quarry. Then follows four chapters that offer a fuller analytical narrative of the half century of African postcolonial itineraries, drawing on the three-cycle periodization in the foregoing overview.

In a final section, I examine a pair of dimensions of postcolonial Africa that have been of crucial importance: internal wars and the politics of identity. The recent wave of rebellions lays bare the fragility of the state and interrogates its capacity to exercise its sovereignty. The contradictions of elevated levels of ethnic consciousness and the astonishing survival capacity of the African state system suggest a naturalization of a territorial nationalism that invites analysis; so also does the enduring vision of pan-Africanism in the face of its multiple disappointments. Both these two issues have captured my attention from the opening moments of my academic journey. As I was completing my first Congo study, the country was swept in by a wave of rebellion that upended many premises. The role of political ethnicity was a key theme of *Politics in the Congo* and has remained a central focus of my research ever since.

The volume concludes with some reflections on the postcolonial state over the first half century. If one relies on the expectations of 1960 as a measure, African state performance overall is clearly disappointing, particularly when compared to most of Asia and, to a lesser extent, Lain America. This outcome beckons one to search for some of the overall factors that might explain the divergence, as well as the wide range of difference in state performance, from Botswana to Somalia. Of particular relevance is whether democratization makes a difference in developmental outcome. As the second half century opens, the improved performance of many states perhaps offsets the disposition to disappointment arising from the shortcomings of earlier decades.

2

In Search of the African State

Not just the management of development belonged to the state, but also its initiation, implementation, and direction. One expected that the state would be not just a gendarme or even a welfare state, but also a demiurge of development.

—Jean-François Médard, 1990

The new state is everything. It must exercise a role of surveillance and control for territorial integrity, public security and application of administrative instructions. It must be the catalyzer of development through the organization of production, harmonization of exchange, nationalization of the means of production and egalitarian satisfaction of the needs of the people.

—Pascal Chaigneau, 1985

The state does not exist in Zaire [Congo-Kinshasa]. It is no more than a skeleton that sustains the illusion.

—Buana Kabwe, 1978

The state is nothing more than organized pillage for the benefit of the foreigner and his intermediaries.

—Declaration of Congo-Kinshasa Bishops, 1981

The epigraphs to this chapter capture the yawning chasm separating once widespread visions of the mission and destiny of the African state, which reached a climax in the early 1970s, and the dispiriting realities of widespread state decline, crisis, failure, or even collapse that became dominant in the later 1980s.[1] The itinerary of the state is central to comprehension of the dilemmas facing contemporary Africa; its analytical capture is a major purpose of this work. Thus we need to suggest a conceptualization of the state, review the diverse interpretations of its nature, and examine its diverse mutations from the decolonization point of departure.

THE STATE AS CONCEPTUAL FIELD

To set the stage for this task, a return to the state as conceptual field is indispensable. I turn first to the idea of the state as a general theoretical category, whose construction builds on a conceptual tradition of remarkable lineage, stretching from such classical political philosophers as Machiavelli, Bodin, Hobbes, and Rousseau to the monumental contributions of Marx, Durkheim and Weber. The vast corpus of recent state theory can be seen if closely inspected to travel along a dual path: a deductive one manifested in successive elaborations of its conceptual superstructure and an inductive one reflected in the extraction of qualities of a small number of countries deemed exemplary: the thorough bureaucratic centralization through its prefectoral instrument of France, the strong but parliamentary regime of the United Kingdom, the effective social democracy of the Scandinavian states, the liberal constitutionalism of the United States, and more recently the state-led developmental achievement of the Asian "tigers." These attributes fuse with the stream of theoretical reflection into abstracted and idealized visions of the model state, which has evolved over time and presented somewhat varying parameters. This normative state, equipped with a Weberian self-image as a rational-legal essence, has pretensions to universality and is accompanied by a corollary premise of exportability irrespective of the cultural specificities of receiving societies.[2]

How then may one win conceptual purchase on the modern state, whose model sets such aspirational parameters for postcolonial Africa? Representing the state usually involves enumerating its characteristics and tends to focus on the institutions of rule and its visible manifestations. However, such a perspective captures only a portion of the state as organism. Beyond its empirical form, Hegelian ghosts lurk; the state is also an idea, engraved in the perceptions and expectations of civil society and its own human agents.[3] The state is also a macrohistorical actor that persists through time, constrained by the path dependencies of its past and engaging the future in its daily action. An important determinant of its purposive behavior is its location in a global universe of 194 sovereign polities, as defined by membership in the United Nations. The webs of internal conflict drive security regimes; patterns of interstate cooperation produce a partial international juridical order. The state at once faces inward toward the populace it rules, a relationship marked by scarcity and thus allocation, and outward toward the international arena, a zone of danger and thus defense.[4]

Early versions of a state can be traced back six millennia.[5] However, the contemporary form flows from the emergence of the absolute state in Europe in the sixteenth century, with France as a critical model. Gradually over the next three centuries, the state acquired the instrumentalities and resources that define its modernity: permanent armies, professional bureaucracies, elaborate fiscal mechanisms. The capacity of emergent modern states in the sixteenth century to replace feudal levies and seasonal mercenaries with permanent armies and navies transformed warfare and the state itself; one recollects the cogent Charles Tilly aphorism that "the state makes war, war makes the state."[6] Also transformational was the rise of a professionalized bureaucracy, skilled in the management of the public realm; through these security and administrative mechanisms, the modern state fulfills its classical Weberian definition as a compulsory association organizing domination, enjoying a monopoly on the legitimate use of coercion.[7] Permanent revenue flows not limited to royal domains, customs, and the whims of Florentine bankers were equally pivotal; Margaret Levi exaggerates only a little in her assertion that "the history of state revenue production is the history of the evolution of the state."[8] Securing the resources now required compelled absolute rulers to concede voice to civil society: hence constitutionalism and liberal democracy, at first with very limited suffrage. In the economic sphere, the ascendance of capitalism and the class politics to which the industrial era gave rise fueled an expansion of the social vocation of the state to include a welfare mission.

The evolution of the liberal democratic state for some decades unfolded in a context that posited the Fascist dictatorships and Soviet-type states as menacing other, framing them as the object of intense global competition for standing as authoritative normative guide. More recently, the market socialism of China and the Islamic state in Iran are also alternative models. Over time, however, the dominant currents in state theory began to be generated internally in Europe, shaped in important measure by the contemplation of the Western state by the philosophers, sociologists, and political scientists preoccupied with the concept.

ATTRIBUTES OF THE STATE

My own reading of the state as concept was initially set forth in *The African Colonial State in Comparative Perspective*, distilled from a wide range of state theory.[9] That model, summarized in table 2.1, proposed to summarize the

complex historic persona of the state by identifying nine defining attributes
and a half dozen behavioral imperatives that shape its action. This frame
proved especially applicable to the African colonial state in its mature form,
stateness in that mature form being underwritten by the power reserves of the
occupying metropolitan nation and the delegated sovereignty being shielded
from popular challenge by the constraints of subject status. These crucial
vectors vanished with independence, and the contemporary African state is a
complex symbiosis of the normative state, the legacy of the colonial state, and
customary precepts of social reciprocities and more personalized concepts of
rule. I retain the conceptualization, largely for its convenience in structuring
later analysis. In the pages that follow, I briefly review the categories, focus-
ing on the African specifics of the attributes and imperatives.[10]

Governing

To begin with the most evident everyday understanding, the state is a government. When I queried students in the opening session of my introductory
course on the state as to their understanding of the meaning of the term, the

TABLE 2.1. State as Concept

Attributes		*Imperatives*	
1 Government	Institutions of rule	Hegemony	Monopoly of legitimate coercion
2 Territory	Land enclosed within boundaries	Autonomy	Minimizing external, internal constraints
3 Population	Inhabitants within territory	Security	Protection from external, internal threat
4 Sovereignty	Ultimate internationally recognized authority	Legitimation	Rightfulness of rule
5 Power	Capacity to exercise authority	Revenue	Resources for exercise of rule
6 Law	Codified standing commands	Accumulation	Expanding economy
7 Nation	People as collectivity		
8 International actor	Membership in global community of sovereign states		
9 Idea	Images, norms, expectations in social imaginary		

great majority responded with "government." Its institutions of rule at both center and periphery constitute the visible expression of stateness. Governing is its most conspicuous function, the function through which the ordinary citizen recognizes and acknowledges its existence. In much of Africa, popular understandings are also shaped by a critique of state performance of its expected functions: policing, defending, adjudicating, educating, social provisioning, taxing, regulating, monitoring, planning, and managing, to offer but a partial roster of governing activities.

Territory

Territory comes next in any list of state attributes. The modern state system is based on clearly demarcated boundaries, pictorially captured in the sharp lines drawn on maps, enclosing differently colored spaces. On the ground the boundary becomes legible by the fences, border officials, and usually formal exit and entry procedures for those traversing the territorial limits. Territoriality was much less clearly defined in precolonial forms of African states. Rule was rather often exercised only at the seat of power, and authority progressively attenuated as one moved outward, becoming only intermittent at the periphery of ill-defined and fluid outer limits. The power of territoriality in the contemporary social imaginary finds full measure in the utter failure of pan-Arab solidarity to overcome the division of the Arab world, mostly through artificial boundaries of imperial imposition, into seventeen sovereign units; so does the persistence of even failed states in Africa, to which we return in chapter 8.

Territoriality assumed singular force in independent Africa with the inscription of existing boundaries as foundational principle of the African state system in the 1963 OAU Charter; territorial integrity was mentioned no less than three times in the document. The 1964 Cairo OAU Summit further reinforced territoriality by declaring by acclamation (though Somalia and Morocco demurred) that all member countries "pledge themselves to respect the borders existing on their achievement of national independence."[11] Rather than vest this engagement in the notion of state succession, postulating the independent state as inheriting the assets, territorial and other, of its colonial predecessor, African jurists imported the doctrine of *uti possedetis* from Latin America. This juridical theory, stipulating the permanence of a territorial frame unless international agreements determined otherwise, enjoyed prescriptive dignity not only for its origins in Roman private law but also for its presumed (but actually debatable) success in preserving territorial integrity and state stability in Latin America.[12] Indeed, territorial attachment even had divine imperative in the famous remark of radical Cameroonian nationalist Ruben Um Nyobe at a 1952 party congress: "Speaking in a Christian manner, the whole world recognizes that GOD created a single Cameroon."[13]

Population

A third and classical attribute is population. The state exercises its authority over a human community enclosed within its frontiers. It regularly counts and codifies its residents, assigning a range of formal statuses. Those classified as full members of the national community are citizens, who have an array of legal rights and responsibilities. Birth normally guarantees citizenship; immigrants may obtain it but typically have to satisfy a roster of requirements, sometimes onerous, to qualify. Others are categorized as alien; though they fall under the authority of the state, their status is precarious and their rights circumscribed.[14] In a number of African states, the concept of citizenship is limited by notions of indigeneity: fully authentic citizens are those descended from an ethnic community resident in the national territory at the time of colonial occupation.[15] States exhibit a compulsive disposition to classify their subjects, conducting periodic censuses that group individuals by such attributes as gender, race, ethnicity, occupation, or income, although a number of African states now avoid enumeration by ethnicity. As James Scott suggests, the exercise of domination impels codification, facilitating state control by simplifying its social domain.[16]

These first three attributes sum to form the established definition of a state in international law, reflected in the 1933 Montevideo Convention that was negotiated to establish the criteria necessary for a political entity to claim recognition as an international person. The minimal requirements for stateness were a permanent population that inhabited a defined territory and that possessed a government demonstrating the capacity to enter into relations with other states. Through international recognition, the aspirant state acquires the critical fourth attribute, sovereignty.[17]

Sovereignty

Sovereignty is the juridical sword of the modern state and a jealously guarded property of the African polity. Its central role for the African state requires more extended discussion. The stupendous doctrine awaited discovery by Jean Bodin in 1576. Earlier authority inhered in rulers, often claiming to be God's delegates; the Bodin formulation first asserted a "high, absolute and perpetual" authority existing outside the mortal body of the king and within a permanent commonwealth. Hobbes glossed the doctrine as a necessary donation of unrestricted power to the leviathan by a populace fleeing the "nasty, brutish, and short" life in the state of nature. Rousseau delved further into the sources of authority, finding sovereignty to be ultimately popular and thus merely exercised by the state. Despite the elusive notion of a "people" enjoying the collective capacity to possess sovereignty, this reading proved enduring, with "people" metaphorically transformed into "nation." The 1791 French Constitution declared: "Sovereignty is one, indivisible, inalienable and imprescriptible. It belongs to the Nation."[18]

The symbolic moment of inscription of sovereignty into international law was the 1648 Treaty of Westphalia, ending the disastrous German civil wars by an agreement barring princes from intervening in the affairs of neighboring states. By the next century the doctrine of sovereignty enjoyed general acceptance in the European state system. The vast Asian, western hemisphere and ultimately African zones that fell under imperial conquest, annexation, or negotiated subjugation were swept under an expansive version of colonial sovereignty.[19] Yet the assertion of sovereignty as coeval with empire was ultimately subverted by the Rousseauvian codicil that its ultimate derivation was from the people.[20] Through this inversion, anticolonial revolt claimed sovereignty to naturally repose in its popular base.

Sovereignty has two faces: external and internal. The Westphalian doctrine incorporated the external dimension. The state as sovereign entity asserted the right to unrestricted supreme authority within its territory; intervention within its boundaries by alien powers was a cardinal sin. The powerful hold of this principle in newly independent countries is well illustrated by the alacrity with which African states sacralized sovereignty as a foundational principle of the OAU.

Naturally, external sovereignty has empirical limits. Power remains the currency of the international system, and weak states cannot avoid trespass by the more powerful actors. Global economic forces operate through the interstices of sovereignty and cannot be readily controlled by the more feeble states. The emergence of structures of global governance and the slow extension of the domain of international law impose further constraints, as has the recent appearance, mostly triggered by African internal wars, of a novel doctrine of an international right to humanitarian intervention. Its contours are uncertain but suggest the shield of sovereignty no longer absolves states culpable of grave abuse of segments of their populace. The establishment of the

International Criminal Court (ICC) empowered to try and punish genocide and other crimes against humanity likewise creates restrictions on sovereignty. To date its case registers have been mostly African and have included even sitting heads of state, such as Omar al Bashir of Sudan, allegedly responsible for mass killings of Darfur civil populations. Such an international "responsibility to protect" was overwhelmingly endorsed at a UN summit in 2005.[21] Indeed, the relative weakness of many African states has given rise to an influential notion that their stateness was defined only by their external recognition; in this view, the laying on of hands by the international community conferred a sovereignty that lacked internal application.[22]

But however circumscribed by internal weakness, external sovereignty remains a priceless attribute whose transactional value is vastly enhanced by the corollary doctrine of sovereign equality of states. As an international legal person, the independent state is the juridical equivalent of any other country; thus sovereignty conjures lilliputian Seychelles as the formal equal of China. As a group, the community of African states can punch above their weight in world affairs through their equal votes in international bodies, often pooled through an African caucus; they constitute over a quarter of the UN membership. Further, the exercise of sovereignty becomes in some instances a commodity, available for sale or other transaction.

On its internal face, sovereignty doctrine accords to the state the right to regulate the behavior of the citizens, to extract their resources through taxation, to expropriate their property, and to conscript them for military service. Only extreme totalitarian states, such as the Soviet Union in the Stalin era, possess the capacity and the will to exercise the plenitude of sovereign authority. In Africa and elsewhere, in well-ordered states the scope of domestic sovereignty in the contemporary state is circumscribed on several fronts. Constitutions are compacts between states and civil societies that set explicit limits upon lawful state action. Representative institutions assert a right of control on the executive agent of sovereignty. Codification of state commands as law sets explicit parameters to state behavior. Constitutional and other public law includes a roster of individual and group rights that can be invoked to oppose state claims. In their design, constitutions normally divide and fragment power in order to safeguard society from unrestricted state power.

In postcolonial Africa, the growing weakness of many states by the 1970s was a huge impediment to full exercise of internal sovereignty. In peripheral zones or rural areas a number of countries were incapable of enforcing the writ of state. But even if the limitless domestic authority conferred on the state by the pure concept of sovereignty is rarely attainable in practice, the doctrine remains serviceable to rulers who wish to extend their authority.

In a stunning new gloss on the doctrine of sovereignty, Pierre Englebert demonstrates its paradoxical vitality even in the weakest African states. The essence of sovereignty in a weak state, he suggests, lies in the internationally sanctioned power of legal command. Local agents of the state enjoy the delegated use of the prerogative. When a weak center loses the capacity to monopolize this power, sovereignty does not disappear but merely filters downward to local agents. Sovereignty thus fragmented becomes a means of accumulation for those possessing its symbols and instruments (for instance, the official stamp required to authenticate the sheath of documents needed to navigate police and other checkpoints).[23]

Power

A fifth attribute is power, closely tied to its rightful exercise or authority. The very core of any state is its security apparatus, the storage center of its physical power. African armies and security agencies project state power, above all internally, and this projection of power is reinforced by the police, who manage in a variety of ways those who defy or resist its edicts. In the semiotics of international relations, countries are "powers," big or small. "Le pouvoir" in French serves as synonym for state or regime. Anthony Giddens usefully summarizes power as accumulated in several containers: in surveillance and information storage and in specialized human skills that are assembled in its organizational structures, in sanctioning capacity through its policing and punishment agencies.[24]

Law

The state speaks through its sixth attribute, law. Its power is systematized and congealed in the corpus of standing commands codified in its legal system. Though modern states insist on the primacy of their legal domain, some degree of legal pluralism may subsist. In much of Africa, customary law may operate, particularly in the civil sphere. Even here, the colonial state and its successor have found a constant impulse to systematize, to capture an oral instrument in writing and monitor its application. In the process, as Martin Chanock argues, the state "changed the nature and use of custom," which "became a resource of the instruments of government, rather than a resource of the people."[25] In regions with significant Muslim populations, the rich heritage of Islamic law continued to shape the legal domain. Overlaid by European legal codes in the colonial period, shari'a within Muslim societies remained operative in the civil sphere and at local level. After independence, Islamic law often expanded its domain, extending to the criminal sphere in Sudan in the 1983 "September laws" and in a dozen northern Nigerian states earlier this decade, as well as becoming a necessary point of reference for all legislation in Egypt. The precarious if not fictive transitional government in Somalia declared shari'a as sole legal instrument in 2009, in a desperate bid for legitimacy. Indeed, in a recent study of policy accommodations to the social reality of ethnic and religious pluralism, legal pluralism was recommended for Africa and Asia as an effective, even indispensable, antidote to the tensions and frictions of cultural diversity.[26] Beyond legal pluralism, a larger issue for many states has been deficiencies in upholding the rule of law, a flaw that detracts from their stateness.

Nation

The first six qualities constitute the state as a bloodless, abstract entity. The seventh, the idea of the nation, transforms an abstraction into a living organism, with a personality defined by the cultures, languages, and historical memories embedded within the populations enclosed within state boundaries. So profoundly has the intertwining of state and nation penetrated the social imaginary that the two terms in everyday discourse are interchangeable, and they are frequently conjoined through hyphenation: nation-state.

The idea of the nation has assumed potent force in the last couple of centuries through its ideological expression: the doctrine of nationalism, appropriated by Africans as ideological armor to confront colonialism. The contemporary ideology of nationalism as assimilated in Africa wove together two potent dogmas: popular sovereignty and self-determination. Through the normative if mostly fictive location of sovereignty in the populace, nation vested in the people as a collectivity an ultimate moral authority; furthermore, it metaphorically transformed the assortment of ethnic groups and religious orientations into a collective person. This metamorphosis allowed African nationalists to draw on the moral resource of the right to self-determination. Postcolonial Africa domesticated popular sovereignty and self-determination by restricting their application to extant territorial units of the decolonization settlement, a crucial point to which I return in chapter 8.[27]

In the contemporary state, the idea of nation is firmly woven into doctrines of legitimation. Older states could usually claim to be a natural embodiment of a constituted national community. For the new states of Africa, nation-hood was conceived as a work in progress, achievable through "nation build-ing." The "normal" polity is a nation-state; the imperfect version is in process of normalization.

Unit in International System

The penultimate state attribute is its membership in a global arena of compa-rable units. The slowly evolving web of international law constitutes the state as a unitary juridical person, formally equal to all other polities. International recognition is a prerequisite for full statehood and for receiving the perqui-sites that accompany membership in the global roster of states: witness the travails of Somaliland, effectively governing its territory since 1991 yet denied the laying on of hands by the world community that would assure external standing.[28] At the same time, prior full international recognition shelters even a failed state, such as Somalia, whose statehood remains externally acknowl-edged for an extended period since its 1991 implosion.

Notwithstanding their sovereign equality, states as international actors vary enormously in the currency of hard and soft power that they bring to their external interactions. In Africa, only the Arab states of North Africa and South Africa have enjoyed a significant endowment of such resources. Coercive diplomacies and the threat of violence remain a vital medium of exchange in international transactions, creating incentives for relatively weak African states to seek the protective cover of dependent partnerships with the more powerful.

As with all forms of identity, the national personality of the state is partly defined by the external other, often as a negative point of reference. In appear-ance, the state most closely approximates a unitary actor in its external rela-tionships, notwithstanding the currents of globalization of recent decades. The operation of a reason of state appears with greater clarity in external rela-tionships than in most internal government operations.

State as Idea

Lastly, and crucially, the state is more than a set of visible institutions of rule. The state exists not only in its physical manifestations but is also deeply imprinted in the minds of its subjects and agents as an array of images, norms, and expectations. In its symbolic form, the state idea is represented by its rit-uals, its artifacts (such as flags and currency), and its monumental architec-ture. Most African offices, public or private, prominently display a picture of the ruler, embodiment of the state. The national football team, through ritual combat in international matches, performs the state.

Throughout Africa, the everyday idea of the state includes an array of expectations as to services it should provide: education, health facilities, roads, clean water, among other social provisions. So also is it assumed to provide mechanisms for conflict resolution. For some the idea of the state may be inseparable from a presumed religious idea: the obligation of a true Islamic state to defend, uphold, and propagate Islam or the notion still encountered in the United States and Europe that the ethos of the state has Christian sources. The idea of the state finds regular reinforcement through its self-celebration in national holidays and the performance of its legitimating values through elections and inaugurations. Indeed, Murray Edelman argues that state behavior is best understood as performance, "constructing the political spectacle."[29]

The pertinence of the idea of the state emerged with particular clarity in Africa in the era of the declining or failed state. Such a notion continues to shape hopes if not immediate expectations in the most dislocated polities and demands for action in recovering countries. Even in anarchic Somalia the power of the idea motivates repeated efforts—fifteen at last count—at resurrection of an institutional form. The Somali state is alive in historical memory, and that memory includes recollections of social functions once performed and a higher order of security than clan and kinship mechanisms can provide.

STATE AS ACTOR: BEHAVIORAL IMPERATIVES

Any roster of characteristics only captures the static aspect of a state, projecting it as frozen in time and space. Yet the very essence of a state lies in its action. The polity is purposive; the daily proclamations of its leaders announce intended moves and promise desirable outcomes. The state through its diplomats attends conferences, enters into accords, forms alliances, exhorts others to collaborate in common goals, or admonishes its adversaries. It trains, equips, and deploys its security forces. The tax collector never sleeps; the police agents make their rounds, arresting those suspected of infraction; courts rule on suspects or adjudicate conflicts. Annual budgets are enacted, prescribing the purposes of and resources available for state action. Longer-term goals are inscribed in electoral platforms, major pronouncements, and the once-fashionable five-year plan. Classical history always privileged the state as primary agent; the enriching new currents of social history cannot elude the state as constituting a field of interactions and relationships. The state is an inescapable macrohistorical actor.

In this role, the state is located in an evanescent present in which action occurs, in perpetual transition from past to future. Decisions are grounded in historical experience and memory. States remember through the voluminous archives that constitute its storage capacity; they draw on accumulated experience as libraries of lessons. Most routine daily actions are predetermined by long-established precedent or rules; economy of decision-making capacity compels limitation of choice. But the most important action is conscious, pointing to the future, conceived in terms of purposive goals. Perhaps most fundamental is the reproduction of the state itself. But state aims reflect the pressures placed on it by powerful economic or political actors and promises made to society at large by its leaders in the pursuit of legitimacy. Though goal driven, the complexity of human events ensures that policies rarely meet full success; thus a continuous process of adjustment mingles with new policy claims.

To recapitulate the operational code that shapes state action, I have suggested that the complex web of interests and requisites that govern the behavior of the state can be reduced to a half dozen imperatives that cumulatively constitute reason of state. These invariably function in combination and are susceptible of differing interpretation and weighting by the leading state agents staffing its summit instruments. But there is an "official mind" in the upper reaches of state bureaucracies that shares a number of assumptions and historical understandings setting parameters to policy debate.[30] In the application of state reason, a notion extracted from Machiavelli in a seminal work by Friedrich Meinecke, power and morality combine, generating constant tension.[31]

Hegemony

The list needs to begin with hegemony, the vocation of domination identified by Weber. Rule-of-law states, and even most of their authoritarian counterparts, insist on the supremacy of the law, or the standing, codified commands of the state. The law may circumscribe the outer bounds of state behavior, but its enforcement requires the professionalized policing agents that are a hallmark of the modern state. Passive resistance or even limited civil disobedience, which acknowledges the law even if declining to follow it, may be tolerated. But overt challenge to the authority of the state and its right to rule will provoke a government response, limited only by its practical capacities.

The notion of hegemony is influenced by its central place in the reworking of Marxism by Antonio Gramsci; in this perspective, uncovering the operation of domination exercised by a ruling bloc is the analytical key.[32] Hegemony becomes effective through an array of ideological, educational, organizational, and other "apparatuses." Robert Fatton follows this path in defining the African state as "the organ of public coercive force that organizes the political domination of the ruling class and disarticulates the unity of subordinate classes."[33] If one sets aside the notion that African societies can be reduced to clearly demarcated economic classes and understands "ruling class" as a congeries of presidential allies, ethnic fractions, wealthy "godfathers," public sector employees, and military combines, then hegemony as exercised in many states may be understood as "disorganizing" and marginalizing some regions and ethnic communities, much of the youth, and urban informal sectors. Even though by the 1980s the reach of hegemony in a number of African states was increasingly limited by weakening institutions and budgetary crises, the ambition to restore it was ever reborn.

Autonomy

Autonomy, the second imperative, has both an external and internal face. The external dimension is most obvious; sovereignty as prized state value mandates that governments resist and block any trespass on their domains by external actors. Even powerful states are restrained by the realities of world politics but nonetheless maneuver to preserve and expand their range of choice. In the African political universe, only the strongest or wealthiest states—arguably Egypt and Libya (before 2011), and South Africa—have had relatively few limitations placed on their external autonomy.[34]

But state bureaucracies equally aspire to unimpeded exercise of their domestic authority. Individuals and groups constantly seek to orient outcomes of administrative process in their favor; a skilled and professional bureaucracy pushes back as agent of state interest. Indeed, academic admirers of the Asian developmental states point to the insulation of the bureaucracy from particularist pressures as a keystone of their effectiveness: these bureacracies have embedded autonomy, in the words of Peter Evans.[35] In seeking lessons for Africa from the dramatic developmental success of South Korea, Thomas Callaghy and John Ravenhill perceive effective autonomization of the state as critical: "Pivotal to this effort was the centralization of political power, the gaining of autonomy from pressures from societal groups, and the institutionalization of centralized decision-making by technocrats who again enjoyed substantial autonomy from societal pressures."[36] From this perspective, insufficient state internal autonomy is a major drag on African development. The opposite view is held in many African quarters; in this perspective, the developmental impasse was a result of inadequate external autonomy. One may cite the lament of Claude Ake, who claims African states were cornered by their external weakness, compelling acquiescence in SAPs that " hardly any [African leaders] believe in" and "that most of them condemn." According to him, they "put up with it to avoid economic sanctions and in the hope of eliciting material support from external patrons."[37] The thread connecting these disparate perspectives is the autonomy imperative.

Security

Security is a third imperative. Indeed, within Africa the northern tier of Arab countries are frequently characterized as *mukhabarat* states, defined by their omnipresent and pervasive security apparatus.[38] In the final years of apartheid in South Africa, the government, fearing what it termed a "total Communist onslaught" from the north, increasingly became a national security state as well. More broadly, cold war competition in Africa led both blocs to assist in the strengthening of armed forces and internal security organs. In the West, the United States and France were particularly active on this front; on the eastern side, East Germany in particular specialized in training secret police forces in ideologically aligned states.

"National security" as policy objective is a staple of political discourse everywhere; so is stirring public fears of insecurity by warning of external dangers or internal subversion. The experience of extended periods of internal war and attendant profound insecurity burns deeply into the public consciousness; only recently has the psychosis of the bitter civil war of the 1930s begun to fade in Spain. For three decades, Mobutu Sese Seko in Congo-Kinshasa relied on the trauma of the 1963–65 rebellions to legitimate the "Mobutu or chaos" theory. In contemporary Liberia and Sierra Leone, the searing memories of the atrocity-laden civil wars of the 1990s induce a powerful longing for domestic peace and internal security. Not the least toxic impact of state crisis or failure in Africa is the likely perversion of security forces into predatory instruments of disorder and insecurity.

Legitimation

Legitimation, the fourth imperative, is a constant necessity for a state. Legitimacy is indispensable to assuring at low cost the habitual consent and obedience of civil society and its respect for state agents. A deficiency in legitimacy makes likely a larger reliance on coercion and fear to motivate conformity to the law. Coercion in turn serves as a gold reserve for the currency of state authority. If constantly deployed, the reserves are depleted and hegemony is devalued. An immediate consequence is a diminished disposition of the populace to everyday deference to state authority and the rules enshrined in its legal code. The reservoir of legitimacy is not fixed or permanent; the frictions inherent in the daily operations of the state are corrosive. The daily replenishment of the stock is the challenge of the legitimation imperative.

Jürgen Habermas suggests that a legitimation crisis can occur for four reasons: the economic system fails to provide the requisite consumable values; the administrative system cannot provide enough rational decisions; the legitimation system does not yield enough generalized motivations; or the sociocultural system is deficient in the production of action-motivating meaning.[39] In sum, a quantum of legitimacy is earned in the daily performance of the state, in its capacity for effective governance. Legitimation is a perpetual referendum on state behavior.

The performance is partly rhetorical. The need to articulate goals that resonate with the public is one aspect. Related is the need to frame policy in terms that win broad support. Until recently in Africa, the capacity to cast goals and policies in some inspirational ideological form—often a version of socialism—was instrumental to legitimation; the global devaluation of explicit forms of socialist ideology since 1990 leaves nationalism as the primary vehicle for portraying the state as an active defender of collective interests. Ritual and ceremonial performance likewise contribute: popular festivals, public displays of military might.

Even more important than discourse is the integrity of state behavior. A powerful vector of delegitimation in Africa has been the scale of corruption in many states. A number of African rulers secreted billions of dollars in offshore accounts; to cite but one example, former military dictator Sani Abacha in Nigeria managed to steal $4 billion in his brief presidency from 1994 to 1999.[40] Regimes originating in military coups inevitably claimed entry legitimacy by cataloguing the sins of their predecessors: venality, incompetence, nepotism, atrocities, subservience to external actors.

State conformity to constitutional limits and requirements is another source of legitimacy, optimally effected through democratic institutions. States manifesting scrupulous respect for their own laws more readily earn willing compliance from the citizenry. The proper functioning of the judicial system also enhances the dignity of the state more broadly. Assuring state accountability through meaningful elections and functioning representative institutions likewise increases legitimacy.

Finally, competent governance, the effectiveness of state action in performance of its expected obligations, reinforces its legitimacy. Management of the economy in ways that visibly enhances prosperity, assures growth, and constrains abuse is one dimension. Another is assuring a functioning legal order, one that provides individual security and protects property rights, as well as reliably delivering of basic social provisions: schools, clinics, safe water, roads. Everyday state competence is a reliable pathway to legitimation, and its conspicuous absence in a number of African states is a vector of delegitimation.

Revenue

In pursuit of the fourth imperative of legitimation, the state acts as a helping profession. The opposite is the case for revenue, the fifth imperative, which pits the state against society in its extraction of sufficient resources to perform its other roles. Society does not readily yield its wealth; no legislation is more painful than tax increases, and no campaign promise is more tempting than the pledge to reduce them. Indeed, the erection of constitutional democratic polities on the absolutist foundations of the early modern state is largely a narrative of successive concessions of authority to representative institutions in return for meeting often war-driven needs for revenue enhancement. The revenue imperative is the most fundamental of all the components to the operational code of the state.

The reasons are obvious enough, well summarized by Levi: "Revenue enhances the ability of rulers to elaborate the institutions of the state, to bring more people within the domain of those institutions, and to increase the number and variety of collective goods provided through the state."[41] The difficulties in collection are directly proportionate to the visibility of the tax to those obliged to pay. Until the twentieth century states tended to rely heavily on taxes on trade; import and export imposts have always been a crucial source in Africa. Income tax collection in particular requires a sophisticated revenue administration, and a reasonable reserve of state legitimacy is needed to induce broad compliance; these state qualities are often lacking in Africa, leading to widespread evasion. Further, the state decline in the 1980s led to a shrinkage of the formal economy and a concomitant growth in the informal sector, outside the reach of the state fiscal net.

A fatal revenue shortfall is crucial to understanding the state crisis that emerged in Africa during the 1980s. External assistance and rents on high-value primary commodities had become dominant sources for many. Revenue shortfall leads swiftly to delegitimating incapacities. Arrearages in public-sector salary payments become endemic, undermining bureaucratic performance and provoking volatile discontent. Funding for basic social provisions dwindles, and schools and clinics function only if their clientele supplants government support with informal payments to replace the salaries of the teachers and medical personnel. State agents monetize their authority by demanding illicit compensation for any service.

Accumulation

The sixth and last imperative is accumulation, intimately linked to the revenue requirement. Only in the age of mercantilism did this dimension of state action become evident. Soon thereafter, it became joined to an emergent idea of progress, reflecting the philosophic optimism of the Enlightenment. The dramatic advances in science and technology in the nineteenth century, and novel vistas of a possible cumulative increase in the level of societal prosperity, gave rise to a new theory of history as a narrative of progress. Perhaps best defined as irreversible ameliorative change, the idea of progress, absorbed into decolonization African nationalism, implies human agency in its realization: thus the idea of the state as overseer of a marshalling of resources and instruments to assure sustained growth.[42]

The notion of progress fused with the concept of development in the early years of the twentieth century to assert more explicitly an accumulation mission for the state—reflected, for example, in the summons of French colonial minister Albert Sarrault in the 1920s to a *mise en valeur* of the colonial estates. In the authoritative words of leading British colonial statesman Lord Hailey, "A new concept . . . had come to be increasingly accepted[:] . . . active State intervention was a necessary lever to the amelioration of social conditions."[43] Development at a redoubled pace was the primary legitimating doctrine of the newly independent states.[44] To achieve this goal, energetic state action to plan, direct, and organize economy and government seemed indispensable: the accumulation imperative in action.

The accumulation imperative in Africa requires a complex and difficult balance of action, with respect to the private economy, especially regarding foreign participation. The effectiveness of state accumulation-directed policies, more than the other imperatives, is subject to an array of measures and indicators: above all the ubiquitous GNP increase statistic. A blend of state intervention, direction, facilitation, and abstention is required. In the first two decades of African independence, consensus favored privileging the first two; since 1980s, the balance has shifted toward encouraging the private sector, to supporting property rights and offering investment inducements.

Needless to say, simultaneous optimization of the entire array of imperatives is impossible. At any given point, aggressive pursuit of one may come at the cost of others. I am reducing the complex processes through which state behavior is determined to this parsimonious list only for reasons of analytical convenience and clarity; key state actors do not consciously pursue their policy calculus within such a simplified framework.

LIMITS TO THE CONCEPT

The portrait of the state sketched in this summary of its attributes and behavioral imperatives, taken alone, inevitably sins through unintended reification. Its conceptual transformation into an apparent unitary rational actor must at once be set aside. At an abstract level, one may perceive an identifiable reason of state. Periodic political statements may castigate a proposal as contrary to state interest or advocate an action as required for state well-being. But rationality fully operates only in the realm of abstraction; in the real world, what Michael Mann calls the "cock-up-foul-up" dimension of state action must enter the picture.[45]

Still, at the end of the day states remain authoritative actors. This is especially evident in the geopolitical realm; states as collective actors do sign accords with other international actors, declare war, form alliances, and take positions in international forums. These acts belong unambiguously to the state, whatever the complexity of the processes through which they were decided on.

Internally, the division of the state into several realms of authority—executive, legislative, and judicial branches, state corporations and central banks, security agencies, among others—both fragments the decision-making process and creates multiple institutional sources of state action. Furthermore, government operates through a nesting hierarchy of territorial subdivisions, with their own functional and often representative organs. Still, once the prescribed procedures for a binding act have been followed, a decision ensues in the name of the state. The decision process encompasses a deliberative, reflective element; as Bertrand Badie and Pierre Birnbaum observe, "The essential function of the state is to think."[46] This observation echoes the Durkheim notion that as organic solidarity takes hold, the state becomes the brain or guiding intelligence for society.[47]

Thus the state acts: yet a paradox remains. In the last analysis, the state is an abstraction; the real actors are the skilled human agents who staff its institutions. Giddens frames the issue well: "All state action is carried on by knowledgeable human agents who both construct the social world through their action, but yet whose action is also conditioned and constrained by the very world of their creation." These agents draw not only on data in state information storage containers but also their on own memories, which they apply to the future-directed purposes at hand.[48] State norms, professional culture, bureaucratic hierarchy, and formal rules all shape and constrain the action of government actors, but they remain subject to their individual identities, interests, and passions. In real policy settings, reason of state is a complex calculus with incomplete information and large uncertainties, yielding some range of possible choice, perhaps inflected by personal dispositions of key actors. In the minds of political leaders, reason of state jostles with the desire to perpetuate their grip on the agencies of rule; the "official mind" most clearly operates at the level of the permanent administrative staffing of the state.

The hegemony and autonomy drives of the African colonial state did place it not only above but largely outside of subject society. The postcolonial successor, even in its most authoritarian moments, could not enforce such a separation. Timothy Mitchell cogently argues that state analysis needs to blur the line between state and society. "The state," he writes, "should not be taken as a free-standing entity, whether an agent, instrument, organization or structure, located apart from and opposed to another entity called society," although the distinction between state and society should nevertheless be taken seriously, as the defining characteristic of the modern political order.[49] The very notion of "civil society" is constituted by the state itself: an analytical collective whose recent rediscovery as a moral actor owes much to the degeneration and delegitimation of the Eastern European states of the former Soviet bloc and of most African states in the 1980s.[50] Various definitions of civil society are on offer; I prefer to regard the concept as referencing the array of associations lying between the household and the state, seeking voice and influence on the public square in that part of their action that operates in a public-regarding domain.[51] Civil society and the state are joined in a web of conflict and cooperation, a constant contest over the boundaries of state authority and over what constitutes the optimal supply of public goods. At the same time, in innumerable more particularistic arenas of encounter, state and society more broadly interact in the realms of identity, resource control, and access to public favor. As I suggest in *The African Colonial State*, "Civil society simultaneously pursues exit, voice, and loyalty at any historical moment; what may vary over time is the valence of each of these factors. The state constitutes, dominates, and rules civil society, which in turn penetrates the state and imprints its collective personality and major cleavages."[52]

There are thus many qualifications to the preceding portrayal of the state as macrohistorical actor whose reproduction over time is guided by a distinctive set of interests. In my reading, reason of state is operative in African polities. In the most debilitated, it is overwritten by competing logics of aggrandizement of rulers or protection of incumbent regimes. But even in these instances a residue remains to which at least a handful of state agents cling. Further, the recent enthronement of good "governance" as supreme developmental virtue in Africa, especially in the eyes of the donor community, can be understood as embodying the elements of stateness I have elaborated.

THE NORMATIVE STATE

Through all of its mutations, the African state dwelled not only in the shadow of its colonial predecessor but also in the normative shadow of external state models: what one may term a "normative state." By this I mean an internationally dominant abstracted concept of the appropriate institutional forms, doctrines, and functions of a sovereign state. This term originates with Ernst Frankel; it was then was adapted by Jens Meierhenrich to frame his careful study of the role of law in the South African transition beyond apartheid. In its original version, "normative" applies only to the supremacy of the law in limiting the prerogative powers of a ruler.[53] I use the concept to suggest an overall model of the effective state.

The very notion of a development gap to be closed in the modern age implied a magnetic tug from idealized external models that purported to fulfill the vision of a life more abundant. Initially, the exemplary nation-state after its post–World War II reconfiguration embodied the Keynesian premises of active economic management and the social pact of a welfare infrastructure; in response, the first-generation postcolonial states adopted indicative planning and rapid expansion of social provisioning. The ideological flow of dependency theory from Latin America in the 1970s pulled state orientation toward expanding its capacities so that it might supplant the economic hold of colonial and international capital.[54] At the same time, the persistent stagnation of advanced economies in the 1970s interrogated the consensus surrounding the welfare state as authoritative model, leading to the revisionist ideology of neoliberalism incarnated by Ronald Reagan and Margaret Thatcher. By the 1980s, the dominant normative state was clothed in the garment of market supremacy, a new master principle that quickly filtered into the operating codes by which international financial institutions and donor communities governed the conditions for assistance to crisis-ridden African states. By the 1990s, the now-ascendant liberal market state model embraced democratization as well as marketization as basic criteria of respectability.[55] Ever since African independence, the primary version of a normative state has always had a major competitor. Initially this was state socialism of Soviet inspiration, characterized by comprehensive state ownership, a command economy, and a densely organized autocracy. As chapter 1 argues, at the moment of independence the Soviet Union and China seemed to march toward progress in seven league boots; this model stood at the pinnacle of its prestige and power, apparently associated with rapid economic growth and transformation of backward societies. In 1960 its African adoption was initially inconceivable, given the institutional legacy of the colonial state and the deep entanglement with the norms, practices, and operating ethos of decolonization. By the 1970s, a handful of states adopted state socialism and attempted to remake the polity on Leninist lines with indifferent success. The 1991 collapse of the Soviet Union and Chinese shift to market socialism removed this alternative vision from the landscape; in its place the remarkable success of East Asian developmental states, which became visible by the late 1980s, provided an new inspiration. Marked by an activist state managing a market economy and guided by a proficient and technocratic bureaucracy and often by semi-authoritarian politics, this model was only temporarily dimmed by the 1997 Asian economic crisis. But by the time the Asian example came into view, the decline of most African states appeared to preclude its adoption. State rebuilding and reform did take hold for a few African countries in the 1990s, and so the allure of the Asian example is still evoked by some, most explicitly by Paul Kagame, Rwandan president since 1994; Singapore has been constantly cited in regime discourse as the exemplary instance of a very small polity that achieved dramatic transformation under authoritarian auspices.[56] By the turn of the century, a resurgent China added a new dimension to the Asian model.

However impaired many states might have become, the normative reach of the primary advanced liberal market state model expanded in tandem with Africa's needs for external support. Whether the profound crisis of the neoliberal state that emerged in its heartland—the United States—in 2008 and that then spread throughout the world through the avenue of globalization will reshape the model modern state is a newly posed and crucial question. Whatever the outcome, the enduring reality is the potency of external models of the efficacious nation-state.

THE DEVELOPMENTAL STATE

Over its five postindependence decades, one can perceive three successive ascendant African state models, corresponding to the three cycles identified in chapter 1. In the immediate postcolonial years, the doctrine of the developmentalist state ruled supreme. This built on but expanded the policy impulses of the terminal colonial state, reconceived in a far more activist mode. At that moment, industrialization was the key passageway to high modernity; marshaling the requisite resources necessitated state planning and initiative. In its most expansive version, Algerian planners, influenced by French radical economist François Perroux, framed this ambition as prioritizing basic heavy industry, especially steel: "industries industrialisants."[57] The fascination with steel mills and giant hydroelectric projects was a mark of the times, not just a unique interest of Africa's. Agriculture was tasked to provide the domestic resource base for development; its surplus was to be transferred to industrial and urban sector needs. Social infrastructure enjoyed similar energetic state backing. The amenities prized by the citizenry—schools and medical facilities above all—expanded impressively in the 1960s, their services often made available for reduced fees or even for free. Indicative planning was held in high esteem and at the time carried the blessing of the international financial institutions; the glossy, bound five-year plan conveyed visions of a prosperous future, with a legitimating subtext of state capacity for fulfillment. A sense of purposive urgency drove the developmentalist state. So also did a relative abundance of resources; withdrawing colonizers at first expanded the public aid to their former African holdings, and independence opened access to a far broader array of external donors, as well as to financing from public and private international institutions.

The activist developmental state needed to concentrate authority to fulfill its ambitions. Thus neutralization of opposition voices in representative institutions was the ransom of progress, as was the expansion of the ruling party into a disciplining mechanism by which to silence the discontented. Authoritarian practice drew on the heritage of the colonial state, which provided an arsenal of legal weapons against dissent. So also did a deeply implanted notion among the ruling elites and bureaucratic cadres that they governed backward societies that required their pedagogical direction. By 1970, of the states then independent, only Botswana, Gambia, and Mauritius had remained within a democratic ambit without interruption.

THE INTEGRAL STATE

By this time, a more ambitious version of the model African state was taking form, influenced by larger ideological currents, especially in the third world. In a number of countries, regimes emerged in the early 1970s laying claim to a far more extended role in management of economy and society. In this system of perfected hegemony, which I and others have termed the "integral state," the state seeks unencumbered domination over civil society. Control is pursued not only via the political realm, usually through the agency of a single party into which all social organization is channeled, but also by the imposition of state suzerainty over the instances of economic accumulation. The integral state falls short of the totalitarian model, requiring only passive subjects, mobilized into sporadic ritual affirmations of deference. It lacks the massive superstructure of coercion and terror of Soviet or Nazi totalitarianism, nor does it fully embrace a totalizing ideology.

The notion of an integral state is found in Gramsci, identified with the success of a ruling "historic bloc" in homogenizing base and superstructure, which renders civil society a merely "gelatinous" condition.[58] The concept appears in the African context in the work of several observers inspired by state developments of the 1970s. Christian Coulon, writing of Senegal in Gramscian terms, perceivsd an emergent effort to transcend the "soft state" with a regime whose "hegemonical apparatuses" would operate more directly on civil society rather than only through political intermediaries (clientelism) or ideological mediation (marabouts).[59] Jean Copans offers a similar portrait of Senegal in the early 1970s: "The objective of the dominant groups in the state apparatus is the control, the maintenance, the augmentation of surplus extraction. . . . The lesson of recent years is the following: the interests of the Senegalese state have triumphed over local private interests[.] . . . [T]his growing role of the state, rendered concrete through the remodeling and multiplication of institutions of control of the peasantry, leads to a new policy. The Senegalese state aims more and more at direct administrative, ideological, and political control over the dominant masses, be they urban or rural."[60]

Bayart, writing about Cameroon a decade before his celebrated discovery of the rhizome state driven by "the politics of the belly," offers a similar portrait of the "hegemonical project" of former president Ahmadou Ahidjo:

From the moment of his accession to office, he held a vision at once precise and vast of the hegemonical quest that it was his task to direct and understood at once that he needed to transcend the clientelistic state he inherited[.] . . . [T]he nomination of Ahidjo as Prime Minister inaugurated in reality a process of autonomization of the state that constituted a global and coherent response, of a Bonapartist stripe, to a structural crisis almost a century old. . . .

. . . The struggle against "under-administration" . . . had always been conceived in terms of encadrement of the population. . . . By means of the development of its structures, the territorial administration pretended, in barely concealed form, to guarantee the essence of social control and political direction of the country.[61]

Several other states of comparable ambition might be noted. Tanzania's abortive project at the time to impose a comprehensive populist socialism reflects a clear integral state thrust. The 1967 Arusha Declaration set forth the platform for state expansion; there followed a wave of measures spreading the net of government control. Through nationalization and construction of a large state enterprise sector, most of the private economy was placed in state hands. Seizure of higher-end and rental urban property at the beginning of the 1970s dispossessed much of the Asian mercantile class. Conversion of an initially voluntary villagization program by 1973 into obligatory resettlement convulsed the countryside with compulsory relocation. Agricultural cooperatives were replaced with state marketing monopolies. An ostensibly decentralizing reform in reality displaced local governments with central government agents; customary chiefs had lost their official roles earlier. The Tanzania *Daily News* observed in 1984, in evaluating the decentralization experiment, that "the bureaucrats had hijacked the power of the people to decide on their own affairs."[62] Thus one observes the unmistakable metamorphosis from the would-be democratic socialist developmentalist state of the immediate postindependence years into a close approximation of an integral state by the late 1970s.

In the extravagant scope of its pretensions, the Congo-Kinshasa regime of Mobutu Sese Seko in its first decade (1965–75) stands out.[63] The 1974 constitution transformed regime ambitions into fundamental law, enshrining "Mobutism" as state doctrine and punishing "deviationism." A single party, the Mouvement populaire de la révolution (MPR), enjoyed exclusive standing; all Congolese were enrolled in it at birth. At the peak of intoxication, in 1973, a law reduced all customary chiefs to mere local administrative agents, who were subsequently all ordered transferred to another jurisdiction. One need hardly add that such a radical measure far exceeded the implementation capacities of the Mobutist state at its integral hour.

In part, the Congo version of the integral state built on the comprehensive scope of the Leopoldian apparatus that preceded it. The first decree founding the state on 1 July 1885 declared all "vacant land" belonged to the state (that is, everything but a small area occupied by Congolese villages). Regalian rights over African labor were asserted through compulsory rubber delivery and conscription for porterage and military service. After Belgium assumed took control from Leopold II in 1908, a comprehensive web of regulations were established that enclosed the African subject: obligatory cultivation, muscular recruitment for mines and plantations. Bruce Fetter sketches an arresting portrait of what he terms totalitarian ascendancy in Belgium's zone of most concentrated dominance, the Katanga copperbelt; the colonial state and its allied hegemonical structures of mining corporations and Catholic missions exerted "full control over its human mileu," a control that extended to virtually all aspects of the life of the African workers.[64] A regime spokesman, interior ,Minister Engulu Baanga Mpolo, referenced the colonial heritage in a major summation of state ideology of the integral era: "The administrative organization of the Colony, the hierarchical military type, was a heritage of the structure established by Leopold II for the occupation of [Congo]. It was founded on the principle of unity of command, which means that, for whatever action, an official receives his orders only from one chief. . . . It was necessary to indicate to the population that authority was one and indivisible."[65]

The majestic potency of the integral state was on display through its chief, represented as a prophet. Engulu declared that "God has sent a great prophet, our prestigious Guide Mobutu . . . our Messiah. Our Church is the MPR."[66] The seductive analogy between the millennial structures of the Catholic Church and the MPR invested the party with the capacity to monopolize doctrinal space and shepherd its following along regime-designated pathways. Another encomium composed by a regime courtesan at the peak of the integral moment suggested that "the majority of Africans believe in the influence of supernatural forces and sorcerers who communicate with the ancestral spirits" and also find enchantment in European science and technology, and so the leader who embodies the two magics "is the greatest magician of all, the greatest sorcerer ever."[67] Mobutu projected a seemingly effortless ascendancy in 1973, spending no less than 150 days in travel abroad.[68] The majesty of the state found illustration in an array of gigantic projects: the Inga dam, the eighteen-hundred-kilometer-long Inga-Katanga direct current power line, huge copper projects, a large steel mill. Serving at the time as a faculty dean at the University of Lubumbashi, I vividly recollect the oft-surrealistic environment, as draconian edicts, national, local, and university, passed across one's desk. Many measures swiftly proved incapable of being put into effect, and the credibility of the integral state began to crumble around the edges by 1975. But it was not revealed to all as a shattered illusion until well into the 1980s.[69]

State expansion well beyond the bounds of the first-generation developmentalist state occurred across the continent. In a number of instances, state-building fell well short of the integral model: in Botswana and Mauritius, where democratic process and liberal economics prevailed, in Nigeria, which was too large and complex for such centralizing impulses to fully succeed, and in Kenya and Ivory Coast, which operated mostly market economies. However, a larger number of countries experienced at least moments of integral state aspirations.

Tunisia was a brief pioneer, during its socialist decade in the 1960s under planning minister Ben Salah, given free rein for a time by President Habib Bourguiba. French land holdings were nationalized in 1964, and Tunisian cultivators were herded into "cooperatives," which in reality were agencies of state control. Commercial enterprises were forced into state parastatals, or government-run cooperatives. In the words of a perennial Tunisian leader, Tahar Belkhodja, this version of integral statehood was operated by a "monstrous bureaucracy" and an "opportunist nomenklatura," which managed "an authoritarian policy with the objective of collectivization of all economic activity in the country." The ruling movement, already a single party, became omnicompetent, omnipotent, and committed to a collectivization that was beyond question.[70] By 1969, a spreading revolt in the countryside forced out Ben Salah and put an end to the integral state venture.

Egypt in the Nasser years likewise operated in an integral state mode, beginning with the nationalization of the Suez Canal in 1956. State takeover of the sprawling mercantile empire of Osman Ahmad Osman, Arab Contractors, followed in 1961. A series of increasingly radical land reforms marginalized the once-dominant landlord class, and the peasant former tenants were organized into state-run cooperatives. At its ideological peak between 1965 and 1967, the Arab Socialist Union was the privileged instrument of state expansion, mandated at that moment of intoxication "to do everything: preempt all other political forces, contain the entire citizenry, and, through its vanguard, turn it into a mobilizational instrument with a cutting edge."[71]

Ambitions faded after the humiliating defeat at the hands of Israel in 1967 and Nasser's death in 1970. The *infitah* (opening) announced by Anwar Sadat in 1974 marked the final rhetorical end of the integral state and the beginning of its dismantlement. As John Waterbury perceptively observes, "Because the initiators were not rooted in any existing set of social or economic interests, they were 'statists'; the state was their chosen instrument of change, and in their vision it was to be self-perpetuating. It would deal with class interests either by creating them or subordinating them, but in no event were these interests to challenge the primacy of the state. The state, as regulator of social and economic activity, would be handed down from generation to increasingly professionalized generation of civil servants and technocrats."[72]

Out of chronological phase, Eritrea following its 1993 independence belatedly followed the integral state path after firmly pledging to avoid the overreaching miscalculations that had so damaged many African polities. Under the leadership of distinguished Eritrean legal scholar Bereket Habte Selassie, an admirably democratic document was completed in 1996. However, rather than implement a carefully drawn constitution, ruler Isaias Aferworki restored the iron military discipline and rigid hierarchy of the Eritrean People's Liberation Movement (EPLF), rebaptized the Popular Front for Democracy and Justice, sweeping populace and economy under the total control of the state.[73] The sheer reach of the state finds measure in its remarkable capacity to enforce tax payment by the large diaspora.

The most bizarre specimen of the integral state genus was surely the Libyan Arab Popular and Socialist Jamahiriyya created by Muammar Qadhafy after his power seizure in 1969.[74] In the Green Book launching his Third Universal Theory in 1975, Qadhafy announced the dissolution of the state and even his title as ruler in favor of basic people's committees and congresses, claiming to incarnate the direct democracy through which the stateless polity would be governed. Relying on Qadhafy's idiosyncratic interpretation of Islam as legitimating doctrine, the *jamahiriyya* eviscerated the existing bureaucracy. The Libyan National Oil Company progressively expanded its control over oil, virtually the sole productive sector; private retail was ended by 1979, and the government controlled what limited agricultural marketing there was. By a curious inversion, the ostensibly dissolved existing state was reborn as an integral, personalized, and highly centralized mechanism of surveillance and control, dominated by the personal rule of Qadhafy. The *jamahiriyya* employed 80% of Libyan workers, confiscated all housing beyond the family residence in 1977, and assumed responsibility for providing the citizenry through its mechanisms the basic necessities of food, housing, and clothing.[75] The all-encompassing centralized personal autocracy of Qadhafy, however pervasive its hold, utterly failed to institutionalize its structures, beginning with its security apparatus core. When the ruler was overthrown in 2011, state structures dissolved into congeries of armed militia linked to regional or clan factions.

Other examples might be cited. Algeria in the Houari Boumedienne years (1965–78) is an evident case. Rulers of even the weakest states, such as Chad, were tempted by the integral model. In the mid-1970s, inspired by the apparent success of the Mobutu regime, François Tombalbaye embarked upon a demented "cultural revolution," which featured, among other excesses, the imposition of initiation rituals for all civil servants into the Yondo cult of the ruler's Sara ethnic community.[76] The magnetic appeal of the idea of the integral state in its momentum of ascendancy is clear.[77]

Several contextual factors operated in its favor. By the late 1960s, a mood of disappointment in the rate of economic progress took hold. Although in retrospect growth statistics appear respectable, achievements fell well short of the transformative aspirations of independence. The appeal of dependency theory to the intellectual elite and ruling circles went hand in hand with a conviction that the invitation to foreign investment most countries issued after independence fell on deaf ears. The solution was to turn inward toward self-reliance and to enlarge the capacity of the state to assume more extended responsibility.

New ideological currents supplied the doctrinal stimulus for state expansion. The more circumscribed theories of "African socialism" in vogue in the first independence years gave way to far more radical versions of socialist orientation. In their more extended form, these regime doctrines drew on orthodox Marxism-Leninism, widely known as Afromarxism in its domesticated form. At the peak in the early 1980s, there were eight regimes that officially embraced Marxism-Leninism as state doctrine. Three—Angola, Mozambique, and (ambiguously) Sao Tome and Principe—issued from the collapse of the Portuguese colonial regime in 1974. Many of these liberation movement leaders had spent formative years in close contact with underground opposition milieux in Portugal, where communist currents were strong; the Soviet Union provided succor for armed struggle refused by Western powers. The other five were regimes originating in military seizure of power: Ethiopia, Somalia, Madagascar, Benin, and Congo-Brazzaville. None of the rulers concerned had any known previous record of Marxist-Leninist conviction; however, they faced the challenge of co-opting an intelligentsia for whom this ideological discourse was common currency.[78] The doctrine of the Leninist state fashioned by the Soviet rulers provided a convenient vessel for the erection of a strong, centralized regime in which exclusive power vested in the ruler and an allied "vanguard." The ideology also offered a formula for building on the already dominant notion of a single party, which further reinforced the tendency to force all corporatist organization within the party framework and to force them to operate according to the norms of "democratic centralism." The Soviet model of the Leninist state also validated the expansion and ideological subordination of the internal security apparatus and the erection of a nomenklatura as ruling caste.[79]

We have lingered over the integral state as modal form, both because of its extraordinary nature and its central role in precipitating the state crisis of the 1980s. The integral state was not only unsustainable but had legacy costs that took years to unwind. The change of mood by 1979 was clear; a consensus of developmental failure, made official by a 1979 OAU summit declaration, had crystallized. African external debt, still negligible in 1970, had reached unbearable proportions. The stage was set for a harsh external critique of the performance of the African state, given official standing by the World Bank's 1981 Berg Report.[80] At the same time, increasingly forceful external voices demanded economic reform that entailed a fundamental reworking of the state itself. Meanwhile, in the industrialized nations outside the "camp of socialism," the global model of the normative state was mutating. The years of stagnation in European and North American advanced economies in the 1970s seriously tarnished the democratic welfare state. Conservative politicians joined a new breed of neoclassical economists to assault the doctrinal foundations of the welfare state: Keynesian economics, social democracy, and liberalism as understood in the 1960s. The private market was enshrined as supreme value; the antistate animus pervading the discourse of singularly influential conservative leaders such as Ronald Reagan and Margaret Thatcher shaped public perspectives, especially in the United States and United Kingdom, and penetrated the official mind. In discourse and practice, market fundamentalism as framed by Reagan and Thatcher and as theoretically elaborated by neoconservative economists was more strongly embraced in the United States and Britain than in continental Europe, where a new infusion of liberal doctrines reshaped but did not erase the normative hold of a social market economy. By the early 1990s, the revised liberal conventional wisdom that took shape during the 1980s had hardened into what became known as neoliberalism, a label at first mainly applied by critics of what Nicolas van de Walle terms a new liberal orthodoxy.[81] The label "Washington Consensus" emerged to characterize the reform agenda expected of African countries that sought international financial institution and donor community aid. Visions of an integral state vanished in the face of World Bank and IMF demands for SAPs, which called for a reduced, remodeled government and enlarged private markets.

New Model: A Liberalized State

As the African crisis deepened in the 1980s at the same time that the available alternatives to accepting the conditions proposed by the World Bank and IMF shrank, leading over time to a revised dominant model for the African state, a liberalized polity. The more radical regimes at first hoped that Soviet camp aid might provide an alternative to the state dismantling otherwise required. However, the "new thinking" associated with Mikhail Gorbachev, who replaced a succession of geriatric rulers in 1985, did not include competing with the international financial institutions in setting the rules for reform.

At first, the standard formula aimed at eliminating imbalances of foreign trade and domestic budgets and enlarging the space for a private economy. In 1979, Senegal received the first IMF loan based conditionally on its effecting certain policy changes; over the following crisis decade nearly all African states faced the necessity of accepting policy-based lending. The scope of the conditions expanded over time; by the time that structural adjustment became known as the Washington Consensus, the standard formula included fiscal discipline, elimination of subsidies, reduction in the public bureaucracy, an end to exchange controls, encouragement of foreign and domestic private investment, privatization of the sprawling parastatal sector, deregulation, and reinforced property rights.[82]

African states found the governance model of the integral era impossible to defend. Public employment had soared, both in the government bureaucracies and state-owned enterprises. Partly this reflected a genuine expansion of social services, particularly the educational system, but much was simply a response to huge pressures for employment; to cite but one example, in Ghana the Cocoa Marketing Board payroll had doubled to 100,000 over the decade stretching from the mid-60s to the mid-70s, but the amount of cocoa being exported had dropped from a 1965 peak of 557,000 tons to 320,000 in 1977.[83] In a number of countries, university graduates were guaranteed government employment; in the mid-70s when I was teaching in Congo-Kinshasa, this was the only career path sought by university graduates. Egypt maintained such a guarantee into the new century, offering employment utterly devalued by nominal pay and meaningless work.

In many countries by the 1970s, governments met budget deficits by inflating the currency, which in turn undermined its exchange value. The standard response of exchange controls invariably failed, becoming an engine of corruption as well as black markets. Countries in the French-managed Communauté financière d'Afrique (CFA) franc zone were shielded from unconvertible currencies and high inflation but often responded to budget shortfall by delaying payments to the public service. In other polities, high inflation savaged the real earnings of civil servants, driving many into survival pursuits and corroding the competence of the bureaucracy. The parastatal sector was enormous; again to cite a single example, Kenya—ostensibly a capitalist state— had accumulated 150 state-owned enterprises and had large shares in 200 more.[84] Across the continent only a handful of parastatals were profitable; the Egyptian Suez Canal Company was an exceptional case of continuous competent management and positive balance sheets. More characteristic was the uneven performance of Algerian scandal-ridden hydrocarbon parastatal SONATRACH, Africa's largest enterprise with a 2010 income of $47 billion.[85]

The response to African pleas for indulgence and self-directed reform, embodied in the 1981 Lagos Plan of Action prepared by the OAU and UN Economic Commission for Africa (UNECA), from the Washington Consensus was stern: there was no alternative to structural adjustment and the impaired sovereignty it implied. Though few denied the need for some reform, many were skeptical of the imposed reforms. Publics at large at first were intensely hostile. Regimes tended to respond by accepting the accords but then only selectively and partially applying the terms. Over the course of the 1980s, economic impasse deepened. African states blamed SAPs; the donor community responded that they had not been fully implemented.[86] But both sides had evolved in their thinking. On the international financial institution side, there was a recognition that the difficulties were far more intractable than had been imagined at the outset of structural adjustment. A few simple prescriptions such as getting prices right and achieving short-term stabilization fell far short of what was required. A less dogmatic approach was needed, one that acknowledged a difficult external environment for African economies and the particularities of the sociopolitical environment. Greater flexibility and more attention to negative social impacts on key groups was necessary. But beyond these changes in perspective, a broader conclusion emerged. The venal and autocratic nature of most extant regimes was an insuperable obstacle to success. Accountability and transparency were indispensable components of recovery. Political as well as economic liberalization was indispensable. Thus democratization came to be seen as critical therapy for ailing African states. By 1989, the concept of "governance" had crept into official discourse, defined by the World Bank as including "a pluralistic institutional structure, a determination to respect the rule of law, and vigorous protection of freedom of the press and human rights."[87] By 1990, major Western donors were expressign a shared commitment to promoting democratization in their assistance programs.

This conceptual evolution coincided with and was reinforced by a wave of popular protest against the patrimonial autocracies ruling most states, beginning with the October 1988 street riots in Algeria that unhinged the regime and forced abandonment of the FLN political monopoly. In Benin another resonating drama opened in late 1989; the urban street in effect seized power, snatching sovereignty from the incumbent regime through the national conference mechanism. Elsewhere most regimes were compelled by the confluence of internal and external pressures to concede political opening, competitive elections, and in most cases new or largely revised liberal constitutions.

These developments produced a moment of consensus among both internal and external actors. The form of state resulting from the decay of the ntegral model was neither sustainable nor desirable. The political aspects of the ascendant global normative state won broad acceptance, whatever the uncertainties about their realization. Many also conceded the necessity of a slimmed but more effective state: "moins d'état, mieux d'état," in the oft-cited slogan of former Senegalese president Abdou Diouf. Some elements of the state apparatus shared much of the economic premises of the neoliberal state, especially top cadres in central banks and finance ministries, many of whom had worked for a time in international financial institutions. Although elements of the intelligentsia remained suspicious of the new orthodoxies, the discrediting of socialist orientation that accompanied the implosion of the Soviet Union in 1991 denied them a ready ideological counter to dominant prescriptions. As in former Soviet lands, "really existing socialism" yielded a daily, lived experience bearing no relation to the ideological visions.

In addition, the thesis of autocracy as necessary shortcut to progress also fell into disrepute; the abysmal performance of the African version of patrimonial autocracy bore telling witness to the shortcomings of authoritarianism.

Democratization was more than a distant ideal; political liberalization was crucial remedy for state decline. Almost overnight, at the beginning of the 1990s, at least ostensible democratic transitions swept the continent. The democratic wave began to recede a few years later, and many liberalized experiments lapsed into semidemocracy (or semiauthoritarianism); however, the constitutional democratic regime remained at least nominally the continental norm. In the international realm, the formal appearance of democratic institutions became the coin of respectability.

The Liberal Polity as Normative State

The dominant state model after the crisis decade thus became the liberal democratic state based on a market economy. Neoliberal economic doctrines remained contested, but the political aspects of the model were much less debated. Indeed, the African commitment to the electoral component of the normative state became codified in the charter of pan-African institutions; the African Union (AU) and its regional counterparts deny recognition and participation to those seizing power by extraconstitutional means. Their active engagement in the political impasses created by such acts in Kenya (2007), Comoros (2008), Niger and Madagascar (2009), and Ivory Coast (2010) attest to this commitment.

In the external side, there was further evolution in the content of the Washington Consensus. Its stipulations became more flexible and reflected greater sensitivity to the political requirements of effective economic reform. A 2008 World Bank report characterizes the doctrine as diagnostic rather than prescriptive; its core elements are described as achieving "reasonably good" governance, maintaining macroeconomic stability, stimulating saving and investment, and providing market-oriented incentives.[88] Transparency and accountability are also mentioned as essential traits of effective governance.

The remaking of the African polity along the contours of the normative liberal state required wrenching adjustments. Credible commitments to the protection of property rights were indispensable but had received short shrift from the integral state. Anne Pitcher found that thirty-eight of the forty-eight current sub-Saharan constitutions, nearly all revised or rewritten after 1990, contained important new provisions offering property guarantees.[89] The terms of engagement with the globalizing economy also required crucial institutional changes to facilitate investment. Indigenous capital, of slender consequence during the first developmental state phase and deeply suspect under the integral state, now merited nurture. Privatization of at least the potentially viable portion of the sprawling parastatal sector was a necessity but strewn with hazards: clientelistic allocation of assets to political cronies, inappropriate pricing, disgruntled state employees facing layoff.[90]

The wide range of outcomes in the third cycle of African state evolution has been underlined in chapter 1. The state crisis years left a number of countries with badly depleted capacities for effectively managing liberalization. Chad, Central African Republic, and Liberia are cases in point. Rentier states with high oil revenues (Angola, Nigeria, Algeria, Libya) had little incentive to vigorously pursue liberalization. A few (Guinea, Guinea-Bissau) were vulnerable to penetration by criminal narcotics combines. Some were so permeated by predatory and neopatrimonial practices by the political class that nominal liberalizing commitment was overwhelmed by everyday practice. A 2005 UN Development Program (UNDP) report on Arab country governance acidly characterized the Arab state as a black hole "which converts its surrounding social environment into a setting in which nothing moves and from which nothing escapes," a colorful judgment perhaps a shade too harsh.[91] On the other hand, Pitcher makes a compelling case that Mozambique managed its transition from Afromarxism to the liberal state with impressive skill. The varying political trajectories in the neoliberal era are examined in more detail in chapter 6.

New economic ideological currents may well emerge from the procrustean bed of populism, following the deep 2008–10 global crisis that originated in the heartland of neoliberalism, the Anglo-American world. British prime minister Gordon Brown announced the death of the Washington Consensus in the April 2009 G20 summit. The requiem may be premature, but the theses of market fundamentalism were damaged. The major Chinese engagement with Africa is another new factor challenging the supremacy of the liberal democratic state as normative model. Another moment of transition in state forms may emerge.

Conceptual Debates

Having sketched my own perspectives on conceptualization of the state and its evolving normative models, I now turn to exploration of the theoretical debates surrounding the postcolonial state. Recently these have centered above all on variants on the neopatrimonial theme. A second main focus concerns the issues surrounding state decline, weakness, and failure. These are central themes in the chapters that follow. However, the first accounts of the postcolonial state focused on its most visible Africanized institution, the political party; bureaucracies still had many Europeans in key posts, and rulers spoke through the parties they led.

Party and State

At the hour of independence, leading Africanists perceived African destiny as bound up in parties, as the sole agency that could lead nation-building, "the primary preoccupation of the leadership of new states" as well as of analysts.[92] But the metamorphosis of political parties from organizational weapon in mobilizing social energies in anticolonial action to instrument of domination on behalf of the independence leadership fundamentally altered their relationship with state and society. The absorption of the dominant parties into the fabric of rule produced party-states in which a rapidly African-izing bureaucracy and political machinery at the service of the ruler tended to fuse. The sharp distinction drawn in initial postcolonial analysis between "revolutionary-centralizing" and "pragmatic patron" parties lost much of its meaning. The rhetorical engagement with "revolutionary transformation" and pan-Africanism of the once-mass parties lost much of its luster, particularly when some of its most compelling spokesmen, such as Kwame Nkrumah, Ben Bella, and Modibo Keita, were unseated by military coups. Tanzania is a partial exception; President Julius Nyerere even left office for several months after independence to devote himself entirely to the building of his party (and did so again in 1985), and its ideological discourse plunged deep and unusually durable roots. More broadly, the radical mobilizing movement heritage of the decolonization moment migrated to the liberation movements of the Portuguese territories and southern Africa, where its revolutionary discourse continued to inspire.[93]

Neopatrimonialism

But the bridge between party-centered analysis and neopatrimonial concepts lay in the role parties came to play as channels of access to state favor: they were essentially political machines of the Chicago type. "The machine," Aristide Zolberg wrote four decades ago, "maintains solidarity among its members by appealing to their self-interest, while allowing for the play of factions."[94] Managing the expectations generated by the promises of decolonization was an immediate challenge for the new states. During much of the 1960s, relatively favorable fiscal conditions and new external aid flows adding to the continuing assistance from the withdrawing powers did permit a substantial expansion in social infrastructure. However, the individual pressures for advancement opportunities weighed heavily; party channels for such requests offered a less rule-bound avenue than the bureaucracy. Employment and contracts were key currency in these linkages; those who commanded local influence or had a clientele to offer enjoyed some advantage.

Rulers of necessity wanted to centralize control over the more important favors at the disposition of the state. In this way, a network of allies in key institutional sectors at the center and distributed through the countryside might be established, rooted in reciprocal advantage. These networks were in constant flux; the ruler needed to create a sense of insecurity in the would-be allies about their relationship. Resources never sufficed to satisfy all claimants. Invariably there were an array of disgruntled influentials pressing for entry or recently ousted from favor. In the 1980s, when in many countries parties were largely eclipsed by "big man" rule, the concept of neopatrimonialism achieved wide currency as the defining property of the African state.[95]

Michael Bratton and Nicolas van de Walle well capture the essence of the neopatriomonial state: "Relationships of loyalty and dependence pervade a formal political and administrative system, and officials occupy their positions less to perform public service, their ostensible purpose, than to acquire personal wealth and status. Although state functionaries receive an official salary, they also enjoy access to various forms of illicit rents, prebends, and petty corruption, which constitute a sometimes important entitlement of office. The chief executive and his inner circle undermine the effectiveness of the nominally modern state administration by using it for patronage purposes and clientelist practices in order to maintain the political order."[96]

The immensely influential and complex portrait of the African state sketched by Jean-François Bayart, although avoiding the neopatrimonial terminology, adds a compelling metaphor in its characterization of the polity as a "rhizome state," through which networks of reciprocity based on family, ethnicity, locality, religion, or other affinity operate both vertically and horizontally to connect the formal institutions and their presidential summit with the social base. Resource leakage from the state is an essential dimension. Official monopolies of formal media notwithstanding, the flow of social communication along these channels is intense.[97]

Although the the notion of state as mere shell for neopatrimonial politics has force, especially in relation to the 1970s and 1980s, it goes too far in erasing the state's formal structures. The caveat of Médard is pertinent here: "In neo-patrimonial societies, although the state is a façade compared to what it pretends to be, it is not only façade, for it is able to extract and distribute resources. For legitimation it refers to public norms and universal ideologies."[98] Alongside neopatrimonial practice there continued to exist segments of the state that operated according to formal administrative norms that are the very heart of the state. Ministries of finance and central banks in particular not only tended to concentrate many of the ablest talents within the bureaucracy but also were subject to the external scrutiny of international financial institutions and the external donor community. Nicolas van de Walle in his seminal critique of African state economic performance notes that "the central bank and key economic ministries can be run with great efficiency even as social ministries are allowed to fall prey to extensive patronage."[99] The massive monograph on the Bank of Uganda by Ugandan historian Phares Mutibwa refutes any supposition that this central bank functioned only by neopatrimonial logic.[100] The debt crisis overwhelming Africa by the late 1970s could never have occurred had external lenders believed that the polity was incapable of rational action, even if widespread venality was well understood.

The top echelon of bureaucrats often had absorbed the culture of administrative probity in the centers of advanced training in Africa or abroad; the portrait by David Leonard of a number of senior Kenyan public servants offers compelling evidence of bureaucratic competence and dedication.[101] Thus the permeation of state operation by clientelism and corruption did not always expunge alternative norms, even if many yielded at times to pressures from above, gave priority to their own kin obligations, or acted on immediate incentives to monetize their office. Higher education was another domain where professional norms and the distinctive culture of the university in many instances persisted in the face of a demoralizing environment, resulting in deteriorating material conditions for the professoriate and political pressure to alter academic outcomes.[102] The complexity of legal process likewise renders the judiciary a sphere in which a premise of neopatrimonialism is inadequate. The judiciary is subject to political intervention and to corruption; the Kenyan aphorism "Why pay a lawyer when you can buy a judge" expresses the widespread lack of public confidence in the integrity of the judiciary. Yet legal norms have stubborn resilience in a sometimes hostile environment; Jennifer Widner in her moving biography of Tanzanian jurist Francis Nyalali provides a compelling example.[103] Peter VonDoepp and Tamir Mustafa offer additional evidence of the partial autonomy of judiciaries and their dedication to legal norms.[104]

The internal security organs are another sphere where efficient operation persists even in states otherwise in disarray. Michael Schatzberg in his monograph on Mobutu's Congo quotes the judgment of sometime regime potentate Nguza Karl-i-Bond: "If there is one thing working very well in [Congo] it is the security police." Schatzberg validates this assertion; the security agency, he concludes, effectively gathers and relates information, as well as intimidates the populace. "In performing its tasks so well, it stands out as a beacon of efficiency in a sea of disorganization and mismanagement."[105] Yet neopatrimonial logic intrudes as well; a competent security agency was a danger as well as an asset. Its control was assured by leadership bound to Mobutu by ethnic ties, and its personnel were disproportionately recruited from his region. The Congo-Kinshasa case illustrates a general phenomenon.

There were other ways in which neopatrimonial realities coexisted with public performance of state norms. Successive regimes compulsively drafted new constitutions to conform to universal standards. National elections regularly were scheduled since 1990 in almost all polities; Swaziland and Libya were rare exceptions. Even in the authoritarian era, competition within the ruling party was sometimes permitted. In countries such as Kenya, Tanzania, Zambia, Malawi, Congo-Kinshasa, Sierra Leone, and Ivory Coast, competing candidates could stand under the banner of the single party in individual constituencies; invariably, a large proportion of incumbents were ousted.[106] Considerable resources were invested in these rites of legitimation; citizen participation was often astonishingly high for presidential balloting that was merely plebiscitary in nature. External presentability weighed on African states, especially by the 1980s as the continent labored under an increasingly negative external image. All the more necessary were regular performances of stateness through enactment of the rituals universally associated with the contemporary liberal polity.

The Hybrid State

The postcolonial state was thus a hybrid creature, and its hybridity took three forms. First, combined within its frame were residues of the colonial state joined to practices of ruling group management of power that drew on customary repertoires. Schatzberg perceptively sketches the cultural dimension of rulership in what he terms the "moral matrix" of state legitimacy: the ruler was a father figure who had parental obligations to nurture and discipline, and power was like "eating"—the president functioned as consumer-in-chief but the populace and bureaucracy were entitled to feeding.[107]

In a second form of hybridization, neopatrimonial practice permeated the political realm, engaging in a predatory extraction of public resources and severely compromising state capacity to function according to normative state precepts. Yet segments of the state do operate following the dictates of Weberian statecraft. The state as public spectacle does perform many of the rites of a civic collectivity, exhibiting a partially and sporadically operative legal order, but parallel structures of reward and punishment function in purely arbitrary fashion.

Though differently inflected forms of neopatrimonialism hybridized with varying degrees of stateness, the proportions varied across time and space. Some time elapsed after independence before new practices of power management took shape; thus monographs from the 1960s do not employ the patrimonial concept. In cases such as Kenya or Ivory Coast, neopatrimonialism became extensive only in the 1980s; until then the common perception of effective governance and impressive developmental performance was well grounded. In Senegal, the pattern was visible earlier, emerging in the tradition of clan politics, but neopatrimonialism never entirely encroached on the state domain. In long-stable polities such as Tanzania, the neopatrimonial dimension was likewise subdued. In some other cases—by the 1980s, in both Congos, Sierra Leone, Central African Republic, for example—neopatrimonialism all but swallowed the state. In a few well-governed polities—Botswana, Cape Verde, Mauritius—neopatrimonialism was virtually absent and can all but be set aside as analytical instrument.

The third version of the hybrid state privileges the blend of democratic norms ostensibly embraced by the state and the reality of a range of authoritarian practices that limit their scope. The emergence by the mid-1990s of the notion of "semidemocracy" or "semiauthoritarianism" as common descriptors reflects this emerging pattern and by 2010 could be said to describe political practice in a majority of African states. Aili Mari Tripp makes deft use of this version of the hybrid state concept to frame her analysis of the Museveni regime.[108]

Even though in most countries a clearly dominant party exists, the opportunity for open electoral competition significantly alters the rules of the game. Staffan Lindberg persuasively argues that repeated competitive elections "foster liberalization and have a self-reinforcing power" and "facilitate the institutional deepening of actual civil liberties," even with a dominant party.[109] Multiparty regimes also enhance the importance of representative institutions. In a comparative study of African legislatures, Joel Barkan shows that overall they are "more powerful and autonomous today than at any time since independence," even though only about a dozen have become major players and effective centers of countervailing power to the executive.[110]

State Weakness

A somewhat different approach to grasping developmental disappointments insists on the weakness of the state. With the dissolution of the Somali state in 1991 and a wave of civil wars that all ravaged states in Liberia, Sierra Leone, Congo-Kinshasa, and Angola, the possibility of state collapse entered the register of outcomes, and the notion of "state failure" entered analytical vocabulary. Even if only a few states collapsed, few would dispute that many if not most African states remain in weakened condition. There are a number of clear exceptions, especially on the northern and southern edges of the continent: the Mediterranean tier of Arab states, South Africa, Namibia, Botswana. Most would view Rwanda and Eritrea as strong states. But varying degrees of weakness characterize most others, a product of severely limited domestic revenue sources and the corrosive legacy of patrimonial autocracy.

Some influential works trace governmental weakness to the colonial state. Though I offer a contrary view in my African colonial state volume, there is some merit in the arguments advanced. Frederick Cooper suggests the contemporary state is best understood as a gatekeeper, whose colonial predecessors had "weak instruments for entering into the social and cultural realm over which they presided, but stood astride the intersection of the colonial territory and the outside world." The postcolonial successor lacked the ability of the colonial state to summon force from the metropole if needed (with the exception of a handful of French intimates in the Françafrique zone); its operation depended on "collecting and distributing resources from the gate itself," notably export-import taxes and foreign aid.[111] The gatekeeper metaphor resembles Robert Jackson's argument that the African state is primarily constituted by its external sovereignty, kept afloat by international recognition rather than the capacity to govern its territory.[112] Jeffrey Herbst takes the weak state argument further, claiming that it began with a colonial apparatus of limited ambitions, a thin presence on the ground, and slender fiscal capacities. Beyond these legacy limitations, the postcolonial successor faced difficult political geographies and relatively dispersed populations, making full administrative occupation of the terrain difficult. Further, the state-building impetus so central to European states, wars, and external security threats was largely absent.[113] The suggestion that more frequent and violent interstate conflict in Africa would have stimulated more effective states in the face of the other factors corroding African states is open to doubt, and I differ with Herbst on the weakness of the colonial state; his other arguments, however, are persuasive.

Another major theme in arguments propounding state weakness is a perceived incapacity to penetrate and control rural society. Goran Hyden advances the most comprehensive explanation in suggesting that an "uncaptured peasantry" lay at the heart of developmental failures. Neither state nor market had incorporated rural producers in a nationally oriented nexus of exchange. The "economy of affection" based on the social reciprocities of the local community insulated the peasantry from the penetrative projects of the state. Whether all rural populations so effectively eluded the embrace of the state as those of Tanzania on which the theory was erected might be debated. But undoubtedly the process of state decline in most areas by the 1980s weakened the governmental hold on the countryside and drove more of the production into an informal economy.[114]

A related avenue to grasping state limits and limitations is through focus on societal linkages. The autonomy imperative can never be fully realized; the state is necessarily a part of society, incorporates its cleavages, and is partly shaped by it. In the words of Joel Migdal, Atul Kohli, and Vivienne Shue, "States may help mold, but are also continuously molded by society." A state's effectiveness in turn is a function of the varied forms in which state-society relations are interwoven.[115] Catherine Boone ably demonstrates the varying capacities of rural areas to resist the hegemonic and extractive drives of the state apparatus depending on the strength of local notables and communal structures.[116]

A parallel argument points to the relative weakness or absence of an African capitalist class necessary both for state and market. As Richard Sandbrook argues, "Increasing state power and capitalist expansion have long been intimately linked."[117] The need for property protection and nationally integrated markets ties bourgeois interests to state construction. But the emergence of an African capitalist class was blocked in colonial times by imperial economic interests, European settlers, and immigrant mercantiles from South Asia and the Mediterranean. Even when this blockage eroded after independence, social mobility for the first postcolonial generation was sought through public sector employment. The state itself became the primary instrument of African class formation; the initial ascendant category was an essentially bureaucratic bourgeoisie. The road to wealth was through political power or access to state favor.

Though in a few countries (notably Kenya, Ivory Coast, and Nigeria) post-independence state ideologies permitted the growth of African capitalism, the more common pattern was hostility to the emergence of an African business class. The long dalliance with socialist orientation in many countries generated a perception that the African private bourgeoisie was a political threat. Preventing its emergence proved well within the capabilities of many states, and at the same time a parasitic neopatrimonial accumulation through diversion of public resources or use of state power to acquire private property achieved growing momentum. In the pungent phrase of John Iliffe, "African governments have shown that they can prevent capitalism; they have not yet shown that they can replace it with anything else that will release their people's energies."[118] However, a substantial but often crony African capitalist class has emerged in recent years. Much of it owes its prosperity to privileged access to state favor: contracts, rigged sales of former parastatals, credit from state-owned or influenced banks.

In a carefully constructed quantitative analysis, Pierre Englebert locates African state decline in a deep deficit of legitimacy. This originates in the exogenous origins of the state and is intensified by poor economic performance. Although he recognizes a large range of variation in developmental outcome, his analysis shows a strong correlation between positive economic management and legitimacy. What might be debated is whether the legitimacy deficit was a causal factor or mainly a consequence of developmental failings.[119]

For a large part of the African intelligentsia, state weakness is indissolubly related to external imposition of SAPs. Its sovereignty diluted by international conditionalities tied to financial advances, the state is stripped of its legitimacy-building capacities. In the eloquent phrasing of Achille Mbembe, "Almost everywhere, the state has lost much of that capacity to regulate and arbitrate that enabled it to construct its legitimacy. It no longer has the financial means, administrative power, and, in general, the sorts of 'goods' that would have enabled it to resolve politically the conflicts that have erupted in the public domain and led, almost universally, to violence previously containable within more or less tolerable limits."[120]

Beyond dispute is the political liability, especially in the urban sectors, of the elimination of price subsidies for basic commodities such as fuel and grain and enforced reductions in government payrolls. Mbembe's observation makes clear why economic reform programs were often reluctantly, half-heartedly, and incompletely adopted by a number of African states. Left unanswered is the matter of how to resolve the fiscal crisis of the state, which is what compelled African states to reluctantly appeal to international financial institutions in the first place. Monetary ruin was the likely alternative for most in the

1980s. A less apocalyptic reading would concede that a number of states found ways to navigate structural adjustment, with beneficial results for government capacity and effectiveness in recent years.[121]

Near the outer limits of state weakness and neopatrimonial analysis lies the thesis of Patrick Chabal and Jean-Pascal Daloz, reducing the political process to the instrumentalization of violence and disorder.[122] In this reading, states are ineffectual not only because of institutional deficiencies but also above all because political elites are mere predatory agents, employing the façade of a government to control and divert resource flows. Deeply personal political relations lie at the heart of seeming formal structures, producing an informalization of governmental action. With disorder a prime resource, political agents have little incentive to nurture institutionalization. Though their volume contains much penetrating observation and reasonably describes Congo-Kinshasa of the 1990s or Nigeria under Sani Abacha from 1994 to 1998, its dismissal of the hybridity of most states goes too far, as I have suggested. Were their analysis as broadly applicable to sub-Saharan Africa as they claim, meaningful development would be unattainable. Yet in the last two decades improved state performance in a number of polities suggests a less pessimistic perspective.

At its farthest extreme—well illustrated by Sierra Leone and Liberia in the 1990s—is what William Reno terms a shadow state. The ruler seeks direct personal control over the rents generated by key productive activity, especially minerals such as diamonds, that normally fund state activity. In return, he endeavors to redeploy these resources exclusively through neopatrimonial channels. To preempt "free riders" who might benefit from state outlays without providing personal loyalty and deference in return, shadow state rulers have an incentive to undermine if not destroy the formal channels of government action. The Reno model, originally based on his compelling exegisis of the political economy of the informalized Sierra Leone diamond trade, helps trace the ultimate logic of unbridled prebendalism, though neopatrimonialism in most instances stops short of the shadow state model.[123]

State Failure

Africa since the 1990s offers several examples of outright state collapse and failure, at least for a time (Somalia, Sierra Leone, Liberia, Congo-Kinshasa, Comoros, and arguably Uganda and Chad earlier). In these instances, a regime able to assert authority across most of the territory ceases to function. What remains of a center no longer controls regional agents. Violence and security are privatized, with warlords emerging controlling local militias, in effect operating protection rackets. Exportable high value resources come under the control of mafia networks; external trade enters the informal sector. A residual state apparatus lacks resources and capacity to maintain public services, which survive if at all on de facto privatization.[124]

Even failed states are capable of revival. Of the examples listed, only Somalia remained in totally collapsed status for more than a decade. Partly this revivalism reflects the preservative instincts of the international community; in 2010 no less than one hundred thousand UN troops served in various African peacekeeping missions. Unlike a bankrupt corporation, whose assets are subject to liquidation, the failed state continues to exist in international law. The international system abhors a vacuum, particularly in the age of terrorism; thus active external nurture soon sets in to restore some form of state. In Liberia, Sierra Leone, Congo-Kinshasa, and Burundi sustained external diplomacy, backed by UN peacekeeping forces, played an indispensable role in restoring a government with generally acknowledged legitimacy. In Comoros, a direct AU military intervention in 2008 restored a more feeble regime threatened by the attempted secession of one of its three main islands.[125]

REGIME AND RULER

Finally, the search for conceptual capture of the African state must grapple with its instability. Frequent power seizures by the security forces or fragments within them, as well as the periodic transitions to restored constitutional order, meant a regular reordering of the basic rules of the game, geographic balances, and dominant coalitions: in other words, regime change. Although the state remained, its nature might alter, even fundamentally. The logic of reproduction of the state as an enduring entity might well conflict with the exigencies of regime survival. Practices that might enhance a given regime—ambitious nationalizations, the reshaping of regional balances, heavy borrowing, patronage practices—could undermine the state over time. Perforce the hunt for the state must accommodate the subsidiary notion of regime.

Nor is acknowledgment of a regime concept sufficient. The potent trend to personalize authority that set in soon after independence introduced yet another dimension: the ruler's imperative. The annals of personal rule make even clearer the possible, even likely, contradiction between reason of state and the calculus of a president. Neopatrimonialism precisely embodies this conflict: the diversion of public resources to lubrication of prebendal networks directly subtracts from the material capacity of the state to meet its own operative imperatives. The powerful disposition of incumbents—undimmed by the democratic openings of the 1990s—to seek to remain in office indefinitely, known as the Robert Mugabe syndrome, was in the long run almost always destructive of the reproductive health of the state.

Regimes

I understand "regime" to refer to a given set of rules of the game that structure political authority and process and define the claim to legitimacy.[126] When political systems remain stable over extended periods, the difference between state and regime dissolves. But in Africa, regime change began almost immediately after independence, and so the change in ground rules, the configuration of power, and the ideological claims legitimating its exercise are crucial. Only in Botswana, Mauritius, Swaziland, and arguably Morocco has regime type been permanent throughout the postcolonial era.

Until 1990, successions of heads of state via established constitutional process were rare: examples include Somalia in 1967, Botswana in 1980, Mauritius in 1982, and Senegal in 1980. (Apartheid South Africa did have successions, but its exclusionary racial order denying participation to the African 85% of the population places it outside the roster of decolonized African states.) In a couple of instances, military regimes permitted a transition to democratically elected regimes (Ghana in 1969 and 1979, Nigeria in 1979, Benin in 1964 and 1972, Burkina Faso in 1970 and 1977) or were compelled by popular uprisings to do so (Sudan in 1965 and 1985), but these successions were in all cases very short lived. Thus a ruler was most frequently displaced through military intervention, inevitably resulting in a change of regime, as those seizing power normally changed the rules of the game in several respects. Often new constitutions were introduced, validated by plebiscites that gave the appearance of legitimacy. Ideological discourse was recast, which permitted the new regime to discred the old one and to issue promises of a new dawn for a disillusioned citizenry. The informal structures of power altered because a new ruler constructed a clientele network whose personal loyalty was rewarded with high office or other governmental favor. When new rulers had different regional provenance, ethnic balances shifted. Regime change thus frequently reordered the political landscape.

Partly for this reason, regimes gave first priority to their own preservation and reproduction. The calculated pursuit of regime self-perpetuation could well conflict with reason of state. The need for resources for neopatrimonial distribution deprived the state of the means to fulfill its normal functions. The urgent quest for entry legitimacy on the part of a new regime of illicit origin gives it incentive to expose, even magnify, the nefarious practices and corrupt habits of the ousted leaders and to claim that a new order is being created; with repetition, the catalogue of denunciation corrodes the credibility of the state itself. Armed forces, before 1990 by far the most frequent launching pads for power seizure, required restructuring to ensure the personal loyalty of inner command circles. Regimes thus normally apply what Cynthia Enloe terms an ethnic security map; regions with communal attachments to the ruler are favored recruitment grounds, while those perceived as opposition strongholds are carefully scrutinized, especially individuals in those areas in the senior officer ranks.[127] The inner security core is likely to have more immediate kinship ties to or related personal affinity with the ruler. The visible application of an ethnic security map carries costs to the morale and competence of the armed forces and breeds disaffection in disfavored regions. Thus regime preservation tactics may over time undermine long-term state security imperatives.

Analysis of regime in Africa has most frequently been framed in terms of typologies. Initially, party system was the primary basis of regime classification. With the swift ascendance of single-party systems, apparent distinctions between them in organization and ambition became the prime diffentiator (pragmatic-pluralist versus revolutionary-centralizing, for example;)[128]. Ruth Collier turns to colonial origin and regime durability as key categorizations in *Regimes in Tropical Africa*. During the ideologically intense 1970s, I suggested regime developmental doctrine as the primary classification basis in *Ideology and Development*, sorting countries into Afromarxist, populist socialist, and African capitalist. John W. Harbeson, Donald Rothchild, and Naomi Chazan propose a more elaborate typology incorporating more than three decades of postcolonial state experience that categorizes by mode of political operation; their tabulation includes administrative-hegemonic, pluralist, party-mobilizing, party-centralist, personal-coercive, populist, and regime breakdown entries.[129]

Rulers

The final conceptual category inviting brief inspection is ruler. From the earliest postcolonial moments the central role of the political leader became apparent. Heroes of the independence movement, the first generation of rulers in many cases wore the mantle of charisma: winning popular adulation through their flamboyant and often courageous challenge to the colonizer.

Kwame Nkrumah, Léopold Senghor, Julius Nyerere, Kenneth Kaunda, Félix Houphouët Boigny, Patrice Lubumba, Habib Bourguiba are all luminous personalities, who embodied in their leadership the theatrics of triumphant anticolonial struggle. Once cast in the ruler role, a subtle metamorphosis took hold, with power consolidation and reproduction supplanting mobilization and struggle. In pursuit of the ruler's imperative, leaders sought to concentrate authority in the presidency; this might be termed "presidential monarchy," to borrow the phrase of Clement Moore, writing of Tunisia.[130] Security services began to whisper of conspiracies taking form, reinforcing tendencies to preempt opposition by denying them sites of challenge. Analysts began to notice that the theoretically parliamentary regimes of decolonization soon exhibited what were initially termed "presidentialist" tendencies, referencing their institutional dimension. As the formal institutions of representative democracy gave way to single-party dominance, restraints on aggregation of personal power shriveled. The exercise of power became increasingly personalized as clientelist networks that evoked the concept of neopatrimonialism began to emerge; Juan Linz and H. E. Chalabi, borrowing another Weberian concept, take the notion one step further in suggesting as conceptual tag "sultanistic" regimes.[131]

Rulership accordingly became far less defined by the formal legal powers enshrined in a constitution than by the skillful deployment of personal ties of clientelism. The "big man" model of politics came into view; the leader as supreme political entrepreneur engineered channels of diverted state flow to reward the loyal and punish the deviant while deploying the coercive apparatus of the state to intimidate and repress.[132] Thus the ruler's imperative cast the leader in a paradoxical role as both state builder and state destroyer. With uncertain legitimacy, the ruler was driven to weaken the state by diverting its resources and corroding its integrity. At the same time, the apparatus of the state was indispensable to ruler survival; thus state-building projects continuously reappear.

Kinship terminology was frequently evoked to convey the personalized nature of the leader role: father of the nation, provider to the following.[133] Wealth was indispensable to fulfilling the expectations of ruler as benefactor; official tours were normally the occasion for distribution of "gifts" to the populace—a school or some other facility or a more immediate means of consumption. Such outlays required resources outside normal budgetary process, inevitably originating in the rents of power. King Hassan II of Morocco and Houpouët-Boigny of Ivory Coast created costly gargantuan religious palaces (the Casablanca mosque and Yamoussoukro cathedral) that were portrayed as their personal gifts to a grateful nation. The strategic use of the resources at the individual disposition of the ruler was an art form. As Howard Wriggins writes, "The unknowns are so numerous that a ruler's choice of one course as against another depends in substantial part upon his own inner dispositions and his own conceptions of the reality with which he deals."[134]

The first generation of rulers began with the party machinery of decolonization, political mobilization and electoral organization, and the reasonably functioning bureaucracies bequeathed by the colonial state. Over the course of the first independence decades, the bureaucracies often lost some of their administrative edge, bloated by rapid recruitment, bypassed by patrimonial transactions, demoralized in a number of countries by relative loss of wage value owing to inflation. As parties transformed into instruments of regime and ruler authority, they lost much of their institutional capacity as well. With the wave of military overthrows of the decolonization regimes, especially beginning in 1965, new military rulers had to improvise mechanisms of rule and legitimation. Given the illegitimacy of their ascent to power, the personal character of rule perforce assumed greater importance. Carl Rosberg and Robert Jackson have developed an influential model of personal rule as a political system. They write that "a personal political system is not structured by impersonal rules that exist to uphold some conception of the public interest or the common good. Personal rule is a system of relations linking rulers not with the 'public' or even with the ruled (at least not directly), but with patrons, associates, clients, supporters, and rivals, who constitute the 'system.' If personal rulers are restrained, it is by the limits of their personal authority and power and by the authority and power of patrons, associates, clients, supporters, and—of course—rivals."[135]

The primacy of personal rule established in most countries by the late 1960s exposed the state in extreme cases to great perils. During the 1970s, in three countries singularly tyrannical rulers came to power and inflicted lasting damage on their states: Francisco Macias Nguema in Equatorial Guinea, Jean-Bedel Bokassa in Central African Republic, and Idi Amin in Uganda. All three utterly lacked credentials for rulership, and their resulting paranoia led to them to engage in ever more extreme acts of atrocity to instill fear in the populace. In Equatorial Guinea, Nguema instituted a reign of terror within months of independence, ordering the murder of nearly half the pre-independence cabinet, two-thirds of the National Assembly, and many senior

civil servants; the majority of the population had fled the country by the time
of his 1979 overthrow. The lethal character of Amin's rule took longer to
emerge but gathered force in his later years; his disastrous rule drove many
skilled elites into exile and decimated state institutions. Bokassa was less murderous but more megalomaniacal; his regime became a theater of the absurd.
His self-coronation as "emperor" in a lavish 1976 ceremony cost $30 million,
a third of government annual revenue at the time.[136]

    This African nightmare ended in 1979, when all three were overthrown:
Nguema by his trusted nephew Teodoro Obiang Nguema (who remained in
power three decades later) assisted by the Moroccan military, Bokassa by
French military intervention, and Amin by the Tanzanian army. The younger
Nguema, after relying on Moroccan troops to perform the execution of his
ousted uncle that no Equatorial Guinean dared carry out, established a more
conventional form of personal rule, venal and inept.[137] The discovery of offshore petroleum in the 1990s and rapid rise of Equatorial Guinea to third
largest sub-Saharan oil producer placed a gusher of revenue in the hands of the
ruler and his inner circle of fellow clansmen (the clan of Mongoma), whose
regime is widely regarded as one of Africa's most corrupt. Central African
Republic has remained unstable and conflict-prone ever since the Bokassa
ouster; only Uganda recovered after several painful years of interregnum and
civil war, restoring something resembling a functioning developmental state
by the 1990s.[138] Though personal rule remains a component of African political practice, no further instances of such grotesque tyranny have appeared.

    Another contradiction between reason of state and a ruler's imperative lies
in the capacity of a single person to make economic choices exposing the polity
to high risk. An important element in the debt crisis that emerged in the 1970s
was the number of large development projects, financed by external debt, that
were promoted by external contractors and interested consulting firms and
abetted by their respective embassies. The seeming attractiveness of these ventures to the ruler was enhanced by the high rents he and his inner clique might
collect on the contracts. A prime example was the Inga-Shaba $2 billion dam
and eighteen-hundred-kilometer-long direct current power line to Katanga
launched in 1972 in Mobutu's Congo-Kinshasa, which is examined in chapter
5; such projects were subject to huge cost overruns and long delays in completion. The external partners and Mobutu made their profit on the transaction;
the state and citizenry bore the risks and heavy costs. Such ventures were a
prime trigger of the debt crisis emerging in the later 1970s, sending the country into a downward spiral from which the economy has never recovered.[139]

The disposition of incumbent rulers to perpetuate their hold on power, unless constrained by the rules of the game, is a near universal axiom of politics; monarchy was the primary model for the early state. An equally strong axiom is that regular succession of leaders is crucial to the health of the state. Here as well we encounter the conflicts between ruler interest and state logic. By the 1970s life presidencies came into view in Africa, as a number of rulers made clear their intent to cling to power indefinitely, and constitutional or other political mechanisms for circulation of elites vanished with the consolidation of single parties or military regimes. The operation of neopatrimonial rule, along with repressive autocracy, rendered rulers over time increasingly vulnerable to charges of corruption or atrocity. With few exceptions, before 1990, death, exile, or prison were the only exits from top office for nearly all heads of state. Those personal rulers who chose retirement in safety, even retaining a measure of public respect and affection, were rare: Senghor (1980) and Nyerere (1985) are the main examples.

Concluding Reflections

By way of conclusion, I offer a few reflections on the vital need for a performing state. In a recent collaborative edited volume, drawing together the contributions of specialists from Africa and the former Soviet Union as well as North American scholars, Mark Beisinger and I conclude:

> The crises of the state in postcolonial Africa and post-Soviet Eurasia are a crisis of stateness itself. They revolve around the capacity of public institutions to rule effectively, to create security within their orbit of territorial sovereignty, to generate legitimacy for their operation, to assure a revenue base adequate for their functioning, and to supply the conditions for a prospering economy and welfare of citizenry. . . .
>
> In the long term, the question that will haunt most of Africa and Eurasia is not whether unreformed autocracies will be forced to initiate change or even whether collapsed states can be pieced back together into weak but intact varieties through skillful statecraft. Rather, it is whether the transitions from state weakness to state effectiveness, from semi-democracy to genuine democracy, and from protracted economic decline to sustained economic growth can be made.[140]

In a thoughtful historical and comparative exegesis of the *longue durée* processes of state-building, Matthew Lange, Dietrich Rueschmeyer, and their collaborators stress not only the indispensable role of an efficacious state, capable of acting in a coherent, corporate way, but the extended time horizon required to achieve such a state. Competent institutions, a supportive normative culture, the coordination of many different actors, the resolution of conflicts, and the overcoming of stalemates are necessary components of a performing developmental state, which can consolidate only gradually.[141] In its 1997 annual development report, the World Bank identified state reconstruction as the central challenge to African development.[142]

I remain persuaded of the thesis that there is no path to a better life for African societies that does not pass through the efficacious state. The somewhat improved economic growth rates for African states overall since 2000 reflects in part better governance for a significant number. Trajectories of decline can be reversed by political and economic reforms; Ghana and Uganda since the 1980s and Liberia since 2007 are striking cases. But state restoration after protracted decline is no simple matter; the continuing dysfunction of the Congo-Kinshasa state is eloquent illustration. Neopatrimonial rule over extended time frames deeply embeds corrupt practice in the behavior of the political elite, who come to assume impunity. In addition to Congo, Nigeria, Kenya, and Cameroon are leading examples—not failed states but, in the apt phrase of John Campbell, "dancing on the brink" of the precipice.[143]

In my reading, some form of synthesis between three essential ingredients of viable and sustainable stateness needs to occur. The universal norms of an idealized vision of an effective state, which derive from an evolving composite model drawn from the most widely admired and best performing polities of the age, are one point of reference. Its elements include universally recognized human rights, constitutional democratic rule, and a liberal economy. This normative state, however, cannot simply be imported. Rather its institutional forms and political operation need rooting in the cultural heritage of a given society to be legible to the citizenry. Finally, the lived experience of a given polity enters the picture. History cannot be erased; societal memory, even its negative and painful dimensions, supplies instructive lessons in statecraft.

PART TWO

Itineraries: Three Cycles of Hope
and Disappointment

3

Decolonization, the Independence Settlement, and Colonial Legacy

COLONIAL PERMANENCE IN QUESTION

With an ever-increasing velocity, the "winds of change" British prime minister Harold MacMillan announced to a stupefied South African Parliament in 1960 swirled through Africa in the 1950s and 1960s. By 1970, only the Portuguese territories, the final white redoubts of southern Africa, and a few scattered microterritories awaited liberation. Only some twenty-five years earlier the premise was that the colonial era in Africa had many decades if not centuries to run.

The purpose of this chapter is to set the stage for the following three chapters detailing the postindependence evolution. I argue the importance of colonial legacy in shaping the postcolonial state; its transmission was shaped by the power transfer process. The nature of the decolonization dynamic established some significant parameters for what followed: the degree of cooperative and planned transition, the role and place of settler communities, the availability of a credible template for evolution. Liberation through armed struggle created a distinctive point of departure for independence. Most studies of decolonization are specific to a given imperial domain; through a comparative inquiry into the range of decolonization patterns and independence settlements, I hope to illuminate both commonalities and divergences in the birth of postcolonial politics.

TERRITORIAL POSSESSIVENESS

Intrinsic to any state is a disposition to territorial possessiveness. Imperial holdings end up being swept into this premise of perpetual sovereign overlordship, a durable article of faith articulated in 1776 by Adam Smith: "To propose that Great Britain should voluntarily give up all authority over her colonies . . . would be to propose such a measure as never was, and never will be adopted, by any nation in the world."[1] This instinctive impulse to territorial preservation might be overridden by successful revolt of the subject (Spanish and English America), by military defeat (Germany after World War I, Italy and Japan following World War II), or other national calamity.

Only Britain before World War II had a formula for reluctantly accepting a voluntary dilution of the overseas imperial domain, but it primarily restricted this loss of power to the kith-and-kin white-ruled territories. Devolution within the empire was conceded for these territories, including by 1910 South Africa, although with an initial vision of imperial federation. The boundaries of dominion sovereignty remained ambiguous even after the 1931 Statute of Westminster appeared to assure independence. Imperial bonds were not fully severed before World War II, and the empire as a security and mercantile community continued, while aiming, in the felicitous words of John Darwin, to "enfold the Dominions in a form of 'imperial nationhood' . . . a kind of 'Britannic nationalism.'"[2] Overall, elsewhere in Africa in the 1930s, the permanence of colonial occupation seemed beyond question. Even in 1945, as Frederick Cooper argues, the colonial powers assumed indefinite prolongation of rule would be possible by coopting the educated elite through the bestowal of enhanced status, winning peasant acquiescence through lower taxes and an end to forced labor, and concocting a new veneer of legitimation with the master concept of development.[3]

However, World War II brought dramatic changes to the international environment, which no longer accommodated the imperial conceits of perpetual proprietorship. The crystallization and accelerating spread of anticolonial nationalism was the most fundamental transformation. But nationalist mobilization now could draw energy from an increasingly supportive global setting. The two superpowers, for different reasons, called for decolonization, even though the real pressure they put on the colonial powers fell well short of their public rhetoric. The new superstructure for international cooperation, the UN system, inscribed the term "self-determination" as a principle in articles 1 and 55 in its 1945 charter. Worse for imperial preservation, article 73 obligated colonizers "to develop the capacity [of colonial subjects] to administer themselves, to take account of the political aspirations of the populations, and to aid them in the progressive development of their free political institutions." In 1960, the UN General Assembly far more forcefully enunciated an obligation of all states "to bring a speedy end to colonialism, having

due regard for the freely expressed will of the peoples concerned."[4] The growing number of once-colonized Asian countries, joined by Latin American
states, congealed into an active anticolonial lobby at the UN and other international forums.

An earlier unexamined assumption that maximal imperial domains were
automatically beneficial came into question; even staunchly Tory prime minister Margaret Thatcher had concluded that the empire "cost more to defend
than it contributed to national wealth."[5] Raymond Cartier, in a series of articles in *Paris-Match* at the beginning of the 1960s, popularized in France the
thesis that colonial holdings were a net drain. The mythologies of unchal-
lengeable colonial strength and beneficence that once underpinned imperial
rule gradually evaporated in the face of the rising costs of resistance to the
angry voice of nationalism.

The Code of Decolonization

One need pursue no further the reasons for the gradual dissolution of the
will to preserve colonial occupation on the part of the metropolitan powers.
During the postwar years, what might be termed a code of decolonization
took form, articulated in part through the UN and in international diplomacy,
reinforced by the various pan-African instances whose assemblies multiplied
in the 1950s, and echoed by the political Left in the imperial homelands, for
whom at this time anticolonialism became everyday rhetorical fare. This
charter of decolonization, formalized as international jurisprudence by the
1960 UN General Assembly resolution on the Granting of Independence to
Colonial Territories and Peoples, had half a dozen elements.

Territoriality

The first and most enduring was territoriality: the elixir of sovereignty hardened the map lines of the colonial partition into a permanent array of containers. This outcome was by no means obvious in 1945, least of all to emergent
African nationalists. The 1945 Pan-African Congress in Manchester denounced
"the artificial divisions and territorial boundaries created by the Imperialist
Powers" as "deliberate steps to obstruct the political unity of the West African peoples."[6] The 1958 Accra All-African Peoples' Conference echoed these
sentiments, again excoriating "artificial boundaries, drawn by the imperialist
Powers to divide the peoples of Africa, particularly those which cut across
ethnic groups and divide people of the same stock," and demanding "the abolition or adjustment of such frontiers at an early date."

However, once normative discourse became defined by states rather than political movements, *raison d'état* dictated the supremacy of existing territorial divisions. Also in 1958, and also in Accra, Ghana president Kwame Nkrumah, a passionate advocate of pan-Africanism, convened the first assembly of independent states, whose consensus he (perhaps reluctantly) summarized: "Our conference came to the conclusion that in the interests of that Peace which is so essential, we should respect the independence, sovereignty and territorial integrity of one another."[7] When the pan-African dream gained organic content in 1963 with the creation of the OAU, "territorial integrity" became a core value inscribed in its charter, as noted in chapter 2.

Worth noticing is that the affirmation of the colonial partition map even sharpened the territorial lines, now an iron grid of sovereign containers. Even in colonial times, the boundaries between the imperial domains of a given colonizer permitted relatively easy interterritorial movement. Moreover, the precolonial safety valve of exit for a dissident community was foreclosed; they became perforce potential recruits for the opposition.

Reason of state was not the only factor in the emergence of a territorial praxis; the momentum of the nationalist struggle also informed it. Though transterritorial political movements had existed earlier in British West Africa, and especially in the sprawling administrative federations of Afrique occidentale française (AOF) and Afrique équatoriale française (AEF), in most settings the imperatives of effective challenge to the colonizer mandated utilization of the territorial frame within which the institutions of domination operated. Thus the nationalist became territorialist *malgré soi*.

On the other hand, the withdrawing colonial powers came naturally to embrace the territoriality principle, which did reflect the operational practices and bureaucratic traditions of the colonial project and especially defined the administrative domain within which the decolonization project could be managed and oriented. To be sure, the British in the interwar period and again following World War II toyed with the idea of creating East and Central African federations. These schemes were fatally flawed by the predominant place accorded to white settler interests. In Central Africa, a Federation of Rhodesia and Nyasaland actually had a brief existence from 1953 to 1964. But the "racial partnership" between an African horse and a white settler rider was doomed from the outset by increasingly bitter African opposition.

A different territorial ambiguity arose in the cases of the former German territories of Togo and Kamerun, which had been partitioned between Britain and France after World War I, with the British portions attached to Gold

Coast and Nigeria respectively. A curious form of ghostly territoriality exca-
vated from German times appeared in the French mandated territories of
Togo and Cameroon, asserting a natural claim to the restoration of the pre-
1914 geographic frame. The doctrine of self-determination, the overarching
normative premise shaping the code of decolonization, came into play, in the
form of referendums in British-administered portions of former German Togo
and Kamerun. In the Togo case, a majority voted for Ghana in a single referendum; in Cameroon, the smaller northern morsel of the Cameroon mandate
administered with Nigeria chose to remain there, while a larger southern segment was lured by a promise of federation to vote for affiliation with the formerly French-ruled Cameroon state.[8]

The failure of the huge colonial federations of AOF and AEF to generate a
sufficiently robust pan-territorial identity to compete with the individual
identities of their respective eight and four component units is an interesting
puzzle. Although Senegal became independent in federation with Mali, the experiment dissolved almost at once. Admittedly, these sprawling bureaucratic
constructs were distant from the subject populace, who were in much more
direct contact with the territorial administrations. However, these multiterrito-
rial federations had long existed, created in 1895 and 1905 respectively (or
longer than Nigeria, unified administratively only in 1914). Particularly in AOF,
the most prestigious political party through much of the 1950s, the Rassemblement démocratique africain, was firmly committed to a vocation of unification, especially for AOF. Naturally, federation sentiment was strongest in the
territories housing the seats of AOF and AEF, Senegal and Congo-Brazzaville,
respectively. In Senegal, a residual nostalgia for the larger entity could still find
expression in an elaborate 1995 official celebration of the centennial of the creation of AOF.[9] However, the most prosperous territories in the two colonial
federations, Ivory Coast and Gabon, long resentful at sharing their revenues
with the more impoverished parts, resisted the supraterritorial frame for decolonization.[10] French officialdom, privately acknowledging by the mid-1950s
that the permanent exclusion of self-government in the African territories
enunciated in the 1944 Brazzaville Declaration was not sustainable, made the
fateful choice in the 1956 Gaston Deferre *loi-cadre* to situate the institutions of
self-rule in sub-Saharan Africa at the territorial level. This crucial legislation
was prepared in collaboration with key African allies such as future Ivory Coast
president Félix Houphouët-Boigny, then a minister in the French government.

The other major exception to the transfer of the territorial frame of the
colonial partition to independent Africa was the split of the Belgian trust

territory of Ruanda-Urundi into its two constituent elements. These two kingdoms were broken off from German East Africa following the First World War; Belgian administration nurtured the separate monarchies under a single bureaucratic frame until decolonization was at hand, using the Tutsi royal castes as intermediaries to rule a large Hutu minority (roughly 85% in both cases). As independence approached, though some African states tried to apply the principle of "territorial integrity" to Ruanda-Urundi, local sentiment overwhelmingly favored separation. Thus Rwanda and Burundi acquired full sovereignty in 1962 as separate countries.[11] A further minor derogation to colonial territorial integrity occurred in 1975, when one of the islands composing the Comoros Republic, Mayotte, voted to accept incorporation into the French Republic (and in 2009 voted by 95% for full departmentalization).[12] Conversely, UN insistence that the two components of Spanish Equatorial Guinea (mainland Rio Muni and the island of Fernando Po) become independent as a single unit in 1968 prevailed over strong sentiment in Fernando Po for separate sovereignty; the indigenous Bubi feared marginalization by the far more numerous mostly Fang on the mainland. These apprehensions proved well justified.[13]

A last apparent exception, which ultimately proved the rule, was the 1960 fusion of the Italian-ruled territory of Somalia, whose independence was prepared under an UN-imposed ten-year deadline when Italy regained administrative control in 1950, and British Somaliland, for which an elected majority legislative council was created only in February 1960. In what D. A. Low characterizes as the "swiftest scuttle from Africa," the British "tumbled over themselves" to respond to requests by Somaliland nationalists to unite with Somalia. An instant decolonization took place in June, "though next to nothing stood ready," and Somali unification immediately followed.[14] Despite the shared Somali identity, the fusion never worked well. Increasingly restive under Somalia sovereignty, Somaliland at once reasserted its territoriality following the collapse of the central institutions and declared independence in 1991.

Representative Institutions

The other five elements of the code of decolonization may be summarized more briefly. A second premise was the central role of representative institutions. The core of the colonial regime was its executive bureaucracy, with its attendant territorial administration and at the lowest levels African chiefly intermediaries; the African colonial state was a pure model of bureaucratic authoritarianism. Until decolonization was well under way Africans were rare in the senior ranks, though in the French and Portuguese cases there was a sprinkling of West Indians or mulattoes.[15] An opening for an African voice could only be acceptable if it came through diverse advisory legislative or territorial councils, not through any dilution of colonial executive authority. Before World War II such bodies had only appointed African members, if any; with limited consultative influence, they were dominated by representatives of colonial interest groups (corporations, missions, settlers). Gradually, African numbers increased after the war, with an initially timid infusion of elected members. At the same time, elected councils were created at the local level, especially by the British. The watershed moment came when the territorial councils acquired elected African majorities and became truly legislative.

The postulate of representative institutions lay at the core of legitimating doctrine for decolonization, except for the pair of colonizers that lacked democratic institutions at home (Portugal and Spain). A tacit pact to this effect joined withdrawing colonizer and emergent African nationalists; for the former, ultimate executive power, though under increasing challenge, was the final redoubt, while for the latter the representative institution provided an indispensable engine for the last assault on alien rule. The supremacy of the representative institution in the hierarchy of legitimating values was fleeting but no less important in its moment.

Universal Suffrage

A third, related element in the decolonization code was majoritarianism based on universal suffrage. Not the least of the ironies of power transfer was the import of a norm that had only recently become applicable in Europe itself; at the time of the colonial partition, working-class suffrage was still incomplete and women's suffrage decades away. Achievement of universal franchise was gradual in Europe but virtually instantaneous in Africa. The universality was unrestricted—there was no requirement of literacy, property, or tax payment nor was any other condition imposed. The various devices to circumscribe or delay universal suffrage in the early postwar years were correctly perceived by African nationalists as schemes to deny the majority its birthright. In East Africa, especially in Kenya and Tanzania, and through the ill-starred Central African Federation, the specious theory of "racial partnership" conceptualized the body politic as composed of corporate communities of Europeans, Asians, and Africans in which the value of equality would apply at the communal level. Tortured formulas emerged for distinct electoral rolls for the different racial communities, perhaps with provision whereby a limited number of Africans of high professional status or service to the colonial order would be included in the top category.[16] In the French case, though the African subject acquired nominal citizenship in the 1946 constitution, dual electoral colleges were established assuring a vastly disproportionate representation to French settlers; the last vestiges of these were finally swept away only in the 1956 *loi-cadre*. In the Belgian case as well, the first colonial elections, held in several cities in 1957, were so structured as to produce a virtual racial codominion at the level of the municipal institutions.[17] Such schemes colored the persistent suspicions of colonial motives that underlay the dialogue of decolonization and reinforced African insistence on universal suffrage majoritarianism, which would automatically restrict the electoral weight of the once-powerful settler communities. Colonial demands that nationalists validate their legitimacy with large majorities backing the independence claim in conjunction with often justified apprehensions that African divisions might be exploited by colonizers to delay decolonization or to favor "moderate" formations sympathetic to imperial interests stimulated the formation of large anticolonial fronts, often forerunners to single parties.

The premise of universal suffrage had important repercussions in a number of territories where a numerically modest population had enjoyed colonial favor or relatively early access to the agencies of social ascension, especially schools. In Sierra Leone, the Freetown creoles, socially and economically ascendant in colonial times, became a marginal electoral factor. So also did the denizens of the four old communes of coastal Senegal (Gorée, Dakar, Rufisque, and Saint-Louis), precociously awarded citizenship in 1871. Buganda and southern Nigeria, regions that supplied the most colonial elites, found themselves outnumbered by suddenly enfranchised voters from other areas.

Political Parties

A corollary of the previous two elements was the centrality of political parties in the decolonization charter. The institution of the political party gave necessary structure to the African voice and provided a vital instrument for using representative institutions. Although other forms of African organization, trade unions in particular, assumed significance after 1945, once the battery of repressive legislation shackling the subject was loosened, the political party became the primordial site of nationalist organization. Through the party, leaders found a mechanism permitting activation of once-isolated rural populations. Indeed, in a number of instances a latent social anger at the innumerable vexations of alien domination crystallized in these populations that the leaders then struggled to channel and control.[18]

Until the decolonization moment, most contentious African politics unfolded at a more local level in the form of struggles within chieftaincies, competition in district councils, and resistance to particular colonial policies (for example, obligatory terracing). The rise of a territorial politics stimulated the creation of political parties. As independence approached, the melodrama of terminal political struggle tended to eclipse (though not erase) the visibility of more localized patterns of politics.

Sovereignty

Fifthly, the doctrine of sovereignty joined territoriality as a defining norm for the independent state. This element in the ideology of the modern state acquired its enduring importance, to which later chapters return, partly as a reaction to early metropolitan visions of colonial self-government as circumscribed by some version of a continuing membership in the imperial family. In the British case, though the dominion formula had eased the path to virtually unencumbered self-rule, the outer boundaries of sovereignty were unclear until 1949, when Ireland officially quit the commonwealth and India entered as a republic recognizing only the "symbolic" place of the British monarch as head of the commonwealth.[19] India provided the model in combining undiluted sovereignty with commonwealth membership, proved in practice by the assertive nonaligned foreign policy pursued by New Delhi, which made commonwealth membership acceptable for all former British holdings in Africa except Sudan (and earlier Egypt). France first tried to contain Morocco and Tunisia within a nebulous French union and wrestled with various ill-defined "federal" formulas for the sub-Saharan territories that were intended to integrate them into an incorporated French family without France having to accept the full consequences of an assimilation doctrine that would have produced a parliamentary majority for the colonized. Algeria, on the other hand, was claimed as an integral part of the French Republic until late in the independence war. In the Belgian instance, in the early 1950s before a nationalist voice was audible, there were vague ruminations of incorporation of the colonial Congo as a tenth province of Belgium or of a fashioning of a permanent partnership through a Belgo-Congolese community, with the colony as a subordinate partner. But at the end of the day, undiluted formal sovereignty for the new African state was a bedrock demand; only after its acknowledgement could mechanisms such as the commonwealth or the informal ties of intimacy linking most sub-Saharan former French territories to Paris be accepted as means of maintaining an association between former colonizer and colonized in the postcolonial period.[20]

Speed

Finally, speed became of the essence. Acceptable timetables were steadily foreshortened. The first decolonization constitutions in Ghana, Nigeria, and Sierra Leone in the 1940s presumed an extended period of tutelage and adaptation; however, the rise of nationalism compelled an abbreviation of the transitions. By 1960, the code of decolonization would tolerate no delays; "immediate independence" became the war cry. In 1958, France held referendums on membership in the French Community proposed by President Charles de Gaulle's Fifth Republic constitution obliging the African territories to choose between instant independence and continued French assistance; only Guinea paid the ransom for immediate sovereignty at that juncture. A mere two years later nearly all others found an escape clause permitting independence with aid. In 1956, the first Congolese political party, the Alliance des Bakongo (ABAKO), seemed extremist in making "immediate emancipation" the centerpiece of its manifesto.[21] In January 1960, Belgium agreed to the instant transfer of power by then demanded by nearly all Congolese parties.[22] By this time, those colonizers accepting negotiated decolonization had lost all appetite for delay.

CONTRAST WITH EARLIER DECOLONIZATIONS

The significance of the code of decolonization is illustrated by the contrast between power transfers after the mid-1950s, by which time it had congealed, and those that occurred earlier.[23] In unifying the English and Afrikaner territories of South Africa and granting them dominion status in 1910, Britain applied the political reason derived from Canada (the Durham Report of 1839 and the British North American Act of 1867), creating the self-governing dominion formula that was subsequently applied to Australia and New Zealand. However, the analogy was incomplete; indigenous populations, mostly overlooked in the new dispensation, were small minorities in Canada and Australia and of modest numbers in New Zealand. In South Africa, the negotiations acknowledged as legitimate claimants only the 25% of the population composed either of British immigrants or the older Afrikaner European population, whose subjugation in the ferocious Boer War between 1899 and 1902 required nearly half a million British (and imperial) troops. The virtual independence within an empire sovereignty gave unrestricted internal power to the white communities, entirely without consideration for the views or rights of the large African majority. The forebodings of that majority were at once validated by the 1913 Land Act, restricting African land rights to 7.3% of the country's total area. The same path was followed in the grant of virtually unrestricted "responsible government" to a proportionally much smaller European settler population in Southern Rhodesia (less than twenty-four thousand) in 1923, who quickly consolidated their seizure of over half the land through the infamous 1930 Land Apportionment Act. Though Southern Rhodesia never achieved dominion status, white minority rule was in practice unencumbered by residual imperial sovereignty; Britain never used its veto power over territorial laws passed by the settler regime.[24]

The other pre–World War II decolonization example was Egypt.[25] It had been occupied and administered by Britain with unreserved imperial suzerainty since 1882, but until 1914 the fiction of ultimate Ottoman sovereignty remained. War with the Ottoman state eviscerated this fig leaf, and Egypt was brought officially within the empire as a protectorate. Egyptian nationalism, spearheaded by the Wafd party, swiftly reacted, and by the end of the war it demanded independence. Serious rioting in 1919 shook the British establishment in Cairo; however, unwilling to concede the demands of the dominant Wafd party for full sovereignty, the British in 1922 unilaterally imposed a nominal independence, denatured by reserved imperial discretionary powers to control defense, to ensure the security of British communications, to protect foreign interests and minorities, and to oversee Sudan. Though a 1936 treaty somewhat diluted London's reserved powers, Britain retained the Suez Canal garrison and dominance in Sudan. Nationalist sentiment was far from assuaged; not until the 1954 Anglo-Egyptian Treaty was the conquest of sovereignty completed in many Egyptian eyes with the final withdrawal of British troops.[26]

Libya is a particularly illuminating example of a postwar decolonization accomplished under an older normative framework. Roger Louis convincingly asserts that the Libyan state at the moment of its 1951 independence was a mere "British creation within the context of Anglo-American collaboration and United Nations sponsorship."[27] By the end of World War II, British forces occupied the north and French the south. After a prolonged postwar stalemate on disposition of the former Italian colonies, the future of Libya was placed in the hands of the UN in 1948.[28] An initial scheme in 1949 provided for division of the country into three separate trusteeships: Cyrenaica (Britain), Tripolitania (Italy), and Fezzan in the southwest (France). This partition plan failed by only one vote in the General Assembly. The Libyan voice divided into two distinct currents: a conventional Arab unitarian nationalist orientation in Tripolitania, led by Beshir Saddawi, and a Cyrenaica-centered religio-nationalist outlook embodied by the Senussi Sufi order, led by Sayyid Idris. But both confronted a struggle of competing imperial visions conducted at the level of high global diplomacy and could play only subsidiary roles in shaping the outcomes. Great-power strategic interests were paramount in the negotiations: air base rights for the United States, a secure strategic foothold for Britain in Cyrenaica, a territorial foothold for the French in Fezzan. Immediate independence eventually emerged as the international least common denominator; in late 1949, a UN agreement took shape by which Libya would become independent by the end of 1951 as a single state. An American, Adrian Pelt, was appointed as UN impresario of decolonization; he cobbled together a federated state, but it was one in which Libyans would be only secondary actors and in which Senussi leader Idris would be the internationally designated monarch. Virtually bereft of resources at that time, the precarious independent state initially relied largely on rents from the giant American Wheelus air base near Tripoli and a small British subsidy. Its total budget at the time was a mere $16.6 million, its exports being worth only a little over $6 million.[29] Never again did independence occur with nationalism and decolonization norms playing so small a role.

In the dialectic of decolonization in the large majority of cases in which negotiation prevailed, one may observe a constant tension between combative mobilization and bargained cooperation. Although nationalist forces gradually gained the upper hand in forcing the pace, paradoxically the withdrawing colonial state was simultaneously strengthening in numbers and governmental capacity even while its authority over the subject populace was weakening. The abundant postwar revenue flow made possible a dramatic growth in state activity, especially in the domain of social and economic infrastructure. Technical and specialized services expanded swiftly, amounting to what John Hargreaves calls "a second colonial occupation," in the form of "a large-scale infusion of technical experts, whose activities not only increased the 'intensity' of colonial government, but seemed to imply its continuance in some form until the new policies had an opportunity to mature."[30] Many of the postwar recruits to colonial service perceived their role to be more as technicians of development than as the agents of command who dominated the prewar ranks. As Cooper argues, "The colonial state that failed in the 1950s was colonialism at its most intrusively ambitious."[31]

PATHWAYS

There was substantial variation in the pathways to independence, which shaped the initial postcolonial physiognomy of the African states. In different ways, the British and French systems alone permitted emergent African elites to acquire a degree of experience and responsibility in the exercise of political power. The phase of "responsible government" in the British case, lasting several years in Ghana but much less time in later power transfers, placed most organs of state (with the significant exception of security agencies) in African hands. In francophone sub-Saharan Africa, from 1946 on modest numbers of political leaders won election to the French National Assembly, and serving in this capacity enabled them to develop networks of intimacy with diverse milieux in Paris that paved the way for the close postcolonial ties of many former French territories with the metropole. The autonomous territorial representative governments created by the 1956 *loi-cadre* soon (except for Guinea) became semi-independent members of the French Community created by the 1958 Fifth Republic constitution, with large majorities approving referendums on membership. By 1960, Ivory Coast under Houphouët-Boigny uncovered a safe path to independence by asking France to transfer to the territories residual sovereign powers in the domains of finance, defense, and law while retaining the levels of aid that France previously pledged to the French Community as inducement for membership.[32]

In both the British and French instances, decolonization left in its wake sufficiently functional state institutions to permit immediate postcolonial stability. Even in the case of Guinea, whose charismatic leader Sékou Touré defied France by rejecting the French Community in favor of instant independence, the territorial government already in place was sufficiently robust to survive the vindictive response of President de Gaulle, who at once carried out the threat to cut off of all French assistance and to withdraw French personnel and assets. However, the flawed Belgian scheme of instant decolonization was a different story and did lasting damage to the postcolonial polity.

The first overt nationalist manifesto in Belgian Congo did not appear until 1956.[33] However, the colonial establishment was aware of an undercurrent of discontent among the still-small, educated elite, whose initial grievances focused on the innumerable affronts they endured owing to the racism that saturated the colonial situation and on the need for a personal status consonant with their educational attainments. "What will be our place in the world of tomorrow," plaintively asked Paul Lomami-Tshibamba in 1945 in a newly launched colonial journal for supervised expression of Congolese opinion;

their wartime loyalty and mastery of European cultural norms called for treatment different from that which might be appropriate for an "ignorant and backward" mass.[34] Thus the initial focus was on defining a special legal status for elites, which proved long past its sell-by date when an edict finally emerged nearly a decade later. A second shibboleth, the need for a cautious, gradual construction of institutions for African participation from the ground up with careful tutelage, led to limited elected urban government in a few cities by 1957. But by then the nationalist genie was out of the bottle, and the pace of political mobilization quickly outstripped the capacity of the ponderous colonial behemoth to adapt. The first official promise of independence was made by King Baudouin in January 1959 but only after several days of tumultuous riots in the colonial capital of Kinshasa just prior dramatized the progressive loss of control by a once omnipotent Belgian administration, popularly known as *bula matari*, or "crusher of rocks."[35] In the months following, the formerly comprehensive administrative control evaporated in several key regions. At home, the Belgian state was much too weak and divided politically to contemplate a repressive response by the dispatch of metropolitan troops to reinforce the badly strained colonial constabulary. The incubus of the Algerian war in France weighed heavily on Belgian policy.

Thus by January 1960, Brussels saw no option but to summon a decolonization conference with the fractious Congolese political parties; to Belgian astonishment, they at once united around the slogan of immediate independence. To create an equivalent bargaining partner, Belgium was represented not only by its government but also by the leading political parties.[36] Though the Congolese representatives were divided in the intensity of their radicalism, in their ethnic and regional attachments, and over issues such as federalism versus unitarism, their unified demand for immediate independence triumphed over divided Belgian views. The final Belgian calculus—the essence of what became known as the *pari congolais* (the Congolese gamble)—was that the goodwill purchased through acceptance of immediate independence would permit a transition process after transfer of sovereignty.[37] At the time, only three of the nearly forty-seven hundred top posts in the colonial bureaucracy were held by Congolese (and they had only been recently named), and the thousand officers of the colonial army were all European.[38] With continued total control of the key armature of the state—its bureaucracy and security forces—Belgian effective tutelage would continue ran the reasoning, while the new Congolese political class would be distracted by the status and perquisites associated with ministerial and parliamentary posts.[39] This precarious formula collapsed within five days of independence, when the army mutinied against its European officers; within a week, most Belgian administrators and officers had fled in panic and the richest province, Katanga, had seceded. A dramatic deflation of state authority ensued, only gradually remedied under veritable UN trusteeship.

European Autocracy and Failed Decolonization

The law of territorial possessiveness examined at the outset of this chapter applied with particular force to the two colonial powers with autocratic regimes at the hour of decolonization, Spain and Portugal. In both cases, the instinctive first response to nationalist challenge was the pretense of complete incorporation of the overseas territories into the metropolitan domain, accompanied by repression. Autocracy insulated the official mind from internal debate on the wisdom of this course and limited the impact of external pressures, especially for Portugal. In different ways, these blockages that dictatorship placed on the course of decolonization had disastrous consequence, and underlined a striking incapacity of authoritarian regimes to manage power transfer.

In the Spanish case, Madrid was first forced to accept decolonization in its Moroccan territory; when France agreed to restore sovereignty in 1956 to the Sharifian monarchy that France had divided with Spain in 1912 there was little option but to accept the unity of the Moroccan territory. At this juncture as well, Spain was seeking an end to the international isolation to which its fascist regime and Axis World War II sympathies had led; only in 1955 did Spain win admission to the UN.[40] In its other main African territories (Western Sahara and Equatorial Guinea), when confronted in the late 1950s by more sustained international pressures and, in Western Sahara, the beginnings of a guerrilla challenge, the first defensive response was assimilation; in 1958 the Spanish African territories were declared integral parts of the Spanish Republic.[41] Thus, Spain informed an incredulous UN that the country no longer had any African colonies subject to article 73. By 1963, however, Spain permitted Equatorial Guinea to become an autonomous territory, still confident of its ability to control its politics in alliance with colonial interests. This illusion evaporated by 1968, under intensified UN pressure and a more assertive nationalist voice, especially from the mainland Rio Muni enclave. A hastily arranged independence soon turned to catastrophe, as the new ruler, Francisco Macias Nguema, soon proved to be a psychopathic and murderous tyrant.[42] However, no disposition was made regarding Western Sahara until long-time despot General Francisco Franco faced imminent death in 1975, at which point Spain faced an uncertain and unsettled political future. A "Green March" (after the color of Islam) to occupy the territory organized by Moroccan king Hassan, which drew over a half million volunteers swarming across the border, led Spain to surrender Western Sahara to Morocco (and Mauritania), even though the International Court of Justice had rejected a Moroccan claim of historical title to the region and a UN mission had called for independence for it after consulting Saharoui opinion.[43]

Far more than Spain, Portugal had elevated its African territories into defining elements in the national mystique, especially following the launching of the Estado Novo (New State) under dictator António Salazar in 1933, perpetuated by his successor Marcelo Caetano from 1968 to 1974. The overseas territories were viewed, much more than in the French case, as integral components of a global Lusitanian polity; in 1961, African subjects became theoretical citizens, even if this status in an authoritarian corporatist framework comported few political rights and practices such as forced labor remained everyday fare on the ground. Innumerable delusional official statements illuminate the depth of Portuguese attachment to the mythology of a unique global multiracial nation. Caetano in 1936, speaking of the Estado Novo, invoked "the supreme flower of the Portuguese language, the symbol of the moral unity of the Empire whose discovery and conquest it sings in imperishable terms." Another imperial bard, Jorge Ameal, sang of "the notion of vast territories over which . . . our flag flies. . . . It is the knowledge that our sovereignty as a small European state spreads prodigiously over three continents and is summed up in the magnificent certainty that we are the third colonial power in the world."[44] As late as 1967, foreign minister Franco Nogueira was asserting that Portugal alone "practiced the principle of multiracialism, which all now consider the most perfect and daring expression of human brotherhood and sociological progress."[45] As the wars of liberation began in the Portuguese African territories in 1961, Salazar insisted that "we will not sell, we will not cede, we will not surrender, we will not share . . . the smallest item of our sovereignty."[46] Thus, for Portugal, decolonization long appeared an intolerable amputation, a severance of several limbs that would mutilate the polity and leave behind a shrunken state of secondary rank.

The normal corrosion of an imperial territorial will by the processes of democratic debate through which slowly accumulating doubts in the public square were reinforced by the dialogic interaction with an increasingly articulate anticolonial nationalism thus never took place in Portugal. Beginning in 1961, faced with Portuguese intransigence, Guinea-Bissau, Angola, and Mozambique nationalists made the difficult choice to engage in armed liberation struggle. A decade later, Portugal had committed over 90% of its available military forces to the three colonial wars, deploying more than two hundred thousand troops and auxiliaries. Kept at bay in Guinea-Bissau and stalemated in Angola and Mozambique, a demoralized army turned on the Estado Novo in 1974, overthrew the regime and acknowledged the necessity of a decolonization that could no longer be choreographed in British or French style. Although in four of the five territories under Portuguese domination clearly ascendant nationalist movements stood ready to assume power, in Angola an enfeebled Portugal was unable to broker a transition and (as with Spain in Western Sahara) simply abandoned the country. On 11 November 1975, the last Portuguese governor announced he was ceding the territory "to the Angolan people," boarded a waiting ship and sailed away, leaving the country to a savage civil war that lasted nearly three decades.

Differentiating Factors

In this extraordinary saga of decolonization, three other differentiating factors require note. First, there was a sharp difference in the capacity of the colonizing states to manage the process of imperial retreat. Second, a number of territories enjoyed particular legal status, either as "protectorates" or UN trust territories. Finally, in eight cases, blocked decolonization led to armed liberation struggles, fundamentally altering the independence settlement equation.

State Capacity

After a number of false starts, Britain and France at the end of the day developed a reasonable mastery of the statecraft of decolonization, with the major exceptions of Algeria, Egypt, and Zimbabwe. In Algeria, France had created an illusion of perpetuity of the colonial tie through departmentalization of the populous coastal regions and large-scale settlement that only the fierce eight-year independence war referenced in chapter 1 could dissolve. In Egypt, the ascendance of a British global reason of empire—the Suez lifeline to India—engendered a meddlesome mentality that constantly clashed with Egyptian sensibilities of sovereignty until 1954. In Zimbabwe, the premature grant of virtually unencumbered autonomy to a small settler minority in 1923 paved the way for a white regime in 1965 to declare unilateral independence; it took fifteen years and a bitter liberation war whose embers still glow for an ultimately negotiated Zimbabwean independence to be effected.

With the exceptions of British Somaliland and Sudan, Britain in its other thirteen African colonies was able to rely on the power transfer template first developed in the old dominions and then adapted for India and Ceylon in the interwar period. The gradual extension of representative institutions, culminating in "responsible government" with an African prime minister under the guidance of a British governor, and then finally independence within the commonwealth defined the pathway. Once the final decision in favor of accelerated independence was made, accumulated experience in power transfer politics facilitated the process.

Despite its increasingly feeble condition, the enduring strength of a state tradition enabled the weakening French Fourth Republic to negotiate its disengagement from Tunisia and Morocco in 1956. That same year, the Deferre *loi-cadre* provided a viable framework elsewhere for territorial autonomy under representative African leadership. Independence was not its intended purpose, but by the same token total sovereignty was not yet being demanded by most of the sub-Saharan African leaders. There proved an almost seamless transition from the fictive "federalism" of the French Community to the subsidized intimacy of *francophonie*, which the much more robust Fifth Republic was able to turn into an enduring French connection. But the Algerian war consumed the Fourth Republic, and its convulsions nearly overturned President Charles de Gaulle; in April 1961 a clique of mutinous generals and army units had seized Algiers and momentarily seemed on the verge of a move on Paris. De Gaulle was forced to plead to the public in a dramatic radio address, begging them to rally to his side and resist the putsch; the moment of peril passed and opened the door to a negotiated peace with the Algerian liberation movement, but it was a narrow escape.[47] The often prickly relations with Algeria in the postcolonial years were largely offset, from a French perspective, by the construction of a large zone of enduring French influence in most of the sub-Saharan territories.

Belgium, however, proved too weak a state to gracefully organize its colonial exit. The underlying cleavages of language (Flemings versus Walloons), religion (Catholic versus anticlerical), and ideology (liberal versus socialist), long obscured by a unitary state dominated by a francophone elite, rose to the surface as the belated nationalist challenge in the colony gained momentum. Indeed, the colonial project and, from the 1920s on, its image as an imperial success had been an important unifying factor in sustaining a Belgian nationalism.[48] However, as the perpetuity of the Belgian Congo came into question by the mid-1950s, imperial solidarity began to dissolve. Flemings demanded equal linguistic status in the colony, anticlerical liberals and socialists challenged the Catholic mission monopoly of the educational system, and the church itself whispered of emancipation. The trauma of an aborted decolonization corroded the exalting sense of triumphant colonial mission; the unitary Belgian state was on a federal path within months of Congo independence, the three major parties split into linguistic segments, and a slow, seemingly unstoppable decomposition of the polity was set into motion that has continued ever since.[49]

In sum, the incapacity of an autocratic state to carry out an effective decolonization is illustrated by the Spanish and Portuguese cases (and further reconfirmed by the collapse of the Soviet Union in 1991 and its postimperial fallout).[50] The striking coincidence of a far-reaching state crisis resulting in regime change (France, Portugal) or fragmentation (Belgium) in the imperial centers that is linked to the traumatic effects of decolonization merits renewed underlining. Only Britain partly stands as a partial exception, though the 1956 fiasco of an Anglo-French-Israeli military effort to seize the Suez Canal, the final chapter in the prolonged and troubled disengagement from imperial entanglement with Egypt, forced the resignation of Prime Minister Anthony Eden.

Differences in Legal Status

The differences in formal colonial status of various territories played some part in the decolonization process. In the three cases where the formal institutions of a well-established precolonial state continued under imperial tutelage and control but with "protectorate" status (Egypt, Morocco, and Tunisia), anticolonial nationalism enjoyed a crucial institutional advantage. Thus, within their respective imperial domains, the early exit of the colonial occupiers was no accident. In the three other polities that were lineal descendants of African states that had voluntarily accepted British rule to protect themselves against South African settler expansionism, Botswana, Lesotho, and Swaziland, decolonization was delayed until the 1960s when South Africa finally abandoned its ambitions to incorporate these territories. Once secure from the threat of annexation, deeply feared by the populations, independence came quickly. The minimalist British colonial presence in the three territories, whose role was essentially limited to preventing South African expansion, meant fewer sources of vexation and grievance for the subjugated, although it did leave the population with an enduring fear of South African aims.

The other important differentiated category of colonial territories were those erstwhile German possessions (Togo, Kamerun, German East Africa and South-West Africa) that became League of Nations mandates following World War I and then UN trust territories after 1945. League mandates were subject to minimal international scrutiny in an international system still dominated by the imperial powers. UN trust territory status, however, was an altogether different story. The UN Charter placed obligations on the mandatory powers that went far beyond the prewar commitment to rule in the best interests of the inhabitants. The UN trust system, devised under the leadership of African American diplomat and Africanist Ralph Bunche, was designed to foster self-government, with independence as an explicit goal.[51] Beginning in 1948, the UN Trusteeship Council sent visiting missions every four years to review the performance of the colonizers and the progress in moving toward self-rule. In 1952, the visiting missions displayed growing impatience with the delays in the transition toward independence, and by 1956 their impatience had intensified.

Particularly in the Togo and Cameroon cases, nationalists made use of the trust territory status effectively to push forward the pace of evolution, in turn dragging in their wake the other sub-Saharan territories under French rule.[52] UN oversight prompted Belgium to hold local elections in the Ruanda-Urundi trust territory before anything comparable could happen in the Belgian Congo. As René Lemarchand has noted, the Trusteeship Council's visiting missions "undoubtedly played a part in hastening the political awakening of the indigenous populations," and "the repeated criticisms voiced against Belgium in the United Nations were equally instrumental in creating a climate of world opinion which had a direct influence on the pace and direction of its trust territory policy."[53] Tanganyika, though initially politically less mobilized than neighboring British territories Uganda and Kenya, wound up securing its independence a year before Uganda, in some part as a consequence of its trust territory status, though primarily because of the effective popular mobilization by the Tanganyika African National Union. South Africa, which endeavored to reject UN trust territory status and annex South-West Africa as a fifth province, was unable in the end to elude the constraints of its international juridical standing. Unrelenting external pressures were placed on South Africa through the UN machinery, which employed as leverage the international legal status of Namibia; the General Assembly formally revoked the mandate in 1968, and then Security Council resolution 435 in 1975 charted a path to independence in spite of South Africa.[54] Though fourteen more years were to pass before the goal was achieved, global jurisprudence and the diplomatic muscle it could evoke eventually overcame tenacious South African resistance.

Armed Liberation Struggle

The last pathway to sovereignty and majority rule to note, when colonial or white minority regime intransigence left no other choice, was armed liberation struggle, a critical factor in eight cases (Algeria, Guinea-Bissau, Angola, Mozambique, Zimbabwe, Namibia, South Africa, and Eritrea). In five other instances, a spiral of urban violence (Egypt, Tunisia, Morocco) or substantial though unsuccessful uprisings (Kenya, Cameroon) accelerated the achievement of independence. But the importance and impact of guerrilla insurrection went far beyond the modest number of actual cases; by tracing a grim portrait for the colonial official mind and metropolitan civil society of the potential costs and consequences of rejecting nationalist demands, armed liberation struggle foreshortened decolonization timetables throughout Africa.

When the nine original leaders ("historicals") launched the Algerian revolution with a series of coordinated raids on 1 November 1954, the odds against success seemed overwhelming. At this moment of symbolic beginning of the saga of armed liberation struggle in Africa, insurgents were few in number, devoid of arms or resources, and lacking in external support. The colonial state had disarmed the African subject. The revolution in rural communication that the cell phone and soon after social network technology would bring a half century later was just beginning with the advent of the transistor radio, but colonial control and censorship of available media made popular mobilization difficult, especially for the adventure of rebellion. Thus the Algerian FLN at first needed to achieve visibility through high-profile exploits, to secure arms by stealing them from security forces, and to fund the purchase of resources by robbing banks. Sustaining the venture was a sense of historic destiny drawing inspiration from the spectacular defeat of the French army by Vietnamese insurgents at Dienbienphu a few months earlier.

Nonetheless, the risks of failure were high. The colonial state in all the armed liberation movement cases except Guinea-Bissau (and Eritrea) could count on strong backing from substantial settler and immigrant populations and had fashioned a network of African intermediaries whose interests were linked to the colonizer. Large numbers of indigenous troops or auxiliaries served the security forces. The older generation among the small numbers of African professionals often remained loyal to the colonial power until late in the game, as did many of the chiefly intermediaries; both were suspicious of the radical young nationalist leaders. However great the grievances, persuading (or forcing) the populace to participate was arduous. Norma Kriger offers compelling evidence that many Zimbabwe villagers had ambivalent feelings about the guerrilla armies and often resented the demands for food supply and other services.[55] The conclusions of Patrick Chabal concerning the three liberation wars against Portuguese rule apply more broadly: "The nationalist movements in three colonies made it plain that they saw war as a last resort in the face of Portuguese intransigence and they were prepared for a cease fire as soon as genuine discussions on independence were offered."[56]

Liberation wars were never won, with the arguable exception of Eritrea, although the Partido africano da independência de Guiné e Cabo Verde (PAIGC) came close.[57] However, with the passage of time, circumstances gradually became more favorable. Growing anticolonial majorities in international forums provided important platforms for generating external pressure. When the Algerian revolution began, only Egypt was available as a base for outside backing and supply. Soon Tunisian and Moroccan independence offered sanctuary for guerrilla fighters. Ghana and Guinea next joined the ranks of active backers of liberation wars; with the creation of the OAU in 1963, African liberation was proclaimed as core value of pan-African cooperation, and the OAU liberation committee became a channel for material and other backing. By 1964, Zambia and Tanzania became available as bases for guerrilla movements, and then with the demise of Portuguese colonialism a decade later the liberation frontier reached South Africa itself. Beyond sanctuary, guerrilla movements also received diplomatic passports for their leadership and funding for external offices, as well as other support.

But in the colonial endgame African liberation needed no Dienbienphu. By avoiding complete defeat and sustaining a costly, protracted stalemate, the guerrilla armies could sap colonial will. By 1960, the French had contained the Algerian forces in the country but could not cope with the sanctuary provided to large guerrilla reserves in Tunisia and Morocco; the struggle could thus continue, if at a reduced level, indefinitely. Similarly, at the time of the 1974 Portuguese military coup aimed at ending the colonial wars, the Angolan liberation movement was split into three and all but paralyzed. The more effectively united Mozambique movement, the Frente da libertação de Moçambique (FRELIMO), was mostly confined in its operations to northern areas, and, Malyn Newitt notes, "only in the final phases of the war, and far too late to make any difference in the outcome, was any attempt made to develop political support among educated Africans in the cities."[58] In

Zimbabwe, though the first guerrilla actions took place in 1966, following the 1964 banning of the two main nationalist parties, actual military successes were few. Although their action was widespread enough to convince many that they could not be defeated, most armed bands contained agents reporting their movements to the settler regime, and the head of Rhodesian intelligence later boasted that penetration of the guerrilla movements was complete.[59] In Namibia, though the South-West African People's Organization launched an armed struggle in 1966, guerrilla action never went beyond the northern Ovambo zone, nor could the military threat seriously challenge the South African Defense Force and its auxiliaries.[60] In South Africa, the odds were even greater against the guerrilla dimension of liberation struggle; though its genesis dates to 1961 and despite eventual substantial external support, its military impact was limited. But as an adjunct to the domestic mobilization intensifying during the 1980s through labor unions and the multiplicity of civic organizations organized under the banner of the United Democratic Front (UDF), its psychological impact was no less tangible. Thus in sum armed liberation struggle was at once marginal in purely military terms, except in Guinea-Bissau, Eritrea and Algeria, and yet a decisive vector in the dynamic of decolonization as a whole. It also had enduring impacts.

The inspiring character of these struggles, and the heroic image of the parties that led them, gave rise to a hope, even expectation, that the most successful in guerrilla groups—the FLN in Algeria, the PAIGC in Guinea-Bissau, the FRELIMO in Mozambique, and the EPLF in Eritrea—would have developed the discipline, mobilizing skills, and unifying ideology to fashion a new state, energetically developmental even if not attracted to liberal democracy. Though these visions of the mobilization polity persisted for a bit after the conquest of independence, over time the habits of rigid military discipline, rigorous hierarchy, and leader monopolization of power so valuable in liberation war proved detrimental to postcolonial state operation.

Although the leaders of guerrilla independence movements were invariably political rather than military figures, the militarization of politics became part of the legacy of colonial occupation, most visibly in Algeria and Eritrea. The heroism of the struggle became central to postcolonial texts of legitimation and a demonstrated liberation role long remained a qualification for leadership. The nature of guerrilla warfare had divisive as well as unifying impacts, especially in the regions where violence was centered. The ideological appeal of independence struggle did not by itself guarantee support; intimidation was part of the picture. Colonial regimes often had allies, especially among the indigenous chiefly intermediaries and others in favorable niches. Large numbers had served in the colonial armies; in Algeria in particular, many paid with their lives or were forced to emigrate. Former guerrilla fighters made extravagant claims on the postcolonial state, even decades later in Zimbabwe. The iron discipline that guerrilla warfare involved led to harsh imprisonment inflicted on those suspected of disloyalty; atrocities toward internees during the struggle years cast a shadow even after the transition to independence on the parties linked to insurgent action in Namibia and South Africa.

The impact of the armed liberation movements in accelerating decolonization reflects the importance of interaction effects. What happened in one territory had important spillover consequences in neighboring countries and even entire regions. The retreating colonial powers had dwindling capacity to insulate one territory from advances toward independence nearby. Decolonization in Africa was far more than a series of disconnected episodes; in a very meaningful sense, it was a continental process. The entangled dialectic found reinforcement in the disposition of the imperial centers to perceive in their African holdings a single policy challenge.

African Nationalism as Decolonization Driver

A powerful connective skein in the decolonization process was the anticolonial nationalism that animated the drive for independence across Africa; though there were regional variations, the commonalities stand out. The demiurge of nationalism, the ultimate motor driving the decolonization process, merits further exploration. Without the popular mobilization inspired by the ideology of nationalism, independence would never have come. Above all, anticolonial nationalism was an organizational weapon. The political party was its primary instrument; the charismatic leader its personification. The manifold vexations, humiliations, and grievances that colonial occupation engendered were woven into a tapestry of protest. Independence, which took on millennial qualities, was the solution. The intellectual elites framed its content; political organizers, often drawn from less lettered milieux, took the simple yet potent message of a possible future beyond colonial subjugation to the four corners of the territory. Persuading a peasantry made risk averse by bitter experience was no easy task. Yet although the colonial state projected an image of strength at its high point, its actual capacity for coercive response to a politically mobilized countryside was circumscribed, except in densely securitized settings such as Algeria or South Africa; in territories such as Nigeria or Uganda, colonial security forces numbered no more than ten thousand.[61] Thus, at a given tipping point, colonial authorities had to come to terms with an incapacity to contain nationalist challenge without costly dispatch of metropolitan reinforcements, as in Kenya faced with Mau Mau or Cameroon confronted with the Union des populations du cameroun (UPC) uprising in the 1950s.[62]

In retrospect, the relative absence of explicit territorial focus stands out in African nationalist semantics, save in countries such as Egypt or Morocco with a powerful historical narrative or countries like South Africa with a unique background. In this respect, anticolonial nationalism contrasts sharply with its contemporary descendant, a point to which I return in chapter 8. Nationalism in colonial Africa was most frequently labeled simply "African"; its geographic referent was a generalized "Africa." Here one may detect an adoption through inversion of a colonial category; the imperial subject was most commonly constituted in colonial discourse as a racial or indigenous other: African, black, native, indigene. The subliminal negativity linked to the categorization in the colonial mind was transformed via ideological metamorphosis into an affirmative image of solidarity. As Ali Mazrui has remarked, "It remains one of the great ironies of modern African history that it took European colonialism to remind Africans that they were Africans."[63] Thus Lord Hailey, an authoritative colonial source, characterized the phenomenon as simply "Africanism" in reaction "against the dominance of Europeans in political and economic affairs," suffused with a call for self-rule.[64] Thomas Hodgkin, in an especially influential monograph at the time, offered an action-oriented definition, terming nationalism "any organization or group that explicitly asserts the rights, claims and aspirations of a given African society."[65] James Coleman as well, in an early seminal article, defined nationalism in African and organizational terms, incarnated by any political organization seeking self-government for recognizable African nations-to-be.[66] In contrast to the idea of nationalism in its European cradle, African nationalism in its anticolonial phase was above all forged in political mobilization rather than intellectual history. The Hodgkin classic, for example, cites only a dozen texts in its exegesis of anticolonial nationalism, half of which were really ethnic charters.[67] At this stage, African nationalism had none of the stigma associated with the bestial elements of older nationalisms, contaminated by racism, fascism, militarism, chauvinism, and aggression. Rupert Emerson, in the most comprehensive study of African and Asian self-assertion at the time, insists on the contrast between European forms as a "disastrous corruption poisoning the political life" and Afro-Asian nationalism that "intrudes itself not only with an aura of inevitability but also as the bearer of positive goods."[68]

Thus framed in the first instance as "African" nationalism, the quest to give content to and historicize the idea turned naturally to older doctrines of pan-Africanism, initially a product of diaspora intellectuals as part of a broader response to racial oppression in the Western world. In its original form, the ideal of pan-Africanism combined a global creed of racial solidarity, a shared purpose in freeing all of Africa from colonial or white minority rule, and ultimately, for most, visionary continental unification. Following the Manchester Pan-African Congress in 1945, a new generation of African intellectuals assumed leadership, led by Kwame Nkrumah of Ghana and Jomo Kenyatta of Kenya.

Several influential African and Caribbean scholars, poets, and statesmen fashioned a refutation of the condescending and scornful colonial views of the African cultural heritage. Cheikh Anta Diop of Senegal inverted the conventional European understanding of classical history, marshaling linguistic evidence to support a claim that a black Egypt was the fount of civilization, whose sources came from deep in Africa. Though disputed in Europe, the Diop theory had an enduring resonance in Africa.[69] A pair of poet-politicians, Aimé Césaire of Martinique and Léopold Senghor of Senegal, discovered within African culture a common tapestry of nonmaterialist, naturalist values, which stood in positive contrast to the materialism and hedonism that pervaded European culture and belied its self-proclaimed superiority. This shared worldview, summarized as *négritude*, provided a natural basis for African solidarity.[70] The thesis of an intrinsic commonality in African culture was translated to the religious realm by the influential text of a Belgian Franciscan missionary, Father Placide Tempels. In his exegesis of the indigenous cosmology he encountered in his Katanga Luba (Congo-Kinshasa) mission station, he proposed an intellectually sophisticated system of religious belief he termed "Bantu philosophy."[71] Two decades after its original publication, a leading Congolese intellectual, Mabika Kalanda, argued its continuing cogency, noting that "educated Africans who . . . have read this book recognize in it their own philosophy[,] . . . the dreamed-of occasion to exalt their *négritude*, the possibility of transcending . . . inferiority inflicted" by colonial racial arrogance.[72]

The profound impact, both individual and collective, of colonial oppression was a common theme in nationalist texts, nowhere more eloquently expressed than in the works of West Indian psychiatrist Frantz Fanon.[73] His medical work during the Algerian war gave unique insight into the trauma experienced by the colonized. His mastery of polemics translated psycho-analysis into populist nationalist text, which included some prescient warn-ings of possible postcolonial betrayal of liberation struggle by the successor elite.

Also noteworthy for their subtlety and empirical grounding were the liberation texts of Amilcar Cabral of Guinea-Bissau. Building on Marxism as intellectual source but not as obligatory epistemology, Cabral drew a careful portrait of the class and ethnic composition of the society for which revolu-tionary struggle was charted. Though Cabral himself apparently saw no spe-cial originality in his thought, its influence extended far beyond the modest dimensions of his country.[74]

Anticolonial nationalism needed more than negation; a vision of a future of shared abundance was indispensable. Freedom could not be its own re-ward; the energies summoned to combat colonialism would be redeployed to conquer ignorance, poverty, and disease. In a decade, Nkrumah claimed, Ghana could become a paradise.[75] Liberation platforms were long on trans-formative vocabulary, evoking revolutionary change and often socialist con-struction, but short on particulars.

Within the overarching commonalities of African nationalist discourse, there were some regional variations. In the northern tier of states in the north, an African attachment was diluted by competing or overlapping Arab iden-tity, and an affirmation of membership in the larger Islamic *umma*. In the cases of Morocco and Algeria, however, the presence of large Berber-speaking minorities (35 and 22% respectively) limited the centrality of Arabhood in Mahgreb anticolonial nationalism.[76] Although Islam was a dimension of iden-tity reference, in the decolonization era there was a clearly secular thrust to any religious framing. The Muslim Brotherhood in Egypt was subject to fierce repression, and currents of religious orientation were marginalized in Tunisia and Algeria by the dominant nationalist movements. The multiple faces of liberation ideology were well captured by Gamal Abdel Nasser in the celebrated summation of Egypt's location at the center of three circles: Arab, Islamic, and African.[77] The racial dimension of the pan-African idea was sub-dued as well in the North African domains.

South Africa was an important though also distinctive center of African nationalist liberation ideology. Here one encounters a complex intertwining of the Africanism of the Pan-African Congress and the "black consciousness" movement of the 1970s and the nonracialism of the ANC 1955 Freedom Char-ter and subsequent doctrine.[78] The interplay of race and class was particularly sharp; overlying this dialectic was the *Herrenvolk* Afrikaner nationalism ascendant politically from 1948 till 1991.

Nationalist intelligentsias often had spent formative years in the imperial centers, particularly in the universities. Paris, London, Lisbon, and Brussels each had distinctive intellectual traditions. Political dialogue, especially with sympathetic leftist milieux, left their mark upon the fermentation of nationalist discourse, reflecting the respective ideological lineages of the different metropoles.

In the final analysis, however, the crucial attribute of African nationalism in its anticolonial moment was its service as driving force for decolonization. Its most essential concept was liberation itself, famously encapsulated in the 1957 Nkrumah aphorism: "Seek ye first the political kingdom, and all else will be added unto you." The political kingdom was indeed conquered, but Africa still awaits fulfillment of the second passage. The cultural content that sustained nationalism as an ideology elsewhere was present only in generalized, abstracted form, with its ethnic elements excised. Vague invocations of medieval African kingdoms could not match the voyage of cultural self-discovery of Indian leader Jawaharlal Nehru in his lyrical *The Discovery of India*.[79] Further, there was a disconcerting disposition to personalize African nationalism as the incarnation of its key leader as founding father and his political discourse: Bourguibism, Nkrumahism, Nasserism, and the like. Nkrumah chose to entitle his autobiography *Ghana*, implying a total fusion of anticolonial nationalism and its political leader. In its more extreme form, such celebration of the heroes of independence fused as well with ancestral cults, verging on deification. Nkrumah assumed the title of "osegyefo" ("redeemer"), a praise name linked to precolonial Ashanti kings. Wale Adebanwi shows how an Awolowo cult in Nigeria elevated "Awo" into at once nationalist avatar and pan-Yoruba ancestral deity.[80] Such conflations ran the risk that any tarnishing of the ruler could swiftly undermine the legitimating doctrine of the new state.

In a review essay on African nationalism in 1986, I concluded that "nationalism as direct orienting focus for ideological discourse or academic analysis is in relative eclipse. The widespread mood of demoralization characteristic of contemporary Africa denies to nationalism the audience to supply it with driving energies." I have since revised this view; nationalism has discovered new roots. Fortunately, I left myself an escape clause: "The possibility of a future confluence of catalyzing circumstance resurrecting nationalism cannot be excluded."[81] I return to the topic of nationalism in chapter 8, examining its place in the key identities driving African politics.

INSTITUTIONAL FRAMES

When the decolonization process reached its final stages in the negotiated transition pathway, there was a natural consensus on the appropriate institutional framework. The metropolitan model served as obligatory reference point: parliamentary for Britain and Belgium, semipresidential in Gaullist France. The compressed transition timetables meant that in most countries there were only one or at most two national elections in which universal suffrage applied and all restrictions on political organization were lifted.[82] But the anointment of a successor regime with at least one fully majoritarian election was critical to both the departing colonizer and the prospective independent government. For the most part, the integrity of the electoral process in the independence elections was assured, and opposition movements were able to challenge the dominant parties that already existed in most countries. Territories in the French orbit had held a number of elections since 1946, though with restricted franchise until 1956; Ruth Collier suggests this facilitated the consolidation of a dominant party. She also finds that, in the British case, the period of multiracialism as decolonization strategy fostered the rise of strongly ascendant African nationalist parties in opposition, especially in Malawi, Zambia, and Tanganyika.[83] Still, by my count in twenty-five (or well over half) of the forty countries whose transition followed the terms of the code of decolonization significant opposition existed at the moment of independence.[84]

Richard Joseph (and others) have argued that much of the outcome of the democracy wave of 1990 in Africa was a product of an intense quest for external presentability.[85] In retrospect, a comparable conclusion is applicable to the transitional independence representative institutions and constitutional arrangements. For the withdrawing colonizer, departure with dignity necessitated leaving behind an institutional frame reproducing the formal arrangements and political values of the metropole. For the nationalist successors, the ostensibly democratic terminal colonial arrangements assured initial international respectability, especially in the Western world, from which aid expectations were at that juncture highest. Further, as argued earlier, the dominant political party, and its leader, needed the voice of a duly elected parliament to push forward and take the final steps to independence. The blessing of sovereignty could thus be feted in mutual celebration.

Several institutional aspects of the bargained independence settlements merit note. With rare exceptions, there was a strongly unitarian cast to the constitutions. Partly this mirrored the institutional heritage of the three negotiating decolonizers, Britain, France, and Belgium. The United Kingdom until the devolution to Scotland and Wales had been a well centralized polity; the Jacobin tradition of the one and indivisible republic was even more pronounced in France. Belgium, although federalized after decolonization, was still a unitary state in 1960. The colonial apparatus was strongly centralized at the territorial levels that became the successor states. Nigeria, where the north had a largely separate administration, and southern Sudan, whose colonial establishment from the 1920s on was insulated from the Arab-speaking north, were the main exceptions.[86]

The unitary preferences ran deep for the dominant political movements everywhere but in Nigeria. Calls for federalism were heard but were audible in only two instances: in the case of regional or ethnic minorities marginal to the ascendant parties and in the case of regions having distinctive interests. The main examples are Sudan, Congo-Kinshasa, Uganda, Kenya, Zambia, and anglophone Cameroon.

In Sudan, decolonization was shaped by the Egyptian interface originating in the pretense that Britain ruled in "condominium" with Egypt. The driving factor was British determination to avoid a power transfer that would meet Cairo hopes for a "unity of the Nile valley," a unity that could be secured by the restoration of Sudan's sovereignty, which Egypt enjoyed at the moment of British occupation in 1882 and vigorously reasserted in 1936 and 1951.[87] British orchestration of terminal colonial politics thus backed those parts of the Khartoum political universe that shared London's antipathy to unification with Egypt, especially the Umma Party descended from the Mahdist movement of the 1880s that originally drove out the Egyptians in 1885.[88] The crucial 1946 conference on constitutional development ignored warnings from administrators in the south, and the protests of the small emergent southern intelligentsia, against accepting a unitary, northern-dominated framework; Sir James Robertson, governor at the time, claimed that any other policy "would be received with great disappointment in the Northern Sudan and would incline many of those who are now supporters of the Sudan Government [colonial administration] to go into opposition and drift across to the Egyptian side."[89] When the radical regime of the Free Officers seized power in Cairo in 1952, and especially after Nasser became ruler in 1954, Britain swiftly conceded the virtually immediate independence demanded by the northern Sudanese political universe, overriding southern fears of marginalization. Thus the stage was set for a southern insurrection that flamed until 1972, then reignited in 1983 and continued until 2005; the first episodes unfolded just before the January 1956 independence, with the mutiny of the southern Equatoria Corps against their northern officers. The consequences have haunted postcolonial Sudan to this day, the country finally breaking up in 2011.[90]

In Congo-Kinshasa, federalist demands came from the two ends of the country, the Kongo ethnic zone in the west and the Katanga region in the southeast. The Kongo, long dominant in the capital, perceived their leading role to be threatened by the unitarist nationalism incarnated by the Lumumbist parties.[91] In southern Katanga, resentment against immigrants from other areas, the lure of monopolizing mining rents, and the complicity of European settler and corporate interests fueled a federalist party that led a secession lasting from eleven days after independence until January 1963.[92] Following the November 1965 creation of the highly centralized regime of Mobutu Sese Seko, federalism was banished from official vocabulary, to partially return only in the 2005 constitution after the decomposition of the state and the brutal civil wars of the 1990s.

In Uganda and Zambia, the demands for federal autonomy came from the well-organized kingdoms of Buganda and Barotseland on which Britain had conferred special treaty recognition and status. In contrast to the settlement negotiated in Sudan and Congo-Kinshasa, some acknowledgment of special standing was part of the agreement, extended in Uganda to three other kingdoms. Postcolonial unitary norms soon overrode these transitional concessions, as well as in anglophone Cameroon. In a few places elsewhere federalist murmurs appeared reflecting apprehensions of postcolonial marginalization, notably from smaller "minority" ethnic groups in Kenya, fearful of the numerical weight of the Kikuyu and Luo, and in Ghana, from Ashanti suspicious of the centralizing intentions of Nkrumah. In the end colonial authorities accepted majoritarian claims for unitary rule. The only example beyond Nigeria of an enduring postcolonial federation was Libya from 1952 till 1963. The exception proves the rule; rather than a mechanism for decentralization responding to internal demands, the federal formula was a device imported by the UN-led external architects to stitch together the disparate parts of Cyreneica, Tripolitania, and Fezzan: a "putting-together federalism" in the terms of Alfred Stepan.[93] As soon as this fragile entity had sufficient revenue flow and central institutions, federalism gave way to the continental unitary currents.

Noteworthy is the rarity of durable constitutional frames in the independence constitutions. Of the forty cases of negotiated decolonizations, only two such examples can be identified: Botswana and Mauritius. Even more striking is the coincident fact that these two states by unanimous judgment currently rank at the top of the continental roster of effective Weberian states: they have had a stable and continuous democracy and a competent administration, and they have shown impressive and sustained economic growth. I return to these two cases in chapter 9.

COLD WAR CONTEXT

A final dimension of the decolonization process requiring note is the larger cold war context. Britain and Belgium especially were keen to marginalize African political leaders or groups suspected of Communist attachments or those who fell in the broader category of "extremists." Colonial security services, greatly expanded in the postwar period, had some capacity to carry out such an aim. In this goal they reflected, and were pushed by, the anti-Communist obsessions of the United States. The battle took place not just in Africa but in the various international organizational forums where competing Western-aligned and Soviet-bloc affiliated movements vied for the participation of young African leaders—labor, youth, and students especially. The Soviet-inspired organizations—the World Federation of Trade Unions, the World Federation of Democratic Youth, the International Union of Students—offered a far more forceful condemnation of imperialism and colonialism, as well as some travel and scholarship opportunities.

Moreover, the Soviet Union and China—in intense rivalry by 1959—were willing to supply arms to liberation movements in return for alignment. But their ability to shape the independence settlements was limited; their primary accomplishment was to instill small currents of Communist orientation among coteries of intellectuals. Especially in the 1970s, African versions of Marxism-Leninism became an important regime option, but the menace perceived in some Western quarters of "Communist penetration" in decolonizations was vastly exaggerated.

BEYOND INDEPENDENCE: COLONIAL LEGACY

Only in Congo-Kinshasa and Equatorial Guinea did the independence settlement instantly unravel; elsewhere the first moments of postcolonial life passed peacefully. On the surface, the youthful contingent of new leaders seemed self-assured. But beneath the surface, darker premonitions lurked. Were the formal institutions of constitutional democracy sufficient to meet the urgent challenges of rapid transformation? Could the ethnic cleavages that electoral competition had frequently politicized be contained within a parliamentary framework? Could the extravagant promises of a life more abundant be translated into tangible improvement in well-being of the ordinary citizen? More immediately, how could the aggressive claims of the political allies assembled for the electoral path to high office be satisfied?

In the event, the most prominent trend of the immediate postcolonial period was the consolidation of power by the independence leaders and their effort to manage politics by constructing political monopolies. Legislatures were marginalized, and the executive inner core of the colonial state under new management returned to its role as the central locus of politics. A clear trend to single-party rule set in quickly, choking off vantage points from which regimes could be challenged. In these processes, one sees the enduring impact of the legacy of the colonial state, whose mentalities, habits, quotidian practices, and operational norms became reproduced in its successor. The immediate postcolonial polity was a hybrid creature in which the deeply rooted heritage of colonial autocracy joined to the shallow constitutional democratic structures of independence. In retrospect, there is little cause for surprise that the former soon triumphed over the latter.

The visible agents of state power—the district officers—continued to wear military-style garments while itinerant or when making public appearances. The shelves of government offices held the statutes bequeathed by the colonial state, including a reservoir of repressive legislation. The new rulers, wrote Jacob Ajayi, "staked their claims to leadership on their superior knowledge" of state management and development pathways; they "took for granted the masses' and the traditional elites's willingness to accept their leadership."[94] In my conclusion to the African colonial state volume, I suggest that "confrontation of the colonial state with a catalogue of its iniquities had earned the right to succession; the elite's rule was justified by a schooled vision denied to the unlettered masses. The schoolroom, however, was the colonial state."[95] I recollect Jean Colin, at that time the Sengalese minister of the interior, telling a colloquium of senior bureaucrats in 1988 that the colonial regime was a "command" state, while its postcolonial successor was based on "encadrement." For the subject, this was a distinction without a difference: in both cases, the task of the administrator was to secure compliance with state instructions in pursuit of its developmental mission.

The imprint of the colonial state was also visible in the organization of government. Government departments became ministries. The basic organizational practices and administrative deontology were transmitted intact. The same remark holds for the military organization and judicial structures.

The army, essentially an internal security force, tended to retain its recruitment patterns and distinct institutional culture; housed in barracks and quarters separated from the population, the military was of insular orientation. The judiciary, which had many expatriate judges in its ranks at independence, internalized in significant ways a culture of the law. Another colonial inheritance was legal pluralism—statutory codes inherited from the imperial center were operative in the cities and modern sector, while customary law was operative in rural areas and shari'a was in effect in Muslim zones.

The new leaders absorbed a vision of the future well characterized by James Scott as "high modernity."[96] As chapter 1 argues, the apparent effectiveness of centrally planned economies in achieving such a goal held a magnetic charm. The democratic strictures of the independence constitutions gave way to interpretations, in the words of Mamadou Diouf, that "served to guarantee the authority of the state and the uncontrollable and uncontrolled exercise of power by the occupants of the state apparatus."[97]

Closing Reflections

Still, when decolonization had run its course with the final liquidation of the apartheid regime in South Africa, a momentous transformation had occurred. This last act in the drama (and trauma) of European occupation of Africa brought to an end an era whose first moments date to 1415, when the Portuguese seized a pair of outposts on the Moroccan coast. Ironically, these enclaves—Ceuta and Melilla, still under Spanish rule—remain the sole remaining traces of direct colonial presence in Africa. The heart of the colonial moment, however, was the eighty-five years between the launch of the partition around 1875 until the zenith of decolonization in 1960.

The varying forms taken by the dialectic of decolonization shaped the independence settlements, the point of departure for postindependence Africa. The divergent pathways, from negotiation to armed liberation struggle, defined the nature of the successor elite. Small states—Belgium and Portugal (as well as Netherlands in Indonesia)—proved especially lacking in decolonization statecraft, which had major postcolonial consequences. Although at the outset of the process, the colonial state held the trump cards, increasingly the growing effectiveness of nationalist mobilization shifted the initiative to the African side. So also did the changing global context, as both great powers backed decolonization, even if for different reasons. The UN became an increasingly important source of pressure, directly through the trust territory system and indirectly as a forum for the expression of anticolonial sentiment.

For the majority of cases, the power transfer pact reflected what I have termed the code of decolonization, which in turn embedded a set of internationalized norms reflected in UN resolutions. Of enduring significance was the sacrosanct status of territorial integrity and sovereignty. The fragile constitutional formulas adopted for independence mostly eroded quickly; they were nonetheless the starting point for postcolonial politics.

The weight of the colonial legacy hung heavily over the African political realm for at least the first three independence decades. Everyday semantics acknowledged this reality in the everyday designation of the African independent state as "postcolonial;" only briefly was the "postindependence" descriptor in vogue. In comparative terms, one may remark that such a label is rarely encountered with respect to Asian or other third world states, an unspoken tribute to the capacity of the African colonial state to reproduce itself in the its independent successor.[98] The bureaucratic authoritarian essence of the colonial state long remained a defining quality of African states, increasingly modified by neopatrimonialism, and perhaps beginning to fade somewhat into the background following the wave of democratization and state remaking beginning in the 1990s.[99]

4

The Road to Autocracy

Breakdown of the Decolonization Settlements

The moment of enthusiasm that accompanied the rituals of independence faded quickly. The first decade of African independence saw a rapid transformation of the political landscape, from governance under the fragile democratic constitutions required by the withdrawing imperial powers as a condition of independence to predominantly autocratic rule, whether under single party or military auspices. Three of the largest countries experienced debilitating civil wars—Nigeria, Sudan, and Congo-Kinshasa. Almost everywhere, by the end of the 1960s military intervention appeared the main alternative to single-party monopolies.

The purpose of this chapter is to explore the main trends of African politics during what chapter 1 suggested was the first cycle of hope and disappointment, largely situated in the 1960s. In my view, the crucial trends were the failure of most of the decolonization constitutional dispensations to endure, the disappearance of autonomous sites of dialogue and debate, the consolidation of single parties fused with the state, and the emergence of military coups as the primary form of regime change. The consequence of these changes was the rise of autocracy as mode of governance. These patterns at first found ideological justification by the rulers and theoretical support from academic observers. By the end of the 1960s, however, the credibility of the single party and military rule was challenged, and the first symptoms of what later became "Afropessimism" were apparent.

Harbingers of what lay in store appeared in the form of three unwelcome developments by 1960, the miraculous year of African independence: the evident drift to autocracy in the two most widely heralded avatars of sovereignty, Ghana and Guinea and the instant postindependence crisis in Congo-Kinshasa. In the Ghana case, after the forceful confrontations of colonial authority in 1948 and 1951 by emergent nationalists, a mostly cooperative and well-crafted transition to independence followed. Though Ghana was not the first African state to gain sovereignty, its celebrated 1957 independence was the key landmark in the decolonization dynamic. But by 1960, a new constitution empowered President Kwame Nkrumah to rule by decree, preventive detention legislation had been adopted, and opposition leader J. B. Danquah was soon headed for prison.

The huge stimulus to African nationalism attending Ghanaian independence was matched by that greeting the abrupt 1958 Guinea independence that followed the epic defiance of France by the radical nationalist leader Sékou Touré. His summons to a "no" vote on the de Gaulle constitutional proposals, offering only autonomy to the African territories, won overwhelming support. This spectacular audacity enjoyed wide admiration in Africa; the Guinea victimization by an immediate and punitive rupture by the colonizer, including withdrawal of all personnel and cessation of aid, evoked a reflex of solidarity. The dominant party, the Parti démocratique de Guinée, earned high esteem for its capacities for mass mobilization, persuasively chronicled by Ruth Schachter Morgenthau among others.[1] But by 1960 there were clear signs that the political monopoly was hardening and that opposition was not being tolerated, and soon dissidents began flowing into exile.

At the time of Ghana and Guinea independence the colonial hegemon in the Belgian Congo still appeared an impregnable fortress. Almost overnight, by the beginning of 1960, *bula matari* dissolved, surrendering its status as leviathan and turning itself into a supplicant to the fragmented Congolese nationalists in order to assure social peace in return for immediate independence: a further fillip to anticolonial enthusiasm and a spectacular warning to all remaining colonial occupants. But the shattering meltdown that began five days after independence eviscerated euphoria: the new state within a fortnight lost control of its mutinous army, its richest province and primary revenue source, Katanga, through secession, and its bureaucracy through the panic flight of most of the Belgian cadres still occupying its top ranks. The global crisis and multiple external interventions that ensued foregrounded new apprehensions about the stability of the new African states, and their vulnerability to outside forces.

The durability of the decolonization settlements thus came into question. In a number of other significant cases, compromise formulas for the independence transition had unraveled by the mid-1960s, resulting in civil wars in Nigeria and Sudan and ugly impasse in Uganda, Burundi, Congo-Brazzaville, and Benin. A clear trend to single-party rule was already evident; so also was a visible drop in mass enthusiasm for once popular independence leaders. Not long after, the military coup emerged as a mechanism for regime change, since the one-party formula made leadership change impossible. The imposition of army rule perhaps solved the problem of political turnover but at the price of a new and unpredictable form of autocracy. Whether through single-party monopolies or military rule, all paths seemed to lead to authoritarianism by the later 1960s. By 1970, only in three independent countries—Botswana, Gambia, and Mauritius—did the ostensibly representative democratic constitutions of the independence transition remain truly operative; elsewhere, nearly 40% of the countries were led by military figures who frequently created their own single parties. In almost all other countries single parties either held legal standing as the sole political organ or were on a path clearly moving in that direction.

THE FATE OF MONARCHIES

Before turning to single-party consolidation and the rise of military rule, I pause for a brief reflection on the virtual disappearance of monarchy as a modality of rule at the territorial state level soon after independence, despite the historical importance of kingship in Africa.[2] In eight countries, at the moment of independence, monarchs served as heads of state. In four—Egypt, Tunisia, Burundi, and Libya—kings were swept aside in favor of single-party or military regimes in the early independence years. Ethiopia and Morocco had a rich history of monarchies of millennial depth; both were lynchpins of the political systems, though the last emperor of Ethiopia was ousted and killed by the army in 1974. Swaziland had a more shallow precolonial history but managed to outwit decolonization constitutionalists and swiftly consolidate royal autocracy. Finally, kingship survived in Lesotho but in a much reduced capacity. These last four cases—Ethiopia, Morocco, Swaziland, and Lesotho—that deviate from continental patterns merit brief scrutiny.

In Morocco, the singular legitimacy of kingship, and the advantage found by sultans in managing a complex society through limited though real political pluralism, resulted in an unusually stable form of rule. Three successive sultans survived serious challenges, both at the time of independence and again in 1971 and 1972 when military coup efforts narrowly failed. The monarchs proved astute political managers, beginning with Mohammed V, king at the moment of 1956 independence, through his successors Hassan II (1965) and Mohammed VI (1999). Though Mohammed V overcame the stigma of royal collaboration with the French by developing ties with emergent nationalists beginning in the 1930s, the critical rehabilitation of the king (sultan) came through his deposition and exile in 1953. Despite strong republican currents in nationalist circles, demand for the return of Mohammed V became the popular rallying cry; confronted with rapidly deteriorating circumstances and a liberation war in neighboring Algeria, the French were compelled to return him to the throne, from which place he then brokered the restoration of Moroccan sovereignty. The sultan maneuvered with consummate skill to prevent the leading nationalist party, Istaqlal, from achieving sole power. Throughout, the monarchy has favored political pluralism, deriving its power from its remarkable capacity to orchestrate diverse social forces: Berber tribes, the restless mountain redoubts (*siba*, or zone of dissidence historically), an organized urban labor force, Islamist currents, and a factionalized bourgeoisie.

In achieving a relative mastery over the Moroccan political landscape, the monarchy drew on a deep historical narrative, dating from the ninth century. The present Alawi line has held the throne since the seventeenth century. Its contemporary kings invoke a potent repertoire of powerfully resonating symbols and beliefs. As sharifs, or presumed descendants of the Prophet, they incarnate intertwined religious and political legitimacy. As commander of the faithful, the sultan also embodies the charismatic supernatural force of *baraka*, the mystical currents of Sufism, and the administrative force of the modern state. John Waterbury appropriately opens his masterful monograph with article 19 of the 1962 constitution: "The King, Commander of the Faithful, symbol of the unity of the Nation, guarantor of the perennity and continuity of the state, watches over the observance of Islam and the Constitution. He is the protector of the rights and liberties of the citizens, and of social groups and collectivities."[3] A more recent study dissecting the performative powers of the monarchy concludes that the "immense capacities of a late twentieth-century technological state, combined with the effective authority of an age-old theocratic-based legitimacy, synthesized to give the regime the capacity to govern with few constraints other than those imposed by economic necessity."[4]

The Swazi kingdom emerged under King Sobhuza only at the beginning of the nineteenth century, in the wake of the Nguni wars in southern Africa and reign of the legendary Zulu conqueror Chaka. Early in the colonial period, kings compromised their legitimacy through extravagant land deals under dubious circumstances; by 1908 some two-thirds of the kingdom was in the hands of foreign concessions. King Sobuza II (1922) launched a land buyback scheme, which recovered a portion of the lost territory; he also irritated the British through repeated demands for recognition as king, not just paramount chief, the habitual colonial designation for a customary ruler. His increasingly prickly relations with the colonizer helped erase the earlier stigma of his predecessor's reckless land cessions and restored the customary prestige of the monarchy sufficiently to allow it to assert regalian claims to postcolonial authority. Though the independence constitution provided for a modicum of representative democracy under royal rule, the royalist party, the Imbokodvo National Movement, won all the seats in the 1967 independence elections (with only 80% of the vote). By 1973, Sobuza II—annoyed by the 1972 election of three opposition Ngwane National Liberatory Congress members—suspended the constitution and began ruling by royal decree. A couple of new constitutions offering some representation through customary channels were subsequently drafted but then quickly set aside, and there was hope for a time that King Mswati III, who ascended the throne in 1986, would institute a less autocratic rule, but today Swaziland remains an autocratic monarchy.[5]

The Ethiopian monarchy, whose antiquity extends back to the sixth century BC, vanished following a military coup in 1974. More than any other African kingdom, the emperor relied on a legendary prominence in classical historical accounts. During two periods of vitality, between the first and eighth and then again from the twelfth to the sixteenth centuries AD, the empire was a regional hegemon. Then after three turbulent centuries of warring factions another moment of renewal came in the mid-nineteenth century. The revival of the empire coincided with the imperial partition of Africa, in which the renovated empire became an important participant, expanding in all directions under Emperor Menelik II in the 1890s. In an epic battle at Adwa in 1896, Menelik's forces inflicted a humiliating defeat on a large Italian army of conquest, a rare event in the annals of colonial occupation memorialized in innumerable popular paintings of this combat.

He was succeeded by the last emperor, Haile Selassie I, in 1930. Under his rule, the empire engaged in a modernization project that ultimately generated a restive military and a radical intelligentsia who took offense at what it perceived as the feudal backwardness of the country. Though under Italian occupation from 1935 to 1941, the imperial throne survived in British exile, from where the emperor led an Ethiopian force in alliance with British units

to restore the kingdom. The new social forces unleashed by the modernization project backed a military coup in 1974 that destroyed the imperial throne
and, with it, most of the landlord class.[6]

Lesotho is the other country that remains a kingdom. Its kings have been
important players, though not the primary rulers. As in Swaziland, the monarchy emerged only in the nineteenth century. Mainstream nationalist parties
were much stronger than in neighboring Swaziland, partly because many
Sotho men spent part of their lives as migrant laborers in the more politicized environment of South Africa. Chiefs as well are an important force
in its unstable politics, and the military has twice intervened. Strikingly,
Lesotho ranked last among the nineteen countries surveyed in the 2008 Afrobarometer study both in support for democracy among the population and
appraisal of government conformity to norms of democracy. The authors of
the study conclude that despite "the façade of parliamentary institutions, the
country's political culture still manifests monarchical and military cultures
from the past."[7]

Kingship had been a central institution both in precolonial and colonial
Africa, though in most cases other than those noted the orbit of monarchy
did not coincide with the territorial demarcations of the colonial partition. In
these instances, colonizers normally recognized kings and other customary
rulers as "chiefs" and incorporated them as intermediaries at the lower echelons of the colonial apparatus. A number remained loyal to the colonizer until
late in the decolonization process, and they were often regarded with suspicion by African nationalist movements. The unitary and centralizing impulses
of the postcolonial states often led to attempts to reduce or even eliminate
the chiefs, an ambition that frequently floundered on the incapacity to replace their influence over rural populations. In some cases, customary rulers
achieved recognition as leaders more august than mere chiefs and had their
kingly titles acknowledged and greater latitude conceded to them (the emirs
of Northern Nigeria, the monarchs of Buganda in Uganda and Barotseland in
Zambia). In the Buganda case, its king (kabaka) served as head of state from
the 1962 independence until 1966. The conflict between their regal claims
and the reach of the sovereignty doctrines embraced by new rulers produced
acute postcolonial conflict in both Uganda and Zambia.

Recourse to a monarchical ethos was to have an unexpected revival later,
when long-ruling auocrats groomed their sons for succession. By 2010, such
dynastic practice had occurred in Togo, Congo-Kinshasa, and Gabon; similar
plans took visible form in Egypt, Libya, Senegal, Niger, Uganda, and Angola.

Public sensibilities were offended by such schemes; even in the successful instances, there was substantial opposition, and especially in Egypt and Senegal clear antipathy to dynasty plans was voiced.

Towards Single-Party Monopolies

These particular instances noted, we may turn to the great majority of cases where the tendency to one-party rule set in, usually swiftly. Though most countries had clearly dominant parties at independence, in many there was significant opposition. In the largest countries—Nigeria, Sudan, and Congo-Kinshasa—no party came close to achieving a majority in the independence elections. In Uganda, the Uganda Peoples Congress, though ascendant, needed a coalition with the Buganda-based Kabaka Yekka to form a government. In francophone Africa, Benin, Togo, Chad, Gabon, and Congo-Brazzaville lacked clearly dominant parties in 1960, though regime measures to impose them soon followed.

Nonetheless, despite these numerous examples of a multiparty reality, the doctrine of single-party rule became continental dogma almost at once. Already in 1959, at a major gathering of African leaders and intellectuals from around the world organized in Ibadan by the Congress for Cultural Freedom, a noted intervention by American scholar David Apter on the political value of an effective opposition encountered almost universal rejection; only a fraction of the Nigerian participants diverged from single-party orthodoxy. Congo-Kinshasa leader Patrice Lumumba argued that "divisions lead to the suicide of Africa;" a Togolese participant warned that "too much freedom kills freedom; too much democracy kills democracy," while others claimed that opposition movements were Trojan horses for imperialism.[8]

An explanation of the swiftness of this trend might begin by noting the shallow commitment to liberal constitutionalism on the part of the new leadership. Doubtless the independence constitutions lacked the iconic status of basic laws in long-established democracies. The colonial state always had "constitutions," which from the perspective of the subject were boundless reservoirs of arbitrary power. One often hears the independence constitutions dismissed as imposed copies of the metropolitan models; there is some truth to this claim, in the sense that the point of departure in the designing of decolonization institutions was inevitably the template provided by the imperial centers: Britain's Westminster model, France's more presidential Fifth Republic, Belgium's parliamentary system. Further, the withdrawing colonizers used the ransom of independence to vest the property rights of colonial interests and in the British case frequently to entrench protection for regions or components of the population to whom it had made special commitments: Barotseland in Zambia, Buganda and the kingdoms in Uganda, smaller communities in Nigeria and Kenya, white settlers in Kenya, Zambia, and Zimbabwe. Though in many respects the independence constitutions were liberal democratic documents, they lacked affective standing for African publics as well as elites; they reflected bargains struck with the colonizer rather than a negotiated compact between state and society. Thus, with little popular outcry, they were quickly subject to amendment or replacement, such revision being a means of restricting opposition and reinforcing what became single-party rule.

New rulers were conscious of the fragility of their power and naturally tended to seek its consolidation; the single party was the favorite mechanism. At the same time, they became swiftly aware of the limits of the single party. The authority of the colonial state ultimately rested upon force, including the hypothetical capacity to summon additional military detachments from the imperial centers. The bureaucracies and colonial constabularies were under secure command of colonial governors, and the local chiefly intermediaries remained for the most part reliable clients. But these coercive capacities did not instantly transfer to the new African leaders. Ostensibly to provide security guarantees, the French army initially set up permanent bases in Senegal, Ivory Coast, Gabon, Central African Republic, and Djibouti, but its intervention in support of regimes was not automatic; Fulbert Youlou in Congo-Brazzaville and David Dacko in Central African Republic made desperate appeals to the French to block coups in 1963 and 1965, respectively, and were turned down. In 1964, the British army put down mutinies in Uganda, Kenya, and Tanzania. But recourse to such security backing was at best a humiliating admission of weakness. The initial postcolonial African armies were small, and they often still had European officers, even commanders, who were reluctant to engage their forces in domestic political conflict. Political activity was off limits for African soldiers and bureaucrats in late colonial times; not only were they mostly not participants in nationalist mobilization, but they were viewed with suspicion as allies of the colonial state and even as agents of repression. Chiefs as well were frequently hostile to nationalist parties, and thus their fidelity to the new order was hardly guaranteed. Thus new rulers could not fully trust the established armature of the state. A common and almost reflexive response was reinforcement of the personal powers of the president, both within state and party.

Presidents soon heard whispered warnings from their entourage of possible conspiracies taking form, contributing to the sense of insecurity surrounding power exercise. Parliaments were difficult to manage, even with apparently secure majorities. Patrice Lumumba, for example, stitched together an alliance of Congolese nationalist parties constituting a large majority of the assembly in pursuit of confirmation as prime minister in June 1960; however, in the actual vote he gathered support from only 74 of 137 members. The discipline of parliamentary parties was far from assured.

Further, in a number of instances political impasses soon emerged. In Senegal in 1962, Prime Minister Mamadou Dia sought to oust President Léopold Senghor by mobilizing the left wing of the ruling Union progressiste sénégalaise (UPS). His attempted parliamentary coup was thwarted by the army and triggered a crackdown on dissidents within and without the UPS, followed by a move to full single-party rule. A similar effort to oust Prime Minister Milton Obote of Uganda through parliamentary maneuver in early 1966 led to a comparable imposition of a single party. In many other instances, ruler fears of constitutional paralysis or opposition conspiracies fueled the move to enforce single-party rule.

Parties achieving dominance in the terminal colonial period necessarily did so as broad alliances spanning regions and ethnic communities; their success as anticolonial national fronts did not erase the regional particularities of the movements. Once established as panterritorial frontrunners, dominant parties did not see the need to make concessions to ethnoregional appeals, thus enabling their competitors to make use of them and thereby gain a foothold. Virtually everywhere the competitive campaign for electoral support to some degree gave new political content to ethnic identity, convincing incumbents of the perils of uninhibited political competition.

The rapid expansion of electorates during the elections immediately preceding independence was important to the ethnic dimension of politics in another way: it introduced numerical strength as an ingredient of power calculus. In the colonial era, communities with early access to missions, schools, urban employment, or other mechanisms of social promotion—Igbo and Yoruba in Nigeria, Ganda in Uganda, Chagga in Tanzania, Kikuyu in Kenya, Luba and Kongo in Congo-Kinshasa, the four old communes in Senegal, the numerically tiny Freetown creole community in Sierra Leone—enjoyed a large advantage in gaining elite representation. Such groups were thus heavily overrepresented in late colonial professional and bureaucratic ranks. The swift introduction of universal suffrage in the decolonization era brought major adjustments in regional voice; in Nigeria, for example, the once "backward" northern region suddenly emerged as a key player, propelled by its demographic strength. Buganda was accustomed to playing a hegemonic role in Uganda from the beginning of colonial rule, but since it only had 20% of the population, universal suffrage and territorial politics ensured its subordination to long-scorned regions. Regional grievances regarding purported neglect by the colonizer added another volatile item to the agenda of rule and supplied another reason to assert the necessity of single-party leadership.

Political ethnicity as an active ingredient in national politics was a novel factor; the difficulty of calculating its impact made it a wild card in decolonization politics, another vector of uncertainty for the new leaders. Jan Vansina recounts his experience as anthropologist-historian at Lovanium University (now University of Kinshasa) at the time of the first Congo national elections; a parade of political organizers sought authoritative information from him as to the exact dimensions and boundaries of their potential ethnic appeal and the nature of affinities that might attract neighboring groups.[9] The electoral patterns often provided early evidence that ethnicity was less fixed and primordial than previously assumed; its parameters proved more fluid and adaptable to instrumental interest and circumstance than conventional wisdom allowed. But it was no less troublesome for that as viewed from the presidential palaces.

In short, assumption of power was surrounded by a host of new uncertainties, perhaps greatest in countries such as Congo-Kinshasa where independence came very suddenly and only recently was even imaginable. Nearly everywhere, no one could be certain what the morrow might bring; a vague sense of lurking danger hovered in the background. A Ghana government white paper concerning an alleged conspiracy in 1961 conveyed a sentiment broadly shared at the time: "The strains experienced by an emergent country immediately after independence are certainly as great as, if not greater than, the strains expressed by a developed country in war time."[10]

Demarcating the Independent State

Thus the legitimation imperative weighed heavily on the new leaders. Beyond the single- party reflex, one common response was the effort on several fronts to demarcate the new state from its colonial predecessor. In the realm of symbols, new flags, banknotes and postage stamps provided visual actualization of new statehood. So did the immediate assertion of an international presence that countries made by joining the UN, by welcoming a flood of embassies to the capital, and by sending their president on overseas tours, especially beyond the imperial capital. The distinctiveness of the new state could also find expression through vocal expression in support of ending colonialism and liberating southern Africa, as well as through participation in "third world" forums and pan-African organizations such as the OAU. The colonial stranglehold on the economy was contested by launching parastatal enterprises and—a few years later—by the nationalization efforts chronicled in chapters 1 and 2. The broad frontal assault on African culture permeating the colonial system found a riposte in the ideological promotion of doctrines celebrating its richness: *négritude*, African personality, authenticity.

An obvious avenue for demarcation was to accelerate Africanization of the visible face of the state through reducing or eliminating the European presence in the bureaucracy and military officer ranks. Vigorous Africanization had the supplementary advantage of enabling the state to reward political clientele. However, there were consequential costs to the speed of Africanization. The large numbers of inexperienced and perhaps underqualified persons catapulted to leading positions took a toll on the administrative capacities of the state in the early years, given that in most countries the pool of university graduates remained small. Moreover, as a general rule the Africanization of the civil service ranks that had once been filled by expatriates was accompanied by retention of the generous perquisites of salary, free housing, and utilities, designed to allow compensation to satisfy presumed requirements for a European lifestyle. These provisions added to the financial burden of a rapidly expanding bureaucracy and soon became a heavy charge on state budgets. A further liability to rapid Africanization was the widespread popular perception that its benefits extended only to a narrow elite.

KEEPING THE PROMISES OF INDEPENDENCE

Fulfilling the promissory notes of the independence movement was another daunting challenge. At the level of the broad public, the demand for social amenities stood foremost. Schools ranked high on the list; the direct link between educational credentials and social ascent was by now apparent to all. Rural health facilities were likewise in high demand; the efficacy of basic modern medicines—pills and inoculations—was highly valued, even if they might be supplemented by customary medicinal practices. Well drilling near settlements spared women the burdensome daily chore of fetching water from stream courses. Rural roads opened farms to commercial outlets for their produce. The terminal colonial state had made major public investments in social infrastructure in its last years; the postindependence successor could suffer by comparison if it failed to keep up the pace of improvement.

Regimes naturally turned to rhetorical devices to complement actual social provisioning. The ubiquitous five-year plan advanced visions of a better prospective future through its listing of an attractive package of projects to be completed during the period. For the most part, such ventures began to lose credibility by the time the second round of plans became due, by which point the large shortfalls in the implementation of the original charters was becoming evident. Huge development spectaculars—above all giant hydro-electric projects and steel mills—had special allure for their high visibility; though a number of the dams, such as Akasombo on the Volta in Ghana and Kainji on the Niger in Nigeria, were effectively completed, steel mills as indus-trial symbols rarely succeeded; the fiascos of Ajaokuta in Nigeria and Maluku in Congo-Kinshasa are cases in point to which I return in chapter 5.

More urgent pressures for the fruits of independence came from the large clienteles fostered by party mobilization and electoral campaigns in the inde-pendence elections. The party cadres and regional notables who had toiled in the party-building efforts were much less interested in regime policies than personal rewards for their investment of time and resources. The party appa-ratus offered only limited means by which to absorb these claimants; revenue from member dues was meager, and alternative ways of diverting flows from the state treasury were not yet available. Only the political superstructure of the state, and its multiplying parastatal auxiliary enterprises, offered a pool of assets with which to satisfy these demands. Over time, as the emergent polit-ical class acquired mercantile resources and interests, it became possible to grant other lucrative favors: government contracts, import licenses, urban property grants. The green shoots of what blossomed into neopatrimonial pol-itics soon appeared, though not initially on a scale dominating the landscape.

For the younger generation, especially those with at least secondary school credentials, accelerating Africanization provided abundant opportunity for entry into the middle ranks of the administration and rapid promotion there-after. The first couple of independence decades witnessed an extraordinary dynamic of state expansion. During the 1960s, in sub-Saharan Africa bureau-cracies grew by 7% annually; by 1970 60% of wage earners were government employees, and up to 80% of the operating budgets were devoted to public sector salaries.[11]

A pair of resulting sociological patterns merit note in passing. First, at the time access to state employment was the key if not the sole path to social promotion for new generations. State agents during this period enjoyed higher remuneration and social respect than their private sector counterparts. Class formation followed the same hierarchy; at the summit appeared an emergent politico-administrative bourgeoisie. The old landed, mercantile, and professional classes established in the Arab tier of states in the north were absent to the south, where the colonial interests, European settlers, or immigrant South Asian or Mediterranean mercantiles stood in the path of African economic accumulation or social ascent, especially outside of West Africa. Access to the state through employment or favor became the primary avenue for economic as well as social ascent. Thus an elective affinity between the dominant postcolonial African class and state expansion took hold.

Second, by the later 1970s this pattern was no longer sustainable, and mechanisms of social closure sprang into place. The life more abundant promised on the decolonization campaign trail accrued above all to that part of a postwar generation positioned by education to seize the sudden opportunities. When fiscal crisis and external debt closed the gates of state expansion, future prospects for an ambitious, young postcolonial generation became far more circumscribed. Further, public service became less attractive as inflation or salary arrearages corroded the value of state employment, transforming civil servants in many lands by the later 1970s into the respectable poor. The political class might still prosper through neopatrimonial channels, but its ranks were subject to turnover with each military coup, and its activities, often on the boundaries of the law if not beyond, carried much more risk than state employment had in the early days of independence. The magnitude of the change finds full measure in the evolving age patterns of the top leadership; whereas at the moment of independence, as chapter 1 noted, new rulers were in their thirties or early forties, by 2010 a number of incumbents were over seventy and some over eighty (Wade in Senegal, Mubarak in Egypt, Mugabe in Zimbabwe). The independence era was an extraordinary moment of high hope for the young, a moment that stands in stunning contrast to the dismal prospects faced by most of their counterparts today that produces the visible social anger of the contemporary youth generation and results in their often desperate efforts to emigrate.

INTERNATIONAL LINKAGES

The new role of independent states as full members of an international system provided opportunities and perils. The nature of the engagement at the end of the day supported the consolidation of single-party rule and accepted without qualms the installation of military regimes. The code of sovereignty required that external powers channel their aid and other attentions through the duly recognized postcolonial regimes. The context of global politics in 1960 ensured that new African states would have eager suitors and that the emergent single-party regimes could draw on external resources to facilitate consolidation of power.

The colonial state largely succeeded in isolating its subject territories from external influences. But the confluence of African independence with the peak of the cold war and the Sino-Soviet split meant that the eager African quest for an international presence intersected a vigorous competition for influence and clienteles. The weapons of the great powers were economic aid, security assistance, and ideological cultivation. The motivations were partly preemptive: the United States sought to block "Communist penetration" or Soviet alignment, and the Soviet Union aimed to prevent alliance with the "camp of imperialism." Maximally, the goals were reliable votes in the UN and other international bodies, security cooperation, and economic management consistent with the competing great-power ideologies.

New African states were invariably attracted to economic aid; the days of the petrostate were well in the future, and none had revenue flows sufficient to fund their ambitions. At first economic assistance was readily available; aid soon became a significant part of most African budgets.[12] Western aid resources vastly exceeded those available from the Soviet bloc, and visible Soviet alignment, especially in the security domain, might threaten assistance flows from the United States in particular. In 1956, this found dramatic illustration when U.S. secretary of state John Foster Dulles abruptly withdrew a commitment to Egypt to help fund the Aswan high dam as punishment for the purchase of arms from Czechoslovakia and other overtures to the Soviets. Conversely, security collaboration with the United States brought aid rewards; through the 1960s Morocco and Libya were generously compensated for hosting major U.S. air bases. Ethiopia was until the 1974 revolution a major recipient of American assistance, military and economic, and had received critical UN backing for its incorporation of Eritrea in 1952 and subsequent annexation in return for housing an important U.S. military base near Asmara.

Initially, many African leaders believed that their states could benefit from cold war competition by playing the two sides against one another and maneuvering between them under the shield of nonalignment. Though the doctrine of equidistance between the global blocs was appealing, its application

proved difficult. For the francophonic states of sub-Saharan Africa, the entanglement with France was extensive; the former colonizer guaranteed the
interterritorial currency, the CFA franc, and was the only donor to provide
direct budgetary support. Many of the first-generation rulers had served in
French parliament or even cabinets; their ties with the Paris political world
were intimate and multiplex, extending even to influence within French
parties. Some, such as Leon Mba of Gabon, sought full incorporation in the
French Republic as a department until 1960.[13] Guinea and Mali, which initially rejected the French community ties, paid a high price in aid access,
by no means offset by Soviet bloc assistance. For others, the legacy connections of the West through higher education, mission-related associations,
and the greater presence on the ground of Western personnel meant closer
natural ties.

Still, the need for demarcation and the importance of radical, often Marx-
ist-tinctured ideological currents among the emergent intelligentsia made the
label of American client state in particular an important liability. Thus at least
nominal nonalignment and links to broader currents of pan-African diplomacy
remained official policy; for the more radical states of the time, an active
engagement in broader third-world movements and the fight for African
liberation were key elements in the quest for legitimation. Indeed, Egypt in
1956, Ghana in the early 1960s, and later Libya all became active sanctuaries for radical opposition and even insurgent movements from other states
deemed too subservient to Western interests.

One more crucial aspect to the international environment at the moment
of the continental shift to single-party systems requires mention. Not only
did new rulers have but a shallow commitment to democracy as a mode
of governance but the erection of single-party monopolies met with no resistance from Western democracies. Some leading academic analysts of the
day—Thomas Hodgkin, Immanuel Wallerstein, Ruth Schachter Morgenthau,
among others—entered a brief in support of the single-party system, provided that it was based on mass mobilization, that many (including myself)
found persuasive in the first moments of independence.[14] Democracy promotion did not have high ranking among American policy goals at the time;
former colonizers were far more concerned about stability and the postcolonial preservation of their interests. The emergence of an active international
human rights movement was still many years away; critical evaluations of
African state performance by such bodies as Freedom House and Transparency International were beyond imagination. Indeed, the view took hold in

policy circles and academic communities that autocracy was a necessary stage for developing countries; this thesis received elegant and influential exposition by Samuel Huntington in 1969.[15]

CONSOLIDATION OF SINGLE-PARTY RULE

The claims by the new leaders that single parties were indispensable instruments for rapid development thus fell on receptive ears internationally. Internally, opposition movements naturally contested the single-party trend, but they were nearly always soon marginalized or eliminated. A number of mechanisms were employed to achieve this end.

Electoral systems could be easily altered. A favorite scheme in francophone Africa was to transform the entire country, or at least large regions, into a single electoral district, with party list voting; thus even a small majority translated into winning all the seats. This manipulative procedure was pioneered in Ivory Coast and Guinea and spread to Mali, Senegal, Benin, Togo and others. Alternatively, opposition ranks could be whittled away by defections brought about by inducements, intimidation, prosecution, or even forced exile. When sufficient majorities were in hand, constitutional provisions could be changed to ban opposition parties, which were at the time legitimated by plebiscites that invariably received overwhelming votes. By the end of the 1960s, one-party rule had juridical standing in most states not yet under military rule.

Another widely employed device to institutionalize single-party supremacy was the forcing of key civil society organizations into the party structure as ancillary organizations. Trade unions, youth, and students, often reservoirs of dissidence, were special targets for such incorporation. Reorganized as agencies of party control, they became instruments of discipline and manipulation rather than vehicles for voice.

The use of arbitrary arrest to silence opposition often required new legislation authorizing preventive detention. Courts could not always be relied on to cooperate with political prosecution; the culture of the law retained its hold on many judges (often still expatriate) long after other components of the state had been placed under party command. The reservoir of arbitrary colonial legislation that remained in force provided other resources for intimidation. Colonies of political exiles soon began to swell, especially in the former imperial capitals and some neighboring countries.

Finally, the communications media needed to be brought to heel. Radio and—as it was introduced—television had always been government monopolies; thus these media were easily transformed into regime mouthpieces.

The press, however, was a different story; especially in West Africa, newspapers and pamphlets were a vital and vibrant source of debate in late colonial times, perhaps alongside a semiofficial government press. The semiofficial government press was transformed into a yet more docile vehicle, and as needed regime papers were launched. For the rest, through legal restrictions, financial pressures, arrests of editors, and outright suppression the independent press in most countries was brought to heel.[16]

THE BRIEF FOR SINGLE-PARTY RULE

Thus, through these and yet other mechanisms single-party rule soon became the near-universal pattern of government.[17] A number of justifications were adduced for the single party, predicated on the reality of its claim to mass mobilization or more minimally on a genuine broad adhesion. These are found in the declarations of leading figures, most importantly those of Kwame Nkrumah and Sékou Touré, and in the writings of academic advocates already cited. The most thoughtful brief for the single party is found in the 1965 Tanzanian report of a widely representative presidential commission to study the feasibility and shape of a democratic single-party state, described in chapter 1.

Thus a genuine mass single party, ran the argument, could bring a truer democracy than the divisive, often ethnic politics of multiple parties. In single-party democracy, membership was open to all; indeed it was often obligatory. Theoretically, decisions were made by the party on the basis of open discussion; thus fractious and adversarial multiparty democracy was replaced by consensual internal party debate. The party could thus claim to generate universal consent and in this way be said to embody a Rousseauvian general will. Candidates could compete within the party for nomination to parliamentary seats and party office; indeed, such competition became widespread and could be found in Tanzania, Kenya, Zambia, Ivory Coast, Congo-Kinshasa, among other countries.

A second cluster of arguments revolved around the urgency of national unity. The single party, through its supreme commitment to the nation, could rise above ethnicity. By barring institutional arenas in which ethnic conflict might occur by eliminating party competition, the party inhibited the harmful politicization of ethnicity and fostered the flowering of a nationalism transcending communal attachments. In short, the single party offered a formula for sidetracking ethnicity through what closely resembled the nation-building project labeled by Nelson Kasfir as "departicipation:" that is, closing down the channels for ethnic mobilization.[18]

A third array of justifications invoked the developmental necessity of a unified regime. There was not a moment to lose nor to waste in sterile debate. Underlying these themes was a curious law of regime energy conservation. The implicit thesis held that developing states possessed a limited quantum of policy energy; any that was consumed in contentious politics or adversarial discussion thus decreased the amount available to the state to act. A single party thus promoted judicious state energy conservation.

Fourth, a single party helped insulate the state from international intervention. Opposition parties readily became instruments of foreign interests. Senegal president Léopold Senghor wrote in 1961 that opposition is "tempted to serve foreign powers. . . . You know it, parties are teleguided from the outside. . . . Our duty is to prevent subversion."[19] Such views were widely held at the time.

Fifth, the single party had an important pedagogical function. In its mobilizational activity, the party provided a primer for the political education of the rural citizenry. Its popular meetings were forums for diffusing an agenda promoting radical change and for arousing the political consciousness of the lower reaches of civil society. Such pedagogy was also carried out by the party ancillary organizations within their respective spheres of activity.

Finally, competing political parties were held to be superfluous in Africa because of the purported absence of established social classes. Multiple parties were necessary where social class and hence conflict existed as a means of structuring and reflecting such fundamental differences. However—an argument particularly dear to Julius Nyerere—African society was in its essence communal. Its unity at the level of political movements was thus organic and natural.

Even by the early 1960s, these theses were losing their credibility, belied by the political realities visible to all. Symptoms of the infirmity of the single-party formula were widespread. Those associated with moderately successful regimes in terms of developmental achievement, such as in Tunisia, Ivory Coast, and Kenya, maintained some of their prestige. Others in which the consent dimension still overshadowed the repressive temptations, such as Tanzania, also retained their élan for another decade. But more often the credibility of the system was wearing thin.

Partly this reflected the de facto fusion of party and state. In the amalgamation, the state was the ascendant partner; as chapter 3 argues, the quiet assimilation of the norms, routines, and practices of the colonial state meant that its authoritarian face was destined to reappear. Parties as distinctive institutions tended to shrivel in postindependence Africa; states had a quotidian role and presence, and parties at the end of the day were above all electoral instruments, elections having been emptied of much of their content save for a plebiscitary function. Party ideology likewise devolved into vacuous slogans. One of my former doctoral students, Soriba Sylla, recounted to me his earlier experiences as an agent of the Ministry of Information in Guinea, sent on tours of villages to give ideological lectures. The villagers dutifully assembled at the summons of the local administrator; they listened politely, although he well understood that they did not believe a word he was saying. He also realized that they knew that he did not believe in the ideological message either.[20]

MILITARY INTERVENTION

By the mid-1960s, the military coup had emerged as the primary vehicle for regime displacement, and it remained so until the wave of democratization in 1990. This pattern—obvious in retrospect—was not foreseen in 1960. At that time, armies inherited from the colonial state were small, a mere ten thousand soldiers for giant Nigeria, and, as noted, with the exception of the Algerian army and the armed liberation movements that later succeeded to power, they had no ties to the nationalist movements. African officers trained in the military academies of Sandhurst and St. Cyr were exposed to very different intellectual views than those that most African university students were confronted with in overseas study, which tended be of radical leftist variety. Thus armies were widely viewed with distrust; Nkrumah was not alone in developing an elite presidential guard outside the military command structure, whose loyalty was assured by the diverse special privileges bestowed on its members.

The first military coup in Africa occurred in Egypt in 1952, when a junta of nationalist officers led by Gamel Abdel Nasser seized power, initially with Muhammad Naguib as front man. Although this military coup did not directly resonate elsewhere in Africa as a model—decolonization on the rest of the continent was still in its early stages—there were several aspects of the coup and the regime that emerged that were harbingers of the military takeover patterns that became institutionalized throughout Africa more than a decade later. First and foremost was the absence of any popular resistance; once a handful of top officers faithful to the old regime were neutralized, the new "Free Officers" junta quickly consolidated control.

The extant regime under King Farouk was utterly discredited by its venality, the greed of the landlord class that underpinned it, its failure to block the emergence of Israel as an independent Jewish state, and its inability to secure the withdrawal of the eighty-thousand British troops occupying the Suez Canal Zone (in violation of the 1936 accord providing for their presence, which capped the number at ten thousand). Farouk himself was a caricature of a modern ruler; as Martin Meredith writes, he had the largest landholding in Egypt, four palaces, two yachts, thirteen private aircraft, two hundred cars, a "gargantuan appetite and endless procession of mistresses."[21] Equally tarnished was the liberal Wafd party, in power since 1922, and dominated by the landlord class.

Though the initial number of officers involved in the conspiracy was small—no more than one hundred—the ability to strike a sudden blow at the heart of the system, to seize the capital, and to convince the public that the old regime was gone sufficed to consolidate power. Farouk was arrested at his summer retreat, compelled to abdicate and depart into exile, thus decapitating the institutions of the ancien régime. The Free Officers articulated a resonating message of radical reform and nationalist assertion that promised a new departure. Proposals to reform land policies for the peasantry, to confront the British garrison in the Suez Canal Zone, and to aggressively pursue funding for the Aswan high dam were wildly popular. So also was the nationalization of the Suez Canal in the wake of the abrupt American withdrawal of its offer of finance for the Aswan project in 1956. When the British and French, in alliance with Israel, sought to reoccupy the Suez Canal in late 1956, the global wave of protest, and intense American pressure compelled a humiliating abandonment of this ill-considered revival of nineteenth-century imperialism. Far more than a mere military autocrat, Nasser now stood at a zenith of global prestige, ennobled as an icon of anti-imperial struggle. Equally important for the future role of the military in Africa were crucial features not recognized at the time: the ready feasibility of the coup mechanism; the possibility of rapid consolidation of a new regime; the availability of a standard narrative of legitimation in cleansing corruption and introducing radical reform.

Thus some key dimensions of the future military coup dynamic were clearly sketched.[22] A sudden strike by a military segment controlling enough force to decapitate the summit of authority could succeed swiftly, especially if the head of state was abroad or distant from the capital and unable to immediately summon loyal forces. Once the key sites of power were captured—the presidency, the parliament building, a handful of core ministries—resistance by incumbents was difficult unless large portions of the security forces rallied to their defense. Quick seizure of the communications nodal points—the radio and television stations, the capital airport—likewise almost always assured success. Unless the conspiracy was betrayed to the incumbents, the plotters failed to seize the key nodal points of power, or external intervention in support of the extant regime occurred, there was little possibility of existing regimes striking back. As in the Egyptian case, the public disaffection that was widespread by the mid-1960s made popular resistance to a junta unlikely, and once the coup seemed a fait accompli the bureaucracy would follow orders. Indeed, almost always the immediate public response was celebration; in this mood of welcome, promises of sweeping away corruption, policy reform and (usually) eventual return to civilian rule and national elections were a passport to entry legitimacy.

Military intervention elsewhere appeared swiftly after independence, although at first each instance was attributable to unique circumstances, and except in Sudan coup organizers at once turned power over to others. Thus there was not yet a perception of an emerging pattern. The distinctiveness of each coup in light of what was to follow merits brief examination.

The next military takeover occurred in 1958 in Sudan, two years after independence. Northern Sudan was fragmented along religious and ideological lines; the two largest parties, the Umma (descendants of the nineteenth-century Mahdiyya) and the Democratic Union Party (later People's Democratic Party, linked to the Khatmiyya sect and Mirghani family), competed with an active Sudanese Communist Party, the political wing of the Muslim Brotherhood (later the National Islamic Front), and radical socialist currents. The south was sidelined in the decolonization arrangements; the British conceded a hasty power transfer to outmaneuver Egyptian claims to restoration of its nineteenth-century sovereignty. The unity of the Nile valley slogan from Cairo had some support from the Khatmiyya but not other northern factions and was strongly opposed in the south. By 1958, paralyzed by the political impasse and faced with the first stirrings of southern insurrection, the Khartoum parties willingly ceded power to the military.[23] This army takeover was little noticed in the excitement of impending independence elsewhere.

Five other brief military interventions took place before the tidal wave beginning in 1965 permanently transformed the environment. In all cases, power was at once turned over to civilians, a clear sign that army rule was not yet in the scripts of African political practice. In these instances, there is little sign of premeditation; the interventions were a product of immediate circumstance.

In September 1960, Colonel Joseph Mobutu temporarily seized power in Congo-Kinshasa, at a moment of total confusion and political impasse; President Joseph Kasavubu had announced the revocation of Prime Minister Patrice Lumumba, who in turn proclaimed the ouster of Kasavubu. Mobutu "neutralized" both and immediately turned authority over to a College of Commissioners composed of university students that he had designated. The army, badly disorganized by the July mutiny, was in no condition to take power, nor would such a move have been welcomed or even permitted by the major external forces then playing a crucial role, the UN and United States in particular.[24]

In Togo, a band of French army veterans, disgruntled by the refusal of President Sylvanus Olympio to incorporate them into a Togolese security force, invaded the presidential compound and assassinated Olympio in January 1963. This murder apparently had little advance preparation, nor was there a plan for what happened next. The assassins turned power over to a civilian national coalition dominated by the parties hostile to Olympio, contenting themselves with incorporation into army ranks and spectacular promotions, perhaps with discreet French guidance.[25] The street was silent rather than festive as it was after most later coups. Though Olympio had imposed an autocratic single-party system, with the north largely marginalized, the regime still had significant support in the capital; a still weak military could hardly have consolidated power.

In August 1963, by contrast, the military was propelled into action by an urban popular revolt in Brazzaville, led by unionists and students. The independence elections were closely contested, and Fulbert Youlou won the presidency by a narrow margin. The politicization of regionalism also produced a high level of ethnic tension, especially in the capital. Street rumor held that Youlou, a defrocked abbot, slept on a golden bed and wore imported Christian Dior soutanes. When Youlou sought to impose a single party, popular demonstrations became a mob march on the presidential palace, immortalized as the *trois glorieuses* days of a revolutionary uprising. A desperate Youlou appeal for French intervention fell on deaf ears, and he was forced to flee; the military intervened to restore order, but rather than taking power it merely brokered the accession to office of Alphonse Massamba Débat, who led a government initially viewed as staffed by "technicians."[26]

Benin was also an early candidate for temporary military intervention in 1963, because of the impasse and paralysis multiparty politics created in a setting where political competition by 1958 had congealed into a three-player ethno-regional game. None of the trio of independence political leaders (Hubert Maga, Magan Apithy, and Justin Ahomadegbe) were able to form any stable coalition; a venture by Maga in imposing single-party rule by the electoral formula of allocating all seats to the leading party led to crisis in October 1963, which the military intervened to calm. However, it began at once to negotiate its exit and organized new elections in 1964.

Finally, in Gabon in February 1964 a military faction aligned with opposition party leader Jean-Hilaire Aubame briefly overthrew President Léon Mba. Aubame and his party, the Union démocratique et sociale gabonaise (UDSG), had initially joined Mba in a coalition regime, but two successive new constitutions concentrated power in the presidency and marginalized the UDSG. Aubame drew much of his support from the Woleu Ntem subgroup of the large Fang ensemble in the northwest of the country rather than from the capital Libreville. This proved a weakness when the French army immediately intervened to reverse the coup in the face of little popular resistance. Mba's heir and successor, Albert-Bernard Bongo (later Omar Bongo Ondimba), completed the consolidation of a single-party rule, setting a record for longevity in office; he held power without serious challenge (and with strong French sponsorship) from Mba's death in 1967 until his own death in June 2009.

Thus before 1965, though in many countries discontents with single-party autocracy were building, military intervention was an isolated and sporadic response to palpable public disaffection. The African political scene altered dramatically from 1965 to 1966, when in the space of a few months nine successful army coups took place in Algeria, Benin, Burkina Faso, Burundi, Central African Republic, Chad, Congo-Kinshasa, Ghana, and Nigeria. Enhancing the shock effect of these coups was the high visibility and broader political importance of several of the countries. In different ways, Ahmed Ben Bella of Algeria and Kwame Nkrumah epitomized the heroic dimension of African liberation; Ben Bella secured his image as a result of his part in the bitter eight-year independence war in the former, and Nkrumah earned his through his towering persona as anti-colonial tribune. Congo-Kinshasa and Nigeria were two of the largest and most important African states. In none of these instances did the military then withdraw in favor of a preferred civilian leader or hold immediate elections to resolve an impasse; from that point until the 1990 democratization wave the army coup became the institutionalized mechanism—indeed, almost the sole means—for incumbent displacement and regime change. This bedrock political axiom became embedded in expectations across the continent.

To be sure, there were a handful of cases during this period in which the military voluntarily withdrew so that electoral democracy and civilian regimes could be restored (Benin, Burkina Faso, Ghana, Nigeria, Sierra Leone, and Sudan). These restorations were either brief or, as in Sierra Leone, soon degenerated into personal rule. In a half dozen cases, an incumbent military regime was ousted by another army ruler (Burkina Faso, Burundi, Chad, Congo-Brazzaville, Ethiopia, Ghana, Nigeria). Throughout the quarter century between 1965 and 1990, at any given point, by my calculation, 30 to 40% of African states were headed by rulers of military origin. Still, worth noting is the fact that nineteen states have never experienced a successful military coup since independence.[27]

As the foregoing suggests, a number of predisposing factors produced the wave of military interventions. A frequent precipitator was paralyzing political impasse, all but beyond resolution by the existing rules. Disillusion with the first-generation regimes was general, whether or not military intervention occurred. Developmental performance, though often respectable in the first independence years, usually fell short of the promises on the campaign trail, especially for the poorer segments of the population. Whispers of corruption in high places began to circulate, and direct experience of extortion by police agents or other officials started to enter daily experience. In a number of countries, European officers had been still atop the military command structure in 1960; by 1965 nearly all were gone.

The spread of discontent was well known to the young officers through their own social networks. In addition—a factor stressed in the influential monograph of Samuel Decalo—corporate grievances on the part of the military along with personal discontents frequently entered the equation.[28] In Ghana, for example, the creation of the President's Own Guard outside the military structure, with special perquisites, angered the regular officers.[29] The small independence militaries were lightly armed infantry units; appetites for more exotic armament—aircraft, tanks, and naval vessels—naturally outgrew budgetary possibilities. Factionalism within the military, personal and ethnic, complicated civilian control. Even if the most senior officers maintained regime loyalty, their junior counterparts might not; the original Nigerian coup was carried out by a handful of mostly Igbo majors. An important dimension of the drama of military intervention was the role of very junior or even noncommissioned officers in power seizure; Sergeant Samuel Doe of Liberia in his 1980 coup is a prime example of what Jimmy Kandeh calls the "lumpen militariat."[30] He cites other examples of subaltern coups in Sierra

Leone (1968, 1992, 1997), Ghana (1979, 1981), Burkina Faso (1983), and Gambia (1994).

The lessons apparent from the earliest military takeovers now seemed applicable on a continental scale. Swift nocturnal seizure of the capital was unlikely to be resisted by the civil population; indeed, with rare exceptions coups were welcomed. Bureaucracies could be expected to transfer their loyalty to the military regimes. Another critical lesson: there was no international sanction. Cold war competition was already intense by the 1960s in Africa; great powers supported their clientele with security assistance while they held office but surrendered to new realities if a successful coup produced a change in external orientation. The French were an exception; with military detachments in place in the countries most critical to French interests, such as Ivory Coast, Gabon, and Senegal, and the capacity, clearly demonstrated in Gabon in 1964, to intervene and reverse a coup, visible French backing for a regime was effective inoculation against conspiracies. So also was the pervasive reach of French intelligence into the security apparatus of states within the Françafrique orbit, making plotting difficult without discovery.

Success for army conspirators was not automatic. The risks of discovery were substantial, requiring that plotter confine the circle of conspiracy to a narrow set of participants strategically situated and possessing the power to

TABLE 4.1. Successful Coups in Africa, 1952–70

Country	Year
Algeria	1965
Benin	1963, 1965, 1965, 1967, 1969
Burkina Faso	1966
Burundi	1966
Central African Republic	1965
Chad	1965
Congo-B	1963
Congo-K	1960, 1965
Egypt	1952, 1954
Gabon	1963
Ghana	1965
Libya	1969
Mali	1968
Nigeria	1966, 1966
Sierra Leone	1969
Sudan	1958, 1969
Togo	1963, 1967, 1967
Uganda	1970

move key units. Defectors might reap attractive rewards for denunciation of the plot. State security organs were on the alert, and foreign intelligence services often had their own networks that might catch the scent of a budding plot. Patrick McGowan has created a data set of all sub-Saharan African coups and unsuccessful coup attempts from 1956 to 2001. He enumerates 108 failed coups, a total that well exceeds the 80 successful ones.[31]

Once coups had succeeded, a standard playbook emerged for transforming the entry legitimacy that disaffection with incumbents usually provided into more enduring patterns of public acceptance. A comprehensive listing of the failings of the outgoing regime normally accompanied the proclamation of the new order. Such rosters of iniquity inevitably included accusations of abuse of power, incompetence, and corruption. A frequent mechanism for translating the coup justification into a veritable "black legend" of the former regime was the swift creation of a commission of inquiry into corruption; inevitably there was ample material to document past predatory behavior, which distracted attention from whatever predatory behavior the incoming rulers might be engaging in. The conspicuous search for the overseas assets of their predecessors accompanied by demands for their return helped keep the misdeeds of their predecessors in the public eye.

Reassuring declarations of the interim, temporary nature of the military mission were also standard fare. The public was usually promised that, once the Augean stables left by the former regime were thoroughly cleansed, a new constitutional order would follow, accompanied by elections and a restoration of civilian rule. The military as national saviors were mere temporary caretakers. To preserve an appearance of continuity, the junta permitted prominent figures from the ousted government, if they immediately rallied to the new order, to hold high office. In Congo-Kinshasa, for example, Mobutu kept the former parliament on salaried employment for a year following his November 1965 coup. Interested external actors, especially those who had the capacity to intervene, were also assured that their interests would be protected. Promises of salary increases for the civil service were likewise a frequent device to consolidate acceptance.

Ideology supplied another avenue for securing legitimacy. New military regimes invariably invoked nationalism as the central dimension of their renovating ambitions. Often, as with Nasser, this reaffirmed nationalism was elevated into a discourse of revolutionary change. The year after seizing power Nasser published his ideological testament as "the philosophy of the revolution."[32] The discursive credibility of the new regime won enhancement when it confronted the British, when it succeeded in nationalizing the Suez Canal in 1956, and when it instituted increasingly radical land reforms. For a time the current of Arab socialism linked to Nasser enjoyed commanding political prestige throughout the Middle East.[33]

Another intriguing use of ideology as a weapon of military legitimation is found in the realm of the Afromarxist state, at one time an important category. The first countries that formally adopted Marxism-Leninism as doctrine—Congo-Brazzaville, Benin, Somalia, Madagascar, and Ethiopia—were all headed by military regimes in search of extended legitimacy. To boot, as noted, the five leaders concerned had no prior known intellectual engagement with Marxism-Leninism; however, the concept of the Leninist state with a security infrastructure at its core was a serviceable vessel for military ambitions. In addition, in all these cases the new military rulers confronted a large and assertive intelligentsia for whom Marxism was orthodoxy. This nettlesome group was outflanked by regime declaration of Marxist-Leninism as official doctrine, which enabled the regime to deftly purloin its ideological clothing.[34]

MILITARY AS RULERS

In the outside academic and policy worlds, a mythology of the unique qualifications of the military as custodians of development took form. However retrograde army rule might be in Europe, the argument went, in the developing world the military had several special institutional characteristics that fashioned armies as midwives of modernization. This thesis had five main components.

First, the mission of the army was to be supreme servant of the nation. More than any other institution, the military was imbued with a national ethos. In the context of the perceived fragility of new African states and their susceptibility to ethnic and religious tensions, the resolute territorial commitment of the military was a critical safeguard against fragmentation.

Second, the army was a more highly professionalized institution than its civilian counterparts. Many of its officers had been trained in military academies or advanced training centers abroad and had internalized a culture of technocratic performance. Action-oriented by nature, the military responded with brisk purpose to the challenge of assigned missions.

Third, armies were based on hierarchy, unity of command, and strict discipline. Thus they were less hampered by onerous procedures and inertial tendencies than bureaucracies. These virtues translated into more energetic and efficacious developmental management.

Fourth, military experience was an academy of leadership. Promotion criteria and processes were strictly merit based, which guaranteed the ability of those rising through the ranks to command positions. These selection procedures rewarded superior talents and screened out the incompetent. High military rank was a certificate of leadership competence.

Lastly, and most importantly, all these qualities permitted armies in power to establish stable patterns of rule, which in turn created the conditions for economic development. The technocratic managerial style of the military organization translated to efficient operation of the state. Stability promoted confidence and the predictability conducive to investment flows.[35]

None of these claims stood the test of time or were borne out by actual experience of military rule. Along with an undoubted national ethos within the military there were ethnic imbalances and tensions mirroring those in the larger society. Colonial constabularies frequently had been recruited primarily from areas lacking in educational infrastructure, especially from certain communities in the hinterland, such as the Tiv in Nigeria, the Kabre in Togo, the Acholi in Uganda, and the Kamba in Kenya. The British in particular imported from India a "martial races" theory for rank and file soldiers, holding that particular communities had special military aptitudes. African officers, late to be recruited, required some secondary instruction and were often of different regional provenance than the rank and file. Thus the new postindependence armies had sharp ethnic imbalances, both in terms of overall demographic composition and representation in the officer corps. Such ethnic disparities were critical factors in the 1955 mutiny of the Sudan Equatoria Corps and the 1966 Nigerian military coups, events leading directly to civil wars. The imbalances in recruitment often increased when armies took power; the top leaders were then influenced by what Cynthia Enloe terms an ethnic security map and favored recruitment in those zones whose loyalty to the military hierarchy might be presumed by their identity affinities.[36]

The professionalism, discipline, and leadership talents of African militaries varied widely. Those armies rarely or never exposed to the temptations of power exercise, such as those in South Africa, Tunisia, Senegal, Botswana, and Zambia, perhaps correspond to the admiring portrait drawn by analysts touting the benefits of military rule in developing countries. In its first years of rule, the Nigerian military drew positive reviews, particularly in its management of reconciliation following the brutal 1967–70 civil war. After extended periods of power, particularly under the rule of the last military autocrat and the most deplorable one, Sani Abacha, it was inevitable that the army leadership would end up being guilty of colossal corruption. Indeed, former U.S. ambassador John Campbell has argued that the key figures in recent decades of Nigerian politics, in particular Olusegun Obasanjo, Ibrahim Babangida, Yakubu Danjuma, and Shehu Yar'Adua, all were positioned following their leadership in the 1967–70 civil war and subsequent rise to general rank to accumulate huge fortunes that would ultimately finance their role as candidates, godfathers, and rainmakers in competitive politics.[37]

Stability as a benefit of army rule is likewise problematic. Some military rulers remained in power for very long periods; Qadhafy in Libya ruled for forty-two years, Eyadéma in Togo for forty, Mobutu in Congo-Kinshasa for thirty-two, and the military lineage in Egypt (Nasser, Anwar Sadat, Hosni Mubarak) for more than a half century, but such longevity usually coincided with gradual corrosion of the state. Though Ellen Trimberger might celebrate the Nasser regime as a prototype of revolutionary development from above in 1978, almost no one would advance a comparable claim for Mubarak in his twilight years.[38] But military regimes by their nature choke off all normal possibilities for leader succession, leaving only a new army coup, revolt in the periphery (Chad 1982, 1990; Ethiopia 1991; Congo-Kinshasa 1997), or eruption of the urban street (Sudan 1964, 1985; Benin 1989; Tunisia, Egypt, and Libya 2011) as a remedy for the inevitable corrosion of power. Of the thirty-four countries experiencing at least brief periods of army rule, only in Gambia was there a successful military intervention whose leader retained power thereafter without further forcible displacement (and in this case dates only to 1994).

The related claims that political stability under military rule ensures successful economic management are likewise difficult to sustain. Any clear overall correlation linking higher levels of economic growth with military management would be difficult to demonstrate. Decalo shreds the claims for superior macroeconomic management in the case of the four countries he explores in depth (Togo, Benin, Congo-Brazzaville and Uganda).[39] Admittedly, there are instances of military rulers, particularly early in their tenure, acquiring a reputation for economic renovation and renewal. Nasser in his early years won wide admiration for his radical land reforms and successful nationalization of the Suez Canal, which has remained one of the rare large African public enterprises to operate profitably and efficiently. From his 1965 power seizure till his 1979 death, Houari Boumedienne in Algeria combined a still legitimating ideology of populist socialism, the mystique of the liberation struggle, and a technocratic statism with the substantial oil revenues fueled by the 1973 and 1979 price booms to produce an image of success. In my 1982 book comparing African ideological pathways, I concluded, based partly on the views of Algerian specialists I consulted, that "the balance of evidence is in many respects positive for the radical populist—and statist socialism in Algeria."[40] Only a few years later, in 1988, this favorable reading was belied by the wave of urban riots reflecting accumulated social anger of the new generations at the stagnation of the politico-military machine and dimming the legitimacy of the liberation mythologies. Congo-Kinshasa ruler Mobutu in his early years enjoyed high prestige internationally and broad support domestically for the stabilization of the economy, the restoration of effective rule, and enchanting prospects of rapid progress.[41] The early admiration for Mobutu rule long ago faded in the face of deepening corruption and public disaffection and colossal policy miscalculations bankrupting the state. There were a few other African military leaders held in high regard until late in their rule, including Sangoulé Lamizana of Burkina Faso, Juvenal Habyarimana of Rwanda, and Yakubu Gowon of Nigeria. But military takeovers have also placed a number of the most catastrophic leaders in presidential palaces: Idi Amin in Uganda, Jean-Bedel Bokassa in Central African Republic, and Samuel Doe in Liberia. Yahya Jammeh in Gambia shows signs of following in their footsteps, as he exhibits increasingly bizarre behavior. Now insisting on being addressed as His Excellency President Professor Yahya Jammeh, he claims to have a secret herbs and a banana medicinal remedy for HIV / AIDS, conducts large-scale witch hunts rounding up hundreds who are coerced into drinking a foul-smelling witch-finding liquid, threatens to behead gays, and has presided over the disappearances and assassinations of journalists.[42]

Despite the promises of a return to civilian rule after a period of cleansing that have normally been made at the time of power seizure from 1965 on, only rarely have army rulers fulfilled such pledges (Ghana in 1969 and 1979, Nigeria in 1979, Sudan in 1965, Burkina Faso in 1971), and in all these instances the newly elected civilian regimes were soon ousted. Rather the military regime changed clothing and ostensibly civilianized itself. A new constitution would permanently extinguish whatever shreds of legitimacy that still clung to the former rulers. A new political party would be launched, embodying the renovation program of the military. The nomenclature of power could also be civilianized; the general became the president in everyday reference. A large fraction of the political class could be recuperated, in return for a place at the table.

This script describes the pattern pursued by most regimes issuing from military coups until 1990. Indeed, it was first drafted by Gamel Abdel Nasser in Egypt following his 1954 takeover, through his Arab Socialist Union (which replaced two previous unsuccessful efforts to form an effective single party, the Liberation Rally and the National Union). Muammar Qadhafy initially modeled his Libyan regime in 1969 on the Nasser design, though he soon abandoned it in favor of his own quixotic "state of the masses" described in chapter 2. In three cases (Algeria, Burundi, Guinea-Bissau), the new military rulers were embedded in an existing single party and preserved it as part of the new fabric. In almost all other cases, the former dominant party was contaminated by its association with the ousted regime, and it would have implied a residual legitimacy of the old order to preserve it; dissolution and erasure were the remedies.

In Ghana and Nigeria, where democratic attachments were not easily stamped out, military rulers sought interim legitimation in the claim that they were in the process of organizing a new elected civilian regime through extended constitutional preparation and broad civil society consultation. In both countries during the 1970s, the military pushed hard to win public assent to a permanent institutionalized role for the military in governance. In Ghana, this took the form of a civil-military diarchy, labeled UNIGOV. Such a scheme never gained tractio, and gave way in 1979 to one of the few honestly conducted if temporary democratic restorations during the era of autocracy.

In Nigeria in the early 1970s, top military officers were sent on speaking tours around the country to promote the notion of army rule as the most suitable form of energetic developmental rule in African conditions. Future president Olusegun Obasanjo in one such sermon in 1972 summarized this brief for military leadership: "[The soldier is] no longer regarded merely as a gun-toting robot. It is his lot to create a world community devoted to stability and socio-economic progress. . . . [Africa should recognize] his role as a nation-builder, his commitment to modernization.[43]

I recollect attending such a lecture by one Brigadier Rotimi, a respected officer, at the University of Ibadan in January 1972. Rotimi drew extensively on the academic literature of the day celebrating the role of the military in political development. The hostile reaction of the student audience mirrored the reception this message received elsewhere in Nigeria. Both the sheer political complexity of Nigeria and its entrenched political culture of democratic attachment posed an enduring problem for legitimation of military rule, even though the army held power more or less continuously from 1965 till 1999 (there was a brief interlude from 1979 to 1983 in the military's reign).[44] The military response was a permanent claim to transition to civilian rule, through a succession of constitutional committees and preparatory electoral consultations.

Whether the ruler was of civilian or military origin, the mechanisms of partial civilianization of army rule over time blurred the distinction between the original form of single-party systems and their military-led counterpart. Presidents of military provenance tended to assure the security apparatus a somewhat greater role, though in nearly all cases, especially after regime consolidation, civilians mostly occupied ministerial and territorial administrative positions. The Arab tier of countries in northern Africa went furthest in constructing national security or *mukhabarat* states, which located the security apparatus at the very center of power. Their policing mechanisms were particularly effective in sustaining regimes until the 2011 "Arab spring." The overriding commonality in all regimes of military provenance was the authoritarian practice of governance. By the 1980s, patrimonial autocracy and life presidencies were firmly established norms, whose consequences I explore in the following chapter.

SUMMATION: THE SIX IMPERATIVES

By way of summation, let us return to the half dozen state imperatives set forth in chapter 2. Hegemony of the new states, through the 1960s, was subject to serious challenge in only three countries: in Nigeria during the civil war, in southern Sudan during the separatist insurgency, and in Congo-Kinshasa, when Katanga seceded in 1960, and during the 1963–65 rebellions. These cases are examined in chapter 7, which covers civil warfare; for the moment we may note that in all three instances central authority prevailed in the form of military action in Nigeria, externally mediated negotiation in Sudan, and decisive intervention by the UN, Belgium, and the United States in Congo-Kinshasa. Independent states in arid and remote areas with small and dispersed pastoral populations that were not economically attractive to the colonizer and subject only to minimal, preemptive administrative control sought without success to extend their effective hegemony; northern Chad, northeastern Uganda, and the Sahara fringes of northern Mali and Niger are examples. But within the zones of effective control in late colonial times, administrative routines continued without serious discontinuity or challenge.

The means by which African countries pursed autonomy altered substantially. The colonial state, by its external nature, enjoyed substantial internal autonomy over the subject populations, who retained a capacity for evasion but little ability to alter policy direction. Anticolonial political mobilization had linked independence movements closely to their supporters, and government agents were far more subject to social pressures, particularly from those with some communal affinity, than their colonial predecessors. The central dynamic this chapter examines consisted of the quest for renewed though differently textured state autonomy. Single-party systems and the autocratic mechanisms deployed by both civilian and military regimes responded to the autonomy imperative. Foreclosure of competitive politics, restoration of arbitrary restrictions and punishments on the unruly, control of the means of communication, central discipline on the parties—these among other measures marginalized civil society.

In its external dimension, the capacity for autonomy quickly proved more circumscribed. The shield formerly provided by the metropolitan power that served as a filter for external influence was gone. Ideological self-assertion and collective protection under the umbrella of the third-world movements and pan-African solidarity served some purpose, but nonalignment offered only limited protection from the active pursuit of clienteles by the great powers, nor was the tactic of playing off West against East a sure guarantee of meaningful autonomy. Countries in the francophone orbit, save Guinea and Mali, were too dependent on France for aid, budgetary support, guarantees for the convertible currency, and security backing to stray far from the *chasse gardée* of Françafrique. Still, cold war competition was less acute in the 1960s than later, the debt crisis had not yet appeared, and the weakening of state fabric that became so apparent by the later 1970s was not yet visible; thus an appearance of a degree of external autonomy persisted.

The nature of the security imperative altered fundamentally after independence. The withdrawal of the metropolitan security blanket placed small and weak African constabularies in a vulnerable situation. External threats within Africa at this juncture were not the issue, though there were a number of instances of minor border disputes and a pair of major ones between Algeria and Morocco and Ethiopia and Somalia. The last two led to brief wars in the early 1960s, and then to a much larger one in 1977–78 between Ethiopia and Somalia. But the swift commitment to maintaining, even sacralizing, the colonial boundaries was instrumental in usually forestalling any sense of direct external security threat. In southern Africa, later to become a vortex of security dilemmas, South Africa did not yet perceive itself under direct threat, protected by the buffer of white-ruled territories to the north; thus the aggressive destabilization projects that so threatened the security of its neighbors by the 1980s were far in the future for it. Pan-Somali irredentism posed a threat to Kenya, Ethiopia, and Djibouti that was contained by pan-African diplomacy and international hostility to any dismemberment of these states.

The anti-imperialist sentiment common to most African nationalisms instilled, particularly in the more radical states, a sense that external security threats were very real. The Congo crisis was a searing memory for many African states, illustrating their potential vulnerability to powerful world forces; the Katanga secession, deeply wounding a new state, received support from Belgian, British, and French colonial interests, suggesting that imperialist conspiracies were alive and well. Even more dramatically, the Lumumba ouster and subsequent assassination, accomplished with the help of Belgium and the United States, sent a shock wave through Africa. For the more moderate states, the belated efforts by the Soviet Union to provide military supply to Lumumbist forces was also threatening. Though at this juncture in the 1960s only Algeria and Egypt could respond with accelerated purchase of heavy armaments, in most cases a reflex reaction of accelerating Africanization of the officer corps was visible.

But the main thrust of the security imperative was internal, directed at the consolidation of hegemony. The inherited colonial constabularies were entirely erected with this objective in mind. But one of the happier legacies of the colonial state was a disarmed population. Only in the few cases of protracted armed liberation struggle had there been a significant influx of weaponry, a situation that stands in striking contrast to the proliferation of armaments by the 1990s.

Response to the legitimation imperative initially rested on the achievement of independence and the promises of expanding social amenities of a prosperity to come encapsulated in the classic Nkrumah pledge to make Ghana a paradise in ten years. Much of the legitimation energies were rhetorical: five-year plans, showcase projects, celebrations of the nation, presidential tours. Gradually shrinking was the aura of governmental rectitude produced by respect for constitutional procedures, as the single-party monopoly took form and the zone of autocracy expanded. Though the novelty of independence soon faded as a legitimating stimulant, and many new rulers lost some of their aura, the legitimacy of the state itself was not at issue, save in the secessionist zones of southern Sudan, the Igbo zone of eastern Nigeria, and Eritrea. The wave of military coups from 1965 on were directed at the salvation of the state, a project of relegitimation, not rejection.

The revenue imperative did not at first seem to seriously constrain African states. Chapter 1 explains the extraordinary fiscal boon that coincided with decolonization; the last colonial decade witnessed a historically unique multiplication of revenue flows, created by the price surge for most African commodity exports, and the meaningful influx of metropolitan public capital. Favorable price regimes continued for many African commodities through much of the 1960s before turning unfavorable in the following decade. The withdrawing colonial powers maintained most of their assistance, and new aid funds became available from the Western donor community, often in grant form at first. However, some ominous clouds appeared on the distant horizon.

The dynamic of state expansion that began in the terminal colonial period redoubled its pace. The expanded pace of social amenity provision, the burgeoning ranks of the civil service, the new parastatal venture to foster industrialization, the reinforcement of security forces—urgent necessities and solemn promises—soon began to outrun revenue capacities. Further, the inherited structure of taxation had liabilities. For most states, the majority of state revenue derived from taxes on foreign trade, particularly export taxes. These in turn had a large impact on agricultural commodities and hence rural producers.

At the time, many development specialists and African leaders firmly believed that industrialization was the key economic growth. The "surplus" needed to fund industrialization could only be found through transfers from the agricultural sector. Thus commodity export revenues had to be increased by control of producer sales by state marketing monopolies, a pattern already set in late colonial times and reinforced after independence. Enhancement of state revenue could be accomplished both through the export tax and by fixing the producer price at a level well below the international market value. The farmers were well aware of the effect of these levies on their incomes, and they were a key source of the discontent that led to the overthrow of Kwame Nkrumah.[45] In interviews with Ugandan farmers in 1966–67, I found that respondents recognized and resented the scale of the fiscal take on their coffee and cotton.[46] Robert Bates in his succinct and masterful 1981 study shows how this revenue reason of state—the belief in the necessity of transferring resources from the rural to a nascent industrial sector combined with a legitimation-driven preoccupation with satisfying the urban sectors whose voice weighed more directly on the political process—wound up defeating its own purposes by undermining over time incentives for production.[47]

With respect to the accumulation imperative, the early independence years in the 1960s were a decade of moderately positive performance. Table 4–2 clearly shows that at first there was no marked discrepancy in economic growth between Africa and other low- and middle- income countries. The table was perhaps set for the difficulties that became apparent in the 1970s and for the outright crisis years of the following decade. Indeed, a seemingly satisfactory performance was far from enough to satisfy the ambitions of African leaders; the time was at hand for a vigorous expansion of the state.

The first signs of a developing divergence between reason of state and logic of regime and ruler began to appear. In the realm of security, especially after the advent of the institutionalized military coup, regimes became very sensitive to the ethnic balances in their armies and above all to the immediate personal loyalty of the top officers. Merit became secondary to political reliability and even kinship affinities. Governments that came to power through coups were driven to assemble a catalogue of iniquities of their predecessors; particularly with repeated use, such stratagems for regime preservation came at some cost to the legitimation of the state. As rulers became committed to remaining in power permanently, the fusion of person and state came at a price for the latter. Construction of personality cults around the president became the central focus of legitimation efforts, providing a perilous diversion from state-building. The growing need to channel public resources into prebends for henchmen and into secret funds for extrabudgetary presidential allocation began to weigh on the state revenue imperative.

All these trends were beginning to attract analytical notice by 1970. They were not yet of a scale to shape overall perspectives on the African state. Although the hour of full-fledged Afropessimism was still in the future, a clear mood of disappointment was evident at the end of the first postcolonial decade.

TABLE 4.2. African and Other Developing Areas Average Annual Growth Rates, 1960–70 (percentage)

Countries	GNP	GNP per capita
Low income countries	4.2	1.8
Sub-Saharan Africa	4.2	1.7
Asia	4.2	1.8
Middle income countries	6.0	3.5
Sub-Saharan Africa	4.8	4.3
Middle East / N. Africa	3.6	1.1
East Asia and Pacific	7.7	4.9
L. America / Caribbean	5.7	2.9

SOURCE: World Bank, *World Development Report 1980* (New York: Oxford University Press, 1980), 99.

5

Anatomy of State Crisis

It is not possible to live in a state where there are killings all the
time. We practically have no state.

> —Antonio Armando, Guinea-Bissau teacher, 2009

The state is in a phase of deliquescence. The state has been
dismantled.

> —Carlos Vamain, former justice minister, Guinea-Bissau, 2009

Already in September the drug traffickers had started moving out
of Guinea-Bissau. The drug traffickers need a certain stability.
They don't need a failed state. They need a weak state.

> —Antonio L. Mazzitelli, UN Office on Drugs and Crime,
> Dakar, 2009

Débrouillez-vous (Fend for yourself).

> —Article 15, Mobutu Congo-Kinshasa Constitution
> (popular version), 2009

A central postulate unanimously shared by political elites,
planners and advisers is that the state must organize and direct
the development effort. Agricultural growth will not come from
the occult workings of an invisible hand, but through the
guidance and stimulation of the political and administrative
structures.

> —Crawford Young, 1971

FROM REVOLUTIONARY EXPECTATION TO
FAILED STATE: GUINEA-BISSSAU

At the zenith of state expansion in 1974, Guinea-Bissau had been a lodestar for
African hopes.[1] Its remarkable liberation struggle from 1961 to 1974 had all but
defeated a Portuguese army that peaked at fifty-thousand. Its extraordinary

leader, Amilcar Cabral, won global admiration for his revolutionary doctrines, rooted in empowerment of rural society and a summons to the petty bourgeois political elites to commit "class suicide."[2] In the latter phases of the liberation war, when Portuguese detachments had been driven back into garrison towns, PAIGC, the revolutionary movement, had created liberated zones in much of the country, establishing people's stores, schools, and clinics. These avatars of triumphant revolutionary transformation attracted admiring commentary from veteran observers of African liberation movements, such as Basil Davidson and Gérard Chaliand, as well as young scholars, who were invited to tour the liberated areas by PAIGC.[3] The state, once torn from colonial grasp and reshaped as revolutionary instrument, could fulfill the guiding mission I and many others anticipated at the time.[4]

But by the end of the 1980s, the illusory nature of transformation projects led by a state incarnating the potent force of the revolutionary liberation movement was clear. A rural civil society, argues Joshua Forrest, had indeed been empowered by the Portuguese loss of authority. But the unusually weak colonial state had never succeeded in fully subjugating peasant society or incorporating its local leadership.[5] The project of rural civil society was local autonomy, not state-led development. The aura of liberation faded and the liabilities of a state with minimal revenue possibilities beyond initially generous external aid, a very slender infrastructure, and unstable politics became evident. Such iconic undertakings as the people's stores had proved to be corrupt, inefficient, even extortionate liabilities rather than vehicles of rural uplift. By 1982 expenditures rising at 19% annually were twice domestic state revenue; the fifteen thousand government employees were 61% of all salaried workers. The array of newly launched state light industrial enterprises were headed for bankruptcy.[6] By the turn of the century, the state became prey to narcotics trafficking and was a prototype of the failed state.

State decline and even failure was the dominant theme of the 1980s. Not all African states succumbed, but many confronted a deep, even existential, crisis by the end of the decade. The anatomy of state decline is the focus of this chapter. In my reading, a core factor was the excess embedded in the state expansion ambitions of the 1970s: what I have termed the integral state project.

Logic of State Expansion

The point of departure is the would-be integral state, whose portrait I sketch in chapter 2. There is no need to add further layers of detail to the schema set forth in that chapter. It is worth recalling, however, that although the 1970s were marked by projects of state expansion almost everywhere, their actual scope varied considerably. But the pattern of overreach was sufficiently general by the 1980s to shape the widespread perception of state crisis afflicting much of the continent. The marriage of the integral state project with the dominant pattern of patrimonial autocracy, whose corrosive effects were becoming fully evident, was a toxic pairing for the African polity. I endeavor in the following pages to unravel the results and consequences of the shattered illusion of the integral state.

The state expansion ambitions that became visible across the continent at the beginning of the 1970s drew inspiration from several sources, some already noted in chapters 1 and 2 but worth underscoring here. Ideology mattered, and a second wave of developmental socialism washed over Africa.[7] In its earlier 1960s version, socialist orientation stressed its singular rooting in African communal values rather than emphasizing confrontation with capitalism.[8] Thus even a robust practitioner of a market economy such as Kenya could represent its guiding doctrine as African socialism in an official document.[9] But second-wave socialism was more rigorous, inflected with Marxism-Leninism. Eight countries made official declaration of Marxism-Leninism as ruling doctrine, five of them the military autocracies examined in the preceding chapter and two more (Angola and Mozambique) issuing from prolonged armed liberation struggles against intransigent Portuguese colonial occupation. In a number of other countries, a discursive radicalization emerged: the call for agrarian revolution in Algeria, *jamahiriyya* (state of the masses) in Libya, the Arusha Declaration in Tanzania, the Mulungushi charter in Zambia, the call for radicalization of the revolution in Congo-Kinshasa, the move to the left in Uganda. In still others, an intensification of nationalist self-assertion was evident in the form of indigenization measures in Nigeria and elsewhere.

The importation of dependency theory from Latin America at this juncture, noted in chapter 1, crystallized diffuse suspicions of the workings of global capitalism into a coherent philosophical critique for many African political elites.[10] Third worldism was at its peak, epitomized by the success of the Organization of Petroleum Exporting States after the 1973 Arab-Israeli war in driving prices upwards more than 500%, following on the heels of the earlier nationalization of the Middle Eastern holdings of the Western oil majors. The Arab oil boycott of Western powers backing Israel in the wake of the war had astonishing short-term impact. A cascade of African diplomatic ruptures with Israel followed the surprising summons to solidarity with Arab brother nations by Congo-Kinshasa president Mobutu Sese Seko at the UN General Assembly on 4 October 1973; "Between a brother and a friend," he declared, "the choice is clear."[11] The Group of 77, formed by the developing nations to achieve a collective voice at the UN, flowed together with the nonaligned movement to formulate the demand for a new international economic order. Among the core theses of the the the new economic order was a sacred right to national ownership of natural resources within the sovereign territory, which served as a doctrinal stimulus to a number of nationalizations of mining corporations in this period.[12]

In the intoxicating moment of state expansion, contagion played no small role. Africa had become an intensely intercommunicating universe. Leaders frequently encountered each other at international events and exchanged regular visits. Informed publics closely followed events in neighboring countries and were often surprisingly attentive to more distant events. My Congolese students at the University of Lubumbashi in 1975 showed astonishingly detailed knowledge concerning the decolonization then unfolding far away on the Comoros Islands and expressed indignation at the success of Mayotte in detaching itself from the other three islands in the archipelago in its attempt to remain in the French fold. Diffusion was such that a successful act of nationalist self-assertion in one country both served as inspirational example and exerted pressure on its neighbors to engage in a comparably energetic defense of national interests.

The ambitious enlargement of the social infrastructure that marked the 1960s continued in the state expansion phase. State budgets still gave priority to schools, rural health facilities, and other social amenities. In turn, state employment figures continued to swell, as personnel to staff these facilities was recruited.

Expansive dispositions also drew sustenance from a brief moment of ready international bank financing for those countries with major resources to serve as implicit collateral. Western economies were entering a decade of relative stagnation, even "stagflation," and major international banks had accumulated large reserves, especially of "Eurodollars," that they were seeking to place. African external debt in 1970 was still very small, and the end of civil wars in Nigeria and Sudan, the restoration of seemingly strong centralized rule in Congo-Kinshasa, and an abundance of ambitious projects in planning ministries made Africa appear a fertile terrain for international bank engagement. Thus funding was available for an array of ambitious development projects in Congo-Kinshasa, Zambia, Sudan, Nigeria, and Gabon, among others.

International bankers were not alone in their sympathy for expansive developmentalism. The World Bank was then led by Robert McNamara, who promoted policies aimed at uplift for the rural poor in the most impoverished countries.[13] Many academic analysts of the day shared the view that the turn to more aggressively expansive development policies, informed by a nationalist commitment, was in keeping with historical necessities.

In such circumstances, the lure of the spectacular giant development project was irresistible. I profile a pair of striking multibillion dollar examples in this chapter, the Inga project in Congo-Kinshasa and the Ajaokuta steel mill in Nigeria. Many major public investment projects became mired in corruption. Nigeria again is an apt specimen. An urgent need in the early 1970s to construct barracks for an army that had swollen from 10,000 to 250,000 during the civil war and that then was to be maintained at 150,000 permanently led to huge imports of cement. For a time, Nigeria accounted for a large fraction of global trade in cement, with cement-laden ships spending one hundred days or more collecting demurrage fees awaiting a berth to discharge the cargo, a good portion of which spoiled on the docks. A morass of corruption surrounded the cement scandal, an initial impetus to a soaring place for Nigeria in the global venality tables.[14]

Another mark of the times was a vigorous enlargement of the parastatal sector. Partly this reflected a systematic effort to displace the colonial enterprise sector with national institutions. Moreover, the absence in most countries of an indigenous capitalist class with resources to launch enterprises meant that sectors earmarked for industrial development projects by planning ministries required state-owned enterprises to fulfill the public ambitions. These in turn needed finance from state development banks, using public capital. Often factories were constructed as foreign contractor turnkey projects. The debt at once became the obligation of the state when the facility was turned over to its operating parastatal. Often prestige played a role in project choice, notably in the instance of national airlines.

The sum of these different factors produced a general pattern of state overreach by the end of the 1970s. The momentum of state expansion had carried it far beyond sustainable levels. A heavy debt burden now overhung the continent, placing a number of countries in virtual receivership; Congo-Kinshasa, for example, had an external debt of $311 million in 1970, which had soared to over $4 billion by 1982. Over the same period, Madagascar's debt rose from $93 million to $1.6 billion and Algeria's from $937 million to $13.9 billion.[15] For most, a turn to the international financial institutions, then in process of designing new "structural adjustment" programs as a condition for assistance, was ineluctable. Embattled rulers could no longer manage politics through minor manipulation of state resource flows as was possible in the early phases of neopatrimonialism; more direct predation now became visible. Social infrastructure began to decay as a consequence of state budgetary crises. The idea that an integral state had been achieved was exposed as an illusion.

Exceptions to State Distress: Ivory Coast and Kenya

By 1980, there were some exceptions to the general pattern of state distress. A few countries had performed reasonably well through the 1970s. One was Cape Verde, which gained its independence in 1975 in union with Guinea-Bissau. Though many Verdeans were involved in the mainland Guinea-Bissau armed liberation struggle from 1961 to 1974, and the two countries were theoretically united, in reality Cape Verde always functioned as a separate state, officially so beginning in 1981. The radical liberation ideology associated with PAIGC did not override the acute sense of the limits of these small, impoverished islands devoid of resources. Thus islanders adopted a cautious rhetorical socialist orientation, and prudent management combined with generous aid flows kept the islands afloat. Contrary to patterns in Guinea-Bissau and in much of Africa, the discipline of self-financing was imposed pon the state enterprise sector.[16] A unique factor for Cape Verde was the size of its diaspora, three times the size of the island population, mostly in the United States. Originating in nineteenth-century recruitment of Verdean hands for whaling vessels, what became a Cape Verde diaspora then took up residence in the whaler ports of origin. The Verdean diaspora retained a strong sense of its identity and an attachment to the islands. Remittances from the diaspora provided an invaluable revenue supplement to the new state.

Ivory Coast and Kenya also avoided state crisis until the 1990s. Though both were within the crosshairs of dependency theorists owing to their robust capitalist orientation, until a series of misadventures in the 1990s both stood out in performance on both economic and social indicators, even though they lost momentum in the 1980s.[17] In the first two independent decades, Ivory Coast had annual growth rates averaging 7–8%. This success was rooted in the agricultural sector and not in high-value mineral or hydrocarbon deposits. A modest industrial sector was built on developmental resources originating in the agricultural sector, often through parastatals, though these were better subject to market discipline than in most countries. A 1978 World Bank study concluded with a ringing encomium to Ivory Coast performance: "Few countries, developed or developing, can match the economic growth record of the Ivory Coast. Its annual growth rate of over 7 % in real terms during the past twenty-five years is unique on the African continent."[18]

Critics hastened to add that the ransom of success was the privileged position of the numerous French expatriates. The single-party rule was mildly authoritarian, though President Houphouët-Boigny until his death in 1993 retained the respect of the populace, in no small part by basking in the success image. Ivory Coast was virtually the sole African polity in the more ideologically charged decades after independence that openly flaunted its commitment to a market economy, and indeed it invites comparison with Ghana in particular and the socialist orientation of Nkrumah. At the same time, Houphouët-Boigny gave voice to elements of integral state reasoning in denying a preference for undiluted market liberalism and favoring instead a planned economy, or what he termed "state capitalism."[19] My concluding judgment in *Ideology and Development in Africa* was that "the economic liberalism that undergirds Ivorian policy is permeated with statism."[20]

Kenya as well merited positive assessment on balance at this point and was widely regarded as a well-governed polity through the first two postcolonial decades, an image badly eroded since that time.[21] Particularly until the 1978 death of Jomo Kenyatta, Kenya managed the biggest challenges of postcolonial adaptation, the disposition of lands occupied by white settlers, with relative skill. A significant fraction of the land went in large blocks to prominent Kenyans, especially Kikuyu, but African smallholders also received substantial amounts; the settlers recuperated their capital and more, and a painfully large number of landless peasants came out empty handed.[22] But African agriculture, the main basis for the Kenyatta success narrative, prospered overall. As in Ivory Coast, the government avoided the temptation to extract its livelihood primarily from the agricultural sector through high export taxes, artificially low state-set prices, or state marketing monopoly profits. State support for rural social provisioning remained strong, with exceptionally high outlays for education and a network of free rural clinics. Students of comparative bureaucracy generally gave high marks to the Kenya administration; the central bank and key ministries had competent technocratic management. In the Kenyatta years, an active nexus between the Nairobi political class and their rural constituencies was maintained both through competitive elections within the dominant party (Kenya African National Union [KANU]) framework and the *harambee* (pull together) movement. In *harambee* sessions, political figures were expected to sponsor some local amenity (a new school, for example) by making substantial personal contributions and by soliciting others to do the same. These virtuous traits declined during the rule of Daniel arap Moi, who succeeded Kenyatta in December 1978. Moi was much less politically secure than Kenyatta and turned KANU into more of a neopatrimonial political machine; cronies replaced technocrats in key government positions. Even diminished in the 1980s, Kenya remained less afflicted by state crisis than most other countries and experienced reduced but still tangible economic growth.[23]

A few other countries in 1980 gave the appearance of relative developmental health. Malawi was sometimes still claimed to be enjoying respectable performance, though its image had been impaired by the harsh autocracy of Hastings Banda and the notorious personal mercantile empire, Press Holdings, which he had assembled.[24] Cameroon as well was still cited by some as an exception to the emerging pattern of stagnation. The Arab tier of states in the north became more clearly defined by their security apparatus, but they were not on the verge of crisis at this time. In addition to these relatively respectable performances, the pair of exceptional success narratives noted in chapter 1, Botswana and Mauritius, again merit notice. I defer until the final chapter an effort to identify the distinctive elements of statecraft that permitted the two to resist the continental temptations of the integral state and avoid the consequent decline.

By the end of the 1970s, harbingers of a darker future for much of Africa were clearly evident. The OAU 1979 summit took formal note of the failure of expansive developmental efforts to produce anticipated results. Yet this summit in Monrovia and the following 1980 conference in Sierra Leone were themselves indicators of the impending crisis; both involved exorbitant expenditures that virtually bankrupted the host states. Lavish new conference sites, residential villas for the fifty-odd heads of state attending these ceremonial spectaculars, plus other sparkling ornamental infrastructure, were a ruinous extravagance. In the Sierra Leone case, the projected outlays for the OAU summit totaled $200 million, or half the state budget.[25]

EARLY EXAMPLES OF STATE FAILURE:
CHAD, GHANA, MOZAMBIQUE

Thus by the beginning of the 1980s, clear signs of the impending crisis were visible in a number of countries. Among them were the three debilitated by the most catastrophic tyrannies of the epoch, briefly profiled in chapter 1: Uganda, Central African Republic, and Equatorial Guinea. These three at the time could be set aside as ghastly but exceptional instances of misrule by paranoid dictators. But warning signals were visible elsewhere in more "normal" polities: Congo-Kinshasa, Tanzania, Somalia, and Mali are examples. Worth further exploration for their illustrative value are three cases in which different forms of state excess had already produced deep crises: Chad, Ghana, and Mozambique.

"In Chad," *Le Monde* reported at the end of 1980, "the modern state inherited from the colonial period no longer exists."[26] Gali Ngothe Gatta, a Chadian economist and former minister, concurred: "Since the combats of February 1979 . . . the Chad state has ceased to exist. . . . However, there does exist a multitude of armed bands that roam about the country and ransom the populations."[27] Indeed, the term "warlords" that gained currency in the 1990s as a label for the leaders of illicit militias first appeared in the context of Chad at this time. William Foltz offers an eloquent and succinct summation:

> As revolt produced reprisal, reprisal in turn produced rebellion—then civil war, coups d'état, foreign military intervention, regional secession, and the division and recombination of alliances and futile governments. No part of the country escaped armed violence; no Chadian family escaped the violence unscathed. State authority collapsed definitively in 1980 when civil war touched virtually every corner of the country, reaching a ferocious peak in the battles fought back and forth across the capital, Ndjamena. Government functionaries—and the entire diplomatic corps—fled the capital. What remained of the administration lost contact with its agents in the countryside: the last government salaries were paid in August 1979. In those few localities where schools and clinics kept their doors open, they did so on local initiative and without supplies. Banks and post offices were looted.[28]

The postcolonial regime led by Ngarta (formerly François) Tombalbaye followed the well-trodden path from securing a narrow 1960 majority to imposing a single party in 1963 and engaging in increasingly personalistic and autocratic rule. His bureaucracy was largely staffed by his Sara coethnics from southern Chad, where most colonial educational facilities had been concentrated.[29] Their arrogant and abusive treatment of the Muslim north, imposition of higher cattle taxation and seizure of herds to enforce payment, and visible corruption provoked localized revolt by 1965, then sustained rebellion and the first guerrilla militia Front de libération nationale du Tchad in 1966, soon followed by a proliferation of armed militias and endemic civil war. In his last years, Tombalbaye, borrowing from the Mobutu script of "nation-building," promoted doctrines of "authenticity" and "Chaditude," buttressed by a delirious scheme to reinforce the personal subordination of state cadres through the obligation to undergo painful initiation rites into a Sara cult known as *yondo*.

Libya occupied the northernmost part of Chad, the Aouzou strip, from 1973 until 1987, and by 1980 it was periodically sending its forces further south, even promoting the idea of unification (that is, Libyan annexation). Sudan, Nigeria, and Congo-Kinshasa were also active players in the Chad civil wars and episodic peace agreements. The restoration of a single ruling leader, Hissein Habré, in 1982 led some to claim that a Chad state had been reborn.[30] Habré did, with French military help, succeed in evicting Libyan forces from Chad by 1986 and in subduing or recuperating most militias. Qadhafy eventually accepted referral of his Aouzou strip claims to the International Court of Justice. The World Court after scrutiny of relevant colonial boundary demarcation documents concluded by 1994 that Chad was the bona fide possessor, and Libya accepted the judgment. However, the legacy of state failure was to endure. Habré proved a singularly sanguinary ruler, accused by a consortium of victims of assassinating as many as forty thousand dissidents, leaving eighty thousand orphans and thirty thousand widows, and of constructing horrendous torture chambers; he stands indicted for crimes against humanity before a Senegalese court authorized by the AU, though there have been long delays in opening the trial.[31] An old adversary from a rival clan of the Zaghawa ethnic cluster of northeastern Chad, Idriss Déby Itno, launched an invasion from Sudan in 1990 that drove Habré into exile and eventual internment, but the pattern of armed factionalism continues. The operations against the Libyan garrisons and other militia resulted in the capture of up to $1.5 billion in modern weaponry, which Chad by 1987 began to sell off to diverse arms merchants, gun smugglers, and neighboring states, a significant element in the huge increase in the armament black market that fed proliferating militias in the African civil wars of the 1990s.[32]

Ghana began its independent life under what appeared to be highly auspicious circumstances. One of Africa's most prosperous states at the time, the country was blessed with large foreign exchange reserves, an expanding cocoa-based economy, and swelling state revenues that grew tenfold in the final colonial decade. A competent bureaucracy had extensive experience in economic management. Under the charismatic leadership of Kwame Nkrumah, Ghana seemed poised for a journey to progress.

By the early 1980s, these hopes had vanished, supplanted by a public mood verging on despair. State revenues sharply dwindled, and the capacity to deliver basic services shriveled. The state suffered a deflation of its legitimacy, authority, and autonomy. Civil society in good part disengaged from the state, seeking shelter in the informal economy (*kalabule*), smuggling, petty crime, or, for about 10% of the population, other lands; in 1980, a million such emigrated Ghanaians were suddenly deported from Nigeria, overwhelming formal and informal coping mechanisms. The public, especially the urban sector, was driven to a variety of survival techniques: what Naomi Chazan terms the "suffer-manage" syndrome.[33]

The downward spiral began soon after independence, originating in a series of policy miscalculations. The original Nkrumah strategy of heavy extraction from the cocoa sector, the leading export commodity, to finance state-led industrial development backfired badly. The real value of the government cocoa purchase price fell by 75% between 1957 and 1965, the result of a combination of reduced payments to producers and new taxes: a "development tax" in 1959 and "forced savings" in 1961. At the same time, world market prices fell sharply during this period. New cocoa plantings all but ceased, and growing amounts were smuggled to neighboring Ivory Coast for hard currency. By 1972, an agricultural survey showed that production of yams, cocoyam, and rice was much more profitable than cocoa, mostly because the state did not control their marketing and had no effective way to tax these crops.[34] Meanwhile, in the acid observation of Douglas Rimmer, socialism was "commonly interpreted to mean personal advancement rather than the abrogation of individual ambition, and no incongruity was seen between private enrichment and adherence to socialist principles."[35]

Nkrumah plunged headlong into the construction of a state corporation empire: Ghana Airlines, Ghana National Construction Corporation, State Steelworks Corporation, State Gold Mining Corporation, Vegetable Oil Mills Corporation, Ghana Fishing Corporation, State Farm Corporation. There were some fifty in all by 1966, most operating with huge losses.[36] The military regime that ousted Nkrumah in 1966 and its elected successor, Kofi Abrefa Busia (prime minister from 1969 to 1972), halted the dynamic of state expansion and even divested a handful of public enterprises, but with the military return to power under Ignatius Acheampong in 1972 a new populist era opened. Inflation, which had reached 40% per annum by the end of the Nkrumah period, returned with a vengeance, averaging 100% during the rest of the 1970s. Per capita income fell by one-third between 1971 and 1980 (in constant 1975 prices).[37] The minimum wage, in real terms, was only 50% of the 1960 level by 1971; in the following decade real wages declined a further 70%.[38] The Cocoa Marketing Board ceased publishing annual reports in 1973, and evidence accumulated that huge amounts were being skimmed by the ruling clique. The weekly *West Africa* calculated that a gap of nearly £500 million existed between reported cocoa export proceeds and the actual world price; Acheampong himself was believed to have diverted $100 million to overseas accounts.[39] The Anin Commission created by Acheampong in 1975 to document the venality of his predecessors issued a blistering report, concluding that "corruption is endemic throughout the whole society," affecting "practically every sector of public life where the possibility of corruption exists." The report cited a distraught bishop who was moved to quote Isaiah: "The devout have vanished from the land; there is not an honest man left."[40]

The deepening anger and despair led to a junior officer coup led by Jerry Rawlings in 1979, which the members of coup followed by unleashing an unprecedented social vengeance, executing the three previous military heads of state, Acheampong, Fred Akuffo, and Okatakyie Afrifa, as well as five other senior military officers. After another brief civilian interlude, Rawlings returned to power at the end of 1981 with a sharply radicalized discourse. Revolutionary change was promised, with workers defense committees and people's defense committees created to mobilize popular support. Vigilantes were let loose in urban markets to force traders to sell at officially set prices; violent assaults on those deemed refractory were frequent. The most chilling atrocity was the murder of three high court judges, attributed to the regime.

But economic catastrophe overwhelmed efforts at populist mobilization. In utter desperation, a delegation of the radical intellectuals then serving as the last redoubt of supporters for the populist socialist phase of the Rawlings regime was dispatched in 1983 to Moscow to plead for Soviet economic rescue. The appeal fell on deaf ears; the Soviet Union was reconsidering its level of support in the fostering of a socialist orientation in Africa and urged the crestfallen delegation to turn to the IMF instead.

By this time, Ghana was in dire straits. A severe drought, rampaging inflation, a breakdown of law and order, the repatriated million citizens expelled from Nigeria: elements of the Rawlings regime came to recognize that populist socialist discourse was an inadequate remedy for political and economic bankruptcy and precipitous state decline. Thus Rawlings dramatically changed course, declared war on "populist nonsense," and embarked on what Jeffrey Herbst termed "the most comprehensive economic reform program on the continent."[41] Although this dramatic change in direction alienated parts of his initial constituency among workers, students, and radical elements of the military, his opening was seized by the international financial institutions as a heaven-sent opportunity to demonstrate the curative powers of their therapy; the World Bank, IMF, and Western donor community underwrote Rawlings and his new coalition with very large resources. The social costs of adjustment were heavy, but by the later 1980s Ghana visibly diverged from the downward trajectory of most of the continent in the "lost decade" and was on the road to recovery from state failure.

The fate of Mozambique was the third harbinger of the continental trend of state crisis by the early 1980s. Like Ghana, its independence was greeted with great expectations within and without Africa. Its armed liberation movement, FRELIMO, was a remarkably unified, coherent, and effective organization. Over the years of armed struggle, from 1964 to 1974, its socialist aspirations and drift to an Afromarxist orientation gradually deepened, though formal endorsement of Marxism-Leninism as regime doctrine awaited the 1977 party congress. The quality of its leadership (Eduardo Mondlane [1962–1969], Samora Machel [1969–1986]), its resolutely national and multiracial orientation, and the formidable organizational weapon forged in the struggle years persuaded many that Mozambique combined the ingredients for successful development on a revolutionary path. For those in Africa and outside whose dreams were vested in discovering an exemplary model of socialist orientation, Mozambique was the last best hope after a chain of disappointments, beginning with Algeria and Ghana. Of the family of Afromarxist states, Mozambique stood out in the coherence of its project. In my 1982 work, *Ideology and Development in Africa*, written before impending crisis was clear, I described Mozambique as the bellwether of a socialist orientation in Africa.[42]

But already by this time storm clouds were gathering. Even though FRELIMO had long disavowed literalist devotion to Marxism-Leninism, ideology was a driving force in fashioning on the ruins of Portuguese colonialism a Leninist version of the integral state. Its leaders, in the telling phrase of Margaret Hall and Tom Young, while "proclaiming from the housetops their reliance on 'experience,' proved to be the prisoners of the most implacable abstractions."[43] Most of the economy was nationalized, partly, in the case of major mining and financial institutions, by ideological prescription, but in the case of the many medium and smaller enterprises abandoned by their

Portuguese owners at independence also by practical necessity. Land was also nationalized; most of the former Portuguese settler estates in the south became state farms. Elsewhere, obligatory resettlement in state-designated villages and state cooperatives, influenced by the (not yet discredited) Tanzanian model, were imposed on much of the peasant sector.

The momentum of liberation enthusiasm, and the organizational energy of FRELIMO, for several years propelled Mozambique forward; until 1981 most macroeconomic indicators were positive. However, by 1980 Machel excoriated the state sector for lagging performance and famously remarked that the state did not need to sell matches. In 1981 the minister of agriculture admitted that not one of the state farms was profitable, despite having received the bulk of agricultural investment.[44] Forced villagization was a clear failure, and the capacity of young party cadres to replace the customary chiefs as custodians of rural comity was limited. Despite FRELIMO action in expanding rural amenities—schools and clinics—peasant disaffection was clearly growing.

By 1981, a pattern of decline was becoming unmistakable. The economy was in free fall, and the state was showing signs of disintegrating. From 1981 to 1985, GDP fell by 8% a year. Marketed output of crops in 1986 was only 25% of the 1980 level, and industrial production was down by half.[45] An escalating level of South African aggression placed growing pressure on FRELIMO; an insurgent challenge emerged with the appearance of Rêsistencia nacional moçambicana (RENAMO) in 1976, at first a creature of the Rhodesian security services intended to serve as a counter to the sanctuary and support Mozambique was providing for the Zimbabwe liberation movements.[46] South Africa took over sponsorship after Zimbabwe achieved independence in 1980, and RENAMO began to find traction in some rural areas, profiting from peasant discontent. Its brutal tactics and extreme violence, as well as its notorious exploitation of often-kidnapped child soldiers, gave the movement a toxic image but nonetheless imposed growing costs on the regimes; by 1984 it was clear that FRELIMO lacked the military capacity to eliminate RENAMO. This led Mozambique to accept an accord with South Africa, trading denial of sanctuary to ANC fighters for an end to South African supply of and support for RENAMO. South Africa, however, only partly respected the 1984 Nkomati accord, and many still see a South African hand in the 1986 plane accident in which Machel perished. Civil war raged on; by 1987 over a million Mozambiquans had fled the unrelenting rural violence to neighboring countries. Mozambique was at bay; the regime could neither feed nor protect its population, putting its stateness in question.

As the crisis first became evident, Mozambique like Ghana sought succor from the Soviet Union. After a Machel pilgrimage to Moscow in 1980, Mozambique applied in 1981 for full membership in the Soviet bloc economic integration mechanism, the Council for Mutual Economic Assistance. Such a Mozambique partnership in the "camp of socialism" would have implied major aid commitments, which the Soviet Union and its East European satellites after some hesitation were not prepared to make. The rebuff of its membership application in 1982 was a critical turning point for Mozambique, forcing a wrenching reconsideration of its orientation. Although official abandonment of Marxism-Leninism occurred only at the Fifth FRELIMO Congress in 1989, by the mid-1980s ideology-driven discourse had vanished. FRELIMO suffered less from Western ostracism than its Afromarxist counterpart Angola, and its overtures over time found a response. American pressure on South Africa facilitated the 1984 Nkomati peace accord; Mozambique joined the IMF the same year, and by 1987 it had accepted the basic parameters of structural adjustment, earning debt relief and opening aid channels. The international community in the coming years played a major role in facilitating the negotiations with RENAMO beginning in 1990 and in securing an eventual settlement in 1992.

Mozambique's trajectory resembled Ghana's in another important respect; although both passed through a phase of evident state failure earlier than most other African states, they both overcame crisis more quickly than their counterparts; by the turn of the century both would figure on any list of the top ten state performers.[47] Mozambique, however, is unique in negotiating the perilous passage from initial celebrated icon of liberation, through the depths of state failure, and back into the ranks of admired models without any change of regime. The remarkable continuity of FRELIMO as ruling party speaks well of its coherence and discipline. The pair of sudden leadership successions occasioned by the 1969 assassination of Mondlane and the 1986 unexplained plane crash that killed Machel were managed by the party without debilitating factional struggle; Joaquim Chissano, who replaced Machel, then retired voluntarily in 2004. Although a hegemonic mentality was continuous, and the popular enthusiasm of the liberation moment never returned, still, the regime never fell into the complete discredit of most of its counterparts. Nor, at least until Chissano retired, was neopatrimonialism or personalist rule a defining element in political life. From Leninist single party to multipartyism, from Afromarxist state-run economy to neoliberalism, FRELIMO maintained its organic identity through extraordinary policy orientation mutations.

Decline in State Capacity, Competence, and Credibility

What then may be identified as the common patterns associated with state crisis and failure? The shrinking ability to perform effectively the core functions that define a state lies at the center. These clearly include the making and implementation of law, the preservation of public order and security, the projection of state authority throughout the territorial domain, the management of the national economy, the protection of property and contracts, and the provision of basic social services, means of communication and exchange, and physical infrastructure.[48]

The state in crisis experiences a sharp drop in its capacity, its competence, and its credibility. The overextended state of the late 1970s experienced a widening gap between its resources and its commitments. The revenue crisis had impacted state performance in multiple ways. The wage bill of the public service became unsustainable, which forced recourse—voluntary or involuntary—to one of two damaging choices. The real wage bill could be reduced by inflation, a widespread solution in the 1970s and 1980s. Or, in the countries of the French-backed CFA zone, where the convertible currency restricted inflationary policies, public sector wages could be paid with delays; in a number of countries these arrearages became a number of months. In either case, civil service morale and integrity plummeted; many diverted part of their energies to private pursuits or sought ways to monetize some aspect of their authority by demanding side payment for performance of their function. Furthermore, governments find themselves unable to meet the payments required to supply public services, provide social amenities, or maintain infrastructure.

This diminished capacity necessarily reduced the reach of the state, particularly in its peripheral areas. Outlying regions were first to experience shortfalls in government commitments. Local administrators found that supplies ceased to find replenishment, and so they had to fend for themselves to meet their operating needs. Government vehicles were out of fuel, in disrepair, or both; district officials were immobilized in their headquarters, pleading with local merchants or missions for transport assistance. In these circumstances the capacity of the state to exercise its routine authority and to perform basic governance functions was inevitably reduced, even if the territorial government buildings still had personnel in their offices for portions of the day.

The reproduction of the legal order and the ability to perform routine law enforcement and conflict regulation were likewise diminished. Though its routine operation might be surprisingly persistent, and while the normative force of a judicial culture provided a degree of insulation, its personnel felt the same survival pressures as other state agents.[49] Thus the administration of justice became more subject to monetary intervention or social power disparities. Police were particularly prone to venal practice, since their daily role as law enforcement agents was so readily monetized.

In the security domain, one frequent consequence of fiscal crisis was budgetary triage for army units. Those close to the capital, whose reliability was most critical, were paid and supplied first; the less favored units, deployed in outlying areas, were last in line for provisions. In effect, as in medieval times, they were forced to forage for food and money. Their uniforms and weaponry facilitated this task but at high cost to the core state function as security provider.

The loss of capacity of the crisis state led to a sharp decline in its everyday competence. The vast array of responsibilities assumed by the expansive state now weighed heavily. The huge state enterprise sector became a heavy drain; often parastatals had acquired heavy debts and could not pay their suppliers, which were frequently other government corporations. It became possible to more easily evade price controls over major consumer items, the issuing of which was a frequent state function dating from colonial times. Goods migrated to the black market. Extensive licensing systems were created as external debts, and trade deficits produced currency crises; regimes sought to maintain exchange value by rationing imports. Such systems created opportunities for top officials issuing the licenses to secure lucrative rents. Port administration and customs services were other key revenue-producing agencies that suffered from a deflation of competence by depriving the state of resources and discrediting it through the high visibility of corruption.

A less competent state meant that the everyday routine encounters with it that few citizens could avoid were more frustrating. Sooner or later there was need for an identity document, a property title, a market license, a driving permit, a vehicle registration, or some other government-issued certificate. Long office waits, the search for the authorized agent, protracted delays, informal fees to accelerate the process: these sharp increases in transaction costs in any interaction with government bred resentment.

Another symptom of a loss of competence was the growing phenomenon of ghost workers on the state payroll in a number of countries, particularly in the educational sector (a huge employer) and the security forces. With centralized payroll systems, if local officials or military commanders managed to retain on the personnel rosters those who had died, retired, or departed or even create fictitious entities, sums of money that were intended to compensate such agents might pass into the hands of those administering salary payments. The ghost-worker phenomenon entered public conversation only in the 1980s, though it may well have originated long before.

The crisis state also faced reduced credibility. Expectations concerning state performance diminished; one may cite as representative of a general pattern the popular rendition of the acronym of the Nigerian Electrical Power Authority, NEPA, as "Never Electric Power Again" or the Congo-Kinshasa adaptation of the state highway office title Office des Routes as Office des Trous (Pothole Office). Fear of the random depredations of its security forces might remain, but confidence in the protective effectiveness of the police and army vanished. Ideological doctrines and charismatic heroes that once supplied a legitimating aura to the state lost their popular hold.

Nicolas van de Walle offers perceptive summary of these processes of decline, concluding that "twenty years of crisis have resulted in a bigger state that does less for its citizens, particularly its poor and rural ones."[50] He adds that evidence suggests that the "capacity of African governments to design, implement, monitor, and evaluate policy actually declined between the early independence eras and the 1990s." The African Governors of the World Bank in a 1996 analysis of state capacity confirmed this conclusion: "Almost every African country has witnessed a systematic regression of capacity in the last thirty years; the majority had better capacity at independence than they now possess."[51]

Deepening Neopatrimonialism

As part of the political dimension of state crisis, neopatrimonialism became increasingly central to state operation, along with its twin partners of nepotism and corruption. I have discussed neopatrimonialism as a modality of rule in chapter 2, and there is no need to retrace those footsteps. Suffice it to recall that abstract Weberian norms of bureaucratic rationality erode in favor of personalized loyalties and monetization of favor. The currency of clientelism was reciprocity of favor: personal loyalty in return for material reward. Rulers selected their key subordinates on a calculus of their personal fidelity. Ethnicity or more immediate kinship was one criterion leaders used when choosing the innermost circle of henchmen on the assumption that they could trust individuals who were related by blood or clan; for the necessary national network of acolytes, prebendal allocation of office assured a hierarchy of cronies whose contingent loyalty depended on a leasehold of authority translatable into personal gain. Presidential control of the neopatrimonial networks relied on maintaining uncertainty among the chain of subordinates; office was never permanent and depended on ever-renewed proof of loyalty to the leader. The very essence of prebendalism was illicit income derived from abuse of office; thus the prebend holder was vulnerable to prosecution for corruption. Gazing into the windows of power were large numbers of aspirant clients. For those who fell from patrimonial grace and faced ouster and even sanction, any temptation to turn to the opposition was mitigated by the tantalizing possibility of a return to favor.

The ascendancy of neopatrimonialism by the 1980s was evident in most countries, along with the inevitable counterpart of state weakening. Rulers of exceptional longevity, such as Eyadéma Gnassingbé of Togo, Paul Biya of Cameroon, Félix Houphouët-Boigny of Ivory Coast, and Omar Bongo Ondimba of Gabon, became masters of neopatrimonial manipulation. Mobutu Sese Seko of Congo-Kinshasa was a particularly skilled practitioner. From 1965 to 1975, of the 212 persons holding ministerial positions or membership in the party political bureau, only 41 lasted five years, and none but Mobutu stayed in office over the ten-year period. Of the 212, 29 went directly from office to prison on political or corruption charges. An additional 26 lost office on grounds of disloyalty or dishonesty, with penal sanctions. Few stayed in jail very long, and many found ways back into high office.[52]

Although the 1980s pattern of state political weakening extended through-out the continent, including South Africa, it was less pronounced in most of the northern tier of states. Particularly in Morocco, Tunisia, and even Egypt, the institutionalization of a bureaucratic tradition was deeper. Above all, the overdeveloped security apparatus of these states did not experience comparable decay, nor was the loss of administrative control of outlying regions as clear. The *mukhabarat* (state security) core to these states became more evident, and the term came into popular use to characterize these polities. Except for Morocco, the rulers by the later 1980s all originated in the security services.

OTHER ASPECTS OF STATE CRISIS

In the social sphere, state crisis brought decay across the board to government services. Schools and health facilities deteriorated, and their irregularly or ill-paid personnel became demoralized. To some extent, these social amenities could still be provided with private support from religious institutions or, in some places, corporate firms. They also might survive through user fees;

local communities often tried to pay teachers in cash or food, and those in urgent need of medical attention might raise modest funds from kin or neighbors. But road maintenance was problematic, and key public utilities had declining service levels. In the 1960s, at least in the towns and cities, power outages were unusual. By the 1980s, they had become daily fare in many countries; aging and poorly maintained equipment could not keep pace with expanding needs as urban populations multiplied. In turn, the operating parastatals found revenue collection more difficult, as customers rebelled against poor service. Power-reliant enterprises had to operate costly private generators.

The slowly accumulating social discontents regarding state performance exploded only at the end of the 1980s, becoming a pivotal factor in the continental clamor for democratization. Even earlier, in the mid-1980s, they became a catalyzing factor in the urban popular mobilization in South Africa that made some large cities almost ungovernable. The animosity of most of the population toward the state in this instance was related to the racial oppression of apartheid rather than state ineffectiveness, but the widespread refusal to pay housing rents, utility charges, and local taxes to the state was central to the sense of township ungovernability that shook the confidence of the state. The assortment of "civics," or emergent civil society bodies loosely coalesced in the UDF, became a potent proxy for the banned ANC, eluding the repressive capacities of the South African state, despite a declaration of a state of emergency in 1986, and signaling an imminent end to the apartheid regime.[53]

The economic dimension of state decline in 1980 was its most visible aspect, especially to the external world. The external debt in the 1970s soared from an inconsequential level to over $300 billion, and for most countries was well beyond their capacity to service much less repay; as a result, further external capital was beyond reach. Also, though the economic growth shortfall was recognized, the full nature of state decay was not; nonetheless, the expansionist state left disabling doubts among investors as to property rights or contract guarantees and the credibility of commitments governments might make.

The international financial institutions, especially the IMF and World Bank, turned to the challenge of designing rescue programs for bankrupt African states. New currents of economic doctrine, later known as neoliberalism, were achieving ascendancy, in the form of the SAPs that both IMF and the World Bank devised to underpin foreign exchange advances or new lending. IMF and World Bank assistance came with extensive policy reform requirements, or "conditionalities," ostensibly agreed on by mutual consent but in reality all but imposed. These included currency devaluation as a means of moving toward convertibility, reductions of budget deficits, elimination of administered prices for consumer goods and agricultural prices so as to provide farmers better returns and curb urban subsidies, and privatization of the state enterprise sector.

Structural adjustment quickly became unpopular among most urban populations. Devaluation led immediately to higher prices for imported goods. An end to price controls for basic commodities had the same effect. The requirement for budgetary reform necessitated sharp reductions in expenditure; given the high percentage of state outlays in many countries devoted to public sector compensation, wage and hiring freezes and layoffs were an inevitable result. The benefits of SAPs in terms of inflation reduction, currency conversion, economic stabilization, and higher farm prices were slow to materialize, while the costs were felt immediately. Students, unions, intellectuals, and segments of the state apparatus, nursing a residual attachment to socialist orientation, economic nationalism, and residues of dependency theory, developed a forceful critique of structural adjustment. They were much less successful in proposing a plausible alternative.

In the economic realm, thus, many African states were caught in a vice: "hemmed in" was the telling title of an incisive collective analysis by leading scholars.[54] The financial situation of many was desperate by this point. Yet accepting the conditionalities of SAPs carried substantial political risks, even if the patrimonial autocracies of the epoch were not accustomed to sensitivity to public opinion. The response in most cases was predictable; IMF and World Bank assistance was accepted, but the conditions were only briefly or half-heartedly respected. The African states could not afford to sever the official participation in structural adjustment, partly because the Western donor community now made such cooperation a requirement for continued aid and in part because the Soviet bloc was clearly withdrawing its support from African states. The international financial institutions had too much invested in rescuing Africa from economic catastrophe to abandon the commitment, even if the terms of partnership had been only partly respected. Thus a series of renegotiated programs marked the 1980s, with African critics claiming failure and the external parties desperately searching for evidence of some success beyond the mere averting of catastrophe.

The emergent consensus view at the end of the decade was that the original SAPs were too shaped by an uncompromising neoliberal ideology and by an excessive confidence in the market mechanisms to quickly heal African economies; as John Ravenhill remarks, "Short-term stabilization and getting the prices rights was a totally inadequate foundation on which to reconstruct Africa's economic trajectory."[55] The IMF and World Bank acknowledged that the social costs of adjustment had been seriously underestimated and that further reform programs needed rethinking to take account of negative impacts on low-income groups.

One of the most contentious aspects of SAPs was the insistence on privatization. The huge size of the state enterprise sector that was a product of state expansion by the 1980s was a major liability. Parastatals were vulnerable to overstaffing, were given unclear and unfunded social mandates, were subject to political pressures, and were often managed by regime cronies. Their external debt was a significant fraction of the African total; domestic bank balance sheets were burdened by nonperforming loans of state-owned enterprises. Interenterprise debt paralyzed many operations, and their accumulated deficits weighed heavily on the state. A survey at this time in a dozen West African states showed that 62% of the state-owned enterprises had net losses and that 36% had negative net worth. Kenya, though it housed more profitable parastatals than almost any other country, had by the early 1980s a net average return of 0.4% on them, even though it had invested $1.4 billion in them. The state-owned enterprises faced irresistible pressures to employ excess staff and were often compelled to charge "social prices" for their output. Thus the pressure to reduce the size of this sector was bound to increase.[56]

Though most African policy makers were disposed to shrink the parastatal sector, privatization had numerous hazards. A number of the enterprises were bankrupt and unviable and really needed to be liquidated. Regime cronies often became beneficiaries of those with profitable prospects via firesale privatizations. Sale to foreign interests carried political risks if the terms were seen as excessively favorable. Accordingly, action on this front was sporadic and half-hearted at best.

Risks of the Giant Development Project: Inga and Ajaokuta

The very nature of the patrimonial autocracy predominant in the 1970s and 1980s rendered states vulnerable to catastrophic economic choices. Decision making was often concentrated in the hands of the ruler, whose voice eclipsed even the narrow circle of intimates who had access to the presidential palace. Gigantic development projects could be undertaken, especially in the early

1970s when loan capital was available, on the basis of data provided by those parties that stood to profit or benefit from its implementation. Lucrative rents accrued to the ruler and a handful of cronies; the foreign contractors received payment up front, with the eventual bill coming due at some future time. Embassies vigorously promoted their national enterprises positioned to participate in the project. The deals were structured so that the participants—the ruling clique, the contractors, the external consultants, the foreign ambassadors—all derived their profit or benefit from the transaction, while all the risk was placed on state and society. African presidents of that time rarely had the economic sophistication to closely calculate the risks, but they were swift to perceive the immediate benefits: the hefty rents and the political attraction of a spectacular development achievement. The critical importance of megaprojects gone awry in the larger pattern of economic decline justifies a detailed examination of a pair of examples. These two instances, the Inga hydroelectric project in Congo-Kinshasa and the Ajaokuta steel complex in Nigeria, well illustrate the huge risks of the giant project.

The ambitious Inga project consisted mainly of two stages of dam construction, a steel mill near Kinshasa and an eighteen-hundred-kilometer-long direct current transmission line to Katanga, linked to major copper mine expansion at the terminus. A number of other hypothetical industrial developments were also promised that never materialized, notably, a large aluminum smelter, repeatedly announced before disappearing from view. There was indeed seductive appeal in the phenomenal energy potential in the three-hundred-meter drop of the vast Congo River between Kinshasa and the port city of Matadi, especially considering that the river at this juncture had a nearly uniform water flow throughout the year. The falls held some 13% of the world's unexploited hydroelectric potential, and there were an array of dry valleys that parallel the river course into which the water flow could be diverted and dammed. Nearly a century before, in the 1920s, the Belgians had explored the possibility of a dam but concluded that the undertaking would be unprofitable. After World War II, the project was resurrected, and an initial, modest dam of 350 megawatts was officially announced in 1957 but then postponed by the drama of belated decolonization.

Mobutu, on seizing power in 1965, immediately dusted off the plans, and by 1968 ground was broken for a first phase of dam development at the Inga site in lower Congo. This project, completed in 1972, was mainly intended to serve the Kinshasa region. Its cost of $140 million was primarily financed by the state development budget and was not burdened by the scale of side payments that accompanied Inga 2. Although the rapidly growing Kinshasa metropolis did provide an immediate market for much of the power, initially over one hundred megawatts was intended for a steel mill upriver from the capital, at Maluku.

A passion for steel mills as emblem of high modernity was then well-nigh universal, and Mobutu was captive to its enchantment. This project dated as well from colonial planning boards, and at first glance it seemed appealing. Several large and rich iron ore deposits had been charted far upriver near Banalia, Isiro, Luebo, and Ubundu. Some poor coal deposits also had been discovered in distant regions. An Italian consulting firm, SICAI, produced feasibility reports containing lyrical visions of the import substitution impact and linkage effects, developmental shibboleths of the day. Investors were skeptical; market prospects and production cost estimates were dubious. Italian contractors financially linked to SICAI offered contractor-financed turnkey construction. Mobutu, trumpeting the technological triumph, committed the state to the $250 million cost.

Construction began in 1972, and the mill came on line in 1975. The illusions of the feasibility study at once became evident. There was no possibility of securing the immense capital required to develop the domestic iron deposits; the mill had to operate with imported scrap. The site chosen was at an inconvenient distance from the river and bulk shipping facilities. Production costs proved to be $660 per ton, rather than the $450–480 promised by SICAI, which was eight times the cost of imported steel. The low-quality product of the mill drew few customers; actual output never exceeded 10% of the 250,000-ton capacity. Maluku virtually ceased operation by 1980 and was shuttered soon after.

The far more ambitious second phase of the Inga dam, with a fourteen-hundred megawatt capacity, required a market that would be provided by planned substantial mining expansion in Katanga to utilize its power. This in turn necessitated the companion project of an eighteen-hundred-kilometer-long direct current transmission line, then the world's longest. At the time, the technology for creating so long a direct current line was not proven and had the major disadvantage of severely limited possibilities for supplying regions along the route. The initial bid by American contractors was only $260 million, but cost overruns eventually pushed the cost close to $1 billion. The commitment was made in 1973, with a promised completion date of 1977; however, the power line came on line only in 1982, well after initial payments on the loan were due. The total cost of Inga 2 and the Inga-Katanga power line was nearly $2 billion, or almost half what had become a crippling external debt. However, beyond the immediate rents he garnered from the contracts, the project had an irresistible attraction for Mobutu: with a flick of his finger, he could darken the sometimes restive and even secessionist province of Katanga.[57]

To make an unhappy situation worse, by the time the power was available, the prolonged slump in copper prices had led to the abandonment of a giant mining project at Tenke-Fugurume, not far from Lubumbashi, where exceptionally rich ore deposits were to be exploited by an American-led consortium stitched together by New York diamond merchant Maurice Tempelsman. Planned expansion by the state mining giant, the Générale des Carrières et des Mines (Gécamines), had likewise been delayed, and ever-increasing presidential diversion of Gécamines's revenues for Mobutu's use began to corrode its production infrastructure; the corporation was starved of resources required for maintenance and yet was charged with responsibility for most of the social institutions in the mining towns. Army looting and expulsions of many of its skilled Kasaien workers in 1991 further corroded Gécamines. The Tempelsman consortium abandoned site development by 1976 after having sunk $200 million. In 1994 copper output fell to 35,000 tons from its 1985 peak of 471,000 tons. By that time, only 18% of the Inga capacity was being utilized.[58]

In the fullness of time, the indisputable potential of the Inga project may be fulfilled. By the turn of the century, some of its power was sold to Zambia. Also, whispers were heard of a giant $80 billion thirty-nine thousand megawatt giant Inga; transmission technology has advanced to make power export as far as South Africa or even Egypt thinkable. By 2007, active South African interest was widely reported; Inga now provides electricity both to the Southern Africa Power Pool and the Central African Power Pool in the north. At that time, the World Bank granted $296 million to rehabilitate Inga 1 and 2, now operating at only 40% of capacity because of poor maintenance.[59] Meanwhile, by 2010 contracts for a forty-five-hundred-megawatt Inga 3 were under negotiation.

The Inga project thus does produce some power, and at some future point it may become a crucial energy asset for the entire region. The Ajaokuta steel mill in Nigeria more closely resembles the Maluku part of the Inga scheme, differing only in the colossal amounts of state capital that it absorbed without ever producing more than token amounts of steel. The saga of Ajaokuta is an even more dispiriting instance of high modernity ambitions processed through prebendal state structures and predatory rulers.[60] The Nigerian weekly *Tell* reported in 2006 that $10 billion in government funds had been sunk in Ajaokuta without a single ingot ever emerging.[61] Repeated obituaries for the scheme have appeared, invariably followed by news of a miraculous rebirth, most recently in a 2010 campaign pledge by President Goodluck Jonathan to make revival of Ajaokuta a priority if he was reelected.[62]

The dreams of a high-tech steel industry date from 1958, shortly before 1960 independence. The ideological perspective driving the commitment to steel development is well captured in an address by Paul Unongo, minister of steel development, to the Nigerian Institute of International Affairs on 24 July 1980: in his speech, he seeks to establish "the inevitability of Nigeria taking a stand in the comity of nations as an arrived nation that must recognize that the role of power broker which seems to be thrust on her by history and that of the indisputable representative voice of black mankind can only be effectively played through the acquisition of a legitimate, indigenous, recognized power status which is conclusively shown to be dependent upon or related to steel development. . . . [T]here is a definite correlation between steel development and national power."[63] At first glance, the dream of a powerful Nigeria undergirded by a major steel industry seemed possible; iron ore deposits were known, coal was mined at Enugu in eastern Nigeria, and the completion of the Kainji dam on the Niger River promised a power supply.

Western corporations explored the possibilities in the early 1960s and concluded that a major steel mill was uneconomic. A disappointed federal government concluded that the former colonizer and his allies were bent on maintaining Nigerian dependence on the West by discouraging industrial development, a resentment deepened by Western refusal to provide arms when Nigeria faced a secessionist war with Biafra in 1967. The Soviet Union, attracted by an opening to influence with a major African nation, won Nigerian gratitude by generous provision of weapons to the federal army. Apparently the Soviets saw an opportunity to cement the new friendship with a key African state by participation in a showcase project; thus Nigeria found a partner for the steel venture.[64] By late 1967, Soviet geologists and technicians were on the ground, prospecting sites for a major steel complex and exploring for further iron ore and coal deposits and ancillary inputs like limestone, manganese, and dolomite. In 1970, Teknoexport signed a contract to carry out geological surveys for another five years.

Soviet mineral surveyors in 1972 discovered a major ore deposit sixty kilometers from the village of Ajaokuta on the banks of the Niger in Kogi state, in south central Nigeria. In 1975, the Soviet state enterprise Tyajpromexport made preliminary commitments to develop a proposal for an integrated steel plant eventually capable of producing 5.2 million tons of flat products and other steel output; a final contract was signed in 1979, with an initial $2 billion Soviet-provided loan capital; some Western firms were subcontracted for parts of the site development and construction. The completion date promised was 1983.[65]

A few small steel plants treating scrap already existed; several other new steel mills were then envisaged as a key cornerstone of Nigerian development, scattered in different parts of the country (Jos, Onitsha, Katsina) to meet the "federal character" test. Though some were actually constructed and briefly operated at a fraction of capacity, only one has recently functioned, the Delta Steel Corporation, which limps along in Warri state after a decade of suspended operation. But the major showpiece complex was planned for Ajaokuta.

Difficulties and infrastructure deficiencies at the site resulted in long delays; one key element promised by the Nigerian government, a rail link to Warri port needed to import the one million tons of coking coal required annually, was never completed, nor was the costly dredging of the Niger river to facilitate ship access to Ajaokuta. The existing Nigerian single-track narrow gauge railway could not carry large volumes of bulky cargo, and no extant line was close to the projected steel complex. The hopes for use of local raw material inputs mostly evaporated; the Itakpe iron mine project languished, and by 1983 all that remained on site was some rusting machinery. Other ores were inadequate, and Enugu coal proved unsuitable for coking, as did other deposits. The key element in the complex, a large blast furnace based on older Soviet technology, never went into production, though some of the ancillary facilities had small output. The sharp drop in oil prices after the 1979–81 boom brought acute foreign exchange shortfalls and made the volume of imported inputs difficult to finance. Some three thousand Soviet technicians and twenty thousand Nigerian workers were on site at the peak of construction; an entire residential town had to be constructed to house expatriate and Nigerian staff. The acute shortage of Nigerian technical personnel was not resolved by short training programs in the Soviet Union; frictions between Soviet staff and Nigerians were constant. Nigeria discovered to its dismay that the Ajaokuta commitment was never inscribed in Soviet five-year plans, a major impediment in a rigid centrally planned system. Further, by then the press was full of allegations of corruption in the many public contracts for site development and ancillary infrastructure.

On several occasions, one or another impasse suspended site work. The target date for completion was repeatedly postponed: 1986, 1989, 1991. By this time, it was evident that technological advances in steel production elsewhere made the blast furnace increasingly obsolete. Press articles suggested that the eventual steel output might be of indifferent quality, and the world's costliest, at least three times the price of imported steel.[66]

Further, as the Soviet Union entered its death spiral in the late 1980s, work on the project was all but paralyzed. Still, the final rupture came only in 1997, when Tyajpromexport formally withdrew from the project, claiming that Nigeria had failed to keep its commitments and had not repaid the $2.5 billion debt accumulated over the two decades of sporadic construction. The facility, it was claimed, was 98% ready, but would still take three or four years to complete. In a murky series of transactions, the Russian contractor sold the unpaid debt for nineteen cents on the dollar in 1998; the debt came into the hands of a shell company controlled by the son of then dictator Sani Abacha. The Nigerian treasury eventually reimbursed the debt at 53% of par, yielding a tidy profit of over $400 million for the Abacha family. Some of the loot was recovered when Nigeria sued the financial companies holding the stolen Abacha funds, including Citibank, 2003.

Ajaokuta appeared to rise from the dead in 2001, when a deal was announced with a little-known American energy company, SOLGAS; the firm pledged new investment of $1.2 billion in a metallurgical plant and $2.4 billion for a power station at Ajaokuta: by now Kainji dam was no longer a reliable supplier.[67] The SOLGAS solution soon proved another illusion; a Nigerian Senate committee concluded the deal was a swindle, and that the company lacked the financial, managerial, and technical capacities to manage the concession. SOLGAS, the committee found, was a minor company that specialized in marketing small capacity generators and had no experience in the steel industry.

By 2004, yet another player had emerged: Global Infrastructure Holdings, linked to the Indian Mittal family, replaced SOLGAS as holder of the Ajaokuta concession and the Delta Steel Corporation. SOLGAS, protesting the annulment of its contract, alleged that the Global Infrastructure deal was a conspiracy in which Gbenga Obasanjo, son of then-president Olusugun Obasanjo, played an integral role. Not long after, accusations flew that Global Infrastructure in turn was cannibalizing the plant and illicitly exporting the iron ore stocks at the site.[68] Still, Ajaokuta Nigerian management announced on 24 April 2006 that the plant was 60% ready for operation, that personnel were still being paid, and that once the blast furnace was finished and the rail link completed, operation could begin.[69] However, Nigeria canceled the Global Infrastructure contract in 2008 but resumed negotiation with the Mittal family in 2009, as a London arbitration court sifted through Global Infrastructure claims that it had invested $450 million.[70] In 2010, renewed initiatives toward exhuming the project were reported; $500 million of new capital would be required.[71]

But in reality the project remained moribund four decades after the first exploratory accords were signed. Nigeria specialist Peter Lewis visited the site in 2007 and saw no sign of activity.[72] Earlier, in 2003, a visitor to Ajaokuta found a desolate scene: "An old weather-beaten signpost . . . proclaims 'Ajaokuta Steel Complex: the path to true industrialization.' The message is evidently lost on a couple of goats grazing absent-mindedly on the grassy slope dotted with remnants of discarded Firestone tires. . . . The empty concrete blocs of its township, the abandoned structures of communication facilities, and the still rolling mills stand exposed to the scorching sun and sand-carrying seasonal winds coming from the Sahara. They stand as silent monuments to the failed ambitions of Nigerian rulers to exorcise by fire and steel the demons of the colonial past."[73]

Inga and Ajaokuta are exemplary instances of the huge liabilities accumulated in the years leading up to the state crisis of the 1980s by the lure of high modernity pursued through gigantic development projects. In both cases, these projects accounted for a significant fraction of the external debts that by the 1980s so burdened the two countries. On projects of this magnitude, in Africa and elsewhere, the costs invariably far exceed the estimates, and the completion dates lag far behind those promised. Many of the parties involved—foreign contractors, political leaders, and others shaping the transaction—may benefit, but the state and society bear the costs. Far from liberating Nigeria from the bonds of dependency, the megaproject led to an unpayable external debt burden, which in turn compelled the country to turn to the London and Paris clubs of private and public creditors and plead for renegotiation of the terms. The invariable response was insistence on recourse to the tutelage of the international financial institutions, which imposed SAPs that were slow to provide relief. Thus the 1970s were a mediocre decade economically for Africa, and the 1980s a disaster. Per capita income growth was 0.8% per annum in the 1970s, then a negative 2.2% through the 1980s. Debt service alone consumed 25% of the African earnings from export of goods and services.[74]

TABLE 5.1. African and Other Developing Areas Average Annual Growth Rates, GNP per Capita, 1965–89

	Average annual growth rate (%), GDP per capita, 1965–89	Average annual inflation rate, 1980–89 (%)
Low and middle income	2.5	53.7
Sub-Saharan Africa	0.3	19.0
East Asia	5.2	6.0
South Asia	1.8	7.9
Latin America & Caribbean	1.9	160.7

SOURCE: World Bank, *World Development Report 1991* (New York: Oxford University Press, 1991), 205.

CONFLICTING REGIME AND RULER LOGICS

During the descent into state crisis, the conflicting logics of state, regime, and ruler came into sharp focus. Regimes shaped by a given ideological commitment might well pursue policies that undermined the interests of the state in its own stable reproduction. A range of economic policies driven by populist nationalism or Afromarxism are cases in point. Nationalizations of broad swathes of the economy committed the state to a scope of responsibilities that were beyond its capacities. High-risk giant projects, influenced by a regime belief that a development spectacular would reinforce its immediate legitimacy, saddled the state with long-term debt commitments that unhinged its financial equilibrium. Agricultural politics shaped by a collectivist bent (state farms, obligatory cooperatives, government marketing monopolies) drove peasants to take evasive measures and disengage from the public economy.

Regimes so structured as to preclude challenge or change responded only to the interests of a given ruling group in its own reproduction. Single-party monopolies, military domination, or neopatrimonial modes of governance were subject to degenerative processes over time that undermined the legitimacy of the institutions of government. By barring societal monitoring of its policy choices, the likelihood of major miscalculations was multiplied.

The contradiction between reason of state and the operative logic of a personal ruler is even more sharp. The autocrat is very likely to employ an ethnic calculus in shaping his inner circle, above all in the security apparatus. With the coup as the sole mechanism for displacement of a personal ruler, conspiracy is sure to flourish, leading to a need for constant vigilance and a high order of trust in the fidelity of the entourage, especially those that control the means of forcible intervention.

Robert Bates reduces the ruler's survival calculus to three variables: the level of public revenue, the potential rewards through predation, and what he terms the "rediscount rate" of the leader. By this he means that if revenue suffices to provide for the modicum of security and prosperity that will assure social peace, then this modality of rule will be preferred. However, if a severe revenue shortfall is at hand, then a predatory capture of resources that can be seized by state power to meet immediate survival needs is likely.[75] Naturally, the length of this volume in contrast to Bates's succinct 174 pages implies a belief that the equation is a shade too simple. But it ably captures an important dimension of the ruler's approach to survival.

Since by the 1980s life presidencies became increasingly frequent, in a number of cases there was a turning point at which the ruler began to appear primarily predatory. In a case like Congo-Kinshasa under Mobutu, I would date this moment to about 1979; until that point, although he had amply enriched himself and his henchmen via their control of the state, he appeared to cling to the illusion that he could at once realize the grandiose dreams for the country that he ceaselessly proclaimed in his frequent travels and divert large sums to his clientele and his individual retirement account. Past that point, personal rule became what Juan Linz, borrowing a Weberian term, labels "sultanism," whereby "personalistic and particularistic use of power for essentially private ends of the ruler and his collaborators makes the country essentially like a huge domain."[76]

Sierra Leone under Siaka Stevens (1967–85) is another apt example. William Reno elegantly documents the progressive evisceration of the formal state and its replacement by what he terms a "shadow state" erected on personal control of the revenues generated by an illicit diamond trade. Stevens was elected in 1967 with broad support on a populist reform platform. However, in the process of consolidating control and sidelining regional big men, he was increasingly driven into an alliance with Levantine and Afro-Lebanese mercantile operators through whom diamond marketing and export took place, increasingly outside official channels. Over time, diminishing levels of rents from diamond exploitation entered the state treasury; by 1984, formal state spending was only a quarter of the 1979 level. The ransom of the Stevens's strategy of exercise of personal rule mainly through a "shadow state" was the decade of violent civil war in the 1990s.[77]

Yet another dimension of ruler interests in conflict with state welfare lay in the potent motivations to cling to power arising from personal security fears. Driven from office, an ousted president is acutely vulnerable to charges of corruption, political assassinations, or other abuses of power. Rare were the Nyereres or Senghors who left office voluntarily in these years and could safely remain inside the country.

SUMMATION: THE SIX IMPERATIVES

Let me again return to the half dozen state imperatives as a device for summary. On the hegemony front, the state expansion era implied setting one's sights higher in order to achieve a more comprehensive subjugation of society. For a time, these ambitions appeared to be on the road to fulfillment; however, the developmental impasse evident by the end of the 1970s soon took its toll on the scope of dominance. As stagnation and decline defined a growing number of polities, there was an uneven but visible shrinkage of state capacity. Even if its roster of public employees remained stable or even increased, their ability to perform the basic functions through which hegemony operated diminished, especially in the periphery. A silent triage operated; the requirements of the capital and the central regions, most critical to regime survival, came first. Society for the most part reacted by disengaging and retreating into the informal economy rather than by directly challenging the state. South Africa was an important exception in the 1980s, as the hegemony of the apartheid regime was undermined by unprecedented levels of civil society mobilization. The growing contradiction between regime and ruler vital interests and state imperatives, first noticed by Bates in 1981, was a major factor; the dilemmas were frequently posed in the ambiguous responses to the economic reform programs imposed by the international financial institutions as a condition for emergency injections of funds.[78] Fully applied, such programs frequently conflicted with more immediate exigencies of regime or ruler survival. With relatively few exceptions, the fabric of state hegemony unraveled during the 1980s.

With respect to autonomy, most expansionist states by the 1970s had perfected and institutionalized systems of patrimonial autocracy. The single-party system, through forcing civil society into corporate structures within the party apparatus, for a time effectively stifled voice. The pressures from below primarily flowed through clientelistic channels, and states were largely insulated from collective claims. But this artificial internal autonomization of the institutions of rule eventually contributed to state decline, as governments lost the affective links with civil society required for stable politics over the longer run.

The early 1970s witnessed the high-water mark of African assertion of its external autonomy aspirations. In this springtime of third-world self-assertion,

African states pushed back against the economic dominance of the industrial world on several fronts. The orbit of effective economic sovereignty expanded through the wave of nationalizations of Western mining and other firms and via indigenization programs targeting immigrant mercantile communities. On the diplomatic front, African states were active players in the formation of the Group of 77 whose purpose was to defend third-world economic interests and to achieve liberation of remaining colonies and white-ruled territories. Politically, the sudden collapse of the Portuguese colonial regime brought overnight independence to five new countries.

By the end of the decade, external debt and domestic fiscal impasse sharply contracted the possibilities of external autonomy. The necessity of seeking financial relief from international financial institutions and the Western donor community as the Soviet Union and China by the 1980s began withdrawing from African aid commitments forced the African state into demeaning rounds of bargaining over conditions for economic rescue. The narrowing of economic options restricted the extent of external autonomy.

On the security front, during the prosperous 1970s, most African states had expanded their armed forces. Some did so as a consequence of major security threats. In particular cases, such as Nigeria and Sudan, internal wars combating secessionist forces drove dramatic army expansions. In Ethiopia and Somalia, conflicting territorial claims, as well as the Eritrean independence struggle in the case of Ethiopia, brought huge enlargements in security force numbers and weaponry; the Ethiopian army peaked at 520,000 in the late 1980s, compared to 41,700 in 1974.[79] Moroccan claims to Western Sahara and Algerian shelter and support for the Saharan independence movement had a similar impact. South Africa, perceiving a growing threat from what was termed "total Communist onslaught" from the north as the Portuguese buffer zone evaporated, likewise reinforced its security apparatus, in turn threatening neighboring states through an aggressive destabilization policy targeting those nearby states sheltering ANC insurgents. Libya invested an important part of its large oil revenues in advanced weaponry; the unusually large size of Egyptian security forces was driven above all by the repeated warfare with Israel.

These important exceptions aside, for most African states the challenge to security was only internal. In a number of instances the military held power and was thus in an unencumbered position to prioritize its presumed needs. For most, a reliable and expanded security apparatus was a necessary pillar of patrimonial autocracy. The cold war and arms sale competition among major powers made credit for weapons purchase readily available into the 1980s.

Thus, until that time the general pattern was military expansion; notable exceptions were the two countries whose rulers enjoyed the most intimate ties with France, Ivory Coast and Gabon. These countries had only small, almost ceremonial, forces. Their security was in effect subcontracted to France, whose military was immediately at hand in local garrisons and whose intelligence services assured effective surveillance of opposition activity and restive officers.

Further, the state crisis decade witnessed a decline in the effectiveness of many African militaries. The empty state treasuries could not assure the maintenance of the heavy equipment acquired in better days, which often fell into disrepair. An American defense intelligence officer describes the lamentable condition of many militaries by the end of the 1980s: "Most African state armies are in decline, beset by a combination of shrinking budgets, international pressures to downsize and demobilize, and the lack of the freely accessible military assistance that characterized the cold war period. With few exceptions, heavy weapons lie dormant, equipment is in disrepair, and training is almost nonexistent. . . . [T]he principal forces of order are in disorder in many countries at a time when the legitimacy of central governments (and indeed sometimes the state) is in doubt."[80]

The quest for legitimation was ideologically driven in the 1970s, with formulations ranging from populist nationalism to Afromarxism to an early version of populist Islamism. Alluring promises of rapid development and large public investment programs, given credibility by the short-lived revenue windfalls from periods of high export prices and easy access to external credit, still had appeal into the mid-1970s. Expansion of basic social provisions also continued at first. As the 1980s wore on, the credibility of the ideological themes diminished along with the states themselves. By late in that decade, the basic legitimacy of most regimes came into question. States became derided as predators, pirates, or vampires. The broad-front deterioration of the public sector and pervasive corruption of the realm drove the public to a mood of cynical despair. The disabled state or its local fragments might still evoke fear; its often unpaid security forces turned to scavenging local communities for their livelihood. Its local agents could still invoke state writ to extort money for a bewildering array of taxes. But these encounters only intensified the fundamental legitimacy crisis confronting many states.

The revenue imperative was the key to all other dimensions of the state crisis. The dramatic inability of most states by the late 1970s to secure an adequate revenue flow from domestic taxes or external aid left rulers with dwindling options and, as Bates has argued, drove many to predation to ensure their own survival, a certain recipe over time for state failure.[81] For many, internal revenue was heavily dependent on customs receipts and other charges on exported commodities; as such, its flow was tributary to fluctuating world market prices. Though there were some periods of very favorable price regimes for many key African commodities (coffee, cocoa, oil, copper, for example) in the early 1970s and again at the end of the 1970s and beginning of the 1980s, thereafter through the decade world markets were mostly unfavorable. The rapidly swelling external debt required growing amounts of foreign exchange merely to service. Africa was indeed cornered financially, and that had negative consequences for its meeting all the other imperatives.

Inevitably, on the accumulation front all the indicators turned negative. Across the continent, growth rates, anemic in the 1970s, deteriorated further in the crisis decade. The burden of external debt weighed heavily on domestic budgets, as did the civil service payroll; there was nothing left for public capital investment. The visible deterioration in state performance measures and rise in predatory behavior by rulers and state elites drove away potential foreign investors, save those who were partners in predation. The optimistic claims of the promoters of SAPs that the magic of the marketplace and "getting prices right" would be immediate remedies proved far from the mark. With few exceptions, by the end of the 1980s the African state faced a far-reaching crisis.

HARBINGERS OF A NEW ERA

Suddenly and unexpectedly, long dormant civil society reacted. The first burst of thunder occurred in Algeria in October 1988, described in chapter 1. A wave of urban street rioting shook the regime to its core; hundreds were killed and many more wounded.[82] The mystique of the Algerian revolution had long since lost its hold, especially on a deeply disaffected youth, which had no memory of the liberation struggle, An even more astonishing turn of events, prefiguring the coming surge of democratization, unfolded in Benin. Long-time ruler and quondam Afromarxist Matthieu Kérékou was at bay; a cornered Kérékou meekly assented to a power seizure by civil society through the mechanism of a "national conference." A new era opened, rendered problematic by the enfeebled condition of the African state. But the events of Algeria and Benin sounded the requiem of patrimonial autocracy as unchallenged mode of rule.

The disparate outcomes that followed are the subject of the chapters 6 and 7. One harbinger of the dangers lurking, little noted at the time, was the crossing into Liberia of a small militia of 250, trained in Libya and led by Charles Taylor, in December 1989. At the time, many Liberian elites regarded him as a deliverance from the venal incompetence of despot Samuel Doe; however, he proved a sanguinary and destructive warlord who brought ruin to most Liberians and to Sierra Leone as well and by 2008 faced a lengthy catalogue of crimes-against-humanity charges before an international criminal court, for which he was ultimately convicted in 2012.

But there were more hopeful omens as well. By 1990, Ghana and Mozambique were well on a path to restored health. They stood as exemplary models of an avenue of state rehabilitation that could be chosen, validating the African proverb that "no condition is permanent."

6

Democratization and Its Limits

> The national conferences appeared as the revelation of a new
> spirit, a flashing rocket, a luminous signal that propels us into
> the future[,] . . . the most important event of our conscious
> history[,] . . . the beauty of something unique, incomparable.
>
> —F. Eboussi Boulaga, 1993

THE THIRD WAVE OF DEMOCRATIZATION

When the urban street erupted in Algeria in October 1988, shattering the
seeming revolutionary élan of a once-invincible regime, few realized that
this was the opening scene of a momentous transformation of the African
political landscape.[1] But a short two years later the surge of democratization
appeared irresistible, and it spread across the continent. Samuel Huntington
captured the supremely mimetic, interactive nature of this dynamic in his
memorable metaphor of a "third wave" of democracy, following on earlier
such moments at the turn of the last century and in the immediate aftermath
of World War II.[2]

The sheer scale of the democratic surge washing over the continent was
stunning. In my reading, only Libya, Sudan, and Swaziland swam against the
current; their respective personalist populist, Islamist and royalist autocracies were little altered, though Sudan and Swaziland did feel constrained to
stage meaningless elections. Initially, the wave lapped more weakly on the
shores of Arab North Africa, before arriving with a vengeance with the 2011
"Arab spring."[3] As chapter 1 argues, for a brief, euphoric moment the elixir of
democracy seemed to offer a means of resurrecting the African state.

But these hopes soon proved illusory. The more canny autocrats gave
ground before the storm and became adept at managing a transition from
patrimonial autocracy to neopatrimonial semidemocracy. Of the incumbent

rulers at the beginning of the democratization surge, no less than seventeen were still in power in 2004. Some projected transitions in key countries (Algeria and Nigeria) soon derailed. In other cases, polities dissolved in disorder and civil war (Somalia, Liberia, Sierra Leone) or were unhinged by ethnic violence linked to the transition (Burundi, Rwanda). By the late 1990s, the most common outcome was what became known as "semidemocracy," a notion given conceptual elaboration by Marina Ottaway: semidemocracies are "ambiguous systems that combine rhetorical acceptance of liberal democracy, the existence of some formal democratic institutions, and respect for a limited sphere of civil and political liberties with essentially illiberal or even authoritarian traits."[4] Others characterized the posttransition polities as "hybrid" regimes or as "semiauthoritarian."[5]

But the rules of the game had changed. Undiluted patrimonial autocracy was permanently discredited. Weakened African states were in desperate need of external presentability; the price of respectability was now at least nominal embrace of democratic norms. The AU, formally launched as a replacement for the OAU in 2002, included in its charter a commitment to democratic governance; member states that experienced coups were suspended from the organization.

Two decades later, some transitions appeared stable and durable, having survived one or more successions of parties or at least rulers (Ghana and Benin are the clearest examples). The most far-reaching of all, South Africa, was a mostly peaceful and truly remarkable constitutional revolution through which real power was transferred to the long-excluded racial majority. But a number of others had been reversed or had had their content eroded. Gambia, one of the three surviving original decolonization democracies, was ousted by a military coup in 1994 and remained trapped in the bizarre despotism of Yahyah Jammeh. However, Botswana and Mauritius, the other two, continued in their stable path; indeed in Mauritius in 1982 and again in 1995 opposition alliances won all sixty-two directly elected seats in parliamentary elections.[6] At the other extreme, Somalia stayed locked in its unending anarchy. In short, after three decades of largely parallel trajectories, African states began to follow widely divergent itineraries.

Survival of Democratic Norms

Democratic norms, despite the failure of nearly all decolonization constitutional settlements, never completely disappeared from Africa. Sudan experienced meaningful though short-lived restorations of democratic rule from 1965 to

1969 and then again from 1985 to 1989. Senegal accepted limited multiparty politics in 1976 and then a fully open field in 1981. Military rulers in Ghana acceded to popular pressures for democratic restoration and held genuinely competitive, close-fought, and well-conducted elections in 1969 and 1979, but in each case army intervention subsequently overturned the civilian regime. The Burkina Faso military permitted democratic elections in 1970 and then again in 1978 but soon restored army rule. Nigeria stands out in the tenacious hold of democratic values on the public mind, even though the military held power thirty-two of the thirty-six years between the initial coup in 1965 and a transition back to civilian rule in 1999. Throughout this protracted period, the military rulers found no road to legitimacy save the claim that they were engaged in organizing a transition to democratic rule.[7] "Permanent transition," Paul Beckett and I have observed, "turns on the paradoxical situation—visible over many years—in which Nigerian military rule is legitimated by a sense of *progress* toward creating its own alternative: civil democratic governance."[8]

During the 1980s, the view slowly took root through various pathways that the drift toward state decline and crisis was not merely economic and could only be reversed by major political reform. Academic observers once in thrall to the premise that rapid development required centralized and uninhibited state authority were dismayed to observe it degenerate into predatory patrimonial autocracy. Many felt that the views Richard Sklar expressed in his U.S. African Studies Association 1982 presidential address devoted to democracy in Africa were visionary. In contrast, Georges Nzongola-Ntalaja's 1988 presidential address issuing a ringing summons to democracy in Africa seemed timely and prophetic. For many in Africa, a remoralization of the public realm and relegitimation of the state required political opening. Many intellectual critics of SAPs rallied to the cry for political opening. Tanzanian scholar Mwesiga Baregu noted that "traditional opponents of the World Bank and the IMF . . . gradually realized that they could not dissuade the government from adopting these policies. . . . Instead, [they] turned their attention to the logical inconsistency in the government's espousal of economic liberalization and its rejection of political liberalization."[9] Long quiescent opposition voices began to challenge single-party monopolies. In the population at large, a responsiveness to political mobilization drew on what Celestin Monga termed the "anthropology of anger," long expressed through "insubordination and indocility, notable and noble signs of the desire for democracy."[10]

PORTENTS OF CHANGE

Another portent of impending change came with the emergence of the "civil society" concept, which first made its appearance in Eastern Europe in the 1980s. This notion, though it had a long historical pedigree stretching from John Locke, Thomas Hobbes, and Alexis de Tocqueville to Hegel and Gramsci, had disappeared from common usage in the postwar years.[11] For East European intellectuals, the Marxist-Leninist Soviet-imposed regimes were an alien excrescence on the body politic, whose authentic identity and virtues were embedded in a society entirely distinct from the state. Their yearning for a "normal" state, comparable to the democratic polities of Western Europe, could be achieved only through accession to power of "civil society."[12] Comparably, in Africa by the 1980s an idea took root holding that the predatory state had become distinct from and alien to society. The vital forces of society, and not the oppressive, derelict state, were the true repositories of legitimacy. To some extent, these intellectual currents also fed on the antistatist perspectives then influential in much of the West, especially Britain and the United States.

Dramatic transformations in the external environment also had a catalytic effect. The cascade of events beginning with the fall of the Berlin Wall in November 1989 that resulted in the collapse of Communist regimes in the Soviet bloc and in 1991 the dissolution of the Soviet Union did not cause the democratization wave in Africa, but its demonstration of the hollow nature of long-standing Soviet bloc autocracies was a potent stimulus, making collective challenge to autocracy thinkable. The spectacle in Romania of perennial dictator Nicolae Ceauscescu overthrown by the street and summarily executed was a chilling spectacle for many in presidential palaces; Ceauscescu had actively cultivated African connections and heads of state, claiming that Romania was a "developing nation" with natural affinities to third-world countries.

The collapse of state socialism in Eastern Europe and the Soviet Union had another critical consequence: the end of the cold war and the attendant global competition for African clienteles. In the early 1980s, the Soviet Union began rethinking its aid commitments in the third world. The withdrawal of Soviet and Cuban forces from Angola in 1988 to facilitate a Namibian settlement and the warning to the Ethiopian client Mengistu Haile Meriam in 1989 that no further arms would be supplied put the final seal on disengagement. Thus, by the time the 1988 Algerian urban riots sounded the death knell for patrimonial autocracy, the Soviet Union had already virtually withdrawn from the cold war competition in Africa. The security-driven American policy calculus in Africa, justifying backing for even such notoriously corrupt and dictatorial regimes as Mobutu's Congo-Kinshasa and Samuel Doe's Liberia, lost its motivating force.

Within international financial institutions and the Western donor community, the conviction grew that economic reform alone was insufficient to restore the African state to health; structural adjustment was denatured by predatory prebendal politics. Within the World Bank for a time, influential voices called for democratization as a necessary counterpart to economic reform.[13] The novel concept of "governance" emerged, given public academic shape in the first instance by Goran Hyden, providing a more antiseptic label for the insertion of political criteria in policy discourse.[14] Governance initially appeared in a World Bank document in 1989 and was defined as "the exercise of political power to manage a nation's affairs," requiring "a pluralistic institutional structure, a determination to respect the rule of law, and vigorous protection of the freedom of the press and human rights."[15] Major donors such as France, the European Union, and the United States indicated that further assistance was conditioned on political opening.

The intensity of external pressures for democratization soon relaxed, as spreading civil conflict restored stability to its throne as supreme value. But the sudden evaporation of external indulgence of autocratic rule sent shock waves throughout Africa. When added to the growing protest mobilization of civil society, the twin detonators of the Algerian riots and the Benin national conference could have their formidable diffusion effect.

I will not add to the millennial theoretical and philosophical debates on the nature of democracy; let me simply endorse the recent thoughtful definitional discussions by Charles Tilly, Staffan Lindberg, and Michael Bratton and Nicolas van de Walle.[16] My understanding of democracy incorporates the "governance" notion and adds the crucial procedural standards of accountable and responsive representative institutions, based on regular, free, and fair universal suffrage elections, multiple parties, a real possibility of political alternation, and guarantees of the organizational freedoms and individual liberties to make competition possible. Democracy also hinges on a constitutional, rule-of-law state (*état de droit*).

NATIONAL CONFERENCE FORMULA

The national conference formula played a critical role in this process. This remarkable device became a mechanism for civil society power seizure by

constitutional coup. Although the national conferences were in reality limited in number and restricted to francophone Africa, their impact extended
far beyond the nine countries (Benin, Chad, Comoros, both Congos, Gabon,
Mali, Niger, and Togo) in which such constitutional assemblies convened. In
just three of these countries (Benin, Congo-Brazzaville, and Niger) were incumbent rulers directly driven from power. But in the euphoric moment of
the democratic wave, the romantic appeal of this resurrection of the French
Revolution Etats-Généraux model was potent.[17]

The Benin example paved the way. By late 1989, the Mathieu Kérékou
regime faced imminent breakdown. The banking system collapsed, undermined by huge unsecured (and naturally "nonperforming") loans to key ministers and large illicit payments to Kérékou's occult counselor, marabout
Mohammed Cissé.[18] Civil servants, after six months of salary arrearages, were
on strike; schools had been closed for a year. Street protests multiplied; France
and the World Bank refused further credit. With the state paralyzed, a desperate Kérékou summoned political and military leaders to announce the abandonment of Marxism-Leninism and the convening of a national conference at
which all sectors of society would be represented to decide on a "democratic
renewal" and frame a new constitution. Once assembled, the delegates, describing themselves as the *forces vives* of the nation, declared their sovereignty,
in effect constituting the assembly as civil society incarnate. Armed with an
asserted sovereignty, the national conference installed a transitional government under Nicéphore Soglo, permitted Kérékou to stay on as a merely ceremonial president, and drafted a new democratic constitution. The newly
relegitimated state with the help of robust external support saw a remarkable
economic recovery; salary arrearages came to an end and a small budget surplus appeared by the end of 1991. These accomplishments burnished the early
image of the national conference formula.[19]

In Chad, Congo-Kinshasa, Gabon, and Togo, incumbent rulers bent before
the wind but in the end outmaneuvered the national conferences and blocked
any sovereignty claims. Multiparty democratic formal rules and new constitutions were conceded, but the rulers involved managed to retain their life
presidencies save for Mobutu in Congo-Kinshasa, driven from power in 1997
by insurgent forces from the periphery. Gnassingbé Eyadéma of Togo and
Omar Bongo Ondimba of Gabon died in office in 2005 and 2009, respectively.
Though proposals for national conferences emerged elsewhere in Africa, incumbent regimes resisted such demands; the Benin example clearly showed
the perils of such an assembly.

New Constitutions

But remarkably widespread was the creation, through more controlled processes, of new constitutions. By my count, there were some thirty-nine across Africa in the early 1990s, and in a half dozen other instances, extensive constitutional revision was undertaken.[20] Invariably these ended single-party systems, included provisions for representative national assemblies, and promised freedom of the press and other civil liberties.

A major innovation was the introduction of term limits for presidents, normally restricted to two. No such provisions were included in the decolonization constitutions; I found no trace of debates on this issue at the time. Partly this reflected the parliamentary nature of the constitutions, which were modeled on the Belgian and British systems, neither of which anticipated executive presidents or single-party systems; even in the French Fifth Republic presidential template used in most francophonic states the risk of the life presidency was not anticipated. By 1990, constitutional assemblies were keenly aware of the dangers of incumbent rulers entrenched in permanent power. By my count, nearly two-thirds of the new constitutions contained provisions designed to prevent life presidencies.[21]

These constitutional processes frequently amounted to optimistic and thoughtful engagements with civil society. In Uganda, a vast consultative process took place in the preparation of the 1995 constitution, beginning in 1988. An extraordinary flow of constitutional seminars and public consultation at all levels followed.[22] In Eritrea, a distinguished constitutional commission led by eminent scholar Bereket Selassie carried out similar grassroots consultations, examined world experience, and drew on an international advisory commission while reflecting at length on the lessons of the failed decolonization constitutions. The resulting 1996 fundamental charter was an impressive accomplishment, making the more disappointing the subsequent refusal of ruler Isaias Afewerki to implement it.

Other Key Transitions: Zambia and South Africa

Influential democratic transitions also took place in Zambia and South Africa. The Zambia political liberalization was the first in anglophone Africa, as well as the first to oust a leader of the nationalist founding generation of African independence. Its immediate antecedents, as in Benin, were a deepening economic crisis, punctuated in mid-1990 by serious urban food riots in response to a doubling of the maize price. The president, Kenneth Kaunda, was less a target of public anger than many other autocrats of his generation; though corruption was rife in his entourage, he was far less personally culpable than most of his fellow presidents. The miscalculations of a statist development agenda had taken a heavy toll, however. After an initial decade of seeming prosperity following 1964 independence, the price of the primary Zambian export, copper, plummeted. From 1975 to 1988 the Zambian economy shrank by an average of 2.1% per year, and annual per capita income fell from $540 in 1964 to $290 in 1988.[23] Inflation intensified in the 1980s, and the half-hearted implementation of SAPs brought no relief. The economic costs of Zambian support for liberation movements in Zimbabwe and South Africa also played a part. By 1985, public sector unrest intensified; there were frequent strikes, and the powerful mine workers union escaped party tutelage and flexed its muscles. In July 1990, energized by the wave of violent urban protest, the Movement for Multi-Party Democracy (MMD) took form, demanding an end to the ruling United National Independence Party political monopoly and early competitive elections. These took place in October 1991, resulting in a sweeping MMD victory with three-quarters of the vote. Kaunda made no effort to rig the elections, and international observers pronounced them free and fair. To his credit, he also made a gracious exit. The transition in Zambia at the time appeared a model of democratic regime change, and intensified pressures elsewhere for political reform.

The South African transition from 1990 to 1994 was the most momentous of all in the scope of the societal transformation involved. Beginning in February 1990 with the liberation of Nelson Mandela and the unbanning of the ANC, the constitutional bargaining was arduous, carried out during a period of serious social unrest, ethnic tension, and violence in the eastern Rand. Though the National Party (NP) had ruled since 1948, elaborating and systematizing the racial apartheid doctrines subordinating and excluding nearly 90% of the population, the European minority continued to enjoy multiparty politics and a parliamentary regime. There was thus a constitutional heritage and deeply implanted legal norms, however circumscribed, on which to build.[24] The negotiation primarily took place between the NP and ANC, leading to a transitional constitution in 1993 mostly incorporating ANC preferences for an elected executive president and unitary government with some quasi-federal provisions. To broker the transition to full majority rule, implying African political predominance and ANC ascendancy, a government of national unity including the NP was established for an interim period. The first universal suffrage elections took place in February 1994; their successful conduct was an inspirational moment in the democratic transition process. It was also the high-water mark in the political liberalization moment; from that point forward the tides of democratization began to recede.

At this stage of political opening, most focus was on the transition dynamics, above all the establishment of multiple political parties and competitive elections.[25] These were the focus of an array of international nongovernmental organizations (NGOs) that sprang into place as democracy advocates, as well as the Western donor community. Others saw in the nurture of civil society the way forward. Many called for a shift in focus, demanding that the role of representative bodies be expanded and that institutions assuring the rule of law be fostered. Yet others perceived human rights, freedom of the press, and associational liberties as the key to effective political liberalization. A multiple array of indices arose seeking to identify and measure dimensions of democratic practice sponsored by such organizations as Freedom House, Afrobarometer, Transparency International, and the World Bank. These brought a clearer picture of the complexities of African democratic transitions, highlighting the limitations of a focus on multiparty elections alone. Influential African intellectuals such as Claude Ake argued that "democracy has been reduced to the crude simplicity of multiparty elections to the benefit of some of the world's most notorious autocrats, such as Daniel arap Moi of Kenya and Paul Biya of Cameroon, who are now able to parade democratic credentials without reforming their corrupt and repressive regimes."[26]

ABORTED TRANSITIONS: ALGERIA AND NIGERIA

Several seriously aborted transitions that inflicted heavy costs on the affected polities likewise dimmed the luster of African democratization. Algeria had been the detonator, but it was also the first to crash and burn. The 1988 urban rioting was violently repressed by FLN rulers, but the regime was shaken to its roots by the realization that its legitimating ideologies of liberation war and revolutionary socialism were sterile slogans, eviscerated of meaning by a sclerotic, clan-ridden, and self-serving military-led autocracy. A disaffected younger generation—a majority of the population—had no personal memory of the independence struggle. The regime moved quickly in 1989 to create a new constitution and to authorize competing parties and electoral competition, still confident in the ability of the FLN machine to manage multiparty politics. To their surprise and dismay, the newly formed Front islamique de salut (FIS) made a stunning sweep of local offices in the first competitive elections in 1989. Paradoxically, FIS was a product of FLN policies in the 1980s to control and capture emergent Islamist currents gaining strength in Algeria and elsewhere; a vigorous program of mosque construction was launched, the idea being that by nurturing an official Islam under firm government tutelage the new religious currents could be co-opted and managed. In the event, discourse in the mosque could not be controlled, and an invigorated Islam became a prime alternative identity for a deeply alienated youth that saw little future for itself in the FLN-led Algeria.

Still, the regime went ahead with plans for parliamentary elections in 1991, hopeful that the inability of FIS-ruled communes to bring much improvement to everyday life would undermine the illusion that "Islam is the answer." But FIS again showed astonishing strength in the first round and seemed headed for a victory that would oust the FLN. Before the second round of voting could take place in early 1992, the military intervened, removed President Chadli Benjedid and installed an overtly military regime. A state of emergency was declared, and FIS was suspended. A civil war soon broke out that during the 1990s produced one hundred thousand deaths by official estimate (twice that in other reports) and tore the country apart. A more militant group, the Groupe islamique armé, broke off from FIS and led a more determined, hydra-headed guerrilla struggle through the remainder of the decade. An even more extreme fragment, the Groupe salafiste de prédication et combat, continued the insurgency, eventually fusing with global terrorism as Al Qaeda in the Islamic Mahgreb (AQIM). Although the army restored the appearance of democracy by holding competitive elections for the presidency in 1995 and generating an amended constitution the following year, the limited competition had circumscribed creditability. The presidential term limits that were inscribed in the revamped constitution were removed in 2008, and the life presidency heritage seems to have been restored under recently reelected Abdelaziz Bouteflika. Still, by 1999 FIS had accepted an amnesty and many of the Islamist fighters had abandoned the struggle.[27] A decade later, the original insurgency was all but moribund, and most of its leaders were dead. AQIM, however, persists, in partnership with dissidents in Mauritania, Mali, and Niger, making sporadic attacks, engaging in lucrative kidnappings of foreigners, and smuggling narcotics.

Another of Africa's largest states, Nigeria, was a second scene of aborted transition. In singular contrast to the sudden, unexpected and abrupt democratizations in most countries, the prolonged and convoluted Nigerian transition extended over nearly a decade, actually culminating in a successful election in 1993 that the military chose to annul. Beyond its longevity, another unique aspect of the Nigerian transition was the protracted effort of the military to blend political elite consultation with elaborate regime orchestration. Beginning in 1985, a study commission largely composed of university faculty and legal scholars labored on proposals for a new democratic order. Federalism, representative institutions, competitive parties and socialism were consensus principles, but the Babangida regime removed the ideological component. A constituent assembly, mostly elected by local government councils, then took over in 1987; two years later, a draft constitution largely based on the 1979 predecessor was proposed, calling for a two-party system, with each required to prove its national character by membership distributed across the country; ethnicity and religion were forbidden forms of organizational discourse. After a failed effort to sort out who would qualify for recognition as a member of one of the two permitted parties, Babangida stepped in to decree that the state would assume responsibility for creating these organisms, one "a little to the left," the other "a little to the right." The state then poured ample resources into its chosen creatures, the Social Democratic Party (SDP) and National Republican Convention (NRC).

A prolonged sequence of elections then followed, beginning in 1990 at the local government level and then ascending to the state and national parliamentary level. Babangida again intervened to suspend the process at the stage of presidential primaries, claiming massive fraud. He launched a new process in 1992, based on indirect elections of delegates to national party conventions, beginning at the ward level and working upward through local government and state echelons. The conventions, each with some five thousand delegates in attendance, duly anointed wealthy Yoruba businessman Moshood Abiola for the SDP and northern financier Alhaji Bashir Tofa for the NRC. Although the elections on 12 June 1993 were far less fraught with spectacular abuse than any prior postindependence national balloting, Babangida stunned the nation by annulling the results even before they were officially proclaimed (but after they had been made public by a democracy advocacy group, the Campaign for Democracy). The NRC initially endorsed the annulment, and its support base in the north and southeast remained quiescent. However, the major centers of SDP support, especially Abiola's home area in the (Yoruba) southwest, reacted with fury and enduring resentment that persisted through the harsh Abacha era. To this day, the reasoning behind the Babangida dissolution of an elaborate and costly democratic transition on which such extravagant resources had been squandered remains murky. The suspicion lurked in some quarters that the entire exercise was never intended as more than political spectacle, concealing a project of indefinite prolongation of power behind the façade of permanent transition.[28]

FAILED TRANSITION AND GENOCIDE: BURUNDI AND RWANDA

Another pair of intertwined aborted transitions in Burundi and Rwanda descended into horrendous genocidal violence. The two countries had similar (but not identical) ethnic demography, overwhelmingly composed of a pair of ethnic categories sharing the same language, Hutu (85%) and Tutsi (15%). In colonial times, both were ruled by Tutsi monarchies with precolonial roots; as chapter 4 notes, both Tutsi monarchies disappeared with independence, though in very different ways: one was supplanted in Burundi by a Tutsi military oligarchy; the other was replaced in Rwanda by a Hutu ethnocracy originating in a 1959 populist uprising against Tutsi ascendancy.

In Burundi, Hutu attacks on Tutsi in communes bordering Rwanda in 1988 brought savage reprisals by the Tutsi army and fifteen thousand fatalities, mostly Hutu. A number fled into Rwanda; most invoked the numbing memories of the 1972 genocidal slaughter by the Tutsi military regime of an estimated one hundred thousand (some claim as many as two hundred thousand), all but a small number Hutu. Though the 1972 genocide attracted meager outside reaction, the altered global environment by 1988 produced an international uproar that brought demands for democratization. The Tutsi regime bowed before the pressures for political opening in 1991, hopeful that its control of the state apparatus and conduct of the elections would assure electoral victory for its party, the Union pour le progrès national africain. Admirably free multiparty elections took place in 1993; although overt ethnic appeals were forbidden, the triumphant Front pour la démocratie au Burundi relied on Hutu mobilization for its sweeping victory (73% of the vote). However, the new Hutu premier, Melchior Ndadaye, faced an entirely Tutsi army officer corps and an overwhelmingly Tutsi administration. A few short months later, in October 1993, an army faction assassinated Ndadaye and several other Hutu leaders, triggering a wave of violence across the country that pitted enraged Hutu against a vengeful Tutsi army. The country descended into a maelstrom of civil strife that continued for a decade until a fragile power-sharing settlement in 2003 and then continued to simmer until the last ethnic militia finally agreed to end the fighting in 2008.[29]

Burundi cast its shadow on Rwanda; its 1972 and 1988 mass ethnic killings reinforced Rwandan regime views that a Hutu political monopoly had to be preserved, views further cemented by harrowing tales of the numerous Burundi Hutu refugees. Under Juvenal Habyarimana (1973–94), Tutsi were rigorously prevented from assuming leading political and military roles; during that period there had been but a single Tutsi minister and army officer.[30]

Through the 1980s, however, the country appeared to the outside world as a relatively well-governed polity; its modest developmental success, at sharp variance with most of Africa, won generous aid flows. Although seven hundred thousand Tutsi had fled the country (outnumbering those staying in Rwanda), the remaining Tutsi could profit in the private sector, and tensions were subdued.

But by the end of the 1980s the corruption in the Habyarimana regime—the pronounced favor enjoyed by Hutu from his northwest region and especially the enrichment of a narrow clique controlling the security apparatus, mostly related to his wife (the *akazu*, or little house)—were becoming visible. Pressures mounted from an internal Hutu opposition and the international community for political opening. In July 1990, Habyarimana conceded the abandonment of the single-party regime; at almost the same moment, a Tutsi refugee army (the Rwandan Patriotic Front [RPF]) that had formed in Uganda, largely from veterans of the insurgent military of Ugandan ruler Yoweri Museveni, invaded their homeland. Over the following four years, a dual-track tragedy unfolded: protracted negotiation for a multiparty coalition leading to elections and an episodic but deadly combat between the Rwandan army, Hutu extremist youth militias (the *interahamwe*), and the RPF. In an atmosphere of deepening ethnic tensions, the assassination of newly elected Burundi Hutu premier Ndadaye in October 1993 added new explosive fuel. The final detonator was the missile destroying a plane bringing Habyarimana and the new Burundi premier back from a Tanzania conference intended to accelerate the stalled transition in April 1994. The author of this catastrophic act remains to this day unproven; initial blame fell on the Hutu extremists that used the pretext to ignite the genocide, though subsequently suspicions of possible RPF responsibility took root.[31] Hutu rage ignited a frenzy of slaughter, led by the *interahamwe* and Rwanda army, leaving a minimum of five hundred thousand dead, mostly Tutsi (according to the most meticulous and cautious count by Alison des Forges; a figure of eight hundred thousand is widely cited by others).[32] Rather than a democratic transition, Rwanda experienced a genocidal regime change, with the RPF seizing power by military force in the wake of the orgy of ethnic killings, for which RPF also had some responsibility. Rather than political liberalization, Rwanda traded one exclusionary ethnic autocracy for another, firmly entrenching the Tutsi minority. Ironically, the major beneficiary is the erstwhile Tutsi diaspora, large numbers of which returned after the RPF victory, and not the resident Tutsi populace targeted by the genocide. The internal Tutsi population at the time numbered only somewhat over six hundred thousand, and was decimated by the slaughter.[33]

MIXED OUTCOME FOR DEMOCRATIZATION

Thus, in different ways the initial powerful surge of democratization soon ran its course. The original interactive momentum faded as the sheer novelty of multiparty elections wore off. Initially intense international pressures slackened, especially as internal wars spread in parts of Africa; the preference for stability replaced an insistence on democracy on the part of external partners. France in particular visibly retreated from its insistence on democracy at the 1990 La Baule francophone summit. "Good governance" tended to supplant democracy in external developmental discourse.[34]

But multiparty elections had become a familiar and expected part of the African landscape. The new constitutions mostly remained in force, and crucial changes in the capacities of civil societies to find voice and organize persisted. The state monopolies of the media ended as an independent press took root, perhaps alongside government mouthpieces. The state broadcasting and television networks faced competition from FM radio outlets and TV satellite dishes. The human rights movement was energized, led by courageous activists and supported by more active international NGOs.

In a significant number of countries, sixteen by my count in 2009, regimes might reasonably qualify as democratic; in all but one of these (Botswana), there had been a change of ruling party since 1990 (see table 6.1). The most common category is the regime type that has acquired currency as semidemocracy; in table 6.1, I subdivide this group into a second set labeled "semiauthoritarian" to suggest a more incomplete degree of political liberalization. Some eight countries figure on my roster of semidemocracies, accepting Ottaway's definition, and seven more in the semiauthoritarian category. These categories and location within them of individual countries are evidently fluid over time.

In several influential cases, long-time autocrats, after facing significant challenge in the initial multiparty elections, adjusted their modes of operation to accommodate limited and controlled competition, especially at election time, but kept in place much of their illiberal political practice. Fear as a weapon returned to the fore; unexplained disappearances or unsolved assassinations of journalists chilled the ardor for political mobilization. Paradigm cases are Burkina Faso under Blaise Compaore, Cameroon under Paul Biya, Gabon under Bongo, and Togo under Eyadéma, the last two recently deceased in office and succeeded by their sons. Biya and Bongo especially faced forceful opposition in the first multiparty elections in 1992 and 1993; Bongo won only narrowly. Co-optation and intimidation returned to the fore thereafter, and

TABLE 6.1. Classification by Regime Type, 2009

Democratic	Semi-democratic	Semi-authoritarian	Autocratic	Transitional	Failed
Benin	Burundi	Algeria	Angola	Guinea	Central African Republic
Botswana	Congo-Kinshasa	Burkina Faso	Djibouti	Ivory Coast	Comoros
Cape Verde	Gabon	Cameroon	Egypt	Madagascar	Guinea-Bissau
Ghana	Kenya	Chad	Equatorial Guinea	Niger	Somalia
Lesotho	Morocco	Congo-Brazzaville	Eritrea	Zimbabwe	
Liberia	Mozambique	Ethiopia	Gambia		
Malawi	Nigeria	Mauritania	Libya		
Mali	Tanzania	Rwanda	Sudan		
Mauritius		Togo	Swaziland		
Namibia		Uganda	Tunisia		
Sao Tome					
Seychelles					
Senegal					
Sierra Leone					
South Africa					
Zambia					

SOURCE: My classification as of 2009, based on Freedom House and other indices, qualitative data from major monographic sources, and interviews. The democratic category includes countries that regularly hold elections generally regarded as relatively free and fair and that are otherwise respectful of constitutional procedures. The semidemocratic group refers to regimes with imperfect elections, limited effective opposition, and impaired respect of civil liberties. Semiauthoritarian regimes are more restrictive of opposition and impose greater limitation on free expression but retain some elements of democratic practice. In the "autocratic" category, even though some token opposition and pro forma elections may exist, rule is essentially repressive. The failed state is lacking undisputed leadership, may be unable to rule over important parts of the country, and is limited in its ability to ensure normal economic operation and to perform basic government functions. The column labeled "transitional" records the 2009 instances where regimes under military or other unconstitutional rule had committed to a transition to democracy.

opposition forces tended to fragment among public disappointment and demobilization.

Even given the initial discredit of most ruling single parties in the initial stages of transition, a number managed to survive the opening round of competition and restore their long-term hegemony; the Chama Cha Mapunduzi in Tanzania is a classic instance, as it used the discipline of party competition to renovate and reform itself. Other parties, born of the political opening, once in power swiftly learned the advantages of control of the state apparatus in electoral competition. Inevitably the exercise of power opened access to invaluable electoral resources: vehicles, money, the media. Thus the number of cases in which beyond the founding elections of the transition moment there was been a change by election of ruling party is limited, comprising Benin, Cape Verde, Ghana, Kenya, Malawi, Mauritius, Zambia, and Senegal. The more common pattern is for a dominant party to enjoy clear ascendancy and a substantial parliamentary majority.

Also increasingly frequent is a move by incumbent rulers to remove the term limits that were enshrined in the transition constitutions, normally two terms. Parliamentary (and civil society) resistance is sometimes effective. Legislatures have blocked such moves in Kenya, Malawi, Nigeria, and Namibia. In Niger in 2009, after parliament and the courts rejected removal of term limits for President Mamadou Tanja, he dissolved these bodies and unilaterally organized a referendum that duly extended his tenure, which soon prompted a military coup reflecting popular antagonism to these moves. In a significant number of other countries—Algeria, Comoros, Chad, Cameroon, Djibouti, Guinea, Togo, and Tunisia—term limits written into transition constitutions were repealed.

The number of interrupted or aborted transitions during the post-1990 period is striking (fifteen by my count), in most cases by military intervention.[35] Despite the anathema on army coups pronounced by the AU and aid cutoffs from the Western donor community, no fully effective inoculation of the still fragile post-transition regimes has taken hold. Especially vulnerable are the semidemocratic (or semiauthoritarian) regimes whose limitations with respect to democratization were apparent. Patrick McGowan argued in 2003 that quantitative analysis over time showed little real drop in military intervention following the democratic wave.[36] Though by my count twelve transitions were interrupted by military power seizure, by 2010 in all cases but Madagascar, army rulers soon had to restore constitutional rule (or in Niger schedule free elections for 2011), even if only semidemocratic or semiauthoritarian in substance or failed in reality (as in my reading, Central African Republic, Comoros, and Guinea-Bissau currently stand). In other cases (Congo-Kinshasa, Ivory Coast, Rwanda) interruptions occurred as a consequence of civil war or illicit civilian power seizures (Ivory Coast in 2010, Madagascar in 2008).

ZIMBABWE CASE

In this roster, Zimbabwe is an all but unclassifiable category (though I list it as a transitional state in 2009). Its evolution occurred in reverse sequence to the continental pattern. The negotiated transition following two decades of insurgent struggle provided for a democratic constitution bearing the imprint of the decolonization model examined in chapter 3. The two liberation movements, the Zimbabwe African National Union (ZANU), led by Robert Mugabe, and the Zimbabwe African People's Union, led by Joshua Nkomo, had different regional bases, reflected in initial electoral returns. A forced marriage in 1987 by the stronger party, ZANU, fused them as ZANU-Patriotic Front (PF) that became a virtual single party, an ascendance reinforced in 1990 by constitutional changes eliminating the twenty reserved white seats that Britain insisted on in the independence bargain as a transitional measure. However, Zimbabwe never became a juridically one-party state. But while most other countries opened in the 1990s Zimbabwe effectively closed, becoming a ZANU-PF political monopoly; in 1995 elections ZANU-PF won all but three national assembly seats. Zimbabwe inherited a strong state and prosperous economy, both consolidated in the first independent decade.[37] Mugabe, despite his personal Marxist-Leninist convictions, left in place the market economy and initially nurtured a difficult reconciliation with the white minority, after a bitter liberation struggle.[38] The record was marred by a vicious repression of unrest in Matabeleland between 1983 and 1986, carried out by the infamous North Korean-trained Fifth Brigade. But far from experiencing the state crisis afflicting most of the continent, Zimbabwe in 1990 was undergoing something that more closely approximated the state expansion moment elsewhere two decades earlier, and before the 1990s was constantly cited as a model African polity.[39]

However, by the late 1990s ominous trends were apparent. Investment shortfalls, unfavorable export prices, and soaring urban unemployment eroded ZANU-PF support, especially in the towns; in the words of William Tordoff, "ZANU-PF had become little more than a Shona peasant party, with little or no urban or union support."[40] The decision to dispatch twelve thousand troops to Congo-Kinshasa in 1998 to help rescue the Laurent Kabila regime, which was faced with an invasion by a new insurgent force organized by Rwanda and Uganda, saved Kabila and brought lucrative business opportunities to top Zimbabwean officers and some Mugabe allies, but the half-decade deployment meant heavy costs for the treasury (an estimated $1 billion).[41] Mugabe attempted to deflect the vocal discontents of some thirty thousand unemployed former guerrilla fighters by making extravagant payoffs in 1997, a further large drain.

By the end of the 1990s, trouble for Mugabe had broken out on new fronts. In 1999, a new opposition party, the Movement for Democratic Change (MDC), emerged and quickly won broad union, urban and Matabeleland support. An effort to reinforce presidential powers by constitutional amendment in 2000 lost badly in a referendum, a humiliating defeat. Mugabe responded by encouraging "war veterans" and ZANU-PF rural youth (Green Bombers) to invade many of the white-owned large farms. According to Scott Taylor, "by 2002 over 80 percent of Zimbabwe's 4,500 white-owned commercial farms had been forcibly seized. The chaotic, corrupt, and violent 'solution' to Zimbabwe's historical landownership disparities has precipitated economic collapse and contributed to the prevailing environment of lawlessness."[42] By 2009, nearly all the white commercial farms had been seized without compensation and a number of farmers killed in the process. Worse, many of the seized farms passed into the hands of Mugabe cronies rather than to African smallholders (though a number did benefit) or to the three hundred thousand African farm workers who were major victims of this lawless operation. Hyperinflation gathered force; life expectancy, an enviable sixty-one in 1991, fell to thirty-nine in 2004. In an environment of rising violence, the ruling party fared poorly in the 2000 parliamentary elections, winning sixty-two seats to fifty-seven for the MDC, which swept the cities. The 2002 presidential elections were far worse; the Mugabe triumph has been described as "a sham, littered with censure, violence, intimidation, presumed vote rigging, and refusal to accept international observers."[43]

In simultaneous parliamentary and presidential elections in 2008, the MDC in the face of a climate of rural violence and intimidation actually won a parliamentary plurality with a small allied fraction, and its leader Morgan Tsvangirai led Mugabe in the first round of presidential balloting. With the Green Bombers on a rampage in the countryside, Tsvangirai felt constrained to boycott the second round, leaving Mugabe with an empty victory on a tiny turnout. By this time, Zimbabwe had become a failed state; schools and many rural clinics were closed because staff salaries were worthless and commercial life was paralyzed by hyperinflation that reached 9,030,000% by mid-2008. The GDP had shriveled by 60% over the previous decade.[44] Millions—perhaps a third of the population—had fled the country. Only an inner core of ZANU-PF securocrats and Mugabe political henchmen remained to exploit the remnants of the state domain.

Mediation by the Southern African Development Community (SADC) finally brought a precarious power-sharing transitional regime into being in early 2009, with Mugabe retaining the presidency and Tsvangirai becoming premier. However, Mugabe has contravened the delicate balance intended by the compromise by retaining full control of the security agencies, arresting MDC parliamentarians, and continuing farm invasions and other rural violence. Still, Tsvangarai has managed to achieve control over the finance ministry, has abandoned the worthless Zimbabwe currency in favor of the dollar and rand, has restored a degree of operationality to schools and clinics, and has brought cautious hope in some quarters that a functioning state outside its security core can be rebuilt. The institutional remains of a once efficacious government can provide the vessel for state restoration; the Zimbabwe descent into a failed polity only occurred during the past decade, and the resource base is ample. For such a restoration to occur, the promised new reformed constitution, internationally credible elections, and an end to the Mugabe grip on ultimate power are preconditions. So also is large-scale international assistance, available only with restoration of a legitimate regime. Democracy once again offers the only exit strategy.

MANAGING ELECTORAL CONFLICT

In one important respect, the Zimbabwe crisis that came to a head with the 2008 contested elections is illustrative of a broader African dilemma: how to manage the high tensions resulting from closely divided or disputed electoral outcomes. Electoral crises shaking the political system to its core have punctuated the postdemocratic transition era in Niger, Nigeria, and Kenya; in 2010 Ivory Coast joined this list. The heated, divisive, and violent episodes that followed bear witness to the possible perils in democratic consolidation. The dramaturgy embedded in electoral process is enacted in a theater of conflict. Political parties acquire collective personalities, perhaps including ethnic, regional, or religious components. The campaign is a ritualized combat, accompanied by a crescendo of expectations and apprehensions. The adversary is readily suspected of violating the rules of battle. In mobilizing supporters, the temptation arises to secure the party with youth militias. The prize—control of the state with its imagined rewards—assumes greater value as the election date nears; defeat means calamitous exclusion. The final moments awaiting the result are thus fraught with tension. Defeat in this mood of escalated competitive tensions inevitably appears cataclysmic; the search for explanation turns quickly to malpractice by the adversary in its numerous possible forms. Acceptance of defeat when the margin is narrow is especially difficult, the more so if the conduct of the election falls short of the "free and fair" gold standard. Given the intrinsic logistical hazards in the complex tasks of registration of voters, supervision of the campaigns, conduct of the balloting, and tabulation of the vote, not to mention infrastructure limitations, the flawless election is probably beyond reach in African circumstances. A remarkable aspect of the democratic transitions is the number of elections that have been relatively well conducted, more than those that have fallen short. But the crises triggered by a failed election impose high costs on the polity.

In Niger, electoral conflicts have produced repeated breakdowns. At issue has been not the conduct of the election but unmanageable divisions ensuing from closely divided results; in the decade that followed the 1991 national conference that drove military ruler Ali Saibou from power, the country experienced no less than four constitutions, three transitions, two military coups, and four heads of state.[45] The initial transition constitution provided for an elected president and a prime minister responsible to parliament. The pretransition ruling party, the Mouvement national pour la société et le développement, won the largest number of parliamentary seats (twenty-nine of eighty-three), with three other parties sharing most of the rest in the first 1993 elections. Although its presidential candidate, Mamadou Tandja, led the presidential poll with 34%, the other parties formed an alliance on the second round to block his victory. As a result, the president and prime minister were from different parties, a prescription for the impasse that swiftly followed. New elections in 1995 reproduced the same impasse, leading to a military coup in 1996 led by Colonel Ibrahim Mainassare Baré. A new constitution was adopted, and Baré created a new party, the Front pour la restauration et la défense de la démocratie. By dubious means, Baré declared himself president following the ensuing elections, a power seizure the opposition refused to accept. After three years of constitutional maneuvering, Baré was assassinated by his presidential guard, and a new army ruler seized power, Major Douada Mallam Wanke.

Finally, with yet another new constitution in place, Mamadou Tandja again contested the presidency, winning 32%; however, on this occasion he found an ally during the second round and became a clearly legitimate head of state. He was reelected for a second term in 2004, this time winning 41% in the first round, securing enough allies in the second to triumph and sustain a working relationship with parliament. During these years of stability and constitutional rule, Niger experienced modest prosperity, and its uranium mining sector has shown signs of growth. However, in 2009 Tandja sought a constitutional amendment to extend his term; when parliament and the constitutional court rejected his request, he dissolved both, rammed through a referendum to approve his power seizure and once again returned Niger to impasse, renewed autocracy, and the likelihood of further instability in the near future. A widely welcomed military coup soon followed; the army rulers have won approval for a new constitution, and by 2011 widely accepted elections had been held and a further democratic transition had taken place.

Even more damaging was the calamitous failure of the 2007 Kenya elections. There was reason to hope that Kenya would serve as model for a political learning process in electoral management. Staffan Lindberg's careful study of African elections, written before the 2007 failure, suggests Kenya is one of several countries where a virtuous cycle of progressively strengthened democracy in reiterated elections through adaptation and learning has been visible. "Elites," he writes, "seem to adjust their behavior and strategies accordingly with increasing experience with elections," as fear and mistrust "is slowly replaced by more-peaceful coexistence, acceptance, and competition."[46] Unfortunately, the Kenyan elites failed to follow this script in 2007.

In the first two multiparty elections in 1992 and 1997, long-time autocrat Daniel arap Moi won electoral mandates as KANU party leader by muscular means but still narrow margins. The 1992 campaign was marred by serious ethnic clashes in the Rift Valley pitting Masai and Kalenjin warriors against Kikuyu settlers. This region, a site of large white settler estates in colonial times, had once been pastoral grazing land. Kikuyu came to the estates initially as squatters in the colonial period and even more came after independence. With land reform providing for individual or corporate ownership, many individuals or land partnerships acquired titles. Top politicians in the Moi entourage fomented the conflict, their lingering Kalenjin resentments at what they regarded as Kikuyu intrusion providing ready fuel. An underlying motivation in provoking these clashes was to demonstrate the dangers of ethnic conflict detonated by electoral competition.[47] This tragedy was re-enacted on a much larger scale following the failed 2007 elections.

A Moi effort to remove the two-term limit in the transition constitution failed, and the 2002 elections took place in an open field and in a reconfigured political party universe. Not only did Moi disappear from the scene, but his KANU party lost power for the first time since 1962 independence. The elderly Mwai Kibaki won the presidency based on an unstable coalition of fifteen parties, the National Alliance Rainbow Coalition (NARC), which broke apart soon after the election. Although money flowed freely in the campaign and the endemic corruption plaguing Kenya was manifest in the competition, the election was free of major flaws and its results enthusiastically accepted. Kenya seemed on a pathway to democratic consolidation.

However, the 2007 election proved instead a major setback; the bitterly disputed result and wave of ensuing violence wreaked havoc on Kenya's political stability and economic prosperity. As the election came onto the political horizon by 2005, the three hundred parties in the competition entered into an ever-shifting set of alliances; most were the personal followings of diverse "big men," with core constituencies that were local and ethnic. The key prize, the presidency, required a plurality plus at least 25% in six of the eight provinces; thus any winning coalition had to have strong support from at least one of the two largest groups, Kikuyu (40%) and Luo (15%). The two leading candidates, Kibaki and the perennial contender Raila Odinga, were allies in NARC in the 2002 election defeating KANU but split soon after; Odinga led a coalition in 2005 that became the Orange Democratic Movement (ODM) and that, in a referendum that year, rejected a Kibaki-tailored proposed new constitution by 57–43%. The main objections were to enhanced presidential powers and to regional decentralization.

The 2007 campaign opened with a large field of contenders, a plethora of parties awaiting regrouping in alliances broad enough to win the presidency. These coalitions were virtually unconstrained by ideological difference, beyond the decentralization issue. As van de Walle has observed, in most African multiparty settings "political cleavages are not well-set, and identity politics typically trumps ideology. As a result, political alliances are more fluid and changing, and individual politicians have a greater degree of autonomy in the deals and alliances they make to gain political power."[48] The final crystallization of leading candidates and coalitions emerged only a few months before the elections. Kibaki assembled the Party of National Unity, comprising KANU and the three wealthiest Kikuyu families linked with the old Kenyatta party.

Odinga reconfigured his ODM to assemble a large fraction of the smaller ethnic groups in western Kenya and the coast.

An important new feature of this competition was the key role played by election polls, which have become salient only in the last decade. Their credibility was greatly enhanced by their remarkable accuracy in predicting the results of the 2005 constitutional referendum. In the weeks leading up to the December 2007 polling, Odinga moved into a narrow lead. In the final survey published by the leading pollster, Odinga had 45% and Kibaki 43%. However, in the results officially announced, these figures were reversed; Kibaki claimed a lead of 230,000 votes out of 9.8 million cast. The ODM at once denounced the results as fraudulent and rigged; its followers took to the streets in violent protest. Ethnic fighting broke out on a large scale, especially in the Rift Valley, this time not only in the countryside but also the towns. Weeks passed before the violence could be tamped down. Over a thousand were killed and a quarter of a million displaced.

The conviction of many Kenyans that the announced results were falsified was intensified by the fact that they were at odds with the final surveys by polling agencies. Also rendering the Kibaki victory claim suspect was his replacement of five of the members of the national electoral commission a few months before the election. As Tom Wolf has observed, one possible impact of the seeming accuracy of the polls was the revelation that the required doctoring of the results was small, the polls offering clear guidance as to how many votes needed to be added. Another poll six months after the election showed that 57% of Kenyans believed that Odinga had won, and only 25% believed that Kibaki had been really elected.[49] This opinion is shared by most international observers.

An imperfect resolution to the crisis took many weeks and the mediation of former UN general secretary Kofi Annan. Kibaki retained a damaged presidency, with Odinga as prime minister. But the harm was done, and an opportunity for democratic consolidation had been squandered. A very harmful precedent was set as well in the country accepting a probably fraudulent outcome. At the same time, this election, like those in Niger and Zimbabwe, illustrated the special tensions arising from hotly disputed contests decided by very narrow margins in a context in which building democracy remains a work in progress.

The 2007 Nigerian elections were yet another body blow to the credibility of the electoral process. Although over time most grudgingly conceded the presidential chair to the announced victor, Umaru Yar'Adua, the European

Union's declaration that the elections were "not credible" echoed the convictions of most observers, Nigerians and outsiders. The announced results showed Yar'Adua with 24.6 million votes, compared to the 2.6 million of runner-up Muhammadu Buhari, a margin too large to dispute the winner, although suspect in its size. But the colossal corruption, disorganization, and thuggery surrounding the conduct of the election denied any legitimacy to the process.

The 1999 transition election that ended military rule and brought former general Obafemi Obasanjo to power as the first southern head of state since 1979 was marred by fraud, like almost all previous postcolonial Nigerian balloting. The Obasanjo reelection in 2003 was more deeply flawed, although the outcome was not contested. But the scale of the malpractice in 2007 was much worse, as "godfathers" who bought and sold entire state legislatures visibly emerged and armed youth militias were incorporated as party auxiliaries.[50] The violent student "cults" that infest university campuses often provided the muscle, as did violent local vigilante groups such as the "Bakassi Boys" in other cases.[51] A vice-presidential candidate explained the mechanism to a Human Rights Watch interviewer: "Earlier I had 20 boys here to see me. If anyone attacks me my boys will unleash terror. . . . I help them to secure a little patronage from government or to start small businesses. . . . It is not possible to start a campaign without your boys."[52]

After protracted deliberation, the high court rejected a challenge to the outcome. However, elections in several states were annulled by the courts. Lacking the standing and mandate that a legitimate election would have provided, Yar'Adua's capacity for leadership of a large and fractious country was compromised and was further diminished when he became seriously ill, dying in 2010. Confronted with endemic violence and well-armed insurgent militias in the oil-producing Niger Delta and violent Islamic sects in the north, an embattled nation has paid a heavy ransom for the inability to manage a credible national election.[53] The 2011 elections, under the able management of electoral commissioner Attahiru Jega, were a substantial improvement.

DEMOCRACY AND DEVELOPMENT

For advocates of a necessary authoritarian passageway to modernity of an earlier epoch, the two clinching arguments were economic development and containment of cultural pluralism. Only a developmental dictatorship could marshal the resources and national energies required to achieve rapid growth. The incubus of politicized ethnicity could only be exorcised by denying it the political space for mobilization. These claims merit revisiting after the experience of two decades of democratic transitions in nearly all of Africa. Although the greatest number of emergent regimes fall into the semidemocratic (or semiauthoritarian) categories, as I have argued, even with circumscribed liberalization the openings for an awakened civil society are sufficient to impose a degree of accountability. Such regimes cannot enjoy the unencumbered autonomy from society anticipated by the bureaucratic-authoritarian state model. In my reading, although ten fully autocratic polities remain (see table 6.1), none of them stand out as exemplars of effective development, although Equatorial Guinea, Angola, and Libya enjoy the huge advantage of large oil revenues and relatively small populations.

A backward glance should suffice to puncture the claims of developmental dictatorships in Africa; during the decades when such patterns of state organization were predominant, economic growth figures continued to decline, culminating in the absolute shrinkage of the 1980s. Between 1977 and 1985, across the continent per capita GDP declined by 15%.[54] The only two countries that clearly and consistently deviated from this trend were Botswana and Mauritius, the sole continuous liberal democracies on the continent. Since 1990, and especially since 2000, African economic performance has improved. Among the most virtuous performers are several from the roster of table 6.1 democracies: Cape Verde, Ghana, Malawi, Namibia, and South Africa. One hesitates to make the contrary assertion that democratic opening clearly fosters improved developmental performance. But statistical analysis by Adam Przeworeski and Fernando Limongi does demonstrate that relatively low levels of economic development are not an insuperable barrier to democratization, though they make consolidation more problematic.[55]

DEMOCRACY AND CULTURAL PLURALISM

The management of cultural diversity within the setting of competitive multiparty politics is a challenge, to which I return in chapter 8.[56] In the post–cold war world in which socialist ideologies have been globally discredited, defining a distinct ideological niche as a means of distinguishing political parties becomes problematic. Perhaps surprisingly, given the negative image of SAPs, parties have by and large avoided populist appeals to reverse economic reform or to a return to statism. Thus ethnic or religious identity stands out as a key marker, readily mobilized for political ends. The likelihood of political competition acquiring an ethnic coloration is enhanced by the sheer dramaturgy of the election process. Though a fluid and ongoing process of social construction, political ethnicity translates into metaphorical kinship, with its powerful emotional tug.[57]

The drafters of the new transition constitutions were keenly aware of this difficulty. In most cases, constitutional prohibitions were erected against formal incorporation of ethnicity or religion as bases for party membership. Various other devices were employed to ensure that a party could not gain power on the basis of a pure regional appeal, such as the Kenyan requirement that presidential candidates win at least 25% of the vote in six of the eight provinces and the similar Nigerian stipulation calling for at least a quarter of the vote in two-thirds of the states. Another mechanism was a proof of broadly distributed membership to secure registration as a political party. Proportional representation was far more widely employed than in the independence constitutions, in the belief that it better assured equitable parliamentary representation for the range of ethnic communities.[58]

In a number of countries, the salience of ethnicity was limited by the existence, even in a multiparty setting, of a single dominant movement; this was the case in Tanzania, Mozambique, South Africa, Namibia, Mali, and Botswana, among others. In several of the clearly democratic countries (Ghana, Mali, Mauritius, and Senegal), multiparty competition including alternation of winning party did not activate intense ethnic animosities. Conversely, in two of the four instances of 2009 failed states in table 6.1, the population is culturally homogeneous (Comoros and Somalia). The fuel for persistent paralyzing conflict lay at a lower level of identity (the three islands for Comoros, the clan hierarchy in Somalia).

Religion as an identity system poses somewhat different challenges. Where the religious proportions of Muslims and Christians are nearly equal (Nigeria, Ethiopia), fears of subordination to the theological dictates of the other readily arise: witness the apprehensions in southern Nigeria triggered by the adoption of shari'a in the criminal codes of a dozen northern Nigerian states following the democratic transition, or the spread of the violent Islamist extremist group Boko Haram in 2011–12. In northern Africa, fears about the democratic commitments of Islamic parties after electoral triumph lie close to the surface and have long operated to keep authoritarian currents flowing among incumbents. Ghassan Salamé argues that such concerns necessitate that transition be accompanied by a firm pact binding the major political forces to guarantee that democratization did not lead to Islamist autocracy.[59] But in most of Africa religious difference has not posed a major challenge to post-transition stability.

DISRUPTED TRANSITIONS

Still, in five of the fifteen cases in which democratic transitions were interrupted or aborted, violent conflicts linked to cultural pluralism were implicated. In Algeria, the 1992 military intervention to block the Islamist party FIS from an electoral victory brought a decade of civil war and one hundred thousand deaths. In Congo-Brazzaville, the street warfare that broke out in 1993 and again in 1997 between three ethnopolitical militias tied to leading politicians led directly to the breakdown.[60] In Ivory Coast, northern soldiers mutinied and seized the northern half of the country in 2002, leading to years of paralysis and to a derailment of a return to an elected government. In Kenya, though constitutional continuity was in the end preserved, the failed 2007 elections triggered the worst ethnic violence since independence.

By far the most serious of the disruptions of democratic transitions were the horrendous genocides in Burundi and Rwanda in 1993 and 1994. The latent risk of violent escalation inherent to ethnic difference was several orders of magnitude greater in these two polities because of the bipolarity of mobilized identities, the historical hierarchy enshrining dominance of the smaller group, and the cultural mythologies surrounding their difference. Dubious racial theories that gained currency in colonial times portrayed Tutsi as a superior stock of Ethiopian origin; Hutu riposted with the claim that Tutsi were an alien race of invaders, usurping the natural rights accruing to indigeneity. Interestingly, the two postgenocide (and postconflict) regimes drew diametrically opposed conclusions from the catastrophic experiences. In Rwanda, a Hutu autocracy was replaced by a semiauthoritarian regime under the tight control of Tutsi immigrants from the refugee diaspora; Paul Kagame rules with limited tolerance for dissent but sustains the indispensable flow of external assistance through careful cultivation of Western guilt over failure to halt the genocide and unusually competent management of the state domain. In Burundi, the former Tutsi regime, after a decade of civil war, was replaced by a delicately balanced consociationalism that established ethnic quotas applicable to the ministries, parliament, the army officers, and top bureaucrats. Parliamentary membership must be 60% Hutu, 40% Tutsi. One national election under this formula was successfully held; the second, in 2010, was the focus of angry controversy. The durability of this formula remains to be seen. The terrible public memories of unending ethnic violence perhaps help sustain a tenuous peace but cannot guarantee that past nightmares will not recur.

Two decades after the democratic transition began, uncertainties remain about its future. Coups still occur: there have been four between 2006 and 2010, in Guinea, Madagascar, Mauritania, and Niger. However, the constraints imposed by the global environment are much greater than in the past. The AU ban on coups and the immediate suspension of countries where they occur from the organization have a certain impact, even if indulgence is shown to the perpetrators if they summon elections. Mauritania is a case in point; the military junta that seized power in 2008 had no intention of subjecting itself to a competitive election until AU mediators led by Senegal compelled it to do so. However, readmission to respectable society at once followed when coup leader General Mohamed Ould Abadallahi easily won the balloting. AU troops invaded Comoros in 2008 to reverse a coup on one of the islands. The AU and SADC refused to recognize the 2009 Madagascar coup and forced the insurgent leader Andry Ralijaona into still unresolved negotiation with ousted president Marc Ravalomanana and other former leaders. Much of the international community as well initially continued to recognize the former ruler and suspended its large assistance program. As noted at the outset, the continuing weakness of most states raises the stakes on presentability. There is a broad range of toleration for semidemocracy or even semiauthoritarianism, but respectability requires at least formal democratization, whose badge is multiparty elections.

Particularly disconcerting was the trend toward subverting electoral outcomes that appeared with the 2007 Kenyan and 2008 Zimbabwean voting. The capacity of incumbents through dilatory maneuver to eventually remain in office despite evident electoral defeat under a "national unity government" formula negotiated with external mediation in effect conferred an international blessing evading voter verdict. These unfortunate precedents likely encouraged Ivory Coast incumbent Laurent Gbagbo to cling to usurped power in November 2010 despite internationally certified election returns showing a clear majority for Alassane Ouattara. This time, however, the international community and most of the AU refused to recognize the Gbagbo usurpation and eventually intervened militarily in April 2011 on the side of Ouattara forces to install the elected president.[61]

THE THIRD WAVE OF DEMOCRACY EVALUATED

Though the evidence if far too mixed for categorical conclusions, nonetheless I would share on balance the cautiously positive overall reading of several recent analysts. A group of Ghanaian scholars in an appraisal of the first decade of democratization after 1993 concludes that "not all needs have been satisfied by the liberal state but it cannot be disputed that peace, stability, transparency, accountability, respect for human rights and the rule of law have been its enduring features."[62] Long-standing Ghana specialist K. C. Morrison finds a stable structure of two-party competition taking root, accompanied by alternating winners in the current constitutional regime.[63] Linda Beck in a carefully qualified monograph on Senegalese politics finds that even though political society is permeated by clientelism the country merits its reputation as a democracy, demonstrated by the graceful acceptance of defeat by long-standing president Abdou Diouf in 2000 and then by his successor Abdoulaye Wade in 2012.[64] The seminal recent study by Lindberg of elections in Africa argues that detailed review of the data gives grounds for "measured optimism." He notes that forty-seven of forty-eight sub-Saharan states were in the process of planning or already holding participatory, competitive, and legitimate elections. Elections, he argues, "not only signify democracy; they breed democracy, through the self-reinforcing, self-improving quality of repetitive elections."[65] Richard Sandbrook concludes his appraisal of democratization by suggesting that, given the obstacles, some impressive successes are evident; even "low intensity democracy" is still an improvement.[66]

These judgments draw support from the survey data provided by Afrobarometer, gathered a decade ago in a dozen countries and now collected in twenty. A 2009 briefing paper found that in the twenty countries surveyed, support for democracy averaged 70%. Military rule, one-party systems, and strongman government were rejected by large majorities. Demand for democracy, although it declined for a time late in the 1990s, is on an upward curve. Some 59% believed that their own countries were substantially democratic. Some of these findings are detailed in table 6.2.[67]

Perhaps the most important lesson to draw from the African "third wave" of democratization is that success over time is possible, and that setbacks are not fatal. Consolidation of democracy is a protracted process, a long march toward a better future. Reversals will continue to occur, but a widespread return to patrimonial autocracy is unlikely. One may recall the puckish response of former president Dawda Jawara of Gambia to an interview question from John Wiseman as to why it was important to maintain a democratic system. "If you look at the alternatives, I think you can see why," replied Jawara, echoing the oft-cited aphorism of Winston Churchill that democracy was the worst form of government except for all the others.[68]

TABLE 6.2. African Perspectives on Democracy, Twenty Countries, 2008
(Percentages)

Country	Support for Democracy	Perceived Extent of Democracy	Rejection of Military Rule
Benin	81	76	73
Botswana	85	91	89
Burkina Faso	58	51	50
Cape Verde	81	71	79
Ghana	78	83	78
Kenya	78	43	94
Lesotho	46	37	75
Liberia	72	63	78
Madagascar	39	36	66
Malawi	74	56	84
Mali	72	60	61
Mozambique	59	59	63
Namibia	64	73	67
Nigeria	72	42	74
Senegal	70	37	69
South Africa	67	48	67
Tanzania	72	74	90
Uganda	79	54	78
Zambia	83	66	91
Zimbabwe	66	14	84

SOURCE: Constructed from data in Afrobarometer Briefing Paper no. 67, May 2009. On "support
for democracy," the question posed was "Which of these three statements is closest to your
own opinion?" (1) Democracy is preferable to any other kind of government. (2) In some
circumstances a nondemocratic government can be preferable. (3) For someone like me, it
doesn't matter what form of government we have.

On "perceived extent of democracy," the question was "In your opinion, how much of a
democracy is your country today?" Included in the percentage figure are responses indicating
that full or almost full democracy exists.

Regarding "rejection of military rule," the wording of the question was "There are many
ways to govern a country. Would you disapprove or approve of the following alternative? The
army comes in to govern the country." The percentage figure includes those disapproving.

As the second half century of the African independence era that began in
1960 opened at the beginning of 2011, the astonishing overthrow of long-
standing dictatorships in Tunisia, Egypt, and Libya by urban popular protest
(followed by armed insurgency in Libya) demonstrated the vitality of democratic aspirations among the citizenry. Once street action gained momentum,
armies declined to intervene in Tunisia and Egypt, and the enormous, detested

security police apparatus proved powerless to halt popular uprisings.[69] Seemingly entrenched and invincible authoritarian regimes can suddenly implode. Still, even the imperfect, hyphenated forms of democracy offer a more hopeful pathway. But so also can apparently successful instances of democratization prove subject to sudden and unexpected reversals, as illustrated by the 2012 military coup in Mali.

In retrospect, one might argue that the essence of the 1990 transition was away from authoritarianism rather than to full democracy.[70] In the new openings for civil society, often courageous human rights activists combat repressive acts. A freer press illuminates regime malfeasance. Judicial institutions acquire more scope to uphold the rule of law. In many small ways, the political and economic liberalization since 1990, however limited in many cases, opens new space for autonomous activity. Even though the democratization surge falls far short of the most optimistic visions of that moment, in my reading its salutary effects are measured in the distance between the despairing pessimism about African prospects at the depth of the state crisis in the late 1980s and the far more sanguine outlook today.

PART THREE

Themes and Conclusions

7

Morphology of Violent Civil Conflict

> Here, then, is one of the reasons for the near indestructibility of
> the idea of the post-colonial state. Those who disarranged and
> nearly destroyed its physical machinery were the most ardent
> bearers of its ideal. It was thus sustained as a focus and an object
> of conflict, even where there seemed to be no limit to the
> disintegration of its material organization and assets.
>
> —Sam C. Nolutshungu, 1996

EXPLORING VIOLENT CONFLICT

Violent civil conflict has been part of the African landscape since the 1950s,
though its forms have radically altered. Armed liberation struggle played
an important role in the drama of African independence, although sustained
guerrilla challenge to colonial rule occurred in only a few territories. In the
first three postcolonial decades, civil wars appeared here and there, a first
wave in the 1960s generated by abortive decolonizations, inadequate postindependence institutional frames, or separatist movements. An additional set
of insurgencies emerged in the 1980s, a product of state crisis. But following
the reconfiguration of global and African political parameters in the 1990s,
with widespread state crisis, the democracy wave, and the end of the cold
war, protracted internal wars ignited over broad stretches of the continent. In
a number of respects, these conflicts were driven by novel factors, reflecting
the changing political landscape since 1960. The at times high levels of violence and the degree of victimization of civil populations often gave a starkly
negative image to the post-1990 rebel movements that stood in bald contrast
to the heroic cast of the liberation movements that led the independence
struggle.[1] The Nolutshungu epigraph points to one of the paradoxes; state
destruction was a frequent consequence but not a purpose of their combat.[2]

This chapter explores the patterns of violent civil war in Africa, primarily those of the last two decades, underlining an array of attributes distinctive to the current political moment.[3] In the 1990s, the number and intensity of such conflicts increased, affecting more than a third of the fifty-three states. Although in some cases (for example, Sudan and Angola), they were continuations of struggles that dated from the independence era, in the majority of instances they were new eruptions. There were a couple of overarching effects of the patterns of the 1980s: a widespread delegitimation of the state and a corrosion of its capacities. I argue that a number of additional novel factors specific to the post-1990 context in both the African and global environment facilitated the outbreak of civil conflict and sustained internal warfare. I explore the nature of these armed conflicts through a detailed examination of a handful of particularly important and protracted instances: Liberia-Sierra Leone, Somalia, Sudan. Some others are briefly covered in chapters 5 (Chad, Mozambique) and 6 (Algeria, Rwanda, and Burundi), and the remainder receive brief treatment here. Since 2000, the spread of such conflicts has notably declined; this as well requires attention. To set the stage, I begin with a backward glance at the episodes of guerrilla combat and African warfare of the earlier period. The chapter then turns to the recent episodes of African armed conflict, seeking out their commonalities as well as their differences.

In terms of the sequencing of political change in Africa that I have employed, the earlier instances of violent conflict fall into three time phases. The majority of them relate to the liberation struggle era. Although the heart of the battle for decolonization took place at the end of the 1950s and early 1960s, the end point of decolonization came only three decades later, when it finally reached the southern African terminus. The decolonization era gave rise to two types of wars. The first was the armed liberation struggle that began in Algeria in 1954, spread to the Portuguese territories in 1961, and then on to Zimbabwe, Namibia, and South Africa shortly after. A second type of decolonization war occurred in the two countries where armed movements in territories with a distinct colonial identity resisted attachment to existing countries, namely, Western Sahara (Morocco) and Eritrea (Ethiopia).

The second phase, the moment of postindependence consolidation, also produced a pair of warfare types. The first arose as a consequence of the failure of the independence settlements to produce a regime capable of governing the entire realm. Into this category falls the 1963–65 Congo rebellions, the sporadic Chad civil wars from 1966 to 1982, and the Angolan civil war that raged from 1975 to 1991 and then reignited from 1992 to 2002. The second, separatist wars in eastern Nigeria (Biafra) and southern Sudan resulted from flawed constitutional dispositions leading important groups to feel excluded (Igbo in Nigeria, non-Arab Christians and other non-Muslims in southern Sudan).

The third phase, in the 1980s, reflected the failure of the integral state project examined in chapters 2 and 5. Two of these insurgencies, the ones in Uganda and Ethiopia, called for the remaking of the state. A third, rather different, instance is the RENAMO rebellion in Mozambique; it likewise found sustenance in the state overreach inherent to the initial Afromarxist ambitions of FRELIMO, although the insurgency was contaminated by its organization and support by the neighboring white minority regimes.

Throughout this pre-1990 era, aside from the ongoing national liberation struggles, at any given moment there were few such internal wars. Thus they always appeared to be the product of unique circumstances and were never seen as forming a pattern. The new states mostly inherited a functioning governmental apparatus, and were not assumed to be ready prey for insurgent challenge. Employing the categorization traced above, I turn first to the national liberation wars.

Liberation Struggles I

Though urban rioting in Cairo in 1919 led to the nominal independence of Egypt in 1922, the role of violent protest in anticolonial politics assumed wider importance only after World War II. Major revolts bringing brutal military repression occurred in Algeria in 1945 and Madagascar in 1947. A handful of urban-centered protest episodes, such as the 1946 railway workers strike in Senegal and the Accra (Ghana) disorders in 1948 were also forerunners. In the early 1950s, sporadic urban violence accelerated the independence of Tunisia and Morocco in 1956. But by far the most resonant guerrilla liberation struggle began in Algeria in 1954. In its scale, the intensity of its liberation ideology, and its capacity over eight years to fight the half-million-strong French army to a standstill and to attract global sympathy and an important flow of external support, the Algerian revolution was an extraordinary drama; it accelerated decolonization elsewhere and served as inspirational model in Portuguese-occupied Africa and white-ruled southern Africa where the doors to negotiated decolonization were long closed.

In 1961, guerrilla movements in Angola took form, followed by uprisings in Guinea-Bissau (1963) and Mozambique (1964), that became a major challenge later in the decade. Also in 1961, the first South African prospective guerrillas sought external training, followed in the mid-1960s by those from what became Zimbabwe and Namibia. Armed liberation struggle thus assumed a central place in the annals of independence, even though in military terms only Guinea-Bissau (and to a lesser extent Mozambique and Zimbabwe) came close to matching the Algerian performance in convincing the colonial armies they could never triumph militarily. In Angola and Zimbabwe, the existence of rival armed liberation movements with different regional bases was a major limitation to the effectiveness of their struggle.

A potent factor affecting the strategy and organization of the liberation movements was the relative bureaucratic strength of the terminal colonial state and its capacity to draw on repressive reinforcement from the colonial centers. This placed a premium on the insurgents' organizational abilities, as well as on the capacity to achieve high commitment from rebel ranks through ideological means and to enforce rigid discipline. In addition, the image of the colonial state was mirrored in the projects to construct a counterstate in liberated areas, especially in Guinea-Bissau, Mozambique, Algeria and later Eritrea.

In all these cases, access to external support and sanctuary was crucial. In the Algerian case, Cairo served as a rear base and organizational center from the outset. With the 1956 independence of Tunisia and Morocco, Algerians acquired neighboring sanctuary, bases, and supply routes; in the latter stages of the war, the bulk of Algerian forces were located in this near abroad. After initial hesitation, the two states bordering Guinea-Bissau, especially Guinea, became key support bases for the guerrilla insurgents. In southern Africa, liberation combat gained momentum only with the opening of borders to independent countries; Tanzania, Zambia, the two Congos, and later Angola were key external sanctuaries. In most instances, a secure retreat for the leadership was crucial to prevent their capture. Over time, it became possible to filter a growing flow of weapons and supplies into the country where the insurgency was taking place, as the global context became steadily more favorable to the liberation agenda.

This in turn reflected the success of liberation movements in establishing the moral legitimacy of their struggle. By skillfully drawing on a normative repertoire of values holding sway in the global community—freedom, liberation, and self-determination—guerrilla violence against the colonial occupation became a virtuous necessity in many external eyes. The movements effectively portrayed themselves as the authentic and unified voice of the subject population, though this was never entirely the case. The more sordid dimensions of insurgent warfare on the ground—violent account settling among guerrilla factions, extortion of supply from villagers, executions of purported colonial collaborators—were veiled from view by the ethical superiority of liberation.[4]

Drawing on this reservoir of moral support, diplomacy became a crucial, indeed decisive, weapon. The inability of the colonial armies to eliminate the insurgencies and prolonged stalemates that usually ensued placed the imperial powers under the pressure of deepening international opprobrium and growing domestic skepticism, deftly exploited by the diplomatic arms of the liberation movements. In South Africa and Namibia, the apartheid regime security forces were able to limit their liberation adversaries to sporadic raids but could never eliminate their external bases. The movements enjoyed access to valuable international forums, especially the UN. The creation of the OAU in 1963, which found a primary unifying focus in completing continental liberation, provided a valuable platform and organizational support. Other African states facilitated the international travel of liberation movement leaders by granting diplomatic passports and often travel funds, an insufficiently recognized advantage. In addition, the more activist states hosted and funded external offices for the movements.

Summing these factors, a crucial element differentiated the decolonization struggle moment from the postcolonial era. Time, history, and global opinion were on the side of the original liberation movements. This was not the case with most postindependence insurgent forces.

Not all terminal colonial uprisings succeeded; two important rural-based violent protest movements in the 1950s were defeated in Cameroon (1955–60) and Kenya (1952–57). In both cases, large reinforcements of metropolitan forces were required; especially in Kenya, the repression was harsh, with massive internment of suspects. The rebel movements—the Union des populations du Cameroun (UPC) in Cameroon, Mau Mau in Kenya—were stigmatized as rooted in ethnic backing (Bassa and Bamileke in Cameroon, Kikuyu in Kenya). Even within their ethnic base, support was far from unanimous; the Mau Mau struggle in Kenya in particular took on the aspects of an intraethnic civil war. Though the UPC did employ a radical, *marxisant* discourse, winning some limited external sympathy, the language and rituals of mobilization for Mau Mau could resonate only within an enclosed Kikuyu universe, and then only partially. Ideology on the battleground proved a decisive resource for the colonial power rather than the protest movement; the UPC was successfully portrayed as a Soviet-inspired "Communist" party, while the British persuaded most outside Kikuyuland that the Mau Mau insurgency was an atavistic and primitive rebellion. Surrounded by still colonial realms, the movements had no possibility of being externally supplied or supported; thus they faced crippling limitations in the armed means of resistance.[5] Their failure further illuminates the core determinants of success in armed liberation movements.

Liberation Struggles 2: Western Sahara and Eritrea

A different form of liberation struggle took place in Western Sahara and Eritrea, two territories joined by the vagaries of decolonization politics to the independent polities of Morocco and Ethiopia, respectively. As noted in chapter 3, Spain in effect simply abandoned Western Sahara in late 1975, confronted with the Moroccan "Green March" of a half million volunteers into the territory. With ruler Francisco Franco on his deathbed and a difficult transition pending, a forceful response was politically impossible. Morocco then initially shared the territory with Mauritania. Meanwhile, in February 1976 the Frente popular para la liberación de Saguia el-Hamra y Río de Oro (POLISARIO) declared Western Sahara a sovereign independent state. Operating from Algeria, its guerrillas initially inflicted serious pain on Morocco and all but drove the much weaker Mauritanian army out of the annexed southern sector. Mauritania abandoned its claim in 1979, and the Moroccan army at once moved into the zone. Even with its army tripled in size, Morocco faced serious internal unrest at the time, making Western Sahara appear indigestible. However, by the mid-1980s, Morocco managed to virtually seal the Algerian border with a wall of sand berms, linked by outposts equipped with electronic surveillance. POLISARIO fighters never found an answer to this strategy, and the guerrilla operations diminished in intensity, all but ceasing by the 1990s.[6] But the diplomatic battle continues.

Moroccan claims to historical sovereignty were rejected by the World Court, and for most of the external world effective Moroccan occupation ever since enjoys tacit acknowledgment but not full recognition. However, the majority of OAU/AU members, and the organization itself, have accorded full diplomatic recognition to Western Sahara; by 1983, fifty-four states, almost all in the third world, officially endorsed Western Sahara sovereignty. More importantly, Algeria has provided sanctuary, arms, and support to POLISARIO since 1975 and currently shelters an exile population estimated by aid agencies at 165,000, perhaps half the Saharoui total.[7]

The Eritrean liberation struggle lasted more than three decades and in its last stages in the 1980s was fought on a large scale. An Italian colony carved out of territory with historic ties to Ethiopia, Eritrea acquired a clear territorial identity in the colonial era under Italian rule, which lasted until 1941. After a complex postwar diplomatic struggle in which Eritreans played little part, agreement was reached by 1952 to join the territory to Ethiopia as an autonomous federated entity with an internationally defined special status. Although the link to Ethiopia initially had some support among Eritreans, opposition to Ethiopian rule gradually built, especially after a unitary state was imposed and all traces of special status erased by 1960. In 1961, the Eritrean Liberation Front (ELF) emerged, drawing most of its support from the Muslim coast. Its first attack in 1961 phased into sporadic skirmishes, at first little different from the armed banditry endemic on the coast, and then transformed into small-scale insurgency. In 1970, a rival movement, the Eritrean Peoples' Liberation Front (EPLF), took the field, its initial core support coming from the highlands. A ferocious civil war ensued from 1971 to 1974 between the two; the EPLF emerged as dominant challenger to Ethiopia at the same time the national army overthrew the monarchy, and a bitter and murderous power struggle unfolded.

A rapid escalation in the scale of hostilities followed, along with a transformation in its nature. An ideologically radical EPLF leadership turned a guerrilla campaign into an all-out people's war, achieving a remarkable degree of unity. With a secure rear base in Sudan, insurgent bands became hardened revolutionary warriors, kept in line by tight discipline and indoctrinated by rigorous ideological schooling. On the Ethiopian side, a regime now committed to Marxism-Leninism and a Soviet alliance pursued a revolutionary agenda and mobilized for full war. The EPLF swiftly expanded, and by the end of 1977 it controlled the key district capital of Nakfa and 90% of the territory.

The Ethiopians responded with major offensives, supported by large Soviet arms flows and reinforced with contingents of Soviet advisors and Cuban auxiliaries. Although an invasion on another front by the Somali army in 1977 was beaten back, EPLF resistance proved impossible to overcome. The sheer scale of the civil war has no parallel in postcolonial Africa; at its peak, the Ethiopian army had 250,000 professionals and an equal number of conscripts; the EPLF fielded over 100,000 warriors. The major engagements were no longer insurgent warfare but major combat between well-armed adversaries. Operation Red Star in 1982, a turning point in the war, pitted in the battle for the EPLF redoubt of Nakfa 84,000 Ethiopian troops with 99 tanks, 94 armored vehicles, 283 artillery pieces, a dozen MiG 21s and MiG 23s plus Mi-24 helicopter gunships, and a contingent of Soviet advisors; they faced

22,000 guerrilla fighters with smaller but significant armament including tanks, armored cars, artillery and mortars, and machine guns.[8] Both sides fought courageously and tenaciously, and there were heavy casualties, but the giant offensive failed, and Ethiopia never again came close to defeating the EPLF.

De facto independence came in 1991, formalized by referendum in 1993. The legacy of the thirty-year struggle was a highly militarized society, unified around the scriptures of revolutionary national liberation. Though instrumental to success in the liberation war, the precepts of enforced unity and iron discipline have shackled the postliberation polity.[9]

FAILED INDEPENDENCE:
ANGOLA, CONGO-KINSHASA, AND CHAD

In three instances, Angola, Congo-Kinshasa, and Chad, failure in power transfer led immediately to widespread disorder or protracted civil war. In the case of Angola as in Western Sahara, a weakened and disorganized colonial power, facing deep internal crisis, simply withdrew without successfully brokering a postcolonial settlement. The vacuum left by the Portuguese abandonment of its residual authority in November 1975 gave rise at once to a civil war that raged from 1975 to 2002. The aborted decolonization and radical deflation of state authority that immediately followed in Congo-Kinshasa set the stage for the wave of rebellions from 1963 to 1965. In Chad, the flawed postcolonial arrangements also led to early political impasse and sporadic civil war from 1966 to 1982.

The Angolan war, which raged intermittently from its anticolonial origins in 1961 until its final end in 2002, went through several metamorphoses, from liberation struggle to cold war–driven combat and then finally resource-driven internal war of the 1990s.[10] In contrast to the relatively unified struggle in Mozambique, the independence war had a quadrangular form. What proved the most important theater had its center in Luanda and its hinterland, homeland to the Movimento para a libertaçâo de Angola (MPLA) that has ruled since independence. Its support drew on the Mbundu ethnic group, the large Luanda community of mestizos, and some radical white settlers. The movement reflecting Kongo aspirations evolved into the Frente nacional para a libertaçâ de Angola (FNLA). The third major movement, whose major support base was the Ovimbundu ethnic cluster in southern Angola, was the Uniâo para a ndependência total de Angola (UNITA). Leadership of the three came from separate Protestant missions (Methodist, Baptist, and Congregationalist, respectively). The ethnic constituencies of the three major groups, Mbundu, Kongo, and Ovimbundu, constituted roughly 25%, 10%, and 40% of the population. A fourth identity zone, giving rise to periodic separatist movements, was the enclave of Cabinda, separated from Angola by a sliver of Congo-Kinshasa. The initial center of oil production, the claims of Cabinda to have once constituted a separate colonial entity entitled by the code of decolonization to independent status found initial support from the neighboring two Congos (attracted to its oil). Needless to say, Angola could never accept the loss of its oil center, and through the 1980s, reinforced with Cuban detachments, the Angolan army was always able to crush revolts in Cabinda.

Liberation struggle was at low ebb in 1974 when the overthrow of the Portuguese dictatorship suddenly brought independence into view. The three main movements sprang into renewed activity; the external patrons of the MPLA (Soviet Union and Cuba) and the FNLA (United States and Congo-Kinshasa) rushed to supply their allies. African diplomacy and the OAU as well as the new Portuguese military regime urgently sought to create a coalition between the three movements, and they briefly succeeded in early 1975. But the accord soon fell apart, and by March 1975 a civil war raged in Luanda, with the MPLA emerging victorious. UNITA found a new ally in South Africa; by October 1975 South African units had crossed the border, advancing up the coastal road with UNITA forces toward Luanda. On 10 November the last Portuguese governor sailed away, abandoning the country to civil war. Cuban forces and Soviet military supply enabled the MPLA to repulse the FNLA and UNITA; by early 1976 South African and Congolese forces had withdrawn.

Though the MPLA won the military battle, it soon proved incapable of effective management of the new state. The Afromarxist ideological enthusiasms of its ruling cadres were not matched by administrative competence. The flight of the Portuguese bureaucrats and the paralysis of the important coffee sector handicapped government operations. A bitter power struggle within the MPLA in Luanda in 1977 brought the capital to the verge of civil war, and then in 1979 MPLA leader Agostino Neto died, replaced by Eduardo dos Santos. Corruption began to appear, and services to the countryside were meager to nonexistent. These developments provided an opening to the Jonas Savimbi-led UNITA to regain momentum.

The FNLA was never again a major player. But UNITA by 1981 found renewed external backing sources from a clandestine American supply through the CIA and more open South African support. The advent of the Reagan administration in Washington, with its more confrontational cold war policy and deep anti-Cuban obsessions, and the new South African "total strategy" destabilization policy toward the African Afromarxist states to its north provided the doctrinal underpinning for the newly aggressive policies.

By the mid-1980s, UNITA had driven the MPLA out of a good part of the south, expanding beyond its Ovimbundu home territory. The fighting increasingly took on the aspects of a conventional war, in which large armies armed with tanks and heavy weaponry were pitted against each other in fixed battles rather than mobile guerrilla warfare. The culmination of this trend was the epic 1988 battle at Cuito Carnavale in which as many as fifty thousand Cubans plus their Angolan allies fought against numerous UNITA fighters reinforced by a substantial South African regular army force. Though there was no decisive winner, the South African-UNITA force failed to drive their adversaries from the major base they had established. Both sides experienced heavy losses, which pushed them toward peace negotiations.

A 1991 peace accord opened the way for the first real peace the tormented country had experienced since independence. The agreement called for the opening of the political arena to competing parties and for national elections, which were held in 1992 and supervised by a UN peacekeeping operation. The elections were peacefully conducted, and observers were unanimous in providing a "free and fair" stamp of approval. But rather than the triumph expected by Savimbi on the basis of his Ovimbundu ethnic base of nearly 40% (whose unity he overestimated), the MPLA won two-thirds of the parliamentary seats, and dos Santos was close to an absolute majority in the presidential balloting. Savimbi refused to take part in the presidential runoff and returned to the bush to resume the armed struggle, which lasted for another decade. I return to this final phase later in the chapter.

In the Congo-Kinshasa case, the national domain of a badly weakened state was restored under international tutelage by UN military suppression of the Katanga secession in January 1963. But the UN peacekeeping operation ended in 1964, exposing a still fragile polity to armed challenges it could not master. Even before, at the end of 1963, rebellion broke out in the Kwilu area of southwestern Congo. Multiple, hydraheaded uprisings then followed in 1964 in eastern Congo; by late that year government authority had vanished from the northeast quadrant of the country. An enfeebled state, widespread in the 1990s but unusual in the 1960s, could not halt a snowballing spread of the rebellion, until its army was stiffened by foreign mercenaries and eventually direct Belgian and American military support.

A few observations relating the Congo rebellions to the 1990s internal wars are pertinent here; the nature of its violence foreshadowed some of the patterns widespread in the contemporary conflicts. The logic of the cold war operated powerfully to precipitate American intervention in partnership with Belgium. They were able to block further the rebels' advance, and subsequently they seized their key base. Although the rebellions were under no initial Soviet influence, they attracted backing from radical African states and Communist sources at a time when they appeared to enjoy some success. Left-leaning African states—especially Algeria and Egypt—attempted to ship arms through Sudan in the fall of 1964, but to the dismay of Khartoum the shipment was intercepted by southern Sudanese insurgents. The misadventure of intervention on the eastern border by a small Cuban expeditionary force under Ernesto "Che" Guevara had no connection with the Soviet Union but readily fit a Western policy template assuming global Communist bloc expansion ambitions.[11]

Whereas the leaders in a number of the 1990s militias had previous army experience, rebel leaders in Congo-Kinshasa in the early 1960s entered the fray with no military knowledge or skills. Nor did they perceive the possibilities so crucial in the 1990s of exploiting the treasure trove of natural resources to finance the rebellions; they did seize and export to Uganda a gold stockpile at the Kilo-Moto mines in the far northeast but never benefited from the proceeds. Insurgent finance relied entirely on liquid resources seized in the towns occupied (especially vehicles and cash), a nonrenewable treasury quickly squandered.

Finally, let us note a consequence of the Congo rebellions that may become visible in contemporary postconflict situations. The human toll of the rebellions was very great; Herbert Weiss estimates a death toll of a million. Folk memories of the terrible costs of the violence and disruption, especially in the affected regions, remained vivid for many years afterward. Many fled the towns and hid in the bush for weeks. The long public quietism in spite of growing dissatisfaction with the Mobutu regime was partly attributable to an abiding fear of renewed violence, an incubus unhappily realized in the east after 1996.[12]

The other instance of civil warfare triggered by early state failure was Chad, already profiled in chapter 5 and needing only brief reference here. Several aspects of the prolonged Chad disorder, like the Congo rebellions, were forerunners of patterns that became widespread in the 1990s. The weakening authority of the state gave rise to a multiplicity of armed bands, surviving by plunder; "warlord politics" were born in Chad. Shifting alignments shaped by clan and ethnicity defined the low-intensity warfare. External players were drawn into the conflicts, especially Libya, Sudan, Nigeria, Congo-Kinshasa, and France. Chad was an early domain for the expansive visions and interventionist dispositions of Qadhafy; he occupied the northernmost part of Chad (the Aouzou strip) in 1973 and by 1980 had sent his units further south in pursuit of a greater Libya, retreating in 1986 after French military backing helped a Chad army to push back and then abandoning his claims on the Aouzou strip. Nigeria led repeated unsuccessful African mediation efforts to create a coalition government before a militia striking from Sudan sanctuary led by Hissein Habré reestablished a single authority in 1982.

Separatist Uprisings: Biafra and Southern Sudan

The Biafran secession (1967–70) arose out of the interplay of the first round of flawed Nigerian elections, ethnoregional party politics, episodes of communal violence, and a deepening sense of exclusion on the part of a major ethnic group, the Igbo. As overlay, an unstable federal arrangement pitted the three major ethnic groups against each other, each dominating one of the three regions. In each of the regions, roughly a third of the population were "minorities," and an electoral arithmetic weighted toward the Hausa-Fulani dominated Northern Region was in place. The innumerable electoral malpractices and venal political behavior of the First Republic had produced serious disenchantment by the mid-1960s. When a group of radical majors tried to seize power in January 1966, much of the public initially applauded; the rebels assassinated the federal prime minister, two of the four regional governors, and a number of senior officers. But the coup unraveled, and a rump cabinet surrendered power to the army commander, General J. T. Ironsi. An ethnic selectivity in leadership and targets became visible. Six of the seven majors were Igbo, and of the seven senior officers assassinated, only one was Igbo, while only non-Igbo regional governors were killed.

General Ironsi, also an Igbo, deepened tensions with insensitive leadership. He relied on an inner core of coethnic senior civil servants; promotions to replace the fallen officers, though based on seniority, saw nine of twelve slots go to Igbo. The sudden declaration of a unitary state in May 1966 was the final detonator; a wave of anti-Igbo riots swept northern cities. In July 1966, another coup took place, this time by northern officers, accompanied by a wave of killings; the victims included Ironsi, 39 officers, and 191 other ranks, mostly Igbo. The remaining Igbo military regrouped in the Igbo-dominated

Eastern Region, along with many ranking professionals and intellectuals. Estimates vary of the fatalities in the attacks on southerners, especially Igbo, in northern cities, ranging as high as fifty thousand; up to two million fled southward. Demands for secession now crystallized, posed in terms of cultural survival. Finally, a sovereign state of Biafra was proclaimed on 30 May 1967.

The separatist claim was always framed in the name of the long-established Eastern Region, never as an ethnic demand for Igbo self-determination. Such a framing was indispensable for possible international acceptance. In addition, this provided the secession with an established set of administrative and political institutions. At the same time, it proved a fatal weakness; the non-Igbo "minorities" in the Niger delta and along the coast were at best reticent and soon defected to the federal side.

More than for any of the other early African postcolonial civil wars, except Western Sahara, the diplomatic front for the Biafran struggle was critical. Nigeria urgently required an arms supply (its army had only seven thousand men and no tanks or aircraft) and denial of international recognition for Biafra. The secession likewise needed weapons and the crucial legitimation that external blessing for sovereignty would supply. Nigeria had the resources and foreign exchange reserves to undertake large arms purchases; the Soviet Union, previously suspicious of Nigeria as a Western client state, now saw an opportunity and was a generous provider. Biafra managed to secure some aging aircraft and other arms, along with a large flow of humanitarian assistance. The Biafran information services, their work abetted by a large and active diaspora, skillfully exploited the claim that genocide awaited the Igbo if the secession failed. Remarkably, Biafra diplomacy did secure formal recognition from four African states (Ivory Coast, Gabon, Tanzania, and Zambia), plus Haiti. But at the end of the day the African state system rallied behind Nigeria; three successive OAU conferences condemned the secession.

So also did the rest of Nigeria. Opinion swung behind the federal cause and its slogan "To Keep Nigeria One Is a Job That Must Be Done." The Nigerian armed forces mushroomed to 250,000 and seized the oil-producing coastal strip of Biafra. But the shrinking Biafran redoubt hung on for thirty months, until the last airstrip permitting resupply was captured. The Biafra war was almost entirely a combat between organized armies; within its diminishing zone of control the secessionist regime operated as a regular government.

However bitter the civil war and the communal violence preceding it had been, the haunting fear of genocide did not materialize, nor did the threatened guerrilla resistance, for which no preparation had been made. On the contrary, federal troops remained disciplined, wreaking no vengeance on the population. The Igbo civilian losses during the war were heavy; there were as many as a million casualties. Igbo elites had lost their leading positions in the federal bureaucracy, as well as much urban property, especially in Port Harcourt in the Niger delta. But the postconflict mood of reconciliation yet stands as a model.[13]

Still, a sense of loss remains among many in the Igbo community; so great a trauma cannot vanish without leaving indelible marks on society. As Daniel Smith observes, especially after the 1999 democratic transition, a renewed Igbo sense of marginalization entered public psychology, fueled by the transformed perceptions of the Nigerian polity and the pathways to wealth since the civil war. Igbo have remained largely absent in the top ranks of the federal government, the military, and the Nigerian National Petroleum Corporation. This exclusion is much more than symbolic; "in Nigeria's military and oil-dominated postcolonial history, controlling the center has translated into controlling the preponderance of the nation's wealth and power."[14] The civil war marked a turning point in this process; corruption made its appearance in the First Republic but on a limited scale and then metastasized in the 1970s. In 2000, a new movement devoted to the cause of a Biafran state was launched: the Movement for the Actualization of the Sovereign State of Biafra (MASSOB). Though a rejuvenated dream of secession is viewed as distant by most Igbo, the movement has a substantial following in the diasporas of the United States and Britain and serves as one focal point for expression of discontent within Nigeria.[15]

The second example of civil war with separatist tonality is the southern Sudan rebellion against the center, which unfolded in two prolonged chapters from 1955 to 1972 and then again from 1983 to 2005. The separatist alternative was always present as a subtext, and many clearly preferred it; it was ultimately realized in 2011. Thus I include southern Sudan as an instance of secessionist warfare, even though during much of the long struggle key insurgent leaders clung to an official goal of a single Sudan in which the ethnically distinct southern regions would have a large degree of autonomy and would be culturally recognized. I discuss the first phase of the civil war here and return to the contemporary act later in the chapter.

The key cleavage in Sudan divides the north, overwhelmingly Muslim with Arabic as vehicular medium (though only 40% of the Sudanese population is Arab by maternal language and genealogy), from the southern third that is of diverse ethnic origin but shares a regional sense of distinctiveness, greatly sharpened by protracted civil war.[16] Anticolonial nationalism was rooted in the Khartoum-centered north, which has completely dominated all postcolonial regimes. From the outset, the embrace of an Arab-Islamic identity for the state by the northern rulers triggered cultural fears in the south, most of whose elites and a growing number of others are Christians. In addition, a deeply embedded historical memory of large-scale nineteenth century slave raiding by armed bands operating on behalf of Khartoum merchants remains alive; so also does a racial scorn of southerners implanted in the northern mentality. Thus a racialized discourse became prevalent, objectifying southerners as "black" or African (even *abid*, or slaves), despite the slender phenotypical differences. Southerners in turn internalized the "African" label as unifying the region, in contrast to an "Arab" north, rejecting Arabism as an assimilative pole.

This consciousness of difference was exacerbated in colonial times by a separate administrative policy for the south pursued by the British. The "Southern Policy," which took form in the 1920s, gave strong encouragement to Christian mission engagement, to which education and health responsibilities could be delegated. Northern presence was discouraged, and after 1929 it was barred when a slave-trading ring was uncovered. In the interwar period, there was some speculative talk about attaching the region to Uganda, perceived by a nascent nationalism in the north as further evidence of British cunning duplicity. The south by 1960 had only three secondary schools, and a mere sixty students at Khartoum University. Southern Sudan was a colonial backwater, with minimal economic development.[17]

By 1947, the decision to move Sudan toward decolonization as a united territory had been made; independence appeared on the horizon far more swiftly than anticipated, amid growing southern apprehensions. These redoubled in 1954 when northern leaders, concerned with restiveness in the south, warned that "they shall use the force of iron in dealing with any southerner who will dare attempt to divide the nation."[18] Shortly after, a list of five hundred nominations for senior government posts slated for Sudanization was published containing only four southern names. With the prospect of postcolonial marginalization thus dramatized, southern political leaders demanded a federal constitution. Although northern parties promised careful consideration of federalism in order to gain southern support for early independence on 1 January 1956, by 1957 the northern-dominated regime was insisting on a unitary state with Arabic as national language and Islam as state religion. The following year, with rumblings of support for federalism audible in the northeast Beja area, Darfur, and the Nuba mountains as well as the south and a fracturing Khartoum political arena, the military assumed power, committed to the unitary formula.

The southern rebellion may be traced to 1955, with a mutiny of the Equatoria Corps, the main security force in the south. Its enlisted ranks were all southern, while most officers were northern. With rumors of mutiny swirling, administrators called for the dispatch of northern troops; a portion of the Equatoria Corps was ordered to Khartoum. Those facing transfer were convinced they would be slaughtered on arrival, amid reports of a massacre of southerners in the main regional center, Juba. This triggered a mutiny against the northern officers; the mutineers disappeared into the bush, soon to form an initial core of the southern insurgency, which began to gain momentum from 1963 on.

The revolt was a loose-knit movement, with multiple centers, fragmented structures, and ambiguous ultimate goals. By 1960, many southern politicians and intellectuals had fled into exile. Legal political parties in the south were banned by the military regime. Many schools were closed, and those remaining were placed under northern schoolmasters; most of these were shuttered in 1964, by which time Christian missionaries were expelled. Oduho and Deng wrote in 1963 that "from the present Northern Sudanese attitude and policies applied to the South, we are irresistibly led to the conclusion that their aim is to destroy the African Negroid personality and identity in the Sudan and to replace it with an arabized and islamicised South."[19] Plans to resettle 1.5 million Arabs in Upper Nile province in the south were announced at the time.

Separate poles of southern resistance took form. The most externally visible were the exile politicians, operating from neighboring countries under a multiplicity of labels. Groups of guerrillas scattered through the south served as energizing centers of rebellion, which acquired the name of "Anya-nya" (guerrilla forces). Their struggle was conducted in almost total isolation; no sanctuary was available, nor were the various groups in close communication. They had very limited armament, consisting in weaponry occasionally captured from the army and a trickle from Israel and Ethiopia late in the game. The actual guerrilla numbers appeared to be no more than ten thousand, though twenty thousand emerged to claim integration into the Sudanese army at the time of the 1972 peace settlement.

Beyond the desire to drive out northern occupation and, for many, to achieve separation, there was little articulated political agenda. Only at the very end did Joseph Lagu, a Madi from Equatoria, emerge as titular leader.

But rebel weakness was offset by the limited capacities of the Sudanese army, which initially numbered only 18,500. With few roads over a vast expanse, Khartoum could control only a few towns and administrative outposts.

The ouster of the military regime in 1965 by a popular uprising in Khartoum brought a brief moment of hope for a negotiated settlement. However, political factionalism in Khartoum, the multiplicity of southern voices, and the hydraheaded nature of Anya-nya at the time made this impossible. However, by 1972 Any-nya had a single voice in Lagu, a new military regime under Jaafar Nimeiri had accepted the fact of stalemate, and the skilled mediation of Ethiopian emperor Haile Selassie had fashioned a settlement. The north won the preservation of a single Sudan; the south gained full autonomy and the right to fashion its own cultural policy. The Anya-nya fighters obtained incorporation into the Sudan army, and Lagu became its deputy commander. The 1972 accord gave the south its only decade of peace since independence before the descent into renewed warfare in 1983 examined later in the chapter.

Reform Insurgencies: Uganda and Ethiopia

During the 1980s, a fourth pattern of pre-1990 insurgency emerged in Uganda and Ethiopia. With tightly disciplined and highly ideological leadership, beginning with a mere handful of fighters, the insurgents proposed an ambitious agenda for remaking states now in crisis. Employing sophisticated methods of guerrilla organization drawn from established liberation movement doctrine, these movements actually succeeded in defeating large and well-equipped though demoralized national armies. In both reform insurgencies, initial radical ideological commitment gave way to conformity to "Washington Consensus" dictates, and an effective state reconstruction project followed military triumph.

In Uganda, after a 1980 election widely believed to have been rigged returned Milton Obote (ruler from 1962 to 1970) to power, several small rebel groups took up arms. The most durable was led by Yoweri Museveni, steeped in the radical ideology then dominant at the University of Dar es Salaam where he had studied and that had guided him when he served as a guerrilla with FRELIMO liberation forces.[20] Developing a base area in Buganda (not his home territory), he expanded his forces with minimal external support, armed them with captured weapons, and developed local councils as a support system offering quasi-governmental structures.[21] Repeated regime offensives failed to dislodge the Museveni National Resistance Army (NRA), though they did produce an estimated three hundred thousand casualties.[22] As word of the brutality of the campaign seeped out, donors disengaged, and the Obote regime became increasingly isolated. A military coup took place in July 1995, but the Acholi generals who replaced Obote were demoralized and discredited; the NRA marched triumphantly into Kampala in January 1986.

The Ethiopian insurgencies of the 1980s took form in the later 1970s but achieved critical mass after 1980. An array of armed movements took the field to resist the military Afromarxist autocracy that had supplanted the imperial dynasty in 1974. The consolidation of its power triggered a murderous power struggle culminating in the "Red Terror" (1975–77). The insurgent leaders were mostly products of the radical Ethiopian student movement, who were steeped in Marxist-Leninist discourse and imagined a society purged of its quasi-feudal structures. The most important was Meles Zenawi, who abandoned his university studies to take part in organizing a revolutionary insurgent movement in his Tigre homeland. His movement, the Tigray People's Liberation Front (TPLF), was the most consequential of the regional insurgencies that also emerged among Oromo, Somali, and other groups to combat the Mengistu regime.

In the words of its best chronicler, Gebru Tareke, "The political success of the insurgent leadership lay in its ability to bridge the gap between its own political ambitions and the material needs of the population. In other words, the ethnonationalist movement was propelled to victory by a combination of the insurgent leaders' frustrated political and educational expectations and popular hopes for the abolition of socially repressive conditions."[23] He adds that in leading the ouster of the Mengistu regime the TPLF "relied on accurate, timely information, secrecy, patience, their intimate knowledge of a landscape that generally did not lend itself to mechanized warfare, the support of the people, their incredible hardiness and stamina and an extraordinary talent for improvisation," all of which contributed to the TPLF's eventual success.[24]

1960–90 CIVIL CONFLICTS: COMPARATIVE REFLECTIONS

A comparative glance at these pre-1990 conflicts yields several general observations. In my view, several common patterns sharply demarcate these struggles from most of the post-1990 civil wars. First, with the sole exception of the Chad conflagration—the only one to which the "warlord" label has been applied—the wars were all linked to a legible normative objective, recognizable not only to the participants but also to the external gaze. The call for separation, whether made in the name of ethnic self-determination or national liberation of constituted colonial partition territories, "reform insurgency" such as that proposed by the NRA in Uganda or the TPLF in Ethiopia, or pursuit of a "second independence," as in Congo-Kinshasa, was rooted in a recognizably moral purpose; so also was the campaign by national governments to uphold the "territorial integrity" of the state.

Second, the grotesque atrocities and human rights abuses so characteristic of contemporary internal warfare were much less in evidence. Insurgents were rooted in a local support base, and they usually were not motivated to assault the populations in their zone of operation. Combat always brings suffering and death to innocent civil populations, and these wars were no exception; the 1963–65 Congo rebellions probably saw more massacres of civilians than any other of this era, and the Biafran struggle produced an abundance of deaths from starvation and disease, but there was much less willful assault on village populations. Rape doubtless occurred but never rose to a level seeming to suggest that it had been intentionally chosen as an instrument of warfare. Nor did one see the deliberate use of child soldiers before the 1980s, when RENAMO auditioned this technique (it was also sometimes used by Museveni's NRA). This tactic and other frequent atrocities gave RENAMO a sulfurous reputation; in this respect the Mozambique insurgency was a precursor of the post-1990 species of rebellion.

Third, the earlier conflicts never turned into resource wars, whereby high-value commodities—gold, diamonds, timber, coffee, coltan—became an instrument of insurgent finance. In part this reflected the availability of other kinds of funding, above all by cold war–driven calculus. The thesis that greed, not grievance, lay at the root of conflict, so widely debated in connection with contemporary civil wars, was not yet "thinkable."[25]

Fourth, at least until the 1980s most African states were not yet weakened to a point that would permit even small insurgent militias to readily operate; only in Congo-Kinshasa and Chad was this the case. Nigerian security forces, once expanded, could overcome the Biafran secession and restore central control, but they proved unable to master a much smaller challenge from Niger delta insurgents in 2003. African armies threatened regimes with coups, not with an inability to cope with small uprisings. The fragility of hinterland administrative presence was not apparent, and the swift collapse of government resistance so evident in the 1990s in Liberia, Sierra Leone, or Congo-Kinshasa was not within the realm of imagination.

Fifth, cold war psychosis induced substantial external financial, military, and intelligence participation in several of the conflicts. In the extreme case, the scale of Soviet and Cuban military backing for the Afromarxist Angolan regime and the importance of resources furnished to its insurgent opposition, UNITA, by South Africa and the United States, seemed at moments to transform the country into a proxy battlefield for a global struggle. Deep American intelligence and other involvement in the 1960 and 1964 Congo-Kinshasa crises played no small part in the outcome.[26] Other national interests besides the cold war shaped external power involvement. In addition to providing military and intelligence protection to much of the sub-Saharan Franco-African zone, France was also a sub rosa supporter of the Biafra secession and an active participant at moments in the Chad civil wars, countering a major Libyan intervention. Libya for some time sought annexation of the northern strip of Chad and in 1980–81 briefly pursued annexation of the entire country.[27]

Sixth, the moral purposes of insurgents attracted some external backing. Scandinavian states saw the case for southern African liberation as providing normative grounds for nonmilitary assistance to some of the movements. Human rights and humanitarian groups in the West responded to the warnings of impending genocide in Biafra with vocal support for the Biafran cause, which constrained (though did not alter) U.S. and UK government tilt toward Nigeria.

However, more important than the limited external backing for some uprisings was the reflexive backing of the international system and global institutions for the national governments in which the insurgencies were occurring, a factor that has continued to operate strongly in the contemporary period. For most, the sanctity of state sovereignty far outweighed any sympathies a given insurgency might attract. Except in Western Sahara, the African state system resolutely backed the territorial integrity of existing countries; as unspoken corollary, this principle included the idea that legitimate authority belonged to existing regimes. A comparable disposition was the natural tendency for the world at large, reinforced by a deference to African positions.

Lastly, another factor common to early and contemporary conflicts was the impact of the ethnic variable. Although the majority of armed liberation struggles managed to unify their constituencies, ethnicity was a visible divider in Angola and Zimbabwe, as well as in Guinea-Bissau and even Mozambique in a more subdued way. Igbo ethnic solidarity drove the Biafran secession but like all other early insurgencies did not overtly frame the struggle. Still, closely inspected, all the postindependence conflicts reveal the entanglement of ethnicity in uprisings even if identity politics was not their original cause, most explicitly in Ethiopia. The stakes are raised for identity in the context of violent conflict, posing daily ethnic security dilemmas. Ethnic consciousness provides a cognitive screen, distinguishing likely friend from possible enemy.

CONTEMPORARY CIVIL WARS: CRUCIAL FACTORS

The political moment around 1990 proved a crucial watershed in the character of African internal wars. Within Africa, the most visible harbinger of a new configuration of political dynamics at the time was the democracy wave examined in chapter 6. That chapter reviews a number of cases in which failures of transition (Algeria, Rwanda, Burundi) or deeply flawed elections (Kenya) led to large-scale violence. But democracy per se was not an intrinsic driver of civil conflict. Indeed, the reverse appears the case; countries with consolidated democratic transitions proved less vulnerable.

Identifying the factors that altered the way conflicts were framed must begin with the end of the cold war and its reconfiguration of the international order. The removal of any projection of great power rivalry onto the African arena transformed the parameters for conflict participants. Soviet withdrawal from Africa was all but complete by 1989; the counter-Soviet premise of American African policy vanished soon after. Once-protected clients such as Mobutu in Congo-Kinshasa or Samuel Doe in Liberia were now on their own. Jonas Savimbi of UNITA could no longer rely on external funding or supply.

Profound mutations in the language of conflict also occurred. Marxism-Leninism evaporated from the discourse of insurgency, as did socialist currents more broadly, erasing a key idiom for legitimating revolt. The 1989 independence of Namibia and 1991 Eritrean triumph over Ethiopia, taken together with the demise of the apartheid regime in South Africa, announced the end of an era of primacy of national liberation struggles and its cognate doctrines; only the isolated and lonely POLISARIO struggle in Western Sahara remained, a long dormant combat.

Ideology reappeared as a conflict driver in a different form: a rise to new salience of radical Islamist currents. In both Algeria and Sudan, these became crucial political vectors in 1989. In Algeria, the emergence of FIS and its electoral force precipitated the 1992 military intervention and ensuing civil war. In Sudan, a military faction linked to the National Islamic Front (NIF, an outgrowth of the Muslim Brotherhood, later the National Congress Party [NCP]) seized power in 1989, and has imposed a more integral Islamic regime that sheltered Osama bin Laden and Al Qaeda until 1996. Throughout Islamic northern Africa, Islamism in the last two decades has been a more potent ideological challenger, vigorously repressed in Egypt, Libya, and Tunisia. The

Qadhafy Green Book and its loose amalgam of ultrapopulism and Islamism had broader reach; it was possible for sub-Saharan radicals to appropriate its populism and leave off the Islamic component.

The range of internal war outcomes widened substantially after 1990, ranging from total enduring state collapse in Somalia to the Rwanda genocide. These two disasters suggested previously unimaginable extremes in the scope of possible catastrophe. A new zone of civil war in Darfur in Sudan in 2003 and the massacres of civil populations by Khartoum-armed irregular marauders that parts of the human rights community (and the US officially) labeled genocidal demonstrated that such tragedies could recur.

The sheer number of substantial violent internal conflicts in the last two decades is striking. By my count, there have been eighteen such cases, listed in table 7.1, in addition to the major interstate war pitting Ethiopia against Eritrea from 1998 to 2000. A map of these conflicts shows two large zones of contiguous conflicts, many interpenetrating. The largest such region extends from the Horn of Africa in a southeastward arc to Angola and the two Congos. The other region covers West Africa, from Senegal to Ivory Coast.

Among the episodes of internal violence, twelve were either of high intensity or long duration or both (Algeria, Angola, Burundi, Congo-Kinshasa, Liberia, Rwanda, Senegal, Sierra Leone, Somalia, Sudan, and Uganda). Two (Senegal and Sudan) involved unresolved claims of separation or regional autonomy. The remaining seven conflicts were briefer and of smaller scale (Central African Republic, Chad, Congo-Brazzaville, Ivory Coast, Mali, Niger, and Nigeria).

Separatism was the motivating factor in only two cases (Senegal, southern Sudan), though regional grievances were important in several others (Central African Republic, Ivory Coast, Mali, Niger, Nigeria, Darfur in Sudan, Uganda). Ethnicity as noted inevitably became implicated in the fabric of violent conflict once ignited and affected the composition of the militias. Although the majority of the wars did not directly involve ethnic agendas per se, Burundi and Rwanda, discussed in chapter 6, are major exceptions; in Mali and Niger, too, regional grievances (on the part of Touareg) provoked the uprisings. In Congo-Brazzaville, the urban warfare primarily involved ethnic militias, and the Casamance separatist struggle in fact mainly featured a single though fragmented ethnic group, but the objective was always couched in regional terms. Still, in the broader pattern of contemporary African conflicts ethnicity cannot serve as master explanatory factor.[28] Ethnicity is salient in most African countries, yet in only a few does it operate as key precipitant of insurgent uprising.

TABLE 7.1. African Civil Wars, 1990–2010

Country	Intensity*	Protracted (over three years active conflict)	Regional autonomy/ separatist	Neighboring state involvement**	Violent conflict continues
Algeria	High	Yes	No	No	No
Angola	High	Yes	No	Yes	No
Burundi	High	Yes	No	Yes	No
CAR	Low	No	Yes	Yes	Some
Chad	Moderate	No	No	Yes	Some
Congo-B	Moderate	No	No	Yes	No
Congo-K	High	Yes	No	Yes	Some
Ivory Coast	Low	No	No	Yes	No
Liberia	High	Yes	No	Yes	No
Mali	Low	No	Yes	No	No
Niger	Low	No	Yes	No	Some
Nigeria	Low	Yes	Yes	No	Some
Rwanda	High	Yes	No	Yes	No
Senegal	Low	Yes	Yes	Yes	Some
Sierra Leone	High	Yes	No	Yes	No
Somalia	High	Yes	Some	Yes	Yes
Sudan	High	Yes	Yes	Yes	Some
Uganda	Moderate	Yes	No	Yes	No

* My qualitative judgment, based on the monographic sources for each conflict.
** Includes providing sanctuary or armed support for insurgents or military intervention in support of government.

To illuminate both general patterns and the range of variation, I turn next to a closer look at the eighteen conflicts, beginning with a summary account of four of the most intense and important civil wars, those fought in Liberia, Sierra Leone, Somali, and Sudan. A condensed overview of several other violent conflicts not previously discussed then follows. Some that are considered in earlier chapters need no further detail here. I return to overall comparative observations in the concluding section. Here I begin with the Liberia and Sierra Leone civil wars, examined jointly because of their inextricable intertwining.

Liberia and Sierra Leone

Among the interpenetrated conflicts in West Africa, by far the most important are the wars in Liberia and Sierra Leone. In many respects, these two brutal and prolonged internal wars defined the character of new conflict patterns in Africa; they have attracted a large volume of academic analysis, often excellent. Their outbreak coincided with the start of the democratic wave in

Africa; the incursion of the initially small band led by Charles Taylor, the National Patriotic Front of Liberia (NPFL), in December 1989 was simultaneous with the summoning of the Benin national conference. The multiplication of armed militias, the scale of the atrocities by all sides, the exploitation of child soldiers, the ideological void surrounding the fighting, the instrumentalization of high-value resources to finance insurgency, and the high degree of external involvement in efforts to halt the combats all foreshadowed patterns that shaped subsequent internal wars.

The striking parallels between the two polities, and the broadly similar chronologies of conflict, reinforce the invitation to paired analysis. Both countries grew out of externally sponsored resettlements of freed slaves, Freetown (1787) and Monrovia (1822).[29] The cultural groupings that emerged from this origin, creoles in Sierra Leone and Americo-Liberians in Liberia, were distinct from the vastly more numerous hinterland populations in their Victorian synthesis of European and African social practices and their habits of entitlement.

Competitive decolonization elections in Sierra Leone shifted power decisively to the hinterland in the early 1960s; a polarity between the two largest ethnic groupings, Mende in the south and east, and mostly Muslim Temne and related groups in the north, became imprinted on the party system from the outset. The two leading political formations, the Sierra Leone People's Party (SLPP) and All People's Congress, had electoral strongholds in south and north respectively, though Jimmy Kandeh's data on the 2002 and 2007 elections show that balloting did not entirely follow ethnic lines.[30]

In Liberia, the state modernization and unification ambitions of longtime president William Tubman (1944–71) gradually extended patronage access and social promotion to some hinterland elites. Ethnic geography was more complex than in Sierra Leone; there were a number of visible groups. Notable were the coastal Kru, well represented in Monrovia, and the Mandingo (elsewhere known as Malinke) Muslim traders prominent in the commercial sphere, widely regarded as alien intruders.[31]

Symptoms of incipient crisis appeared in both states by the later 1970s. In Liberia, the increasingly contested rule of William Tolbert (1971–80) was shaken by rice riots in 1979, triggered by a sharp price rise accompanied by suspicion of profiteering and corruption, and by generalized resentment over an austerity program.[32] Master Sergeant Samuel Doe and a small band of conspirators assassinated Tolbert in 1980, seized power, and then executed thirteen Tolbert henchmen on the Monrovia beach. Among them was Tolbert's son, wed to a goddaughter of Ivory Coast president Houphouët-Boigny, an

affront Houphouët-Boigny never forgave. Initially acclaimed as a savior acting on behalf of the hinterland majority, Doe soon lost his luster as he expanded on the patronage system of his predecessors, developed profitable
mercantile ties with the Mandingo traders, and embezzled state funds with
impunity—an estimated $300 million over his decade of rule, or half the 1989
GDP.[33] He also relied heavily on his Krahn coethnics (only 5% of the population), or more accurately, on two of the sixteen Krahn clans, in his military.[34]
The levels of brutality in his rule far exceeded previous norms. Nonetheless,
he enjoyed the sponsorship and protection of the United States as a reliable
cold war (and anti-Libyan) client; his notorious rigging of a 1985 election was
endorsed by Washington.

In Sierra Leone, Siaka Stevens, initially elected to power in 1967 as a progressive reformer, ruled until 1985 (after a military interlude in 1967–68). He
maneuvered to impose a political monopoly and single-party rule by 1973
and then constructed an increasingly venal neopatrimonial system by securing personal control over the flow of diamond exports, accumulating a fortune estimated at $500 million in the process. The value of diamonds flowing
through formal, taxable channels, once an important state revenue and foreign exchange source, had dwindled to $100,000 by 1987. The remainder was
illegally marketed, mostly through private Lebanese channels, in networks
linked to Stevens. State institutions, well organized and provisioned in the
1960s, were starved of resources and deteriorated. Far from seeking to build a
state, Stevens's strategy aimed above all to deny resources to rival strongmen,
which had the result of in effect equipping his private controlled networks
with sovereignty and setting the stage for a modality of rule that became
characteristic of the age of warlord politics.[35] He installed a pliant officer,
Joseph Momoh, to succeed him in 1985; Momoh was powerless to alter the
system. The deepening public frustrations and social anger first flowed into
pressures for multiparty elections, to which Momoh conceded by 1991. But
before these could occur the Revolutionary United Front (RUF) took form
in Liberia and invaded, and in January 1992, Momoh was ousted by junior
officers led by Valentine Strasser.

The era of guerrilla warfare punctuated by moments of relative calm thus
opened in 1989 (Liberia) and 1991 (Sierra Leone). The wars flowed together
from the outset and remained interwoven until their termination in 2002
(Sierra Leone) and 2003 (Liberia). Both countries had periods of remission in
1996–97, during which internationally monitored and astonishingly peaceful
national elections took place that won endorsement as free and fair by large

international observer teams. However, civil war soon reignited with re-newed ferocity, further brutalizing society, displacing millions, and destroy-ing state infrastructure. From the very outset of the two internal wars, the international community mobilized to send peacekeepers and seek diplo-matic settlements; in both cases, mediated negotiations produced a series of seeming accords that soon unraveled. But finally agreements leading to suc-cessful elections in Sierra Leone (2002) and Liberia (2005) produced stability and relatively credible regimes that restored a more lasting peace.[36]

The two initial guerrilla armies, Taylor's NPFL and Foday Sankoh's RUF, both had a core of leaders that had undergone training in Libyan camps near Benghazi and had a joint ambition to overthrow the two incumbent regimes. Included in the Libyan camps were a handful of radical university students inspired by the Qadhafy Green Book and anti-imperial doctrine. At the time, the Libyan leader's mood with respect to his Western adversaries was bel-ligerent, and he hosted a number of guerrilla training sites.

In the Liberian case, the NPFL also benefited from the availability of groups of former soldiers once linked to Thomas Quiwonkpa, mastermind of the original Doe coup but then estranged and marginalized. Quiwonkpa led an unsuccessful coup attempt in 1985; his mutilated corpse was dragged through the streets of Monrovia, enraging his followers and his Gio commu-nity. Taylor himself, partly of Americo-Liberian descent, was tied through marriage to the Quiwonkpa group. On returning from university training in the United States, he was appointed by Doe to a government procurement agency, a ready conduit for corruption. In 1983, he absconded to America with $900,000; charged with embezzlement, he was arrested in Massachusetts but escaped in 1985 and made his way back to West Africa.[37]

By the late 1980s, the Liberian diaspora in the United States and West Africa was desperate to eliminate the Doe regime. Ivory Coast and Burkina Faso were likewise keen to see the elimination of Doe; with their facilitation, Taylor was able to enter Liberia from Ivory Coast with a small band of one hundred fighters, to be welcomed by the local population. Troops, mostly made up of Krahn, sent to repel the invaders engaged in indiscriminate slaughter, redoubling the support for Taylor and ensuring a flow of new re-cruits, who were soon joined by former Quiwonkpa soldiers. Future interim ruler Amos Sawyer and president Ellen Johnson-Sirleaf collected small amounts of funds to back the Taylor insurgency.

The snowballing expansion of the NPFL was matched by the melting of Doe's support. Regime corruption had exceeded the limits of toleration for his major foreign aid supporter, and the imminent end of the cold war erased any motivation to continue overlooking it. Doe had increasingly followed the Stevens pathway of seeking resources outside the state channels, all but abandoning the bureaucracy. Little stood in the way of the Taylor advance; the NPFL was at the gates of Monrovia in August 1990, when Nigeria mobilized West African states to prevent his takeover. An ECOMOG intervention force blocked their path.

Shortly thereafter, an NPFL splinter led by Prince Johnson managed to capture Doe. Johnson personally conducted his execution in macabre circumstances. ECOMOG installed an interim Monrovia government under respected scholar and American university professor Amos Sawyer; this regime had little authority but did retain the crucial resource of international recognition and sovereignty. The Taylor forces, however, occupied much of the hinterland and gained control over the key tradable resources: diamonds, timber, and rubber. Thus by 1991 the NPFL had ample revenues to pay its forces and purchase weapons. Meanwhile, Taylor declared himself head of a "Greater Liberia," in which he included portions of Sierra Leone and Guinea. This would have encompassed a major part of the Sierra Leone diamond fields, a good part of whose output was smuggled through Liberia by Mandingo traders. He also facilitated the organization of the RUF in zones he controlled and expedited its 1991 invasion of Sierra Leone.

Meanwhile, assaults on ethnic groups that were beneficiaries of the Doe regime multiplied, and many were killed. In response, Krahn and Mandingo clamored for weapons. Soon a movement responding to their security pleas, the anti-Taylor United Liberation Movement of Liberia (ULIMO), led by Mandingo Alhaji Kromah, arose and carved out a sphere of operation along the Guinea border. The Krahn elements soon broke off into a separate faction under Roosevelt Johnson known as ULIMO-J; Kromah's group was called ULIMO-K. ULIMO-J acquired control of some diamond mining areas and tapped into illicit trading nets in Sierra Leone. ULIMO-K derived its revenue from Mandingo control of transit trade into Guinea. A further ULIMO splinter, the misnamed Liberian Peace Council (LPC), emerged in 1993, and acquired control of some rubber estates.

Warlord politics now became institutionalized. Taylor and his NPFL was the most important in size and revenue, as well as the most notorious for its atrocities. The recruitment of child soldiers gained momentum, as did the brutalization of society through pillage and rape, with all militias culpable. The various factions plundered the vital substance of the Liberian economy in an effort to sustain their unending militia warfare; an estimated 150–250,000 fatalities resulted, and by 1996, half the population was displaced.[38]

A series of unsuccessful peace conferences outside the country took place. In 1993, Nigeria served as the lead negotiator as well as primary ECOMOG participant and helped establish the Transitional National Government under a succession of heads, but like its predecessor, this government had no authority outside Monrovia. In 1996, agreement was reached whereby all the major factions would be incorporated in the government, all militias would be disarmed, and national elections would be held in 1997. Miraculously, though disarmament was at best partial, the elections took part in a peaceful climate; Taylor defeated his main opponent, Johnson-Sirleaf, with 75% of the vote. The outcome was accepted by all parties, and the election conduct won the blessing of the international community. Peace for a shattered country seemed at hand.

But events in neighboring Sierra Leone cast their shadow. The RUF force that had organized in Liberia under Taylor's sponsorship invaded in 1991 and found initial welcome as well as ready recruits from a rural population whose disaffection with the Freetown elite and national government was by now intense. Stevens distrusted the Sierra Leone army and so had kept it small (it had three thousand members at the time of RUF invasion). It recruited using ethnoregional criteria, and it was poorly equipped; Stevens satisfied his security needs with private militias operating in the diamond fields or militias maintained by the mining companies (iron ore and rutile, or titanium dioxide). The military, like the population at large, was seething with discontent and had little capacity to rout the RUF, initially a small force.

Taken by surprise, the Freetown regime desperately recruited new troops to confront the rebels; as Momoh after his 1992 ouster lamented, training and discipline was lacking, and "a large number of undesirables, waifs, strays, layabouts and bandits may now be in the nation's uniform."[39] Deployed in the countryside, this ragged force spent more time terrorizing the local population than attacking the RUF; for villagers, those in uniform became known as "sobels," or, in Kandeh's phrase, soldiers "who took the guise of rebels to pillage, rape, maim and murder."[40]

In this deteriorating situation, junior officers led by Captain Valentine Strasser ousted Momoh in 1992, establishing the National Provisional Ruling Council and promising national elections in 1996 after the "clean up" of corrupt rule and defeat of the RUF. The customary postcoup euphoria sustained the young officers, most of whom were in their twenties and many of whom were high school dropouts, for a few months. With the help of Guinean and Nigerian troops, the RUF was pushed back from most of the areas it had over-run in 1993. But the combat became more complex, as some soldiers defected to the RUF, others operated semiindependently as sobels, and a new commu-nal self-defense militia, the Kamajors, at first composed of initiation groups and hunters, took form in Mende areas in the south. A number of Liberian youths joined the RUF or other militia forces as well.

Yet a further complicating factor was government recourse to mercenary fighters, initially Gurkhas (Nepalese) discharged from the British army and then South African professionals (mostly former special forces or white-officered black soldiers used in destabilizing neighboring states) employed by Executive Outcomes. Though the Gurkhas were ineffective, Executive Outcomes helped repel a 1995 RUF effort to attack Freetown and once again drove them out of most areas they occupied. The presence of these profes-sional soldiers helped provide the window of security that made 1996 elec-tions possible.

Though the Strasser provisional regime appeared for a moment to improve the economy, lowering inflation substantially and winning a debt reduction from the international financial monitors, the formal economy was corrod-ing. Official diamond mining vanished, replaced by illicit artisanal digging and smuggling. Control of the output became the major target for all par-ties and the payment source for Executive Outcomes. By 1995, the insecure environment surrounding the iron, bauxite, and rutile (titanium oxide) mines forced their closure.

Rebellion tapped a deep reservoir of alienation that those outside Free-town and the ruling institutions experienced. Declining rural well-being during the Stevens and Momoh regimes, combined with the conspicuous wealth of the political elite, spawned a sense of exclusion felt most keenly by the young. Escape from rural poverty by education or formal employment seemed foreclosed, as schools deteriorated and the formal economy declined. The oppressive behavior of local government agents and chiefs added to the undercurrents of disaffection, which meant that state forces could not count on national loyalty as a resource against rebel forces.

The RUF was never an ethnic movement; even though its leader Sankoh was a northerner, the majority of its fighters came from the south and east. Nonetheless, Kamajor leaders presented it as an alien force, and many of the Freetown elite perceived it in geoethnic terms.[41] Although the RUF dis-course spoke vaguely of revolutionary aims, and its manifesto bore the title

"Footpaths to Democracy," any ideological content to the movement's purposes disappeared in the maelstrom of violence its agents unleashed on local populations. Little effort was made to win local support or, for that matter, to administer areas that it occupied at times. Some rural youths might join in the hope of securing a survival livelihood or because the loss of their families left them no other choice; the power provided by a gun perhaps attracted others. Many were urban marginals or former soldiers. But many other recruits were obtained locally by coercion or abduction, and villages were forced to provide food and supplies or were simply pillaged. The pattern of atrocities—amputations, rape, burning of villages—appeared early in the game and remained a permanent feature, reinforcing the local hostility that the RUF often encountered. RUF forces resided in forest camps, which served as bases for plunder expeditions; for the most part, they were roving rather than stationary bandits.[42]

Thus by 1995 diverse military forces—the national army, sobels, RUF, Kamajors, Executive Outcomes, and ECOMOG, among which numbered fighters having floating loyalties—were operating in many areas of the country. Strasser by then had developed an appetite for power and reneged on his promise not to run for office. To block his ambitions, a rival member of the Strasser junta, Julius Bio, overthrew him in January 1996 and announced that elections would go forward. An Executive Outcomes offensive produced a moment of remission in the combat, and miraculously the first multiparty elections since 1967 took place later in 1996, with strong international support. Inadequate security required use of a national proportional representation system rather than constituency-level tabulation. Still, even more remarkably, the conduct of the voting met minimum standards of respectability, permitting international observers to bless the outcome. The SLPP, led by Ahmad Tejan Kabbah, whose primary base was in the south, emerged as the leading party among five significant contenders. With a Liberian peace accord also in place and election preparations proceeding on schedule for a July 1997 vote, at the beginning of 1997 the West African nightmare seemed to end.

But merely for an instant: only the first chapter in a two-part internal war in both countries was concluded; an equally deadly second part was about to begin, this time opening in Sierra Leone. Kabbah pursued negotiations with the RUF, which did not participate directly in the elections, signing an accord with Sankoh at a 1996 peace conference in Abidjan. For the first time, RUF thus received international legitimation, even though Sankoh reneged on the agreement in short order. The army again seized power in May 1997, installing Major Johnny Paul Koroma as head of a new junta, the Armed Forces Revolutionary Council (AFRC), composed mainly of northern and western members; shortly before, Kabbah had ended the Executive Outcomes contract, thereby losing a part of his protection. The RUF was invited to join the government; Sankoh would be appointed deputy president and several RUF officials would receive posts.

The international community, heavily invested in restoring constitutional rule, was infuriated. The brief rule of the AFRC/RUF coalition proved entirely predatory, and Sankoh in power made no contribution to peace. ECOWAS met in Conakry in June 1997 and determined to overturn the coup, authorizing an ECOMOG force and proposing a comprehensive embargo. After efforts to return Kabbah to power by negotiations failed, an ECOMOG force, mostly Nigerian, ousted Koroma by force in February 1998, and Kabbah resumed office. However, the AFRC army defected to the rebels.

Efforts followed to create an entirely new security force and to encourage the emergence of local civil defense forces on the Kamajor model. A new mercenary contract was signed with Sandline, a British outfit tied to diamond merchants that employed many former Executive Outcomes personnel; Sandline was apparently promised a diamond concession in return. In the face of international objections, Sandline soon disappeared from the scene. Security remained precarious, dramatized by a January 1999 raid in Freetown by RUF and ex-army fighters; the capital was looted and six thousand civilians killed before the invading force was driven out, mainly by ECOMOG. The enfeebled condition of the government was starkly evident. At this juncture, the UN Security Council authorized a peacekeeping force for Sierra Leone, UNAMSIL. Slow to arrive, by mid-2000 UNAMSIL forces numbered eighty-seven hundred.

The shock of the Freetown devastation brought pressure for a renewed settlement with RUF. Yet another peace conference convened in Lomé, Togo, in May 1999; a disastrous accord resulted, inscribed ever since as a paradigmatic instance of imprudent conflict resolution. The Kabbah delegation held a very weak hand; at that juncture an estimated 70% of the country escaped its control, and the RUF along with allied former soldiers occupied the diamond mining zones. The RUF was absolved of all past crimes and given four key cabinet posts, and Sankoh was named to a position that in practice placed him in charge of the diamond trade.[43] In the eyes of the many Sierra Leonean victims of RUF violence, the highest rewards went to the worst criminal.

The Lomé settlement was short lived. Sankoh overreached in May 2000; the RUF seized five hundred UN peacekeepers as hostages and again attacked the capital. British forces were sent to rout the RUF; Sankoh and other RUF leaders in Freetown were imprisoned, and UNAMSIL joined in an offensive with ECOMOG. Thereafter RUF was in retreat. International pressure on Taylor to cease his supply and support of RUF increased. An RUF incursion into Guinea to attack encampments of anti-Taylor militias brought heavy losses, and the Guinea army pursued the RUF into Sierra Leone. British forces secured Freetown and took over training of a new Sierra Leone army. The Kamajors received growing support, and became a larger threat to RUF. The RUF lost control of the diamond fields, and its smuggling operations were constrained by new international measures on "blood diamonds." A process of disarming combatants and providing them some compensation for their surrender gained momentum; in the end some seventy-two thousand emerged. A number of RUF fighters slipped across the border into Liberia, accompanied by Sankoh deputy commander Sam "Mosquito" Bockarie, who was to join Taylor's forces.[44] Sankoh by 2003 was indicted by a newly created Special Tribunal for Sierra Leone; he died in prison, and Bockarie perished in Liberia not long after.

Although it was not immediately evident, by January 2002 the war had completely ended, enabling preparations to go forward on schedule for national elections in that year. Kabbah won reelection, and the RUF, running as a political party, received only 2%. No part of Sierra Leone had escaped the terrible ravages of internal warfare; only slowly did the semblance of a functioning state take form around the political superstructure legitimated by successful elections.

In Liberia, the false peace of 1996 leading to the fear-driven 1997 landslide election of Charles Taylor as president soon came apart. Despite the legitimacy conferred by respectable elections, his predatory past cast doubt on the likelihood of his behaving appropriately in office. And, indeed, his warlord habits soon reappeared in his assertion of personal control over state revenues, his continued backing of the RUF, and his management of an ongoing illicit diamond trade. Moreover, his violent attacks on opponents resumed, especially those presumed sympathetic to such former rival militias as the defunct ULIMO factions or the LPC; he had told a Monrovia Baptist congregation that "I will be ferocious."[45] Indeed he was, and by 1999 opposition militias began to reform.

By 2000, the most active groups—Liberians United for Peace and Democracy (LURD) and the Movement for Democracy in Liberia, which had core ethnic constituencies among the Mandingo and Krahn, respectively—had become significant irritants to Taylor.[46] Some Liberian dissidents took refuge in neighboring Guinea; Taylor dispatched his army to attack their camps, in alliance with the RUF. This reinforced Guinean support for LURD, as well as triggering its army incursions into Sierra Leone. As a rogue tyrant, Taylor found himself being undermined by growing international opprobrium. The marginalization of his RUF ally by 2002 was a further blow.

Thus, when LURD insurgents greeted him at the gates of Monrovia in 2003, he was isolated and unable to resist external demands for his ouster. Already under secret indictment for war crimes by the Special Tribunal for Sierra Leone, he was promised safe exile to Nigeria in return for his resignation and departure. Despite the amnesty promise, under international pressure and perhaps reflecting the concerns of the newly elected Liberian government, Taylor was extradited in 2006 to face the Special Tribunal for Sierra Leone sitting in The Hague, Netherlands. After his 2012 conviction, the lethal legacy of Charles Taylor finally appears to have been eliminated from the Liberian scene. A two-year interim regime was created, leading up to a successful transition to democratic rule in 2005 and the election of Ellen Johnson-Sirleaf. The elections featured a mainly new roster of political parties, the legacy of the civil war militias mostly vanishing.

Thus the long nightmare of unending internal war appeared to end. Several years of peace may be consolidating civility in society. Sierra Leone had a second round of postconflict elections in 2007 that resulted in alternation of ruling party, a positive measure of political normalization. Johnson-Sirleaf, with her long background of international experience and newly demonstrated political skills, enjoys a particularly favorable external reputation. Honored with a Nobel Prize, she was reelected in 2011, though not without controversy. An unusual attribute of postconflict Liberia is the exceptionally large leadership role of women, who hold a substantial fraction of cabinet posts and parliamentary seats.[47]

Still, the obstacles are enormous. The legacy of warlord politics is not easy to eradicate, and the exploitation of key commodities is difficult to cleanse of criminal practices. The decay and destruction of infrastructure takes years to repair. Above all, the utter brutalization of society over an extended period leaves wounds that require extended convalescence. No part of either country escaped unscathed; the intertwined Liberian and Sierra Leonean wars stand alone among the internal wars surveyed in this chapter in the penetration of violence to all corners of both polities, including the capital cities. Thus engulfed in combat, few in either country were able to stand outside the conflicts. Most citizens experienced violence either as victims or perpetrators, and in many cases they found themselves in both roles. Thus in everyday life one must live with the knowledge of past transgressions of friends and neighbors, with all the fears, animosities, and insecurities embedded in social memory.

Women and children were special victims of the violence. The horrendous scale of violence against women and widespread use of rape as an instrument of terror, humiliation, and control left deep wounds. According to one international human rights legal specialist who interviewed many victims, most women in Liberia were raped during the internal wars.[48] The sinister RENAMO innovation of systematic use of child soldiers was utilized on a large scale, above all by Taylor and the RUF. Many were abducted and often compelled to commit acts of violence against their family or neighbors to sever their links with their home communities. Others joined voluntarily for the reasons already noted—perhaps offered the promise of power or a means of survival or as a last desperate measure in the wake of the loss of one's family. Most rural youth and urban marginals felt socially excluded to an extreme degree and resented the venal prosperity of the political class, which gave some appeal to the vague warlord slogans of revolutionary intent and elimination of corrupt rulers.

Extensive postconflict interviews with former child soldiers reveal the multiplicity of motives. A study by Paul Richards reports that 87% of those interviewed had originally been abducted, though many cited promises of jobs, cash, or food.[49] Mozambique's experience, based on the first systematic postconflict effort to reincorporate former child soldiers, suggests that reasonable success is possible with a combination of invocation of customary mechanisms for community reconciliation and meaningful opportunity.

Both countries borrowed the Truth and Reconciliation Commission formula that originated in South Africa to come to terms with hurtful memories and foster forgiveness and healing, with mixed results. The Sierra Leone commission was better conducted and more useful than its Liberian counterpart, which fell into the hands of opponents of President Johnson-Sirleaf. They discredited its labors by issuing a wildly excessive call to ban her from political office for thirty years for the small sums she and diaspora colleagues had contributed to Taylor when he was organizing his rebellion in 1989.

Even at the height of the civil war, states never disappeared; their remnants continued to operate in Freetown and Monrovia during the first phase and then again in that moment of conflict remission in 1996–97. They remained important as the points of intersection with the international community, whose role was great in providing aid, humanitarian relief, and peacekeeping forces. Further, the shards of sovereignty invoked by diverse parties momentarily claiming state authority were one dimension of the complex fabric of disorder. The idea of the state remained fully alive in the social imaginary, as a presence that would return once the conflict ended; the numerous interim peace accords that punctuated the warfare continually reawakened expectations that fighting might soon stop. And the historically rooted state template persisted, running from the chiefly institutions that remained in place through the permanent government buildings in the district seats that were perhaps sacked but not demolished to the array of more ambitious structures that housed the central place of state rule. The possibility of normal politics going forward is enhanced by the relatively muted role of ethnic and religious difference in the internal wars. Some Liberian militias had ethnic constituencies, as did such Sierra Leone civil defense forces as the Kamajors. But the wars were never about ethnicity or religion.

Somalia

The Somalia conflict is both the most prolonged and intractable of contemporary wars, resisting almost two decades of efforts at resolution. There have been numerous successive "transitional regimes" cobbled together with extensive external mediation, most recently primarily through the Inter-African Governmental Agency for Development (IGAD), a cooperative forum for negotiation drawing together the states of northeast Africa. After the dissolution of an organized central authority in 1991, a complex amalgam of clan and subclan rivalries, warlord politics, Islamist mobilization and ineffectual if not counterproductive external intervention sustained an unending state of war, ebbing and flowing in intensity. Yet Somalia had once been hailed as a culturally unified society, whose state was legitimated by a robust Somali nationalism. It was the sole postcolonial African state to have an electoral change of leadership (in 1967) until Mauritius in 1982. After the assassination of the elected president in 1969, a military regime ruled with initial apparent success; Siad Barre at first basked in an external reputation as a progressive enlightened despot presiding over an apparently strong state with a widely admired developmental record. Well-regarded *Le Monde* correspondent Philippe Decraene, writing in 1975, declared that, "the transformations of Somali society now in course promise to be more profound than those of any other African society."[50]

Despite the shared language and culture, the deeply rooted clan identities trumped territorial national attachment in the ongoing struggle for access to state resources and then became even more sharply divisive when political competition degenerated into armed conflict. The half dozen maximal clan families (Darood, Hawiye, Isaaq, Digil, Reyanweyn, and Dir) and especially the much larger roster of clans and subclans provided a core template for alignments.[51] The depth of clan attachments was remarkable; young boys learned to recite the genealogy back some twenty generations to an eponymous ancestor. The nested hierarchy of kin-based identity segments had enduring force in defining the social geography for most Somalis; emergent factions, whatever their original motivation, quickly acquired the clan identity of their leader. Still, other bases of social affinity operated. Merchants, warlords, elders, Islamist militants, youth, and women had different interests and various links to contending factions; competing personal ambitions added another dimension. So also did the contradictions arising from separate colonial traditions in Italian-ruled Somalia and in British Somaliland, uneasily amalgamated in 1960. Tensions arose from the outset; Isaaq clans that had dominated Somaliland found their importance greatly diminished in the larger Somalia arena. Divergent educational, administrative, and legal practices added further complications.

The disastrous invasion of Ethiopia in 1977 was the turning point for the Somali state, and the regime had degenerated into a clan-based tyranny by the late 1980s. In clear decline, the narrow clan base of the regime (popularly referenced as "MOD" for Marehan, Ogaden, and Dulbuhante clans of the Darood family) became increasingly clear. In the words of Somali scholar Hussein Adam, Siad Barre "went beyond shouting about treason to bombing villages, towns, and cities, destroying water reservoirs vital to nomads in what he called enemy territories," engaging in "indiscriminate jailings, utilizing terror squads and assassination units, and intensifying interclan wars."[52] Hargeisa, capital of Somaliland, was especially hard hit by aerial attacks. The descent into anarchy began when one clan-based insurgency, the United Somali Congress (USC), with Hawiye roots, drove Barre into exile in 1991, but its leaders (Mohammed Farah Aideed and Ali Mahdi) immediately split in a struggle for power in the capital Mogadishu. Another armed faction, the Somali National Movement (SNM) composed of Isaaq, took control of the north, declaring the independence of Somaliland later that year. Yet another, the Somali Salvation Democratic Front (SSDF), led by Abdullahi Yusuf, (made up of Majerteen and Harti of the Darood family, created another separate state in the northeast region of Puntland in 1998, though without declaring formal secession.[53]

Three other new vectors came into play. The first was intervention by the international community, especially the UN, the United States, and the neighboring states, horrified by the appearance of ungoverned space. By 1992 the UN had mounted a large humanitarian relief program as well as an international force (UNOSOM), in which the United States initially participated. In 1993, the UN organized the first ineffectual state restoration project, following a conference of clan elders, militia leaders, and civil society representatives, from which emerged a transitional national council. However, the disaster overtaking US military involvement in 1993, dramatized in the film *Blackhawk Down*, led to American withdrawal, and UNOSOM itself was terminated in 1995. Again internationally organized conferences to restore the semblance of a state took place in Cairo in 1995 and Djibouti in 2000. On each occasion, an assemblage of Somali personalities presumed to speak for the major clans, militias, and other identifiable parapolitical forces, including growing numbers of diaspora participants, traced the outlines of a decentralized state, and designated personnel to occupy its top offices. The Fifteenth Peace and Reconciliation Conference held in Kenya in 2004, now under the primary auspices of IGAD, laid the groundwork for the present Transitional Federal Government (TFG), nearly all whose finance comes from the international community. The AU promised a peacekeeping contingent, deployed in Mogadishu. Much smaller than initially anticipated, with only fifty-one hundred Ugandan and Burundian troops by 2010, the AU force could control only the airport and port.

The Al Qaeda attack on the New York World Trade Center on 11 September 2001 injected a further external element: the "war on terrorism" and the American preoccupation with Islamist movements. When by 2006, the Islamic Courts Union (ICU), some of whose more extreme members had jihadist sympathies, emerged as the dominant faction in Mogadishu and organized the closest approximation to a functioning government in the capital since 1991, the Ethiopian army with American encouragement intervened to drive them out. The deep-seated antagonism of most Somalis toward Ethiopia proved a liability for the TFG; the force was withdrawn in 2009, by which time the authority of the TFG was limited to a small part of Mogadishu. Meanwhile, new dimensions to external intervention opened as American security forces carried out operations aimed at purported jihadist Al Qaeda allies and escalated its military aid to the TFG.[54] Eritrea further complicates the situation by providing bases, sanctuary, and arms to Islamist insurgents in Somalia, in the face of AU and UN sanctions.

The second new dimension was the rise of Islamist sentiments. In the Afro-marxist phase of the Siad Barre regime, secular currents were strong enough to produce a very liberal family code in 1975; ten leading Muslim clerics were executed for their forceful denunciation of the legislation as an affront to Islam, with no visible protest.[55] In the 1980s, underground Islamist factions coalesced, emerging openly during the most intense phase of civil war in 1991–92. Most had similar points of ideological reference, including radical Egyptian thinkers like Sayyid Qutb and Muslim Brotherhood founder Hassan al Banna. One, al Itihaad al Islami, developed its own militia, made up of urban youth. Others, in the face of governmental collapse, organized schools and health services, with the support of Middle Eastern NGOs. Merchants organizing new mercantile channels in the region found affiliation with Islamist organizations a useful credential.

By 1994, amid continued anarchy, insecurity, and banditry in Mogadishu, one faction leader, Ali Mahdi, gave his blessing to the creation of Islamic courts with militias and judges to restore some degree of order. Over the following years, the scope and role of Islamic courts ebbed and flowed; they were opposed by a number of clan militia. But the role of Islamic charities in urban centers expanded over time in the vacuum left by statelessness. In the face of the failure of the 2004 TFG, headed by Puntland leader Abdadallahi Yusuf, to establish its presence in Mogadishu or most other areas, the Islamic courts movement (now renamed as ICU) gained strength and by 2006 dominated Mogadishu and a number of other parts of the country, triggering the Ethiopian intervention. Under intense external mediation, the leader of the moderate wing of the ICU, Sharif Sheikh Ahmed, became TFG head. He had hoped to create a broader coalition, but the more radical elements regrouped around a pair of Islamist militias, Al Haraka al Shabaab el Mujahideen and Hizbal Islam, whose most visible leader is Sheikh Hassan Dahir Aweys. In 2010, these merged under al Shabaab. Dominant in south central Somalia, al Shabaab seeks a Somali caliphate; beneath the surface, however, clan politics percolate.

The entirely new saliency of Islamism produced by the internal warfare in Somalia has multiple faces. One is Islamic law and its tribunals, which satisfy a popular craving for order and security that are lacking in the absence of a state-provided judicial system. Another is the network of social services that operates through Islamic structures, drawing on support from Middle Eastern sources, the diaspora, and some of the international humanitarian funds.

Yet another face is the Islamic militias, some of whom are guilty of intimi-dation, beheadings, and other atrocities to enforce their will. A small number of foreign fighters and jihadists with links to global terrorist franchises (Al Qaeda) are found at the fringes.

The third new vector in the age of anarchy is the enhanced role of the dias-pora. Expanded in numbers by chaotic circumstance in Somalia, there are now well over a million Somalis in the Middle East, Europe, North America, and Australia. Their remittances, estimated by the World Bank at $1 billion by 2010, flow not only to relatives but also to political factions, warlords, and social service agencies;[56] one may compare this figure to the approximately $10 million monthly customs proceeds from Mogadishu port, which are the sole domestic revenue for the TFG.[57] They are actively involved in Somalia factional rivalries; a significant fraction of the TFG parliament members come from the diaspora, which has always been well represented at the successive peace conferences. In recent times, they have tended to divide in support or opposition to the TFG; this overlapped a Darood (TFG) versus Hawiye clan polarity.[58]

As the internal warfare in Somalia nears its third decade, no end is in sight. Beneath the recent surface appearance of a contest between the internation-ally backed TFG and Islamist insurgents, the reality is far more complex. Out-side of Somaliland and Puntland, no group exercises real control over much territory, although some militias can deny access to a given region to others. Taxable nodal points of commerce—ports, airports, boundary zones between clans—provide locations for revenue extraction. Substantial funds flow into the country from external sources: the diaspora, international aid agencies, the international community, neighboring countries in the region. These resources finance some humanitarian undertakings and are inevitably subject to some diversion by various militias. They also fund the multiplicity of parties to the conflict that aim to influence the ultimate outcome. By 2007, a wholly new source of revenue became visible with the rapid development of piracy on the northern coast, which press estimates suggest may have generated over $100 million annually. During 2009, some 214 ships were attacked and 47 suc-cessfully captured and held with their crews for ransom.[59] Indeed, if one sums the five important new sources of revenue, the piracy ransoms, the diaspora remittances, aid to the TFG, $100 million for the African intervention force, and humanitarian relief, the external sums flowing into the Somali economy may come close to the amounts in the 1980s. Various "suffer-manage" mech-anisms spring up to supplant state structures. An informal banking system manages currency transactions, facilitated by the recent spread of cell phones. Clandestine trade in livestock, narcotics (*qat*, a widely used narcotic produced in Ethiopia and Yemen), and other commodities flourishes.

Nonetheless, the costs to the population of permanent statelessness are heavy. Chronic insecurity affects both urban and rural livelihoods. Many are forced into refugee camps by disorder or drought, and aid deliveries are uncertain. Although NGOs, Islamic charities, and others provide some social services, these are inevitably sporadic and irregular. The armed youth that populate the militias intimidate, extort, and abuse. Although existence in the prolonged anarchy of Somalia is several steps above the classic Hobbesian forecast of life in the state of nature as "nasty, brutish, and short," few long for the perpetuation of statelessness. Yet the stubborn fragmentation of Somali society militates against any one faction gaining sufficient strength to enforce the erection of a new state. Nor is it conceivable that any international actors would have the will or capacity to do so.

Still, there have been important limits to the degree of violence. After an initial moment of intense civil war in the first two years of state collapse, military combat became more scattered and sporadic. The casualty toll over two decades is far less than in Sudan or Congo-Kinshasa. Some atrocities have occurred, but they fall well short of ghastly crimes directed against civilian populations in Sierra Leone, Liberia, Congo-Kinshasa, Sudan, and Mozambique during their internal wars. Mass rape has rarely been a weapon of Somali conflict.

The large stretch of ungoverned space will continue to bedevil neighboring states and the international community more broadly. Various criminal and terrorist enterprises can find operating bases, provided that they can blend into the social environment. Thus the recently developed piracy industry, now operating on an industrial scale, offers coastal Somali groups a lucrative franchise, far more rewarding than their previous fishing livelihoods. The invasion of their fishing grounds by factory ships had threatened their way of life and supplied a grievance that could justify the turn to piracy in local eyes. To date the enterprise has been relatively low risk; a few pirates have been killed and a small number captured, but difficult issues of a reliable venue for prosecution and punishment and legal grounds for trials elsewhere limit the effectiveness of deterrence by possible interception and confinement by the various navies now patrolling the offshore zone. Ship owners, once the seized vessel is brought into a Somali port, invariably negotiate down the ransom demanded and pay to secure release of their vessel and crew. Warlords and militias operating in the area doubtless share in the profits.

Beyond piracy, the abiding fear of terrorist cells with Al Qaeda links joining forces with the radical Islamist militias to secure operating bases continues to motivate Western, and especially American, policy. Successive efforts to fund and supply cooperating warlords, to promote a TFG security capability, or to carry out strikes against terrorist suspects have been inconclusive or even counterproductive; Somali specialist Bronwyn Bruton argues that such efforts "have alienated large parts of the Somali population, polarized the country's diverse Islamist reform movement into moderate and extremist camps, and propelled indigenous Salafi jihadist groups to power."[60] The sporadic operations of the Western Somali Liberation Front in the Ethiopian Ogaden and their cross-border links and a broader Ethiopian apprehension of radical Islamism continuously draw in Ethiopian security forces. The Eritrean regime, though it detests domestic jihadists, eagerly supports them in Somalia as a proxy weapon against the Ethiopian foe. The vacuum created by protracted anarchy is a permanent attraction to external interventions in pursuit of agendas unrelated to Somali welfare.

Meanwhile, the empty shell of the collapsed Somali state continues to enjoy international sovereignty. But not all space is ungoverned; the northwestern segment, coterminous with former British Somaliland, declared independence in 1991 following a clan conclave; though interclan fighting continued until 1993, a further gathering of clan and community leaders adopted a provisional constitution, provided for a bicameral parliament incorporating clan heads, and negotiated a more enduring peace among the clan and community leaders. The SNM militia commanders, who had initiated the revolt against Siad Barre's exactions in 1988, were set aside in favor of an institutionalized state structure featuring civilian leaders, a formal bureaucracy, and a new currency; by 1997, regularized elections were held, and Somaliland took on the attributes of stateness. The unrecognized state did face dissidence in its eastern precincts, populated by Harti subclans resentful of Isaaq dominance of the new institutions, but it otherwise attracted admiring comment from visiting observers for its well-ordered institutions.[61]

Still the critical attribute of international sovereignty eluded Somaliland. Repeated efforts to breach this barrier, in spite of the relative effectiveness of its government, failed to overcome the embedded antagonism of the international system to nonconsensual fragmentation of one of its constituent units.

As one international law specialist put the matter: "Firstly, governments are protected by a presumption in favor of their effectiveness and continuity. Therefore, the temporary ineffectiveness or absence of a government . . . does not affect statehood. Secondly, state identity also enjoys legal protection by a presumption in favor of its continuity and against extinction."[62]

As noted, in 1998, Puntland along the northeast coast of Somalia followed suit by creating a regional array of state institutions. Civil war was much less intense here than further south and mostly ended by 1993. A militia linked to the Darood clans dominant in the area, the SSDF, led by Abdullahi Yusuf (later to become TGF head from 2005 to 2009), was the most prominent force. Though committed to a united Somalia, the prolongation of anarchy eventually generated local pressures to create a functioning regional administration. In 1998, a clan-based conclave, similar to those in Somaliland, erected a set of institutions largely modeled on those of Somaliland. With the support and participation of Harti clan elders, a regularized administration emerged, with a paid bureaucracy, offering a modicum of state-like governance. In search of legitimacy, carefully avoiding invocation of a clan name for the region, the Puntland leadership appropriated the storied name of Punt from classical Egyptian sources (though the wondrous land of incense visited by Egyptian voyagers was probably well to the northwest). But Puntland remained committed to membership as an autonomous unit in a federated revived Somalia state.[63] A long wait is in prospect.

But the Nolutshungu citation that opens the chapter has singular application to Somalia; the idea of the state appears indestructible, despite the disappearance of its physical manifestations outside of Somaliland and Puntland. In strife-torn southern Somalia, populations painfully adapt to permanent disorder. The resilience of the clan structures provides some shelter, a basis for local solidarities, and mechanisms for coping with quotidian conflicts. Many even profit from disorder; any number of merchants, warlords, pirates, and militia members carve out lucrative niches, finding benefit from the absence of state regulation and attendant taxation. But the dream of a reborn state lives on in the social imaginary.

Sudan

I turn next to completing the narrative of the Sudan internal war, a combat that resumed in southern Sudan in 1983 and then acquired a crucial new dimension with the lethal warfare in Darfur beginning in 2003. The era of good feeling between south and north that opened with the equitable peace settlement of 1972 gradually eroded, as did the authority of the Nimeiri regime in Khartoum. The promised autonomy for the south was diluted, and divisions within the region encouraged. Tensions also mounted over natural resource issues. Oil was discovered in the south about 1976; by the early 1980s, Nimeiri had taken steps to ensure that the crude oil would go north by pipeline and then be refined and exported from Port Sudan. He also pushed through the controversial Jonglei Canal project to assure greater Nile flow to the north (and Egypt), impacting the pastureland of southern cattle herders; the Jonglei project was begun but interrupted by renewed rebellion, and it remains unfinished. But the immediate precipitant of renewed civil war came when the by-now embattled ruler tried to restore his flagging legitimacy in 1983 with the sudden proclamation of the September Laws, imposing a rigorous version of shari'a on the entire country. He also unilaterally abrogated the Southern Regional Constitution, dividing the south into three administrative zones and expunging the 1972 guarantees of southern taxation rights on natural resources. One of the SPLA commanders, Lual Diing Wol, described the impact of the September Laws: "In the past, our people never used to talk about being African or Christian or non-Arab because they did not need to prove to anyone what their identity was. . . . But since 1983, it has become a question of showing the government and its Muslim zealots that we are proud of our identity and do not want anybody to change us. This insistence of northern rulers that one must become Arab or Muslim has only created a sense of extremism to prove the opposite."[64]

By the late 1970s, as Nimeiri erosion of the 1972 accord was becoming evident, scattered revolt by veterans of the earlier insurgency emerged in the south, under the label Anya-nya 2. By 1983, a high-ranking southern officer in the Sudan army, John Garang, had defected and launched a new and more sustained insurgent movement, the Sudan People's Liberation Movement (SPLM), with a military wing (SPLA), absorbing and marginalizing Anya-nya 2, whose main support was in Equatoria bordering Ethiopia. The SPLM was a far more coherent movement than its Anya-nya predecessors; it was only an indirect successor of Anya-nya 1, whose commander, Lagu, remained in Khartoum. Garang was a radical intellectual (and holder of an American doctorate), whose primary aim at the outset was to create a new Sudan, shorn of Islamism and Arabism as state ideologies. Garang held that a thus renovated Sudan could then tackle the underlying issues of inequality between north and south. Once a member of the Sudanese Communist Party, he had served as minister of southern affairs under Nimeiri and had not been involved with the earlier Anya-nya.[65] After the 1972 accord, he had been absorbed into the army, rising to the rank of colonel. His core support was among his ethnic community, the Dinka, a very large umbrella identity whose subgroups, mainly cattle-herding agriculturalists, populated a sizable part of the south. However, initially the SPLA/M enjoyed broad backing in the south. The period following 1972 had been marked by massive Christian conversion in parts of the south, making the September Laws the more offensive.[66] The SPLA by the late 1980s had eliminated Khartoum's authority in much of the south.

The desperate gambit by Nimeiri of reinventing himself as an Islamist leader failed in the face of growing popular unrest, and he was ousted by a military junta in 1985. The army agreed to elections and a return to civilian rule in 1986; the enduring alignment patterns reflecting the followings of the major Islamic brotherhoods, the Ansar (heirs to the Mahdi movement that ruled Sudan from 1885 to 1898) and Khatmiyya, represented by the Umma and Democratic Unionist Party (DUP), respectively, and the National Islamic Front (NIF), emanation of the Muslim Brotherhood. The NIF received only 17% of the vote. The two largest parties, Umma and the DUP, formed a coalition under Sadiq El-Mahdi; by 1989, this group was close to arriving at a negotiated settlement with the SPLM that would have ended shari'a implementation in the south and restored a regional government.

The prospect of such an accord triggered a coup by an officer clique linked to the Muslim Brotherhood led by Omar al Bashir; its initial mentor was the enigmatic Islamist scholar Hassan al-Turabi. Political parties were banned and a state of emergency was declared; a reign of terror followed, driving opposition far underground and ending negotiation with the SPLM. The NIF supplied the cadres and doctrine for the Bashir regime, which sought presentability through a new constitution tailored to Islamist standards; 1996 elections in the north, boycotted by the opposition, were widely viewed as a sham. Turabi himself was ousted from power in 1999 and then imprisoned for a time the following year.

Through the 1990s, the Islamist regime was driven by a jihadist dream of state-imposed religious unity and purification for all of Sudan. But its project foundered on the everyday corrupt practices of the military regime, its struggle to monopolize and reproduce political power, and the deep contradiction between its vision and the diversity of Sudanese society. Islamist doctrines became conflated with Arabism, offending the piously Muslim non-Arab periphery of the north—Darfur, Kordofan in the west, and the Beja northeast—in addition to the south. By the end of its first decade the Bashir regime had become little distinguishable from other military autocracies, whose main preoccupation was retaining power. Alex de Waal and A. H. Abdel Salam provide a persuasive summation of its limitations: "Islamism in Sudan is in an impasse. It cannot move forward: it is not equipped with the political imagination or state practice to make sense of the modern world, or to run a state. Islamism's appeal ultimately relies on what cannot be explained: an ethical transformation among human beings or the direct intervention of the Almighty. . . . [I]t is a philosophy of deceptive promise and fatal weakness."[67]

Beyond seeking to enforce Islamism, the Bashir regime was also determined to crush the SPLA. Its resolve was reinforced by the imminent prospect of oil revenues from the discoveries in the south, promising an exit from the recurrent Sudan brushes with bankruptcy. The army was greatly expanded by conscripts from the rural areas and the floating urban marginals in Khartoum who had fled insecurity elsewhere. Though control was maintained in the main southern towns, an effective reoccupation of the southern countryside, a vast region with almost no paved roads, was impossible. A strategy of outsourcing military repression to local, mostly ethnic, militias did pressure the SPLA while exploiting rivalries within the south, especially between the two largest groups, the Dinka and Nuer. But the effect was devastating; groups such as the Baqqara Arabs adjacent to Dinkaland were licensed to loot, ravage, and kill. Much of the mayhem in the south in the 1990s was attributable to the subcontracting of violence; indeed, the Sudan army was only a secondary actor in the bulk of the fatalities in military encounters during the southern revolts.

Particularly damaging to the south was the split in the SPLM/A in 1991; a separate, mainly Nuer, faction under Riek Machar and Lam Akol (a Shilluk) broke off, initially demanding that Garang abandon the goal of a united Sudan in favor of southern separation. The following year, Machar succumbed to solicitations from Khartoum and allied with the regime against the SPLA in return for military supplies, an alliance of circumstance that lasted a decade. Akol split with Machar in 1992, forming his own militia, the SPLA-United. At the same time, the 1991 overthrow of the Mengistu regime in Ethiopia closed a supply source to Garang, which the regime had provided in retaliation against the Sudanese for offering sanctuary to the rear bases of the Eritrean EPLF. This drove several hundred thousand Sudanese refugees back into Sudan; their camps became a major recruitment center for all parties. Several years of ghastly internecine warfare ensued in Dinka and Nuer territory; southern Sudanese scholar Francis Deng records that the Riek militia "rampaged through Dinkaland with unprecedented brutality, massacring people and loot-ing for cattle. The SPLM/A retaliated with commensurate ruthlessness."[68]

Machar headed a mostly-Nuer militia under a succession of names that in 1997 became the Southern Sudan Defense Force (SSDF), loosely incorporating several small militias that had been armed by the Sudan army military intel-ligence to combat the SPLA. In an irony that continues to baffle, in a Khar-toum agreement negotiated with the SSDF, the Sudan government agreed to an eventual referendum on self-determination for the south. Independence was the ultimate goal for Machar at the time rather than the reformed Sudan officially advocated by Garang and the SPLM. Elements of the SSDF occu-pied some key oil fields, permitting the concession holders to bring them into production on behalf of Khartoum and generating major new revenue streams not long thereafter. The deal with the SSDF also permitted Khartoum to con-struct new paved highways into the south; the primitive road network had long constrained national army deployments in the region.[69]

As the internal war dragged on, and its terrible toll on civil populations became more visible to the outside world, more external support became available to the SPLA. The Islamist character of the Khartoum regime was unappealing to Western powers, especially after its shelter of Al Qaeda and Osama bin Laden became known (Bin Laden was invited to leave in 1996 under outside pressure). Bashir regime complicity in the 1993 World Trade Center bombing and a failed assassination attempt on Egyptian president Hosni Mubarak in 1995 in Addis Ababa also gave rise to reprobation.[70] The fate of southern Christian communities activated humanitarian support for SPLA, especially from American churches. Human rights activists mobilized protest against Western oil companies engaging in petroleum exploitation in the south (and expelling local populations from production zones with the help of Sudanese security forces and allied southern militias).[71] Their action, combined with the insecurity, eventually compelled the Western companies to withdraw; they were quickly replaced by Chinese and other Asian enter-prises.[72] By the early 1990s, Uganda, frustrated by the sanctuary provided in Sudan to its rebel Lord's Resistance Army (LRA), was providing military sup-ply to the SPLA.

Among the many negative consequences of the prolonged southern insur-gency was the militarization of ethnicity. Sharon Hutchinson documents the ways in which the culture of the gun impacted social values and hierarchies in Nuer country. Not only did young men with guns acquire abusive author-ity but the lived experience of ethnic difference was transformed by the new security dilemmas arising from violent communal combat.[73] Women were major victims in the environment of chronic warfare.

By the end of the 1990s, it was apparent that neither side would triumph; external and other pressures mounted on southern groups to unite sufficiently for full negotiations and on the Sudan government to seek a settlement. The Khartoum tactics of outsourcing repression, soon to be repeated in Darfur, had run their course in the south. They could inflict great damage but not enforce the Khartoum writ. The SSDF was an uncertain and fragmented ally, who never abandonned its goal of self-determination even during its marriage of convenience with the Sudan regime. Worse, endemic insecurity was inhibiting the opening of a number of oil fields and threatened the security of existing pipelines. For the SPLA, though an aggressive strategy of extending its reach to Darfur and other disaffected parts of the periphery seemed at moments to hold promise and at times the capture of the southern capital of Juba appeared within reach, external supply was always episodic and uncertain, and achieving its aims militarily an elusive hope.

By 2003 more active international diplomatic mediation began to make headway, resulting in a peace settlement in 2005. The accord mirrored some of the 1972 provisions, constituting an autonomous southern regional government and giving the SPLM/A a place in the Khartoum regime while permitting the SPLA to provide the security force for the south. There were also novel new provisions: a 50–50 formula for southern share in the oil revenues, a 28% share for the SPLM in the Khartoum government (along with 52% for the NIF, now renamed as the NCP), Garang as national vice president, joint administration of disputed areas along the north/south dividing line, UN peace monitors, a pledge of national elections in 2009, and a referendum in the south on possible independence in 2011. Garang and his lieutenants were able to secure the agreement of the large number of lower-level SPLM cadres and followers, who strongly preferred secession, through the referendum promise. His own ambitions for Sudan might find realization if the SPLM could win national power in Sudan-wide voting by forming a coalition with the disaffected populations of western and northeastern areas. The agreement was saluted as a triumph for international mediation, though many were skeptical as to whether Khartoum would respect its provisions over time, especially with relation to open elections and the independence referendum.

Significantly, the SSDF was not a party to the accord, which provided for incorporation of all southern militias into the SPLA. A subsequent 2006 Juba accord between the SPLM and SSDF produced an agreement in principle to accept integration. However, this has been only partially accomplished; some SSDF elements have refused incorporation, invoking a need to retain a military capacity until southern independence is assured. Some militias continued to be armed as allies of the Khartoum army.[74]

One of the most remarkable aspects of the southern war was not only the educational credentials of the top southern leadership (Garang, Machar, and Akol all had overseas doctorates) but also their chameleon-like behavior. Garang had served the Khartoum regime as minister during the first southern uprising and never backed Anya-nya 1; he was a ranking officer in the national army until his 1983 defection to launch the SPLM/A. Machar and Akol were initially key lieutenants of Garang but defected and formed their own insurgency in 1991. Akol subsequently created his own separate militia in 1992. Not long after, Machar's faction became a subcontracted auxiliary force for Khartoum against the SPLM/A before returning to the insurgent fold in 2002 as peace negotiations were about to begin. After the 2005 accord, Garang became initial head of the Southern Regional Government but was killed later in 2005 in an aircraft crash. Machar and Akol took up Khartoum posts representing the SPLM as vice president and foreign minister, respectively; at times they seemed to be enthusiastic regime spokesmen. However, Machar claimed to represent southern interests above all by insisting on reasonable terms for the 2011 referendum; in the end, Khartoum did back down from demanding a high majority for independence. By 2010, few doubted that a referendum would yield a large majority for independence; Salva Kiir, Garang's successor in the SPLM and southern regional president, firmly endorsed separation for the south. In the end, mostly peaceful elections voted nearly unanimously for separation; South Sudan became the fifty-fourth independent African state in July 2011.

The south has endured unending warfare that waxed and waned for all but eleven of the forty-three years between independence and conclusion of the 2005 peace accord. By 1995, casualties were commonly reported to have reached two million, and there have been perhaps another five hundred thousand since (in addition to a similar number in the earlier civil war).[75] Isolation and insecurity blocked economic development; the region remains starved of infrastructure and social amenities.

No sooner was a resolution of the long and bitter southern war in sight than a new center of insurgent resistance broke out in 2003 in Darfur in western Sudan. I do not offer a detailed summary of this phase of internal warfare but instead suggest a few of its key aspects.[76] The discontents that produced the rebellion reflect a sense of marginalization in the peripheral regions of northern Sudan, as well as the south. Darfur, long neglected in colonial times, was largely absent from decolonization politics and had little representation among the Khartoum elite. Indeed, in the 1990s a group of Darfur intellectuals assembled a widely circulated "black book" that examined the regional origins of top Sudan government officials over time, demonstrating the overwhelming predominance of Nile valley Arabs centering around greater Khartoum.[77]

The inadequacy of the perception that conflict in Sudan was essentially a north-south division was illuminated by the framing of identities when the warfare taking place in Darfur erupted into the global media in 2003, where it was represented as a humanitarian disaster of genocidal proportions. Fur and other western rebel groups became racialized as "Africans" or blacks, confronting "Arabs," though a phenotypical difference was nonexistent, all shared in Islamic piety, and Arabic was a shared lingua franca. The "bandits on horseback" (janjawid) armed by Khartoum to attack the insurgents were drawn from mostly nomadic arabophone tribes, though some held local identities distinct from the broader "Arab" category.

Although AU and international mediation produced a peace accord in 2006, the splintering of the two main rebel movements and continuing attacks by the Khartoum-sponsored "Arab" militias prevented full application. AU and other peacekeepers helped diminish the intensity of conflict, but no real peace returned. The damage was immense: at least two hundred thousand fatalities, hundreds of thousands displaced, a zone of scorched earth, and a legacy of bitter animosities.

The folly of subcontracting security operations to local militias found further demonstration in both Darfur and the south. In arming irregular armed factions to assault insurgents, one provides these uncontrollable elements a license to loot, rape, and kill. The terror they may sow rarely works to effect the willing submission of disaffected regions harboring insurgent fighters to a national authority. The hatreds they create, the redoubled insecurity arising from the multiplication of weaponry in the countryside, and the risk that, thus empowered, they become in turn rogue forces finding a livelihood in continuing local violence are destructive outcomes far outweighing any short-term benefit.

Thus Sudan remains an imperiled polity, with many unresolved problems arising from the secession of the south. The NCP regime rests on a narrow ideological and political base. Its president faced indictment by the ICC for crimes against humanity and bears responsibility for the breakup. The oil revenues have showered the Khartoum area with highly visible prosperity, which does not extend to the periphery of the country. The solution to its current dilemmas is difficult to see, and the legacy of its two major internal wars weighs heavily.

OTHER MAJOR INTERNAL WARS

Congo-Kinshasa

The most complex of the internal wars took place in Congo-Kinshasa from 1996 to 2003, leaving in place an intricate web of disorder that has plagued the eastern border regions ever since. No less than eight African armies became involved in some point in the hostilities, dubbed Africa's world war. I leave the details to several masterful accounts and offer only a condensed summary.[78]

The Mobutu regime was in utter dereliction by the mid-1990s, expelled from the IMF, abandoned by its external patrons, afflicted with hyperinflation and administrative decay. Neighboring Rwanda and Uganda, angered by the sanctuary that the Congolese gave to fugitive soldiers of the ousted Rwandan Hutu regime and to armed Uganda rebel militias, sponsored the amalgamation of four small factions into the Alliance des forces democratiques pour la libération du Congo-Zaire (AFDL), with veteran Lumumbist insurgent Laurent Kabila, a holdover from the mid-1960s Congo rebellions, emerging as its leader in fall 1996. Although the AFDL enlisted a number of disaffected youths from the eastern region, its primary military force was the Rwandan army. The demoralized Mobutu forces offered only scattered resistance, and the AFDL swept across the country, marching into Kinshasa in 1997 and installing Kabila as president.

Kabila soon tired of Rwandan tutelage, which was resented by the Congolese public. In July 1997, he suddenly expelled all the Rwandan military advisors and troops. The Rwandan regime reacted immediately, again in partnership with Uganda, and promoted the launching of a new rebel force, the Rassemblement congolais pour la démocratie (RCD). An audacious Rwandan airborne operation in August 1998 aimed at seizing the capital nearly succeeded, but forceful intervention of the Angolan and Zimbabwean armies stymied the maneuver. However, RCD recruits won control of the eastern borderlands.

The RCD soon splintered, but the Rwandan and Ugandan military forces entered the fray, occupying large areas of the east and north. The SADC responded to an appeal from Kabila for armed support; Namibian units joined the Angolans and Zimbabweans. Chad and—furtively—Sudan were also briefly involved; Burundi units crossed the border to attack their own Congo-based Hutu rebels. Thus the Congo wars became exceptionally internationalized.

The mosaic of violence became yet more complex by 1999 when another Congolese insurgent group, the Mouvement pour la libération du Congo emerged, carving out a zone in the northern fringe, armed and supplied by Uganda. Remnants of the Rwandan Interahamwe and former army, deeply implicated in the 1994 genocide, re-formed as a lethal force estimated at twenty thousand and created a zone of control in north Kivu, the Forces démocratiques pour la libération du Rwanda (FDLR). Managing artisanal mining provided survival revenues; the FDLR became enrooted in this part of Kivu. Throughout the east, local, usually ethnic, self-defense forces proliferated; this loosely connected assortment of militias became collectively known as Mai-Mai (meaning "water," after the supernatural protective potions these militias employ).

Various parties to the conflict fastened on the abundant resource base in the east, especially gold, coltan, and coffee.[79] Rwanda and Uganda both financed their military operations in good part through plundered precious materials; they backed different rebel factions and came into violent conflict with each other in Kisangani in mid-1999, partly over control of diamond smuggling. A UN panel of experts in 2002 reported that an elite network of Congolese and Zimbabwean political-military interests had "transferred ownership of at least $5 billion of assets from the State mining sector to private companies under its control with no compensation or benefit for the State treasury of the Democratic Republic of the Congo."[80]

The international community anxiously engaged by 1999, facing a costly and confused stalemate on the ground. The UN, OAU, SADC, South Africa, United States, and Libya all competed in mediation efforts. A UN mission appeared on the scene; initially, the members of the team functioned only as observers, but by 2003 the mission had become a substantial peacekeeping force reaching twenty thousand. A ceasefire negotiated at a mid-1999 Lusaka conference immediately collapsed. Serious steps toward ending the great African war came only after the January 2001 assassination of Laurent Kabila, who was replaced by his son Joseph.[81] The younger Kabila was far more willing to cooperate with international mediation. After tortuous negotiations, the major factions came to an agreement in South Africa in 2003, providing for a framework for a power-sharing transitional regime and parliament. Rwandan and Ugandan troops withdrew, a new constitution was drafted, and a relatively successful election in 2006 confirmed the presidency of Joseph Kabila.

But armed factions continue to operate in the eastern borderlands. The Congolese army, cobbled together in good part from insurgent factions, has limited capacities and discipline. The costly international venture in post-conflict state-building has had only limited therapeutic effect.[82] The human toll, widely estimated at six million, the entrenchment of exploitative smuggling rackets plundering the resources of the eastern borderland, and the intractable obstacles to restoration of effective governance in the affected areas all bear witness to the terrible costs of the Congo wars.

Uganda

The Ugandan insurgency of the LRA that began soon after Museveni's NRA seized power in 1986 is still ongoing, as residual elements continue to sow mayhem in neighboring countries. Its Ugandan operations, as well as attempts at suppression by the Ugandan army, largely took place in Acholiland in the northern region. For two decades, the afflicted region experienced atrocity-laden military operations and massive population displacement.[83]

The predisposing conditions for the Acholi war originate in the singular dynamic of regime displacement in Uganda and in the ethnic strategies employed in army recruitment. The Museveni march into Kampala in 1986 marked the second time in seven years that armies from the periphery had ousted incumbent rulers; the Tanzanian army with allied Ugandan exile fighters chased Idi Amin from the presidential place in 1979. A number of former Amin and Obote soldiers re-formed into rebel militias; at one point in its early years, Museveni's Uganda People's Defense Force (UPDF) was fighting twenty-seven different armed factions.[84] Obote favored northerners from Acholiland and his neighboring Lango homeland for recruitment; most of the soldiers involved in the murderous campaign against the Museveni insurgent bastion in Buganda in 1982–83 were Acholi. As the Museveni regime moved to consolidate its power in 1986, the new-formed UPDF was largely recruited in the south. Acholiland had ample reason to fear vengeance. Their woes multiplied when neighboring pastoral warriors from Karamoja, heavily armed with weapons looted from an abandoned armory, engaged in devastating cattle raids that decimated Acholi herds.[85]

In this climate of fear and uncertainty, a prophetess, Alice Auna Lakwena, formed the Holy Spirit Movement, offering a mystical message combining Christianity with supernatural elements. Her appearance as a spirit medium gave resonance to her call to save Acholiland by a march on Kampala to overthrow Museveni. The ragtag army that answered her call advanced to within fifty miles of Kampala before being defeated at the hands of the UPDF and disintegrating.

The politico-spiritual energies Lakwena had unleashed found a new incarnation in another spirit-possessed leader in 1987, Joseph Kony, a bizarre, enigmatic, and brutal figure who has constantly eluded contact with outsiders. His movement, soon known as the LRA, was not a direct successor to the Lakwena militia, but the LRA adopted her spiritual discourse and ritual initiation and cleansing ceremony. Kony offered a vague agenda, based on the Ten Commandments, promising a new Acholi people and a society cleansed of evil.[86]

Though the LRA purported to speak for the ravaged Acholi population, in fact its daily operations soon deeply antagonized the great majority. The forcible recruitment the Lakwena movement had used on a limited scale became intensified, and spread to the systematic kidnapping of children to serve as soldiers or sex slaves. By some estimates, the LRA had abducted as many as twelve thousand boys and girls by 1997; Heiki Behrend suggests that a child had been stolen from almost every extended family.[87] The kidnapped children were often compelled to commit atrocities on their families or communities as a means of enforcing their severance from their home society. Violence exacted on the village population multiplied, as the LRA looted food supplies and other goods.

In turn, the army response compounded the distress. Unable to protect rural populations and seeking to deny LRA access to supply, by the early 1990s the Museveni regime had compelled much of the population to regroup in displaced persons camps; at the peak, 1.8 million were confined to these settings. Some were able to return by day to their fields, but many were cut off from their homes and livelihoods. Although the camps were provided survival rations by the government and humanitarian relief organizations, the conditions were deplorable.

Early on, the LRA insurgency got caught up in a proxy war between Sudan and Uganda. Museveni offered supplies to the SPLA, while Khartoum riposted with sanctuary and arms flow to the LRA. In 1999, Sudan and Uganda agreed to cease and desist the proxy war, an accord only partly implemented. In 2002, Khartoum authorized the Uganda army to operate in southern Sudan in pursuit of the LRA. In 2005, the Sudan Comprehensive Peace Accord facilitated joint operations by the SPLA and UPDF. By this time, the LRA had been driven out of Uganda and had retreated to remote redoubts in ungoverned areas of Sudan, Central African Republic, and northeast Congo-Kinshasa.

Sporadic efforts to mediate a settlement never bore fruit. The reclusive Kony was a difficult negotiating partner, mostly insisting on discussing through intermediaries. A settlement briefly appeared possible in 2006, when distinguished African mediators appeared to have struck a deal with LRA negotiators, mostly from the diaspora. Kony, however, failed to appear for the signing ceremony. His 2004 indictment by the ICC for crimes against humanity is cited by some as one impediment to concluding a settlement.

The LRA is no longer a threat in Acholiland, and by 2009 all but 190,000 of the 1.8 million once interned had left the camps and resumed rural lives. But the long war in the north devastated and impoverished Acholiland and a brooding resentment toward the Museveni regime remains. Most of the LRA commanders have been killed, and only a few hundred fighters remain, still enough to terrorize the remote areas where they shelter in the neighboring states of Congo-Kinshasa, Central African Republic, and Sudan.

Angola

The Angolan war reignited in 1992. One measure of the impact of the war was the place of scrap metal among top exports by the 1990s, a product derived from destroyed military vehicles and armament. By the 1990s, the original ideological content of the war had long vanished; the combat pitted the "totalitarian savagery" of insurgent leader Jonas Savimbi against the "totalitarian presidentialism" of Angolan president José Eduardo dos Santos. In the summation of David Birmingham, the war was a "depraved conflict between a corrupt government mesmerized by an inhuman opposition obsessed by power."[88] UNITA could no longer count on external support, but Savimbi quickly gained control of key diamond mines, whose revenues sustained large-scale military operations for a decade.

The final decisive blow came in 2002 when the Santos regime succeeded in identifying Savimbi's location and mounted a commando raid to assassinate him. Savimbi's rule over UNITA had become increasingly tyrannical, punctuated by executions of close collaborators suspected of disloyalty. The diamond mines he controlled were worked by what amounted to forced labor, and the cumulative impact of his brutalities toward villagers in the regions under his control eroded his former support. Thus the sudden removal of Savimbi from the equation brought the war to an abrupt halt. Other UNITA leaders returned to Luanda, where they were permitted to find mercantile niches.

Though the return of peace was universally welcomed, the cost to the country of three decades of war was immense. Angola's large army, hardened by many years of combat and Soviet-Cuban nurture, is a strong institution, but the texture of governance overall has deteriorated. Long vanished are the high-minded ideals of Afromarxism; since the 1990s, an authoritarian regime fueled by the oil wealth that entered the system from the top has entrenched itself in its place, a regime that bears some resemblance to the Mobutu mode of rule but with much more money. Rural areas benefit little from the oil revenues. The ruling entourage has accumulated vast wealth, much of it in Brazil or elsewhere overseas. The IMF tried to compel Angola to account for several billion dollars of missing oil revenues in the 1990s, but the scale of petroleum receipts permits the regime to ignore disciplinary pressures from the international community.

OTHER LESS INTENSIVE WARS

Of the remaining seven civil wars not otherwise summarized, all were of limited intensity and consisted of episodic clashes between rebel militias and government forces. Central African Republic was an exceptionally weak state with a slender presence in the northern areas where rebel forces carved out pockets of autonomy. In the northern reaches of Mali and Niger, Tuareg unrest was a recurrent challenge, flaring in the 1990s into open rebellion, with sporadic skirmishing since that time, revolving around grievances related to their marginal status in the national political realm, a challenge that became far more serious at the end of 2011 with the collapse of the Qadhafy regime and the influx of former Tuareg soldiers from the Libyan army and a large flow of weaponry. In Mali a weak and divided army was unable to contain a 2012 revolt by a pair of rival rebel movements, one reviving Tuareg separatist demands and a more extreme Al Qaeda linked Islamist force. An ill-considered military coup in response overturned a seemingly consolidated democratic order, with unforeseeable consequences. In Ivory Coast, the internal battles between 2002 and 2006 involved regional factions of the military; northern troops attempted to seize power in Abidjan by ousting President Laurent Gbagbo and then retreated to create an autonomous bastion in their region. French forces kept the two sides apart, and a UN peacekeeping mission endeavored to hold the ring while interminable negotiations took place for holding national elections that would provide a mechanism for ending the conflict. Burkina Faso mediation produced a compromise interim regime; the long-awaited election was delayed until 2010 by arguments over voter registration and eligibility. Credible elections did take place in November 2010, but

Gbagbo refused to admit his clear electoral defeat. Forces aligned with the electoral victor, Alassane Ouattara, spearheaded by French and UN forces, finally ousted and arrested Gbagbo in April 2011, with AU and widespread international backing.

Congo-Brazzaville and Nigeria were both essentially petro states, oil providing the great majority of state revenue. In Congo, oil revenues nourished the growth of a remarkably overdeveloped state whose population and activity was concentrated in the capital. The civil service roster swelled from thirty-six hundred at independence to eighty-five thousand at the outbreak of civil war; Congo was the sole instance in which the civil strife was concentrated in the capital and essentially amounted to an urban power struggle pitting three ethno-regional youth militias in open combat, especially in 1993–94 and 1997. Angolan military intervention in 1997 in support of one faction, led by Denis Sassou-Nguesso, was decisive; he still held power in 2010.

In Nigeria, a simmering anger in the Niger delta over the environmental destruction of the region by oil exploitation and the meager benefits to its population produced deepening unrest and violence by the 1990s and militia uprisings by 2004. The armed groups, mostly ethnic, acquired substantial weaponry from "bunkered" (that is, stolen) oil; the disaffection of most of the local population and corruption of the military and government made elimination of the armed gangs difficult. Negotiated settlements, most recently in 2009, foundered on the multiplicity of groups and mutual distrust.

The Casamance insurgency in southern Senegal, separated from most of the country by the Gambia enclave, is rooted in a long-standing sense of marginality and exclusion on the part of the Diola and some other related small groups from the national community. What Diop and Diouf call the Islamo-Wolof sociocultural integrative model operative elsewhere does not extend to Casamance.[89] The Mouvement des forces démocratiques de Casamance (MFDC) launched an independence struggle in 1982. When the Senegal army moved in, elements of the MFDC formed guerrilla bands in the forested countryside. Although the disciplined and effective army easily contained the movement, eradicating its forest bases proved difficult and costly. The difficulties were compounded by the spillover of Diola populations into neighboring Gambia and Guinea-Bissau, which offered sanctuary and supply opportunities.[90]

The fissiparous nature of Diola society, which had long blocked incorporation of the region into the national patronage networks, made resolution of the insurgency problematic.[91] A peace accord granting autonomy was reached with the MFDC in 1991, but only the leadership accepted the settlement. Since then, there has been a regular pattern of accords irrigated with financial rewards to MFDC leaders, followed by further splintering and renewed small-scale violence. However, with the independence claim mostly abandoned, the peripheral nature of the insurgency and the capacity of the well-ordered Senegalese state to isolate and contain rebel factions meant that the Casamance rebellion had little effect on the country as a whole. By 2010, only one small faction with a few hundred fighters continued the independence struggle.

Contemporary Civil Wars in Perspective

A number of overall observations arise from this comparative excursion. The first striking point is the contrast between the number of internal wars and the infrequent outbreak of interstate combat. Setting aside the brief skirmishing over disputed borders that took place pitting Algeria against Morocco and then Somalia against Ethiopia in 1963 and 1964, the only major interstate battles involved (again) Somalia and Ethiopia in 1977–78 and Ethiopia and Eritrea from 1998 to 2000. Somalia since independence has always laid claim to Somali-populated areas of Ethiopia, Kenya, and Djibouti; in 1977, spotting a moment of Ethiopian weakness, the huge Somali army invaded but was driven back by large Soviet and Cuban reinforcements in supply and troops. This humiliating defeat began a downward spiral for the Barre regime in Somalia, leading to the 1991 collapse; the failed invasion is likely the final requiem for the Somali irredentist project. The Ethiopian-Eritrean war was also fought by very large armies, over small areas of disputed territory; its bitterness was a carryover from the Eritrean liberation war. Thus interstate wars have been relatively rare, have occurred within a single theater, and have been of limited duration compared to the decades of combat in some internal wars.

The second is the diversity of the contemporary conflicts, ranging from the large-scale warfare involving heavy weapons in Angola in the 1990s to the low-intensity regional violence in Senegal and the Niger delta. A number of common patterns may be identified, but few if any apply to the entire universe of contemporary conflict.[92] Some of the aspects most firmly implanted in the international imagery—mass rape, astonishing levels of brutality, exploitation of child soldiers, blood diamonds—applied to a number but not all the wars. Ethnicity or religion—passe-partout explanations for African conflicts—were central only in a few cases.

A factor common to nearly all cases was the weakening of the fabric of stateness, which rendered central institutions incapable of coping with uprisings that were initially of small size. The predatory turn of many states by the 1980s, the spread of neopatrimonial modes of power management, and the associated high levels of corruption delegitimated governments and undermined bureaucratic institutions. Thus an undercurrent of grievance was invariably present; the state as experienced daily by much of the population bore little resemblance to the legal-rational national entity described in constitutional texts.[93] Rebelling against a fragmented and weakened state tended to produce movements that mirrored these characteristics, as in Liberia, Sierra Leone, and Congo-Kinshasa.[94]

But widespread grievance alone did not make recruitment of followings easy; elementary prudence, mistrust of rebel motives, fear of violence all cautioned reticence. Major urban centers, especially capital cities, tended to remain under closer government control. In rural areas, peasants in most areas had secure access to land and the minimal subsistence it provided; they were especially resistant to recruitment by rebel militias from outside their area.[95] But generalized disappointment if not disaffection toward state institutions made insurgency possible. Their often weak hold on the rural periphery made rebellion thinkable.

In particular, the disaffection of a large fraction of the youth is a major factor.[96] The 1950s and 1960s were an era of rising hopes for social ascension, as the multiplication of schools and a momentum of strong economic expansion provided the young generations, especially the educated, ample opportunity. By the end of the 1970s, states had reached their outer limits of public sector expansion and began to restrict new recruitment; the onset of economic crisis shriveled employment possibilities. The rapid growth of cities during this period created a large pool of unemployed youths surviving in the informal economy, the urban "lumpens" highlighted by Jimmy Kandeh and Ibrahim Abdullah as prime militia recruits in Sierra Leone and elsewhere and the thugs widely utilized by political parties in electoral competition.[97] But discontents over repressive state behavior, the corrupt enrichment of the political elite, and the social closure youth faced also affected young generations in rural areas.

The momentum of population expansion in several countries (especially Rwanda and Burundi), along with environmental changes, intensified tensions over livelihoods. These tensions were sometimes further complicated by conflicting needs of herders and cultivators (especially in Sudan and eastern Congo-Kinshasa but also in Mali and Niger) and poisoned by doctrines of indigeneity (Ivory Coast, Senegal, Congo-Kinshasa). Under such doctrines, immigrant agriculturalists or even internal migrants had acquired land rights in a setting of growing scarcity. Although ethnicity per se was infrequently determinant, in a few instances communal solidarities fed into the equation of conflict (especially in Rwanda and Burundi but also in Casamance, Niger delta, Niger, Mali, Sudan, and both Congos, and locally in Sierra Leone and Liberia). Religious ideology was at issue in Algeria, Sudan, and Somalia.

Some critical new factors came into play with the momentous transformations in global politics marking the end of the cold war, whose overall significance I have already stressed. A major side effect of the collapse of the Soviet bloc was that vast inventories of armaments were left in the hands of bankrupt successor states with cash-starved security forces. For a time, especially in the Russian Federation, Ukraine, and Bulgaria, weapons warehouses became mercantile bazaars, where black market arms dealers could obtain at fire sale prices large stocks of the basic armament so useful in the new African wars, especially AK47s and ammunition.

The new pattern of power seizure by armed rebels from the periphery created another huge source for the black market in weapons; this began with Uganda in 1979, followed by Chad in 1982. The pattern was repeated in Uganda in 1986, Chad again in 1990, Somalia and Ethiopia in 1991 (with two of the largest armies in Africa), both Congos in 1997, Central African Republic in 2003, and Libya in 2011. The dissolution of existing armies that resulted meant that weaponry in good part vanished into the bush. Automatic weapons became readily and inexpensively available on black markets, in contrast to the earlier postcolonial moments when few arms were obtainable in the countryside.

A corollary consequence of dissolution of existing armies was diffusion of basic military knowledge through substantial numbers of unemployed former soldiers who retreated to the countryside and whose only marketable skill was fighting. Among them were some former officers who had received advanced military training and thus some valuable skills in warfare. In the Algerian, Mali, and Niger cases, there were a small number of "Afghans" (veterans of the anti-Soviet struggle in the 1980s) who offered rebel militias knowledge and experience applicable to guerrilla combat.

New forms of communication available to insurgents in remote locations added another dynamic, especially when cell phones became widely available. From the forest redoubt, negotiations could be conducted with black market weapons dealers or commodity merchants. Rebels were no longer isolated from the outside world.

Rebel organizers faced two key dilemmas: how to recruit, motivate, and discipline followers and how to finance the uprising.[98] The risky choice of enlistment normally required a motivation more specific than antipathy toward a dysfunctional state; the oft-heard promise of democracy, an end to corruption, and social provisions was unlikely to suffice. A sentiment of regional or ethnic marginalization operated in a number of cases (Niger delta, Casamance, Uganda, Rwanda, Burundi, among others). Hope of assured subsistence might be a more direct incentive. Once incorporated into a rebel militia, isolation from the home community, fear and intimidation were potent deterrents to defection.

One of the solutions to the recruitment challenge was the kidnapping of child soldiers, first visible on a large and deliberate scale by RENAMO in Mozambique in the 1980s. Child soldiers were honed into a formidable instrument in several cases (above all Uganda, Liberia, and Sierra Leone, although they were used in several other conflicts); they became a defining feature of the new conflicts, especially in external eyes. Adults might be more risk averse, with more to lose by abandoning farm, home, and community for the adventure of insurgency. Adolescents had much less to lose, and some children might find it attractive for the several reasons already noted. But they could also be abducted, and they were on a large scale in the cases cited; once severed from their communities, indoctrinated, perhaps drugged and guaranteed supernatural protection, they could be fearless and brutal soldiers.

Novel as well was the solution to the finance challenge. Rebel militias discovered new ways to finance their struggle through seizure of an array of marketable commodities of relatively high value. This almost never happened in earlier rebellions, which were funded by external assistance, confiscation of government or other assets, or support from local communities. For many of the post-1990 insurgents, traffic in diamonds, gold, tin, coltan, timber, or coffee could assure a revenue flow for rebellion. The warlords leading insurgencies became skilled operatives in illicit commerce.

In several places—Angola, Congo-Kinshasa, Liberia, Sierra Leone, Niger delta—the sums raised by looted commodities accruing to rebel militias was remarkably high. Though lucrative returns went to many intermediaries and some principals in the smuggling rackets, for the militias themselves the resources exploited were instrumental to the violence rather than its explanation. The once-fashionable "greed not grievance" thesis has a number of convincing rebuttals.[99]

A striking characteristic of the new African wars was their structural stalemate; once begun, they were painfully difficult to end. In only two instances— Algeria and Angola—was the regime capable of military triumph on its own. In Rwanda in 1994 a rebel militia seized power by its own efforts, and in both

Congos in 1997, incumbent regimes were ousted with decisive support from neighboring armies. But in all other cases where insurgents aspired to seize power nationally, there was no possibility of success, nor did state rulers have the capacity to eliminate them by force. Where sustained conflict has ended, external mediation has played a key and indispensable role (or a modest one at least in the case of Mali and Niger).

In several respects, the insurgencies were self-limiting. A few had only regional objectives (Mali, Niger, Nigeria, Senegal, and Sudan). In other instances, their extraordinary violence and atrocities alienated populations. The absence of a compelling ideological discourse, beyond ousting a corrupt and unpopular regime, limited their appeal, although in Algeria and Somalia a call to jihadism and integral Islam motivated some insurgents. In contrast to national liberation movements of an earlier period, the new movements made little effort to create "liberated zones" or to actually administer territory not under any state control.

In cases where insurgency continued over extended time, internal dynamics often altered its character.[100] For example, in Uganda, the LRA initially had wide support in its Acholi home base, but over time its violent behavior and kidnapping of children led to disaffection and facilitated repressive action by the Ugandan army. Driven into Sudan sanctuary, the LRA increasingly became a rogue movement reflecting the bizarre character of its leader, Joseph Kony. A similar degeneration is visible in Congo-Kinshasa; the original protagonists fragmented, which provoked emergence of local defense forces (Mai-Mai). Thus a shifting alignment of militia forces emerges, their warlord commanders becoming elements in a criminal network of plunder of high-value minerals. The Liberian and Sierra Lone cases followed a similar trajectory. Invariably, the evolving nature of conflict was driven a complex of micro-level variables.[101]

Neighboring states pursuing their own objectives were an important source of militia supply in several cases (Central African Republic, Chad, Somalia, Sudan, Uganda, and, to a limited extent, Senegal). States would supply militias usually either in retaliation for the warring country's suspected funneling of arms to internal dissident militias (Chad, Sudan, Uganda) or as participant in a proxy war directed at a third-party antagonist (Eritrea, for example, armed Islamist rebels in Somalia as an anti-Ethiopian gambit). Whatever the motive, the inevitable consequence was prolongation of the internal war.

The multiplication of internal wars in Africa—and the intense media attention generated by the instances of extraordinary insurgent violence (above all Liberia and Sierra Leone)— attracted high levels of international attention. So also did the spectacle of complete state dissolution in Somalia in 1991 that led to a humanitarian emergency and the 1994 Rwanda genocide. Both African and international mobilization followed, aimed at blocking insurgent take-overs, introducing peacekeeping forces, and pursuing active mediation in search of conflict resolution. ECOWAS peacekeepers played an important role in Ivory Coast, Liberia and Sierra Leone; African forces were also assembled for Central African Republic, Somalia, and Sudan. A remarkably extensive roster of UN peacekeeping forces were mounted: at some stages of conflict, the UN deployed in Angola, Burundi, Central African Republic, Congo-Kinshasa, Ivory Coast, Liberia, Mozambique, Rwanda, Sierra Leone, Somalia, and Sudan, as well as along the Eritrean-Ethiopian border. The Rwandan and Somali interventions ended badly and the inadequacies in Congo-Kinshasa were widely criticized, but in the other instances the UN played a helpful role. In Central African Republic, Chad, and Ivory Coast, French forces operated to contain conflicts or bloc insurgent takeover and then in 2011 to spearhead the Ouattara-UN operation to end the Gbagbo usurpation. A dramatic new form of external intervention unfolded in 2011, when NATO forces under UN mandate in Libya provided air cover to insurgents, eventually facilitating their victory.

Brokering peace settlements in complex emergencies had intrinsic difficulties, which bedeviled the mediators in several cases. Ending an internal war locked in stalemate inevitably involved inviting to the conference table—and thus in some respects legitimating—movements like the RUF, the NPFL, and RENAMO that were guilty of crimes against humanity. Only RENAMO really abandoned violence and accepted a minority role in civil politics. Also inherent but problematic in such bargained end to conflict is the need to incorporate some insurgent fighters into the security forces, a source of continued indiscipline, instability, and predation in the Congo-Kinshasa army.

The global preoccupation, if not obsession, with international terrorism after 2001 and the ability of its most noteworthy practitioners, Al Qaeda, to franchise regional subsidiaries intensified concerns with ungoverned space in whose interstices such groups could operate. In all these cases, lawless zones were linked to internal warfare. Somalia, southern Algeria, Tuareg regions of Mali and Niger all offered such sanctuary. Other criminal enterprises could also flourish: for example, piracy rapidly emerged and became professionalized in Somalia and to a lesser degree in lawless regions in the Niger delta, as did trans-Saharan narcotics smuggling.

The interwoven nature of the African political universe came more sharply into view in the contemporary internal warfare. A spillover effect is visible in virtually all the cases, save perhaps the Niger delta. The reciprocal entanglement of the genocidal conflicts in Rwanda and Burundi stands out;

so does the participation at one stage or another of the Congo wars of eight other African armies. The protracted Angolan war against the UNITA insurgency motivated Angolan involvement in both Congos and Ivory Coast, where Savimbi had enjoyed sanctuary and support from given regimes. The linkages between some fragments of the dissidence in Tuareg regions in Mali and Niger with AQIM and the trans-Saharan narcotics trade drew in Algeria and Mauritania. Chad, Uganda, and Ethiopia were drawn into Sudan's civil wars to the extent that they provided sanctuary and support to insurgents.

The particular activism of Libya merits special note. With an ample flow of oil revenue, a small population to service, and few if any domestic constraints on his personal diplomacy, Qadhafy enjoyed the latitude to pursue his continental visions. By the later 1970s, once his early pan-Arab ambitions were thwarted by the reticence of partner Arab states, he turned to Africa as a field for his quixotic leadership. The insurgent training camps he sponsored in Libya produced a number of the early participants in the Liberian and Sierra Leonean rebellions. His hand was also visible in internal conflicts in Chad, Central African Republic, Uganda, and Sudan, among others. More recently he had cast himself as a peacemaker, tribune, and financier of a rejuvenated pan-Africanism through the AU, subsidizing at one time or another nearly half the members.

Finally, a survey of the present African landscape reveals several positive signs. The number of active conflicts has significantly diminished from a peak in the 1990s. Not only are there fewer internal wars but they are smaller, involve fewer direct encounters by large forces, and occur in the periphery of affected countries. The insurgents tend to be more fragmented, and they are also often less disciplined fighting forces.[102] Between 2000 and 2010, the only major new centers of conflict have been Ivory Coast and Nigeria; the former was resolved in 2011, and the Niger delta violence is now much reduced. Mozambique appears to be far beyond its civil war and to have healed most of its wounds. Liberia and Sierra Leone have now enjoyed several years of genuine peace, if not full reconciliation. Only Somalia currently appears beyond any hope of resolution. The Darfur conflict is likewise still at impasse in Sudan; the projected southern independence transition is fraught with perils as well as high hopes. One might suggest that there is a reverse spillover effect in the reduction of the number of active civil wars. The settlement of one relieves the pressures on neighboring states.

Civil society groups have played an important part in the reduction of levels of violence and in mitigating its effects on the population. Human rights groups, women's organizations, peace groups, churches, and other organizations were active voices in the quest for ending the violent conflicts that imposed such high human costs on civil populations. They were also helpful participants in peace settlement negotiations.

By way of coda to this chapter, one may ask what is the legacy of an era of proliferating internal wars? At the beginning of the chapter, I mention the Tilly thesis of the historical importance of warfare in the building of the modern state. His reasoning did not apply to internal war, which does not unify and mobilize a citizenry against an external foe nor stimulate the institutionalization of a revenue-generating capacity or an enhanced administrative capability; on the contrary, institutional capacities are likely to be degraded as a state loses its control or even presence in important parts of the country and as mechanisms of plunder of natural resources that may survive the end of conflict become established. The two states that defeated insurgencies, Algeria and Angola, emerged from conflict with greatly strengthened security forces but also with habits of autocracy reinforced. They are perhaps stronger states but not necessarily in ways conducive to sustainable development or societal well-being. The two interstate wars to which the Tilly hypothesis might apply, Somalia-Ethiopia and Ethiopia-Eritrea, left in their wake arguably reinforced states in Ethiopia and especially Eritrea. In Somalia, the failed irredentist war of 1977–78 began the long decline and decay of the Siad Barre regime, leading to the 1991 state collapse. The Tilly thesis rests on European historical evidence; its exportability remains to be demonstrated.

The human costs, however, are clear. The fatality toll as direct or indirect consequence is sobering: an estimated six million in the Congo-Kinshasa wars, perhaps three million in Sudan; though these statistics are estimates rather than verified head counts and include deaths from disease, starvation, or displacement as well as military action, that the impact on the directly affected regions was calamitous cannot be doubted. The Algerian, Sierra Leonean, Liberian, Angolan, Mozambican and Somalian wars likewise saw elevated casualty figures. Especially in Angola and Mozambique, land mines were indiscriminately sown and continue to maim peasants today. Civil populations were frequent targets of militias as well as government forces. Endemic insecurity in the combat zones leaves its own traumatic legacy and a decaying public infrastructure. Only many years of renewed peace can mend the wounds.

8

Africanism, Nationalism, and Ethnicity

The Ambiguous Triple Helix of Identity

Africans, all over the continent, without a word being spoken,
either from one individual to another or from one African country
to another, looked at the European, looked at one another, and
knew that in relation to the European they were one.

—Julius Nyerere, 1960

We are dancing the frontier.

—Kivu youth group (Congo-Kinshasa), 2003

Nigerian nationality for me and my generation was an acquired
taste. . . . Being a Nigerian is abysmally frustrating and
unbelievably exciting.

—Chinua Achebe, 2010

The Three Pillars of Identity

The introductory citations point to the three pillars of identity this chapter
will explore: Africanism, territorial nationalism, and ethnicity.[1]

I recollect sitting in a Wellesley College audience in 1960 mesmerized
by the eloquent charisma of future president Julius Nyerere when he uttered
the words cited in the epigraph. They draw attention to a pair of aspects of
Africanism: its original reference point of identity formation in the European
other and its racial subtext. The visibility of the difference came not just from
subjugation but also from phenotype.

The Kivu dance troupe was encountered by a pair of American academics
crossing from Rwanda into Congo-Kinshasa in 2003, at the moment when an
accord that promised to bring peace and reunification to the tormented country had been signed. Asked why they were dancing, the young men replied

that they were "dancing the frontier," adding that once they had completed the ritual at this crossing they planned to continue to other frontier posts to repeat the ritual. In their dance, they were performing the nation, suggesting a deeply naturalized attachment to the vast territory created by the imperial diplomacy of Belgian King Leopold II in 1885. Their performance not only celebrated a territorial "self" but also demonstrated a marked antagonism to the national "other" beyond the frontier, Rwanda. Unspoken but embedded in the ritual was a pronounced hostility toward the external enemy within, namely, populations of Rwandan origin, especially Tutsi, established within the Kivu region.

Achebe in his autobiography captures the ambivalent grip of territorial nationalism.[2] Nigeria was not a compelling category in his childhood in the 1930s. It became so only with the rise of anticolonial nationalism in his youth. After a literary lifetime exposing the country's dysfunctions in a brilliant series of novels while also celebrating his Igbo origins and after momentarily transferring his loyalty to the abortive Biafra secession, he finds his renewed Nigerian attachment "unbelievably exciting."

This chapter explores these three pillars of identity, Africanism, territorial nationalism, and ethnicity. These frames have provided the discursive categories of the state and much of the political process. Yet each of them, closely inspected, contains important ambiguities. As activated modes of consciousness, all three are products of the last two centuries. In terms of the triple helix metaphor, territorial nationalism operates as connecting middle strand, intertwined both with pan-Africanism and ethnicity, though the last two have little direct connection.

One might suggest that these elements correlate with a threefold constitution of the subject by the colonial state. The colonizer had various labels signifying the racial otherness and presumed inferiority of the subject: African, black, native, indigene (or the delectable Belgian colonial census categorization "homme adulte valide" [able-bodied adult male, or unit of labor]). For other purposes, the colonizing country applied the territorial designation, usually solely to reference the indigenous population. Even within a given colonial domain of contiguous territories, distinct ordinances and administrative provisions operated, evoking a territorial label (Congolese, Nigerian, Senegalese). Further, ruling the subject population required sorting it into legible cultural categories; the master premise of colonial occupation was that Africa was "tribal." Africans internalized each of these categorizations and transformed them into a discourse of solidarity: pan-Africanism, territorial nationalism, and ethnic community. This chapter explores each of these axes of identity and their ambiguity.[3]

Hovering in the background is a critical question arising from the preceding chapter: what can explain the astonishing persistence of the African territorial map of independence, in the face of widespread state crisis by the 1980s and the proliferation of internal wars in the 1990s and beyond? This puzzle is stated in stark terms by Pierre Englebert in his insightful search for an answer. Most African states, he argues,

> have not brought about or facilitated much economic or human development for their populations since independence. . . . Parasitic or predatory, they suck resources out of their societies. At the same time, weak and dysfunctional, many of them are unable or unwilling to sustainably provide the rule of law, safety, and basic property rights that have, since Hobbes, justified the very existence of states in the modern world. . . . Yet . . . for all their catastrophic failures, weak African states are still around. With the partial exception of Somalia, state collapse has yet to lead to state disintegration on the continent. There have been almost no changes to African boundaries since 1960.[4]

This triple helix of identity has played a critical role in defining the political itineraries of African states; thus an inquest into the nature and origins of the three strands is an indispensable component of an overall analysis. Pan-Africanism, whatever its limits, is the essential cement of the African state system. The idea and doctrine of territorial nationalism is the foundation of the survival of African states in the face of periods of decline and crisis. No inquiry into African political dynamics can elide the issue of ethnicity or ignore its central place in the social imaginary.

PAN-AFRICANISM AS CONTINENTAL UNIFICATION

Chronologically the first form of ideological expression of African identity evolved into the doctrine of pan-Africanism, briefly treated in chapter 3. Since independence, Africanism has been partially eclipsed by territorial and ethnic forms of consciousness, but despite its capture by the postcolonial state system it remains a force. This ideology of racial solidarity originated in the nineteenth century, mostly in the diaspora. The searing experience of slavery, the sight of the despoiling of the African continent through imperial seizures of land and resources, and the racial scorn and marginalization imposed by the dominant white society on diaspora Africans provided the template for the call to racial solidarity as a means of combating injustice. Its essence was captured in the classic passage from the autobiography of the major leader of the early pan-African movement, W. E. B. Du Bois: "As I face Africa I ask myself: what is it between us that constitutes a tie that I can feel better than I can express? Africa is of course my fatherland. Yet neither my father nor father's father ever saw Africa or knew of its meaning or cared overmuch for it. . . . But the physical bond is least, and the badge of color relatively unimportant save as a badge; the real essence of the kinship is its social heritage of slavery; the discrimination and insult; and thus heritage binds together not simply the children of Africa, but extends through yellow Asia and into the South Seas. It is this unity that draws me to Africa."[5] Various heroes of diaspora African resistance to the repression of dominant society became emblematic symbols: Toussaint Louverture, the leader of the successful slave revolt in Haiti, Marcus Garvey, who in the 1920s started the back-to-Africa movement, and later Martin Luther King and Malcolm X, among many others.

With the exception of Liberia and Freetown as locations of return, diaspora pan-Africanism had no territorial attachments. Few in the diaspora had any notion of their actual place of origin; racial solidarity was a generalized sentiment linked only to an abstract Africa: more specifically, that part of it that was the source of the slave trade. The first institutionalization of this idea came through a series of pan-African conferences held from 1900 to 1927, which Du Bois organized. The first five such gatherings denounced racial oppression, excoriated European land seizures, and demanded African rights in colonized territories, but they did not call for independence. In 1935, the Italian invasion of Ethiopia marked a turning point in mobilizing diaspora intellectuals in support of an independent African state.

However, the rooting of pan-African ideology in the continent and its liberation awaited the Sixth Pan-African Congress in Manchester in 1945. Though Du Bois was still honored with the chair, a new generation of young African nationalists took the lead, including two future presidents (Kwame Nkrumah and Jomo Kenyatta). From its diasporic antecedents came an ideology of liberation through self-determination, which called for a metamorphosis that initially privileged a continental rather than territorial vision.

In the years leading up to the surge to independence, pan-Africanism as a cultural ideology continued to engage some diaspora intellectuals, especially centered those around the journal *Présence Africaine* in Paris. However, its main energies gradually shifted to Africa; some (though far from all) nationalist leaders shared the continental unification dreams of Ghanaian Kwame

Nkrumah. The 1955 Bandung conference and subsequent assemblies situated the anticolonial solidarity of pan-Africanism in the larger anti-imperial frame of Afro-Asian alignment. But, as I argue in chapter 3, the tactical imperatives of independence struggle drove political leaders to embrace the territorial frame as the primary basis for action.

But even as territory shaped political organization, nationalist discourse had a robust African content (except in North Africa). The first major studies of emergent nationalism in Africa invariably characterized it as "African nationalism."[6] The primary rhetorical other for the anticolonial activist was not just the specific territorial administration but the colonial power and European rule more broadly and those immigrating in its baggage trains: white settlers and the South Asian and Mediterranean mercantiles who usually dominated commerce. After independence, the African focus on the idea of nationalism shifted, "nation-building" imperatives intervening, bit by bit to territory. This new focus fundamentally reshaped the parameters of pan-African doctrine. The swelling ranks of sovereign states now stood between the populace and the intellectual dream of a continental imagined community. Pan-Africanism in the process was captured by the new African state system, unified and sustained by the imperative of liberating southern Africa. In this metamorphosis, its racial and cultural content faded, though the idea lived on for a time in such sites as the periodic pan-African festivals. Another enduring legacy was the monumental eight-volume history of Africa, undertaken by UNESCO in the 1970s and mostly published in the 1980s that was explicitly committed to an Africa-centered focus redolent of pan-African doctrine. But overall its inspirational force clearly diminished.

A project of continental unification as a federation of states took the place of pan-Africanism. Its first forerunner was the abortive 1959 Ghana-Guinea Union, which Mali briefly joined in 1960, intended as a platform of broader African unification. Though Nkrumah's ambitions for a brief moment seemed like they might realized when Congo-Kinshasa prime minister Patrice Lumumba signed a secret accord in August 1960 joining the Guinea-Ghana Union, the fleeting agreement was never published and vanished into the maelstrom of the Congo crisis.[7] The union evaporated not long after, giving way to plans for what became the OAU in 1963, which was in turn supplanted by the AU four decades later. But these frameworks for continental collaboration by independent African states never came close to achieving the dream of a pan-African federation absorbing the sovereignty of participating nations.

As pan-Africanist ideology migrated from its diasporic roots back to Africa, communities of African descent elsewhere became absorbed in other agendas. The incomplete but important battles fought by the civil rights movement in the United States and elsewhere diminished the intensity of racial oppression as a global signifier. The Afro-Caribbean, whose intelligentsia had contributed so much to pan-African cultural expression and thought, for the most part also achieved independence and became engrossed in postcolonial politics. A large and articulate new generation of African emigrants joined the diaspora in America and Western Europe, but now they came equipped with territorial attachments and orientations. An active cultural discourse continued in the enlarged and transformed diaspora, but pan-Africanism was no longer a salient trope.

As pan-Africanism was assimilated into the institutional frame of continental interstate cooperation, the idea of a natural community defined by racial solidarity faded in favor of a more diffusely geographic sense of affinity. The transformation of South Africa by 1995 from an exclusionary white oligarchy to a government defined by a multiracial "rainbow" form of African identity and its sudden mutation from primary target of pan-African solidarity to major player in continental affairs put into question the continued pertinence of racial affinity as basis for shared purpose. So also did the ambiguities of Arab state identification with the original themes of pan-African solidarity. As Ali Mazrui points out, the British never referred to their Egyptian subjects as "Africans" or natives. They were merely Egyptians.[8]

In his 1953 political testament, *The Philosophy of the Revolution*, Egyptian leader Gamal Abdel Nasser does include Africa as one of his three circles of transnational identification englobing his nation. However, he links the affinity to shared geography and to Egypt's paternal obligation as guardian and bearer of uplift: "We cannot under any condition, even if we wanted to, stand aloof from the terrible and terrifying battle now raging in the heart of that continent between five million whites and two hundred million Africans. We cannot stand aloof for one important and obvious reason—we ourselves are in Africa. Surely the people of Africa will continue to look to us—we who are the guardians of the continent's northern gate, we who constitute the connecting link between the continent and the outer world. We certainly cannot, under any condition, relinquish our responsibility to help to our utmost in spreading the light of knowledge and civilisation up to the very depth of the virgin jungles of the continent."[9] Nasser places the African circle on the same plane with the Arab and Islamic ones, but the affinity is geographic rather than grounded in identity; proximity dictates the obligation to bring uplift to the "virgin jungles"; the emotive resonance of shared Arabhood or Islam is an entirely separate form of connection not shared by those in the heart of darkness.

However, from the outset of the continental quest for pan-African institutions, Arab states, initially especially Tunisia and Egypt, were active participants. During their experience as colonized populations, the Arab tier of northern African states experienced a degree of racialization as a less civilized "other," yet as heirs to the classical civilization of the Mediterranean and the golden age of Islamic flourishing, the Maghrib or Egyptian indigene did not suffer the full indignity of cultural dismissal as mere savages. Nor was the consciousness of difference from the colonizer refracted through a prism of color. Though Senegalese intellectual Cheikh Anta Diop among others invoked a mythical black Egypt as a reference point for a celebration of the African cultural heritage, the reverse was never true. On the contrary, the history of Arab connections with the sub-Saharan lands was burdened by the long-standing precolonial trans-Saharan and Nile valley slave trade, whose memories are still sharp in Sudan. Thus the vision of an eventual continental federation of African states of necessity came to rest on ideological foundations other than the original doctrines of a solidarity of the black world in the face of racial oppression.

By the turn of the twenty-first century, the OAU faced a growing barrage of criticism within Africa for its limited effectiveness. The end of the era of anticolonial liberation marked by the South African transition to majority rule removed its most important unifying cause. For much of the African public, the OAU had long appeared a mere self-protective cartel of heads of state rather than an emanation of the popular will. The majority of states were delinquent in their dues, and the secretariat struggled with limited finances. Less well funded than the other two major continental institutions, UNECA and the African Development Bank (ADB), the OAU had a weak staff and limited institutional capabilities. UNECA and ADB were vehicles to a degree for African economic nationalism, but they were not incarnations of pan-Africanist doctrine.

The disappointments with the OAU engendered a revived effort to achieve a continental polity, beginning with a 1999 summit conference summoned by the quixotic Libyan leader Muammar Qadhafy. His earlier dreams were of pan-Arab unity, but a series of abortive schemes with Egypt, Sudan, Tunisia, and Morocco demonstrated the unfeasibility of that idea, prompting a turn to pan-Africanism. William Zartman well captures the essence of the Qadhafy-led campaign for a renovated and empowered new pan-African framework: "The dynamo behind the negotiations was Qadhafy, and the form of the Union with its parliament, court, and many state-like (and European Union-like) institutions reflected his insistence and his purse in encouraging support. A group of moderate, sound-thinking leaders supplied the substance of the Union, which in working essence is much like its predecessor but animated by a new sense of purpose and order."[10] Although the AU, formally launched in 2002, is more ambitious in its institutional design, it is likely to founder on the same tenacious attachment of existing states to their sovereignty and to face the same the circumscribed means that restricted the ambit of the OAU.

And yet the durability of the pan-African project is striking. Beyond the AU, an array of regional bodies for inter-African cooperation (ECOWAS, SADC, and other regional organizations) demonstrate an attachment to Africa as interstate frame. African states at the UN have a formalized caucus and often achieve joint positions. A new array of slogans and structures bear witness to an engagement with continental uplift—the African Renaissance, the New African Partnership for Development (NEPAD). The OAU frequently played a consequential role in mediating interstate conflicts or resolving internal wars, and the AU has followed in its footsteps. Recently in Somalia and Darfur African peacekeeping forces under AU command and mandate have deployed. The penalty of suspension for those seizing power by force has been applied to a number of countries, notably Mauritania, Togo, Guinea, Central African Republic, and Madagascar. Though the required elections to legitimize rule do not necessarily result in a new leader taking the reins, they do set some limits to military interventions. In a very different mode, the intensely symbolic realm of international football (soccer) offers another venue for the performance of pan-Africansm. During the 2010 World Cup competition, once Ghana became the last surviving African team, the huge pool of avid football fans across the continent fixed their passions on what became the emblem of all of Africa.[11]

AFRICANISM AS RACIAL BELONGING

Once it was removed from the domain of an intellectual discourse of populist resonance and was captured by the state system and its leadership, pan-Africanism as an identity-forming ideology lost much of its force among the population at large.[12] But Africanism—a sense of racial belonging and affiliation—remains embedded in the popular psyche. African travelers and emigrants of sub-Saharan origin are perceived in Europe, North America,

Japan and China as racial others, even if the stigma attached is much attenu-ated from the early days of pan-Africanism. Within Africa, the visible role played by expatriate executives and resident racial minorities sustains an African consciousness. A racial subtext to the idea of the nation shaped decol-onization debates about the extension of citizenship to settled European, Asian, or Levantine populations. To this day their claims to a right to belong to the nation remains a contentious issue in a number of countries; oppo-nents cite their privileged standing in the colonial hierarchy, their mainte-nance of external citizenship, and their presumed contingent loyalty.[13] The "rainbowism" that is the official nation-building metaphor of multiracial part-nership in South Africa has not come close to erasing the conviction of a good part of the African majority that its impoverishment and oppression under the apartheid regime call for a more African-centered ideology of nationhood. Race may be a mere social construct, but phenotype as social signifier remains embedded within Africa and in the world at large.

Explaining State Persistence

More surprising than the rise and decline of pan-Africanism is the naturaliza-tion of what can only be understood as territorial nationalism. I alluded to the remarkable fact of state persistence in Africa in the face of widespread dys-functionality and decline, not to mention the wave of civil wars in the 1990s. As chapter 7 demonstrates, a Somalia continues to exist in the social imagi-nary even in the circumstances of more than two decades of virtual anarchy in much of the country and the absence of really functioning institutions of rule. A significant number of African states are so weak that they would be unable to resist or overcome a determined effort by a segment of its citizenry to secede, yet secessionism is surprisingly rare. Of the eighteen recent internal wars examined in chapter 7, in only two, those in Senegal and Sudan, were separatist agendas explicitly on the table (at times more ambiguously auton-omy or even independence figured in Touareg rebel discourse in Mali and Niger); after fifty years of independence, the only actual secession was South Sudan in 2011. A significant part of the explanation for the astonishing persis-tence of the postcolonial state lies, I believe, in the crystallization of a territo-rial attachment that belongs to the ideological genus of nationalism. In other words, states persist because their citizenry expect and prefer that they do.

Those skeptical of this assertion point to other factors that inhibit state fragmentation; these have unquestionable validity and require examination before I turn to the sources of the perhaps surprising attachment to territorial nationalism. The pronounced hostility of the international state system to the fragmentation of countries is indeed a critical element in accounting for the persistence of African states. Although any number of new states emerged in the wake of World War I, from World War II until 1990 decolonization was the only widely accepted avenue to sovereignty. In the first three postwar decades, the only postcolonial exceptions to this rule were the consensual withdrawal of Singapore from the Malaysian Federation and Bangladesh's separation from Pakistan, midwived by the intervention of the Indian army. The sanctity of the territorial integrity of the states issuing from decolonization received increasingly robust affirmation, notably in the UN General Assembly 1960 Declaration on the Granting of Independence to Colonial Countries and Peoples; this insisted that the right of all peoples to self-determination did not include "the partial or whole disruption of the national unity and territorial integrity of a country," which would be "incompatible with the purposes and principles of the charter of the United Nations."[14] Sacralization of territorial integrity is enunciated more emphatically still in the 1970 Declaration on Principles of International Law Concerning Friendly Relations and Cooperation among States in Accordance with the Charter of the United Nations. After issuing a ringing declaration of the sacred right to self-determination, the document states that "nothing in the foregoing paragraphs shall be construed as authorizing or encouraging any action which would dismember or impair, totally or in part, the territorial integrity or political unity of sovereign and independent States. . . . Every State shall refrain from any action aimed at the partial or total disruption of the national unity and territorial integrity of any other State or country. . . . The territorial integrity and independence of the State are inviolable."[15]

For a brief moment at the beginning of the 1990s, the floodgates appeared to open, as the fifteen component "republics" of the Soviet Union all withdrew, to the dismay of parts of the international community. The "velvet divorce" of the Czech Republic and Slovakia soon followed, then the violent breakup of Yugoslavia. Eritrea benefited from this breach in the walls of the state integrity principle to make good its escape from Ethiopia, though only after winning the thirty-year civil war. The international system quickly repaired this break in the dam; an international commission headed by French jurist Robert Badinter appointed by the European Union gave retroactive blessing to the existing separations but erected a new barrier to any others by restricting any separations to existing autonomous administrative units, whose own borders were sacrosanct.[16]

By ricochet, the Badinter report reinforces the operative code of African decolonization set forth in chapter 3. Only constituted colonial territories with a distinct administrative personality were entitled to succeed to internationally recognized sovereign status.[17] The small number of separatist movements of significance that have developed have invariably invoked a claim to a territorial standing of colonial origin, never ethnic self-determination (for example, Katanga, Biafra, Casamance, Zanzibar, Cabinda, Anglophone Cameroon), or to special standing as kingdoms that enjoyed a privileged treaty relationship with the colonial occupant (Buganda in Uganda, Barotseland in Zambia).

The African state system reinforced this international jurisprudence with its own charter affirmations of the sanctity of existing boundaries and state integrity. In articles 3 and 5 of the OAU's charter, which was drawn up at the first conference in 1963, stipulated that all member states were obligated to respect the sovereignty and territorial integrity of every African state.[18] Although four African states appeared to subvert this principle by recognizing Biafra (Ivory Coast, Gabon, Tanzania, and Zambia), the Nigerian triumph in the civil war erased this breach in the African international legal order. The blessing of sovereignty could only pass to distinct and separate colonial territorial entities, which justified the recognition of Western Somalia by most African states. But Eritrea, which also met this standard, was accepted into the African community of nations only after its independence was won militarily, acknowledged by Ethiopia, and validated by an internationally supervised referendum.

Somaliland further illustrates the force of territorial integrity doctrine. Though de facto separation from the anarchy of Somalia was proclaimed in 1991, in deference to the united African front against external recognition not a single country has acknowledged the living reality of an independent state. Even though as British Somaliland the territory had a separate colonial antecedent, its freely made choice in 1960 to unite with Somalia was deemed irrevocable. The acute disabilities faced by the forlorn unrecognized polity find compelling demonstration in the Somaliland example. Lacking the grace of sovereignty that only comes with the ritual laying on of hands by the international state system through formal recognition, Somaliland cannot participate in international institutions, access external aid, win acceptance of its currency or identity documents such as passports, or borrow from the international financial institutions or banks.

The insistence on territorial integrity and border sanctity closes another historical pathway to state reconfiguration elsewhere: partial or total absorption of weak units by a more powerful neighbor. The Ethiopian attempt to acquire Eritrea by decolonization diplomacy ultimately failed; the Moroccan annexation of Western Sahara still lacks full international recognition. Consensual amalgamations at the moment of decolonization were accepted: British Somaliland and Somalia, anglophone Cameroon with its larger francophone neighbor, and British Togoland with Ghana, all legitimated by referendum or assembly vote. The only enduring postcolonial expansion by absorption of a smaller unit was the 1964 incorporation of Zanzibar by then-Tanganyika, which became Tanzania in the process. This territorial amalgamation occurred at a moment of political turmoil in Zanzibar and was supported by the incumbent island leadership; thus the African state system overlooked this transgression of its charter. Zanzibar was granted disproportionate standing in the central institutions; elements on both the island and the mainland periodically question the union even yet.

Another illuminating example of the impracticality of state expansion by incorporation is found in the failed confederation of Senegal and Gambia from 1982 to 1989. Political disorder in Gambia triggered Senegalese army intervention in 1981, and the confederation scheme was designed to bring the Gambian microstate, entirely surrounded by Senegal, under the protective cover of a more powerful state and to facilitate economic ties. Gambia however proved a troublesome and indigestible junior partner; Senegal unilaterally ended the confederation. The failed Senegal-Gambia union, taken together with the periodic tensions in the Tanzania conglomeration and the stubborn tenacity of Zanzibar particularism, illustrates what might be termed the East Timor syndrome: the intractable difficulties in securing a compliant acceptance of the new territorial identity that was proposed by Indonesia when the former Portuguese territory was forcibly seized at the moment of collapse of Lisbon imperial will in 1974–75. After enduring a prolonged and costly insurgency, Indonesia was compelled by international pressure to abandon its annexation. Though historically powerful states pursued territorial expansion projects with sublime confidence in their capacity to absorb new populations, within the contemporary ideological, social, and communications environment, acquisition of new territory and unwilling subjects guarantees endless costs and few benefits.

The persistence of African states then finds powerful reinforcement in the jurisprudential doctrines underlying the international system. The most important such precept is the doctrine of sovereignty, whose crucial role as an attribute of statehood is underlined in chapter 2. The weakened condition of many African countries illuminates the gap between the extraordinary reach of sovereignty as concept (absolute and unitary in the eyes of international law) and the real capacity of states to project power internally. Robert Jackson in an influential work suggests that many African (and other third-world) polities are mere "territorial jurisdictions supported from above by international law and international aid. . . . In short, they often appear to be juridical more than empirical entities: hence quasi-states."[19] Quasi states or not, they enjoy the blessing of internationally recognized sovereignty, whose inertial force acts as agent of reproduction of the existing roster of state units.

A second major factor driving the embrace of the colonial partition as the basis for the postcolonial state system, in spite of the artificiality and historical illegitimacy of the territorial entities thus created, is the absence of any viable alternative. Nyerere famously declared that "precisely because African boundaries were so absurd, it was essential to maintain them."[20] Though reworking the state system as a solution to the travails of Africa has at times been suggested by academics, none provide a persuasive formula.[21] Ethnonationalism might serve as basis for revamped states in the former Soviet Union or Yugoslavia, but cultural geography in Africa is far too complex and interpenetrated for this to serve, and the political implications remain much too explosive. Nor is a multiplication of micropolities an appealing option, either to the world state system or within Africa. Initiatives to form larger regional units exist (for example, the commitment of Tanzania, Kenya, Uganda, Rwanda, and Burundi to establish a federation by 2015), but bigger states such as Sudan, Congo-Kinshasa, and Nigeria have faced some of the most intractable difficulties in governance. Thus there is no audible African conversation about a reconfigured cartography, leaving reproduction of the extant polities the likely outcome absent some drastic precipitating circumstances beyond the ken of contemporary imagination.

A third explanation, redolent of rational choice theory, situates the explanation in the shared interest of political elites in preserving extant polities on whose rents they rely for their livelihoods. Through mechanisms termed "reciprocal assimilation of elites" by Bayart and "hegemonial exchange" by Rothchild leaders resolve their own differences by summit transactions assuring minimally satisfying access to state resources by regional barons and factional big men.[22] Even those in a dissident role are acutely conscious of the high risks associated with espousing separation; externally, the international system will provide neither succor nor hope of recognition, while internally such a step exposes those participating to the capital charge of treason. Reno takes the argument a step further in suggesting that even where warlord politics prevail, the preservation of a shadow state is indispensable to give the cover of international sovereignty to the predatory operations of militia leaders.[23]

In short, the elite interest thesis explaining state persistence argues that the diffusion of neopatrimonial modes of state management that gained momentum in the 1970s normally operates to assure servings of the "national cake" to enough regional elites to guarantee continuity of the polity. In a large country like Nigeria that is home to intense ethnic and religious contestation, elites recognize that without access to the Niger delta oil revenues controlled by the center, their prosperity would vanish. In Congo-Kinshasa, whose endowment is more scattered, regional elites in the resource-bearing areas of Katanga, Kasai, and Kivu are better able to profit from this bounty under the cover of an enfeebled sovereignty than from within a new state, given the international uncertainties that a secession effort might bring.

Englebert takes this line of argument several important steps farther in teasing out the full implications of the doctrine of sovereignty in its local applications. External sovereignty derives from the international system; internally it confers a monopoly of legal command. In everyday terms, even when the central capacities of the state are impaired, the many local agents who operate in its name even in failed states continue to benefit from the fragments of sovereignty operative at the ground level. The pervasiveness of regulatory activity undertaken under the cover of legal command, particularly in urban settings, continues even if few if any services are provided. As Englebert suggests: "Survival is not infrequently predicated upon following procedures. There appears to be, for example, an endless series of circumstances when one will need a birth certificate or some evidence of nationality, including enrollment in school, matrimony, voter registration, or starting a business. These documents will have to be obtained at some agencies of the state and produced to some other agencies as evidence of one's status. If nothing else, the ubiquity of police and military roadblocks puts a significant premium on the necessity of official documents."[24]

Possession of the ubiquitous official stamp validating such documents is a valuable asset. Theodore Trefon, in an engaging study of administrative process in Lubumbashi in Congo-Kinshasa notes the handicaps facing local agents: they have no resources, phones, computers, office material; they oscillate between predation and constraint yet at the same time are empowered by the shards of delegated sovereign legal authority embodied in the official stamp.

Even external providers—NGOs, aid agencies—can only operate through the local state apparatus.[25]

Thus regardless whether the rule of law is circumscribed, its commands can be a useful instrument in interpersonal conflict. One option available, widely used in Lubumbashi and vividly documented by a Congolese sociologist who served as participant-observer in a police station for a week, is denunciation of an adversary to the police, which can result in the incarceration of the victim. Once jailed, a complex interplay of police, judges, and litigants comes into play; money inevitably changes hands, and usually the victim reemerges, poorer for the episode.[26]

The pertinence of the Englebert argument is reinforced by the fact that even rebel forces clothe themselves in the appropriated local sovereignty of the state by establishing their own tax collection mechanisms and document enforcement practices in the name of laws and regulations inherited from the ousted administration, notably by levying "customs" on the illicit export of seized resources. The rebel militia commanders rely on a predation dependent on the borrowed sovereign command of the state. Beyond "hegemonial exchange," counterhegemonial appropriation of state attributes also operates to preserve at least the fiction of a persisting state.

Territorial Nationalism

The preceding explanations all have substantial validity, and Englebert makes a noteworthy contribution to the debate. Yet taken together they do not fully explain why African citizenries remain attached to an idea of an imagined nation, even if the state that enshrouds itself in this vision has lost most of its legitimacy and barely functions. In the final analysis, African states persist because most of their populations want them to do so, and they will nor hear the few voices proposing their fragmentation. Not only is the discourse of the nation firmly assimilated into elite discourse but a perhaps diffuse attachment to the extant territorial frame has become an unreflected everyday part of the lifeworld of the mass of the population. The political language that describes this orientation is grounded in the global doctrine of nationalism. Thus, while acknowledging its specific contours in the African setting, one must perforce identify this phenomenon as territorial nationalism, an indispensable element in unraveling the puzzle of state persistence.

Congo-Kinshasa is an illuminating point of departure. Though the deliquescence of the polity was overwhelming by the early 1990s, and a civil war originating in 1996 continues episodically to this day, few voices have been raised contesting the preservation of a Congo. Lifelong Congo specialist Herbert Weiss and a collaborator provide persuasive evidence that "the identification of the Congolese with the Congolese nation over the last forty years has become stronger, despite predatory leaders, years of war and political fragmentation, devastating poverty, ethnic and linguistic diversity, and the virtual collapse of state services."[27] This conclusion is buttressed by survey data collected in 2002 in five cities scattered around the country (Kinshasa, Kikwit, Gemena, Goma, and Lubumbashi). Overwhelming majorities agreed with the statement that "the Congo must remain unified, even if the use of force is necessary to achieve this" and that "the unity of the Congo is more important than the interests of any particular group or ethnicity."[28] Most Congolese believe that the long and predatory rule of Mobutu Sese Seko, however destructive to state institutions and economic well-being, had one merit: its nation-building effect. In a series of Afrobarometer surveys in ten democratic African states in the late 1990s and early 2000s, 94% agreed with similar statements, demonstrating a level of national attachment exceeding that of any other region (Latin America came in second with 91%).[29] Francis Deng, a leading southern Sudanese scholar, reports that in surveys he directed in the early 2000s, as many as 47% of southerners interviewed likewise agreed with such a statement, suggesting that the late SPLM leader John Garang was not alone in seeking a formula for salvaging a single Sudan.[30]

Another measure of this territorial attachment is the insistence of all Congolese insurgent groups on the notion that is reflected in their choosing names for their parties that invoke the nation, for example, Alliance démocratique pour la libération du Congo, Rassemblement congolais pour la démocratie, and Mouvement pour la libération du Congo, even though their original following was distinctly regional. Even more striking is the nomenclature of a pair of rebel militias locking in a bloody battle for control of the northeastern city of Bunia in 1999 and the years following, that resulted in fifty-thousand casualties. Although each party represented an ethnic contender for urban dominance, both concealed their communal projects under names proclaiming a fidelity to nation: the Union des patriotes congolais (Hema) and the Front des nationalistes intégrationistes (Lendu). This contrasts with the independence elections in 1960, when any number of parties adopted without hesitation ethnic labels (Alliance des Bakongo, Balubakat, Union des Mongo).

The same pattern holds true elsewhere. In the African civil wars of the 1990s, virtually all contenders, even those in Sudan, relied on such nomenclature: the Sudan People's Liberation Movement led the second southern revolt. The main Darfur rebel movements bear the names of Sudan Liberation Movement and Justice and Equality Movement. The Revolutionary United Front in Sierra Leone, the National Patriotic Front of Liberia, the Forces nouvelles of Ivory Coast, the diverse fragments in Somalia all follow the same mode. The major exception is the Mouvement des forces démocratiques de Casamance in Senegal, initially a rare explicitly separatist (Diola) uprising.

These illustrations of the vitality of territorial attachments suggest the need to seek their origins in a now globalized doctrine of nationalism and its importation into Africa. "Nation" as one of the defining attributes of the state was introduced in chapter 2. Metaphorically, it transforms the state from an arid abstraction, whose corporeal representation is found in the institutions of rule, into a living organism embodying its human population. Students of nationalism agree that the ideology took form in Europe, and most date its visible emergence to the French Revolution.[31] In its initial forms, the idea of the nation was intertwined with the cultural personality of its core ethnic group. With few exceptions, across the Eurasian land mass from Ireland to Japan nations are defined in name and content in terms of their dominant ethnonational group. When by the nineteenth century "nation" rather than dynasty identified a country, populations transformed from subjects of the king into a "people." The people in turn, through the alchemy of the doctrine of popular sovereignty, became the nation as wellspring of state legitimation.[32]

The idea of nationalism then diffused throughout the world, mutating in form to respond to particular circumstances: it yielded the doctrine of unification for the principalities of Italy and Germany, and it brought explosive challenges for the three vast multinational empires, the Russian, Austro-Hungarian, and Ottoman. In Japan, China, and Thailand, ruling groups seized on nationalism as a doctrine of self-strengthening to resist imperial expansion. In the Western hemisphere, populations immigrated from the imperial centers but required a script of difference to justify revolt; this they found in territorially grounded ideals of liberty, though they simultaneously denied such rights to slave and indigenous populations. Civic political values also became defining elements in some versions of nationalism: secular republicanism in France, parliamentary rule in United Kingdom, constitutional federalism in the United States.[33] These liberal or civic forms of nationalism gave rise to distinctions contrasting these virtuous forms and the more pathological ethnic nationalisms of Eastern Europe.[34] But in all the early versions of nationalist ideology a project of homogenization lurked: the premise of the nation as one and indivisible.

Nationalism as global force thus evolved as a potent yet protean construct; it had varying content and took divergent pathways, and the valence of its symbolic resources differed from one country to the next. For Africa, the crucial genetic adaptation of the idea of nationalism was its fusion with anticolonial revolt in tandem with its embrace of the doctrine of self-determination. Initially in the Americas, then in Asia and the Middle East, and finally in Africa, independence struggle assimilated the idea of nationalism as its doctrinal foundation. In the process inhabitants of a colonial territory became a people.

The colonial state never invested resources in fostering such an outcome, offering only a subordinate role in imperial administration to the educated African; indeed, the French and Portuguese sought with some success to inculcate the metropolitan identity by promising assimilation to schooled Africans who adopted the cultural repertoire of the colonizer. In the French case, such a prospect held attraction for elements of the elite until late in the colonial period. In the late 1930s, subsequent Algerian nationalist leader Ferhat Abbas could still write, "If I had encountered the Algerian nation, I would be a nationalist, and, as such, have nothing to be ashamed of. Men who have died for a patriotic ideal are honored and respected every day. . . . And yet I will not die for the Algerian fatherland, for this fatherland does not exist. I have not encountered it. I have questioned history. I have questioned the living and the dead. I have visited the cemeteries. No one has spoken to me of such a thing."[35]

In the sub-Saharan territories under French rule, some form of federated autonomy within a French ensemble was still the ostensible objective of much of the political leadership as late as 1958. A British Colonial Office document in 1944 noted that with growing contacts and travel educated Africans had "a dawning realization of themselves as Africans, even as 'nationals' of a territory."[36] But even in 1947, leading Nigerian politician Obafemi Awolowo could famously declare, "Nigeria is not a nation. It is a mere geographic expression."[37]

However, the accelerating dynamic of decolonization forced the African nationalist into the territorial compartment. When the campaign for liberation succeeded more quickly than most anticipated, the colonial territory became sovereign state. The colonial occupant as negative focus for mobilization receded into the background, and the legitimation of the newly conquered institutions of rule became paramount. Appropriation of a territorial interpretation of the idea of nationalism was critical to consolidation of the rule of the postcolonial successor elites: in a word, nation-building became a critical project.

The now universalized international state system had come to rest on a premise that its individual components were "nations." In everyday language, "state" and "nation" were interchangeable terms. If states fell short of corresponding to a recognizable version of nationhood, then they were summoned to improve themselves. African states thus required nation-building not only for internal legitimation but also for international respectability.

In the classical definitions, the original "nations" were based on such shared attributes as culture, language, ancestry, history, myths, narrative, memory, territory, or religion. Around these symbolic resources, the pioneers of nationalist ideology erected a dogma of commanding emotive resonance. In its fullest forms, the nation claimed the supreme loyalty of its subjects, obligating them to fight, even die, in its defense. In his classic study of Afro-Asian nationalism, Rupert Emerson writes: "In the contemporary world the nation is for great portions of mankind the community with which men most intensely and fervently identify, even to the extent of being prepared to lay down their lives for it, however deeply they may differ among themselves on other issues."[38] As nationalism became a global export, not all the original constitutive elements were available, yet the idea proved amenable to different circumstances. The crystallizing global premise that states should be nations fostered its diffusion. Once assimilated, "nation" transformed the arid, juridical state into a warm, living collective person. Through the alchemy of the nation, civil society acquired a vocation of unity.

In the African adaptations of nationalism, many of the raw materials were not available. A deep historical narrative is found only in three states: Morocco, Egypt, and Ethiopia. Neither shared culture nor language could play the same role as they did in polities lacking relative ethnonational homogeneity, found only in the Arab states, Somalia, and a few of the smaller polities (Cape Verde, Sao Tome and Principe, Comoros, Lesotho, Botswana, and Swaziland). Nor was religion necessarily a useful component. Religious diversity was the most frequent pattern; even in the overwhelmingly Muslim states of northern Africa, divisive understandings of Islam make it a problematic defining element of the nation. Thus territorial identity itself became the primary component, erected with few exceptions on a shallow historical narrative, recent shared memories, and a limited repertoire of common icons: major episodes of resistance to colonial occupation, the anticolonial struggle, epic political leaders like Nkrumah, Senghor, Nyerere, or Bourguiba for some, unique historical events such as the national conferences for others.

Acutely conscious of the potential fragility of their polities, the postcolonial leadership resolutely embarked on the path of nation-building. The pedagogical resources available the state for such purposes are considerable; Africa in part merely retraced a path followed in the heartlands of older nationalisms. Eugen Weber persuasively demonstrates that even in the French cradleland of nationalism, a consciousness of French national identity was far from permeating peasant consciousness even in the late nineteenth century. Deliberate nation-building by the center was central to its diffusion; the prime instruments were the republican schoolhouse and universal military conscription.[39] The oft-cited adage of the founders of the Italian state could apply to many others: "We have created Italy; now we must create Italians." One may cite as well the place of the common school in the United States in fostering the assimilation of successive generations of immigrants. These ventures in national construction were grounded on the premise of homogenization; the modern nation required for its collective purposes a standardization of culture and a common idiom.

However, in a crucial respect creating Nigerians or Congolese differed from fabricating Italians, French, or Americans: for most countries outside the Arab north, homogenization was not just problematic but downright perilous. Some small island polities enjoyed a creolized homogeneity, but most were multiethnic. Only five countries bear the name of a preponderant group or, in erstwhile Soviet parlance, a "titular nationality" (Botswana, Lesotho, Swaziland, Somalia, Comoros).[40] Most African versions of nation-building needed to project cultural neutrality, a territorial consciousness devoid of ethnic referents, and so avoid drawing on the extensive cultural resources of a nation-forming group. And African states did have at their disposal a number of resources to achieve this purpose.

The celebration of the liberation movement is one such resource, often personified by the leader of the independence movement. Armed liberation movements provided a particularly compelling script, when they were unified and effective. The iconography derived from the dramaturgy of struggle is well illustrated by the obelisk and statue of the unknown liberation fighter in Namibia at Heroes' Acre in Windhoek.[41]

Everywhere in Africa, school systems were rapidly expanded after independence. Curriculums were reformed in the name of "Africanization," although its real content was territorialization. School systems once largely the domain of missions were often nationalized or at least brought under closer supervision of education ministries, who prescribed the curriculum and texts. The schoolhouse assiduously promoted an attachment to the new nation. Its buildings were adorned with national symbols: flags, maps, portraits of the national leader. Daily routines included rituals of national affiliation, such as singing the newly created national anthems. Even after the early years, the national language (usually the former colonial tongue) was the medium of instruction. The educational system was an important instrument in the construction of national attachments.

Seemingly banal symbolic resources also operated. The iconography of currency, stamps, and flags communicated a silent message of state presence. The ubiquitous presidential portraits decorated the walls of government buildings, and even shopkeepers found it imprudent to fail to display the official photograph. Uniformed state personnel were widely visible. Many enterprises bore the country designation: airlines and many parastatals. Most countries had obligatory identity cards of government issue; travelers had to have passports. Thus placed in the citizen's pocket, the state could hardly fail to also find a way to his or her head.

The nation is also present in many domains of popular culture. International matches of the national soccer team attract intense excitement, especially the global competitions of the World Cup or its African counterparts. The movie *Invictus* captures the role of rugby as a reinforcing emblem of a multiracial South African nation in a world competition. In symbolic terms, the national team performs a ritualized, regulated limited war against the external other, capturing as a surrogate collective self, in the process, the mobilized identity of the citizenry. A symbolic pedagogy is found in various other cultural domains: local films, street literature, such territorially specific art forms as Congolese urban popular painting or Senegalese glass paintings. Distinctive genres of urban popular music are likewise subliminal registers of national identity.

Even though the territorial nation has shallow historical roots, there has been a gradual accretion of memory now for more than a century. No living person can remember a different territorial frame. Successive sedimentary layers of shared experience enter historical recollection. The territory becomes the location for social memory and for recording the major events defining the past. As such, at an unconscious level it becomes an assumed, unreflected identification, or what Michael Billig perceptively terms banal nationalism: "In so many little ways the citizenry are reminded of their national place in the world of nations. However, this reminding is so familiar, so continual, that it is not consciously registered as reminding. The metonymic image of banal nationalism is not a flag which is consciously waved with fervent passion; it is the flag hanging unnoticed in the public building."[42]

The African project of nationhood is usually compelled to differentiate itself from ethnicity. At first, leaders normally assumed that ethnicity was an artefact of a traditional worldview and that the relentless march of modernity would reduce its importance. For example, Guinean leader Sékou Touré declared at the time of independence that "in three or four years, no one will remember the tribal, ethnic or religious rivalries which, in the recent past, caused so much damage to our country and its population."[43]

Such illusions did not long survive, but the nation-building project generally did succeed in representing territorial nationalism as a higher form of identity distinct from ethnicity, existing on a different identity track. Ethnicity was deemed legitimate within a purely cultural and private kinship realm but not as a discourse of statehood. In the linguistic realm, sub-Saharan states invariably retained the language of the colonizer as official medium. In the unusual cases in which a single lingua franca had currency throughout the territory (most notably Tanzania), it could assume the role of state language, but elsewhere the linguistic distancing that came with adopting the colonizer's language as the official language insulated the nation from having to identify with its largest groups. The corresponding cost was identification of the state with a medium that a number of citizens could not speak.

Nonetheless, the exceptional place of multilingualism in African societies provides an important support for territorial nationalism. The widespread pattern described by David Laitin of a three-layered linguistic universe, each with distinctive domains, diffuses the tensions often generated by language diversity elsewhere. Maternal language operates as medium for hearth and local community. A regional lingua franca, now spoken by most, facilitates urban and marketplace communication. The European language operates as medium for government and high politics. The everyday reality of multilingualism inhibits the crystallization of aggressive forms of language ideologies.[44]

In the first decades, the single-party system of rule was another mechanism of state containment of ethnicity. Even after political opening in the 1990s, many countries retained a constitutional prohibition on party organization based on ethnicity or religion. Such rules could not entirely succeed, and in instances where a particular region or ethnic community was perceived as unduly dominating the state apparatus, groups sensing exclusion expressed their resentment, though generally without withdrawing their identification with the territorial nation.

In arguing the thesis that the internalization of a form of territorial identity among African citizenries partly explains state persistence, I do not wish to overstate its weight, force, or even its necessary permanence. In states afflicted with unending crisis and prolonged failure, a progressive detachment of the abandoned citizen from a territorial attachment is conceivable; whether the young men in Kivu will still dance the frontier ten years from now if there is no return to peace and security in eastern Congo-Kinshasa is uncertain. Indeed there is some recent evidence in that country of higher levels of ethnic or regional assertion in Katanga and the Kongo areas.[45] The recent reappearance of an Igbo separatist movement, MASSOB, discussed in chapter 7, is another symptom of potential restiveness, even though few Igbo view secession as a realistic possibility.[46] But, except for Sudan, there is no evidence of a widespread defection from the territorial nation as yet.

The territorial nationalism thus normalized has some limits. In terms of its emotional intensity, perhaps it falls short of the more assertive and deeply rooted versions of nationalism in the world such as the American, French, Japanese or Chinese forms that are equipped with vibrant historical narratives mostly lacking in Africa. We find little comparable to the 1389 "field of blackbirds" that served as a foundational mythology for Serbian nationalism, nor such lyrical historical epics like Nehru's *Discovery of India* that inspired Indian nationalism.[47] Rather than an active, aggressive consciousness, territorial nationalism is a more passive, unreflected attachment.

Englebert provides a more scathing indictment of the limits of African territorial nationalism: "While the paradoxical spread of nationalism in Africa is often perceived as one of the few notable achievements of African leaders, a closer look at some of its dimensions reveals a propensity for alienation that certainly rivals its unifying qualities. . . . Nationalists live a lie in Africa more than anywhere else. African elites relentlessly engineer nationalist sentiments to downplay the exogenous origins of their state, conceal the private nature of state theft, and remove exit from the politically thinkable. As such they sacralize colonial structures whose intrinsic absolutism and arbitrariness make for poor conduits for individual emancipation."[48]

One finds here the essence of the paradox of territorial nationalism in Africa; state and nation do not operate as elsewhere like interchangeable terms identifying the same entity. In a number of African states the predatory behavior of given regimes and their inability to provide elementary security or basic social provisions, as well as the marginalization of some regions, have left the legitimacy of the formal institutions of rule in tatters. But this delegitimation does not erase an attachment to the imagined community of the territorial nation, nor the hope that it may give birth to a reformed state. Some once dysfunctional failed states have recovered (for example, Ghana, Mozambique, Liberia, Sierra Leone, and Uganda). Absent any evidence that the total dissolution of a failed state would improve the prospects for its populace, there is benefit in its territorial survival in the hope of better days, so long as the citizenry retains any expectation that these may come.

THE THREE DIMENSIONS OF ETHNICITY

The third axis of identity in Africa is ethnicity, a far more variable and complex form of self-ascription than Africanism or nationalism. Ethnicity is intimately tied to high politics at the state level; both juxtaposed to and intertwined with territoriality, it operates as a cognitive screen through which political process and state action acquire social meaning. Contemporary patterns of ethnicity are in part a product of the categorizations employed by the colonial state. Ethnicity as political variable occupies a central place in postindependence state calculus, as well as that of political actors, and thus demands close scrutiny.

Ethnic and territorial maps of the continent do not overlap, yet the state system imposes bounded arenas within which active competition and cooperation occur. Africanism and territorial nationalism are relatively stable variables; ethnicity is a fluid and shifting identifier and signifier, producing changing patterns of affiliation and conflict. Its complexity is mirrored in the diverse modes of interpretation it has generated.

Ethnicity may be usefully understood as based on three dimensions.[49] First, it is based on a variable list of common attributes, usually including language, shared cultural practices and symbolic resources, belief in common ancestry, and historical narratives. Second, ethnicity is defined by the shared consciousness of belonging to a named group. Third, ethnicity presumes the "other"; such awareness rests on the boundary that demarcates the collective self from a visible outsider. Each of these aspects merits brief examination.[50]

The roster of common properties varies with the group and does not necessarily include all the factors I have cited. Language is usually but not always a marker. The shared speech code provides the basis for instant mutual recognition and intimate communication and the means by which we think about our existence and action; these qualities reinforce an awareness of difference from those speaking incomprehensible tongues. Especially when equipped with a written form, standardized with dictionaries and grammars and endowed with published literatures, language can become the focus of intense emotional attachments. Leading sociolinguist Joshua Fishman well captures this maximal form of linguistic identity: "The beloved language represents the moral order. It functions similarly to that order in ennobling human life and, in addition, it is co-constitutive of that order. . . . It is also, for some, the heart of morality itself."[51]

But ethnic identity does not necessarily require the contrast with an other who speaks a different language. The intense ethnic polarization and violence in Rwanda and Burundi is between groups sharing the same language (as, in reality, do Serbs and Croats). The widespread multilingualism in Africa dilutes the connection between language and identity, especially with the spread of regional affiliations based on a lingua franca. In Tanzania, for example, where Swahili has received strong government promotion as national medium, some groups are giving up their maternal language in favor of Swahili.[52]

Shared cultural practices include such elements as the mode of calculating kinship and descent (patrilineal, matrilineal, or bilateral), the customary prescriptions regarding marriage, and common culinary or sartorial practices. Ethnicity is subconsciously performed in the customs surrounding other aspects of everyday living. Localized understandings of the sacred and the supernatural are another bond. A shared culture gains added force when systemized in written form; the anthropologist, suggests Jean-Loup Amselle, "writes culture," providing it with an authoritative text.[53]

Historical narratives are potent foundations of identity. Myths of origin, eponymous ancestors, and chronicles of migration identify the group. The 1897 *History of the Yoruba* by churchman Samuel Johnson was foundational to the cultural unity of the Yoruba. At the turn of the twentieth century, the legendary Protestant Katikiro (prime minister of the Buganda kingdom), Sir Apolo Kagwa, published in Luganda a series of historical chronicles of the realm that served as a bible of identity; nearly a century later, Christopher Wrigley notes, copies of the Kagwa history of the kings of Buganda can still be found in most villages.[54]

Consciousness is a second defining feature. Collective awareness is necessary for a group to operate as a social entity. Often expressed in the language of kinship, brothers and sisters, consciousness is historicized as a theory of shared ancestry. Though descent may be molded to conform to contemporary social or ideological requirements, the mythology of ancestral origin retains its hold on the social imaginary. Deng cites the example of self-identified Arab populations in northern Sudan, who originate from small numbers of Arab migrants who crossed the Red Sea more than a millennium ago.[55] Intermingling with indigenous African women through marriage, Arab social dominance and patrilineal descent rules led over time to erasure of the African ancestry. Now enrooted in social consciousness is the firm belief in authentic Arab identity.

Boundaries are the third defining element of ethnicity. Awareness of the self as situated in an identity group assumes full meaning through knowledge that beyond a social boundary there exist different identity groups. Humans, argues Henri Tafjel, are inherently disposed to categorizations of the other.[56] Collective and individual consciousness is defined by who one is not, as well as who one is, an awareness reinforced by interactions at the frontier. Though the "other" may not be hostile, often they compete for the same resources or are suspected of seeking dominance. There is a tendency for stereotypical categorizations of groupings that extend beyond the social boundary to heighten the sense of otherness, often cast in negative terms.

Modes of Understanding of Ethnicity

In recent comparative analysis of cultural pluralism, a distinction is made between three interpretive modes: primordialism, instrumentalism, and constructivism.[57] The oldest and long ascendant frame was primordialism, which postulated ethnic identity as a timeless essence. This perspective gave rise to frequent explanations in the media of violent ethnic conflicts in Rwanda or former Yugoslavia as the product "ancient tribal hatreds"; as all-purpose explanation, such a theory dissolves on close historical inspection demonstrating the essential modernity of most ethnic violence.[58] For example, before World War II neither Hutu and Tutsi nor Serbs and Croats ever fought each other. But, still, the primordial dimension as an element in conceptual purchase over the ethnic phenomenon is too readily dismissed in some recent treatments. The continuing pertinence of this aspect of identity finds validation in the fact that most ethnic actors are instinctive primordialists, likely to behave as if ethnic consciousness did indeed existe outside of time and to be little disposed to interrogating its origins.

The second mode of interpretation, instrumentalism, became salient in analysis in the 1970s but acquired the name only in the 1980s.[59] This approach perceives ethnicity as a political variable that assumes importance as a weapon in the competitive pursuit of material advantage and the struggle for power. The instrumentalist perspective finds expression in the representation of politics as "slicing the national cake," a metaphorical image originating in Nigeria but now encountered elsewhere. Power in Africa, as Michael Schatzberg observes, "has much to do with 'eating' (and other forms of consumption.)"[60] The "national cake" metaphor raises the ante of the imagery by its focus on the most delicious part of the meal. The state and its revenues, in this imaginative metamorphosis, assume the form and properties of a cake, divisible by slicing and whose consumers are ethnic groups. The relative size of the shares is clearly visible. Those groups receiving disappointingly small portions look with angry envy at their rivals whose plates are heaped with outsized, icing-laden slices. The competitive clamor for equitable slices directs attention to the hand that holds the knife; the presumption on all sides is that the ethnic preferences and affiliation of the slicer will influence the relative shares.

Reflection on the national cake metaphor as a representation of state political process directs our attention to the competitive nature of ethnic politics, and its two key dimensions, domination and distribution. What fuels ethnic competition is the ambition to maximize group returns. The political realm is determinant, and the outcomes are shaped by the relative power position of the ethnic contenders. Dominance in state institutions guarantees the safeguard of the material interests of the ethnic community thus situated. In turn, mobilization of ethnic solidarity is a necessary strategy, both to have instrumental effect and to overcome the "free rider" problem: the disposition of some to remain aloof from group action because they anticipate sharing the benefits even if they do not participate. The visibility of ethnic group membership facilitates leadership monitoring and enforcement of the obligations of solidarity.

Instrumentalist understandings of ethnicity are particularly applicable in settings that activate group consciousness. Competitive elections in which competing parties take on ethnic coloration are one such setting; the dramaturgy of the process is inherent to the election mechanism, with its ritualization of combat, gradual intensification of the emotional engagement of the audience, and the disposition in the late stages to elevate the perceived stakes in the outcome. The outbreak of violent conflict raises the stakes in a different way if social understanding interprets the fighting as defined by ethnic lines; acute security dilemmas then arise, driving ethnic actors into the protective shelter of communal solidarity.

The speed with which instrumentalist perspectives dethroned primordialism invites explanation. As independence approached, one could hardly fail to hear the ethnic voices framing the emergent political competition for power and material advantage. Furthermore, the instrumentalist premise offered a bridge for ethnicity to two influential paradigms, Marxism and rational choice theory. Once removed from the domains of culture and psychology and situated in a materialist realm, currents of Marxist theory could acknowledge ethnicity as a "real" but misguided substitute for class consciousness. For the rational choice theorist, the logic of politics grounded in the choices of the self-interested, rationally calculating individual could be extended to the group. In the words of one of its leading practitioners, Russell Hardin, in ethnic competition "self-interest can often successfully be matched with group interest."[61]

A third analytical orientation that took form in the 1980s came to be known as "constructivism." A Ugandan pastor in a 1992 Christmas address in Biguku parish gave unwitting summary to the central premise of constructivism in prosaic terms; "God," he pointed out, "has not created all these ethnicities. God created a single person. People created ethnicity later."

To some extent, constructivism arose out of instrumentalism. If, as the instrumentalism suggested, ethnicity was situational and contingent on immediate circumstances for its activation and saliency, then one might benefit from seeking out its origins and sources. If ethnicity were in its essence circumstantial, some doubt would be cast on the premises of primordialism. A particularly influential work charting this analytical path is Benedict Anderson's classic *Imagined Communities*. Although he addresses nationalism, his reasoning applies equally to ethnicity. In directing attention to the macrohistorical processes that produced the invention of a nation for millions who could only envisage their membership through imagining its existence, Anderson calls for the exploration of the processes of formation of ethnic consciousness. If ethnicity is indeed a collective human act of creative imagination rather than a timeless essence, then important questions concerning its origins and evolution come to the fore. Constructivism adds to the situational and circumstantial stress of instrumentalism the view of ethnicity as contingent, fluctuating, and fragmented.

The search for the origins and historical construction of given ethnic identities quickly led to the colonial state. Its need for cost-effective modes of administrative organization gave rise to classification schemes, institutionalized through the census, that simplified the cultural landscape, making it more legible. Linguistically similar groups were amalgamated into a larger category. Missions faced with the urgency of translating the scriptures into local speech codes also needed an economy of categories. The promotion of literacy for evangelical purposes motivated the creation of a unified form for closely related dialects, producing in its wake a shared ethnonym. Administrators and anthropologists assiduously collected ethnographic information, similarly made more intelligible once it was situated in larger categories. Once an ethnic monograph was published, accessible to the schooled, its codification of custom fed back into oral libraries of self-knowledge. Academic identification of these cultural histories led to studies proclaiming the invention of ethnicity.[62]

Invention, however, is a misleading term; social construction requires vibrant cultural resources for its assembly. The focus on colonial codification likewise requires modification; African agency played an important part.[63] Colonial chiefs were frequently beneficiaries of enlarged ethnic domains and took part in their promotion. In emergent cities, ethnic associations helped overcome the quotidian challenges of death, marriage, employment, housing, and schooling. When political parties took form in the 1950s, they moved to take advantage of the vote banks such associations offered.

Constructivism became for a time a dominant interpretive voice, perhaps aided by a predisposing intellectual climate. A partial explanation lies in its distant kinship with the various currents of postmodernism arising in the 1980s, especially influential in anthropology, that privileged contingency and fragmentation of meaning in human agency. Also worth noting is the parallel appearance in international relations theory of an approach bearing the same name. Although the content of constructivist international relations approaches differ from that of studies of ethnicity, many of its assumptions and vocabulary are similar.

The momentary predominance of constructivist approaches quickly produced challengers. Their most compelling objection was that constructivism existed only in the eye of the conceptual beholder; the ethnic actor was an innate primordialist. In the words of one leading critic, Alexander Motyl, "Social constructionism is a social construction, that is, a social science concept 'imposed' on the non-self-consciously constructivist of people, who by and large do not believe themselves engaging in construction."[64]

Most contemporary analysis of cultural pluralism avoids exclusive allegiance to any one of these approaches. Seeking an understanding the tragic episodes of ethnic violence in Burundi and Rwanda that began in 1972 and reached a paroxysm of communal killings in 1993–94 in both countries illustrates the need to draw on all three perspectives. In the genocidal moments, these conflicts evoked such deep fears and anxieties that members of each group could only achieve a sense of security by demonizing the other and could only feel safe when among ethnic kin; journalists reporting these events invoked the "ancient tribal hatreds" thesis partly because those they interrogated on the ground spoke in such primordialist terms. In earlier moments of postcolonial politics, Tutsi-Hutu ethnic encounters more closely fit the instrumentalist perspective as a struggle over distribution and domination defined by ethnic consciousness. And an integral grasp of the cultural dynamics requires exploration of the nineteenth-century origins of Tutsi and Hutu as social categories, which hardened into primary identities under the impact of colonial and mission policies and then degenerated into what Jowitt termed "barricaded identities," "dogmatically and hysterically defined and defended."[65]

COMPLEXITY OF ETHNIC IDENTITY

Conceptual capture of the ethnic phenomenon requires consideration of two further dimensions: the inherent complexity of ethnic consciousness and its variant levels of intensity. Ethnic groups are not closed corporate communities, bouncing off each other like billiard balls; rather they are permeable at the margins and entangled with "the other" in numerous ways. Ethnic consciousness can vary widely in intensity, depending on the depth of cultural resources on which it draws and its degree of mobilization.

The enjoinder of the late Aidan Southall four decades ago bears repeating: "To hammer home the importance of interlocking, overlapping, multiple collective identities is one of the most important messages of social and cultural anthropology."[66] In the first place, ethnic consciousness is often multilayered. Somalia is an important case in point. An umbrella ethnonational identity is shared by nearly all inhabitants of Somalia and by ethnic Somalis in the neighboring states of Djibouti, Ethiopia, and Kenya, as well as by those in a swelling diaspora in the Middle East, Europe, and North America. The pan-Somali layer of identity rests upon a potent cultural ideology grounded in shared language with a recently standardized script, a rich literary heritage of oral poetry, a common religion, and legend of origin. But for most social purposes and political conflict alignments, the operative identity is located in a hierarchy of nested segments, extending downward from a half dozen clan families to clan, subclan, and lineage group through which ancestor descent is traced.

Another illuminating example is found in the Yoruba in Nigeria. Since the 1930s Yoruba cultural mobilization has weighed on Nigerian social dynamics and political process. Yoruba consciousness became salient in the nineteenth century when churchman Samuel Crowther used the Oyo regional dialect to unify the language, which was then diffused through the mission schools.[67] The mythology of an eponymous ancestor, Oduduwa, and a narrative of a primeval creation complete the cultural foundations. In recent times, Yoruba cultural organizations such as the Egbe Omo Oduduwa in the terminal colonial years and more recently Afiniferi and the more militant cultural organization Oodua People's Congress have fostered pan-Yoruba identity. Yoruba consciousness in the numerous diaspora is sustained by such religious cults as Candomble in Brazil and Santeria in Cuba. Yet within Nigeria the pan-Yoruba identity often comes second to ancestral town attachments, which frequently defines rivalries and competition.[68]

Another variant in the multilayering phenomenon arises in instances in which colonial ethnic classification schemes grouped together a number of related small groups under a new category. The label "Bantu Kavirondo" in Kenya was applied to a congeries of similar decentralized communities, later relabeled as Luhya. The larger label became naturalized, especially in the towns and national politics, though the smaller constituent identities remained the major identifiers in localized settings. A similar pattern is found among Kalenjin in Kenya and Mongo in Congo-Kinshasa. Among many other examples are Bamileke, a pivotal element in Cameroon politico-ethnic geography; Bayart captures their identity complexity: they are "a composite group from the point of view of their modes of political organization and language. They have diverse origins and offer a now classic example of ethnogenesis: Bamileke is a 'frontier' society . . . constructed by emigrants, or pioneers who came from various places."[69]

In urban areas, groups of closely related ethnic origin may amalgamate under a broader, even novel ethnonym. In Kinshasa, those migrating from the upper river and using Lingala as lingua franca became known as "Bangala," and over time internalized the ethnonym.[70] Across the river in Brazzaville, "Mbochi" is a comparable constructed entity, drawing together culturally similar migrants from the north around an ethnic category that in its rural homeland is very small.[71]

For many everyday social purposes, instrumentalization of identity requires a proximity more intimate than an ethnic category of millions. Membership in a more immediate kinship group or village community is more likely to facilitate access to administrative favor or material succor in moments of need than ethnic solidarity of the maximal group. In urban settings, innumerable hometown associations, burial groups, rotating credit clubs, or other such shared endeavors are based on a narrower affinity than the entire ethnic community. The lower layers of identity do not always compete with the summit ethnicity, and much less do they erase it. But they are frequently the bottom echelon of clientelistic networks, and they often form the basis for factional struggle.

Another form of identity layering occurs, especially in national political competition, in the alliances that form around a major lingua franca. Congo-Kinshasa has four such vehicular languages that have provided in large urban or national contexts an orienting identity: Kongo, Lingala, Luba, and Swahili. In the 2005 national elections, a clear pattern emerged in the outcome, with voting alignments largely shaped by the Lingala (west) versus Swahili (east) axis. Daniel Posner elegantly shows the impact of regional language-based political coalition building in the context of national politics in Zambia. Census orthodoxy dating from colonial state codifications lists seventy-three ethnic groups in Zambia. However, there are only four major languages (Bemba, Nyanja, Lozi and Tonga), each based in an identifiable ethnic community, but of regional currency for urban and other inter-ethnic utilization. The lingua franca serves as orienting frame for the indispensable ethnic coalition-building required by national level politics. However, in the contest for constituency choice of candidate, the seventy-three groups come back into play as fulcrum of competition.[72]

Significantly, the importance of territorial nationalism finds further illustration in the rareness of cross-border mobilization of identity. Transnational Arab identity and Somali irredentism are the most important exceptions. Transterritorial Kongo ethnic identity at first glance might appear another exception, but more striking is the subordination to territoriality of an identity narrative tracing its origin to a major fifteenth-century kingdom spanning contemporary Angola and the two Congos; its legendary conversion to Christianity, formal ties to the Vatican, and high stature in the early phases of Portuguese colonial expansion gave it unique prestige in Europe at the time. Although at the moment of decolonization there were some murmurs of revival of the old kingdom (as the first Congo-Brazzaville president Fulbert Youlou notably put it, "Tous ceux qui se ressemblent, se rassemblent" ("Those who resemble each other regroup together"), yet these nostalgic longings were swiftly submerged by the territorial politics of the two Congos and Angola. Another example is the separate political paths taken by Ewe, divided between Ghana and Togo; though at the time of decolonization, some voices called for group unification under a single sovereignty, Paul Nugent found that by the 1980s "informants strenuously identified with something called Ghana."[73]

William Miles persuasively shows the decisive impact of the international border dividing Hausaland between Niger and Nigeria, placing a large community sharing a common language and well-rooted historical consciousness into distinct sovereign jurisdictions. Differing colonial traditions and contrasting postcolonial experiences do not erase shared consciousness, but they do suppress any disposition to joint action. Even in the religious domain, Islamic theology has evolved along different paths. Though the border is porous and merely a line on the map often little visible on the ground, its effect is profound. Miles gives engaging summary of the paradox symbolized by the lonely boundary marker: "Incongruously, provocatively, it towers on high: a fifteen-foot metal pole, springing out of the dirty brown Sahelian sand. No other human artifact is to be seen in this vast, barren, flat savanna; only an occasional bush, a tenacious shrub, a spindly tree break upon the monotonous, infinite landscape. . . . But there it stands: a marker of an international boundary, a monument to the splitting of a people, a symbol of colonialism, an idol of 'national sovereignty.'"[74]

Indeed, boundaries at times create different ethnonyms for virtually identical groups. Konjo in Uganda are the same group as Nande in Congo-Kinshasa. Kiga in southwest Uganda are similar to those who became classified as Hutu in northern Rwanda.

Beyond national politics, the phenomenal growth of urban centers since World War II created critical arenas for social competition and identity construction; before 1940, few African towns exceeded one hundred thousand, but today such megacities as Kinshasa, Lagos, Abidjan, or Nairobi have many millions, and in many countries a third or more of the population is urban. The difficult struggle for livelihood is intensely competitive, creative of social solidarity needs and newly negotiated affinities with similar others within the kinship metaphor. In the recent years of deep economic crisis, those unemployed workers forced to retreat to the countryside face a different challenge: renegotiating their identities and relationships with their home communities. The difficulties of this task are well demonstrated by James Ferguson in the Zambia case.[75]

Communal identity is thus situational and multilayered. Many everyday social encounters are devoid of ethnic content, such as sharing a public conveyance or engaging in a marketplace transaction. The activation of ethnic consciousness requires a context in which an outcome is perceived as determined by communal motivations. Although this occurs with special visibility in electoral competition or appointments to high office, everyday experience provides other cues for ethnic response: for example, in selecting a local authority, in trying to gain access to school or employment, or in attempting to assert control over land.

VARIATIONS IN INTENSITY

Ethnicity varies widely in intensity. Some groups have sharply delineated cultural profiles; others have more diffuse identities that are less readily mobilized. To my mind, the most decisive factor differentiating levels of intensity of ethnic attachments relates to the bonding power of the cultural ideology defining the group. In turn, the living force of the ideology depends on the same constituent elements that define nationalism: above all language, shared culture, historical narrative.

The valence of language as ideological foundation depends heavily on its acquisition of a written form. In the contemporary world, purely oral languages risk eclipse and even erasure in the face of the spread of the lingua franca. The transcription of a language standardizes its usage and widens its currency, enabling its use in the school system. The compilation of dictionaries enriches its vocabulary and connects it to the broader linguistic universe by facilitating translation. The print medium opens the path for a published literature to become a cultural endowment that confers prestige on the group. Oral literatures can provide an important expressive role, illustrated by the legendary place of oral poetry in Somali culture, which until the 1970s lacked an agreed-on written form. But print literature takes cultural ideology a step further.

The shared culture also gains stature through its formal codification. Ethnography was long the primary domain of the anthropologist. Though its colonial phase was scorned by some as mere instrument of subjugation, the classic ethnic monographs were major sources of self-learning for the young generations of schooled Africans. Few of them were derogatory in tone; in translating the cultures they studied to the conceptual categories of the discipline, most anthropologists were engaging in a project of validating "their" people. Thus the ethnic monograph could serve as important source for construction of an ideology of collective self-worth. In urban settings, cultural associations proliferate, providing a forum for performance of and debate on the ethnic heritage as well as for the collection of materials related to it.

Another basis for cultural self-pride lies in exceptional success in social ascension. In colonial times, in a number of countries a particular ethnic group acquired the prestige of exceptional prowess in "modernization." Group mobility usually originated in precocious access to schooling or unusual entrepreneurial and commercial dispositions. Prominent examples include Igbo in Nigeria, Kasai Luba in Congo-Kinshasa, Chagga in Tanzania, and Bamileke in Cameroon. Strikingly, in each of these cases, colonizers in ambiguous admiration compared their talents for education and commerce to the stereotypical Jewish success narrative. The intensities of identity rested both in the internalized self-image of masters of modernity and in the fears aroused by the hostile envy of others. Such fears were well justified; Bamileke, writes Cameroonian scholar Jacques Kago Lele, "are marginalized, excluded from the society and rejected by the national community," even encountering calls for their extermination.[76] Igbo suffered pogroms in northern Nigeria in 1965, and Luba-Kasai were repeatedly expelled from Katanga.

Historical narrative is a crucial source for cultural construction. The rediscovery or embellishment of a glorious past energizes ethnic consciousness. Zulu ethnonationalism finds rich source material in the Shaka myth: the heroic tale of an all-conquering leader who transformed a minor chiefdom into a powerful state at the beginning of the nineteenth century.[77] Zulu warriors then inflicted one of the rare major defeats on a colonial army in 1879 in humiliating a British unit. Buganda ethnonationalism is erected on the narrative of a kingdom engaged in continual expansion in the nineteenth century that accepted British overrule in a treaty of near equals in 1900, contrasting sharply with the subordination through conquest of most other Ugandan groups. Buganda in colonial times enjoyed special status, and its institutions served as model for the rest of the country. Its remarkable cultural architects early in the colonial era, Sir Apolo Kagwa and Ham Mukasa, contributed to the narrative of a powerful kingdom with a rich history, Kagwa through his reconstruction of monarchical chronology, Mukasa through publication of collected proverbs attesting to the invincibility, strength, and terrifying power of the kabaka. The reigning kabaka at the time of independence, Mutesa II (ousted and exiled in 1966), wrote that "we were accepted as the most civilized and powerful of the kingdoms," whose "integrity and superiority" was "fully recognized" in the 1900 treaty with Britain.[78] The binding force of Zulu and Ganda historical narratives is reflected in the unusual salience of these identities in South African and Ugandan national politics.

Groups weakly endowed with an elaborated cultural ideology were likely to have less intensely expressed identities, especially groups that were small and peripheral to high politics. Those such as Karimojong in northeastern

Uganda, Turkana in northwestern Kenya, or the various small groups in southwestern Ethiopia have an ethnic consciousness that is less reflected in mobilized identities. If the group is isolated from the center of postcolonial politics and weakly represented among the intellectual elites, the possibility of it constructing a strong cultural ideology is circumscribed.

A cultural ideology in itself is merely raw political material. Its activation depends on agents I have in previous work characterized as cultural entrepreneurs and political brokers. The cultural entrepreneur performs the tasks of codification, self-study through membership in associations that group together dedicated intellectuals, and promotion. The political broker translates these identity-building materials into a competitive organizational weapon.[79]

John Lonsdale offers a further useful gloss on the contrast between identity as cultural resource and political weapon. Within the group, ethnicity defines a moral community, within which a matrix of social responsibility exists. Lonsdale calls this "moral ethnicity": the positive solidarity of a shared normative order that operates to assure a protective framework of disciplined and cooperative social interaction. As weapon in the struggle for national power and resources, ethnicity loses its moral force and becomes mere political tribalism, an instrument in a ruthless combat for power and pelf.[80]

A final dimension of variation of identity intensity inviting reflection is the interface with gender. There is some evidence that men and women experience and enact ethnicity differently. Given the near universality of patriarchal norms embedded in societal structure, one may ask whether the resulting asymmetries influence ethnic consciousness.

Triggering this interrogation is a thesis advanced in some recent feminist scholarship that nationalism (and by logical inference ethnicity) is inherently gendered.[81] The ideology of nationalism in its language and symbolism is masculinized by its salient references to conflict and warfare; its demands of exclusive loyalty reinforce the authority of usually male leadership. The woman is portrayed as protector of the home and producer of children to fill the nationalist ranks. In this perspective, nationalism becomes yet another strand in the fabric of patriarchy.

This logic is not entirely transposable to the language of ethnicity. But ethnic practice may well implicate gender inequality. The predominant patrilineal descent norm in much of Africa results in the social erasure of female ancestry. Most patrilineal ideologies assume endogamy in which men's lineal identity is fixed whereas women's is, by definition, fluid as she must cross lineage boundaries to marry and raise another lineage's children.[82] Various female disadvantages in land rights, inheritance, and property control are often claimed as cultural heritage. Vail makes a cogent argument of the consequences: "An emphasis on the need to control women and a stress on the protection of the integrity of the family came to be intrinsic to both ethnic ideologies and the actual institutional practices. . . . Ethnicity's appeal was strongest for men, then, and the Tswana proverb to the effect that 'women have no tribe' had a real—if unintended—element of truth."[83]

Surely it has an element of truth, but it is not the whole truth: evidently in highly polarized contexts, conflict situations will constrain men and women to ethnic choices in similar ways. Nonetheless Aili Tripp in her monograph on Ugandan women's associations offers compelling evidence that women are more successful than their male counterparts in sustaining cooperation across ethnic lines in their organizations.[84] Her findings received normative echo during the 1994 constitutional debates in a passionate denunciation by an outstanding woman leader, Wyinnma Banyema, of politics reduced to equitable ethnic shares in the proverbial "national cake": "I find discussion around sharing and eating the cake childish at the very least and irresponsible, selfish and parasitic at worst. . . . Values which we women care about such as caring, serving, building, reconciling, healing and sheer decency are becoming absent from our political culture. This eating is crude, self-centered, egoistic, shallow, narrow and ignorant[,] . . . a culture which we must denounce and do away with if we are to start a new nation."[85]

Arab identity is in a class of its own through its transterritorial spread, its intimate link with religion as a provider of a scriptural language for Islam, and its robust ideological formulation.[86] The historical link between Arabhood and Islam and the wave of Arab conquest and migration bringing the rapid early spread of Islam gave rise to a millennial process of incorporation of dominated populations that continues to this day. As the language of power and medium of religious observation, Arab identity had exceptional assimilative powers. Its boundaries have always been permeable, and most of those now proclaiming Arab identity in the Maghreb or Sudan are products of such an incorporative process. Only recently has the construction of competing identities—for example, various categories of Berber (Tamazigt) speakers in Algeria and Morocco—gained momentum. Since the nineteenth century, Arabhood has acquired added cultural resources through the appropriation of the idea of nationalism. As an ideology of pan-Arab territorial unification, the doctrine—powerful in the 1950 and 1960s—has, like pan-Africanism, fallen victim to territorialism, even though virtually all the present boundaries of the seventeen Arab states in the Middle East and Africa were drawn by an imperial hand. However, Arabhood is an integral component of the text of territorial nationalism in the half dozen majority Arab African states (Mauritania, Morocco, Algeria, Tunisia, and Libya), as well as Sudan, where the 1956 census counted only 39% self-ascribed Arabs but a substantial majority for whom Arabic was lingua franca. Arabic is also a major lingua franca in Chad and Eritrea, both of which have small ethnic Arab minorities. Although the dialectical variation is substantial, the uniformity of its classic sacred texts and the contemporary emergence of a modern standard Arabic widely used in the schools and media are unifying instruments. But only at the cultural and communicative levels: interstate rivalry and at times conflict between African Arab states is a constant, illustrated by the tussle between Algeria and Morocco over the status of Western Sahara that has been ongoing since 1976. A more banal example was the violence and verbal warfare between Egypt and Algeria in 2009 over a World Cup qualifying soccer match.[87]

ETHNIC GROUP VERSUS INDIVIDUAL ACTOR

Finally, in grasping ethnicity one needs to unravel the difference between group behavior and individual action. In the analysis of ethnicity, even in its vocabulary, the inarticulate major premise reigns that cultural communities behave as groups. At moments of peak mobilization such may be the case, but at most times actions or interests imputed to the group do not equally engage all its members. Indeed, the very term "ethnic group" can, on close inspection, be seen to have problematic aspects. The intensity of identification with a group varies among ethnic subjects. At any given moment, many may have immediate interests at variance with those articulated by group spokesmen. The multiple identity repertoires (occupation, gender, religion, residence, among many others) held by most individuals may mean that cross-cutting interests are at play. If performing ethnic solidarity carries social costs in a given setting, the actor may hesitate, perhaps with the secret hope of being a "free rider." Max Weber long ago suggested the necessary qualification to perceiving ethnic group as collective actor: "Ethnic membership does not constitute a group; it only facilitates group formation of any kind, particularly in the political sphere."[88]

In the final analysis, much social action occurs at the individual level; group behavior ultimately depends on large numbers making simultaneous identical choices. Through the conscious (or unconscious) performance of ethnicity by the actor, communal awareness achieves social visibility. Such performance can occur in a range of activities from participating in a group customary ritual to weighing marital choices, seeking employment, angling for a government favor, and voting in an election. In all these contexts, not all persons attach equal importance to ethnic solidarity; all competitive election studies show that even when ethnicity visibly textures the competing parties, the balloting does not completely align with communal divisions.[89] The multilayered nature of ethnicity enters the equation. So also does the possibility of multiple cultural identities, a product of intermarriage (fairly common in urban areas), migration, or the ambiguity of ethnic boundaries. An apt example is supplied by Jean Bazin in pointing to the multiplicity of identities at play within the Bambara category in Mali: "Misled by the reassuring rigor of the colonial taxonomies and their internalization as a form of knowledge widely shared within urban milieux and amongst educated elites in Mali today, one cannot imagine the extreme variety of those who in one way or another, according to the context, the conjuncture, and the point of view of the interlocutor, in the past or recently, have found themselves designated, inventoried, honored, feared, insulted, mistreated, exterminated under this name."[90]

While acknowledgment of the element of individual choice in performance of ethnicity is necessary, so also is recognition that the options may be constrained. Although ethnicity is in part the assertion of the individual, the actor also encounters the ascription of identity by others. When ethnicity is salient in the social landscape, one's actions may be interpreted by the other as ethnically motivated, whatever their intent. All persons are assumed to have an ethnic identity, usually known by those in socially proximate locations. Even if one aspires to ethnic anonymity, numerous cues are available to others to read ethnicity: name, language, visible social practices, dress, and sometimes facial scarifications. The ethnic attachment of major political figures is inevitably known to most, who readily attribute a communal orientation to parties or organizations they lead. Accordingly, the choices open to Africans in identity performances are far more constrained than the "ethnic options" Mary Waters engagingly explores for Euroamericans.[91]

States at first usually responded to newly politicized ethnicity by projects of containment. A central claim of the single-party system was its purported capacity to cage ethnicity within the obligatory structures of the national movement, thus eliminating incentives for ethnic mobilization. State managers preoccupied with hegemony and legimation imperatives publicly excoriated "tribalism" while privately deploying it in ramifying neopatrimonial apparatuses. Rather than being regarded as an integral dimension in the social and moral order, ethnicity was negatively viewed; it was seen as a sin especially practiced by others and as an obstacle to the territorial nation. In the era of single-party and military autocracies, ethnicity was banned from the public square, and ethnic associations were outlawed. Yet as state capacity shrank by the 1980s, ethnic solidarity became an important shelter for many. Banned but not erased, ethnic currents flowed just beneath the surface of patrimonial autocracy. They periodically broke through the surface in many countries; Nigeria and Kenya are notable examples of inflamed and public ethnic politics during this period.

The democratic moment around 1990 largely ended the illusion that even if it could not be eliminated, ethnicity could be at least confined within an underground private sphere. Around the world, national integration projects based on assimilative premises gave way to a realization that on close inspection most polities are culturally plural. The accommodation of diversity required its acknowledgment rather than denial and called for multicultural strategies that were adapted to the circumstances rather than single-track integrative doctrines.

Within Africa, ethnicity slowly became more respectable. African intellectuals who once equated "tribalism" with backwardness read the trends and reframed their discourse to accord legitimacy to ethnic solidarity. The late Claude Ake wrote for a generation in declaring that a genuine African democracy "will have to recognize nationalities, subnationalities, ethnic groups and communities as social formations that express freedom and self-realization and will have to grant them rights to cultural expression and political and economic participation."[92] Still, states and political leaders viewed ethnicity warily; Uganda president Yoweri Museveni wrote in 1997: "A leader should show the people that those who emphasize ethnicity are messengers of perpetual backwardness."[93] In most countries, laws regulating political parties proscribe the use of ethnicity or religion as a basis for organization.

Viewed comparatively, ethnicity in Africa stands out for its greater fluidity and less rigid self-conceptualizations. Its instrumentalist and constructivist dimensions are more salient, and its primordial aspects are less powerfully expressed than in major ethnonational formations in Europe or Asia. Indeed, most African ethnicity does not borrow the scripts of nationalism in its expression. The critical distinction between nationalism and ethnicity as ideologies of solidarity lies in the nature of the political claims arising from the identity. A fundamental precept of nationalism is the right to self-determination, the prerogative of creating an independent or at least highly autonomous political unit. Ethnic agendas point to cultural self-preservation and enhancement in social and economic spheres; members of the groups seek relative shares within a polity rather than separation from it.

Some versions of ethnicity verge on ethnonationalism: the Zulu and Buganda cases come to mind. In Nigeria in the last couple of decades ethnic claims have frequently been labeled "the national question." But only Ethiopia has reconstituted itself around the premise of ethnonationalism, reconfiguring itself into six ethnic provinces and three multiethnic ones without a single dominant group. To some extent, this ethnic federalism bears the imprint of imported Soviet nationality theory during the Afromarxist Mengistu regime (1974–91). More significantly, the main insurgent movements that drove out the Derg were (except for the Eritreans) ethnic armies. Thus constitutionalizing ethnonationalism with a theoretical right to self-determination and secession was a consequence of the dynamics of decay and demise of the Mengistu regime. The actual exercise of power remains highly centralized under the rule of Meles Zenawi, though in some domains, such as language policy, provincial autonomy may gradually deepen the "federal character" of Ethiopia; in addition, the Tigre leadership at the core of the state has eroded the Amharic cultural personality of the historic Ethiopian state.[94]

Indigeneity Battles

The era of at least nominal democratization introduced another new dimension to the ethnic phenomenon: intensified battles over citizenship and indigeneity. African citizenship legislation stands out for its tendency to imply that there is a necessary tier of ethnic membership by which a person gains automatic entitlement to nationality. Many constitutions stipulate membership in ethnic communities geographically present at the time of territorial creation as prerequisite for natural citizenship.[95] In a number of countries—notably Ivory Coast, Congo-Kinshasa, Kenya and Uganda—intense battles discussed in chapters 6 and 7 over rural land rights pitted immigrant or internal migrant cultivators against the home community. These violent contests spawned toxic doctrines of indigeneity: *ivoirité*, for example, in Ivory Coast. Indigeneity is claimed as exclusive basis for land rights and is invoked to question the legitimacy of the residence of "strangers" in the area.[96]

Doctrines of indigeneity appear in a different form in Nigeria, where residents of the 36 states and the 774 odd local government authorities claim exclusive entitlement to employment, contracts, services, and other facilities;

above all, they assert control over "their" areas. This precept of special entitlement for those indigenous to states and local government areas entered
juridical language in the 1979 constitution, as a component to the "federal
character" of the nation. Indigeneity doctrine and its discriminatory impact
on long-resident migrants has become a source of bitter dispute in many areas
and has led to several violent episodes in Jos, in which seven hundred were
killed in 2008 and then three hundred more in 2010. Its workings are summarized by Philip Ostien, who led an inquiry into the serious 2008 Jos violence:
"Administration of all [locally administered resources] is by a system of 'indigene certificates' issued by local governments. Access to indigene certificates
and the resources depending on them is directed primarily towards members
of the ethnic or subethnic group controlling the [local government]."[97]

CONCLUSIONS

In sum, the three master identities defining African polities—Africanism, territorial nationalism, and ethnicity—operate on different tracks.[98] Any potential conflict between pan-African and national loyalties was eliminated at the
outset of independence by the capture of pan-Africanism by the state system.
Territorial nationalism usually does not compete directly with ethnicity; in
contrast to what happens Europe, in Africa ethnic groups are never referred
to as "national minorities" juxtaposed to a titular nationality. Most Africans
perceive these identities as operating in separate spheres. Ethnicity has only
infrequently been framed as ethnonationalism; the prevalence of multilingualism lowers the temperature of language issues that are so volatile in India, Sri
Lanka, Turkey, Belgium or Canada.

All three of these overarching identities contain major ambiguities. The
evolution of pan-Africanism from the shared consciousness of the subordinated and victimized African to a more geographical and interstate cooperative sphere removes a good deal of its original emotional charge. But the
logic and value of the perennial quest for more effective pan-African institutions is rarely challenged. At another level, Africanism lives on in the cultural
personality of states. A subliminally racial African component to territorial
nationalism finds reflection in the ambivalence toward citizenship for those
immigrating from other continents.

Territorial nationalism has become embedded in the quotidian subcon-
scious of most Africans. Nothing else could fully explain the extraordinary
persistence of African states, even in circumstances of failure. This form of
nationalism doubtless remains limited in the depth of the attachments it can

command by its original sin of derivation from the colonial partition and its shallow historical narrative. But its enduring reality finds irrefutable proof in the insistence of nearly all warring parties in the many civil conflicts of the 1990s that they, like the young men in Kivu dancing the frontier, were defending the territorial nation.

The seeming simplicity of commonly accepted ethnic mappings dissolves on realization of their multiple layerings, permeability, and interpenetration, as well as their flux and contingency. Yet in the competitive struggle for relative shares in state institutions and resources, decolonization and postindependence politics politicized ethnic identities, particularly among the larger groups whose numbers amplified their voice. The changing situations of and interplay between regional, ethnic, and subgroup categories illuminate the premise that social construction never has a fixed end point.

Returning to the overall themes of this volume, I would suggest that analytical capture of these three pillars of identity are prerequisite to an overall understanding of the postcolonial state. The Africanism dimension is a constitutive element in the African state system through the superstructure of pan-African institutions. It also finds expression in the meaningful sense of affinity that transcends borders. The growth of an unreflected affective attachment to the originally artificial territorial containers assures an overall stability to the state system, irrespective of the dysfunctions of a number of its units. An adequate conceptualization of the complex phenomenon of ethnicity is essential to an informed reading of state political dynamics.

If one accepts that a healthy and functioning state, adapted to the evolving norms of the global state system, is an ineluctable element in a better future for Africa, then the counterintuitive naturalization of territorial nationalism is in my view a positive force. So is the reconciliation of state and ethnicity, which the growing acknowledgment that cultural pluralism is a natural condition, not unique to Africa, has led to. Though pan-Africanism has a far more limited role than in the dreams of its pioneers, its place as venue for interstate cooperation and joint action has value. The ambiguous triple identity helix of Africanism, nationalism, and ethnicity endures and continues to shape the political landscape.

9

The African Postcolonial State

Concluding Reflections

> By and large, the states of sub-Saharan Africa are failures.
>
> —Pierre Englebert, 2009

> There is no reason to downplay the progress that African
> countries have made in the past two decades under very difficult
> circumstances. The distance they have covered is considerable in
> many instances.
>
> —Goran Hyden, 2006

These contrasting conclusions capture the spectrum of perception of a half century of African independence. Both authors are distinguished scholars of African politics who have immersed themselves in researching a number of states over most of this period. The disparity in their positions reflects the complexity and contradictions of the African state in its postcolonial journey.[1]

Closely inspected, the evaluative disparity is less complete than the quotations might suggest. Englebert concedes that there are some exceptions to his stark indictment, though he finds the modal pattern to be one of states that are "parasitic or predatory" yet also "weak and dysfunctional." Hyden devotes a chapter to "the problematic state," which he defines as the state that has a far weaker hold on an elusive society and its informal moral economy than its counterparts in other regions.

Part of the divergence also lies in time perspective. Hyden restricts his point of reference to the last two decades. If one measures recent performance against the depth of the state decline in the 1980s, then a more optimistic reading of the postcolonial state is possible. Although several of the most derelict states have stagnated or even regressed, the condition of the majority of countries has improved. But a 1960 benchmark poses a sterner test.

From Developmental Disappointments
to Mixed Recovery

Beyond doubt, the African state failed to achieve the march to modernity that many hoped and mainstream development economists forecast when independence dawned. Although a leading textbook at the time ranked Africa's development potential well above East Asia, real per capita GDP did not grow over the 1960 to 1990 period; in East Asia and the Pacific, by contrast, there was a 5% per annum per capita increase,while in Latin America, there was 3% growth.[2] The level of disappointment finds measure in the Congo-Kinshasa case; its legendary resources appeared in 1960 to promise a bright future. Five decades later, a meticulous study of contemporary state rebuilding efforts concludes that, with stability and competent economic management, the population might regain the average level of 1960 well-being by 2030.[3]

Two decades ago, the verdict of failure was well-nigh universal; the very concept of "state failure" derived from the predicament facing most African states at the time. The striking diversity of state itineraries since 1990 produces a variety of outcomes in terms of political form, developmental performance, and quality of governance, ranging from the relatively positive in Ghana, Namibia, or Tanzania to the anarchy of Somalia. Overall, in economic terms, prospects seemed somewhat improved. Since 2000, African economies have fared better than any time since the 1960s. In 2008, the IMF forecast that sub-Saharan African economic growth would slow to 6% after several years of a higher figure; though the global recession undermined this estimate, African countries fared better in resisting the crisis than advanced economies.[4] Although a semiauthoritarian drift has gained momentum in recent years, the political opening produced by the 1990s democratization surge is far from being erased.

There remains an underlying volatility to African politics that requires acknowledgment in anyone's overall conclusions. Zimbabwe in 1997 ranked high on most criteria of effective governance; from that point forward, the situation deteriorated, rapidly from 2000, relegating the country for a time to the failed-state category. The political alternation in Kenya produced by the 2002 elections brought hopes of a renovated polity cleansed of the culture of corruption and impunity, a dream tarnished by the growing evidence that only the beneficiaries changed and dashed by the ethnic violence triggered by the disputed 2007 balloting.[5] Madagascar was the first state to qualify for the American Millenium Challenge Grants, a reward earned by competent and democratic governance. By 2009, the model performance had been compromised by the spectacle of a proliferating mercantile empire accumulated by President Marc Ravolamanana.[6] The sudden 2009 overthrow of the constitutional order by a thirty-three-year-old mayor of Antananarivo, Andry Rajoelina, unhinged politics, cut off access to most foreign aid, and isolated the country. Most dramatic of all, three game-changing events in 2011 altered the African political landscape: the "Arab spring" and the overthrow of seemingly impregnable long-ruling autocrats by street action in Tunisia and Egypt; the ouster by international action of rulers in Ivory Coast and Libya, supporting internal insurgent challenge to Laurent Gbagbo's usurpation and the Muammar Qadhafy's forty-two-year dictatorship; and the first successful secession in South Sudan after more than three decades of armed revolt. Equally unexpected was the 2012 military intervention in Mali, ousting a seemingly democratic regime and accompanied by rebel occupation of the north.

Not all African polities are subject to this degree of volatility. Indeed, there has been a striking stability of political orders in the southern portions of the continent (except for Zimbabwe), as well as the small offshore island states (save for Comoros). Elsewhere, a substantial number of countries that may have known episodes of turbulence have had stable if perhaps only semidemocratic regimes over an extended period: Ghana, Senegal, Benin, Tanzania, and Mozambique come to mind. Still, my concluding reflections are tempered both by the divergent pathways of the last two decades and the possibility of abrupt change in any individual case.

In the closing subjective observations that follow, I focus only on the segment of the total picture that has been the subject of this volume: state politics, pathways, and performance, especially those dimensions that have been at the center of my previous work. By extracting this dimension both from the international domain of a globalizing world in which Africa occupies a subordinated position and the complex sociopolitical processes of ground-level life I necessarily offer only a selective and partial portrait.

COLONIAL STATE LEGACY

The first question that arises is the extent to which postcolonial politics are shaped by the legacy of the colonial state. In 1994, I wrote in *The African Colonial State in Comparative Perspective* that "a genetic code for the new states of Africa was already imprinted on its embryo within the womb of the African colonial state."[7] The essence of the legacy was what Achille Mbembe termed the *principe autoritaire*: the arbitrary discipline of the subject by a state that "aspires to the exercise of a symbolic hegemony over indigenous societies signified by its claim to a monopoly of legitimate vision" and that incorporates into that exercise of power a vocation of "modernizing the nation and civilizing the society."[8] The developmental ideology assimilated into reason of state in the final colonial period and given new urgency by the successor elites appeared to require a command government staffed by an educated ruling caste convinced of its superior knowledge. New political superstructure directed by the triumphant nationalist leaders was bolted onto the sturdy frame of colonial autocracy. The voice briefly available to the subject at the decolonization moment was extinguished by single-party monopolies constructed to concentrate all national energies on combatting the legendary demons of poverty, ignorance, and disease. In many silent ways, the mentalities and routines of the colonial state were absorbed into the quotidian action of its postcolonial successor.

The reproduction of this dimension of colonial state legacy was fundamental to the physiognomy of the first postindependence generation of polities. Its overarching common attributes far outweighed any differences that might be detected in regimes issuing from different colonial powers.[9] Nonetheless, in a few cases institutional discontinuities resulting from failures in orderly decolonization impacted colonial state heritage. In the small number of cases where liberation armies directly succeeded to power and the colonial establishment evaporated at independence (Algeria, Guinea-Bissau, Mozambique, and Angola), the dynamic was different and military institution more central, but the authoritarian practices of the colonial state were reproduced in new form. The Belgian adventure in instant decolonization examined in chapter 3 produced immediate state failure, though once Mobutu consolidated power in 1965 the *bula matari* colonial state model clearly inspired the new order. Other variant cases include the three Arab states whose precolonial bureaucratic armature was modified but not dissolved under colonial rule—Egypt, Tunisia and Morocco—where imperial legacy mingles with an older state heritage. South Africa is also an outlier, having an essentially colonial relationship with the African majority even as it functioned as a liberal constitutional state for its white minority; a far more autonomous society and economy resulted. For most states in the early independence years, however, the overall commonality of colonial state legacy stands out.

The authoritarian patterns and practices of rule inherited from the colonial state had one offsetting merit: their usefulness as tools of governing. Most of the African colonial states had achieved impressive developmental momentum in the last imperial decade, and by the 1950s, they had effective institutions of rule as well. Thus, new rulers had at their disposition a functioning governmental infrastructure. In the small number of countries where the colonial administrative hold was especially weak (Guinea-Bissau, Central African Republic, Chad, Comoros), the *principe autoritaire* joined to a feeble state was a prescription for an ailing postcolonial polity. Another dimension of imperial legacy worthy of note is that the colonial state bequeathed a disarmed population, and so the new states inherited a Weberian monopoly on the means of coercion.

The ambitions of the independence generation of rulers went far beyond those of the colonizer. Chapters 2 and 5 examine the emergence by the 1970s of what I have termed a project to build an integral state. Government command of the economy expanded through nationalizations of colonial enterprises and parastatal management of most extractive and other industries, as well as agricultural marketing. The seeming unencumbered dominance over civil society was enforced by comprehensive instruments of social control through single parties and administrative encadrement, an atmosphere of fear sustained by a pervasive security apparatus, and state monopoly over print and other media.

Embedded within the integral state project were certainly elements of the colonial state legacy. However, novel practices emerged. Personalization of power by the ruler was common currency. In institutional terms, this was expressed as presidentialism visible from early independence days in the form of the unitary executive. However, the formal hierarchies of command could not be maintained except by establishing more personal linkages to influential intermediaries. In the clientelistic networks thus emerging, loyalty was exchanged for material advantage. The formal structures of sovereign state command could not suffice; parallel webs of prebendal linkage were needed to underwrite ruler authority. In short, the would-be integral state was completed—and ultimately subverted—by its growing neopatrimonial nature.

At the summit, the ruler required a clientele encompassing the regional and ethnic diversity of society. At the base, affinity of locality, clan, or ethnicity shaped the chain of linkages. In contrast to the formal structures of the state, the neopatrimonial networks were inherently unstable. The sorts of rewards the ruler could dispense to his clientele were usually in kind and necessarily finite: a government position, contracts, commissions on foreign investments, diversion of other state resources, land or other property subject to presidential allocation. Thus the ruler had reason to maintain some uncertainty among his clients as to the permanence of the prebends; he could not afford to retain all aspirant clients. He would drive some out, but the possibility of a reversal of fortune might be dangled before them. This disaffection, communicated to the following as a marginalization of the group, might well spread to their ethnic clientele.

The growing reliance on neopatrimonialism as instrument of rule was a postcolonial innovation. Although it reinforced the hand of long-standing rulers, it also corroded the formal institutions of the state. By the 1980s, the predatory nature of neopatrimonial rule became increasingly prevalent, reflected in the scale of corruption. In turn, the capacity of the state to sustain its social provisions and basic services became constrained, subverting its legitimacy.[10]

In sum, the explanatory power of colonial legacy, initially compelling, becomes less central as time goes by. The half century of postcolonial existence now matches the historical duration of effective colonial rule; a dwindling number of Africans have a personal recollection of "being colonized."[11] Although I retain the "postcolonial" descriptor in this work, in a 2004 article I queried its continuing pertinence:

New historical experience reshapes social memory and begins to obscure the colonial past . . . Deeper continuities with pre-colonial social and political patterns, and novel experiences of coping with the realities of state decline in recent decades, combine to close a set of parentheses around the post-colonial as a defining condition[,] . . . [which are] progressively overwritten by new defining events, political practices and agendas. The tides of globalization wash over the continent, depositing sedimentary layers of social exposure and economic impact. The rise of significant diaspora populations from many countries produces novel forms of international linkage. As these many processes work their way into institutional forms, political patterns, and social memory, the explanatory power of the post-colonial label erodes.[12]

COMPARING AFRICAN STATE PERFORMANCE
WITH OTHER REGIONS

One last element in the colonial legacy problematic merits exploration: its comparative dimension. In my African colonial state volume I argue for the distinctiveness of the imperial institutions of rule on the continent in comparison with their counterparts in other world regions. Although colonial occupation in Africa occurred in a more compressed time frame than in Asia, Latin

America, or the Caribbean, its social, cultural, and economic impact was unusually intense. Beginning and ending later, the technologies of domination in communications and weaponry facilitated erection of a more elaborated apparatus of hegemony. The historical artificiality of the territorial units issuing from colonial partition far exceeded that of other postimperial states and yielded an especially complex ethnicity; in colonized Asia, for example, except for Indonesia and the Philippines, the units of sovereignty were grounded in historicized identities. Perhaps only nineteenth-century Latin America compares in possessing a colonial legacy steeped in authoritarian practice whose adaptation to independence posed intractable difficulties to the successor states. Without exception the independent Latin American states were plagued by instability, punctuated by episodes of military or caudillo dictatorship; only a few achieved stable democratic forms in the first century of independence.

The single instance of imperial rule implemented by a dense, penetrative occupation of the subject population whose autocratic legacy over time translated into dynamic developmental states is Japan, particularly in Korea and Taiwan. Japanese administration in these territories involved a thorough bureaucratic implantation, in whose structures large numbers of the subject populace found places in the lower echelons. Although the harshness of Japanese rule generated intense Korean nationalist antagonism (though much less in Taiwan), extensive educational and economic infrastructure intended to permanently link the colonized territories to the imperial center well served the developmental purposes of successor states. A systematic land registration facilitated postwar land reforms that analysts have identified as key economic propellants.[13]

Beyond the issue of colonial legacy, a few other comparative reflections may be offered. The disappointments of postcolonial African state performance by developmental measures weighs the more heavily on rulers and citizens by the unfavorable contrast with other developing regions. Since the 1980s, the East Asian developmental state has had seductive allure. An influential school of analysis has taken form, stressing the embedded autonomy enjoyed by a highly trained bureaucracy as a key to dynamic management of a capitalist economy under state leadership.[14] By the late 1980s, a group of senior African policy advisors were drawn to searching examination of the Korean experience, hoping for an epiphany; although they concluded that "nothing suggests that the social and political regimes" in Africa are "much different from [those in] other countries," the possibilities of the African state replicating the capacities of their East Asian counterparts are slim.[15] Only South Africa is a remote candidate.

The emergence of China as a different emblem of extraordinary state-led economic success provides a new lodestar. The explosive growth rates once the economic reforms beginning in 1978 had taken hold draw envious glances, and the deepening Chinese engagement in African infrastructure and mineral extraction offers an attractive alternative to the traditional donor community imposition of human rights and democratic practice as conditions for receiving assistance. Authoritarian market socialism with Chinese characteristics is not for the moment an export commodity, but the giant loans and investments devoid of accompanying lessons in good governance is welcome in many capitals.

Africans correctly point out that the comparison with East Asian "tigers" is not entirely fair. Their ascent is partly the result of their having some advantages not available to Africa: the large early flow of American aid to South Korea and Taiwan, the huge resources flowing into the region as a consequence of the Korean and Vietnamese wars, and an already educated population. A deep tradition of stateness, a homogeneous and supportive cultural heritage, and a large entrepreneurial class were also facilitative factors, reinforcing a performing state. More to the point might be a comparison to other developing countries, whose political systems and social environments more closely resemble the African context. The authors who have most systematically endeavored such comparison are Atul Kohli and Peter Lewis.[16]

Of the four countries selected by Kohli as regional paradigmatic cases (South Korea, India, Brazil, and Nigeria), South Korea is, in terms of developmental performance, in a class by itself, Nigeria is clearly at the bottom, and India and Brazil are in between. India is riven by the world's most complex array of cultural divisions of religion, language, and caste and is subject to regular episodes of communal violence. The initial socialist engagement mingled with the imperatives of coping with cultural complexity to produce a regulatory state and a mediocre growth record: the "license raj" superintending the "Hindu rate of growth." Persistent low-intensity Maoist Naxalite insurgency, ongoing since 1967, now impacts rural zones in a half-dozen Indian states and has a presence in several others.[17] On the eve of the surprise emergence of India as a politico-economic giant on the global stage at the turn of the twenty-first century, leading specialists, while admiring the capacity of India to hold together in a democratic frame, arrived at pessimistic conclusions about developmental prospects. Paul Brass perceived "a decline of authoritative institutions in Indian politics[,] . . . the ever-declining effectiveness and the ever-increasing corruption of the bureaucracy, and the demoralization of the police and other state security forces and their direct involvement at times in the perpetration rather than control of violence."[18] Kohli concluded that the highly interventionist state was beset by "growing incapacity" and "relative ineffectiveness."[19] Lloyd and Suzanne Rudolph note that the Indian state "directly controls a significant proportion of physical and financial capital and employs a majority of workers in the organized economy" and is thus position "to serve itself and, like other self-interested actors, to be a source of exploitation and injustice."[20] The future, once again, is another country; economic reforms that were implemented in the 1990s have elevated India's developmental prospects, and a newly energized private sector has emerged that responds to the opportunities at the same time that the state preserves democratic structures. The reservoirs of bureaucratic skill and competence, especially at the summit, have come to the fore, even if slothful and venal habits at the base have persisted.

Brazil as well has in recent years begun to fulfill the promise implied by its resource base and continental scale. Perennially hampered by incoherent politics, formless and personality-driven parties, weak national economic management, repeated bouts of hyperinflation and military interventions, Brazil long lingered in the ranks of the underperforming polities. Consolidated democracy, improved political structuration, and effective national leadership since the 1990s, especially under the presidencies of Fernando Cardoso and Luiz Inácio Lula da Silva, have given new standing to the Brazilian polity as major international actor and developmental state. India and Brazil now rank as major "emerging economies," whose prospects appear well above those of most of Africa, although the Afro-optimist might suggest that the recent surge of a number of African economies after decades of stagnation is a harbinger for at least some African states.

Indonesia is a particularly pertinent case for African comparison; its cultural complexity, regional imbalances, and colonial origins as a territorial entity closely resemble the profile of larger African states. In 1976, I joined with Indonesian specialist Donald Emmerson in organizing a course and seminar comparing Congo-Kinshasa and Indonesia, whose postcolonial itineraries at that moment seemed closely parallel. Both countries experienced a disorderly decolonization and an initial high instability. In the mid-1960s, both suffered cataclysmic violence: the wave of rebellion in Congo examined in chapter 7 and the mass killings of alleged communists in Indonesia. In the wake of these trauma, military rulers seized power in 1965 in both countries, pledging recentralized authority and establishing the "new regime" and "new order," respectively. Both Mobutu and Suharto won initial admiration for restoring peace and seeming prosperity, even though by 1976 clear symptoms of corrosive corruption afflicted both regimes.

From that point forward, the pathways dramatically diverged in ways that we did not foresee. Rent seeking and crony capitalism pervaded both countries; by the 1990s Suharto's fortune was estimated at $16 billion, dwarfing the $5 billion attributed to Mobutu at his peak.[21] Yet in spite of high levels of corruption over the following decades, Indonesia sustained an impressive level of growth, industrialization, and economic diversification, while Congo entered a prolonged period of state decline, leaving a polity in ruin when Mobutu was finally ousted in 1997 at almost the same time as Suharto. Indonesia experienced an acute economic crisis in 1997–98 but engineered a prompt recovery and a successful democratic transition; the post-Mobutu political order managed to achieve constitutional redemption and successful national elections only after an eight-year civil war and without a concomitant restoration of effective stateness.

Lewis contrasts the Indonesian performance, however flawed, with Nigerian outcomes. Even though Nigeria had a far more functional state than Congo, its record nonetheless compared unfavorably with Indonesia. Lewis concludes:

> Beginning from very similar foundations, the two countries deviated sharply in the 1970s and 1980s, as Indonesia recovered from early economic crisis, successfully adjusted from the leading distortions of the resource windfall, and embarked on a period of sustained growth and competitive development. By the middle of the 1990s, Indonesia appeared to be a promising economy with prospects of sustained high performance, an evaluation supported by the enthusiastic responses of international investors to the Indonesian market. Indonesia's dynamism was starkly contrasted by Nigeria's path from modest recovery after the civil war to the pathologies of the 1970s oil boom, through the post-windfall crash of the 1980s and the predatory decline of 1990s. Nigeria's sustained decline pushed the country to the margins of the global economy as investment diminished, non-oil production withered, growth slowed, and poverty mounted.[22]

Lewis attributes the difference to the inability of Nigeria to sustain effective economic governance, make credible commitments to the private sector, and constrain rent seeking. Though crony capitalism pervaded Indonesia, a proficient technocratic core to the state apparatus was better able to assure effective management of the political economy. Another differentiating factor was the role of the large entrepreneurial community of Chinese ancestry, whose Indonesian presence is often generations deep. Of the 140 top businesses in 1997, only 40 were controlled by indigenous Indonesians, 16 of these by the Suharto family. The economic calculus of Sino-Indonesians is inevitably influenced by the resentment they encounter, and their resultant insecurity; they nonetheless contribute precious entrepreneurial skills.[23]

Some broad parallels with Latin American evolution in the last half century may be discerned. A wave of populist nationalism influenced by dependency theory shaped political economies, while the roster of liberal democratic regimes shriveled in the 1960s; Costa Rica is the sole Latin American regime with uninterrupted democracy since 1948.[24] The ascendant mood of state expansion was frequently manifest in military juntas constructing bureaucratic-authoritarian regimes on corporatist foundations, a trend for which some writers perceived a colonial state legacy.[25] Like Africa, after strong growth in the 1960s Latin America experienced a decade of economic crisis and stagnation in the 1980s, discrediting the populist authoritarian path. After Spain, Portugal, and Greece, Latin America was the primary site for the swelling wave of democratization in the 1980s, which became global by 1990. Political liberalization there, unlike in Africa, was relatively enduring, with democratic process rooted in growing numbers of stable and institutionalized party systems.[26] The shift to more outward-looking market economies produced modest improvements as well.[27]

A recent major collaborative inquest into African developmental performance in the first four decades of independence, sponsored by Harvard University and Oxford University, drew together a team of distinguished analysts, with extensive experience in the international financial institutions. Its problematic was the same as that of this chapter: how to assess the disappointments of African performance in comparison with other developing regions.[28] They conclude that "the record is profoundly unsettling. Non-African growth consistently outpaced African growth after 1960, with the result that Sub-Saharan real incomes fell by over 35 percent relative to incomes in other developing regions and by nearly half relative to industrial countries. . . . Africa's cumulative progress was insufficient, by 2000, to reach the levels of human development the rest of the developing world had already attained."[29]

TABLE 9.1. Sub-Saharan African Economic Growth in Comparison, circa 1960–2000

	Annual growth (%), real per capita GDP	Adult illiteracy (%), 1970	Adult illiteracy (%), circa 2000	Life expectancy at birth (years), circa 1960	Life expectancy at birth (years), circa 2000
Sub-Saharan Africa	0.56	55.8	41.2	41.1	47.8
Latin America	1.44	17.4	11.1	56.4	70.8
South Asia	2.10	55.5	45.2	45.3	63.8
East Asia and Pacific	3.41	20.4	11.4	50.6	69.6
Middle East, North Africa, Turkey	2.61	42.3	27.8	51.7	70.6

SOURCE: Data is drawn from Benno J. Ndulu, Stephen A. O'Connell, Robert H. Bates, Paul Collier, and Chukwuma C. Soludo, *The Political Economy of Economic Growth in Africa, 1960–2000*, 2 vols. (Cambridge: Cambridge University Press, 2008), 1:4.

The authors take due note of some major environmental constraints imposing differential disadvantage on Africa. Many African nations suffer from difficult political geography, a constraint underlined by Jeffrey Herbst in his diagnosis of state crisis.[30] Fifteen are landlocked, and many have inadequate transportation infrastructure. Electricity shortfalls and blackouts afflict many, even the relatively prosperous such as South Africa. Malaria, tuberculosis, and other devastating diseases overwhelm deficient health facilities. Africa has been especially cursed by the HIV-AIDS epidemic, which has sharply reduced life expectancies in the most afflicted countries. At the same time, pressures mount on the population front, which has expanded fourfold in a number of states since 1960. Only North Africa (especially Tunisia) has begun to experience the demographic transition to longer lives and smaller families. The limited range of export commodities for most renders them vulnerable to sudden price shifts on global markets.

The prevalence of internal war, especially in the 1990s, is an evident block to development. When localized in a peripheral region, as in Senegal, Mali, Niger, and even Uganda, its economic impact may be limited. Even in these circumstances, though, precious resources are diverted into defense expenditures, as table 9.2 suggests. But Angola, Sudan, Congo-Kinshasa, Liberia, and Sierra

Leone experienced severe developmental damage. Civil peace is an obvious facilitating condition.

The authors conclude, however, that deficiencies of governance are a major factor in African developmental disappointments. Although authoritarianism characterized East Asian regimes until the late 1980s, its effects were less harmful. The high discretion in deployment of state resources available to African rulers freed of institutional constraints opened the door to large amounts of those resources being diverted, both to support neopatrimonialism and to enrich the inner presidential clique. The negative impact was multiplied by the command role attributed to the state and the scope of the economy in government hands at the peak moment of integral state visions.[31]

An extended debate on the possible link between ethnic diversity and developmental performance opened in 1997 with an influential article by William Easterly and Ross Levine suggesting that high orders of ethnic fractionalization were closely correlated with flawed policies.[32] Their data was drawn from Soviet measures from the early 1960s that imposed a highly primordialist template on the identification of ethnic diversity. They reason that ethnic diversity produces competitive rent seeking and struggles over shares of the "national cake" that divert resources from the common pool available for developmental purposes. Ethnic groups as collective actors are inherently self-aggrandizing.

There is little doubt that cultural diversity in Africa is exceptionally marked, and as chapter 8 argues the territorial units with few exceptions were arbitrary products of the colonial partition lacking a historical narrative. The accommodation of racial, religious, and ethnic diversity requires state acknowledgment of difference and distributive policies that recognize that relative equities of state action find measure in many eyes in communal shares. However, there are a wide range of policy choices that can contribute to this end, once models of ethnic dominance or homogenization goals are set aside.[33] The fractionalization index has been queried, as has the assumption that sheer numbers of groups necessarily correlate with instability. Two of Africa's most stable polities, Tanzania and Zambia, have high fractionalization figures. Cultural pluralism challenges statecraft, but in my reading it cannot be the prime explanation for developmental disappointments.

Comparing State Performance

By way of organizing an overall comparison of state performance, I draw on the half dozen imperatives of state reproduction outlined in chapter 2. These broadly framed parameters during the era of patrimonial autocracy become operative at the level of regimes or rulers; as chapter 2 stresses, choices made in these dimensions of state action may reflect survival calculations of autocrats—Mobutu and Mugabe are prime examples—that are destructive of the long-term health of the polity. The political opening around 1990, when the ultimate equilibrium was democratic or even semiauthoritarian, tended to resituate the logic of reproduction in the state itself.

Hegemony

In terms of hegemony, the first disposition of new states was to seek its reinforcement, often with initial success, as chapter 4 records. The first postcolonial rulers were at once newly conscious of the perils of sovereignty and determined to demand discipline of the subject. The colonial state was satisfied with the passive deference of the subject to its authority; its successor insisted on the active loyalty of the citizen.

The excesses of the command state and its inability to expand its most valued social services at the rate promised by anticolonial nationalism led to the beginnings of disaffection. So also did perceptions that ruling parties favored regions that had provided them support while marginalizing others and restricting their access to the state. The limits to effective hegemony of the weakest states, such as Guinea-Bissau or Central African Republic, were evident within a few years of independence.[34]

The prolonged state crisis of the 1980s produced a contraction of the reach of government. It concentrated its resources more on the capital and a few core areas; in the periphery, its agents were bereft of operational resources—means of transport and office supplies—and often only irregularly paid. They were thus driven to local predation as a survival mode. Sensing abandonment, civil society rechanneled its energies into the underground economy, illicit cross-border trade, artisanal mining, and other productive activities based on evading residual state hegemony. Rulers, meanwhile, increasingly diverted public resources into parallel prebendal networks, even at the cost of eviscerating the hegemony of the formal state in favor of the "shadow state" illuminated by William Reno.[35] Although far from all regimes evolved in this direction, for a time it was the dominant pattern.

The differentiated itineraries after 1990 in the more successful polities—Ghana, Uganda, Benin, Tanzania, among others—permitted some restoration of state authority. Hegemony appeared robust until the 2011 protest wave in the Arab tier of states in the north, as well as in southern Africa. In the lands between, the broad weakening of the fabric of state hegemony and the loss of the monopoly of the means of coercion through the weapons influx opened a breach of state authority through which insurgent militias found room for operation. The virtual absence of the state in a number of regions, a social backdrop of generalized disaffection, and innovations in resourcing and arming insurgencies created new possibilities for revolt.

Security

The postcolonial security imperative was inward looking. Interstate warfare was remarkable for its absence, save only in the Horn of Africa, the brief Algerian-Moroccan conflict, and the Egyptian battles with Israel in 1948, 1956, 1967, and 1973. The only large-scale interstate wars pitted Somalia in irredentist battle with Ethiopia in 1976–77 and Ethiopia in bitter warfare with Eritrea over disputed territory from 1998 to 2000. The logic driving creation of most security forces was the threat of internal disorder. Most were of modest size, as table 9.2 shows, supplied with armament mostly appropriate for infantry units. The main exceptions were armies issuing from liberation struggle, apartheid South Africa, post–civil war Nigeria, the Horn, and Egypt. For most, the extreme constraints imposed by the meager revenue flow limited the size of security forces. The small offshore island states, facing a minimal external security threat, operate with the tiniest of armies.

The internal security equation was modified when the military coup became, starting in 1965, the major vehicle for regime displacement. Rulers of military derivation were instinctively self-aggrandizing actors who expanded army budgets and were prone to purchasing costly high-end equipment such as fighter jets, advanced tanks. Whatever prestige ensued was often offset by the incapacity to assure maintenance or replacement parts. All leaders found close attention to the ethnic security map indispensable and sought immunization against coups by establishing personal affinities, securing the loyalty of key commanders, and restricting recruitment in regions of suspect fidelity. The lurking threat of a military coup persuaded a number of longtime rulers to distrust their armies, leading them to keep the armies relatively small; Félix Houphouët-Boigny of Ivory Coast, Omar Bongo Ondimba in Gabon, and Zine el Afidine Ben Ali in Tunisia are cases in point. Ben Ali relied primarily on a huge internal security apparatus of secret police, informers, contract enforcers and thugs numbering 600,000 according to Henry and Springborg, eclipsing the mere 35,800 military in 2007.[36] The North African states all stood out for the sprawling dimensions of their security police.

In some cases, the security imperative was partly outsourced to foreign protectors, especially during the cold war when the major powers sought strategic clientele. During the first independence decades, the intimate partners of Françafrique could count on French garrisons that had been placed in Senegal, Ivory Coast, Gabon and Djibouti as well as on the efficient French intelligence networks on site to forestall conspiracy. The United States had long-standing intimate security ties with Liberia, Congo-Kinshasa, Egypt, and (until 1974) Ethiopia. The Soviet Union partnered with Cuba in providing major security assistance to Angola and Ethiopia under the Derg; the proficient East German security service trained domestic intelligence forces in several Afromarxist states in the 1970s and 1980s.

Although external security was infrequently subject to serious threat, southern Africa became a zone of insecurity from the moment that the 1974 Portuguese coup dissolved the colonial protective barrier insulating apartheid South Africa from African liberation forces. Suddenly ANC guerrillas, once safely remote in Tanzania, had access to neighboring states. South African securocrats, believing that a "total Communist onslaught" was at hand, launched aggressive destabilization campaigns directed at any neighboring state sheltering ANC insurgents.[37] In Angola and Mozambique, active supply and encadrement was provided to UNITA and RENAMO. The security obsessions of South Africa, along with their consequences for neighboring states, finally dissolved only with the Namibia settlement in 1989 and withdrawal of Cuban troops from Angola.

The wave of civil wars in the 1990s brought the security imperative to the fore in much of Africa. The French disposition for engagement diminished; Paris declined to intervene to reverse the first military coup experienced in Ivory Coast in 1999. The end of the cold war ended interventionist logic for the United States, and the Soviet Union vanished; marines remained just offshore when American client Samuel Doe was assassinated in 1990. But the spectacle of the macabre violence attending some of the internal wars and the fear of contagious insecurity led to international intervention through the UN and AU in a striking number of cases. Interventions of international forces had taken place in no less than sixteen countries by 2010, which included twelve UN operations since the 1980s.[38] The interpenetration of a number of civil wars with neighboring country political dynamics and frequent use by rebel militias of bordering territories for shelter further complicated the security dilemma. Still, in 2008 sub-Saharan African states spent only 1.51% of their GDP on defense.[39]

TABLE 9.2. African Defense Expenditures, 2007

Country	GDP ($ billions) 2007	Defense expenditure ($ millions)	Armed forces (numbers)
Algeria	131	3,690	147,000
Angola	48.3	2,290	107,000
Benin	5.7	57	4,750
Botswana	12.3	283	9,000
Burkina Faso	7.2	101	10,800
Burundi	1.0	46	35,000
Cameroon	20.1	324	14,100
Cape Verde	1.4	8	1,200
Central African Republic	1.8	18	3,150
Chad	7.5	72	23,350
Comoros	NA	NA	NA
Congo-Brazzaville	10.6	97	10,000
Congo-Kinshasa	9.1	181	134,484
Djibouti	0.8	17	10,950
Egypt	130	3,040	468,000
Equatorial Guinea	10.8	NA	1,320
Eritrea	1.4	NA	201,750
Ethiopia	16.6	330	138,000
Gabon	11.2	NA	4,700
Gambia	0.8	1.6*	800
Ghana	14.8	104	13,500
Guinea	4.8	52	12,300
Guinea-Bissau	0.4	16	9,250
Ivory Coast	20.5	300	17,050
Kenya	25.5	355*	24,120
Lesotho	1.6	34	2,000
Liberia	1.0	NA	2,400
Libya	56.9	807	76,000
Madagascar	7.8	385	13,500
Malawi	2.4	21	5,300
Mali	7.1	162	7,350
Mauritania	3.8	19	15,870
Mauritius	7.9	20	2,000
Morocco	71.8	2,470	195,000
Mozambique	8.1	57	11,200
Namibia	7.2	248	9,000
Niger	4.4	47	5,300
Nigeria	136	988	80,000
Rwanda	3.3	62	33,000
Sao Tome	NA	NA	NA
Senegal	13.5	173	13,620
Seychelles	0.5	10	200

TABLE 9.2. (*continued*)

Country	GDP (*$ billions*) 2007	Defense expenditure (*$ millions*)	Armed forces (*numbers*)
Sierra Leone	1.7	25	10,500
Somalia	NA	NA	NA
South Africa	277	3,840	62,334
Sudan	44.8	579	109,300
Swaziland	NA	NA	NA
Tanzania	15.1	173	27,000
Togo	2.6	43	8,550
Tunisia	35.2	500	35,800
Uganda	11.6	226	45,000
Zambia	11.3	243	15,100
Zimbabwe	3.1	155*	29,000

* 2006 figures
SOURCE: Data drawn from International Institute for Strategic Studies, *The Military Balance 2008* (London: Routledge, 2008).

Autonomy

Like security, the autonomy imperative has both external and internal dimensions. Externally, the primary weapon was the doctrine of sovereignty, enshrining a normative entitlement to unencumbered and exclusive right to command within a state's borders. The blessing of international recognition confirms external sovereignty. Although in theory this is conditioned on the capacity to rule the people and the territory enclosed in a sovereign unit, the Somalia case examined in chapter 7 demonstrates that a fictive state subsists in international law even though for two decades now it has had no empirical existence. Even before Somalia, analysts who were puzzled by the persistence of weak states even in the face of their practical failure to provide effective government suggested that many African polities were merely juridical states, not empirical ones.[40]

In the first two postindependence decades, before such weakening was detected, forceful assertion of sovereignty dominated state discourse. Active African engagement in anti-imperial third-world forums such as the Afro-Asian solidarity conferences and Group of 77 reflected this commitment. So also did the foundation of the OAU, whose core vocation is to foster continental liberation and solidarity.

Regimes and rulers following the script recited in chapter 4 pursued internal autonomy with equal vigor. As the ruling elite claimed exclusive knowledge of the secrets of development, they at the same time imposed single parties and military regimes to restrict the public at large to the duty of acclamation of decisions taken. The corporate structures of civil society—trade unions, merchant chambers, lawyer associations, and others—were forced into the framework of the single party. Government monopolies on the media held public debate within narrow limits. For a number of years, states enjoyed a substantial autonomy from society at large. Perhaps more than anything else, their underlying economic weakness set growing limits on state autonomy. This was magnified by the state expansion project of the 1970s.

The severe limits that the slender revenue base imposed on many states became fully evident at the end of the 1970s. Earlier, most former French-ruled countries had accepted the constraints of the franc zone and accompanying Paris fiscal tutelage in return for the guarantee of a convertible currency, which was a valuable shield against the hyperinflation that often took place elsewhere. However, by 1980 African external debt had reached unsustainable levels, leaving international bankruptcy as the only alternative to accepting the SAPs imposed by international financial institutions and backed by the Western donor community. In the first decade of such programs, which were ideologically rooted in the most rigorously neoliberal version of the "Washington Consensus" on an economic reform template, the conditionalities on budget discipline were severe, forcing painful cutbacks in government expenditure, including social provisions.

Although by 1990, international financial institutions realized the necessity of buffering the social costs of adjustment, even with an easing of the terms the limits on autonomy imposed by the continuing debt burden were substantial. Further, a substantial number of countries became habituated to very large and enduring aid flows, which provided half or more of their resources; Senegal, Ghana, Uganda, and Mozambique are examples. The shackles of structural adjustment have not entirely foreclosed state avenues for autonomous escape. Nicolas van de Walle documents the extent to which many states have evaded the conditionalities through selective observation or half-hearted application.[41]

Another measure of the limits to state autonomy is their circumscribed capacity to monitor the financial transactions of foreign corporations; a recent study by Global Financial Integrity shows that between 1970 and 2008 the staggering sum of $850 billion was lost to Africa by diverse tax evasion schemes engineered by external economic operatives. If all transfer pricing devices and mispricing of trade in services were included, the loss to Africa might total

$1.8 trillion; even the smaller figure is twice the amount of aid received. The director of Global Finance Integrity adds that "this massive flow of illicit money out of Africa is facilitated by a global shadow financial system comprising tax havens, secrecy jurisdictions, disguised corporations, anonymous trust accounts, fake foundations, trade mis-pricing and money laundering techniques. These figures dwarf the capital loss to Africa through clandestine export of corruptly obtained funds by top government officials."[42]

Legitimation

The legitimation imperative found its first response in independence itself. "Seek ye first the political kingdom," Ghana leader Kwame Nkrumah famously declared, and all else will be added unto you. He spoke for a generation in claiming that the dream of independence that powered the anticolonial nationalist movement would be self-fulfilling. But legitimation was also built on a negation: the colonial state, with its multiple vexations, inexpungible racism, and barriers to African advance. A discourse of development soon broadened the language of legitimation, in many cases completed with a patina of vaguely defined socialist aspiration.

The military power seizures that followed a few years later recast the negation of colonialism by repudiating the policies and practices of the regimes they ousted. A host of evils was discovered in their actions: corruption, tribalism, incompetence, and servitude to foreign interests were frequent entries to the articles of indictment, which commissions of inquiry were swiftly appointed to document. Especially for the first episode of military intervention, denunciation of the ousted regime often sufficed to secure entry legitimacy, when the military claims to integrity, national commitment, discipline, and efficiency had not faced a reality check. But entry legitimacy was only that, a wasting asset soon superseded by the sterner test of performance. In a number of instances, successor rulers for a few years confirmed these hopes; Yakubu Gowon and later Ibrahim Babangida in Nigeria, Juvenal Habyarimana of Rwanda, even Mobutu are examples. But over time, above all in patrimonial autocracies that lack rules for succession, other modes of legitimation are necessary.

In the 1970s, a renewed and more systematic recourse to socialist orientation served this purpose. In its most advanced Afromarxist forms, the ideology had important appeal to intellectuals and students, habitually in the forefront of vocal opposition even under the constraints of neopatrimonial authoritarianism. Diverse indigenization projects transferred resources to the autochtonous; these projects rewarded the immediate beneficiaries and responded to widespread popular resentments of the Levantine, South Asian, and other Mediterranean mercantiles who dominated large commercial sectors.

By the 1980s, a deep deficit of legitimation was woven into the fabric of state decline and crisis. Patrimonial autocracy as modality of rule had run its course. In the face of deteriorating well-being for most of the populace, a change of military rulers could no longer secure even entry legitimacy. The turn to democratization was a cathartic shift, at its peak seeming to sweep the tables clean and open the polity to a new and more stable path to legitimation. Negation once again was an integral part of the process: witness the painstaking briefs of the misdeeds of the antecedent regimes assembled by the national conferences. But liberalization promised an entirely new political dispensation that would be rewarded by a renovated legitimation. A moment of enthusiasm attended the constitution writing and competitive elections that heralded a democratic rebirth.

Though the political rebirth of the African state examined in chapter 6 proved enduring in a modest number of instances, the more frequent outcome was semidemocracy with an entrenched ruling party or else a partial autocratic restoration. Even if there was more political space for civil society action and opposition expression, the relegitimation of the democracy wave faded, and a palpable popular disengagement took hold. Two decades after the 1990 political earthquake, even though African state performance had shown some improvement in the aggregate, undercurrents of unease tinging on disaffection flowed in many lands, underscored by the wave of protest in North Africa in 2011.

Spanning these periods are elements of the compelling portrait of African concepts of legitimacy sketched by Michael Schatzberg, derived from a careful reading of popular culture in what he terms middle Africa. Authority is viewed within a metaphoric template of the family writ large on the nation in what he terms a "moral matrix" of legitimation. The ruler in the popular mind takes on the attributes of the father-chief. "As long as he nurtures and nourishes, his legitimacy is maintained. The father-chief may eat, but not while people are hungry. In providing for his political children, he is entitled to gratitude for the debt incurred."[43] At the same time, the father-chief is not entitled to perpetual rule; eternal power is inherently illegitimate, and some mode of alternation is indispensable.

Recasting this aspect of the moral matrix, one might suggest that an implicit distinction lurks in the public mind between the nation-state as a permanent entity, on the one hand, and rulers and regimes, on the other. The massive disaffection encountered by most rulers by the late 1980s was a repudiation of regime but not state. Alternation as a thinkable political event opens the possibility of a new order in which the normative vision of state as impartial and efficacious provider of security and social provisions might be achieved. Even in long troubled lands like Somalia or Congo Kinshasa, such a state still abides in the social imaginary, however remote in empirical reality. This observation applies with even greater force to the remarkable popular attachment to the territorial nation, even in the face of prolonged dereliction of the really existing state. I reflect at length on this paradox in chapter 8, joined by a number of other analysts. Pierre Englebert in his critique of African state performance notes that "students of African politics share a common puzzlement at the success that African countries have demonstrated at developing national identities in contrast to their failure at constructing actually functioning states."[44] Patrick Chabal adds that "there is little doubt that Africans do identify, never more strongly than when football is at stake, with their country of origin. Whatever differences may separate individuals within a particular country, there is clearly a vibrant bond that joins them together when it comes to expressing or defending national interests."[45]

Revenue

The fifth imperative, revenue, is central to grasping the African state crisis of the 1980s, and the ongoing constraints it imposes. The ceaseless quest for revenue is "the bedrock postulate of state behavior."[46] Robert Bates broke new ground in identifying the revenue imperative as core driver to postcolonial politics.[47] The search for money is the shorthand answer to the classic query by Goran Therborn: what does the ruling class do when it rules?[48]

Initially this did not appear problematic. Chapter 3 details the exceptional revenue expansion across the continent in the 1950s, whose momentum carried through much of the first independence decade. New access to external aid and continuing public capital flows from the withdrawing colonizer kept treasuries afloat. Well into the 1970s, international banks and donors lent Africa into the debt crisis. Ever since, serious revenue shortfalls have plagued the African state, with destabilizing consequences: inflation, inability to compensate civil servants, the starving of social and other infrastructure. The bitter medicine of often harsh SAPs was the ransom of temporary relief from the international financial institutions.

The impasse originates in the revenue patterns inherited from the colonial state. The primary central sources of government finance were levies on external trade, weighted to bear heavily on rural African incomes. On the import side, products aimed at Africans often carried higher duties than those destined for Europeans.[49] On agricultural products, African producers bore both the customs duty plus "stabilization" charges aimed at generating a reserve to maintain the state-fixed producer prices when international markets were unfavorable but in reality usually diverted to other uses. In addition, different forms of capitation taxes, used mainly to fund local government in the late colonial period, though apparently small, could be a significant fraction of a peasant cash income; one careful study in Uganda demonstrated the small rural producers paid half their cash incomes in one form or another.[50] Expatriate sectors of the economy were relatively lightly taxed.

Naturally, colonial fiscal arrangements came under challenge after independence. Use of state agricultural marketing monopolies as an instrument to generate developmental resources was challenged over time; by the 1990s such practices had largely disappeared. Embattled regimes gradually abandoned the capitation tax. Meanwhile, the larger commercial sector, immigrant or indigenous, proved difficult to tax. Income taxes on prosperous merchants or leading politicians are beyond the capacity of most states to collect. This leads some to experiment with a value added tax.

Rents on high-value commodities whose export channels can be readily monitored do produce substantial revenues; oil is the prime example. The emergence of Africa as a major oil producer is entirely postcolonial; only a small beginning was made in Algeria, Nigeria, and Angola before independence. Reliability of mineral rents on more readily smuggled commodities (diamonds and gold, for example) is more problematic. African states lack the technology to organize the exploitation of most minerals on their own. The urgency of securing the revenue flow reduces their leverage in bargaining with external corporations on terms of exploitation; long tax holidays, customs exemptions, and limited royalties have been the frequent result.

In the recent conflict zones or in circumstances of extreme state weakness, operational risks become too high for mainstream international corporations, who are arguably more likely to follow conventional protocols in their arrangements with African counterparts. In these circumstances, a horde of buccaneering operatives, willing to operate outside the normal rules, accept high risks in the expectation of comparably large returns while contributing little to state coffers. Congo-Kinshasa has been a particular magnet for such enterprises in recent years. Their activities are a significant element in the dispiriting figures reported by Global Financial Integrity.

But the critical overriding fact is that most African states have a patheti-cally small domestic revenue flow. The best endowed government, South Africa, ranked only thirty-first in a world ranking by state internal revenue in 2007. At that time, only thirteen African countries appeared among the top hundred globally in this respect, mainly either North African states or major oil exporters. Most African states cluster at the bottom end of the world scale. Only fourteen countries had government outlays exceeding the $4 billion 2010 budget of the University of Wisconsin System. In dramatic contrast stands the paltry domestic revenue that Congo-Kinshasa has at its disposal to govern its nine hundred thousand square miles and over sixty million people: $2 billion in 2005, over $3 billion in 2010.[51]

Accumulation

The limits to the accumulation capacities of most African states with the exception of northern Africa and South Africa is thus evident. The patheti-cally small domestic revenue base of the more impoverished African states provide little scope for public investment except from external sources. The major oil producers that do enjoy ample revenue appear singularly suscepti-ble to corrupt diversion of the oil revenues entering state coffers; Nigeria, Angola, Equatorial Guinea, and Algeria all rank near the top in Transparency International corruption perception scores. They also tend to have large mil-itaries, equipped with high-end weaponry, a further constraint on resources for public investment (see table 9.2).

The global discredit of socialist orientation by the late 1980s and the failure of the integral state as instrument of accelerated development produced a far-reaching recalculation of the avenues to accumulation. With the global recasting of developmental doctrine and the emergence of the period of predominance of neoliberal policy reason, most African states accepted the premise of a market economy (although Seychelles clung to socialist orienta-tion until 2009). By the late 1990s, access to foreign capital improved, an im-portant factor in the modest enhancement in developmental measures. In the following decade, the massive Chinese influx of mineral investment, often accompanied by funds for major infrastructure projects, altered the profile of foreign capital. Tourism was another significant sector for foreign invest-ment. A number of countries negotiated major write-downs of their external debts, reducing the crippling burden of debt service. As Nigerians were quick to point out, the sums paid in mere service of the debilitating debt that reached $37 billion well exceeded the original value of the borrowed funds; a

2005 deal forgave $18 billion in return for a payment of $12 billion, reducing the external debt to a manageable $7 billion.[52] In 2010, Congo's $13 billion external debt originating with the Mobutu regime was mostly written off.

Measures of State Performance

In the 1990s and 2000s, a number of indices emerged permitting a ranking of African state performance on various important criteria. One of the most ambitious and interesting is sponsored by Sudanese billionaire Mo Ibrahim, whose fortune of very recent vintage is rooted in his leading role in the spectacular spread of cell phones in Africa, especially in the first decade of the twenty-first century.[53] He commissioned a working group led by Robert Rotberg in 2006, who developed a scoring system combining some fifty-seven variables, whose main components included sustainable economic opportunity, human development, safety and rule of law, political participation, and human rights. The resulting annual index attracts great attention in Africa and elsewhere. Table 9.3 lists the top and bottom performers in 2010.

Table 9.4 undertakes a variant of this exercise by combining along with the Mo Ibrahim Index four other rankings that endeavor a measurement of important aspects of state performance: Freedom House's Freedom in the World; UNDP's Human Development Index (which measures social factors such as life expectancy, school enrollments, and adult literacy), Transparency International's Corruption Perceptions Index, and the Failed State Index, developed by *Foreign Policy* and Fund for Peace and based on a dozen indicators tapping instability, delegitimation, conflicted elites, refugees, and external interventions. For the Freedom House scale, the lowest score means highest

TABLE 9.3. Top and Bottom Ten Countries, 2010 Mo Ibrahim Index

Top 10	*Bottom 10*
Mauritius	Ivory Coast
Seychelles	Guinea
Botswana	Equatorial Guinea
Cape Verde	Central African Republic
South Africa	Sudan
Namibia	Eritrea
Ghana	Zimbabwe
Tunisia	Congo-K
Lesotho	Chad
Egypt	Somalia

SOURCE: *Africa Confidential*, 8 October 2010.

level of freedom; for the other measures, the higher figures record more virtuous performance according to the respective criteria of the scale. The fifty-three African states are listed in the table in the order of their overall average ranking across these five comparative scales.

A number of limitations to this exercise are apparent from the outset. To begin with, there is some overlap in the contents of the indicators used to construct these indices; the overall ranking conveys at best only an approximate portrayal of relative performance. Further, in the middle part of the rankings the differences in score are small; thus the real significance lies at the upper and lower ends of the scale.

More important questions arise concerning the most highly ranked North African states, whose dysfunctions became fully evident only when mass uprisings suddenly appeared at the end of 2010. The macro-indicators appearing to demonstrate a performing state failed to capture the flaws so starkly revealed, for example, in the protest movement against the Ben Ali regime in Tunisia. Other seeming anomalies appear in the rankings. For example, Comoros, widely regarded as an infirm, unstable, and feeble polity, implausibly ranks above Kenya, Rwanda, or Uganda, although its standing perhaps reflects the first democratic transition since 1975 independence in 2006, and significant improvement in IMF evaluations of its economic governance. Liberia seems more highly ranked than its still dilapidated condition might justify; clearly here the indices are partly capturing improvement under President Johnson-Sirleaf from a very low base.

Notwithstanding these limitations, a number of pertinent observations arise from contemplation of table 9.4. Perhaps the first striking correlation is size of polity and overall performance. With the exception of Comoros, the small offshore island polities all rank near the top. Only Mauritius has highly salient ethno-racial diversity among this group; I return below to the particulars of this case. All but "partly free" Comoros dwell in the "free" category of Freedom House, and all earn high scores on the human development index. Cape Verde, Mauritius, and Seychelles have enjoyed high stability. Insulated by their geography, they require only tiny security forces.

At the other end of this spectrum, the largest African states appear encumbered by their sheer scale and human complexity, contrary to conventional wisdom that bigger is better. If one sets aside relatively homogeneous Algeria, much of whose geographic expanse is little populated, the three giant polities are Sudan, Congo-Kinshasa, and Nigeria. All three have been theaters of civil war and high ethno-regional tensions. Internal war raged in southern Sudan for

TABLE 9.4. Comparative African State Performance, 2009

Country listed in order of average of rankings in in the five scales	Freedom House 2009	Mo Ibrahim 2009	Human Development Index 2009	Transparency 2009	Failed State Index* 2009
Mauritius	1.5	82.83	0.804	5.4	53
Seychelles	3.0	77.13	0.845	4.8	49
Cape Verde	1.0	78.01	0.708	5.1	40
Botswana	2.5	73.59	0.694	5.6	48
South Africa	2.0	69.44	0.683	4.7	51
Namibia	2.0	68.81	0.686	4.5	43
Ghana	1.5	65.96	0.526	3.9	52
Tunisia	6.0	65.81	0.769	4.2	50
Sao Tome	2.0	60.23	0.651	2.8	42
Morocco	4.5	57.83	0.654	3.3	41
Benin	2.0	58.20	0.492	2.9	44
Lesotho	3.0	61.18	0.514	3.3	32
Senegal	3.0	55.98	0.464	3.0	46
Gabon	5.5	53.92	0.755	2.9	45
Madagascar	5.0	58.37	0.543	3.0	33
Tanzania	3.5	59.24	0.530	2.6	34
Algeria	5.5	58.36	0.754	2.8	36
Zambia	3.5	55.30	0.481	3.0	30
Mali	2.5	54.55	0.371	2.8	39
Egypt	5.5	60.09	0.703	2.8	23
Libya	7.0	53.69	0.847	2.5	47
Malawi	3.5	53.03	0.493	3.3	17
Swaziland	6.0	49.43	0.542	3.6	31
Gambia	5.0	55.13	0.456	2.9	38
Comoros	3.5	48.58	0.574	2.3	28
Burkina Faso	4.0	51.58	0.389	3.6	21
Djibouti	5.0	46.04	0.520	2.8	37
Mozambique	3.5	52.38	0.402	2.5	35
Liberia	3.5	44.92	0.442	3.1	20
Kenya	4.0	53.74	0.541	2.2	9
Rwanda	5.5	48.53	0.460	3.3	24
Togo	4.5	40.83	0.499	2.8	27
Uganda	4.5	53.57	0.514	2.5	12
Mauritania	5.5	50.57	0.520	2.5	25
Sierra Leone	3.0	48.91	0.365	2.2	19
Nigeria	4.5	46.46	0.511	2.5	10
Angola	5.5	41.02	0.564	1.9	29
Niger	4.5	46.59	0.340	2.9	13
Congo-B	5.5	42.79	0.601	1.9	18
Ethiopia	5.0	45.59	0.414	2.7	11

TABLE 9.4. *(continued)*

Country listed in order of average of rankings in in the five scales	Freedom House 2009	Mo Ibrahim 2009	Human Development Index 2009	Transparency 2009	Failed State Index* 2009
Cameroon	6.0	47.00	0.523	2.2	15
Equatorial Guinea	7.0	39.39	0.719	1.8	26
Guinea-Bissau	4.0	43.50	0.396	1.9	16
Eritrea	7.0	36.96	0.472	2.6	22
Burundi	4.5	45.27	0.394	1.8	14
Ivory Coast	5.5	36.61	0.484	2.1	8
Central African Republic	5.0	35.00	0.369	2.0	6
Sudan	7.0	33.45	0.531	1.5	3
Guinea	6.5	40.41	0.435	1.8	7
Zimbabwe	6.0	31.29	NA	2.2	2
Congo-K	6.0	33.25	0.389	1.9	5
Chad	6.5	29.86	0.392	1.6	4
Somalia	7.0	15.24	NA	1.1	1

SOURCE: www.freedomhouse.org/uploads/fiw/FIW.2010_Tables_and_Graphs.pdf, accessed 28 May 2010; Mo Ibrahim Index www.moibrahimfoundation.org/en/section/the-moibrahimindex/ scores-and-ranking, accessed 28 May 2010; United Nations Development Program Human Development Index, *Jeune Afrique*, special issue 24, May 2010, 88–168; Transparency International www.transparency.org/policy.research/surveys.indices.cpi/2009/table; Failed State Index, *Foreign Policy* May–June 2009. I am indebted to research assistants Brandon Kenthammer and Laura Singleton for the initial data collection and conceptualization of this table and to Estelle Young and Eva Young for assistance in its construction.

thirty-nine of the fifty-four postcolonial years and recently spread to Darfur; its breakup is imminent. Congo struggles to overcome a failed decolonization, the predatory rule of Mobutu, endemic violence in its eastern regions, and a debilitated state. Nigeria navigates from one crisis to another, despite its high oil revenues; though often remarkable political ingenuity has held the polity together in spite of the multiplicity of ethnic and religious fracture lines, its performance ranks in the bottom third of table 9.4. Herbst and Mills point out that in 1999, these three had a per capita GDP of less than $300, compared to $2,200 for countries with less than two million inhabitants (the island polities plus the microstates of Gambia, Equatorial Guinea, Djibouti, and Swaziland). The giant states also fared poorly on the Human Development Index.[54]

The countries at either end of the continent fared distinctly better than others in the rankings; all lay in the top half. In the southern African complex

(South Africa, Namibia, Botswana, Lesotho, and Swaziland), they all fall in the Freedom House "free" category and rank highly in the Mo Ibrahim index, except for Swaziland. South Africa since the transition to majority rule and Namibia and Botswana since independence have been stable democracies that perform well on all measures.

The Arab tier of northern African states reflect a different profile. Their relative rankings owe nothing to democratic virtue; only Morocco , which has relatively open and competitive elections and is a mostly law-abiding state, fits the "partly free" category. At the center of the law, however, is the palace, the fount of authority and ultimate manager of the political realm. The other four Arab tier countries (Algeria, Tunisia, Libya, and Egypt) have been mostly authoritarian states. They also have revenues that vastly exceed those of most sub-Saharan states. All but Libya have tolerated some impotent and divided opposition groups and periodic but mostly sham elections. The regimes were frozen in power, protected by a powerful security apparatus, surrounded by predatory sycophants and greedy families.[55]

Libya is a category of its own. During his four decades of highly personalized autocracy, Muammar Qadhafy offered an extraordinary blend of sultanism, revolutionary populism, and idiosyncratic Islamism.[56] His *jamahariyya* doctrine essentially gave ideological cover to an *mukhabarak* state like its northern African counterparts, differing above all in the institutionally personalized nature of power exercise. Although he entirely monopolized authority, he used no formal title of office, other than his military rank of colonel and his favored informal designation as "guide" of the "Libyan revolution." Although he drew on traditional norms of rural Libyan tribal culture in his patrimonial rule, his legitimating ideology was an original blend of anti-imperial nationalism, popular socialism, and his distinct exegesis of Islamism. As chapter 3 explains, Libya began independence with a virtual vacuum of governance; the Italian colonial state left little behind after it was extinguished in World War II.[57] However, vast oil revenues, providing Libya with the third highest state revenue in Africa, and a small population of six million assured the means for four decades of Qadhafy's quixotic personal rule. His paradoxical antipathy to state-building combined with his destruction of the private economy created a bizarre polity, entirely patrimonial at the summit but statist at the base, with housing, food distribution, and retail trade left in government hands.[58] Oil revenues also funded Qadhafy's shifting but extravagant ambitions in the international realm from early ventures in Arab state unification (Egypt, Tunisia) to trans-Sahara expansion (a short-lived ambition to annex

Chad) to more recent pan-African ambitions (his role in launching the AU and leadership aspirations, his self-appointment as "king of kings" at an assembly of African chiefs). His costly penchant for a visionary and revolutionary African and global role led to his hosting in the 1980s a wide range of insurgents, from the Irish Revolutionary Army to the rebel leaders in Liberia and Sierra Leone, to his seeking nuclear weapon technology from North Korea (a project he abandoned in 2003), to his downing of American and French passenger aircraft. To these reckless actions one may add the multiple interventions in violent conflicts in Sudan, Somalia, Ethiopia, Uganda, Mali, Niger, and Chad. Nonetheless, sufficient resources remained to earn Africa's highest rating in the UNDP Human Development Index. Still, the scale of the 2011 uprising that overthrew him revealed the depth of popular antagonism toward his dictatorship.

The authoritarian pattern dominant in the North African states was not in itself necessarily a barrier to developmental performance in other respects. Tunisia in particular by economic measures appeared to be an effective state, whose growth rate had consistently averaged almost 5% since independence. The poverty rate had diminished from 75% to 3% and per capita GDP multiplied tenfold.[59] The initial ruler, Habib Bourguiba, was never interested in wealth and lived a modest life. His plan for transforming Tunisian society was ambitious; he insisted on universal education; when he left power, almost all adults were literate and all children were enrolled in school. Within three months of his accession, he had promulgated a remarkably progressive family code, assuring the equality of women and education for girls; he arranged for his tomb in Monastir to bear the inscription "liberator of the Tunisian woman." Although Tunisia has only small hydrocarbon revenues, a competent bureaucracy had effectively managed available resources and the substantial external assistance its positive image and careful diplomacy had assured. However, the increasingly sclerotic autocracy of Zine el Abidine Ben Ali, who ousted Bourguiba in 1987, and the immense mercantile empire seized by his family had been a source of intense frustration for the intelligentsia; regime critics long decried an inequitable distribution of the fruits of growth.[60]

Any inference of a correlation between authoritarian rule and positive developmental performance vanishes on examination of the countries in the bottom half of the rankings. Some may be classified as semidemocratic and others as in the midst of precarious democratic transition following civil war (Sierra Leone, Liberia, Congo-Kinshasa), but most are primarily authoritarian. The utter discredit of neopatrimonial autocracy below the Sahara by 1990 is not reversed by any observable performance in the last two decades. There is in contrast a striking correlation between degree of democracy and positive performance.

Another relationship worth noting concerns those polities with high levels of oil export. Even in notoriously corrupt countries whose rulers are beneficiaries of high levels of offshore wealth, such as Equatorial Guinea or Angola, the UNDP's Human Development Index figures are well above those of the most debilitated states. Even after a predatory levy has been collected on the oil revenues at the summit, enough remains to better sustain social expenditures than in the revenue-deprived polities.

LEADERSHIP AS VARIABLE

Turning to other differentiating factors explaining relative state performance, I would place leadership high on the list. The pervasive presidentialism of the postcolonial regimes multiplied the impact of the leader on the polity. Perhaps this vector operated with special force in the founding years; the most remarkable leaders created an enduring array of norms governing state behavior and a pattern of voluntary withdrawal from power that path dependency reproduced in succeeding rulers. Among noteworthy examples, I would mention Julius Nyerere of Tanzania, Léopold Senghor of Senegal, and Nelson Mandela, hero of the South African transition.

Nyerere and Senghor both made consequential miscalculations in developmental orientation, drawn for a time into the temptations of the integral state. Forced villagization in Tanzania and rural animation in Senegal were unsuccessful policies. But the leaders came to recognize the failings of this model and did not oppose policy changes by their successors. The single-party monopolies they erected provided more channels for voice than most others. Their framing of socialist orientation as rooted in African heritage was far from universally convincing, but it was less denatured by unrestrained oppression and visible predation under a socialist façade than in many other countries. Two peaceful constitutional successions have taken place in Senegal and South Africa, three in Tanzania. Nyerere, Senghor, and Mandela especially are inscribed in popular memory as revered founding fathers who all left office voluntarily. All of them bequeathed to their countries a secured national identity.

Some others might be added to the roster of able and effective leaders who left a legacy of prosperity; many would include Félix Houphouët-Boigny of Ivory Coast, president for thirty-three years. Especially during his first two decades, the country enjoyed remarkable economic success, and his paternal

autocracy was never as harsh as that of many of his contemporaries. However, his successors, especially Laurent Gbagbo, have not proved worthy of
his legacy.

In 2006, the Mo Ibrahim Foundation established an annual Prize for Leadership Achievement, whose emoluments exceed those of the Nobel Prize.
The award is intended to recognize meritorious presidential performance
and constitutional departure from office; Joaquim Chissano of Mozambique
won the first prize in 2007, and Festus Mogae of Botswana won the second
in 2008. No prize was awarded in 2009 and 2010; Pedro Pires of Cape Verde
was honored in 2011. In retrospect, beyond Nyerere, Senghor, and Mandela,
one might find few credible nominees for such a prize from earlier decades.
Otherwise put, outstanding leadership could make a difference; however,
only a modest number of countries had rulers who left an enduring positive
legacy.

The emergence of the pattern of life presidency by the late 1960s, with the
military coup being the sole avenue of incumbent displacement, figured prominently in the catalogue of discontents surfacing during the 1990 moment of
democratic enthusiasm. Most African states adopted new constitutions at this
time, two-thirds of which included provisions limiting presidential terms to
two.[61] As chapter 3 indicates, none of the independence constitutions had
such a provision. They had been closely modeled on the political institutions
of the colonizer; terms limits were alien to European parliamentary systems,
and the newly installed presidentialist French Fifth Republic had yet to confront this issue.

As the democratic wave receded a decade later, moves to eliminate term
limit provisions began to accelerate. Thus far, term limit repeal has taken place
in Guinea (2001), Tunisia and Togo (2002), Gabon (2003), Chad and Uganda
(2005), Cameroon and Algeria (2008), and Djibouti (2010). In several of these
cases, repeal was fiercely opposed, and in Nigeria, Malawi, and Zambia it was
blocked by parliaments and civil society. I find this repeal trend regrettable;
the lessons of five decades of African politics speak eloquently to the advantages of periodic alternation. The longer a ruler holds power, the more difficult disengagement becomes. The accumulation of repressive acts, including
arbitrary imprisonments and even assassination of journalists or other vocal
critics, make the ruler vulnerable to prosecution if an opposition party ever
wins power. So also does resort to neopatrimonial or prebendal practices to
sustain loyalties. The threat is not only to the ruler but also the inner circle
of henchmen, likely partners in predation, who insist on prolongation of his

rule. Perpetuation in power also tends to consolidate security clienteles tied to the ruler by ethno-regional affinities. The congealing ethnic alignments may advantage some, but they may permanently marginalize others to the ultimate cost of the polity: this is one of the lessons of the recent spread of internal wars. The certainty of rotation from office that term limits enforce makes presidential power accountable to a degree and imposes a constraint on predation and repression. To be sure, a countervailing incentive may exist if there is a deadline for translating power into wealth, but at the cost of likely self-exile on leaving office.

I have argued that in the period since 1990, there has been a striking variation in pathways, in contrast to the largely parallel state itineraries of the first three decades, from total state collapse to relatively effective political and economic liberalization. Beyond leadership, the relative strength and capacity of states facilitated successful transition, although as Ivory Coast illustrates, it did not assure it. The weakest states, such as Central African Republic or Guinea-Bissau, were especially vulnerable. Although protracted civil wars, as chapter 7 argues, had a range of specific causes, they usually exacted a toll on state capacity and performance even after relative peace returned, and they frequently had spillover effects on adjoining states. Financial vulnerability and severity of revenue constraints varied. Neopatrimonialism was more deeply entrenched in some countries and thus more strongly persistent. Some forms of patrimonial autocracy were more destructive than others; Bongo in Gabon was much less damaging to the polity than Mobutu in Congo-Kinshasa. But no list of overall determinants provides a full explanation of the contemporary divergence of itineraries; much of the difference lies in the particular events, sequences, and configurations of particular countries.

Top Performers: Botswana and Mauritius

The evidence strongly suggests that a democratic rule-of-law state over time makes a large difference. Negatively put, extended periods of internal war or disorder, tyrannical rule, or high levels of corruption impose lasting damage; a lost decade is difficult to overcome. To illuminate this thesis, I return to the striking cases of Botswana and Mauritius. Chapter 3 takes note of the arresting fact that of the fifty-three African states they are alone in preserving an uninterrupted constitutional democratic framework since independence. This enduring attachment to a liberal political order and related stability must surely figure prominently in any explanation of their place at the top of the rankings of state performance in table 9.4, and it merits further reflection.

Chapter 3 also points to the particular nature of colonial occupation and legacy in both cases.[62] For different reasons, the colonial state in these two countries was, relative to most of Africa, a minimal presence. In Botswana, British rule until the era of decolonization was a holding operation in anticipation of eventual South African incorporation. The Tswana chiefs, who had originally accepted British overrule to avert such a fate, were trusted intermediaries, whose cattle herds prospered. From their ranks came much of the first generation of postcolonial leaders, including the founding president, Seretse Khama of distinguished ancestry. Minimalist colonial occupation had its costs: slender physical and human infrastructure (twelve kilometers of paved roads, twenty-two university graduates at independence).

Though Khama died in office in 1980, he had made careful provision for a constitutional succession, placing Quett Masire, of chiefly derivation from another of the eight Tswana subgroups, as vice president. Festus Mogae was elected president in 1998 when Masire stepped aside and was replaced in turn by Ian Khama, son of Seretse and chief of the largest Tswana subgroup as well as Botswana Defense Force commander, in 2008. His military background, his critics murmur, finds reflection in a political style less consensual than that of his predecessors.

The ruling Botswana Democratic Party (BDP), which initially enjoyed the favor of the withdrawing colonizer, has remained continuously in office for more than four decades. This entrenched domination in some eyes dilutes the seductiveness of Botswana's performance. However, the BDP ascendancy has survived nine postindependence elections whose integrity has not been challenged. Its electoral majority in the last two polls in 2004 and 2009 was 52% and 53%, respectively. The single-member district majoritarian electoral system, combined with a divided opposition, translates these figures into large parliamentary majorities. Although Freedom House ranks Botswana below Cape Verde, Mauritius, and Ghana in its freedom scale, BDP hegemony does not rely on repression.

Rather, stable and open politics, joined to wise leadership, facilitated the crafting of a performing developmental state built on the modest institutional legacy of its colonial predecessor. At the local level, the customary structures of indirect rule served as the basis for regional administration. The legitimacy of the chiefly class was less impaired by its colonial associations than in most other states. The *kgotlas*, or local councils, retained a role in fostering consensus. To an unusual degree, the modern state was an organic growth rooted in Tswana historical culture.

The chiefly core of the postcolonial elite provided cohesive leadership for a modernization project, even though there were rivalries between the groups as well as significant subject populations within the Tswana zones.[63] Perhaps because of the local rooting of the chiefly elite and customary sources of its social standing, Botswana never yielded to the temptations of socialist orientation or the integral state. A market economy was the clear choice, and it was made at the time of 1966 independence, under the guidance of an autonomous state apparatus. Somali scholar Abdi Samatar provides a penetrating exegesis of Botswana's success: "To fully understand the nature of the postcolonial [Botswana] state, its role and ability to transform the economy, requires an appreciation of the motives and agendas of two groups: those dominant-class members who occupy strategic positions in the state apparatus and those bureaucrats who provided the leadership with technical advice. . . . This leadership recognized the importance of disciplined and technically competent public institutions for systematic capitalist development."[64]

The professionalism of the state managers finds measure in the unusually low incidence of corruption. The Transparency International Corruption Perceptions Index in table 9.4 rates Botswana as the least corrupt country in Africa. One plausible explanation offered for the exceptional integrity of the state lies in the fact that the core chiefly elite's wealth comes from their own cattle and land; political power was not a unique pathway to wealth. Further, a performing state guaranteed a stable livelihood for the public service; thus Botswana never experienced the evisceration of the real value of civil service salaries through high inflation or extended pay arrearages that forced government employees in many states into survival-driven corrupt practices.

At the moment of independence, Botswana had meager receipts and was completely a tributary to the South African economy. The main sources of income were cattle, a modest part of which came from beef exports, and remittances from its migrant workers in the South African mines. The new state further commercialized its cattle herds and expanded its meat-packing industry through a well-run parastatal.[65] Mineral good fortune blessed Botswana independence; the development of a copper mine and the providential discovery of a rich diamond pipe transformed the revenue equation, and began to provide a resource base for developmental investment. The crucial differentiator was the insulation of the windfall from predation. Revenues flowed into state-building, infrastructure, and social provisions, creating an enduring developmental momentum.

I have underlined the lasting significance of the norms of leadership instilled by exemplary founding presidents. Seretse Khama, who had a modest
style that starkly contrasted with the flamboyant lust for power often visible
elsewhere, set a standard of conduct that had a lasting effect. Michael Crowder
offers an insightful portrait: "Personally he was equable, a good listener with
a keen sense of humor. He was the most unpompous of men and disliked that
trait in others. He was unostentatious—like most Batswana, who were chiefs
or commoners—and was happiest when on his farm or cattle post."[66]

Critics of the Botswana example are not without some pertinent caveats
to its model status. Though leaders have changed, the BDP remains a fixture
in power, even if it can argue that its effective rule merited continuous reelection. Though not by predation, the chiefly elite has prospered during its
decades of political ascendancy. Even if inequality in Botswana is far from the
extremes of kleptocratic states, there is enough to validate the grumbling from
the less favored. The rents from the giant diamond mine are turning downward; new mineral sources to sustain state revenue will soon be needed. Projects to develop new mines in the Kalahari region populated by San groups
have generated protests. HIV/AIDS hit Botswana hard, reducing life expectancy from nearly seventy to forty by 2003; however, Botswana has the resources and capacity to organize a public health campaign to combat this
plague and reduce its incidence. Even acknowledging the limits of success, I
find Botswana's performance admirable.

Mauritius, the other polity that has seen continuous postindependence
constitutional democracy, differs in many key respects from Botswana. The
small geographic dimensions of the island polity and absence of high-value
natural resources are a first obvious distinction. Even more striking is the
demographic difference; in utter contrast to the relative homogeneity of
Botswana, Mauritius has a remarkably complex cultural pluralism. From its
first eighteenth century settlement as a slave-based sugar plantation, mostly
French planters drew on the servile labor of Africans from the eastern coast
and Madagascar. Under British rule from 1810 to 1968, emancipation of slaves
in 1834 led the planters to seek an alternative labor supply through importation of indentured workers from south Asia. Later, a small Chinese mercantile
population completed the demographic kaleidoscope. Although a number of
Franco-Mauritian large sugar estates remain, a good part of the land passed
into the hands of the Indian indentured servants, who became a small and
medium planting class. Over time, a creolization occurred amongst the African

population and those of mixed race. As in Botswana, the colonial state rested lightly upon Mauritius, small in scale and minimal in its functions.

Mauritius faces the challenge of managing a complex cultural pluralism sharply defined along the distinct axes of race, ethnicity, and religion. Nearly 70% are Indian, of whom 80% are Hindu; Chinese and Franco-Mauritians are small minorities, and the remainder are of African or mixed ancestry. As a census and—in practice—political category, whites, coloreds, and Africans are combined under the label "general population," who make up 30% of the total. Cultural identities are strong; serious rioting along identity lines accompanied independence. But communal polarization has been held in check, in good part through the play of democratic politics structured by ingenious constitutional engineering.

The sixty-two elected parliamentary seats are mostly contested in three-member districts, in which each voter chooses three candidates, not necessarily from the same party. Parties can run multiple candidates; the three securing the most votes are elected, irrespective of party. The electoral districts are carefully drawn to take account of communal geography; the goal is to obtain a parliamentary demography reflecting the cultural diversity of the country. To ensure the approximation of this goal and prevent any group from feeling like it is being culturally excluded, eight additional seats are allocated to "best losers" with an eye to overall balances.

The national parties run slates of candidates that represent all major groups. Electoral geography and a multiparty system mean that no party can expect to win a majority alone; thus coalitions are the rule. By custom, the heads of government usually come (except for Paul Berenger [2003–5]) from the largest group, Hindus, though from different parties. There have been three heads of state since independence: Seewoosagur Ramgoolam (1968–82), Aneerod Jugnauth (1982–95), and Navinchandra Ramgoolam (1995–2003, since 2005). The two most important parties over time have been the Mauritian Labor Party, a centrist formation, and the Mouvement militant mauricien, created as a class-based leftist party in 1969 by Franco-Mauritian radical Paul Berenger but moderating when in governing coalitions. All parties have been subject to periodic splits, creating a fluid political alignment and frequent realignment of coalitions. On two occasions (1982 and 1995), incumbent coalitions lost virtually all the elected seats, though the triumphant alliance won less than two-thirds of the votes.[67] To a striking degree, political families have supplied the rulers; the initial key players, Seewoosagur Ramgoolam,

Aneerod Jugnauth, and Gaëtan Duval, have been replaced by their respective sons, Navinchandra, Pravind, and Xavier-Luc.

Contrary to pessimistic expectations at the time of independence, the developmental performance matches the political.[68] Entirely a sugar plantation economy at independence, Mauritius made creative use of an export-processing zone to build a light industrial base, especially textiles, long benefiting from privileged access to the European Common Market. Tourism also provided substantial revenue and employment. Sugar production expanded, enjoying a period of high prices in the 1970s and occasionally since. More recently, financial services have joined the list. Although the textile sector in particular has come under heavy pressure recently from Chinese competition and the export-processing zone is less successful than at first, state initiatives to diversify the economy have built a more secure economic foundation. Even though ruling coalitions have often been unstable, prudent policy, a competent bureaucracy, and a rule-of-law state offset the limits of the natural endowment. Mauritius ranks well at the top of the Mo Ibrahim governance index and second only to Botswana in Transparency International measures of state integrity.

FINAL REFLECTIONS

These two cases serve as a fitting coda to this volume. Even if perhaps idiosyncratic and not representative of the continental landscape, they do illustrate another future that is open to Africa other than the stagnation and decline predominant in the first three postcolonial decades. The last two decades provide encouraging evidence that the top two performers may be joined by a significant number of countries.

I share the view of David Leonard and Scott Straus that the developmental impasse was linked in the first instance to politics: the neopatrimonial autocracy and personal rule that were its primary expression in the first decades, joined to the pathologies of the integral state project and illusions for a number of state socialism experiments.[69] But politics is also a learning process, and the bitter lessons of state crisis and failure are inscribed on the historical tablets informing recent deliberations on governance. Recent evidence would indicate that political learning has taken place, that sectors of competence at the heart of states have somewhat enlarged, and that developmental performance has improved, not only through favorable commodity prices in recent years. The "official mind" operating at the inner core of many states has a far more informed and realistic grasp of the global political economy and the choices available. There is a larger consensus on the value of democratic politics and market economics than existed in the early decades, grounded in the lessons drawn from the excesses of the 1970s and 1980s; this is reflected in the nature of recent constitutional debate, as well as AU projects such as NEPAD.

But as I stress in the opening chapter and elsewhere, the recent phase of African political evolution shows a striking divergence of itineraries. Neopatrimonial habits are not erased, and continue to dominate in a distressing number of states, especially the weakest performers in Table 9.4. The subordinate location of Africa in the global arena and its high vulnerability to external shocks still shackle the continent. The sad chronicle of Haiti two centuries after 1804 liberation is a salutary reminder that there is nothing linear or inevitable about progress and that reproduction of state failure over an indefinite period is a real possibility for the most dysfunctional polities.[70]

Coinciding with some overall positive trends are several unforeseen vectors of change. The scale of diaspora remittances was first recognized only in the 1990s; in recent years, it has exceeded the flow of official aid. Chinese economic engagement with Africa has dramatically expanded and has now reached a scale sufficient to weigh substantially on future development. The balance of advantage, particularly of the huge mineral quest, remains for the future to determine, but China will be a major player. The new salience of developmental models different from the neoliberal postulates of the "Washington Consensus" offers both choice and modest leverage in external dealings.

At the base, even in the most deteriorated and dysfunctional polities, African society has demonstrated remarkable capacities for adaptation and survival. Theodore Trefon, in the context of a deeply pessimistic assessment of state-rebuilding efforts in Congo-Kinshasa, insists that the disappointments of reform do not imply a failure of society, which in contrast to the state "is strong, innovative and dynamic."[71] The populace of Somalia, dwelling in a stateless environment and perpetual warlord politics for two decades, find ingenious avenues of survival, operating the political economy of anarchy.

The shelters for survival are situated in the informal sector, whose emergence was first noted only in 1972.[72] Informal sectors during the 1980s crisis decade exploded to engulf much of the economy in many countries. Their size and resistance to government capture in the weaker polities both provide social protection and constrain the state.

Other changing parameters merit passing note. The crisis years particularly blighted the hopes of the youth generation, who found their prospects for social ascension blocked. Their frustration and discontents found eloquent voice in the protest movements sweeping North Africa at the end of 2010, as well as in the sometimes desperate attempts to emigrate to Europe. They do not share the social memory of winning independence, and most have grown up under repressive and corrupt regimes. The contrast with the independence moment is stark; at that moment, the rising young generation, particularly its educated members, found their nationalist enthusiasm rewarded by expectations of social advance. The first generation of nationalist leaders were mostly under forty; in recent years few rulers were young, and a number were octogenarians (Mubarak, Mugabe, Wade).

The rapid spread of new forms of communication have already had a dramatic effect, cell phones in particular. The social media that follow in their wake are only beginning to make their impact felt; internet penetration remains limited in many countries. But these new technologies will knit civil society together in novel ways and open the door to different forms of collective action.

Another momentous change is the greatly expanded role and influence of women in the political process, ably documented by Aili Tripp and others.[73] In part stimulated by the landmark UN conferences on women in Nairobi (1985) and Beijing (1995), women have claimed and won a place in political leadership mostly absent in 1960. Women now hold over 30% of parliamentary seats in Rwanda, Mozambique, South Africa, Uganda, Tanzania, and Burundi, and a woman holds the presidency in Liberia. Many entered the ministerial ranks and play a crucial role in civil society and mediation of violent conflicts.

No country is more crucial to the future of Africa than South Africa. Its remarkable transition from apartheid to nonracial constitutional democracy was an epochal event. It is by far the strongest economy and polity in Africa, and thus by example and engagement its regional and continental leadership is a critical trump card. Two successions following Mandela later, its essential strength is intact. But the difficulties that lie ahead are daunting. The huge inequalities that are a legacy of apartheid remain, resistant to early reduction. Less saintly leadership than Mandela was doubtless inevitable, but Jacob Zuma has faced growing contestation, as did Thabo Mbeki before him. Tensions within the ruling ANC are growing, and the challenge of balancing prudent macroeconomic management of a capitalist order and satisfying populist pressures from its base is huge. South Africa is a growing contributor to the economies to its north and has been an energetic mediator in African civil conflicts, though it perhaps has disappointed many in its toleration for Mugabe's destructive rule in Zimbabwe and its support for Gbagbo's usurpation despite his clear electoral defeat in Ivory Coast; it has been a positive influence in most cases. The continuing success of South Africa as a political economy will shape the future far beyond its borders.

Hope for a better future thus is daily reborn. The path to redemption and recovery has been found in an encouraging number of instances. Not all will find and follow this trail in the years ahead, but I believe that enough states will do so to build on the positive recent overall trends in political and economic liberalization. Returning to the conclusion of chapter 2, my reading of the last half century is that the most certain avenue to a performing, efficacious state is through constitutional democratic rule-of-law governance that is respectful of universal values of human rights and authenticated by a grounding in an African heritage.

Notes

CHAPTER I. A HALF CENTURY OF AFRICAN INDEPENDENCE

1. Other earlier dates of at least nominal independence might be noted: 1847, when Liberia shedded the tutelage of the private American Colonization Society; 1910, when South Africa won dominion status and power was transferred almost exclusively to its white minority; 1922, when Egypt gained heavily circumscribed sovereignty, although Britain retained important defense, foreign policy, and financial powers; 1941, when the brief Italian occupation of Ethiopia was thrown off; and 1951, when a jerry-built Libyan state was launched unaware of its oil riches by the United Nations. None of these earlier developments had any broader African impact.

2. From 1960 until 1971, Congo-Kinshasa was known as the Republic of the Congo; from 1971 to 1997, it was rebaptized Zaire. The formal title of the country was again changed in 1997 to Democratic Republic of Congo, often shortened to DRC or DR Congo. Until a new constitution was adopted in 2005 and internationally monitored national elections were held in 2006, this was a misnomer; the regime founded by Laurent Kabila as self-proclaimed president was neither democratic nor republican, since Joseph Kabila succeeded his assassinated father in 2001. Though the country now formally conforms to its title, for purposes of clarity and consistency, I use "Congo-Kinshasa" to refer to it during the entire postcolonial period, and I use "Congo-Brazzaville" for the neighboring Republic of Congo, whose capital is Brazzaville.

3. G. N. Sanderson, "The European Partition of Africa: Origins and Dynamics," in *The Cambridge History of Africa*, vol. 6, ed. J. D. Fage and Roland Oliver (Cambridge: Cambridge University Press, 1985), 96–102.

4. Ali A. Mazrui, introduction, *General History of Africa*, vol. 8, ed. Ali A. Mazrui and Christophe Wondji (Oxford, UK: Heinemann, 1993), 9–10.

5. Jan Vansina, *Paths in the Rainforest: Toward a History of Political Tradition in Equatorial Africa* (Madison: University of Wisconsin Press, 1990).

6. Diverse examples include W. E. Abraham, *The Mind of Africa* (Chicago: University of Chicago Press, 1962), Kwame Anthony Appiah, *In My Father's House: Africa in the*

Philosophy of Culture (New York: Oxford University Press, 1992), and Kwame Gyekye, *Tradition and Modernity: Philosophical Reflections on the African Experience* (New York: Oxford University Press, 1997).

7. Julius Nyerere, *Ujamaa: Essays on Socialism* (London: Oxford University Press, 1968); Léopold Senghor, *On African Socialism* (New York: Praeger, 1964).

8. Michael G. Schatzberg, *Political Legitimacy in Middle Africa: Father, Family, Food* (Bloomington: Indiana University Press, 2001).

9. Crawford Young, *The African Colonial State in Comparative Perspective* (New Haven, CT: Yale University Press, 1994).

10. Daniel R. Headrick engagingly shows how the steamboat, the machine gun, the telegraph, and quinine were powerful force multipliers for colonial conquest. See *Tools of Empire: Technology and European Imperialism in the Nineteenth Century* (New York: Oxford University Press, 1981).

11. Young, *The African Colonial State*, 280.

12. A fifty-fourth state entered the African roster in 2011, South Sudan.

13. For example, David Apter notes that the average age of ministers in the first Ghanian government was forty-four; the average age of assembly members was forty. Ghana had an unusually well established political elite. See *Ghana in Transition*, 2nd ed. (Princeton, NJ: Princeton University Press, 1972).

14. Bertrand Badie, *L'état importé: Essai sur l'occidentalisation de l'ordre politique* (Paris: Fayard, 1992).

15. John Campbell, *Nigeria: Dancing on the Brink* (Lanham, MD: Rowman and Littlefield, 2011); 12; Chinua Achebe, "Nigeria's Promise, Africa's Hope," *New York Times*, 16 January 2011, WK12.

16. Goran Hyden, *African Politics in Comparative Perspective* (New York: Cambridge University Press, 2006); William Tordoff, *Government and Politics in Africa*, 4th ed. (Bloomington: Indiana University Press, 2002); Victor T. Le Vine, *Politics in Francophone Africa* (Boulder, CO: Lynne Rienner, 2004); René Lemarchand, *The Dynamics of Violence in Central Africa* (Philadelphia: University of Pennsylvania Press, 2008); Patrick Chabal, *Africa: The Politics of Suffering and Smiling* (London: Zed, 2009).

17. The term derives from Jean Copans, *Les marabouts et l'arachide: La confrérie mouride et les paysans au Sénégal* (Paris: Sycamore, 1980), 248; see also Christian Coulon, *Le marabout et le prince: Islam et pouvoir au Sénégal* (Paris: Pedone, 1981), 289. I draw on this concept in "Zaire: The Shattered Illusion of the Integral State," *Journal of Modern African Studies* 32.2 (1994): 249–63, and *The African Colonial State*, 287–88.

18. Hyden, *African Politics*, 26–37.

19. For an excellent account, see Anthony Low, "The End of the British Empire in Africa," in *Decolonization and African Independence: The Transfers of Power 1960–1980*, ed. Prosser Gifford and W. Roger Louis (New Haven, CT: Yale University Press, 1988), 33–72.

20. Cited in Crawford Young, "Decolonization in Africa," in *Colonialism in Africa 1870–1960*, vol. 2, ed. L. H. Gann and Peter Duignan (London: Cambridge University Press, 1970), 452.

21. With the exceptions of Algeria, whose armed struggle for independence succeeded only in 1962, and the microstates of Comoros and Djibouti, which became independent in 1975 and 1977 respectively.

22. In the words of his biographer, Brian Urquhart; see *Hammarskjold* (New York: Knopf, 1972), 382.

23. Martin Meredith, *The Fate of Africa: From the Hopes of Freedom to the Heart of Despair* (New York: Public Affairs, 2005), 29.

24. Alistaire Horne, *A Savage War of Peace: Algeria, 1954–1962* (London: Macmillan, 1977), 538–40.

25. Horne, *A Savage War of Peace*, 13–14.

26. Young, *The African Colonial State*, 213.

27. Meredith, *The Fate of Africa*, 66.

28. Kwame Nkrumah, *I Speak of Freedom: A Statement of African Ideology* (New York: Praeger, 1961), 117.

29. See Tony Killick's *Development Economics in Action* (London: Heinemann, 1978), an insightful review of the impact of development economics of the 1950s in framing the radical (and ultimately flawed) strategy of Nkrumah's Ghana,.

30. W. W. Rostow, *States of Economic Growth: A Non-Communist Manifesto* (Cambridge: Cambridge University Press, 1960); Albert Hirschman, *Journeys Toward Progress: Studies of Economic Planning in Latin America* (New York: Twentieth Century Fund, 1963); Albert Waterston, *Development Planning: Lessons of Experience* (Baltimore, MD: Johns Hopkins University Press, 1965); Andrew W. Kamarck, *The Economics of African Development*, 2nd ed. (New York: Praeger, 1967).

31. Crawford Young, *Politics in the Congo* (Princeton, NJ: Princeton University Press, 1965), 402; the original source is *Staff Problems in Tropical and Subtropical Countries* (Brussels: International Institute of Differing Civilizations, 1961), 174.

32. Thomas Hodgkin, *African Political Parties* (Baltimore, MD: Penguin, 1961); Ruth Schachter Morgenthau, *Political Parties in French-Speaking West Africa* (London: Oxford University Press, 1964); James Coleman and Carl Rosberg, eds., *Political Parties and National Integration in Tropical Africa* (Berkeley: University of California Press, 1966).

33. Important examples include Aristide Zolberg, *One-Party Government in the Ivory Coast* (Princeton, NJ: Princeton University Press, 1964), Apter, *Ghana in Transition*, and Herbert Weiss, *Political Protest in the Congo: The Parti Solidaire Africain During the Independence Struggle* (Princeton, NJ: Princeton University Press, 1967).

34. Goran Hyden, *Political Development in Rural Tanzania: TANU Yajenga Nchi* (Nairobi: East African Publishing House, 1969).

35. Crawford Young, "United States Policy toward Africa: Silver Anniversary Reflections," *African Studies Review* 27.3 (1984): 1–17.

36. Apter, *Ghana in Transition*, ix.

37. For detail on the Nkrumah turn to repression, see Meredith, *The Fate of Africa*, 179–92.

38. Notably Morgenthau, *Political Parties in French-Speaking West Africa*; Immanuel Wallerstein, *Africa: The Politics of Independence* (New York: Vintage, 1971).

39. Lionel Cliffe, ed., *One Party Democracy: The 1965 Tanzania General Election* (Nairobi: East African Publishing House, 1967), 467. Substantial extracts from the 1965 report are reprinted in this volume.

40. Aristide Zolberg, *Creating Political Order* (Chicago: Rand McNally, 1966).

41. Wallerstein, *Africa*; Immanuel Wallerstein, "The Decline of the Party in Single-Party African States," in *Political Parties and Political Development*, ed. Joseph LaPalombara and Myron Weiner (Princeton, NJ: Princeton University Press, 1969), 201–14.

42. Qtd. in Dennis Austin, *Politics in Ghana, 1946–1960* (London: Oxford University Press, 1964), 411.

43. René Dumont, *L'Afrique noire est mal partie* (Paris: Seuil, 1962); Albert Meister, *L'Afrique: Peut-elle partir?* (Paris: Seuil, 1966).

44. Martin Kilson, "Authoritarianism and Single-Party Tendencies," *World Politics* 15.2 (1963): 262–94.

45. W. Arthur Lewis, *Politics in West Africa* (New York: Oxford University Press, 1965), 63.

46. Lewis, *Politics in West Africa*, 32.

47. The size of the literature on the 1960–61 Congo crisis bears witness to the magnitude of the drama. The most invaluable single source remains the annual documentary volumes published from 1959 to 1967 by the former Centre de recherches et d'informations socio-politiques in Brussels, especially Benoît Verhaegen and Jules Gérard-Libois, *Congo, 1960*, 2 vols. (Brussels: CRISP, 1961). Other especially invaluable guides include Jean-Claude Willame, *Patrice Lumumba: La crise congolaise revisitée* (Paris: Karthala, 1990), Thomas Kanza, *Conflict in the Congo* (Harmondsworth, UK: Penguin, 1972), and, on the international dimensions, Madeleine G. Kalb, *The Congo Cables: The Cold War in Africa from Eisenhower to Kennedy* (New York: Macmillan, 1982). Larry Devlin, CIA station chief in Kinshasa at that time, has recently published his Congo autobiography, which sheds some new light on the CIA role in ousting Lumumba; see *Chief of Station Congo: A Memoir of 1960–67* (New York: Public Affairs, 2007).

48. Influential contributions include Robin Luckham, *The Nigerian Military* (Cambridge: Cambridge University Press, 1971), and Dennis Austin and Robin Luckham, eds., *Politicians and Soldiers in Ghana, 1966–1972* (London: Frank Cass, 1975). One might recollect that a wave of mutinies, ultimately put down by British troops afflicted Kenya, Tanzania, and Uganda in 1964, another indicator of the possible fragility of new power.

49. See especially the splendid two-volume *Rébellions au Congo* (Brussels: CRISP, 1966, 1960); other accounts include Catherine Coquéry-Vidrovitch, Alain Forest, and Herbert Weiss, eds., *Rébellions-révolution au Zaire, 1963–1965*, 2 vols. (Paris: L'Harmattan, 1987), and Crawford Young, "Rebellions and the Congo," in *Protest and Power in Black Africa*, ed. Robert I. Rotberg and Ali A. Mazrui (New York: Oxford University Press, 1970), 969–1011.

50. Of special value on the Nigerian civil war are Anthony Kirk-Greene, *Crisis and Conflict in Nigeria*, 2 vols. (London: Oxford University Press, 1971), on the internal dimension, and John J. Stremlau, *The International Politics of the Nigerian Civil War, 1967–1970* (Princeton, NJ: Princeton University Press, 1977).

51. Francis Deng offers a sensitive and discerning exegesis in *War of Visions: Conflict of Identities in the Sudan* (Washington, DC: Brookings Institution, 1995).

52. E.-Xavier Ugeux, "La diplomatie agissante de Mobutu," *Remarques Africaines* 16–30 September 1973, 49–70. Jean-Claude Willame at the time joined in the sanguine appraisal, although he subsequently became a stinging critic; see *Patrimonialism and Political Change in the Congo* (Stanford, CA: Stanford University Press, 1972). See also Crawford Young and Thomas Turner, *The Rise and Decline of the Zairian State* (Madison: University of Wisconsin Press, 1985).

53. Richard L. Sklar, "Crisis and Transitions in the Political History of Independent Nigeria," in *Dilemmas of Democracy in Nigeria*, ed. Paul A. Beckett and Crawford Young (Rochester, NY: University of Rochester Press, 1997), 21–22.

54. Deng, *War of Visions*, 158.

55. These arguments appear in a number of influential works; among them are Morris Janowitz, *The Military in the Political Development of New Nations* (Chicago: University of Chicago Press, 1964), John J. Johnson, ed., *The Role of the Military in Underdeveloped Countries* (Princeton, NJ: Princeton University Press, 1962), and Claude Welch, *Soldier and State in Africa* (Evanston, IL: Northwestern University Press, 1970).

56. Samuel Huntington, *Political Order in Changing Societies* (New Haven, CT: Yale University Press, 1968).

57. Samuel Decalo, *Coups and Army Rule in Africa: Studies in Military Style* (New Haven, CT: Yale University Press, 1976).

58. Crawford Young, *Ideology and Development in Africa* (New Haven, CT: Yale University Press, 1982), 132–33.

59. These extraordinary measures and their disastrous consequences are described in Young and Turner, *The Rise and Decline of the Zairian State*, 326–62.

60. Cited in Thomas J. Biersteker, *Multinationals, the State, and Control of the Nigerian Economy* (Princeton, NJ: Princeton University Press, 1987), 75.

61. Young, *Ideology and Development*, 106.

62. Of the voluminous writings of Samir Amin, especially relevant to this intellectual moment are *Accumulation on a World Scale: A Critique of the Theory of Underdevelopment* (New York: Monthly Review Press, 1974) and *Unequal Development* (New York: Monthly Review Press, 1977). The powerful polemic by the able historian Walter Rodney, *How Europe Underdeveloped Africa* (London: Bogle L'Ouverture, 1972), had particular resonance among the African intelligentsia.

63. Eight by my count: Congo-Brazzaville, Benin, Somalia, Madagascar, Ethiopia, Mozambique, Angola, and Sao Tome and Principe.

64. "The State and the Small Urban Center in Africa," the 1977 paper, was published in *Small Urban Centers in Rural Development in Africa*, ed. Aidan Southell (Madison: African Studies Program, University of Wisconsin–Madison, 1979). The life history of this project contained in miniature the mood shift in the second cycle from hope to despair; when the venture began in the mid-1970s, the small urban center was seen as the vital nexus between the developmental center and the rural periphery. By the time of publication, regional centers were viewed as mechanisms of extraction by the center. See also Crawford Young, "Zaire: The Unending Crisis," *Foreign Affairs* 57.1 (1978): 169–85.

65. Robert H. Jackson and Carl G. Rosberg, *Personal Rule in Black Africa* (Berkeley: University of California Press, 1982), 17–19.

66. Willame, *Patrimonialism and Political Change.*

67. Jean-François Médard, "The Underdeveloped State in Africa: Politicial Clientelism or Neo-Patrimonialism?" in *Private Patronage and Public Power*, ed. Christopher Clapham (London: Pinter, 1982), 162–92; Jean-François Médard, "L'état néo-patrimonial en Afrique Noire," in *États d'Afrique noire: Formation, mécanismes et crises*, ed. Jean-François Médard (Paris: Karthala, 1994).

68. David J. Gould, *Bureaucratic Corruption and Underdevelopment in the Third World: The Case of Zaire* (New York: Pergamon, 1980), 49.

69. Stanislas Andreski, *The African Predicament: A Study in the Pathology of Modernization* (London: Michael Joseph, 1968), 92–109. For one such example of indulgent academic treatment, see James C. Scott, *Comparative Political Corruption* (Englewood Cliffs, NJ: Prentice-Hall, 1972).

70. *New York Times*, 14 June 2002. For an insightful and detailed exegesis of contemporary corruption, see Daniel Jordan Smith, *A Culture of Corruption: Everyday Deception and Popular Discontent in Nigeria* (Princeton, NJ: Princeton University Press, 2007).

71. World Bank, *Accelerated Development in Sub-Saharan Africa: An Agenda for Action* (Washington, DC: World Bank, 1981).

72. World Bank, *Sub-Saharan Africa: From Crisis to Sustainable Growth* (Washington, DC: World Bank, 1989), 221.

73. Young, *Ideology and Development*, 6.

74. Richard Sandbrook, *The Politics of African Economic Stagnation* (Cambridge: Cambridge University Press, 1985); Crawford Young, "Zaire: Is There a State?" *Canadian Journal of African Studies* 18.1 (1984): 80–82.

75. Naomi Chazan, *An Anatomy of Ghanaian Politics: Managing Political Recession, 1969–1982* (Boulder, CO: Westview, 1982), 334–35.

76. Robert H. Jackson and Carl G. Rosberg, "Why Africa's Weak States Persist: The Empirical and the Juridical in Statehood," *World Politics* 35.1 (1982): 1–24; Robert H. Jackson, *Quasi-States: Sovereignty, International Relations, and the Third World* (Cambridge: Cambridge University Press, 1990).

77. Johnathan H. Frimpong-Ansah, *The Vampire State in Africa: The Political Economy of Decline in Ghana* (London: James Currey, 1991).

78. Samuel P. Huntington, *The Third Wave: Democratization in the Late Twentieth Century* (Norman: University of Oklahoma Press, 1991).

79. See, for example, "Governance, Cultural Change, and Empowerment" (*Journal of Modern African Studies* 30.4 [1992]: 543–67) by World Bank official Pierre Landell-Mills.

80. For further elaboration, see Crawford Young, "Africa: An Interim Balance Sheet," in *Democratization in Africa*, ed. Larry Diamond and Marc F. Plattner (Baltimore, MD: Johns Hopkins University Press, 1999), 63–79.

81. For detail, see Luis Martinez, *The Algerian Civil War, 1990–1998*, trans. Jonathan Derrick (New York: Columbia University Press, 2000), and William B. Quandt, *Between Ballots and Bullets: Algeria's Transition from Authoritarianism* (Washington, DC: Brookings Institution Press, 1998).

82. I am indebted to research assistant Geraldine O'Mahoney for the assembly of this data.

83. President Isaias Afeworki, to the disappointment of many admirers of the thirty-year Eritrean struggle for independence, chose never to bring the constitution into force; among other critical works, see Kidane Mengisteab and Okbazghi Yohannes, *Anatomy of an African Tragedy: Political, Economic and Foreign Policy Crisis in Post-Independence Eritrea* (Trenton, NJ: Red Sea Press, 2005).

84. Marina Ottaway, *Democracy Challenged: The Rise of Semi-Authoritarianism* (Washington, DC: Carnegie Endowment for International Peace, 2003), 3.

85. William F. Case, "Can the 'Halfway House' Stand? Semidemocracy and Elite Theory in Three Southeast Asian Countries," *Comparative Politics* 28.4 (1996): 437–64.

86. Richard Joseph, "The Reconfiguration of Power in Late Twentieth-Century Africa," in *State, Conflict, and Democracy in Africa*, ed. Richard Joseph (Boulder: Lynne Rienner, 1999), 57–80; see also Richard Joseph, "War, State-Making, and Democracy in Africa," in, *Beyond State Crisis? Post-Colonial Africa and Post-Soviet Eurasia in Comparative Perspective*, ed. Mark R. Beissinger and Crawford Young (Washington, DC: Woodrow Wilson Center Press, 2002), 241–62.

87. I return to this issue in chapter 6. One may note at this point particularly influential works on democratic transitions in Africa by Michael Bratton and Nicholas van de Walle, *Democratic Experiments in Africa* (Cambridge: Cambridge University Press, 1997), *Democratization in Africa*, John A. Wiseman, *Democracy in Black Africa: Survival and Renewal* (New York: Paragon House, 1990), and Staffan I. Lindberg, *Democracy and Elections in Africa* (Baltimore, MD: Johns Hopkins University Press, 2006).

88. I employ the term "polyarchy" as defined by the most influential single contemporary work on defining democracy: Robert Dahl's *Polyarchy: Participation and Opposition* (New Haven, CT: Yale University Press, 1974). Any list of third-wave transitions is subject to debate; mine includes Benin, Botswana, Cape Verde, Ghana, Lesotho, Malawi, Mali, Mauritius, Namibia, Sao Tome and Principe, Senegal, Seychelles, Sierra Leone, South Africa, Tanzania, and Zambia.

89. A team of Ghanaian scholars in a careful study of the first decade of full liberalization make a persuasive case for combined political and economic success; see Kwame Boafo-Arthur, *Ghana: One Decade of the Liberal State* (London: Zed, 2007).

90. Countries experiencing serious insurgencies during at least part of the post-1990 period include Algeria, Angola, Burundi, Central African Republic, Chad, Congo-Brazzaville, Congo-Kinshasa, Ivory Coast, Liberia, Mali, Mozambique, Niger, Nigeria, Rwanda, Senegal, Sierra Leone, Somalia, Sudan, and Uganda.

91. John F. Clark, ed., *The African Stakes of the Congo War* (New York: Palgrave Macmillan, 2002). For further elaboration on the wave of insurgency, see in this volume Crawford Young, "Contextualizing Congo Conflicts: Order and Disorder in Postcolonial Africa," 13–31.

CHAPTER 2. IN SEARCH OF THE AFRICAN STATE

1. Jean-François Médard. "L'État patrimonialisé," *Politique Africaine* 39 (September 1990), 25; Pascal Chaigneau, *Rivalités politiques et socialisme à Madagascar* (Paris: CHEAM,

1985), 112; Buana Kabwa, *Citoyen Président: Lettre ouverte au Président Mobutu Sese Seko . . . et les autres* (Paris: L'Harmattan, 1978), 23; cited in David J. Gould, *Bureaucratic Corruption and Underdevelopment in the Third World: The Case of Zaire* (New York: Pergamon Press, 1980), 49.

2. Among the vocal critics of the "imported state," Bertrand Badie stands out; see *L'état importé: Essai sur l'occidentalisation de l'ordre politique* (Paris: Fayard, 1992), 70–72.

3. On the Hegelian theory of the state, still useful are Zbigniew A. Pelzcynski, ed., *The State and Civil Society: Studies in Hegel's Political Philosophy* (Cambridge: Cambridge University Press, 1984), and Shlomo Aveneri, *Hegel's Theory of the Modern State* (Cambridge: Cambridge University Press, 1972).

4. Gianfranco Poggi, *The Development of the Modern State: A Sociological Introduction* (Stanford, CA: Stanford University Press, 1978).

5. The rise of states is traced recently in a pair of monumental histories, S. E. Finer, *The History of Government from the Earliest Times*, 3 vols. (Oxford: Oxford University Press, 1997), and Michael Mann, *The Sources of Social Power*, 2 vols. (Cambridge: Cambridge University Press, 1986, 1993).

6. Mann, *The Sources of Social Power*, 2:402–40; Charles Tilly, *Coercion, Capital, and European States, AD 990–1992* (Oxford, UK: Blackwell, 1990), 67–92.

7. Max Weber, "Politics as a Vocation," in H. H. Garth and C. Wright Mills, eds., *From Max Weber: Essays in Sociology* (New York: Oxford University Press, 1958), 77–128.

8. Margaret Levi, *Of Rule and Revenue* (Berkeley: University of California Press, 1988), 1.

9. No comprehensive listing of sources is proposed, but let me cite some of the works not otherwise noted that I have found especially influential: Anthony Giddens, *A Contemporary Critique of Historical Materialism: Power, Property, and the State* (Berkeley: University of California Press, 1978); Anthony Giddens, *The Nation-State and Violence* (Berkeley: University of California Press, 1987); Martin Carnoy, *The State and Political Theory* (Princeton, NJ: Princeton University Press, 1984); David Held, *Political Theory and the Modern State: Essays on State, Power, and Democracy* (Stanford, CA: Stanford University Press, 1989); Leslie Green, *The Authority of the State* (Oxford, UK: Clarendon, 1988); Anthony de Jesay, *The State* (Oxford, UK: Blackwell, 1985); Roger King, *The State in Modern Society: New Directions in Political Sociology* (Chatham, NJ: Chatham House, 1986); Linda Weiss, *The Myth of the Powerless State* (Ithaca, NY: Cornell University Press, 1998); Mohammed Ayoob, *The Third World Security Predicament: State Making, Regional Conflict, and the International System* (Boulder, CO: Lynne Rienner, 1995); Rodney Barker, *Political Legitimacy and the State* (Oxford, UK: Clarendon, 1990); Barry Buzan, *People, States, and Fear: The National Security Problem in International Relations* (Chapel Hill: University of North Carolina Press, 1983); Martin van Creveld, *The Rise and Decline of the State* (Cambridge: Cambridge University Press, 1999); Matthew Lange and Dietrich Rueschmeyer, *States and Development: Historical Antecedents of Stagnation and Advance* (New York: Palgrave Macmillan, 2005); Pierre Manent, *A World Beyond Politics? A Defense of the Nation-State* (Princeton, NJ: Princeton University Press, 2006); Christian Reus-Smit, *The Moral Purpose of the State: Culture, Social Identity, and Institutional Rationality in International Relations* (Princeton, NJ: Princeton University Press, 1999); Peter J. Steinberger, *The Idea of the State* (Cambridge: Cambridge University Press, 2004); Jacqueline Stevens,

Reproducing the State (Princeton, NJ: Princeton University Press, 1999); Blandine Kriegel, *The State and the Rule of Law*, trans. Marc A. LePain and Jeffrey C. Cohen (Princeton, NJ: Princeton University Press, 1995); Karen Berkey and Sunita Parikh, "Comparative Perspectives and the State," *Annual Review of Sociology* 17 (1991): 523–49; Lars-Erik Cederman, *Emergent Actors in World Politics: How States and Nations Form and Dissolve* (Princeton, NJ: Princeton University Press, 1997); Brian M. Downing, *The Military Revolution and Political Change: Origins of Democracy and Autocracy in Early Modern Europe* (Princeton, NJ: Princeton University Press, 1992); David K. Leonard and Scott Straus, *Africa's Stalled Development: International Causes and Cures* (Boulder, CO: Lynne Rienner, 2003); Thomas Ertman, *Birth of the Leviathan: Building States and Regimes in Medieval and Early Modern Europe* (Cambridge: Cambridge University Press, 1997); James C. Scott, *The Art of Not Being Governed: An Anarchist History of Upland Southeast Asia* (New Haven, CT: Yale University Press, 2011); Philip J. Roeder, *Where Nation-States Come From: Institutional Change in the Age of Nationalism* (Princeton, NJ: Princeton University Press, 2007).

10. For a fuller discussion, see Crawford Young, *The African Colonial State in Comparative Perspective* (New Haven, CT: Yale University Press, 1994), 25–40.

11. Onyeoro S. Kamanu, "Secession and the Right of Self-Determination: An OAU Dilemma," *Journal of Modern African Studies* 12.3 (1974): 371–73. See also Saadia Touval, *The Boundary Politics of Independent Africa* (Cambridge, MA: Harvard University Press, 1972).

12. In its Roman version, *uti possedetis* asserted the right of a holder of immovable property to retain lawful permanent possession unless some negotiated transfer took place. Territorial stability in Latin America was much less assured than the OAU framers assumed, nor were Latin American boundaries mere replications of colonial geography. See Carlos A. Parodi, *The Politics of South American Boundaries* (Westport, CT: Praeger, 2002). A pair of twentieth-century wars over disputed territory took place: the Chaco War between Bolivia and Paraguay from 1933 to 1936 and the Peru-Ecuador war of 1941, in which Ecuador lost over 40% of its territory (Kalevi J. Holsti, *The State, War, and the State of War* [Cambridge: Cambridge University Press, 1996], 154).

13. Richard A. Joseph, *Radical Nationalism in Cameroun* (Oxford, UK: Clarendon, 1977), 208. Um Nyobe was arguing for the God-given sanctity of the original colonial partition version of a Cameroon.

14. See the valuable discussions in Rogers Brubaker, *Nationalism Reframed: Nationhood and the National Question in the New Europe* (Cambridge: Cambridge University Press, 1996).

15. The notion of indigeneity, of growing importance in Africa, receives incisive treatment in Peter Geschiere, *The Politics of Belonging: Autochtony, Citizenship, and Exclusion in Africa and Europe* (Chicago: University of Chicago Press, 2009).

16. James C. Scott, *Seeing Like a State: How Certain Schemes to Improve the Human Condition Have Failed* (New Haven, CT: Yale University Press, 1998), 53–83.

17. Daniel Philpott, *Revolution in Sovereignty: How Ideas Shaped Modern International Relations* (Princeton, NJ: Princeton University Press, 2001), 92.

18. Lucien Jaume, "Citizen and State under the French Revolution," in *States and Citizens: History, Theory, Prospects*, ed. Quentin Skinner and Bo Strath (Cambridge: Cambridge University Press, 2003), 133.

19. Jane Burbank and Frederick Cooper, *Empires in World History: Power and the Politics of Difference* (Princeton, NJ: Princeton University Press, 2010).

20. Rousseau was not the first to trace sovereignty to the people, though his rendition attracted wide attention. Althusius in 1603 wrote of "the absolute inalienability of the sovereignty of the People" (F. H. Hinsley, *Sovereignty* [London: C. A. Watts, 1966], 132).

21. *Africa Confidential*, 6 March 2009, 4; the enthusiasm for the principle still flags when the need for application arrives. This restriction on the doctrine of sovereignty finds useful treatment in Francis M. Deng, Sadikiel Kimoro, Terrence Lyons, Donald Rothchild, and I. William Zartman, eds., *Sovereignty as Responsibility: Conflict Management in Africa* (Washington, DC: Brookings Institution, 1996). Stephen D. Krasner elaborates various of the limitations to the full exercise of external sovereignty in *Sovereignty: Organized Hypocrisy* (Princeton, NJ: Princeton University Press, 1999). See also Philpott, *Revolutions in Sovereignty*.

22. Robert H. Jackson, *Quasi-States: Sovereignty, International Relations, and the Third World* (Cambridge: Cambridge University Press, 1990). Omar al Bashir's Arabic name is also often rendered as Omer el Beshir.

23. Pierre Englebert, *Africa: Unity, Sovereignty, and Sorrow* (Boulder, CO: Lynne Rienner, 2009).

24. Giddens, *The Nation-State and Violence*, 9–17.

25. Martin Chanock, *Law, Custom and Social Order: The Colonial Experience in Malawi and Zambia* (Cambridge: Cambridge University Press, 1985), 47.

26. Yash Ghai, "Decentralization and the Accommodation of Ethnic Diversity," in *Ethnic Diversity and Public Policy: A Comparative Inquiry*, ed. Crawford Young (New York: St. Martin's, 1998), 31–71.

27. Among other works, see Lee C. Buchheit, *Secession: The Legitimacy of Self-Determination* (New Haven, CT: Yale University Press, 1978), Benyamin Neuberger, *National Self-Determination in Postcolonial Africa* (Boulder, CO: Lynne Rienner, 1986); Allen Buchanan, *Secession: The Morality of Political Divorce from Fort Sumter to Lithuania and Quebec* (Boulder, CO: Westview, 1991), and Crawford Young, "Self-Determination Revisited: Has Decolonization Closed the Question?," in *Conflict in the Horn of Africa*, ed. Georges Nzongola-Ntalaja (Atlanta, GA: African Studies Association Press, 1991).

28. See the remarkably prescient analysis by Markus V. Hoehne, "Mimesis and Mimicry in the Dynamics of State and Identity Formation in Northern Somalia," *Africa* 79.2 (2009): 252–81.

29. Murray J. Edelman, *Constructing the Political Spectacle* (Chicago: University of Chicago Press, 1988).

30. Michael Barnett offers an eloquent example in describing his experience with the American delegation to the UN in 1994 at the time of the Rwanda genocide. At that moment, in the shadow of the 1993 American debacle in Somalia, the conviction that

any military involvement to counter the unfolding genocide was contrary to national interests set firm parameters to policy debate. Barnett found himself a prisoner of the official mind at that moment, a position he later came to deeply regret. See his "The UN Security Council, Indifference, and Genocide in Rwanda," *Cultural Anthropology* 12.4 (1997): 551–78, and his *Eyewitness to Genocide: The United Nations and Rwanda* (Ithaca, NY: Cornell University Press, 2002).

31. Friedrich Meinecke, *Machiavallism: The Doctrine of Reason of State and Its Place in Modern History*, trans. Douglas Scott (New Haven, CT: Yale University Press, 1957).

32. Christine Buci-Glucksman, *Gramsci and the State* (London: Lawrence and Wishart, 1980).

33. Robert Fatton, *Predatory Rule: State and Civil Society in Africa* (Boulder, CO: Lynne Rienner, 1992), 2.

34. The insurrections overthrowing long-standing regimes in Egypt and Libya in 2011 may reduce their capacity for relative autonomy.

35. Peter B. Evans, "The State as Problem and Solution: Predation, Embedded Autonomy, and Structural Change," in *The Politics of Economic Adjustment*, ed. Stephen Haggard and Robert Kaufman (Princeton, NJ: Princeton University Press, 1992), 139–81. See also Alice H. Amsden, *Asia's Next Giant: South Korea and Late Industrialization* (Oxford: Oxford University Press, 1992), and Robert Wade, *Governing the Market: Economic Theory and the Role of Government in East Asian Industrialization* (Princeton, NJ: Princeton University Press, 1990).

36. Thomas M. Callaghy and John Ravenill, "How Hemmed In: Lessons and Prospects of Africa's Responses to Decline, in *Hemmed In: Responses to Africa's Economic Decline*, ed. Thomas M. Callaghy and John Ravenhill (New York: Columbia University Press, 1993), 548.

37. Claude Ake, *Democracy and Development in Africa* (Washington, DC: Brookings Institution, 1996), 41.

38. Clement Henry Moore and Robert Springborg call them "bunker" and "bully praetorian" (*Globalization and the Politics of Development in the Middle East*, 2nd ed. [Cambridge: Cambridge University Press, 2010]).

39. Jürgen Habermas, *Legitimation Crisis* (Boston: Beacon Press, 1973), 49.

40. The most thorough account of pervasive corruption in Africa is the monograph on Nigeria by Daniel Jordan Smith, *A Culture of Corruption: Everyday Corruption and Popular Discontent in Nigeria* (Princeton, NJ: Princeton University Press, 2007).

41. Levi, *Of Rule and Revenue*, 1–2.

42. See the various essays in Gabriel A. Almond, Marvin Chodorow, and Roy Harvey Pearce, eds., *Progress and Its Discontents* (Berkeley: University of California Press, 1977), especially Nanerl Keohane, "The Enlightenment Idea of Progress Revisited," 21–40, and Crawford Young, "Ideas of Progress in the Third World," 83–105.

43. Lord Hailey, *An African Survey* (London: Oxford University Press, 1957), 203.

44. E. A. Brett provides a compelling exegesis of development theory and a robust defense of its necessity; see *Reconstructing Development Theory: Institutional Reform and Social Emancipation* (New York: Palgrave Macmillan, 2009).

45. Mann, *The Sources of Social Power*, 23–24.

46. Bertrand Badie and Pierre Birnbaum, *Sociologie de l'état* (Paris: Bernard Grasset, 1979), 27–37.

47. Roger King, *The State in Modern Society: New Directions in Political Sociology* (Chatham, NJ: Chatham House, 1986), 60.

48. Giddens, *A Contemporary Critique*, 32–68.

49. Timothy Mitchell, "The Limits of the State: Beyond Statist Approaches and Their Critics," *American Political Science Review* 85.1 (1991): 95.

50. A landmark volume in the resurrection of civil society as a concept in African politics is John W. Harbeson, Donald Rothchild, and Naomi Chazan, eds., *Civil Society and the State in Africa* (Boulder, CO: Lynne Rienner, 1994).

51. I wrestle with the definitional conundrums in "In Search of Civil Society," in *Civil Society and the State*, 33–50.

52. Young, *The African Colonial State*, 25.

53. Ernst Frankel, *The Dual State: A Contribution to the Theory of Dictatorship* (New York: Oxford University Press, 1942), 107; Jens Meierhenrich, *The Legacies of Law: Long-Run Consequences of Legal Development in South Africa, 1652–2000* (Cambridge: Cambridge University Press, 2008).

54. A key work in embedding dependency theory in state reason was Walter Rodney, *How Europe Underdeveloped Africa* (Washington, DC: Howard University Press, 1972); also important were the numerous works by Dakar-based Egyptian political economist Samir Amin, such as *Le développement inégal* (Paris: Minuit, 1973). Long after dependency theory lost its theoretical allure for most, it continued to have resonance among in some African leadership circles; see Nicolas van de Walle, *African Economies and the Politics of Permanent Crisis, 1979–1999* (Cambridge: Cambridge University Press, 2001).

55. I use the term "liberal market" interchangeably with "neoliberal." The term "neoliberalism" has the disadvantage of its frequent use with intended negative connotations. Also, the full neoliberal model is particularly associated with Anglo-American post-1970s capitalism; though European states moved in this direction, their social market orientation was more pronounced. Through the agency of international financial institutions, the Anglo-American version tended to shape the normative state promoted by the donor community.

56. The East Asian developmental state has received influential admiring treatment from Wade, *Governing the Market,* and Amsden, *Asia's Next Giant.*

57. Henry and Springborg, *Globalization and the Politics of Development,* 122–24.

58. Buci-Glucksman, *Gramsci and the State,* 90–91.

59. Christian Coulon, *Le marabout et le prince: Islam et pouvoir au Sénégal* (Paris: Pedone, 1981), 289–90.

60. Jean Copans, *Le marabout et l'arachide: La confrèrie mouride et les paysans du Sénégal* (Paris: Sycamore, 1980), 248.

61. Jean-François Bayart, *L'état au Cameroun* (Paris: Presses de la Fondation Nationale des Sciences Politiques, 1979), 52, 222.

62. Dean E. McHenry, *Limited Choices: The Political Struggle for Socialism in Tanzania* (Boulder, CO: Lynne Rienner, 1994), 62.

63. For details, see Crawford Young and Thomas Turner, *The Rise and Decline of the Zairian State* (Madison: University of Wisconsin Press, 1985).

64. Bruce Fetter, "L'union Minière du Haut-Katanga, 1920–1940: La naissance d'une sous-culture totalitaire," *Cahiers du CEDAF* 6 (1973): 38.

65. Engulu Baanga Mpongo, speech to the Makanda Kabobi Institute for party ideological instruction, N'sele, 1974, cited in Crawford Young, "Zaire: The Shattered Illusion of the Integral State," *Journal of Modern African Studies* 32.3 (1994): 261.

66. Cited in Young and Turner, *The Rise and Decline of the Zairian State*, 169.

67. Manwana Mungonga, *Le générale Mobutu Sese Seko parle du Nationalisme Zairois Authentique* (Kinshasa: Editions Okapi, n.d. [1972?]), 85–86.

68. Young and Turner, *The Rise and Decline of the Zairian State*, 368–69.

69. Young, "Zaire," 247–64.

70. Tahar Belkhodja, *Les trois décennies Bourguiba* (Tunis: Arcantères Publisud, 1999), 75–84.

71. John Waterbury, *The Egypt of Nasser and Sadat: The Political Economy of Two Regimes* (Princeton, NJ: Princeton University Press, 1983), 322. On the Nasser version of the integral state, see also Raymond William Baker, *Sadat and After: Struggles for Egypt's Political Soul* (Cambridge, MA: Harvard University Press, 1990), Patrick O'Brien, *The Revolution in Egypt's Economic System* (London: Oxford University Press, 1966), and Robert Marbro, *The Egyptian Economy, 1952–1972* (Oxford, UK: Clarendon, 1974).

72. John Waterbury, *Exposed to Innumerable Delusions: Public Enterprise and State Power in Egypt, India, Mexico, and Turkey* (Cambridge: Cambridge University Press, 1993).

73. I am indebted to Eritrean specialist Sara Dorman for the insight linking the integral state concept to postliberation Eritrea. For an anguished account of the integral drift of the Eritrean state by a pair of Eritrean scholars, see Kidane Mengisteab and Okbazghi Yohannes, *Anatomy of an African Tragedy: Political, Economic and Foreign Policy Crisis in Post-Independence Eritrea* (Trenton, NJ: Red Sea Press, 2005). On the massive conscription of youth for public works and military service, see Gaim Kibreab, "Forced Labour in Eritrea," *Journal of Modern African Studies* 47.1 (2009): 41–72.

74. There are numerous transliterations of the Arabic name of Muammar Qadhafy. I arbitrarily choose one of the many on offer. Qadhafy felt obligated to repeat the charade in 2009, when the dissolution of a regrown state was again announced, with all oil wealth purportedly to go directly to the people ("Libya: Power to the People," *Africa Research Bulletin,* Political, Social and Cultural Series, 46.2 [2009]: 17858–59).

75. See especially Dirk Vandewalle, ed., *Qadhafy's Libya, 1969–1994* (New York: St. Martin's, 1995, and Lillian Craig Harris, *Libya: Qadhafy's Revolution and the Modern State* (Boulder, CO: Westview, 1986).

76. Abderrahman Dadi, *Tchad: L'état retrouvé* (Paris: L'Harmattan, 1987); Sam C. Noloshungu, *Limits of Anarchy: Intervention and State Formation in Chad* (Charlottesville: University Press of Virginia, 1996).

77. The integral state vision is also found in the utopian Japanese imperial project in Manchuria in the 1930s; see Louise Young, *Japan's Total Empire: Manchuria and the Culture of Wartime Imperialism* (Berkeley: University of California Press, 1998).

78. Dawit Giorgis provides a compelling personal portrait of the pervasive hold of Marxism-Leninism on Ethiopian students by the 1970s; see *Red Tears: War, Famine and Revolution in Ethiopia* (Trenton, NJ: Red Sea Press, 1989).

79. Marina Ottaway and David Ottaway, *Afrocommunism* (New York: Africana Publishing Company, 1986); Edmond J. Keller and Donald Rothchild, eds., *Afro-Marxist Regimes* (Boulder, CO: Lynne Rienner, 1987); Arnold Hughes, ed., *Marxism's Retreat from Africa* (London: Frank Cass, 1992); John Markakis and Michael Waller, *Military Marxist Regimes in Africa* (London: Frank Cass, 1986); Crawford Young, *Ideology and Development in Africa* (New Haven, CT: Yale University Press, 1982), 22–96.

80. World Bank, *Accelerated Development in Sub-Saharan Africa: A New Agenda for Action* (Washington, DC: World Bank, 1981).

81. See van de Walle's masterful volume on African economic reform, *African Economies*.

82. The term "Washington Consensus" is said to have first been used by economist John Williamson in 1990; see Todd J. Moss, *African Development: Making Sense of the Issues and Actors* (Boulder, CO: Lynne Rienner, 2007), 108, for Williamson's roster of elements.

83. Crawford Young, Neal P. Sherman, and Tim H. Rose, *Cooperatives and Development: Agricultural Politics in Ghana and Uganda* (Madison: University of Wisconsin Press, 1981), 173.

84. Moss, *African Development*, 102.

85. Henry and Springborg, *Globalization and the Politics of Development*, 120; *Jeune Afrique*, special issue 26, December 2010, 107.

86. See the competing 1989 documents, World Bank, *Sub-Saharan Africa: From Crisis to Sustainable Growth* (Washington, DC: World Bank, 1989), and UNECA, *African Alternative Framework to Structural Adjustment Programmes for Socio-Economic Recovery and Transformation* (Addis Ababa: ECA, 1989). See also the excellent analysis by John Ravenhill in "A Second Decade of Adjustment: Greater Complexity, Greater Uncertainty," in *Hemmed In*, 18–53.

87. World Bank, *From Crisis to Sustainable Growth*, 61.

88. Henry and Springborg, *Globalization and the Politics of Development*, 11.

89. M. Anne Pitcher, *Party Politics and Economic Reform in Africa's Democracies* (Cambridge: Cambridge University Press, 2012). Her study offers a masterful comparative summary of the institutional challenges of liberalization.

90. Roger Tangri, *The Politics of Patronage in Africa: Privatization and Private Enterprise* (Trenton, NJ: Africa World Press, 1999).

91. Henry and Springborg, *Globalization and the Politics of Development*, 73.

92. James S. Coleman and Carl G. Rosberg, introduction, *Political Parties and National Integration in Tropical Africa*, ed. James S. Coleman and Carl G. Rosberg (Berkeley: University of California Press), 8. See also Aristide Zolberg, *Creating Political Order: The Party-States of West Africa* (Chicago: Rand McNally, 1966).

93. In his insightful reflections on postcolonial politics, Goran Hyden stresses the enduring significance of the movement heritage of the first generation of mass parties; see *African Politics in Comparative Perspective* (New York: Cambridge University Press, 2006).

94. Zolberg, *Creating Political Order*, 160.

95. An influential early use of "neopatrimonialism" as concept can be found in Samuel N. Eisenstadt's *Traditional Patrimonialism and Modern Neopatrimonialism* (London: Sage, 1972). Also influential in reviving the Weberian concept was Guenter Roth, "Personal Rule, Patrimonialism and Empire-Building in the New States," *World Politics* 20.2 (1968): 194–206.

96. Michael Bratton and Nicolas van de Walle, *Democratic Experiments in Africa: Regime Transitions in Comparative Perspective* (Cambridge: Cambridge University Press, 1997), 62. See also Christopher Clapham, *Third World Politics: An Introduction* (Madison: University of Wisconsin Press, 1985.

97. Jean-François Bayart, *The State in Africa: The Politics of the Belly* (Harlow, UK: Longman, 1993), 218–29.

98. Jean-François Médard, "The Underdeveloped State in Tropical Africa: Political Clientelism or Neo-Patrimonialism?," in *Private Patronage and Public Power: Political Clientelism in the Modern State*, ed. Christopher Clapham (New York: St. Martin's, 1982), 180.

99. van de Walle, *African Economies*, 54.

100. Phares M. Mutibwa, *The Bank of Uganda, 1966–2006: A Historical Perspective* (Kampala: Bank of Uganda, 2006). Though this is an official history, and so it may elide some less creditable episodes, its detail is nonetheless convincing in portraying an institution mostly true to its formal mission, even during the Idi Amin era.

101. David Leonard, *African Successes: Four Public Managers from Kenyan Rural Development* (Berkeley: University of California Press, 1991).

102. I well recollect from my years as Lubumbashi faculty dean a number of occasions when Congolese colleagues resisted at some personal risk pressures from ranking politicians to help out a relative. Most made great effort to assure that the university functioned according to academic norms. In Uganda, Makerere continued to operate as a university even during the moral disorder of the Amin era.

103. Jennifer A. Widner, *Building the Rule of Law: Francis Nyalali and the Road to Judicial Independence in Tanzania* (New York: Norton, 2001). Lynn S. Khadiagala notes that women farmers in western Uganda found in the courts an avenue for enforcing their property rights in the face of unsupportive customary norms and male hostility; see "Law, Power, and Justice: The Adjudication of Women's Property Rights in Uganda" (PhD diss., University of Wisconsin–Madison, 1999).

104. Peter VonDoepp, *Judicial Politics in New Democracies: Cases from Southern Africa* (Boulder, CO: Lynne Rienner, 2009); Tamir Mustafa, *The Struggle for Constitutional Power: Law, Politics, and Economic Development in Egypt* (Cambridge: Cambridge University Press, 2007).

105. Michael G. Schatzberg, *The Dialectics of Oppression in Zaire* (Bloomington: Indiana University Press, 1988), 49.

106. On the continuing importance of elections prior to the 1990 political opening, see Fred M. Hayward, ed., *Elections in Independent Africa* (Boulder, CO: Westview, 1987).

107. Michael G. Schatzberg, *Political Legitimacy in Middle Africa: Father, Family, Food* (Bloomington: Indiana University Press, 2001), 24–30.

108. Aili Mari Tripp, *Museveni's Uganda: The Paradoxes of Power in a Hybrid Regime* (Boulder, CO: Lynne Rienner, 2010).

109. Staffen I. Lindberg, *Democracy and Elections in Africa* (Baltimore, MD: Johns Hopkins University Press, 2006), 2.

110. Joel D. Barkan, "African Legislatures and the 'Third Wave' of Democratization," in *Legislative Power in Emerging African Democracies*, ed. Joel D. Barkan (Boulder, CO: Lynne Rienner, 2009), 2.

111. Frederick Cooper, *Africa Since 1940: The Past of the Present* (Cambridge: Cambridge University Press, 2002), 5, 156–57.

112. Jackson, *Quasi-States*.

113. Jeffrey Herbst, *States and Power in Africa: Comparative Lessons in Authority and Control* (Princeton, NJ: Princeton University Press, 2000).

114. The original thesis is found in Goran Hyden, *Beyond Ujamaa in Tanzania* (Berkeley: University of California Press, 1980). Hyden reaffirms and elaborates his case in *African Politics in Comparative Perspective* (Cambridge: Cambridge University Press, 2006).

115. Joel S. Migdal, Atul Kohli, and Vivienne Shue, *State Power and Social Forces: Domination and Transformation in the Third World* (Cambridge: Cambridge University Press, 1994), 2–3. See also Joel S. Migdal, *Strong Societies and Weak States: State-Society Relations and State Capabilities in the Third World* (Princeton, NJ: Princeton University Press, 1988).

116. Catherine Boone, *Political Topographies of the African State: Territorial Authority and Institutional Choice* (Cambridge: Cambridge University Press, 2003).

117. Richard Sandbrook, *The Politics of Africa's Economic Stagnation* (Cambridge: Cambridge University Press, 1985), 29.

118. John Iliffe, *The Emergence of African Capitalism* (Minneapolis: University of Minnesota Press, 1983).

119. Pierre Englebert, *State Legitimacy and Development in Africa* (Boulder, CO: Lynne Rienner, 2000). Robert Jackman also joins in, linking legitimacy to state capacity in his broad comparative study *Power without Force: The Political Capacity of Nation-States* (Ann Arbor: University of Michigan Press, 1993).

120. Achille Mbembe, *On the Postcolony* (Berkeley: University of California Press, 2001), 76.

121. See the various cases examined in the ambitious collective work by a number of African and other political economists, Benno J. Ndulu, Stephen A. O'Connell, Robert H. Bates, Paul Collier, and Chukwuma C. Soludo, eds., *The Political Economy of Economic Growth in Africa, 1960–2000*, 2 vols. (Cambridge: Cambridge University Press, 2008).

122. Patrick Chabal and Jean-Pascal Daloz, *Africa Works: Disorder as Political Instrument* (Oxford, UK: James Curry, 1999).

123. William Reno, "Mafiya Troubles, Warlord Crises," in *Beyond State Crisis? Postcolonial Africa and Post-Soviet Eurasia in Comparative Perspective*, ed. Mark R. Beissinger and Crawford Young (Washington, DC: Woodrow Wilson Center Press, 2002), 105–27; William Reno, *Corruption and State Politics in Sierra Leone* (New York: Cambridge University Press, 1995).

124. Robert I. Rotberg, ed., *When States Fail: Causes and Consequences* (Princeton, NJ: Princeton University Press, 2004); I. William Zartman, ed., *Collapsed States: The*

Disintegration and Restoration of Legitimate Authority (Boulder, CO: Lynne Rienner, 1995); Robert H. Bates, *When Things Fell Apart: State Failure in Late-Century Africa* (Cambridge: Cambridge University Press, 2008).

125. Eliphesis Mukonoweshuro, "The Politics of Squalor and Dependency: Chronic Political Instability and Economic Collapse in the Comoro Islands," *African Affairs* 89.357 (1990): 555–77. Bereft of resources and suffering endemic mediocrity in political leadership, the author argues that this micropolity survives by auctioning its sovereignty to France, South Africa or the Gulf States. Remittances from the diaspora provide 24% of GDP, and a third of the population of Mayotte, a Comoran island that chose incorporation into France, have fled from Comoros. Still, after nineteen successful or failed coups in its first three decades of independence, and despite a secession attempt by one of its three island territories (thwarted by the AU), Comoros had its first electoral change of ruler in 2006. Recent reports on its performance by the IMF have been more positive. *Africa Research Bulletin*, Economic, Financial, and Technical Series, 49.2 (2012): 19486.

126. The thoughtful definitional discussion in Naomi Chazan, Peter Lewis, Robert A. Mortimer, Donald Rothchild, and Stephen John Stedman, *Politics and Society in Contemporary Africa*, 3rd ed. (Boulder, CO: Lynne Rienner, 1999), and Ruth Berins Collier, *Regimes in Tropical Africa: Changing Forms of Supremacy, 1945–1975* (Berkeley: University of California Press, 1982), is helpful is conceptualizing regime.

127. Cynthia Enloe, *Ethnic Soldiers: State Sovereignty in Divided Societies* (Athens: University of Georgia Press, 1980).

128. Coleman and Rosberg, *Political Parties and National Integration*, 5–111.

129. Chazan et al., *Politics and Society in Contemporary Africa*, 137–58.

130. Clement Moore, *Politics in North Africa: Algeria, Morocco, and Tunisia* (Boston: Little Brown, 1970); Clement Moore, *Tunisia since Independence: The Dynamics of One-Party Government* (Berkeley: University of California Press, 1965).

131. H. E. Chalabi and Juan J. Linz, eds., *Sultanistic Regimes* (Baltimore, MD: Johns Hopkins University Press, 1998).

132. Médard was an early contributor to the "big man" concept; see "L'état patrimonialisé," 25–36. In *Paths in the Rainforests: Toward a History of Political Tradition in Equatorial Africa* (Madison: University of Wisconsin Press, 1990), Jan Vansina shows the deep historical roots of a "big man" tradition; periodically in stateless settings an extraordinary individual would arise who was able to build a small-scale polity through his skills in assembling resources and in weaving customary worldviews into discourse that legitimated his personal leadership and by his savvy in acknowledging the exercise of local rule.

133. Schatzberg skillfully documents the ubiquity of the father metaphor in *Political Legitimacy in Middle Africa*.

134. W. Howard Wriggins, *The Ruler's Imperative: Strategies for Political Survival in Asia and Africa* (New York: Columbia University Press, 1969), 12.

135. Robert H. Jackson and Carl G. Rosberg, *Personal Rule in Black Africa: Prince, Autocrat, Prophet, Tyrant* (Berkeley: University of California Press, 1982).

136. Samuel Decalo offers chilling comparative portraits in *Psychoses of Power: African Personal Dictatorships* (Boulder, CO: Westview, 1989).

137. Robert Klitgard's engaging memoir of his experiences as an international aid worker, *Tropical Gangsters: One Man's Experience with Development and Decadence in Deepest Africa* (New York: Basic Books, 1990). See also Max Liniger-Gomez, *La démocradura: Dictature couflée, démocratie truquée* (Paris: L'Harmattan, 1992).

138. Among the many works on Uganda in the Museveni age, see Crawford Young, "After the Fall: State Rehabilitation in Uganda," in *Beyond State Crisis?*, 465–86; Phares Mutibwa, *Uganda since Independence: A Study of Unfulfilled Hopes* (Kampala: Fountain, 1992), Justus Mugaju and J. Oloka-Oloyango, eds., *No-Party Democracy in Uganda: Myths and Realities* (Kampala: Fountain, 2000), and Tripp, *Museveni's Uganda*.

139. Young and Turner, *The Rise and Decline of the Zairian State*, 276–325. Another example was the $6 billion liquefied natural gas project in Nigeria, of which former Haliburton subsidiary Kellogg, Brown and Root was the prime contractor. In February 2009, KBR and Haliburton were forced to pay $579 million in criminal and civil penalties under the Foreign Corrupt Practices Act for bribes paid to dictator Sani Abacha and his two successors from 1995 to 2005 ("Nigeria: Seize the Moment," *Africa Research Bulletin*, Economic Financial and Technical Series, 46.2 [2009]: 18160).

140. Mark R. Beissinger and Crawford Young, "The Effective State in Postcolonial Africa and Post-Soviet Eurasia: Hopeless Chimera or Possible Dream?," in *Beyond State Crisis?*, 465, 483.

141. This is the thesis of Lange and Rueschmeyer's *States and Development*.

142. World Bank, *World Development Report 1997: The State in a Changing World* (Washington, DC: World Bank, 1997).

143. John Campbell, *Nigeria: Dancing on the Brink* (Lapham, MD: Rowman and Littlefield, 2010). See also Smith, *A Culture of Corruption*; Michela A. Wrong, *It's Our Turn to Eat: The Story of a Kenyan Whistle-Blower* (New York: HarperCollins, 2009).

CHAPTER 3. DECOLONIZATION, THE INDEPENDENCE SETTLEMENT,
AND COLONIAL LEGACY

1. Cited in David Fieldhouse, "Arrested Development in Anglophone Africa," in *Decolonization and African Independence: The Transfers of Power, 1960–1980*, ed. Prosser Gifford and William Roger Louis (New Haven, CT: Yale University Press, 1988), 135–36.

2. John Darwin, "The Third British Empire? The Dominion Idea in Imperial Politics," in *The Oxford History of the British Empire*, vol. 4, ed. Judith M. Brown and William Roger Louis (Oxford: Oxford University Press, 1999), 70.

3. Frederick Cooper, *Africa since 1940: The Past of the Present* (Cambridge, MA: Cambridge University Press, 2002), 36–38.

4. In the 1960 General Assembly Declaration on the Granting of Independence to Colonial Countries and Peoples; see Hurst Hannum, *Autonomy, Sovereignty, and Self-Determination: The Accommodation of Conflicting Rights* (Philadelphia: University of Pennsylvania Press, 1990), 33–36

5. Cited by Anthony Clayton, "'Deceptive Might': Imperial Defence and Security, 1900–1968," in *The Oxford History of the British Empire*, 280. In reality, Britain benefited greatly from the export earnings of its African colonies during World War II and squeezed them energetically from 1945 to 1951 to finance postwar recovery; both Britain and

France drew heavily on African military manpower. However, the "balance sheets of imperialism" suggested at best ambivalent evidence on the profitability of colonies. By 1957, Prime Minister Macmillan queried the Colonial Office on the cost-benefit ratio of seeking to defer independence; the "official mind" consensus was that there was no economic case for delay, and the strategic arguments were not compelling (David K. Fieldhouse, *Black Africa, 1945–80: Economic Decolonization and Arrested Development* [London: Allen and Unwin, 1986], 8).

6. Saadia Touval, *The Boundary Politics of Independent Africa* (Cambridge, MA: Harvard University Press, 1972), 21.

7. Touval, *Boundary Politics*, 54–57.

8. In the Togo case, the main driver for rejoining British Togoland with French-administered Togo was Ewe ethno-nationalism, which in the long run was trumped by territoriality. Over time an initially precarious attachment of Ghanaian Ewe to a Ghana nationality deepened, and the border deepened their differences with Togolese Ewe. At the same time, the border and shared ethnicity facilitated a prosperous commerce, both legal and illicit. For detail see Paul Nugent, *Smugglers, Secessionists and Loyal Citizens on the Ghana-Togo Border: The Life of the Borderlands since 1914* (Oxford, UK: James Currey, 2002). On Anglophone Cameroon, see Piet Konings and Francis Nyamnjoh, "The Anglophone Problem in Cameroon," *Journal of Modern African Studies* 35.2 (1997): 207–29.

9. Part of the observation of the centennial was a major conference in Dakar, where the sense of loss was palpable. See the collected papers in Charles Becker, Saliou Mbaye, and Ibrahima Thioub, eds., *AOF: Réalités et heritages: Sociétés ouest-africaines et ordre colonial, 1895–1960* (Dakar: Direction des Archives du Sénégal), 1997. The best study of the breakup of AOF is Joseph-Roger de Benoist, *La balkanization de l'Afrique Occidentale Française* (Dakar: Nouvelles Editions Africaines, 1979).

10. As Raymond Pourtier points out, Gabon territorial identity, whose negative point of reference was Brazzaville and the AEF institutions, took form very early, initially among European settlers and soon spreading to the first generation of educated Gabonese (*Le Gabon*, vol. 1 [Paris: L'Harmattan, 1989], 76). Pourtier also notes that a 1937 decentralizing reform of AEF provided "the spatial dynamic which led to the independence, not of AEF, but of its constituent territories" (131).

11. On the power transfer in Rwanda and Burundi, see especially René Lemarchand's classic *Rwanda and Burundi* (London: Pall Mall, 1970) and the various works of Jean-Pierre Chrétien, particularly *The Great Lakes of Africa: Two Thousand Years of History*, trans. Scott Straus (New York: Zone, 2003). During the colonial period, the Ruanda-Urundi trust had been administratively integrated with the Belgian Congo. Into the mid-1950s, some Belgians and early Congolese nationalists assumed that the territories would remain united with the Belgian Congo. Retrospectively, following the genocidal ethnic strife in both countries, some counterfactual speculation suggested that had Tutsi and Hutu remained within the larger territorial frame of colonial Tanganyika as successor to the rest of German East Africa, the sharpness of the ethnic confrontation might have been diluted (Ali Mazrui, personal communication).

12. The dismal postcolonial performance of Comoros reinforced Mayotte preference for the French connection; by 2008 the island was clamoring for total incorporation as

a full overseas department of France, subsequently confirmed by referendum and implemented (*Le Monde*, 29 August 2008).

13. Randall Fegley, *Equatorial Guinea: An African Tragedy* (New York: Peter Lang, 1989); Max Liniger-Goumaz, *Small Is Not Always Beautiful: The Story of Equatorial Guinea* (London: Hurst, 1988).

14. D. Anthony Low, "The End of the British Empire in Africa," in *Decolonization and African Independence*, 43.

15. Morocco, Tunisia, and Egypt, which had well-developed state institutions before colonial occupation, were an exception.

16. The bizarre gymnastics of franchise manipulation as a means of marginalizing the overwhelming African majority in an ostensibly "democratic" decolonization constitution reached ludicrous heights in the Central African Federation, which established different devices in each of its component territories. For franchise details, see David C. Mulford, *Zambia: The Politics of Independence* (London: Oxford University Press), on Zambia (Northern Rhodesia) and Colin Leys, *European Politics in Southern Rhodesia* (Oxford, UK: Clarendon, 1959), on Zimbabwe (Southern Rhodesia).

17. For detail on the Congo Statut des villes and its application, see Crawford Young, *Politics in the Congo* (Princeton, NJ: Princeton University Press, 1965), 106–9.

18. A compelling example of this phenomenon is provided by Herbert Weiss, *Political Protest in the Congo* (Princeton, NJ: Princeton University Press, 1967).

19. Ireland in a number of respects was a pacesetter in the annals of decolonization; see Deirdre McMahon, "Ireland and the Empire-Commonwealth," in *The Oxford History of the British Empire*, 138–62.

20. Joseph-Roger de Benoist, a scholar-journalist in Dakar closely connected to the AOF political universe, argues that until the last minute most of the political elite (though not radical intellectuals and students) still preferred some loose federated attachment to France to full independence (personal communication and *La balkanization*).

21. Many believed that ABAKO President Joseph Kasavubu had explicitly demanded independence. Benoît Verhaegen shows that his actual words were "immediate emancipation," although the term was clearly a code word for independence (*L'ABAKO et l'indépendance du Congo Belge: Dix ans de nationalisme kongo (1950–1960)* [Paris: L'Harmattan, 2003], 151–62).

22. Young, *Politics in the Congo*, 140–83.

23. The earliest example is perhaps Liberia in 1847, though it was not strictly speaking decolonized. The American Colonization Society, a private body created in 1816 that received some indirect state assistance to promote African settlement of freed slaves, was the umbrella authority from the first settlement in 1822 until 1847. A convention of Americo-Liberians then simply declared independence and drafted its own constitution. See Tom Shick, *Behold the Promised Land: A History of Afro-American Settler Society* (Baltimore, MD: Johns Hopkins University Press, 1980), D. Elwood Dunn and S. Byron Tarr, *Liberia: A National Polity in Transition* (Metuchen, NJ: Scarecrow Press, 1988), and J. Gus Liebenow, *Liberia: The Evolution of Privilege* (Ithaca, NY: Cornell University Press, 1969).

24. See, inter alia, Leys, *European Politics in Southern Rhodesia*, 8–40.

25. I omit the case of Ethiopian independence, which occurred following its liberation from Italian occupation in 1941 by British-led forces. Italian colonial ambitions in Ethiopia lasted a mere six years, and following Italy's expulsion there was a simple restoration of the former regime rather than a decolonization.

26. For a succinct account, see M. W. Daly, "Egypt," in *Cambridge History of Africa*, 8 vols., ed. J. D. Fage and Roland Oliver (Cambridge: Cambridge University Press, 1975–84), 7:743–54.

27. William Roger Louis, "Libyan Independence, 1951: The Creation of a Client State," in *Decolonization and African Independence*, 159.

28. The other two Italian colonies, Eritrea and Somalia, also had their fate determined by great-power politics and UN maneuvering. Eritrea, through the confluence of astute Ethiopian diplomacy, American geopolitical interests, and international bargaining became an appendage of Ethiopia, soon to perceive itself, as chapter 7 details, as subordinated in a quasi-colonial relationship leading to a three–decade-long liberation war. Somalia was returned temporarily to Italian tutelage in 1950, but it was given a firm international deadline of ten years to prepare for independence.

29. This and other encyclopedic detail on the UN-administered creation of a Libyan state is found in Adrian Pelt, *Libyan Independence and the United Nations: A Case of Planned Decolonization* (New Haven: Yale University Press, 1970), 673–74. See also Lisa Anderson, *The State and Social Transformation in Tunisia and Libya, 1830–1960* (Princeton, NJ: Princeton University Press, 1986).

30. John D. Hargreaves, *The End of Colonial Rule in West Africa* (London: Macmillan, 1979), 41.

31. Cooper, *Africa since 1940*, 4.

32. This somewhat simplifies the path from the 1958 referendums to 1960 independence; for details, see Keith Panter-Brick, "Independence, French Style," in *Decolonization and African Independence*, 73–104.

33. Jan Vansina cites earlier little-known evidence of *évolué* discontents during World War II, in the form of a letter to "the US army" invoking the Atlantic Charter as a basis for a claim to Congolese rights; see *Being Colonized: The Kuba Experience in Rural Congo, 1880–1960* (Madison: University of Wisconsin Press, 2010), 270–71.

34. Paul Lomami-Tshibamba, "Quelle sera notre place dans le monde de demain?," *La Voix du Congolais* 2 (March–April 1945): 47–51. A widely-known tract of *évolués* in 1944 also had asked for due recognition for their wartime loyalty and mastery of colonial linguistic and cultural norms, insisting that the educated elites could not be treated like "the ignorant and backward masses" (Young, *Politics in the Congo*, 74–75, 274–75).

35. For more on *bula matari* as a metaphor for the Belgian colonial state, see Crawford Young and Thomas Turner, *The Rise and Decline of the Zairian State* (Madison: University of Wisconsin Press, 1985), 1–40.

36. At a crucial point in the negotiations, a leading opposition representative, Senator Henri Roland, joined the Congolese in arguing that independence had to be complete

and unqualified; in the metaphor utilized, "all the keys to the trousseau" had to be handed to the new Congolese regime on independence day.

37. Many years later a key Congolese participant confirmed rumors prevalent at the time that the two leading Congolese leaders, Patrice Lumumba and Joseph Kasavubu, were mandated by their colleagues to suggest a delay in independence, with immediate formation instead of a provisional Congolese government for a couple of years. Belgium insisted that by that point there was no turning back. Justin-Marie Bomboko, "Vers l'indépendance: Perceptions congolaises," in *Congo 1960: L'échec d'une decolonization*, ed. Colette Braekman (Brussels: GRIP, 2010), 81.

38. Young, *Politics in the Congo*, 402, 443–46.

39. This calculus was not entirely wrong, as confirmed by one of the most gifted intellectuals in the first Congolese government, Thomas Kanza: "The first meetings of our Council of Ministers were unforgettable. Our discussions were of the most desultory kind. All of us were happy, or at least cheerful and satisfied, at being ministers. . . . We argued about offices, about suitable and available sites for them, and how they could be shared among us. We discussed the allocation of ministerial cars; the choosing and allotting of ministerial residences; arrangements for our families and their travel. . . . Though we sat so comfortably in our sumptuous official cars, driven by uniformed military chauffeurs, and looked s though we were ruling this large and beautiful country, we were in fact ruling nothing and a prey to whatever might happen" (*Conflict in the Congo* [Harmondsworth, UK: Penguin, 1972], 31–32).

40. Spain, though ostensibly neutral in World War II, was suspected of Axis sympathies, which led to an extended diplomatic quarantine. The first break in its international isolation came with the establishment of American air bases in 1953; however, European states blocked entry into NATO until 1982, and European Community membership was granted only in 1986.

41. Spain also held minor territories in Africa: the small enclave of Ifni on the southern Morocco coast, ceded back to Morocco in 1969, and the tiny Mediterranean coastal settlements of Ceuta and Melilla, which remain under Spanish rule over Moroccan protest to this day.

42. Fegley, *Equatorial Guinea*, 41–58; Samuel Decalo, *Psychoses of Power: African Personal Dictatorships* (Boulder, CO: Westview, 1989), 42–48.

43. Full detail may be found in Tony Hodges, *Western Sahara: Roots of a Desert War* (Westport, CT: Lawrence Hill, 1983). Mauritania was initially a junior partner in partitioning the Spanish Sahara; however, its small army and meager finances proved totally inadequate in the face of the insurgent Polisario challenge; The first and long stable postcolonial regime of Mokhtar Ould Daddah was fatally undermined by its humiliation in this territorial seizure and was overthrown by the military in 1978; the latter abandoned its share of the Western Sahara to Morocco in 1979.

44. Cited in James Duffy, *Portuguese Africa* (Cambridge, MA: Harvard University Press, 1959), 270.

45. Basil Davidson, "Portuguese-Speaking Africa," in *The Cambridge History of Africa*, 8:758.

46. Davidson, "Portuguese-Speaking Africa," 760.

47. For valuable detail see Alistaire Horne, *A Savage War of Peace: Algeria, 1954–1962* (London: Macmillan, 1977), 415–62.

48. King Leopold II, whose gargantuan imperial appetite was joined to a consummate skill in the diplomacy of the colonial partition, created the Congo as a personal fiefdom. He was obsessed with the notion that only a colony could secure Belgian national identity and settled on central Africa only after peering at China, the Philippines, Fiji, and other possible sites. The famous medallion presented to a reluctant finance minister, inscribed "Il faut à la Belgique une colonie" ("Belgium must have a colony"), reflected this conviction. It was a conviction shared by few Belgian leaders at the time, and that made it necessary for him to assume personal rule over this vast domain. The uninhibited plunder and scandalous atrocities that soon followed made the king's fief a national embarrassment by the time that Belgium assumed responsibility for the territory in 1908. Once the worst abuses had been remedied by the 1920s, and the sweet scent of economic expansion was in the air, Belgians of all descriptions found a role in the swelling ranks of the administration, colonial corporations, and Catholic missions. By the early 1950s, the colonial Congo seemed embarked on a march to prosperity; it was an "oasis of peace" or "empire of silence" untroubled by nationalist agitation. On the role of Leopold, see especially Guy Vanthemsche, *La Belgique et le Congo: L'impact de la colonie sur le metropole* (Brussels: Le Cri, 2010), Adam Hochschild, *King Leopold's Ghost* (Boston: Houghton Mifflin, 1998), Neal Ascherson, *The King Incorporated* (London: Allen and Unwin, 1963), Jean Stengers, "La Belgique et le Congo," in *Histoire de la Belgique contemporaine* (Brussels: La Renaissance du Livre, 1974), and Roger Anstey, *King Leopold's Congo* (London: Oxford University Press, 1969). On the construction of the colonial Congo in the Belgian national imaginary, see Kevin C. Dunn, *Imagining the Congo: The International Relations of Identity* (New York: Palgrave Macmillian, 2003).

49. For a vivid and moving account of this gradual but relentless process, see Renee C. Fox, *In the Belgian Chateau: The Spirit and Culture of a European Society in an Age of Change* (Chicago: Ivan R. Dee, 1994). She concludes that the reality of Belgium as a nation and a social community was disappearing into the past, its breakup a subject of serious discussion. Vanthemsche adds that "the loss of the Congo reduced the possibilities for imagining a Belgian nation by Walloons and Flemings and must be considered as among the factors leading to decentralization and regionalism in Belgium after 1960" (*La Belgique et le Congo*, 89).

50. See the contributions in Mark R. Beissinger and Crawford Young, eds., *Beyond State Crisis? Postcolonial Africa and Post-Soviet Eurasia in Comparative Perspective* (Washington, DC: Woodrow Wilson Center Press, 2002).

51. See Herschelle S. Challenor, "The Contribution of Ralph Bunche to Trusteeship and Decolonization," in *Ralph Bunche: The Man and His Times*, ed. Benjamin Rivlin (New York: Holmes and Meier, 1990), 109–57, and Brian Urquhart, *Ralph Bunche: An American Life* (New York: Norton, 1990).

52. For detail, see Marc Michel, "The Independence of Togo," in *Decolonization and African Independence*, 291–319, Georges Chaffard, *Les carnets secrets de la decolonization*

(Paris: Calmann-Levy, 1965), Victor T. Le Vine, *Politics in Francophone Africa* (Boulder, CO: Lynne Rienner, 2004), and Bernard Chidzero, *Tanganyika and International Trusteeship* (London: Oxford University Press, 1961).

53. Lemarchand, *Rwanda and Burundi*, 79.

54. Gretchen Bauer, "Namibia: Limits to Liberation," in *Politics in Southern Africa: State and Society in Transition*, ed. Gretchen Bauer and Scott D. Taylor (Boulder, CO: Lynne Rienner, 2005), 205–36; Lionel Cliffe, *The Transition to Independence in Namibia* (Boulder, CO: Lynne Rienner, 1994).

55. Norma J. Kriger, *Zimbabwe's Guerrilla War: Peasant Voices* (Cambridge: Cambridge University Press, 1992).

56. Patrick Chabal et al., *A History of Postcolonial Lusophone Africa* (Bloomington: Indiana University Press, 2002), 4.

57. Of the substantial and sometimes hagiographic accounts of the Eritrean liberation war, I find especially useful Ruth Iyob, *The Eritrean Struggle for Independence: Domination, Resistance, Nationalism, 1941–1993* (Cambridge: Cambridge University Press, 1995), and Michela Wrong, *I Didn't Do It for You: How the World Used and Abused a Small African Nation* (London: Harper Perennial, 2005). Worth noting is that Ethiopia, like the European colonial powers, was traumatized by the long Eritrean independence war, whose end coincided with a collapse of the preceding Ethiopian regime.

58. Malyn Newitt, "Mozambique," in *The History of Postcolonial Lusophone Africa*, 190.

59. Ken Flower, *Serving Secretly: An Intelligence Chief on Record—Rhodesia into Zimbabwe* (London: John Murray, 1987), 105–15.

60. For a sympathetic but critical examination, see Colin Leys and John S. Saul, *Namibia's Liberation Struggle: The Two-Edged Sword* (London: James Currey, 1995).

61. Robin Luckham, *The Nigerian Military* (Cambridge: Cambridge University Press, 1971); Amii Omaru-Otunno, *Politics and the Military in Uganda, 1800–1985* (New York: St. Martin's, 1987).

62. The realization that colonial hold on the populations was vanishing was particularly acute in the Belgian Congo in 1959; Belgian constitutional law made it difficult to envisage sending metropolitan units with conscripts to fight a colonial war, as did popular mobilization against dispatch of troops to defend "Union Minière."

63. Ali A. Mazrui, introduction, *UNESCO General History of Africa*, vol. 8, ed. Ali A. Mazrui and Christophe Wondji (London: Heinemann, 1993), 10.

64. W. M. Hailey, *An African Survey: A Study of Problems Arising in Africa South of the Sahara* (London: Oxford University Press, 1957), 252–53.

65. Thomas Hodgkin, *Nationalism in Colonial Africa* (London: Frederick Muller, 1956), 23.

66. James S. Coleman, "Nationalism in Tropical Africa," *American Political Science Review* 48.2 (1954): 404–26.

67. Hodgkin, *Nationalism in Colonial Africa*.

68. Rupert Emerson, *From Empire to Nation: The Rise to Self-Assertion of African and Asian Peoples* (Cambridge, MA: Harvard University Press, 1960), 379.

69. Cheikh Anta Diop, *Nations nègres et culture* (Paris: Présence Africaine, 1965). Following his death in 1986, the distinguished University of Dakar was renamed in his honor.

70. Aimé Césaire, *Cahier d'un retour au pays natal* (Paris: Présence Africaine, 1956); Léopold Senghor, *African Socialism* (London: Pall Mall, 1964).

71. Placide Tempels, *La philosophie bantoue* (Elisabethville: Lovanie, 1945). An English translation was published in 1969 by the journal *Présence Africaine*.

72. Mabika Kalanda, *La remise en question: Base de la decolonization mentale* (Brussels: Remarques Africaines, 1967), 150–51.

73. See especially Frantz Fanon, *Peau noir, masques blancs* (Paris: Seuil, 1952), and Frantz Fanon, *Les damnés de la terre* (Paris: Maspero, 1963).

74. Amilcar Cabral, *Revolution in Guinea: An African People's Struggle—Selected Texts* (New York: Monthly Review Press, 1969). For a valuable appraisal, see Patrick Chabal, *Amilcar Cabral: Revolutionary Leader and People's War* (Cambridge: Cambridge University Press, 1983).

75. For Nkrumah's vision, see in particular his collection of policy addresses: *I Speak of Freedom: A Statement of African Ideology* (New York: Praeger, 1961). I recollect this pledge being cited when I visited Ghana in 1958 and 1984.

76. These estimates are from several decades ago and may no longer be accurate owing to a millennial slow drift to Arab identity among Tamazigt (Berber) communities. See Charles F. Gallagher, "North African Problems and Prospects: Language and Identity," in *Language Problems of Developing Nations*, ed. Joshua Fishman, Charles A. Ferguson, and Jyotirindra Das Gupta (New York: John Wiley, 1968), 129–50. In Algeria at the liberation war stage, another limit to Arabhood was the limited mastery of the language by much of the intellectual elite. I recollect attending North African student congresses in the late 1950s; in Morocco and Tunisia, these were conducted in Arabic, but the Algerians had to use French, as too many lacked fluency or even knowledge of Arabic.

77. Gamal Abdel Nasser, *Egypt's Liberation: The Philosophy of the Revolution* (Washington, DC: Public Affairs Press, 1955). Egyptian nationalism had an older pedigree than most; British intervention in 1882 was partly stimulated by the nationalist challenge of native Egyptian officers led by Ahmad Urabi to the dynasty of Albanian rulers founded by Muhammed Ali in 1805 after Napolean's withdrawal. Egypt was also unique in the extraordinary historical depth of continuous alien rule (by Persians, Greeks, Romans, Byzantines, Arabs, Mamelukes, the French (briefly), Albanians, and then the British), from 332 BC till 1922.

78. Among other sources, I find especially useful Gail M. Gerhart, *Black Power in South Africa: The Evolution of an Ideology* (Berkeley: University of California Press, 1978).

79. Jawaharlal Nehru, *The Discovery of India* (New York: Meridian, 1946).

80. Wale Adebanwi, "The Cult of Awo," *Journal of Modern African Studies* 46.3 (2008): 335–60.

81. Crawford Young, "Nationalism, Ethnicity, and Class in Africa: A Retrospective," *Cahiers d'Etudes Africaines* 26.3 (1986): 438.

82. Invaluable detail is provided in Roth Berins Collier, *Regimes in Tropical Africa: Changing Forms of Supremacy, 1945–1975* (Berkeley: University of California Press, 1982).

83. Collier, *Regimes in Tropical Africa*, 63–94.

84. "Significant opposition" is defined as winning at least 25% of the vote and gaining some parliamentary representation: the countries who meet this standard include Benin, Burkina Faso, Chad, Congo-Brazzaville, Congo-Kinshasa, Equatorial Guinea, Gabon, Gambia, Ghana, Kenya, Lesotho, Madagascar, Mauritius, Namibia, Nigeria, Senegal, Seychelles, Sierra Leone, Somalia, South Africa, Sudan, Togo, Uganda, Zimbabwe, and Zambia. Egypt, Ethiopia, Liberia, Morocco and Tunisia did not have preindependence elections. Data from Dieter Nohlen, Michael Krennerich, and Berhard Thibaut, *Elections in Africa: A Data Handbook* (New York: Oxford University Press, 1999.

85. Richard A. Joseph, "The Reconfiguration of Power in Late-Twentieth Century Africa," in *State, Conflict, and Democracy in Africa*, ed. Richard A. Joseph (Boulder, CO: Lynne Rienner, 1999), 57–80.

86. For detail see I. F. Nicolson, *The Administration of Nigeria 1900–1960: Men, Methods, and Myths* (Oxford, UK: Clarendon, 1969), and Francis M. Deng, *War of Visions: Conflict of Identities in the Sudan* (Washington, DC: Brookings Institution, 1995).

87. Robert O. Collins, *A History of Modern Sudan* (Cambridge: Cambridge University Press, 2008), 46–59. In the 1936 treaty with Egypt, Britain formally recognized Egyptian sovereignty over Sudan. In 1951, King Farouk abrogated previous treaties and declared the "unity of the Nile" under the king.

88. The major party favoring unification with Egypt at the time was the Democratic Unionist Party rooted in the Khamiyya Sufi order and the Mirghani family. The other major political currents, the Muslim Brotherhood and the Communists, were also anti-Egyptian. None of these movements had any presence in southern Sudan.

89. Peter Woodward, "The South in Sudanese Politics, 1946–1956," *Middle Eastern Studies* 16.3 (1980): 178–92.

90. A succinct and convincing account is found in M. W. Daly, "The Transfer of Power in the Sudan," *Decolonization and African Independence*, 185–97; see also Deng, *War of Visions*, Muddathir 'Abd al-Rahim, *Imperialism and Nationalism in the Sudan* (Oxford, UK: Clarendon, 1969), and Robert O. Collins, *Shadows in the Grass: Britain in the Southern Sudan, 1918–1956* (New Haven, CT: Yale University Press, 1983).

91. Verhaegen, *L'ABAKO*.

92. Jules Gérard-Libois, *Katanga Secession*, trans. Rebecca Young (Madison: University of Wisconsin Press, 1966).

93. Alfred Stepan, *Arguing Comparative Politics* (Oxford: Oxford University Press, 2001), 316–34.

94. J. F. Ade Ajayi, "Expectations of Independence," *Daedalus* 111.2 (1982): 2.

95. Young, *The African Colonial State*, 284.

96. James C. Scott, *Seeing Like a State: How Certain Schemes to Improve the Human Condition Have Failed* (New Haven, CT: Yale University Press, 1998).

97. Mamadou Diouf, personal communication.

98. Although Asian states are rarely if ever described as "postcolonial," the recent field of "postcolonial studies" is dominated by Asian diasporic intellectuals. I am indebted to Aili Mari Tripp for this observation.

99. So I argue in "The End of the Post-Colonial States in Africa? Reflections on Changing African Political Dynamics," *African Affairs* 103.410 (2004): 23–49.

CHAPTER 4. THE ROAD TO AUTOCRACY

1. Ruth Schachter Morgenthau, *Political Parties in French-Speaking West Africa* (London: Oxford University Press, 1964), 219–64.

2. See René Lemarchand, ed., *African Kingships in Perspective: Political Change and Modernization in Monarchical Settings* (London: Frank Cass, 1977).

3. John Waterbury, *The Commander of the Faithful: The Moroccan Political Elite—A Study in Segmented Politics* (New York: Columbia University Press, 1970), xviii. His analysis stands the test of time remarkably well.

4. Rahma Bourquia and Susan Gilson Miller, *In the Shadow of the Sultan: Culture, Power, and Politics in Morocco* (Cambridge, MA: Harvard University Press, 1999), 12. See also the section on globalizing monarchies in Clement Moore Henry and Robert Springborg, *Globalization and the Politics of Development in the Middle East*, 2nd ed. (Cambridge: Cambridge University Press, 2010), 212–60.

5. Robert H. Davies, Dan O'Meara, and Sipho Dlamini, *The Kingdom of Swaziland: A Profile* (London: Zed, 1985).

6. Among many sources, Edmond J. Keller, *Revolutionary Ethiopia: From Empire to People's Republic* (Bloomington: Indiana University Press, 1988), provides a lucid account. See also the marvelously insightful though lightly fictionalized portrait in Ryszard Kapuscinki, *The Emperor* (London: Quartet, 1983).

7. "Neither Consolidating Nor Fully Democratic: The Evolution of African Political Regimes, 1998–2008," Afrobarometer Briefing Paper no. 67, May 2009.

8. Aristide Zolberg, *Creating Political Order: The Party-States of West Africa* (Chicago: Rand McNally, 1966), 49–50.

9. Jan Vansina, personal communication.

10. Zolberg, *Creating Political Order*, 42.

11. Naomi Chazan, Peter Lewis, Robert A. Mortimer, Donald Rothchild, and Stephen John Stedman, *Politics and Society in Contemporary Africa*, 3rd ed. (Boulder, CO: Lynne Rienner, 1999), 55.

12. On the dimensions and impact of foreign aid, see especially Carol Lancaster, *Aid to Africa: So Much to Do, So Little Done* (Chicago: University of Chicago Press, 1999), and Nicolas van de Walle, *African Economies and the Politics of Permanent Crisis, 1979–1999* (Cambridge: Cambridge University Press, 2001).

13. See the detailed review of Gabon political leadership in the obituary of Omar Bongo Ondimba in *Jeune Afrique*, 14–20 June 2009, 18–41.

14. Thomas Hodgkin, *African Political Parties* (Baltimore, MD: Penguin, 1961); Immanuel Wallerstein, *Africa: The Politics of Independence* (New York: Random House, 1961); Morgenthau, *Political Parties in French-Speaking West Africa*.

15. Samuel P. Huntington, *Political Order in Changing Societies* (New Haven, CT: Yale University Press, 1969). The issue, argues Huntington, was not what kind of government but how much government; achieving development required a strong state.

16. The process of marginalizing the independent press is well chronicled by William A. Hachten in *Muffled Drums: The News Media in Africa* (Ames: Iowa State University Press, 1971).

17. For a more complete discussion, see Zolberg, *Creating Political Order*, 66–127, and Ruth Berins Collier, *Regimes in Tropical Africa: Changing Forms of Political Supremacy, 1945–1975* (Berkeley: University of California Press, 1982), 95–151.

18. Nelson Kasfir, *The Shrinking Political Arena: Participation and Ethnicity in Africa, with a Case Study of Uganda* (Berkeley: University of California Press, 1984).

19. Léopold Senghor, *Nation et voie africaine du socialisme* (Paris: Présence Africaine, 1961).

20. Soriba Sylla, personal communication. Such tours were reminiscent of the sessions ("barazas") that touring district commissioners once held in colonial times to deliver government messages to (obligatorily) assembled local communities.

21. Martin Meredith, *The Fate of Africa—From the Hopes of Freedom to the Heart of Despair: A History of Fifty Years of Independence* (New York: Public Affairs, 2005), 30.

22. See Edward Luttwak's engaging primer of military coup preparation and implementation, *Coup d'état: A Practical Handbook* (London: Allen Lane, 1968).

23. Useful detail on decolonization politics is provided by John Obert Voll and Sarah Potts Voll in *The Sudan: Unity and Diversity in a Multicultural State* (Boulder, CO: Westview, 1985), by Peter Woodward in "The South in Sudanese Politics, 1946–1956," *Middle Eastern Studies* 16.3 (1980): 178–92, and by Robert O. Collins in *A History of Modern Sudan* (Cambridge: Cambridge University Press, 2008).

24. CIA station chief Larry Devlin provides new details on this complicated era of multiple external interventions in his memoir, *Chief of Station Congo: A Memoir of 1960–67* (New York: Public Affairs, 2007).

25. Comi M. Toulabor offers an incisive account; see *Le Togo sous Eyadéma* (Paris: Karthala, 1986), 15–71. Olympio based his power on his Ewe ethnic community in the south, and after independence he was quick to impose a single-party monopoly. He was a vocal critic of France; his replacement, Nicolas Grunitzky, enjoyed close ties with France. The army, soon joined by the mutineers, was still only in what Toulabor terms "embryonic form" and, like the army in Congo-Kinshasa, was little prepared to assume power.

26. Rémy Bazanguissa-Ganga, *Les voies du politique au Congo: Essai de sociologie historique* (Paris: Karthala, 1997).

27. Angola, Botswana, Cameroon, Cape Verde, Djibouti, Eritrea, Kenya, Malawi, Morocco, Mozambique, Namibia, Sao Tome and Principe, Senegal, South Africa, Swaziland, Tanzania, Tunisia, Zambia, and Zimbabwe. Several, notably Kenya in 1982 and Morocco in 1970, had nearly successful coup efforts.

28. Samuel Decalo, *Coups and Army Rule in Africa: Studies in Military Style* (New Haven, CT: Yale University Press, 1976).

29. Coup leader Colonel A. A. Afrifa in his account (*The Ghana Coup, 24th February 1966* [London: Frank Cass, 1967]) stresses the sense of suffering and anger in his village over shortages of key commodities and regime looting of the cocoa sector. See also Dennis Austin and Robin Luckham, eds., *Politicians and Soldiers in Ghana, 1966–1972* (London: Frank Cass, 1975).

30. Jimmy Kandeh, *Coups from Below: Armed Subalterns and State Power in West Africa* (New York: Palgrave Macmillan, 2004).

31. Patrick McGowan, "African Military Coups d'état, 1956–2001," *Journal of Modern African Studies* 41.3 (2003): 339–70.

32. Gamel Abdel Nasser, *Egypt's Liberation: The Philosophy of the Revolution* (Washington, DC: Public Affairs Press, 1955).

33. On ideological currents in the Middle East at the time, see Kemal H. Karpat, ed., *Political and Social Thought in the Contemporary Middle East* (New York: Praeger, 1968).

34. Other Afromarxist states such as Angola and Mozambique were by formal self-ascription, products of national liberation wars. In these instances, the doctrinal commitment ran deeper than in the military cases. Some add Zimbabwe to the list, on the basis of the personal intellectual perspective of President Robert Mugabe, even though he was never able to impose Marxism-Leninism as regime ideology. Sao Tome and Principe is another ambiguous candidate. On this regime type, see David Ottoway and Marina Ottoway, *Afrocommunism* (New York: Africana Publishing Company, 1981), Edmond J. Keller and Donald Rothchild, eds., *Afro-Marxist Regimes: Ideology and Public Policy* (Boulder, CO: Lynne Rienner, 1987), and Crawford Young, *Ideology and Development in Africa* (New Haven, CT: Yale University Press, 1982).

35. This listing is distilled from some of the influential works contributing to the theory of the military as agents of development: Samuel Finer, *The Man on Horseback: The Role of the Military in Politics* (London: Pall Mall, 1962); Morris Janowicz, *The Military in the Political Development of New Nations* (Chicago: University of Chicago Press, 1964); John J. Johnson, ed., *The Role of the Military in Underdeveloped Countries* (Princeton, NJ: Princeton University Press, 1962); Claude E. Welch, *Soldier and State in Africa* (Evanston, IL: Northwestern University Press, 1970); W. F. Gutteridge, *Military Regimes in Africa* (London: Methuen, 1975).

36. Cynthia Enloe, *Ethnic Soldiers: State Sovereignty in Divided Societies* (Athens: University of Georgia Press, 1980).

37. John Campbell, presentation on Nigerian politics to African Studies colloquium, African Studies Program, University of Wisconsin–Madison, 13 November 2007; John Campbell, *Nigeria: Dancing on the Brink* (Lanham, MD: Rowman and Littlefield, 2011).

38. Ellen Kay Trimberger, *Revolution from Above: Military Bureaucrats in Japan, Turkey, Egypt, and Peru* (New Brunswick, NJ: Transaction, 1978).

39. Decalo, *Coups and Army Rule in Africa.*

40. Young, *Ideology and Development in Africa*, 141.

41. For an example of an initially largely positive reading of the Mobutu regime by a leading specialist who later became a sharp critic, see Jean-Claude Willame, *Patrimonialism and Political Change in the Congo* (Stanford, CA: Stanford University Press, 1972).

42. His autocratic drift and bizarre behavior are well known to frequent Gambia visitors; see also *New York Times*, 21 May 2009. The Amnesty International 2008 State of the World's Human Rights report alleges at least one thousand "witch" kidnappings and a string of illegal detentions, disappearances, and torture cases ("The Gambia: Witch Hunt," *African Research Bulletin*, Political, Social, and Cultural Series, 46.3 [2009]: 17900).

43. Ian Campbell, "Military Withdrawal Debate in Nigeria: The Prelude to the 1975 Coup," *West African Journal of Sociology and Political Science* 1.3 (1978): 318.

44. Crawford Young, "Permanent Transition and Changing Conjuncture: Dilemmas of Democracy in Nigeria in Comparative Perspective," in *Dilemmas of Democracy in Nigeria*, ed. Paul A. Beckett and Crawford Young (Rochester, NY: University of Rochester Press, 1997), 65–82.

45. For chapter and verse, see Bjorn Beckman, *Organizing the Farmers: Cocoa Politics and National Development in Ghana* (Uppsala: Scandinavian Institute of African Studies, 1976).

46. Crawford Young, Neal P. Sherman, and Tim H. Rose, *Cooperatives and Development: Agricultural Politics in Ghana and Uganda* (Madison: University of Wisconsin Press, 1981).

47. Robert H. Bates, *Markets and States in Tropical Africa: The Political Basis of Agricultural Strategies* (Berkeley, CA: University of California Press, 1981).

Chapter 5. Anatomy of State Crisis

1. The first three quotations in the epigraphs come from *New York Times*, 28 June 2009.

2. See Cabral's revolutionary testament: *Revolution in Guiné* (London: Stage 1, 1969), and the valuable exegesis of his thought in Henry Bienen, "State and Revolution: The Works of Amilcar Cabral," *Journal of Modern African Studies* 15.4 (1977): 555–68.

3. See especially Basil Davidson, *The Liberation of Guiné* (Baltimore, MD: Penguin, 1969), Lars Rudebeck, *Guinea-Bissau: A Study of Political Mobilization* (Uppsala: Scandinavian Institute of African Studies, 1974), Patrick Chabal, *Amilcar Cabral: Revolutionary Leadership and People's War* (Cambridge: Cambridge University Press, 1983), and Gérard Chaliand, *Armed Struggle in Africa: With the Guerrillas in Portuguese Guinea*, trans. David Rattray and Robert Leonhard (New York: Monthly Review Press, 1969).

4. Crawford Young, "Agricultural Policy in Uganda: Capability and Choice," in *The State of the Nations*, ed. Michael F. Lofchie (Berkeley: University of California Press), 141–42.

5. Joshua Forrest, *Lineages of State Fragility: Rural Civil Society in Guinea-Bissau* (London: James Currey, 2003). See also his earlier work, *Guinea-Bissau: Power, Conflict and Renewal in a West African Nation* (Boulder, CO: Westview, 1992).

6. Rosemary E. Galli and Jocelyn Jones, *Guinea-Bissau: Politics, Economics and Society* (Boulder, CO: Lynne Rienner, 1987), 117–19. A ray of hope appeared in July 2009, when, to general astonishment, successful elections following constitutional script took place after the political assassinations of the head of state and army commander. An elder statesman, Malam Bacai Sanha, won an election, whose conduct was validated by

international observers, in which 61% of the electorate participated. Sanha won on a second round with 63% over former president Kumba Yala, who accepted the results. Sanha is from a smaller ethnic group, while Yala is a Balante, one of two large groups, each of which comprises 25% of the population *Jeune Afrique*, 2–8 August 2009, 10–11). These brief hopes were again shattered in 2012 by a military coup disrupting new elections necessitated by the death of Sanha.

7. Carl G. Rosberg and Thomas M. Callaghy, eds., *Socialism in Sub-Saharan Africa* (Berkeley: Institute of International Studies, 1979).

8. For a valuable overview of this phase of African socialism, see William H. Friedland and Carl G. Rosberg, eds., *African Socialism* (Stanford, CA: Stanford University Press, 1964).

9. Sessional Paper no. 10, Kenya Parliament, in *African Socialism and Its Application to Planning in Kenya* (Nairobi: Government Printer, 1965).

10. In addition to key intellectual sources cited in chapter 1, Nigerian scholar Claude Ake's *A Political Economy of Africa* (Harlow, UK: Longman, 1981) was an influential work. Colin Leys also published a powerful critique of Kenyan capitalism grounded in dependency theory: *Underdevelopment in Kenya* (Berkeley: University of California Press, 1974).

11. Crawford Young and Thomas Turner, *The Rise and Decline of the Zairian State* (Madison: University of Wisconsin Press, 1985), 389. Congolese observers quietly noted the applicability of this Mobutu obiter dictum to his domestic political management.

12. For valuable coverage of the NIEO movement, see Steven D. Krasner, *Structural Conflict: The Third World Against Global Liberalism* (Berkeley: University of California Press, 1985), and Robert I. Rothstein, *The Weak in the World of the Strong: The Developing Countries in the International System* (New York: Columbia University Press, 1977).

13. Intellectual support for McNamara's ideas was found in writings of economists with World Bank ties; see Hollis Chenery, *Redistribution with Growth* (London: Oxford University Press, 1974).

14. Jimi Peters, *The Nigerian Military and the State* (London: I. B. Tauris, 1997), 144.

15. World Bank, *World Development Report 1984* (New York: Oxford University Press, 1984), 248–49.

16. Among the rare monographs on Cape Verde is Colin Foy's *Cape Verde: Politics, Economics and Society* (London: Pinter, 1988).

17. Jennifer A. Widner, *The Rise of a Party-State in Kenya: From Harambee! To Nyanyo!* (Berkeley: University of California Press, 1992); Yves Fauré and Jean-François Médard, eds., *État et bourgeoisie en Côte d'Ivoire* (Paris: Editions Karthala, 1982).

18. Bastiaan A. den Tuinder, *Ivory Coast: The Challenge of Success* (Baltimore, MD: Johns Hopkins University Press, 1978), 3.

19. Cited to this effect in Alexander G. Rondos, "Ivory Coast: The Price of Development," *Africa Report* 24.2 (1979): 4.

20. Crawford Young, *Ideology and Development in Africa* (New Haven, CT: Yale University Press, 1982), 192.

21. Among the abundant works covering postcolonial Kenya politics up to the democratic transition, I find especially valuable Widner, *The Rise of a Party-State in Kenya*.

22. Some 17%, according to S. E. Migot-Adholla, "Rural Development Policy and Equality," in *Politics and Public Policy in Kenya and Tanzania*, ed. Joel D. Barkan and John J. Okumu (New York: Praeger, 1979), 164.

23. For detail on Kenya's diminished performance in the 1980s, see Marilee S. Grindle, *Challenging the State: Crisis and Innovation in Latin America and Africa* (Cambridge: Cambridge University Press, 1996).

24. Despite Banda's siphoning from Press Holdings funds, partly to fund his elite secondary school, the Kamuzu academy, after restructuring the conglomerate became profitable in the mid-1980s and was privatized by 1998. Jan Kees van Donge compares the sprawling enterprise to the South Korean "chaebols"; see "The Fate of an African 'Chaebol': Malawi's Press Corporation after Democratization," *Journal of Modern African Studies* 40.4 (2002): 651–81.

25. William Reno, *Corruption and State Politics in Sierra Leone* (Cambridge: Cambridge University Press, 1995). The folly of grandiose state investment in luxurious facilities for the brief encounter of an OAU summit began in 1965, when Nkrumah committed £10 million for the infamous "Job 600," building a sumptuous conference center and residential facilities for heads of state at a moment when the Ghana economy was already in free fall.

26. *Le Monde*, 30 December 1980.

27. Gali Ngothe Gatta, *Tchad: Guerre civile et désaggrégation de l'état* (Paris: Présence Africaine, 1985).

28. William J. Foltz, "Reconstructing the State of Chad," in *Collapsed States: The Disintegration and Restoration of Legitimate Authority*, ed. I. William Zartman (Boulder, CO: Lynne Rienner, 1994), 15.

29. The Sara are less a single ethnic group than a congeries of related though culturally and linguistically distinct groupings that came to share a collective ethnonym during colonial times. The French viewed them as a "docile and passive" but handsome "race," particularly valuable as a manpower reservoir. Sara politicians were able "to create a political myth [of Sara identity] with sufficient historical truth to give it credibility" (René Lemarchand, "The Politics of Sara Ethnicity: A Note on the Origins of the Civil War in Chad," *Cahiers d'Eudes Africaines* 20.4 [1980]: 449–71).

30. See, for example, Chad scholar Abderahman Dadi's *Tchad: L'état retrouvée* (Paris: L'Harmattan, 1987). This is also the thesis of Foltz, "Reconstructing the State of Chad," 15–32. Other valuable works on the Chad civil wars include Sam C. Nolutshungu, *Limits of Anarchy: Intervention of State Formation in Chad* (Charlottesville: University Press of Virginia, 1996), Virginia Thompson and Richard Adloff, *Conflict in Chad* (Berkeley, CA: Institute of International Studies, 1981), and Robert Buijtenhuis, *Le Frolinat et les revoltes populaires du Tchad, 1965–1976* (The Hague: Mouton, 1978).

31. Scott Straus, African Studies colloquium, African Studies Program, University of Wisconsin–Madison, 30 November 2006. The Senegal government pleads the necessity of international funding to carry out the judicial proceedings.

32. Foltz, "Reconstructing the State of Chad," 29.

33. Naomi Chazan, *An Anatomy of Ghanaian Politics: Managing Political Recession* (Boulder, CO: Westview, 1982), 191–202.

34. R. A. Kotey, L. Okali, and E. E. Rourke, *The Economics of Cocoa Production and Marketing* (Legon: University of Ghana, 1975), 53. On the cocoa political economy, see also Gwendolyn Mikell, *Cocoa and Chaos in Ghana* (New York: Paragon House, 1989), and Bjorn Beckman, *Organizing the Farmers* (Uppsala: Scandinavian Institute of African Studies, 1976).

35. Douglas Rimmer, *Staying Poor: Ghana's Political Economy, 1950–1990* (New York: Pergamon, 1980), 28.

36. Martin Meredith, *The Fate of Africa: From the Hopes of Freedom to the Heart of Despair—A History of 50 Years of Independence* (New York: Public Affairs, 2005), 185.

37. Jeffrey Herbst, *The Politics of Reform in Ghana, 1982–1991* (Berkeley: University of California Press, 1993), 27.

38. Rimmer, *Staying Poor*, 129–33.

39. *West Africa*, 17 July 1978, 1775.

40. Ghana, *Final Report of the Commission of Enquiry into Bribery and Corruption* (Accra: Ghana Publishing Corp., 1975).

41. Herbst, *The Politics of Reform in Ghana*, 30.

42. Young, *Ideology and Development in Africa*, 89–95.

43. Margaret Hall and Tom Young, *Confronting Leviathan: Mozambique since Independence* (Athens: Ohio University Press, 1997), 68.

44. Hall and Young, *Confronting Leviathan*, 109. Also especially useful on the socialist experiment among the many works devoted to Mozambique is Patrick Chabal et al., *A History of Postcolonial Lusophone Africa* (Bloomington: Indiana University Press, 2002), Edmond J. Keller and Donald Rothchild, eds., *Afro-Marxist Regimes: Ideology and Public Policy* (Boulder, CO: Lynne Rienner, 1987), Joseph Hanlon, *Mozambique: Who Calls the Shots?* (London: James Currey, 1991), and Allen Isaacman, *Mozambique: From Colonialism to Revolution, 1900–1982* (Boulder, CO: Westview, 1983).

45. Hall and Young, *Confronting Leviathan*, 196.

46. Alex Vines, *RENAMO: Terrorism in Mozambique* (Bloomington: Indiana University Press, 1991); William Finnegan, *A Complicated War: The Harrowing of Mozambique* (Berkeley: University of California Press, 1992).

47. For persuasive evidence, see M. Anne Pitcher, *Transforming Mozambique: The Politics of Privatization, 1975–2000* (Cambridge: Cambridge University Press, 2002).

48. Recent attempts at definition of state failure include Robert I. Rotberg, ed., *When States Fail: Causes and Consequences* ((Princeton, NJ: Princeton University Press, 2005), I. William Zartman, ed., *Collapsed States: The Disintegration and Restoration of Legitimate Authority* (Boulder, CO: Lynne Rienner, 1995), and Robert H. Bates, *When Things Fell Apart: State Failure in Late-Century Africa* (Cambridge: Cambridge University Press, 2008).

49. Lynn S. Khadiagala in her research on rural women and their encounters over property rights with local judicial instances in southwestern Uganda found that even during the devastated state of the late Idi Amin period local courts continued to function and show surprising respect for legal norms in upholding the rights of female litigants ("Law, Power, and Justice: The Adjudication of Women's Property Rights in Uganda" [PhD diss., University of Wisconsin–Madison, 1999]).

50. Nicolas van de Walle, *African Economies and the Politics of Permanent Crisis, 1979–1999* (Cambridge: Cambridge University Press, 2001), 66.

51. van de Walle, *African Economies*, 130.

52. Young and Turner, *The Rise and Decline of the Zairian State*, 165–66.

53. Among other valuable accounts, see Tom Lodge, Bill Nasson, Steven Munson, Khekla Shubane, and Nokwanda Sithole, eds., *All Here and Now: Black Politics in South Africa in the 1980s* (London: Hurst, 1992); Chris Alden, *Apartheid's Last Stand: The Rise and Fall of the South African Security State* (Houndmills, UK: Macmillan, 1996).

54. Thomas M. Callaghy and John Ravenhill, eds., *Hemmed In: Responses to Africa's Economic Decline* (New York: Columbia University Press, 1993). This volume includes the contributions of a number of the ablest students of the African economic crisis. See also Carol Lancaster, *Aid to Africa: So Much to Do, So Little Done* (Chicago: University of Chicago Press, 1999), and van de Walle, *African Economies*.

55. John Ravenhill, "A Second Decade of Adjustment: Greater Complexity, Greater Uncertainty," in *Hemmed In*, 48.

56. See John R. Nellis, "Public Enterprises in Sub-Saharan Africa," in *State-Owned Enterprises in Africa*, ed. Barbara Grosh and Rwekaza S. Mukandala (Boulder, CO: Lynne Rienner, 1994), 3–24. See also Roger Tangri, *The Politics of Patronage in Africa: Parastatals, Privatization and Private Enterprise* (Trenton, NJ: Africa World Press, 1999).

57. Indeed, the potency of such a weapon was demonstrated in 1998, when an airborne Rwandan army contingent backing a Congolese insurgent movement briefly captured the Inga site, momentarily cutting off the power supply to Kinshasa.

58. See Jean-Claude Willame's invaluable monograph *Zaire: L'épopée d'Inga, chronique d'une prédation industrielle* (Paris: L'Harmattan, 1986); see also Young and Turner, *The Rise and Decline of the Zairian State*, 296–304, and Crawford Young, "Zaire: The Anatomy of a Failed State," in *History of Central Africa: The Contemporary Years*, ed. David Birmingham and Phyllis M. Martin (London: Longman, 1998), 119–21.

59. "Bio-fuels: Nigeria, South Africa," *Africa Research Bulletin*, Economic, Financial and Technical Series, 44.5 (2007): 17428.

60. I am indebted to my former research assistant Ric Tange for assembling documentation on the Ajaokuta project.

61. http://www.tellng.com/news/articles/060110-13/news/biz, accessed 23 September 2009. Daniel Jordan Smith cites the slightly lower figure of $8 billion in his exegesis of Nigerian corruption; see *A Culture of Corruption: Everyday Deception and Popular Discontent in Nigeria* (Princeton, NJ: Princeton University Press, 2006), 50.

62. http://234next.com/CSP/sites/Next/Money/565 6518-147/jonathan_promises -to-revive-ajaokuta-steel.esp, accessed 3 March 2011.

63. Proceedings of the colloquium on the Ajaokuta steel project, Nigerian Institute of International Affairs, Lagos, 1981.

64. Gbolahan Alli-Balogun provides a useful account of the early history of the project; see "Soviet Technical Assistance and Nigeria's Steel Complex," *Journal of Modern African Studies* 26.4 (1988): 623–37.

65. Technical details on the project are provided in Matthew O. Esholomi, "Industrial Technology Transfer and Steel Production in Nigeria," booklet published by Eshalomi and Associates, Lagos, January 1983.

66. Alli-Balogun, "Soviet Technical Assistance and Nigeria's Steel Complex," 632.

67. http://www.nigeriafirst.org/article_1161.shtml, accessed 11 September 2006.

68. *New York Times*, 3 December 1998.

69. *This Day* (Lagos), 24 April 2006.

70. "Nigeria Gears to Lead Steel Production in Africa," 10 June 2009, http://www.afrol.com/articles/29309, accessed 23 August 2009.

71. *Sunday Punch* (Lagos), 12 April 2010.

72. Peter Lewis, personal communication.

73. Maxim Matusevich, *No Easy Row for a Russian Hoe: Ideology and Pragmatism in Nigerian-Soviet Relations, 1960–1991* (Trenton, NJ: Africa World Press, 2003), 189.

74. Ravenhill, "A Second Decade of Adjustment," 18.

75. Bates, *When Things Fell Apart*, 15–29.

76. Juan L. Linz, "Totalitarian and Authoritarian Regimes," in *Handbook of Political Science*, vol. 3, ed. Fred I. Greenstein and Nelson Polsby (New Brunswick, NJ: Transaction 1978), 240. See also H. E. Chelabi and Juan L. Linz, eds., *Sultanistic Regimes* (Baltimore, MD: Johns Hopkins University Press, 1998).

77. Reno, *Corruption and State Politics*. The shadow state bears some resemblance to what Achille Mbembe terms "private indirect governance"; see *On the Postcolony* (Berkeley: University of California Press, 2001), 66–101.

78. Robert Bates, *Markets and States in Tropical Africa: The Political Basis of Agricultural Politics* (Berkeley: University of California Press, 1981).

79. Gebru Tareke, *The Ethiopian Revolution: War in the Horn of Africa* (New Haven, CT: Yale University Press, 2009), 111–31.

80. William G. Thom, "An Assessment of Prospects for Ending Domestic Military Conflict in Sub-Saharan Africa," *CSIS Africa Notes* 177 (1995), 3, cited in Herbst, *States and Power*, 19.

81. Bates, *When Things Fell Apart*.

82. William B. Quandt, *Between Ballots and Bullets: Algeria's Transition from Authoritarianism* (Washington, DC: Brookings Institution Press, 1998), 45.

CHAPTER 6. DEMOCRATIZATION AND ITS LIMITS

1. See my "Democratization in Africa," *Economic Change and Political Liberalization in Africa*, ed. Jennifer A. Widner (Baltimore, MD: Johns Hopkins University Press, 1994), 230–50, "Africa: An Interim Balance Sheet," in *Africa: Dilemmas of Development and Change*, ed. Peter Lewis (Boulder, CO: Westview Press, 1998), 341–58, and "The Third Wave of Democratization in Africa: Ambiguities and Contradictions," in *State, Conflict, and Democracy in Africa*, ed. Richard Joseph (Boulder, CO: Lynne Rienner, 1999), 15–38.

2. Samuel P. Huntington, *The Third Wave: Democratization in the Late Twentieth Century* (Norman: University of Oklahoma Press, 1991).

3. Ghassan Salamé argues that the Muslim Arab world more broadly initially missed out on the third wave, owing to the entrenched power of its security apparatus, the rentier character of many of its polities, and the challenge of incorporating political Islamist movements into a competitive electoral framework; see "Introduction: Where Are the Democrats?," in *Democracy without Democrats? The Renewal of Politics in the Middle East*, ed. Ghassan Salamé (London: I. B. Tauris, 1994), 1–20.

4. Marina Ottaway, *Democracy Challenged: The Rise of Semi-Authoritarianism* (Washington, DC: Carnegie Endowment for International Peace, 2003), 3.

5. Aili Mari Tripp offers an extended application of this notion in *Museveni's Uganda: Paradoxes of Power in a Hybrid State* (Boulder, CO: Lynne Rienner, 2010).

6. Monique Dinan, Vidula Nababsing, and Hansraj Mathur, "Mauritius: Cultural Accommodation in a Diverse Island Polity," in *The Accommodation of Cultural Diversity: Case-Studies*, ed. Crawford Young (Houndmills, UK: Macmillan, 1999), 72–102.

7. The striking theme of permanent transition is central to a pair of edited volumes on Nigerian politics in the mid-1990s Larry Diamond, Anthony Kirk-Greene, and Oyeleye Oyediran, eds., *Transition Without End: Nigerian Politics and Civil Society under Babangida* (Boulder CO: Lynne Rienner, 1997), and Paul A. Beckett and Crawford Young, eds., *Dilemmas of Democracy in Nigeria* (Rochester, NY: University of Rochester Press, 1997).

8. Beckett and Young, "Introduction: Beyond the Impasse of 'Permanent Transition' in Nigeria," in *Dilemmas of Democracy*, 4.

9. Mwesiga Baretsu, "The Rise and Fall of the One-Party State in Tanzania," in *Economic Change and Political Liberalization*, 168.

10. Celestin Monga, *The Anthropology of Anger: Civil Society and Democracy in Africa* (Boulder, CO: Lynne Rienner, 1996), 115.

11. For a brief intellectual history of the concept, see Crawford Young, "In Search of Civil Society," in *Civil Society and the State in Africa*, ed. John W. Harbeson, Donald Rothchild, and Naomi Chazan (Boulder, CO: Lynne Rienner, 1992), 33–50; see also John Keane, ed., *Civil Society and the State: New European Perspectives* (London: Verso, 1988).

12. These perspectives were eloquently expressed by East European intellectuals at a 1991 conference organized in Bellagio, Italy, by Bogumul Jewsiewicki and Prosser Gifford comparing state crisis in African and Eastern Europe.

13. See, for example, Pierre Landell-Mills, "Governance, Cultural Change, and Empowerment," *Journal of Modern African Studies* 30.4 (1992): 543–67.

14. Goran Hyden first developed the notion in *No Short Cuts to Progress: African Development Management in Comparative Perspective* (Berkeley: University of California Press, 1983), which he then more fully elaborated in *Governance and Politics in Africa* (Boulder, CO: Lynne Rienner , 1992), coauthored with Michael Bratton.

15. World Bank, *Sub-Saharan Africa: From Crisis to Sustainable Growth, a Long-Term Perspective Study* (Washington, DC: World Bank, 1989), 61.

16. Charles Tilly, *Democracy* (Cambridge: Cambridge University Press, 2007); Staffan I. Lindberg, *Democracy and Elections in Africa* (Baltimore, MD: John Hopkins University Press, 2006); Michael Bratton and Nicolas van de Walle, *Democratic Experiments in Africa: Regime Transitions in Comparative Perspective* (Cambridge: Cambridge University Press, 1997).

17. As suggested by the epigraph to this chapter from F. Ebussi Boulaga, which comes from *Les conférences nationales en Afrique: Une affaire à suivre* (Paris: Karthala, 1993), 9.

18. Chris Allen, "Democratic Renewal in Africa: Two Essays on Benin," Centre of African Studies, University of Edinburgh, Occasional Papers no. 40, 1992, 6.

19. Richard Westebbe, then a World Bank official closely involved in Benin negotiations, provides an excellent account; see "Structural Adjustment, Rent-Seeking and Liberalization in Benin," in *Economic Change and Political Liberalization*, 80–100. See also Samuel Decalo, "Benin: First of the New Democracies," in *Political Reform in Francophone Africa*, ed. John F. Clark and David E. Gardinier (Boulder, CO: Westview, 1997), 43–61, Richard Banegas, "Retour sur une 'transition modéle': Les dynamiques du dedans et du dehors de la démocratization au Bénin, in *Transitions démocratiques africaines*, ed. Jean-Pascal Daloz and Patrick Quantin (Paris: Karthala, 1997), 23–94, and Bruce A. Magnusson, "The Politics of Democratic Regime Legitimation in Benin: Institutions, Social Policy, and Security" (PhD diss., University of Wisconsin–Madison, 1997).

20. I am indebted to my research assistant, Geraldine O'Mahoney, for collecting data on this point.

21. Again I rely on data collected by O'Mahoney. Tripp, using several sources, counted thirty-eight new constitutions.

22. For a detailed account, see Oliver Furley and James Katalikawe, "Constitutional Reform in Uganda: The New Approach," *African Affairs* 96.383 (1997): 243–60.

23. For this and other detail on the Zambian transition, see Michael Bratton, "Economic Crisis and Political Realignment in Zambia," in *Economic Change and Political Liberalization*, 101–28.

24. This argument is convincingly made by Jens Meierhenrich in *The Legacies of Law: Long-run Consequences of Legal Development in South Africa, 1652–2000* (Cambridge: Cambridge University Press, 2008).

25. Special tribute is due to the editors of the immensely valuable documentary record of all elections in African states: Dieter Nohlen, Michael Krennerich, and Bernhard Thibaut, eds., *Elections in Africa: A Data Handbook* (Oxford: Oxford University Press, 1999).

26. Claude Ake, *Democracy and Development in Africa* (Washington, DC: Brookings Institution, 1996), 130.

27. Especially valuable for this period in Algeria is Luis Martinez, *The Algerian Civil War, 1990–1998*, trans. Jonathan Derrick (New York: Columbia University Press, 2000). Martinez, a pseudonym for an Algerian scholar, conducted extensive interviews with guerrilla participants in the civil war.

28. Richard Sklar provides a cogent account of the failed transition; see "Crisis and Transition in the Political History of Independent Nigeria," in *Dilemmas of Democracy*, 15–44. See also Eghosa E. Osaghae, *Nigeria since Independence: Crippled Giant* (London: Hurst, 1998).

29. Excellent accounts are provided by René Lemarchand in *Burundi: Ethnocide as Theory and Practice* (Washington, DC: Woodrow Wilson Center Press, 1994), in "Burundi at a Crossroads," in *Security Dynamics in Africa's Great Lakes Region*, ed. Gilbert M. Khadiagala (Boulder, CO: Lynne Rienner, 2006), 41–58, and in *The Dynamics of Violence in*

Central Africa (Philadelphia: University of Pennsylvania Press, 2009). See also Jean-Pierre Chrétien and M. Mukuri, eds., *Burundi: La fracture identitaire* (Paris: Karthala, 2002).

30. Gérard Prunier, *The Rwanda Crisis: History of a Genocide* (New York: Columbia University Press, 1995), 5.

31. The first published allegation that RPF leader and current president Paul Kagame was responsible came from RPF defector Abdul Ruzibiza in his *Rwanda: L'histoire secrete* (Paris: Panama, 2005). French investigating magistrate Paul Bruguière in a 2008 indictment accused Kagame and other RPF leaders of shooting down the plane, based on extensive though circumstantial evidence (Lemarchand, *The Dynamics of Violence*, 105). Ruzibiza subsequently repudiated his allegations, and France did not pursue the Bruguière indictment.

32. Alison des Forges, *"Leave None to Tell the Tale:" Genocide in Rwanda* (New York: Human Rights Press, 1999). Lemarchand, also a careful scholar, uses the figure of eight hundred thousand (*The Dynamics of Violence*, 73).

33. In addition to sources already cited, among the abundant works about the Rwanda genocide, the best include Timothy Longman, *Commanded by the Devil: Christianity and Genocide in Rwanda* (New York: Cambridge University Press, 2006), Mahmood Mamdani, *When Victims Become Killers: Colonialism, Nativism, and the Genocide in Rwanda* (Princeton, NJ: Princeton University Press, 2001), Filip Reyntjens, *La guerre des Grands Lacs: Alliances mouvantes et conflits extra-territoriaux en Afrique Centrale* (Paris: L'Harmattan, 1999), and Scott Straus, *The Order of Genocide: Race, Power and War in Rwanda* (Ithaca, NY: Cornell University Press, 2006).

34. Rita Abrahamson elaborates at length on this point in *Disciplining Democracy: Development Discourse and Good Governance in Africa* (London: Zed, 2000).

35. From 1900 to 2010, interrupted or aborted transitions occurred in Algeria, Burundi, Central African Repblic, Comoros, Congo-Brazzaville, Congo-Kinshasa, Gambia, Guinea-Bissau, Guinea, Ivory Coast, Madagascar, Mauritania, Niger, Nigeria, and Rwanda.

36. Patrick McGowan, "African Military Coups d'état, 1956–2001," *Journal of Modern African Studies* 41.3 (2003): 339–70.

37. On the early years of Zimbabwe independence, see Jeffrey Herbst, *State Politics in Zimbabwe* (Berkeley: University of California Press, 1990), and Colin Stoneman and Lionel Cliffe, *Zimbabwe: Politics, Economics and Society* (London: Pinter, 1989).

38. As one example, Mugabe chose to keep on the intelligence chief of the settler regime, Ken Flower, who later wrote in his memoir that "Mugabe was reconciliation personified, and as we got to know each other he proved to be the most appreciative of all the Prime Ministers I had served" (*Serving Secretly: An Intelligence Chief on Record—Rhodesia into Zimbabwe 1964 to 1981* [London: John Murray, 1987], 273).

39. In his widely heralded 1986 BBC series, Ali Mazrui made Zimbabwe the paradigm of the virtuous African polity of the early 1980s.

40. William Tordoff, *Government and Politics in Africa*, 4th ed. (Bloomington: Indiana University Press, 2002), 201.

41. For an analysis by a Zimbabwean scholar sympathetic to the initial intervention, see Martin R. Rupiya, "A Political and Military Review of Zimbabwe's Involvement in

the Second Congo War," in *The African Stakes of the Congo War*, ed. John F. Clark (New York: Palgrave Macmillan, 2002), 91–105.

42. Scott D. Taylor, "Zimbabwe: State and Society in Crisis," in *Politics in Southern Africa: State and Society in Transition*, ed. Gretchen Bauer and Scott D. Taylor (Boulder, CO: Lynne Rienner, 2005), 177.

43. Lindberg, *Democracy and Elections in Africa*, 87.

44. *Africa Confidential*, 4 July 2008.

45. For detail see Leonardo A. Villalon and Amdourahmane Idrissa, "Repetitive Breakdowns and a Decade of Experimentation: Institutional Choices and Unstable Democracy in Niger," in *Fate of Africa's Democratic Experiments: Elites and Institutions*, ed. Leonarda A. Villalon and Peter VonDoepp (Bloomington: Indiana University Press, 2005), 27–48.

46. Lindberg, *Democracy and Elections in Africa*, 147.

47. As a member of a study team visiting Kenya to study the electoral process in 1994, I can attest that available documentation and interviews left no doubt as to the responsibility of leading political figures in fomenting the ethnic clashes.

48. "Tipping Games: When Do Opposition Parties Coalesce?," in *Electoral Authoritarianism: The Dynamics of Unfree Competition*, ed. Andreas Schedler (Boulder, CO: Lynne Rienner, 2006), 84.

49. Tom P. Wolf, "'Poll Poison?' Politicians and Polling in the 2007 Kenya Election," typescript, 2009.

50. American ambassador John Campbell, a close observer of the 2003 and 2007 elections, characterized the latter as a complete sham, a mere "election-like event" (*Nigeria: Dancing on the Brink* [Lanham, MD: Rowman and Littlefield, 2011], 97–113).

51. For detail on the Bakassi Boys, see Daniel Jordan Smith, *A Culture of Corruption: Everyday Deception and Popular Discontent in Nigeria* (Princeton, NJ: Princeton University Press, 2007), 166–90.

52. Human Rights Watch, "Criminal Politics: Violence, 'Godfathers,' and Corruption in Nigeria," Human Rights Watch Reports 19.16(A) (2007): 30.

53. For detail on these elections, I rely on *African Research Bulletin* and *Africa Confidential*.

54. Michael Bratton, Robert Mattes, and E. Gyimah-Boadi, eds., *Public Opinion, Democracy, and Market Reform in Africa* (Cambridge: Cambridge University Press, 2005), 10.

55. Adam Przeworski and Fernando Limongi, "Modernization: Theories and Facts," *World Politics* 49.2 (1997): 155–83.

56. Valuable recent contributions on this theme include Daniel N. Posner's *Institutions and Ethnic Politics in Africa* (Cambridge: Cambridge University Press, 2005), Joshua B. Forrest's *Subnationalism in Africa: Ethnicity, Alliances, and Politics* (Boulder, CO: Lynne Rienner, 2004), and Donald Rothchild's *Managing Ethnic Conflict in Africa* (Washington, DC: Brookings Institution Press, 1997).

57. See the thoughtful contributions in Bruce Berman, Dickson Eyoh, and Will Kymlicka, eds., *Ethnicity and Democracy in Africa* (Oxford, UK: James Currey, 2004).

58. See K. M. de Silva, "Electoral Systems," in *Ethnic Diversity and Public Policy: A Comparative Inquiry*, ed. Crawford Young (Houndmills, UK: Macmillan, 1998), 72–107, and Andrew Reynolds, *Electoral Systems and Democratization in Southern Africa* (Oxford: Oxford University Press, 1999).

59. Salamé, "Introduction: Where Are the Democrats?," 6.

60. For exhaustive detail see Remy Bazenguissa-Ganga, *Les voies du politique au Congo: Essai de sociologie historique* (Paris: Karthala, 1997).

61. For a succinct account stressing the African diplomatic role, see Thomas J. Bassett and Scott Straus, "Defending Democracy in Côte d'Ivoire," *Foreign Affairs* 90.4 (2011): 130–40.

62. Kwame Boafo-Arthur, "A Decade of Liberalism in Perspective," in *Ghana: One Decade of the Liberal State*, ed. Kwame Boafo-Arthur (Dakar: CODESRIA Books, 2007), 18.

63. Minion K. C. Morrison, "Political Parties in Ghana through Four Republics: A Path to Democratic Consolidation," *Comparative Politics* 36.4 (2004): 421–42.

64. Linda J. Beck, *Brokering Democracy in Africa: The Rise of Clientelist Democracy in Senegal* (New York: Palgrave Macmillan, 2008). For similar findings by a lifelong scholar of Senegalese politics, see Sheldon Gellar, *Democracy in Senegal: Toquevillian Analytics in Africa* (New York: Palgrave Macmillan, 2005).

65. Lindberg, *Democracy and Elections in Africa*, 143–44.

66. Richard Sandbrook, *Closing the Circle: Democratization and Development in Africa* (London: Zed, 2000).

67. Three of the major leaders at Afrobarometer, Michael Bratton, Robert B. Mattes, and Emmanuel Gyimah-Boadi, draw evidence from the first round of these surveys that overall public opinion is supportive of democracy, though with qualification; see their *Public Opinion, Democracy, and Market Reform*.

68. John A. Wiseman, *Democracy in Black Africa: Survival and Renewal* (New York: Paragon House, 1990), 182.

69. In the Tunisian case, although the army numbered only thirty thousand, diverse police groups totaled six hundred thousand for a population of only ten million (Clement Moore Henry and Robert Springborg, *Globalization and the Politics of Development in the Middle East*, 2nd ed. [Cambridge: Cambridge University Press, 2010], 196).

70. This argument is well made in Tripp, *Museveni's Uganda*, 193–95.

CHAPTER 7. MORPHOLOGY OF VIOLENT CIVIL CONFLICT

1. For an earlier essay exploring this theme, see my "Contextualizing Congo Conflicts: Order and Disorder in Postcolonial Africa," in *The African Stakes of the Congo War*, ed. John F. Clark (New York: Palgrave Macmillan, 2002), 13–32.

2. Sam C. Nolutshungu, *Limits of Anarchy: Intervention and State Formation in Chad* Charlottesville: University Press of Virginia, 1996), 280–81.

3. The finest comparative study of this topic is William Reno, *Warfare in Independent Africa* (Cambridge: Cambridge University Press, 2011), which became available only after this manuscript was in press.

4. For examples, see Alistaire Horne, *A Savage War of Peace: Algeria, 1954–1962* (London: Macmillan, 1977), and Norma Kriger, *Zimbabwe's Guerrilla War: Peasant Voices* (Cambridge: Cambridge University Press, 1992).

5. On the UPC, the sympathetic account by Richard Joseph, *Radical Nationalism in Cameroun: Social Origins of the UPC Rebellion* (Oxford, UK: Clarendon, 1977), remains a basic source. On Mau Mau, among an abundant literature see Carl G. Rosberg and John Nottingham, *Kenya: The Myth of Mau Mau* (New York: Praeger, 1966), David F. Gordon, *Decolonization and the State in Kenya* (Boulder, CO: Westview, 1986), and Frank Furedi, *The Mau Mau War in Perspective* (London: James Currey, 1989). The brutality of British repression is eloquently documented by Caroline Elkins in *Imperial Reckoning: The Untold Story of Britain's Gulag in Kenya* (New York: Henry Holt, 2005) and by David Anderson in *Histories of the Hanged: The Dirty War in Kenya and the End of Empire* (New York: Norton, 2005).

6. See in particular Tony Hodges, *Western Sahara: Roots of a Desert War* (Westport, CT: Lawrence Hill, 1983).

7. *Jeune Afrique*, 20–27 September 2009, 36–37. Algeria claims the number is 165,000.

8. These figures are provided by Gebru Tareke in *The Ethiopian Revolution: War in the Horn of Africa* (New Haven, CT: Yale University Press, 2009), 229. This remarkably detailed military history of the Ethiopian wars of the 1970s and 1980s is based on information culled from the Ministry of Defense archives, which Tareke was given access to.

9. The extraordinary militarization of Eritrean society that was a product of the intensity of the societal mobilization the liberation war inspired was maintained in the form of an obligatory eighteen-month military conscription. However, Gaim Kibreab shows that in the wake of the 1998–2000 war with Ethiopia, the Eritrean regime has now indefinitely extended the conscription period, transforming the military recruits into a forced labor contingent ("Forced Labor in Eritrea," *Journal of Modern African Studies* 47.1 [2009]: 41–72).

10. In my view the best single account of the multiple phases of the Angolan wars is the masterful Angola chapter by David Birmingham in Patrick Chabal et al., *A History of Lusophone Africa* (Bloomington: Indiana University Press, 2002). Also valuable for its broad sweep of the different war phases is W. Martin James, *A Political History of the Civil War in Angola, 1974–1990* (New Brunswick, NJ: Transaction, 1992).

11. See his autobiographical account, *The African Dream: The Diaries of the Revolutionary War in the Congo* (London: Harvill, 1999).

12. Herbert Weiss, "Zaire: Collapsed State, Surviving Society, Future Polity," in *Collapsed States: The Disintegration and Restoration of Legitimate Authority*, ed. I. William Zartman (Boulder, CO: Lynne Rienner, 1995), 157–70. See also the comprehensive review of Congo internal wars in Emizet François Kisangani, *Civil Wars in the Democratic Republic of Congo: 1960-2010* (Boulder, CO: Lynne Rienner, 2012).

13. On the Nigerian civil war, crucial sources are Anthony Kirk-Greene, *Crisis and Conflict in Nigeria*, 2 vols. (London: Oxford University Press, 1971), and John J. Stremlau, *The International Politics of the Nigerian Civil War, 1967–1970* (Princeton, NJ: Princeton University Press, 1977).

14. Daniel Jordan Smith, *A Culture of Corruption: Everyday Deception and Popular Discontent in Nigeria* (Princeton, NJ: Princeton University Press, 2007), 192.

15. Smith, *A Culture of Corruption*, 193–94.

16. John Obert Voll and Sarah Potts Voll, *The Sudan: Unity and Diversity in a Multicultural State* (Boulder: Westview Press, 1985), 7–8; Robert O. Collins, *A History of Modern Sudan* (Cambridge: Cambridge University Press, 2008).

17. For contrasting perspectives on the colonial backdrop to southern insurgency, see Mohamed Omar Beshir, *The Southern Sudan: Background to Conflict* (London: William Blackwood and Sons, 1968), and Joseph Oduho and William Deng, *The Problem of the Southern Sudan* (London: Oxford University Press, 1963). See also Crawford Young, *The Politics of Cultural Pluralism* (Madison: University of Wisconsin Press, 1976), 489–501.

18. Quoted from the report of the Commission of Inquiry into Southern Sudan disturbances, August 1955, in K. D. D. Henderson, *The Sudan Republic* (London: Ernest Benn, 1965), 173.

19. Oduho and Deng, *The Problem of the Southern Sudan*, 38.

20. Yoweri Museveni, *Sowing the Mustard Seed* (London: Macmillan, 1997).

21. Amii Omara-Otunnu, *Politics and the Mlitary in Uganda, 1890–1985* (New York: St. Martin's, 1987). On the subsequent functioning of the local councils, see Gina M.S. Lambright, *Decentralization in Uganda: Explaining Successes and Failures* (Boulder, CO: First Forum Press, 2011).

22. Thomas Ofcansky, *Uganda: The Tarnished Pearl of Africa* (Boulder, CO: Westview, 1996), 52.

23. Tareke, *The Ethiopian Revolution*, 82.

24. Tareke, *The Ethiopian Revolution*, 92.

25. This thesis is initially attributed to Mats Berdal and David Malone, eds., *Greed and Grievance: Economic Agendas in Civil War* (Boulder, CO: Lynne Rienner , 2000). The notion was then employed by Paul Collier and others at the World Bank utilizing quantitative data.

26. The scope of American intelligence involvement in Congo-Kinshasa in the 1960 crises is documented in Madeleine G. Kalb, *The Congo Cables: The Cold War in Africa from Eisenhower to Kennedy* (New York: Macmillan, 1982). Larry Devlin, CIA Kinshasa station chief during a good part of this period, adds new detail in his recent autobiography, *CIA Station Chief Congo, 1960–67: A Memoir* (New York: Public Affairs, 2007).

27. Nolotshungu, *Limits of Anarchy*, 145–72.

28. I elaborate on this point in "Deciphering Disorder in Africa: Is Ethnicity the Key?," *World Politics* 54.4 (2002): 532–57.

29. See the engaging comparative analysis by Christopher Clapham in "The Politics of Failure: Clientelism, Political Instability and National Integration in Liberia and Sierra Leone," in *Private Patronage and Public Power: Political Clientelism in the Modern State*, ed. Christopher Clapham (New York: St. Martin's, 1982), 176–92.

30. Jimmy D. Kandeh, "Sierra Leone's Post-Conflict Elections of 2002," *Journal of Modern African Studies* 41.2 (2003): 189–216; Jimmy D. Kandeh, "Rogue Incumbents,

Donor Assistance and Sierra Leone's Second Post-Conflict Elections of 2007," *Journal of Modern African Studies* 46.4 (2008): 603–36.

31. Stephen Ellis, *Mask of Anarchy: The Destruction of Liberia and the Religious Dimension of an African Civil War* (New York: New York University Press, 1999), 38–39.

32. A saying on the street at the time held that Tubman gave you ninety cents on the dollar, while Tolbert gave you only ten. The investment of large sums in a marble palace in his small home town symbolized regime excess. A 1988 visit to the site found the palace looted and surrounding infrastructure in decay.

33. Ellis, *Mask of Anarchy*, 64.

34. Ellis, *Mask of Anarchy*, 56.

35. My account here relies on the seminal analysis of William Reno, *Warlord Politics and African States* (Boulder, CO: Lynne Rienner, 1998), 113–45, and William Reno, *Corruption and State Politics in Sierra Leone* (Cambridge: Cambridge University Press, 1995).

36. In addition to works already cited, I have found especially valuable David Keen, *Conflict and Collusion in Sierra Leone* (Oxford, UK: James Currey, 2005), Morten Bøås and Kevin C. Dunn, eds., *African Guerrillas: Raging against the Machine* (Boulder, CO: Lynne Rienner, 2007), especially William Reno's "Liberia: The LURDs of the New Church," 69–80, Jimmy D. Kandeh, *Coups from Below: Armed Subalterns and State Power in West Africa* (New York: Palgrave Macmillan, 2004), Yusuf Bangura, "Strategic Policy Failure and Governance in Sierra Leone," *Journal of Modern African Studies* 38.4 (2000): 551–79, Paul Richards, *Fighting for the Rain Forest: War, Youth and Resources in Sierra Leone* (London: International African Institute, 1996), and Paul Richards, "To Fight or to Farm? Agrarian Dimensions of the Mano River Conflicts (Liberia and Sierra Leone)," *African Affairs* 104.417 (2005): 571–90.

37. Ellis, *Mask of Anarchy*, 66–68.

38. David Harris, "From 'Warlord' to 'Democratic' President: How Charles Taylor Won the 1997 Liberian Elections," *Journal of Modern African Studies* 37.3 (1999): 436.

39. Quoted in Kandeh, *Coups from Below*, 148.

40. Kandeh, *Coups from Below*, 149.

41. Bangura, "Strategic Policy Failure," 553.

42. I employing here a distinction originally articulated by Mancur Olson relative to Chinese warlords between those who relied on a permanent base and were motivated by curry favor with local populations (stationary bandits) and those who were itinerant and thus indifferent to popular support (roving bandits), a notion used with telling effect by Thandika Mkandiwire in his excellent comparative analysis of African guerrillas, "The Terrible Toll of Post-Colonial 'Rebel Movements' in Africa: Towards an Explanation of the Violence Against the Peasantry," *Journal of Modern African Studies* 40.2 (200): 181–216.

43. Keen, *Conflict and Collusion*, 249–66; Bangura, "Strategic Policy Failure," 564–65.

44. Morten Bøås provides a sympathetic biography of Bockarie in "Marginalized Youth," in *African Guerrillas*, 39–54.

45. Reno, "Liberia," 73.

46. David Harris, "Liberia 2005: An Unusual African Post-Conflict Election," *Journal of Modern African Studies* 44.3 (2006): 376.

47. In 2008 interviews with women leaders in Liberia, Aili Mari Tripp found not just their numbers but their real influence in state management exceptional, concluding that this was a positive omen for postconflict consolidation.

48. According to data collected by international human rights law specialist Jeremy Leavitt, who worked with the Liberian Truth and Reconciliation Commission, in "Illicit Peace: Violence, Conflict Resolution, Peace Settlements, and Gender," presentation at University of Wisconsin Law School, 9 October 2009.

49. Richards, "To Fight or to Farm," 576. See also Laurel Stovel, "'There's No Bad Bush to Throw away a Bad Child': Tradition-Inspired Reintegration in Post-War Sierra Leone," *Journal of Modern African Studies* 46.2 (2008): 305–24.

50. Philippe Decraene, "Specificités somaliennes," *Revue Française d'Études Politiques Africaine* 10.115 (1975): 29–40. See also his more extended monograph, *L'expérience socialiste somaliennes* (Paris: Berger-Levrault, 1977); for a more critical perspective, see Ahmed Samatar, *Socialist Somalia: Rhetoric and Reality* (London: Zed, 1988).

51. I. M. Lewis, *A Pastoral Democracy: A Study of Pastoralism and Politics among the Northern Somali of the Horn of Africa* (London: Oxford University Press, 1961), remains the classic source on the structure of Somali society.

52. Hussein M. Adam, "Somalia: A Terrible Beauty Being Born?," in *Collapsed States*, 73.

53. Marcus V. Hoehne provides a valuable guide to northern Somalia in "Mimesis and Mimicry in Northern Somalia," *Africa* 79.2 (2009): 252–81.

54. For an analysis of what he views as counterproductive American strategies in Somalia, see Bronwyn Bruton, "In the Quicksands of Somalia," *Foreign Affairs* 88.6 (2009): 79–94.

55. Roland Marchal, "Islamic Political Dynamics in the Somali Civil War," in *Islamism and Its Enemies in the Horn of Africa*, ed. Alex de Waal (Bloomington: Indiana University Press, 2004), 119. The essay provides a valuable account of the rise of Islamism in Somalia during the crisis years.

56. *Africa Research Bulletin, Economic, Technical and Financial Series* 47, 9 (16 September–15 October 2010), 18845.

57. *Economist*, 18–24 February 2011, 74.

58. Ladan Affi, "State Collapse, Civil War, and the Role of Diaspora Somalis," African Studies colloquium, University of Wisconsin–Madison, 25 March 2009.

59. *New York Times*, 30 December 2009; Jeffrey Gettleman, "The Pirates Are Winning," *New York Review of Books*, 14 October 2010, 35–36.

60. Bruton, "In the Quicksands of Somalia," 79.

61. An excellent account is found in Hoehne, "Mimesis and Mimicry."

62. Riikka Koskenmäki, "Legal Implications Resulting from State Failure in Light of the Case of Somalia," *Nordic Journal of International Law* 73.1 (2004), 1–36, cited in Hoehne, "Mimesis and Mimicry," 255.

63. Again, I rely on Hoehne, "Mimesis and Mimicry," 261–66.

64. Jok Maduk Jok, *Sudan: Race, Religion, and Violence* (Oxford, UK: Oneworld, 2007), 78. Other useful sources on the second civil war include Ruth Iyob and Gilbert M. Khadiagala, *Sudan: The Elusive Quest for Peace* (Boulder, CO: Lynne Rienner, 2006), and

Lam Akol, *Southern Sudan: Colonialism, Resistance and Autonomy* (Trenton, NJ: World Sea Press, 2007).

65. Francis Deng, *War of Visions: Conflict of Identities in the Sudan* (Washington, DC: Brookings Institution, 1995), provides biographical detail on Garang.

66. Sharon Hutchinson, *Nuer Dilemmas: Coping with Money, War, and the State* (Berkeley: University of California Press, 1996), 144.

67. Alex de Waal and A. H. Abdel Salam, "Islamism, State Power and *Jihad* in Sudan," in *Islamism and Its Enemies*, 112. The authors paint a compelling intellectual portrait of Turabi, holder of a Paris doctorate, whose Islamist philosophy contains echoes of extremist Sayyid Qutb yet also suggests a compatibility with women's rights and democracy.

68. Deng, *War of Visions*, 233. Hutchinson (*Nuer Dilemmas*, especially 103–57) further attests to the extraordinary brutality and devastation. She conducted field research in the Nuer areas during the early 1990s.

69. For a thorough account of the extreme complexity of southern militia divisions and alliances, see Matthew B. Arnold, "The South Sudan Defence Force: Patriots, Collaborators or Spoilers?" *Journal of Modern African Studies* 45.4 (2007): 489–516.

70. Collins, *A History of Modern Sudan*, 194–99.

71. The original oil corporation that developed the southern deposits was Chevron, which departed in the mid-1980s because of the insecurity, abandoning substantial investments in the oil fields to a succession of consortiums, which eventually came to be dominated by Chinese and Malaysian operatives.

72. Hutchinson was part of a team that assembled documentation and filed a lawsuit against a Canadian oil firm for the ethnic cleansing of the Nuer population in one of the oil fields.

73. Sharon Hutchinson and Jok Madut Jok, "Gendered Violence and the Militarization of Ethnicity: A Case Study from South Sudan," in *Postcolonial Subjectivities in Africa*, ed. Richard Werbner (London: Zed, 2002), 84–108; Sharon Hutchinson and Jok Madut Jok, "Sudan's Prolonged Second Civil War and the Militarization of Nuer and Dinka Identities," *African Studies Review* 42.2 (1999): 124–45.

74. Sharon Hutchinson, personal communication.

75. Sharon Hutchinson, personal communication.

76. For valuable summaries, see Gérard Chaliand, *Darfur: The Ambiguous Genocide* (Ithaca, NY: Cornell University Press, 2005), Iyob and Khadiagala, *Sudan*, and Oystein H. Rolandsen, "Sudan, the Janjawid and Government Militias," in *African Guerrillas*, 151–70.

77. de Waal and Abdel Salaam, "Islamism," 198.

78. The Congo wars are richly documented; see especially Filip Reyntjens, *The Great African War: Congo and Regional Geopolitics, 1996–2008* (Cambridge: Cambridge University Press, 2009), Gérard Prunier, *Africa's World War: Congo, the Rwandan Genocide, and the Making of a Continental Catastrophe* (Oxford: Oxford University Press, 2009), Thomas Turner, *The Congo Wars: Conflct, Myth and Reality* (London: Zed, 2007), Kisangani, *Civil Wars*, and Jean-Claude Willame, *La guerre du Kivu: Vues de la salle climatisée et de la veranda* (Brussels: GRIP, 2010).

79. Coltan is an amalgam of two rare minerals, columbium and tantalite, whose value soared thanks to its use in cell phones and some other electronic goods.

80. UN Security Council, "Final Report of the Panel of Experts on the Illegal Exploitation of Natural Resources and Other Forms of Wealth of the Democratic Republic of the Congo," S/2002/1146, 16 October 2002, 7.

81. The Kinshasa rumor mill flooded with reports that Joseph was only an adopted son, whose real parentage was Rwandan. Erik Kennes provides convincing refutation of this persistent rumor in his remarkably detailed biography of the elder Kabila, *Essai biographique sur Laurent Désiré Kabila* (Paris: L'Harmattan, 2003).

82. See the scathing critique by Theodore Trefon in *Congo Masquerade: The Political Culture of Aid Inefficiency and Reform Failure* (London: Zed, 2011).

83. The war in Acholiland is also well documented. See especially Aili Mari Tripp, *Museveni's Uganda: Paradoxes of Power in a Hybrid Regime* (Boulder, CO: Lynne Rienner, 2010), Heiki Behrend, *Alice Lakwema and the Holy Spirits: War in Northern Uganda, 1986–97* (Oxford, UK: James Curry, 1999), Sverker Finnström, *Living with Bad Surroundings: War, History, and Everyday Moments in Northern Uganda* (Durham, NC: Duke University Press, 2008), Kevin C. Dunn, "Uganda: The Lord's Resistance Army," in *African Guerrillas*, 131–49, and Ruddy Doom and Koen Vlassenroot, "Kony's Message: A New *Koine,*?" *African Affairs* 98.390 (1999): 5–36.

84. Tripp, *Museveni's Uganda*, 149–79.

85. Mustafa Mirzeler and Crawford Young, "Pastoral Politics in the Northeast Periphery of Uganda: AK47 as Change Agent," *Journal of Modern African Studies* 38.3 (2002): 407–30.

86. Finnström did extensive interviewing in Acholiland and spoke with both friends and foes of the LRA. He challenges the widely held opinion regarding the vacuity of the LRA political agenda, arguing instead that manifestoes he has seen have some substantive content, beyond pledges to eliminate witchcraft and find inspiration in the Ten Commandments, including a commitment to human rights, multitparties, federalism, and an end to corruption (*Living with Bad Surroundings*, 100–22).

87. Behrend, *Alice Lakwena*, 194.

88. Birmingham, "Angola," 182–83.

89. Momar Coumba Diop and Mamadou Diouf, *Le Sénégal sous Abdou Diouf* (Paris: Karthala, 1990).

90. Vincent Foucher, "The Resilient Weakness of Casamançais," in *African Guerrillas*, 171–98.

91. Catherine Boone, *Political Topographies of the African State: Territorial Authority and Institutional Choice* (Cambridge: Cambridge University Press, 2003), 116–140; Linda J. Beck, *Brokering Democracy in Africa: The Rise of Clientelist Democracy in Senegal* (New York: Palgrave Macmillan, 2008), 153–95. The authoritative source for the armed conflict and factional struggle within the Casamance rebellion is Jean-Claude Marut, *Le conflit de Casamance: Ce que dissent les armes* (Paris: Karthala, 2010).

92. A particularly insightful analysis of contemporary African conflicts is offered by Morten Bøås and Kevin C. Dunn in "African Guerrilla Politics: Raging against the

Machine," in *African Guerrillas*, 9–38, as well as by the case studies in the volume. For an earlier useful comparative treatment, see Christopher Clapham, ed., *African Guerrillas* (Oxford, UK: James Currey, 1998). Also of special value is Jeremy M. Weinstein, *Inside Rebellion: The Politics of Insurgent Violence* (Cambridge: Cambridge University Press, 2007), and Reno, *Warlord Politics* and *Warfare in Independent Africa*.

93. In "African Guerrilla Politics," Bøås and Dunn give rational grievance a central role in their explanation of the "rage against the machine." See also Jean-Claude Willame, *La guerre du Kivu* (Brussels: GRIP, 2010), who captures this contrast in perspective as the difference between the air-conditioned capital office, from which the diplomatic community and aid agencies perceive the state, and the veranda, where the actual dysfunctionality of formal institutions is encountered by the citizenry.

94. William Reno, personal communication.

95. This point is stressed by Mkandiwire in "The Terrible Toll."

96. This factor receives particular emphasis in Edna G. Bay and Donald L. Donham, eds., *States of Violence: Politics, Youth, and Memory in Contemporary Africa* (Charlottesville: University of Virginia Press, 2006).

97. Kandeh, *Coups from Below*; Ibrahim Abdullah, "Bush Path to Destruction: The Origin and Character of the Revolutionary United Front / Sierra Leone," *Journal of Modern African Studies*, 36.2 (1998): 203–36.

98. Weinstein explores these dimensions with admirable clarity, drawing on the African cases of Museveni's NRA and RENAMO in Mozambique in *Inside Rebellion*. See also Reno, *Warlord Politics*.

99. For example, in very different analytical modes, Weinstein, *Inside Rebellion*, Bøås and Dunn, eds., *African Guerillas*, Keen, *Conflict and Collusion in Sierra Leone*, Stathis N. Kalyvas, Ian Shapiro, and Tarek Masoud, eds., *Order, Conflict, and Violence* (Cambridge: Cambridge University Press, 2008), and James D. Fearon and David D. Laitin, "Ethnicity, Insurgency, and Civil Wars," *American Political Science Review* 97.1 (2003): 75–90.

100. This point emerges from the study of 117 armed conflicts worldwide from 1989 to 2003 by Christopher Cramer; see *Violence in Developing Countries: War, Memory, Progress* (Bloomington: Indiana University Press, 2006).

101. This is a core argument of Stathis N. Kalyvas in *The Logic of Violence in Civil Wars* (Cambridge: Cambridge University Press, 2006). An elegant illustration of this point in relation to the Rwandan genocide is found in Scott Straus, *The Order of Genocide: Race, Power, and War in Rwanda* (Ithaca, NY: Cornell University Press, 2006).

102. This is a major finding of current comparative study of African conflicts by Scott Straus.

CHAPTER 8. AFRICANISM, NATIONALISM AND ETHNICITY

1. The triple helix metaphor is borrowed from Michael G. Schatzberg, *Political Legitimacy in Middle Africa: Father, Family, Food* (Bloomington: Indiana UniversityPress, 1995), though he uses the image in a different sense.

2. Chinua Achebe, *The Education of a British Protected Child* (London: Allen Lane, 2010), 45.

3. The issue of ethnicity and its encounter with nationalism has been a central focus of my research and teaching since my first work on decolonization politics in Congo-Kinshasa. I first formulated the problematic in *Politics in the Congo* (Princeton, NJ: Princeton University Press, 1965) and then extended it to a comparative frame in *The Politics of Cultural Pluralism* (Madison: University of Wisconsin Press, 1976). My most recent contribution on this topic is "Nation, Ethnicity, and Citizenship: Dilemmas of Democracy and Civil Order in Africa," in *Making Nations, Creating Strangers*, ed. Sara Dorman, Daniel Hammett, and Paul Nugent (Leiden: Brill, 2007), 241–64.

4. Pierre Englebert, *Africa: Unity, Sovereignty and Sorrow* (Boulder, CO: Lynne Rienner, 2009), 1.

5. Colin Legum, *Pan-Africanism: A Short Political Guide* (New York: Praeger, 1962), 24.

6. For example, in the foundational works, James S. Coleman, "Nationalism in Tropical Africa," *American Political Science Review* 48.2 (1954): 404–26, and Thomas Hodgkin, *Nationalism in Colonial Africa* (London: Frederick Muller, 1956).

7. Jean-Claude Willame, *Patrice Lumumba: La crise congolaise revisitée* (Paris: Karthala, 1990), 353.

8. Ali A. Mazrui, "On the Concept 'We Are All Africans,'" *American Political Science Review* 57.1 (1963): 91.

9. Legum, *Pan-Africanism*, 39.

10. I. William Zartman, "Inter-African Negotiations and Reforming Political Order," in *Africa in World Politics: Reforming Political Order*, 4th ed., ed. John W. Harbeson and Donald Rothchild (Boulder, CO: Westview, 2009), 228.

11. The Ghana player who scored the winning penalty kick against Serbia to make his team the last surviving African competitor declared that his goal was for all of Africa. I am indebted to Michael Schatzberg for this savory detail.

12. One measure of the eclipse of pan-Africanism is the relative absence of major works devoted to its institutional expression; after a flurry of interest in the 1960s and 1970s, the OAU all but vanished from the academic bookshelves. William B. Ackah's *Pan-Africanism, Exploring the Contradictions: Politics, Identity and Development in Africa and the African Diaspora* (Aldershot, UK: Ashgate, 1999) is a rare exception. Earlier studies include, in addition to Legum's *Pan-Africanism*, Vincent Bakpetu Thompson's *Africa and Unity: The Evolution of Pan-Africanism* (London: Longman, 1998), Yassin El-Ayouty's *The Organization of African Unity after Ten Years* (New York: Praeger, 1975), and Berhanykun Andemicael's, *The OAU and the UN: Relations between the Organization of African Unity and the United Nations* (New York: Africana Publishing Company, 1976).

13. Tanzania is a case in point; Ron Aminzade documents the intense opposition of Africanist currents to independence leader Nyerere's insistence on a cosmopolitan definition of nationality and recurrent resurrection of the issue in postcolonial politics ("Nationalism and Exclusion: Race, Foreigners and Citizenship in Tanzania," ms. in progress).

14. Cited in Sally Healy, "The Changing Idiom of Self-Determination in the Horn of Africa," in *Nationalism and Self-Determination in the Horn of Africa*, ed. I. M. Lewis (London: Athaca Press, 1963), 93–109.

15. Cited in Hurst Hannum, *Autonomy, Sovereignty, and Self-Determination: The Accommodation of Conflicting Rights* (Philadelphia: University of Pennsylvania Press, 1990), 35–36.

16. Badinter's dictum resembles Philip G. Roeder's argument that new nation-states only spring from autonomous segments of extant polities (*Where Nation-States Come From: Institutional Change in the Age of Nationalism* [Princeton, NJ: Princeton University Press, 2007]).

17. There had been a number of territorial alterations over the course of European rule, all of which originated in the late nineteenth-century colonial partition, especially with the redistribution of the territories seized from Germany during World War I. Burkina Faso (the colonial Haut Volta) was attached to Ivory Coast from 1932 to 1948. Rwanda and Burundi were amalgamated as a single administrative unit under Belgian occupation from World War I till their independence in 1962, although the two kingdoms remained distinct.

18. Andemicael, *The OAU and the UN*, 12.

19. Robert H. Jackson, *Quasi-States: Sovereignty, International Relations, and the Third World* (Cambridge: Cambridge University Press, 1990), 5.

20. John A. Hall, "Introduction: Nation-States in History," in *The Nation-State in Question*, ed. T. V. Paul, G. John Ikenberry, and John A. Hall (Princeton, NJ: Princeton University Press, 2003), 19. Nyerere did at first harbor illusions of merging Tanzania into a large East African Union, but these visions foundered.

21. For one important example, see Jeffrey Herbst, *States and Power in Africa: Comparative Lessons in Authority and Control* (Princeton, NJ: Princeton University Press, 2000), 257–72.

22. Jean-François Bayart, *The State in Africa: The Politics of the Belly* (London: Longman, 1993), 150–79; Donald Rothchild, *Managing Ethnic Conflict in Africa: Pressures and Incentives for Cooperation* (Washington, DC: Brookings Institution Press, 1997), 25–58.

23. William Reno, *Warlord Politics in African States* (Boulder, CO: Lynne Rienner, 1999).

24. Englebert, *Africa*, 64.

25. Theodore Trefon, *Parcours administratifs dans un État en faillite: Récits populaires de Lubumbashi (RDC)* (Paris: L'Harmattan, 2007).

26. Olivier Kahola, "Une semaine d'enquêtes ethnographiques dans les commissariats de Lubumbashi," *Civilisations* 54.1–2 (2006): 25–32.

27. Herbert F. Weiss and Tatiana Carayannis, "The Enduring Idea of the Congo," in *Borders, Nationalism, and the African State*, ed. Ricardo René Larémont (Boulder, CO: Lynne Rienner, 2005), 135.

28. Weiss and Carayannis, "The Enduring Idea of the Congo," 163–64.

29. Englebert, *Africa*, 197–98.

30. Francis M. Deng, "Sudan's Turbulent Path to Nationhood," in *Borders*, 65–73. The significance of this figure is doubtless vitiated by the fact that the southerners interviewed were located in Khartoum, Cairo, and Washington. Had conditions permitted surveying in the south, the figures would surely have been lower.

31. Among a vast literature, some of the most influential contributions are Ernest Gellner, *Nations and Nationalism* (Oxford, UK: Blackwell, 1983), Eric Hobsbawm, *Nations and Nationalism since 1780* (Cambridge: Cambridge University Press, 1990), Benedict Anderson, *Imagined Communities: Reflections on the Origin and Spread of Nationalism* (London: Verso, 1983); Montserrat Guibernau and John Hutchinson, eds., *Understanding Nationalism* (Cambridge, UK: Polity Press, 2001), John Breuilly, *Nationalism and the State* (Manchester, UK: Manchester University Press, 1982), and Anthony D. Smith, *Nations and Nationalism in a Global Era* (Cambridge, UK: Polity Press, 1995). Smith differs from the others in perceiving a more distant origin for the idea of nationalism; he is joined by Adrian Hastings in *The Construction of Nationhood: Ethnicity, Religion and Nationalism* (Cambridge: Cambridge University Press, 1997).

32. See the illuminating contribution of Bernard Yack, "Nationalism, Popular Sovereignty and the Liberal Democratic State," in *The Nation-State in Question*, 29–50, and Bernard Yack, *Nationalism and the Moral Psychology of Community* (Chicago: University of Chicago Press, 2012).

33. Thus originates the debate between "civic" and "ethnic" nationalism, stressed by Liah Greenfeld in *Nationalism: Five Roads to Modernity* (Cambridge, MA: Harvard University Press, 1992).

34. In accounts of nationalism by such leading analysts as Hans Kohn, John Plamenatz, and others; see Yael Tamir, "Theoretical Difficulties in the Study of Nationalism," in *Theorizing Nationalism*, ed. Ronald Beiner (Albany: State University of New York Press, 1999), 67–90.

35. Cited in Michael Clark, *Algeria in Turmoil* (London: Thames and Hudson, 1960), 17.

36. Mazrui, "On the Concept 'We Are All Africans,'" 92.

37. Young, *The Politics of Cultural Pluralism*, 274.

38. Rupert Emerson, *From Empire to Nation: The Rise to Self-Assertion of Asian and African Peoples* (Cambridge, MA: Harvard University Press, 1960), 95.

39. Eugen Weber, *Peasants into Frenchmen: The Modernization of Rural France, 1870–1914* (London: Chatto and Windus, 1979).

40. Uganda also bears the name of the Ganda, dominant in the creation and early administration of the colony but representing only 20% of the population and minoritized by universal suffrage.

41. See Heike Becker's intriguing article "Commemorating Heroes in Windhoek and Eenhana: Memory, Culture and Nationalism in Namibia," *Africa* 81.4 (2011): 519–43. Interestingly, the symbolism is not without ambiguities; some Namibians from the center and south point out that the physical features of the "unknown soldier" statue bear a striking resemblance to independence leader Sam Nujoma and are characteristic of northern Namibians (Ovambo).

42. Michael Billig, *Banal Nationalism* (London: Sage, 1995), 5.

43. Sékou Touré, *Towards Full Reafricanisation* (Paris: Présence Africaine, 1959), 28.

44. This point is effectively developed in David Laitin, *Language Repertoires and State Construction in Africa* (Cambridge: Cambridge University Press, 1992).

45. The recent emergence of a Kongo ethnonationalist religious cult Bundu dia Kongo and the sizable 2010 Lubumbashi demonstration (dispersed by the military) to "celebrate" the fiftieth anniversary of the Katanga secession are straws in the wind; see Denis M. Tull's insightful article "Troubled State-Building in the DR Congo," *Journal of Modern African Studies* 48.4 (2010): 643–61.

46. Daniel Jordan Smith, *A Culture of Corruption: Everyday Deception and Popular Discontent in Nigeria* (Princeton, NJ: Princeton University Press, 2007), 193–94.

47. Jawaharlal Nehru, *The Discovery of India* (New York: Meridian, 1946).

48. Englebert, *Africa*, 198.

49. My most complete recent discussion of the ethnicity phenomenon can be found in *Ethnicity and Politics in Africa* (Boston: Boston University African Studies Program, 2002).

50. For a valuable methodological discussion on analytical capture of ethnicity, see Rawi Abdelal, Yoshiko M. Herrera, Alastair Iain Johnston, and Rose McDermott, eds., *Measuring Identity: A Guide for Social Scientists* (Cambridge: Cambridge University Press, 2009). See also Kanchan Chandra, "What Is Ethnic Identity and Does It Matter?," *Annual Review of Political Science* 9 (2006): 375–95.

51. Joshua A. Fishman, *In Praise of the Beloved Language: A Comparative View of Positive Ethnolinguistic Consciousness* (Berlin: Mouton de Gruyter, 1997), 20.

52. Aili Mari Tripp and Crawford Young, "The Accommodation of Cultural Diversity in Tanzania," in *Ethnopolitical Warfare: Causes, Consequences, and Possible Solutions*, ed. Daniel Chirot and Martin E. P. Seligman (Washington, DC: American Psychological Association, 2001), 259–74.

53. Jean-Loup Amselle, *Logiques métisses: Anthropologie de l'identité en Afrique et ailleurs* (Paris: Fayot, 1990), 30.

54. Christopher Wrigley, *Kingship and State: The Buganda Dynasty* (Cambridge: Cambridge University Press, 1996).

55. Francis Deng, *War of Visions: Conflict of Identities in the Sudan* (Washington, DC: Brookings Institution, 1995).

56. Henri Tafjels, *Human Groups and Social Categories* (New York: Cambridge University Press, 1981). See also Richard Jenkins, *Social Identities* (London: Routledge, 1996).

57. Although "instrumentalism" and "constructivism" are implicit aspects of interpretation in my *Politics of Cultural Pluralism*, it only occurred to me only to approach ethnicity through these three explicit analytical categories when I was preparating my introductory chapter, "The Dialectics of Cultural Pluralism," in *The Rising Tide of Cultural Pluralism: The Nation-State at Bay?*, ed. Crawford Young (Madison: University of Wisconsin Press, 1992), 3–35.

58. An argument well made by Stuart J. Kaufman in *Modern Hatreds: The Symbolic Politics of Ethnic War* (Ithaca, NY: Cornell University Press, 2001).

59. This perspective informed my first major work on cultural pluralism, *The Politics of Cultural Pluralism*, though without the conceptual designation. Susan Olzak and Joane Nagel, eds., *Competitive Ethnic Relations* (Orlando, FL: Academic Press, 1986), was one of the first to hone this perspective into a systematic conceptual frame.

60. Schatzberg, *Political Legitimacy in Middle Africa*, 26.

61. Russell Hardin, *One for All: The Logic of Group Conflict* (Princeton, NJ: Princeton University Press, 1995), 5.

62. An influential example is Leroy Vail, ed., *The Creation of Tribalism in Southern Africa* (Berkeley: University of California Press, 1989).

63. The essays in *The Creation of Tribalism*, also stress this aspect.

64. Alexander J. Motyl, "The Social Construction of Social Construction: Implications for Theories of Nationalism and Identity Formation," *Nationalities Papers: The Journal of Nationalities and Ethnicity* 38.1 (2010): 64.

65. Kenneth Jowitt, "Ethnicity: Nice, Nasty, and Nihilistic," in *Ethnopolitical Warfare*, 28.

66. Aidan Southall, "The Illusion of Tribe," *Journal of Asian and African Studies* 5.102 (1970): 37.

67. A persuasive account of Yoruba ethnogenesis is provided by J. D. Y. Peel in *Religious Encounter and the Making of the Yoruba* (Bloomington: Indiana University Press, 2000).

68. The key role of ancestral town identity in Yoruba politics is well documented by David Laitin in *Hegemony and Culture: Politics and Religious Change among the Yoruba* (Chicago: University of Chicago Press, 1996).

69. Jean-François Bayart, *The Illusion of Cultural Identity* (London: Hurst, 2005), 2.

70. For details on Ngala ethnogenesis, see Young, *Politics in the Congo*, 242–45.

71. John F. Clark, *The Failure of Democracy in the Republic of Congo* (Boulder, CO: Lynne Rienner, 2008), 121–22.

72. Daniel N. Posner, *Institutions and Ethnic Politics in Africa* (Cambridge: Cambridge University Press, 2005). Posner's excellent monograph is an example of pure instrumentalist analysis, informed by rational choice theory.

73. Paul Nugent reports arriving in Ghanian Eweland in 1985 expecting to find strong cross-border identity, but, despite the weakness of the Ghana state at the time and notwithstanding the fact that much trade and smuggling was taking place across the frontier, he discovered that villagers "regarded Togo as a foreign land where unpredictable (and often unpalatable) things were likely to happen" (*Smugglers, Secessionists and Loyal Citizens on the Ghana-Togo Border: The Life of the Borderlands since 1914* [Oxford, UK: James Currey, 2002], 7).

74. William F. S. Miles, *Hausaland Divided: Colonialism and Independence in Nigeria and Niger* (Ithaca, NY: Cornell University Press, 1996), 1.

75. James Ferguson, *Expectations of Modernity: Myths and Meanings of Urban Life in the Zambian Copperelt* (Berkeley: University of California Press, 1999).

76. Jacques Kago Lele, *Tribalisme et exclusions au Cameroun* (Yaoundé: CRAC, 1995), 6. Lele also reports that in 1966, a professor at the national school of administration publicly called for Bamileke's extermination (17). Though he was dismissed from his position by President Ahidjo, the incident shows that Bamileke had good reason to fear the animosity of others and react with enhanced identity intensity.

77. Carolyn Hamilton, *Terrific Majesty: The Powers of Shaka Zulu and the Limits of Historical Invention* (Cambridge, MA: Harvard University Press, 1998).

78. The Kabaka of Uganda (Sir Edward Mutesa II), *The Desecration of My Kingdom* (London: Constable, 1967), 78–79.

79. I elaborate further on this point in *The Politics of Cultural Pluralism*, 45–46.

80. John Lonsdale, "Moral and Political Argument in Kenya," in *Ethnicity and Democracy in Africa*, ed. Bruce Berman, Dickson Eyoh and Will Kymlicka (Oxford, UK: James Currey, 2004), 73–95. This distinction resembles the contrast drawn over three decades ago by Peter Ekeh in a classic article distinguishing the moral community and normative order operative at the ethnic level from the amoral realm of the state; see "Colonialism and the Two Publics in Africa: A Theoretical Statement," *Comparative Studies in Society and History* 17.1 (1975): 91–112.

81. Examples include V. Spike Peterson, "The Politics of Identity and Gendered Nationalism," in *Foreign Policy Analysis: Continuity and Change in its Second Generation*, ed. Laura Leack, Jeanne A. K. Hey, and Patrick J. Hanay (Englewood Cliffs, NJ: Prentice Hall, 1995), 167–86, and Nira Yuval-Davis, *Gender and Nation* (New York: Routledge, 1997).

82. I am indebted to Thomas Spear for this point.

83. Leroy Vail, introduction, *The Creation of Tribalism*, 15.

84. Aili Mari Tripp, *Women and Politics in Uganda* (Madison: University of Wisconsin Press, 2000). In a subsequent collaborative work, she reinforces this point by extending it to other African states; see Aili Mari Tripp, Isabel Casamiro, Joy Kwesiga, and Alice Mungwa, *African Women's Movements: Changing Political Landscapes* (Cambridge: Cambridge University Press, 2009).

85. Constituent Assembly proceedings of 5 August 1994, quoted in Aili Mari Tripp, "Women's Movements and Challenges to Neopatrimonial Rule: Preliminary Observations fro Africa," *Development and Change* 32.1 (January 2001): 33–54.

86. I offer an extended treatment of Arab identity in *The Politics of Cultural Pluralism*, 373–427.

87. The Egyptian press scornfully dismissed the Algerians as not only territorial others but as pseudo-Arabs, whose innate Berberhood was concealed under a thin veneer of Arabism (*Jeune Afrique*, 15–21 November 2009, 24–28).

88. Cited in Jowitt, "Ethnicity," in *Ethnopolitical Warfare*, 28.

89. For some examples among many, see the pair of articles by Jimmy D. Kandeh on the 2002 and 2007 Sierra Leone elections, "Sierra Leone's Post-Conflict Elections of 2002," *Journal of Modern African Studies* 41.2 (2003): 189–216, and "Rogue Incumbents, Donor Assistance, and Sierra Leone's Second Post-Conflict Elections of 2007," *Journal of Modern African Studies* 46.4 (2008): 603–36, as well as Peter Arthur, "Ethnicity and Electoral Politics in Ghana's Fourth Republic," *Africa Today* 56.2 (2009): 45–74.

90. Jean Bazin, "A chacun son Bambara," in *Au coeur de l'ethnie: Ethnies, tribalisme et état en Afrique*, ed. Jean-Loup Amselle and Elikia M'Bokolo (Paris: Découverte, 1985), 97.

91. Mary C. Waters, *Ethnic Options: Choosing Identities in America* (Berkeley: University of California Press, 1990). Most Euroamericans are only loosely if at all constrained in their ethnic options, as their ancestries are often scrambled and they may have scant knowledge of the origins of their forebears.

92. Claude Ake, *Democracy and Development in Africa* (Washington, DC: Brookings Institution, 1996), 132. See also Joshua B. Forrest, *Subnationalism in Africa: Ethnicity, Alliances, and Politics* (Boulder, CO: Lynne Rienner, 2004).

93. Yoweri Museveni, *Sowing the Mustard Seed: The Struggle for Freedom and Democracy in Uganda* (London: Macmillan, 1997), 189.

94. Excellent treatments of the national question in Ethiopia are provided by Edmond J. Keller, "Making and Remaking State and Nation in Ethiopia," in *Borders*, 87–134, David Turton, ed., *Ethnic Federalism: The Ethiopian Experience in Comparative Perspective* (Oxford, UK: James Currey, 2006), and Katsuyoshi Fukui and John Markakis, *Ethnicity and Conflict in the Horn of Africa* (Oxford, UK: James Currey, 1994).

95. In one of the rare studies of citizenship in Africa, Jeffrey Herbst shows in a survey of forty constitutions the predominance of jus sanguinis principles (*States and Power in Africa*, 227–48).

96. The insidious effect of indigneity doctrines where they have achieved prominence in Ivory Coast, Cameroon, and Congo-Kinshasa receive incisive treatment in Peter Geschiere, *The Perils of Belonging: Autochtony, Citzenship, and Exclusion in Africa and Europe* (Chicago: University of Chicago Press, 2009).

97. Philip Ostien, "Jonah Jang and the Jasawa: Ethno-Religious Conflict in Jos, Nigeria," *Muslim-Christian Relations in Africa*, www.sharia-in-africa.net, August 2009, accessed 8 April 2012.

98. Finnström in his numerous interviews with young Acholi in Uganda finds ample evidence of the coexistence of the three identity tracks that echo many of my conversations with Africans in many countries: "In everyday life, my informants would refer to themselves as Ugandans just as often as they portrayed themselves as Acholi or Luo. It all depends on context. Often, young informants referred to themselves as Africans more than anything else. In the present situation, with war, social breakdown, ethnic tensions, and political turmoil, these young men and women found inspiration and hope from pan-Africanist ideas" (*Living with Bad Surroundings: War, History, and Everyday Movements in Northern Uganda* [Durham, NC: Duke University Press, 2008], 37).

CHAPTER 9. THE AFRICAN POSTCOLONIAL STATE

1. Pierre Englebert, *Africa: Unity, Sovereignty and Sorrow* (Boulder: Lynne Rienner, 2009), 1; Goran Hyden, *African Politics in Comparative Perspective* (Cambridge: Cambridge University Press, 2008), 271. By a different line of reasoning, Robert Bates also suggests that state failure is a dominant outcome for sub-Saharan Africa; see *When Things Fell Apart: State Failure in Late-Century Africa* (Cambridge: Cambridge University Press, 2008).

2. William Easterly and Ross Levine, "Africa's Growth Tragedy: Polities and Ethnic Divisions," *Quarterly Journal of Economics* 112.4 (1997): 1203.

3. Theodore Trefon, introduction, *Réforme au Congo (RDC): Attentes et désillusions*, ed. Theodore Trefon (Paris: L'Harmattan, 2009), 15.

4. "AFDB/IMF/World Bank: Divergent Predictions," *Africa Research Bulletin*, Economic Financial and Technical Series, 46.10 (2009), 18451.

5. High hopes were vested in the designation of John Githongo as presidential deputy to document and prosecute corruption; he was driven into exile after unraveling the infamous Goldenberg, Anglo-Leasing, and other notorious scandals. He was a major source for Michela Wrong's appalling chronicle of malfeasance, *It's Our Turn to Eat: The Story of a Kenyan Whistle-Blower* (New York: HarperCollins, 2009)

6. See Richard R. Marcus's excellent "Marc the Medici? The Failure of a New Form of Neopatrimonial Rule in Madagascar," *Political Science Quarterly* 125.1 (2010): 111–31.

7. Crawford Young, *The African Colonial State in Comparative Perspective* (New Haven, CT: Yale University Press, 1994), 283.

8. Achille Mbembe, *Afriques indociles: Christianisme, pouvoir et État en société postcoloniale* (Paris: Karthala, 1988), 128–43.

9. In her careful study, Ruth Collier does identify some contrasts in party type and system in the politics of decolonization and initial independence; see *Regimes in Tropical Africa: Changing Forms of Supremacy, 1945–1975* (Berkeley: University of California Press, 1982). These differences soon faded.

10. Bates offers a more elaborated sketch of state failure in *When Things Fell Apart.*

11. I here borrow the title Jan Vansina's masterful *Being Colonized: The Kuba Experience in Rural Congo, 1880–1960* (Madison: University of Wisconsin Press, 2010).

12. Crawford Young, "The End of the Post-Colonial State in Africa? Reflections on Changing African Political Dynamics," *African Affairs* 103.410 (2004): 48–49.

13. Among the analysts pointing to the developmental legacy of Japanese colonial rule is Atul Kohli in *State-Directed Development: Political Power and Industrialization in the Global Periphery* (Cambridge: Cambridge University Press, 2004). More generally on the Japanese colonial legacy, see Ramon H. Myers and Mark R. Peattie, eds., *The Japanese Colonial Empire, 1895–1945* (Princeton, NJ: Princeton University Press, 1984).

14. Classic exponents of the developmental state model include Alice Amsden, *Asia's Next Giant: South Korea and Late Industrialization* (New York: Oxford University Press, 1989), and Robert Wade, *Governing the Market: Economic Theory and the Role of Government in East Asian Industrialization* (Princeton, NJ: Princeton University Press, 1990).

15. Thomas M. Callaghy and John Ravenhill, "How Hemmed In? Lessons and Prospects of Africa's Response to Decline," in *Hemmed In: Africa's Responses to Decline*, ed. Thomas M. Callaghy and John Ravenhill (New York: Columbia University Press, 1993), 585.

16. Kohli, *State-Directed Development*; Peter M. Lewis, *Growing Apart: Oil, Politics, and Economic Change in Indonesia and Nigeria* (Ann Arbor: University of Michigan Press, 2007). See also David Bevan, Paul Collier, and Jon Willem, *Nigeria and Indonesia* (New York: Oxford University Press, 1999).

17. The striking spread of Naxalite presence is mapped in *Economist*, 19 August 2006.

18. Paul Brass, *The Politics of India since Independence*, 2nd ed. (Cambridge: Cambridge University, 1994), 350.

19. Atul Kohli, *Democracy and Discontent: India's Growing Crisis of Governability* (Cambridge: Cambridge University Press, 19090), 378–79.

20. Lloyd I. Rudolph and Susanne Hoeber Rudolph, *In Pursuit of Lakshimi: The Political Economy of the Indian State* (Chicago: University of Chicago Press, 1987), 400.

21. Theodore Friend, *Indonesian Destinies* (Cambridge, MA: Harvard University Press, 2003), 247; Crawford Young and Thomas Turner, *The Rise and Decline of the Zairian State* (Madison: University of Wisconsin Press, 1995), 178–82.

22. Lewis, *Growing Apart*, 270.

23. Friend, *Indonesian Destinies*, 233.

24. Deborah J. Yasher, "Civil War and Social Welfare: The Origins of Costa Rica's Competitive Party System," in *Building Democratic Institutions: Party Systems in Latin America*, ed. Scott Mainwaring and Timothy R. Scully (Stanford, CA: Stanford University Press, 1995), 72.

25. Claudio Veliz, *The Centralist Tradition in Latin America* (Princeton, NJ: Princeton University Press, 1980); James Lang, *Commerce and Conquest: Spain and England in the Americas* (New York: Academic Press, 1975). The bureaucratic-authoritarian state model originates with Guillermo O'Donnell in *Modernization and Bureaucratic-Authoritarianism* (Berkeley: Institute of International Affairs, University of California, 1973). Influential comparative analysis capturing the authoritarian moment includes David Collier, ed., *The New Authoritarianism in Latin America* (Princeton, NJ: Princeton University Press, 1979), and James M. Malloy, ed., *Authoritarianism and Corporatism in Latin America* (Pittsburgh, PA: University of Pittsburgh Press, 1979).

26. Mainwaring and Scully, eds., *Building Democratic Institutions*.

27. Barbara Stallings and Wilson Peres led a team of political economists who evaluated Latin American economic reform; they found it brought some improvement, though less than its most fervent advocates expected (*Growth, Employment, and Equity: The Impact of the Economic Reforms in Latin America and the Caribbean* [Washington, DC: Brookings Institution Press, 2000]).

28. Benno J. Ndulu, Stephen A. O'Connell, Robert H. Bates, Paul Collier, and Chukwuma C. Soludo, eds., *The Political Economy of Economic Growth in Africa, 1960–2000*, 2 vols. (Cambridge: Cambridge University Press, 2008).

29. Benno J. Ndulu et al., introduction, *The Political Economy of Economic Growth in Africa*, 1:5.

30. Jeffrey Herbst, *States and Power in Africa: Comparative Lessons in Authority and Control* (Princeton, NJ: Princeton University Press, 2000).

31. Benno J. Ndulu and Stephen A. O'Connell, "Policy Plus: African Growth Performance, 1960–2000," in *The Political Economy of Economic Growth in Africa*, 1:3–75.

32. William Easterly and Ross Levine, "Africa's Growth Tragedy: Policies and Ethnic Divisions," *Quarterly Journal of Economics* 112.4 (1997): 1203–50.

33. Some of these are examined in Crawford Young, ed., *Ethnic Diversity and Public Policy: A Comparative Inquiry* (Houndmills, UK: Macmillan, 1998).

34. Joshua B. Forrest, *Lineages of State Fragility: Rural Civil Society in Guinea-Bissau* (Oxford, UK: James Curry, 2003); Pierre Kalck, *Central African Republic: A Failure in Decolonization* (New York: Praeger, 1971); Andreas Mehler, "The Shaky Foundations, Adverse Circumstances, and Limited Achievements of Democratic Transition in Central African

Republic," in *The Fate of Africa's Democratic Experiments: Elites and Institutions*, ed. Leonardo A. Villalon and Peter VonDoepp (Bloomington: Indiana University Press, 2005), 126–52.

35. William Reno, "Mafiya Troubles, Warlord Crises," in *Beyond State Crisis? Postcolonial Africa and Post-Soviet Eurasia in Comparative Perspective*, ed. Mark R. Beissinger and Crawford Young (Washington, DC: Woodrow Wilson Center Press, 2002), 105–28.

36. Clement Moore Henry and Robert Springborg, *Globalization and the Politics of Development in the Middle East*, 2nd ed. (Cambridge: Cambridge University Press, 2010), 196.

37. Among other sources, see Chris Alden, *Apartheid's Last Stand: The Rise and Fall of the South African Security State* (Houndmills, UK: Macmillan Press, 1996), Robert M. Price, *The Apartheid State in Crisis, 1975–1990* (New York: Oxford University Press, 1991), Annette Seegers, *The Military in the Making of Modern South Africa* (London: I. B. Tauris, 1996), and Joseph Hanlon, *Beggar Your Neighbors: Apartheid Power in Southern Africa* (Bloomington: Indiana University Press, 1986).

38. UN forces have been deployed in Angola, Burundi, Central African Republic, Congo-Kinshasa, Eritrea-Ethiopia, Ivory Coast, Liberia, Rwanda, Sierra Leone, Somalia, and Sudan. An EU force served in Chad, and the AU sent forces to Comoros, Sudan, and Somalia. Senegal intervened unilaterally in Gambia and Guinea-Bissau, and South Africa in Lesotho.

39. International Institute for Strategic Studies, *The Military Balance 2008* (London: Routledge, 2008).

40. This thesis was first set forth by Robert H. Jackson and Carl G. Rosberg in Why Africa's Weak States Persist: The Empirical and the Juridical in Statehood," *World Politics* 35.1 (1982), 1–24. See also Robert H. Jackson, *Quasi-States: Sovereignty, International Relations and the Third World* (Cambridge: Cambridge University Press, 1990), and Englebert, *Africa: Unity, Suffering and Sorrow* (Boulder, CO: Lynne Rienner, 2009).

41. Nicolas van de Walle, *African Economies and the Politics of Permanent Crisis, 1979–1999* (Cambridge: Cambridge University Press, 2001.

42. "Africa: Illicit Outlfows," *Africa Research Bulletin*, Economic, Financial, and Technical Series, 47.3 (2010): 18631.

43. Michael G. Schatzberg, *Political Legitimacy in Middle Africa: Father, Family, Food* (Bloomington: Indiana University Press, 2001), 212.

44. Englebert, *Africa*, 197.

45. Patrick Chabal, *Africa: The Politics of Suffering and Smiling* (London: Zed, 2009), 97.

46. Young, *The African Colonial State*, 38.

47. Robert H. Bates, *Markets and States in Tropical Africa: The Political Basis of Agricultural Politicies* (Berkeley: University of California Press, 1981), 12–19.

48. Goran Therborn, *What Does the Ruling Class Do When It Rules? State Apparatuses and State Power under Feudalism, Capitalism and Socialism* (London: NRB, 1978).

49. For an example, see Vali Jamal, "Taxation and Inequality in Uganda," *Journal of Economic History* 38.2 (1978): 418–38.

50. E. H. Winter, *Bwamba Economy* (Kampala: East African Institute of Social Research, 1955), 34–35.

51. This draws on a table of African government revenue constructed by Michael Schatzberg from CIA World Factbooks.

52. CIA, *The CIA World Factbook 2009* (New York: Skyhorse Publishing, 2008), 480. The debt-relief accord reflected in good part the credibility at the time of the Economic and Financial Crimes Commission, then led by Nuhu Ribadu, and the skills of the finance minister, Ngozi Okonjo Iweala.

53. Ken Auletta provides an engaging profile in "The Dictator Index," *New Yorker*, 7 March 2011, 48–55.

54. Jeffrey Herbst and Greg Mills, "Africa's Big Dysfunctional States: An Introductory Overview," in *Big African States*, ed. Christopher Clapham, Jeffrey Herbst, and Greg Mills (Johannesburg: Wits University Press, 2006), 1–15. See also Alberto Alesina and Enrico Spolaore, *The Size of Nations* (Cambridge, MA: MIT Press, 2003).

55. In the Egyptian case, Tamir Mustafa shows that there was some latitude for the press in the 1990s, and the judiciary enjoyed surprising autonomy until the turn of the century, with litigation the most effective channel to challenge the regime (*The Struggle for Constitutional Power: Law, Politics, and Economic Development in Egypt* [Cambridge: Cambridge University Press, 2007]).

56. For a model of contemporary sultanism, see H. E. Chalabi and Juan J. Linz, eds., *Sultanistic Regimes* (Baltimore, MD: Johns Hopkins University Press, 1998). In my view, Qadhafy more closely resembles this model than any other perennial African ruler.

57. Lisa Anderson argues that the "devastating experience of state destruction combined with the country's continued and growing dependence on external sources of revenues to create a pattern of persistent hostility to the notion of the state, to bureaucratic organization" (*The State and Social Transformation in Tunisia and Libya, 1830–1980* [Princeton, NJ: Princeton University Press, 1986], 230).

58. Dirk Vandewalle, ed., *Qadhafi's Libya, 1969–1994* (New York: St. Martin's, 1995).

59. *Jeune Afrique*, 4–10 April 2010, 22–36.

60. A very critical article in *Le Monde* (24 October 2009) evoked furious riposte from the regime and led to instant arrest and expulsion of the journalist, reflecting its acute sensitivity to criticism.

61. I am indebted to research assistant Geraldine O'Mahoney for collecting this data.

62. For a contrary argument attributing postcolonial success to the British colonial legacy, see Matthew Lange, *Lineages of Despotism and Development: British Colonialism and State Power* (Chicago: University of Chicago Press, 2009).

63. According to Motsamai Keyecwe Mpho, these subordinated groups are actually a majority; see "Representation of Cultural Minorities in Policy Making," in *Democracy in Botswana*, ed. John Holm and Patrick Molutsi (Athens: Ohio University Press, 1989), 58–73.

64. Abdi Ismail Samatar, *An African Miracle: State and Class Leadership and Colonial Legacy in Botswana Development* (Portsmouth, NH: Heinemann, 1999), 96. Steven Levitsky and Lucan A. Way relegate Botswana (unconvincingly) to the "competitive authoritarian"

category, based on the uninterrupted rule of the BDP; *Competitive Authoritarianism: Hybrid Regimes after the Cold War* (Cambridge: Cambridge University Press, 2010). The elections have been of undisputed integrity and fairness, the opposition has won a significant percentage of the vote, and has had a parliamentary voice. The BDP majorities are magnified by the single member district electoral system. For another positive appraisal of Botswana (and Mauritius), see Pita Ogabea Agnese and George Klay Kieh, eds., *Reconstituting the State in Africa* (New York: Palgrave Macmillan, 2007).

65. John Stephen Morrison, "Divergence from State Failure in Africa: The Relative Success of Botswana's Cattle Sector" (PhD diss., University of Wisconsin–Madison, 1987).

66. Michael Crowder, "Botswana and the Survival of Liberal Democracy," in *Decolonization and African Independence: The Transfers of Power, 1960–1980*, ed. Prosser Gifford and William Roger Louis (New Haven, CT: Yale University Press, 1988), 464.

67. For detail from a trio of Mauritian scholars, see Monique Dinan, Vidula Nababsing and Hansraj Mathur, "Mauritius: Cultural Accommodation in a Diverse Island Polity," in *The Accommodation of Cultural Diversity: Case Studies*, ed. Crawford Young (Houndmills, UK: Macmillan, 1999), 72–102. Electoral detail can be found in Dieter Nohlen, Michael Krennerich, and Bernhard Thibaut, eds., *Elections in Africa: A Data Handbook* (Oxford: Oxford University Press, 1999), 603–22. See also Larry Bowman, *Mauritius: Democracy and Development in the Indian Ocean* (Boulder, CO: Westview, 1991).

68. Adele Smith Simmons writes that the "economic chaos that was expected to follow independence did not materialize" (*Modern Mauritius: The Politics of Decolonization* [Bloomington: Indiana University Press, 1982], 190).

69. David Leonard and Scott Straus, *Africa's Stalled Development: International Causes and Cures* (Boulder, CO: Lynne Rienner, 2003).

70. For depressing portraits, see Robert I. Rotberg, *Haiti: The Politics of Squalor* (Boston: Houghton Mifflin, 1971), and Robert Fatton, *Haiti's Predatory Republic: The Unending Transition to Democracy* (Boulder, CO: Lynne Rienner, 2002).

71. Trefon, introduction, 18.

72. International Labour Office, *Employment, Incomes and Equality* (Geneva: International Labour Office, 1972), was the seminal work that discovered the significance of the informal sector.

73. Aili Mari Tripp, Isabel Casamiro, Joy Kwesiga, and Alice Mungwa, *African Women's Movements: Changing Political Landscapes* (Cambridge: Cambridge University Press, 2009).

Index

Page numbers in italics indicate figures, tables and maps.

Africa and the Diaspora:
History, Politics, Culture

THOMAS SPEAR, DAVID HENIGE, AND MICHAEL SCHATZBERG

Series Editors

Spirit, Structure, and Flesh: Gendered Experiences in
African Instituted Churches among the Yoruba of Nigeria
DEIDRE HELEN CRUMBLEY

A Hill among a Thousand: Transformations and Ruptures in Rural Rwanda
DANIELLE DE LAME

Defeat Is the Only Bad News: Rwanda under Musinga, 1897–1931
ALISON LIEBHAFSKY DES FORGES; EDITED BY DAVID NEWBURY

Power in Colonial Africa: Conflict and Discourse in Lesotho, 1870–1960
ELIZABETH A. ELDREDGE

Nachituti's Gift: Economy, Society, and Environment in Central Africa
DAVID M. GORDON

Intermediaries, Interpreters, and Clerks:
African Employees in the Making of Colonial Africa
EDITED BY BENJAMIN N. LAWRANCE, EMILY LYNN OSBORN,
AND RICHARD L. ROBERTS

Naming Colonialism: History and Collective Memory in the Congo, 1870–1960
OSUMAKA LIKAKA

Mau Mau's Children: The Making of Kenya's Postcolonial Elite
DAVID P. SANDGREN

Antecedents to Modern Rwanda: The Nyiginya Kingdom
JAN VANSINA

Being Colonized: The Kuba Experience in Rural Congo, 1880–1960
JAN VANSINA

The Postcolonial State in Africa: Fifty Years of Independence, 1960–2010
CRAWFORD YOUNG